EVIDENCE

EVIDENCE

Inns of Court School of Law
Institute of Law, City University, London

OXFORD
UNIVERSITY PRESS

OXFORD

UNIVERSITY PRESS

Great Clarendon Street, Oxford OX2 6DP

Oxford University Press is a department of the University of Oxford.
It furthers the University's objective of excellence in research, scholarship,
and education by publishing worldwide in

Oxford New York

Auckland Bangkok Buenos Aires Cape Town Chennai
Dar es Salaam Delhi Hong Kong Istanbul Karachi Kolkata
Kuala Lumpur Madrid Melbourne Mexico City Mumbai Nairobi
São Paulo Shanghai Singapore Taipei Tokyo Toronto

and an associated company in Berlin

Oxford is a registered trade mark of Oxford University Press
in the UK and certain other countries

Published in the United States
by Oxford University Press Inc., New York

A Blackstone Press Book

British Library Cataloguing in Publication Data

Data available

Library of Congress Cataloging in Publication Data

Data available

ISBN 0-19-925502-4

1 3 5 7 9 10 8 6 4 2

Typeset by Style Photosetting Limited, Mayfield, East Sussex
Printed in Great Britain
on acid-free paper by
Ashford Colour Press, Gosport, Hampshire

FOREWORD

These manuals are designed primarily to support training on the Bar Vocational Course, though they are also intended to provide a useful resource for legal practitioners and for anyone undertaking training in legal skills.

The Bar Vocational Course was designed by staff at the Inns of Court School of Law, where it was introduced in 1989. This course is intended to equip students with the practical skills and the procedural and evidential knowledge that they will need to start their legal professional careers. These manuals are written by staff at the Inns of Court School of Law who have helped to develop the course, and by a range of legal practitioners and others involved in legal skills training. The authors of the manuals are very well aware of the practical and professional approach that is central to the Bar Vocational Course.

The range and coverage of the manuals have grown steadily. All the manuals are updated annually, and regular reviews and revisions of the manuals are carried out to ensure that developments in legal skills training and the experience of our staff are fully reflected in them.

This updating and revision is a constant process and we very much value the comments of practitioners, staff and students. Legal vocational training is advancing rapidly, and it is important that all those concerned work together to achieve and maintain high standards. Please address any comments to the Bar Vocational Course Director at the Inns of Court School of Law.

With the validation of other providers for the Bar Vocational Course it is very much our intention that these manuals will be of equal value to all students wherever they take the course, and we would very much value comments from tutors and students at other validated institutions.

The enthusiasm of the publishers and their efficiency in arranging production and publication of the manuals is much appreciated.

The Hon. Mr Justice Elias
Chairman of the Advisory Board of the Institute of Law
City University, London
August 2002

CONTENTS

PREFACE

The law of evidence regulates the means by which facts may be proved in courts of law. It is for this reason that mastery of its basic principles and rules is essential to the practitioner. All too often, both before a trial and during its conduct in court, evidence law has to be applied on the spur of the moment, without the opportunity to consult books or articles. Perhaps instructions have been belatedly received. Perhaps a problem arises at the trial itself: during examination in chief, cross-examination or re-examination; when the admissibility of an item of evidence is suddenly questioned; or when it becomes necessary to deal with a judicial intervention or to make submissions about the contents of a summing-up.

This Manual, by its combination of text, materials, examples and problems, aims to develop not only a knowledge of evidence law, but also understanding of the ways in which it is applied in practice.

The law is stated on the basis that all provisions of the Youth Justice and Criminal Evidence Act 1999 are fully in force.

TABLE OF CASES

TABLE OF STATUTES

TABLE OF RULES AND REGULATIONS

ONE

INTRODUCTION

> I know a parrot who can learn the rules of evidence in half an hour and repeat them in five minutes.

That was the view of Edmund Burke at the trial of Warren Hastings. But that was in 1794. Today, over two centuries later, evidence is anything but a straightforward subject to learn. Part of the difficulty stems from the fact that it is highly integrated: individual topics are often incomprehensible without reference to some other topics which are, in turn, incomprehensible when viewed in isolation. Another difficulty is the absence of a code: evidence is a set of common-law principles interlaced with a variety of statutory provisions, a combination which often does little to promote either coherence or clarity. A third problem is that evidence has more than its fair share of seemingly irreconcilable judicial decisions. A fourth problem is that evidence, like many other parts of the law, is potentially affected by the European Convention on Human Rights. The Convention was incorporated into English law by the Human Rights Act 1998. It has already had a substantial impact on evidence law, especially in relation to reversals of the burden of proof in criminal trials, the interpretation of s. 41 of the Youth Justice and Criminal Evidence Act 1999, the right to silence, and illegally or improperly obtained evidence. On the interpretation of the Convention generally, see *Brown* v *Stott* [2001] 2 All ER 97 and *Heaney and McGuinness* v *Ireland* [2001] Crim LR 481.

Evidence cuts across the whole field of substantive law, regulating the means by which facts may be proved in courts of law. But its application is erratic. Evidence is applied to its fullest extent in criminal trials by jury in the Crown Court. It has far less impact on civil trials, where rules of exclusion have been much relaxed, and in some arbitrations and tribunals the strict rules of evidence may have no application at all.

A thorough mastery of all the basic principles of evidence is essential to the practitioner because there is rarely time to consult a book and look up rules, statutes or cases. Evidential problems can arise in court without warning and, when they do, must be resolved instantly. For example, questions put to a witness which seek to elicit inadmissible evidence require a speedy objection to prevent the witness from answering before the issue of admissibility has been considered by the court. Similarly, objections made to questions which have been put to a witness require the speedy formulation of an answer to the objection.

Evidential problems also arise in the preparation of cases and must be considered before the trial even begins. Knowing that your client has a valid claim or defence is not enough: counsel must also know how, or how best, to prove it. Witness statements in a criminal trial must be scrutinised to identify any material which is considered to be inadmissible. If that material is crucial to the prosecution case, admissibility will have to be determined as a preliminary issue immediately after the jury has been empanelled and, if the material is excluded, the prosecution may be forced to offer no evidence. In many cases, advance notice must be given to an opponent before evidence can be adduced.

Evidence also deals with the instructions that judges either may or must give to juries in criminal trials where evidence that may be misused, overrated or even underrated has been admitted. Advocates today are expected to make submissions to judges, where appropriate, about the contents of the summing-up, and knowledge of this part of evidence law is essential to do so effectively.

The materials on evidence in this Manual are designed to help students of the subject to do two things: first, to acquire a thorough knowledge of all the principles of evidence (to the level that would be expected of a barrister in the early years of practice); and secondly, to be able to apply that knowledge practically. All major areas of the subject are covered. Broadly speaking, the material is of two kinds.

(a) The first is text accompanied by authorities, including statutory materials and extracts from leading judgments and the Civil Procedure Rules. This material, originally designed for the benefit of students attending the evidence lectures at the Inns of Court School of Law, is also free-standing: in addition to summarising all the leading principles, it provides a framework for private research into a variety of subsidiary case-law and other material. In appropriate circumstances, diagrams and charts are employed; and 'transcript' is provided to show how the rules are actually used in court. One of the best ways of approaching the subject is to consider first the sorts of questions which it seeks to answer. For this reason, at the start of each chapter a series of questions is posed to alert you to the critical relevance which the law of evidence has to practice.

(b) The second is a variety of problems and questions specifically designed to ensure that you have not only acquired the relevant knowledge, but are also in a position to apply it realistically.

TWO

PRELIMINARY MATTERS

What facts, if any, have to be proved by a party to litigation?

Can such facts be established without adducing evidence?

May the other party admit such facts and, if so, how?

May a party adduce evidence of other facts from which it is possible to infer the facts which that party seeks to prove?

May you adduce evidence of facts affecting the credibility of your opponent's witnesses, that is, to show that such witnesses are not worthy of belief?

What are the types of evidence by which facts are open to proof or disproof?

What is meant by the concepts of relevance, admissibility and weight?

Does the judge have any *discretion* to admit or exclude evidence or is the judge entirely bound by rules of *law?*

Which questions, relating to the evidence, are for the judge and which for the jury?

2.1   What is Evidence?

'Evidence' can be used to refer to information presented to a court or tribunal in order that it may decide on the probability of some fact asserted before it, i.e. information by which facts tend to be proved or disproved. 'Evidence' can also be used to refer to what is said in court by a witness (e.g. 'You heard the evidence of the defendant'); to refer to a relationship between certain facts (e.g. 'His torn coat was evidence that he had been involved in a struggle'); and to refer to information that is legally admissible at a trial (e.g. 'You must not tell us what the soldier, or any other man said; it's not evidence').

2.2   The Fact-Finding Process

Approaching this subject for the first time, you would be forgiven for thinking that it is relatively straightforward: the two parties come before the court with their versions of the facts in dispute, whereupon the court embarks upon a discovery of the truth by taking into account all available evidence which is relevant. This, however, would be to make two enormous errors. First, it assumes, wrongly, that there is a scientific investigation for the discovery of the truth. Secondly, it is to ignore the fact that much of the English law of evidence comprises rules which exclude relevant evidence.

2.2.1   FACT-FINDING AND THE DISCOVERY OF THE TRUTH

A number of factors intrinsic to any fact-finding process and common to all legal systems militate against a scientific investigation of the truth.

3

(a)   The facts in question may be witnessed by no one.

(b)   The facts in question may be witnessed, but the capacity of the witnesses for accurately observing and remembering them may be weak.

(c)   The witnesses' capacity for accurate observation and recall may be strong but they may have no desire to tell the truth.

(d)   The tribunal of fact is limited to the evidence adduced by the parties to the litigation — it cannot inform itself by adducing its own evidence.

(e)   The tribunal of fact has no training in the investigation of facts.

(f)   The tribunal of fact may prefer to be at work (earning money) or at home (and, say, watching the Wimbledon semi-finals).

(g)   The parties, who are hardly impartial, decide what evidence to adduce and what evidence to withhold.

(h)   The evidence may be inadequate or inconclusive but the court must nonetheless come to a decision.

(i)   Time.

(j)   Cost.

(k)   Emotions — fact-finding is a human, and not a purely intellectual exercise.

2.2.2   EXCLUSIONARY RULES

The reasons for the mainly exclusionary nature of the English rules of evidence are partly historical and partly based on policy considerations extrinsic to the efficiency of the fact-finding process.

2.2.2.1   History
The scales used to be loaded against the defence; and the judicial desire to protect the accused resulted in the adoption, by the judiciary, of a paternalistic attitude towards the jury. At common law therefore, much evidence, the significance of which the jury may overrate, such as evidence of out-of-court statements, evidence of the accused's bad character and evidence, by non-experts, of opinion (as opposed to fact), is inadmissible. The exclusionary mentality has been further nurtured by a near-obsessional fear, on the part of the English judiciary, of the deliberate manufacture of evidence by parties and their witnesses.

2.2.2.2   Policy
Policies extrinsic to the efficiency of the fact-finding process, when accommodated by the law, result in the exclusion of relevant evidence.

(a)   Relevant evidence may be excluded if its disclosure would be injurious or prejudicial to the public interest (national defence, good diplomatic relations etc.): see **14.3**.

(b)   The client of a lawyer has a privilege not to reveal communications between himself and his lawyer, the policy being to encourage full and frank communication in the obtaining and giving of legal advice see **14.2**.

In order to understand the law of evidence, it is necessary to begin with a number of preliminary matters of general importance. First, what are the facts which may be proved or disproved in an English court?

2.3 Facts Open to Proof or Disproof

Under English law the facts open to proof (or disproof) are facts in issue, relevant facts and collateral facts.

2.3.1 FACTS IN ISSUE IN CRIMINAL CASES

Facts in issue in criminal cases are those which it is necessary for the prosecution to prove if it is to succeed in the prosecution together with those which it is necessary for the defence to prove if it is to succeed in the defence.

In *R v Sims* [1946] KB 531, CCA, Lord Goddard CJ said (at p. 539):

> Whenever there is a plea of not guilty, everything is in issue and the prosecution has to prove the whole of their case including the identity of the accused, the nature of the act and the existence of any necessary knowledge or intent.

Evidence which can directly establish a fact in issue is often referred to as direct evidence (as opposed to circumstantial evidence — see **2.3.5**).

2.3.2 FACTS IN ISSUE IN CIVIL CASES

Facts in issue in civil proceedings should be identifiable from the statements of case, the whole point of which is to set out the parties' allegations, admissions and denials so that before the trial everyone knows exactly what essential matters are left in dispute and therefore open to proof or disproof.

Under Civil Procedure Rules 1998 (CPR), r. 16.4(1), particulars of claim must include a concise statement of the facts on which the claimant relies. Rule 16.5(1) states:

> *In his defence, the defendant must state—*
> *(a) which of the allegations in the particulars of claim he denies;*
> *(b) which allegations he is unable to admit or deny, but which he requires the claimant to prove; and*
> *(c) which allegations he admits.*

As a general rule, a defendant who fails to deal with an allegation shall be taken to admit it: r. 16.5(5).

As in criminal cases, evidence which can directly establish a fact in issue in a civil case is often referred to as direct evidence — see **2.3.5**).

2.3.3 FORMAL ADMISSIONS

A fact which is formally admitted ceases to be in issue. Evidence to prove such a fact is neither required nor allowed.

2.3.3.1 Civil cases

CPR, r. 14.1, provides as follows:

> *(1) A party may admit the truth of the whole or any part of another party's case.*
> *(2) He may do this by giving notice in writing (such as in a statement of case or by letter).*
> *. . .*
> *(5) The court may allow a party to amend or withdraw an admission.*

In civil proceedings, therefore, a fact may be formally admitted in a variety of ways. In addition to an express admission in a defendant's defence (see r. 16.5(1)(c), above at **2.3.2**), a fact may be admitted by default, i.e. by a defendant failing to deal, in the defence, with an allegation made by a claimant (see r. 16.5(5) above at **2.3.2**), or by either party in response to a notice to admit facts (see r. 32.18) or in response to a written request, or court order, to give additional information (see rr. 18.1 and 26.5(3) and PD 18).

As to admissions before or at the trial by the parties or their representatives, see *Ellis* v *Allen* [1914] 1 Ch 904 (an admission in a letter written by a legal adviser), *Urquhart* v *Butterfield* (1887) 37 ChD 357, CA (an admission at the trial itself) and *H. Clark (Doncaster) Ltd* v *Wilkinson* [1965] Ch 694, CA (an admission in interlocutory proceedings).

2.3.3.2 Criminal cases

A plea of guilty obviously amounts to an admission of the offence charged, but it is *not* an admission of the facts stated in the depositions: *R* v *Riley* (1896) 18 Cox CC 285.

Criminal Justice Act 1967, s. 10, provides as follows:

(1) *Subject to the provisions of this section, any fact of which oral evidence may be given in any criminal proceedings may be admitted for the purpose of those proceedings by or on behalf of the prosecutor or defendant, and the admission by any party of any such fact under this section shall as against that party be conclusive evidence in those proceedings of the fact admitted.*

(2) *An admission under this section—*

(a) *may be made before or at the proceedings;*

(b) *if made otherwise than in court, shall be in writing;*

(c) *if made in writing by an individual, shall purport to be signed by the person making it and, if so made by a body corporate, shall purport to be signed by a director or manager, or the secretary or clerk, or some other similar officer of the body corporate;*

(d) *if made on behalf of a defendant who is an individual, shall be made by his counsel or solicitor;*

(e) *if made at any stage before the trial by a defendant who is an individual, must be approved by his counsel or solicitor (whether at the time it was made or subsequently) before or at the proceedings in question.*

(3) *An admission under this section for the purpose of proceedings relating to any matter shall be treated as an admission for the purpose of any subsequent criminal proceedings relating to that matter (including any appeal or retrial).*

(4) *An admission under this section may with the leave of the court be withdrawn in the proceedings for the purpose of which it is made or any subsequent criminal proceedings relating to the same matter.*

The phrase 'any fact of which oral evidence may be given in any criminal proceedings' in subsection (1) makes it clear that s. 10 cannot be used to admit evidence which would otherwise be excluded because, for example, irrelevant, or inadmissible opinion, or hearsay: *R* v *Coulson* [1997] Crim LR 886, CA.

2.3.4 JUDICIAL NOTICE

No evidence is required to establish facts that are judicially noticed.

2.3.4.1 Judicial notice without enquiry

In both criminal and civil proceedings, a court may take judicial notice of a fact if it is so notorious or of such common knowledge as to be beyond serious dispute, in which case the tribunal of fact may then be directed to treat it as having been established despite the absence of proof. Celebrated examples include the following: *R* v *Luffe* (1807) 8 East 193 (two weeks is too short a period for human gestation); *Huth* v *Huth* [1915] 3 KB 32 (a postcard is the sort of document which anyone might read); and *Nye* v *Niblett* [1918] 1 KB 23 (cats are ordinarily kept for domestic purposes).

Foreign law, usually being a question of fact (see **2.9.4.4**) is not generally the subject of judicial notice, but there are exceptions in the case of the common law of Northern Ireland (*Re Nesbitt* (1884) 14 LJMC 30) and Scots law in civil cases, of which judicial notice may be taken by the House of Lords.

Judicial notice of some facts is expressly required by statute. For example, evidence is not generally required to prove the contents of Acts of Parliament or that they were passed by both Houses of Parliament: see Interpretation Act 1978, ss. 3, 22(1) and sch. 2, para. 2, whereby every Act passed after 1850 is a public Act and to be judicially noticed as such unless the Act makes express provision to the contrary. (At common law, judicial notice is taken of public Acts passed before 1851.)

See also European Communities Act 1972, s. 3(2): judicial notice is to be taken of the European Community Treaties, the Official Journal of the Communities and decisions of the European Court.

2.3.4.2 Judicial notice after enquiry

Facts which are neither notorious nor of common knowledge may also be judicially noticed, after enquiry, i.e. after the judge has consulted sources such as learned works, authoritative reference books or even the oral statements of witnesses. The enquiry, however, is not proof by evidence in the ordinary sense because (a) the rules of evidence do not apply (b) evidence to rebut the judge's findings is not admissible and (c) the judge's decision is usually treated as a binding legal precedent.

In *McQuaker* v *Goddard* [1940] 1 KB 687, CA the question arose whether camels are wild or domestic animals. The judge consulted books and listened to expert evidence on oath concerning the behaviour of camels. The Court of Appeal, upholding the judge's decision that camels are domestic animals, held that judicial notice could be taken of the matter and that the evidence received was not evidence in the ordinary sense but was tendered to assist the judge in forming a view.

Less exotic and more typical examples are when a judge refers to a diary to determine on what day of the week a certain date fell, or when a judge refers to an authoritative atlas to determine the latitude and longitude of a certain place. Judicial notice after enquiry has also frequently been taken of facts of a political nature. For example, in *R* v *Bottrill, ex parte Kuechenmeister* [1947] 1 KB 41 the Court of Appeal, accepting as conclusive a certificate of the Foreign Secretary that the country was still at war with Germany, judicially noticed that fact. See also *Duff Development Co.* v *Government of Kelantan* [1924] AC 797 (that Kelantan was an independent State and the Sultan its sovereign ruler) and *Engelke* v *Musmann* [1928] AC 433, HL (membership of the staff of the German ambassador).

2.3.5 RELEVANT FACTS

Relevant facts are those that tend to prove or disprove, either directly or circumstantially, facts in issue. Classic examples of direct evidence include:

(a) testimony by a witness about his own perception of a fact in issue, for example, that he saw the defendant stab the deceased;

(b) the production to the court of some object, the existence of which is in issue, for example, a lease or a policy of insurance.

Circumstantial evidence does not involve the immediate perception of the existence of a fact in issue, but is evidence from which the existence of a fact in issue can be inferred.

Classic examples of circumstantial evidence include:

(a) evidence of opportunity, i.e. evidence of presence at the time and place of the acts in question;

(b) certain varieties of evidence of identity, for example expert evidence that samples taken from an accused's body or clothing match samples found at the scene of the crime or on the victim;

(c) evidence of facts providing a motive for a person to have done a particular act (because relevant to the likelihood that he or she did indeed perform that act); and

(d) evidence of a person's plans to do a particular act (because relevant to the question whether he or she did subsequently perform that act).

As to adverse inferences that may be drawn from the words, conduct or silence of the accused (for example, lies told, refusal without good cause to allow an intimate body sample to be taken, failure to mention facts when charged, and failure to give evidence or to call witnesses), see generally **Chapter 11**.

In *Teper* v *R* [1952] AC 480, PC Lord Normand said:

Circumstantial evidence must always be narrowly examined.

However, see also *R* v *Exall* (1866) 4 F & F 922 *per* Pollock CB at p. 929:

It has been said that circumstantial evidence is to be considered as a chain, and each piece of evidence as a link in the chain, but that is not so, for then, if any one link broke, the chain would fall. It is more like the case of a rope composed of several cords. One strand of the cord might be insufficient to sustain the weight, but three stranded together may be of quite sufficient strength.

Thus it may be in circumstantial evidence — there may be a combination of circumstances, no one of which would raise a reasonable conviction, or more than a mere suspicion; but the three, taken together, may create a conclusion of guilt with as much certainty as human affairs can require or admit of.

2.3.6 COLLATERAL FACTS

Collateral facts are not relevant to the existence of facts in issue, but are relevant to one of the following matters:

(a) The credibility of a witness. Evidence of bias, for example, will be relevant to credibility. See *Thomas* v *David* (1836) 7 C & P 350, where the witness was the mistress of the party for whom she was testifying. Whether evidence is relevant to credibility alone, or also to a fact in issue, may be difficult to determine. See **5.2.4.3**.

(b) Legal ability to testify (the 'competence' of a witness). For example, whether a child satisfies the conditions set out in Youth Justice and Criminal Evidence Act 1999, s. 53(3). See **4.1.2.3**.

(c) Whether a pre-condition for admitting an item of evidence has been satisfied. For example, under Police and Criminal Evidence Act 1984, s. 76(2)(a), whether a confession by a defendant may have been obtained by oppression. See **10.1.2**. This type of collateral fact is sometimes referred to as a 'preliminary' fact.

2.4 Types of Judicial Evidence

The types of evidence by which facts are open to proof or disproof are known collectively as judicial evidence. The principal labels given to the varieties of judicial evidence are as follows.

2.4.1 TESTIMONY

Testimony means the statements of a witness made orally in court and presented as evidence of the truth of what he or she states.

2.4.2 DIRECT TESTIMONY

Direct testimony means the statements of a witness about a fact of which he or she has or claims to have direct, personal or first-hand knowledge.

2.4.3 HEARSAY

Hearsay means any statement, other than one made by a witness in the course of giving his/her evidence, offered as evidence of the truth of its contents.

The rule against hearsay is complex — see **Chapter 8**.

2.4.4 ORIGINAL EVIDENCE

Original evidence means evidence of an out-of-court statement tendered for any relevant purpose other than that of proving the truth of the facts contained in it, e.g. simply to prove that the statement was made or to prove the state of mind of its maker — see **Chapter 8**.

2.4.5 REAL EVIDENCE

Real evidence usually takes the form of a material object produced for inspection by the court, either to prove that the object in question exists, or to enable the court to draw an inference from its own observation as to its physical condition or value.

2.4.6 DOCUMENTARY EVIDENCE

Documentary evidence consists of documents produced for inspection by the court, either as items of real evidence or as hearsay or original evidence.

2.4.7 PRIMARY EVIDENCE

Primary evidence means evidence of the best or highest kind, applied, e.g., to the original of a document.

2.4.8 SECONDARY EVIDENCE

Secondary evidence is evidence of an inferior kind, applied, e.g., to a copy of a document or a copy of such a copy.

2.5 Relevance

The most fundamental and important rule of the English law of evidence is that all evidence of facts in issue and all evidence which is sufficiently relevant to prove or disprove facts in issue is admissible *unless* one or more of the exclusionary rules applies or the evidence in question is excluded as a matter of discretion.

According to art. 1 of Stephen's *Digest of the Law of Evidence*, 'relevance' means that:

Any two facts to which it is applied are so related to each other that according to the common course of events one either taken by itself or in connection with other facts proves or renders probable the past, present or future existence or non-existence of the other.

In *DPP* v *Kilbourne* [1973] AC 729, Lord Simon said (at p. 756):

Evidence is relevant if it is logically probative or disprobative of some matter which requires proof. It is sufficient to say, even at the risk of etymological tautology, that relevant (i.e. logically probative or disprobative) evidence is evidence which makes the matter which requires proof more or less probable.

For the importance of generalisations in constructing arguments about relevance, see *R* v *Bracewell* (1978) 68 Cr App R 44.

In *Beresford* v *St Albans Justices* (1905) 22 TLR 1, it was held that evidence of a driver's speed at a particular point in time was relevant to the issue of the speed at which that driver was driving a few moments later. The question, however, is one of degree: the evidence would not be relevant if what was in issue was the speed at which the driver was driving an hour earlier or an hour later.

In cases where it is necessary to decide whether certain conduct complies with an objective standard of behaviour, is it relevant to know how others would have behaved in the same or similar circumstances? In *Noble* v *Kennoway* (1780) 2 Doug KB 510 the issue was whether underwriters were entitled to repudiate liability on the insurance of a ship's cargo because of unreasonable delay in discharging it in Labrador. The plaintiffs asserted that there was a practice of delaying the discharge of cargo in certain circumstances and it was held that they could call evidence of such a practice in the Newfoundland trade because it was relevant to show that a similar practice existed in Labrador. Buller J was of the opinion that if it could be shown that the time of the delay would have been reasonable in Newfoundland, that was of some relevance in showing that it was reasonable in Labrador.

Turning to examples of what has been rejected as insufficiently relevant, in *Hart* v *Lancashire & Yorkshire Railway Co.* (1869) 21 LT 261, a negligence action, the fact that the company, after the accident, had altered and improved its practice concerning the method of changing the points, was held to be irrelevant to the question whether the accident was caused by the Company's negligence. In *Hollingham* v *Head* (1858) 27 LJ CP 241, where the defendant sought to show that a contract was made on certain special terms and wanted to call witnesses to show that the plaintiff had entered into contracts with other customers which contained such special terms, the Court of Common Pleas held such evidence to be irrelevant: it afforded no reasonable inference as to the terms of the contract in dispute.

In *R* v *Blastland* [1986] AC 41, the accused, B, was charged with the buggery and murder of a boy. At the trial, B admitted that he had met the boy and had engaged in homosexual activity, but said that when he had seen another man nearby, who might have witnessed what he had done, he panicked and ran away. B's description of the other man corresponded closely to M, and B said that M must have committed the offences charged. At the trial, the prosecution made formal admissions (see **2.3.3.2**). Some of the admissions related to M's movements on the night in question and others showed that M had been investigated by the police after the murder and that M was known to have engaged in homosexual activities in the past with adults. B wanted to call a number of witnesses to say that before the victim's body had been found M had said to them that a boy had been murdered. The trial judge held this to be inadmissible and B was convicted. In the House of Lords, B submitted that although the statements made by M were inadmissible hearsay if tendered for the truth of any fact stated, they were admissible as original evidence to prove the state of mind of their maker, i.e. to show M's knowledge of the murder before the body had been found. Lord Bridge held that original evidence of this kind was admissible only if relevant. The issue at the trial, his lordship said, was whether B had committed the offences and what was relevant to that was not M's knowledge, but how he had come by it. Since he might have done so in a number of different ways, there was no rational basis on which the jury could infer what the source of that knowledge was or conclude that M and not B was the offender. On that basis, it was held that the evidence had been properly rejected, because it was irrelevant.

The House of Lords took a similarly strict and equally controversial stance in *R* v *Kearley* [1992] 2 AC 228, holding that in a trial for possession of drugs with intent to supply, evidence of telephone calls and visits to the flat in which the callers asked to speak to the accused and asked for drugs was irrelevant to the issue of whether the accused intended to supply drugs. *R* v *Keast* [1998] Crim LR 748, CA, provides another example of what may be criticised as an unduly strict approach. In that case it was held that unless there is some concrete basis for regarding the out-of-court demeanour and state of mind of a victim of sexual abuse as confirming or disproving the occurrence of such abuse, it cannot assist a jury bringing their common-sense to bear on who is telling the truth. See also *R* v *Akram* [1995] Crim LR 50, CA.

In *Hui Chi-ming* v *R* [1992] 1 AC 34, the Privy Council held that where two criminal trials arise out of the same transaction, evidence of the outcome of the first is *generally* irrelevant to the issues in the second. See also *R* v *H* (1989) 90 Cr App R 440, CA and *R* v *Hudson* [1994] Crim LR 920, CA.

The question of relevance has given rise to particular problems in cases of possession of drugs with intent to supply. This is because very often evidence which is relevant to the issue of intent to supply will be highly prejudicial, as when it also indicates past dealing or dealing generally — as we shall see (**Chapter 6**), evidence which tends to show that the accused is disposed to commit the kind of offence with which he is charged is generally inadmissible to prove the offence charged.

In *R* v *Batt* [1994] Crim LR 592, for example, the Court of Appeal held that evidence of the discovery of £150 in the accused's house was inadmissible on the grounds that it had nothing to do with intent to supply in the future the drugs actually found, but had a highly prejudicial effect as evidence of propensity to supply generally. However, it seems that the case has not laid down a general rule that evidence of possession of money is never admissible on a charge of possession with intent to supply (see *R* v *Morris* [1995] 2 Cr App R 69, CA and *R* v *Nicholas* [1995] Crim LR 942, CA). It has also been suggested that the case should be regarded as confined to its own facts, bearing in mind that £150 is too small a sum to be the hallmark of present and active drug dealing (see *R* v *Okusanya* [1995] Crim LR 941, CA). In *R* v *Wright* [1994] Crim LR 55, CA, it was held that drug traders need to keep by them large sums of cash and therefore evidence of the discovery of £16,000 could have given rise to an inference of dealing and tended to show that the drugs found were for supply, an approach which was followed in *R* v *Gordon* [1995] Crim LR 142, CA. In *R* v *Grant* [1996] 1 Cr App R 73, CA, it was held that the jury should be directed to regard the finding of the money as relevant only if they reject any innocent explanation for it put forward by the accused; and that if they conclude that the money indicates an ongoing dealing in drugs, they may take account of the finding of it, together with the drugs, in deciding the issue of intent to supply. It is also particularly important, in cases in which the evidence is admitted, to direct the jury clearly that they must not treat it as evidence of propensity: see *R* v *Simms* [1995] Crim LR 304, CA.

According to some authorities, where possession of drugs is in issue, evidence of the possession of money or drugs paraphernalia can never be relevant to that issue (see *R* v *Halpin* [1996] Crim LR 112, CA and *R* v *Richards* [1997] Crim LR 499, CA). In *R* v *Guney* [1998] 2 Cr App R 242, the Court of Appeal declined to follow these authorities. It was held that although evidence of possession of a large sum of cash or enjoyment of a wealthy lifestyle does not, on its own, prove possession, there are numerous sets of circumstances in which it may be relevant to that issue, not least to the issue of knowledge as an ingredient of possession. The real issue in the case was whether G was knowingly in possession of nearly five kilos of heroin or whether it had been 'planted', the defence having conceded that if possession were to be proved, then it would be open to the jury to infer intent to supply. It was held that in all the circumstances, evidence of the finding of nearly £25,000 in cash in the wardrobe of G's bedroom and in close proximity to the drugs, was relevant to the issue of possession. *Guney* was applied in *R* v *Griffiths* [1998] Crim LR 567, CA. See also *R* v *Edwards* [1998] Crim LR 207, CA, where it was said that in some cases it would be contrary to common sense for the jury to be told to ignore evidence of the possession of money or drugs paraphernalia in relation to possession and it would be preferable for them to look at the overall picture and to draw such inferences as seemed proper. Thus it was said that where an accused is shown to be conducting a flourishing business as a drugs dealer, it may be reasonable to infer that he has knowledge of and control over drugs found at his premises, although such evidence would not be conclusive and there may be other evidence showing that such an inference should not be drawn or that it is unsafe to draw it. See also *R* v *Scott* [1996] Crim LR 652, CA. In that case, intent to supply could be inferred from the quantity of drugs found; either Scott or his co-accused was in possession of the drugs, or both of them were; and they conducted cut-throat defences. It was held that the co-accused was entitled to rely on evidence of Scott's possession of money and drug paraphernalia, as affecting Scott's credibility.

2.6 Admissibility

The admissibility of evidence is a question of law for the judge. Evidence, as we have seen, must be sufficiently relevant to be admissible, but it does not follow from this that all sufficiently relevant evidence is admissible. An item of relevant evidence is not admissible if it is excluded by any of the exclusionary rules of evidence or if it is excluded by the judge in the exercise of his or her discretion. Thus if an exclusionary rule does apply, it matters not how relevant, or indeed how cogent and reliable, the item of evidence in question may be: it will be inadmissible. The exclusionary rules are based on considerations other than relevance. The principal exclusionary rules relate to:

(a) the incompetence of certain witnesses — see **Chapter 4**;

(b) evidence of previous consistent statements — see **Chapter 5**;

(c) evidence of the accused's previous convictions, bad character or disposition towards wrongdoing — see **Chapters 6 and 7**;

(d) hearsay — see **Chapter 8**;

(e) non-expert opinion evidence — see **Chapter 13**;

(f) evidence privileged from disclosure — see **Chapter 14**; and

(g) evidence withheld as a matter of public policy — see **Chapter 14**.

2.6.1 MULTIPLE ADMISSIBILITY

If an item of evidence is, under the rules of evidence, admissible for one purpose but inadmissible for another, it remains admissible for the former purpose. The principle is referred to, somewhat inappropriately, as 'multiple admissibility'. For example, a confession which implicates both its maker and a co-accused is admissible for the truth of its contents as against its maker (by way of exception to the hearsay rule), but is no evidence against the co-accused.

2.6.2 CONDITIONAL ADMISSIBILITY

Sometimes an item of evidence by itself appears to be irrelevant, but in conjunction with another item of evidence can be shown to be relevant. If the other item has yet to be admitted, the judge will admit the first item on the undertaking of counsel to show its relevance at a later stage, failing which the tribunal of fact will be directed to ignore it. The evidence is said to be admitted conditionally or *de bene esse*.

2.7 Weight

The weight of evidence is its quality, cogency or probative value in relation to the facts in issue. Like relevance, it is a question of degree and a notion dependent on common sense. In determining the weight of evidence, one may take into account a multiplicity of factors including:

(a) other evidence given in the case;

(b) the fact that a party has failed to bring to court the best available evidence but has instead relied on inferior evidence;

(c) in the case of testimony, the demeanour, credibility and plausibility of witnesses;

(d) in the case of documentary evidence, authenticity.

Statute may also make provision as to the relevant factors to be taken into account in assessing the weight to be attached to specific types of evidence. See, for example, in the case of civil hearsay, Civil Evidence Act 1995, **Chapter 9**.

The fact that evidence may be of varying degrees of cogency has led to more labels.

'Insufficient evidence' means evidence which is adduced by a party to prove a particular fact but which, even if uncontradicted, is so weak that it could not justify a finding on that fact in that party's favour — see **2.9.3**.

'Prima facie evidence' is usually used to refer to evidence of a fact which is sufficiently weighty to entitle but not to require a reasonable person to find in a party's favour on that fact.

'Conclusive evidence' means evidence which is conclusive in relation to a fact in issue: the court cannot hear contradictory evidence, but must find the fact in question to have been established.

Weight must be distinguished from admissibility: the former is a question of fact for the jury or tribunal of fact, the latter a question of law for the judge. It does not follow, however, that the judge in a criminal trial can ignore the weight of the evidence. He or she must form an opinion on the weight of the evidence for a variety of different purposes:

(a) in deciding whether preliminary facts have been established as part of his or her general function to decide all questions of admissibility — see **2.3.6**;

(b) in commenting to the jury on the weight of the evidence; and

(c) in deciding whether to withdraw an issue from the jury or to uphold a submission of no case to answer — see **2.9.3**.

2.7.1 THE BEST EVIDENCE RULE

This exclusionary rule, which operates to prevent the admissibility of evidence where better evidence is to hand, is now virtually defunct. See *Omychund* v *Barker* (1745) 1 Atk 21.

The only remaining instance of the rule is that a party seeking to rely on the contents of a document must rely on primary evidence, secondary evidence being admissible only exceptionally: *Kajala* v *Noble* (1982) 75 Cr App R 149, DC. See also *R* v *Governor of Pentonville Prison, ex parte Osman* [1989] 3 All ER 701, QBD at p. 728.

For a rare example of the application of the best evidence rule in modern times, see *Greenaway* v *Homelea Fittings (London) Ltd* [1985] 1 WLR 234.

2.8 Discretion

2.8.1 INCLUSIONARY DISCRETION

There is no judicial discretion to include evidence that is relevant, but legally inadmissible. See, e.g., *Sparks* v *R* [1964] AC 964, PC, where the Privy Council held that highly relevant evidence of identification had been properly excluded because it was inadmissible hearsay, and *Myers* v *DPP* [1965] AC 1001, HL (both at **8.3**). But see also *R* v *Ward, The Times*, 2 February 2001, CA.

2.8.2 EXCLUSIONARY DISCRETION

An exclusionary discretion is a power to exclude as a matter of discretion evidence which is admissible as a matter of law.

2.8.2.1 Civil cases

Prior to the introduction of the Civil Procedure Rules, there was some authority to suggest that the judge had a discretionary power to allow a witness to refuse to reveal information where (a) its disclosure would be a breach of some ethical or social value, e.g. a confidence between a doctor and patient, priest and penitent or banker and customer, and (b) its non-disclosure would be unlikely to cause serious injustice: see *per* Donovan LJ in *Attorney-General* v *Mulholland* [1963] 2 QB 477, CA. However, in *D* v *National Society for the Prevention of Cruelty to Children* [1978] AC 171, HL, two members of the House of Lords took the view that although the judge can certainly exercise moral pressure to stop the questioning, when it comes to the forensic crunch, the judge had no such discretion.

CPR, r. 32.1(2), has introduced a general exclusionary discretion in civil cases. Rule 32.1 provides as follows:

> (1) The court may control the evidence by giving directions as to—
> (a) the issues on which it requires evidence;
> (b) the nature of the evidence which it requires to decide those issues; and
> (c) the way in which the evidence is to be placed before the court.
> (2) The court may use its power under this rule to exclude evidence that would otherwise be admissible.
> (3) The court may limit cross-examination.

When the court decides to exercise its power to exclude evidence under r. 32.1(2), then as when exercising any other power given to it by the rules, it must seek to give effect to their 'overriding objective' (see r. 1.2), which is to enable the court 'to deal with cases justly' (see r. 1.1(1)). Rule 1.1(2) provides as follows:

> (2) Dealing with a case justly includes, so far as is practicable—
> (a) ensuring that the parties are on an equal footing;
> (b) saving expense;
> (c) dealing with the case in ways which are proportionate—
> (i) to the amount of money involved;
> (ii) to the importance of the case;
> (iii) to the complexity of the issues; and
> (iv) to the financial position of each party;
> (d) ensuring that it is dealt with expeditiously and fairly; and
> (e) allotting to it an appropriate share of the court's resources, while taking into account the need to allot resources to other cases.

It is submitted that it would be undesirable, and probably of little real assistance, for the courts to go beyond the wording of r. 1.1(2) itself, with a view to providing additional general guidance as to the way in which the discretion under r. 32.1(2) should be exercised, because circumstances vary infinitely. For the same reason, it would seem that exercise of the discretion is only likely to be impugned on appeal if perverse in the *Wednesbury* sense (*Associated Provincial Picture Houses Ltd* v *Wednesbury Corp.* [1948] 1 KB 223), i.e. where the court reaches a decision which no reasonable court could have reached.

2.8.2.2 Criminal cases

In criminal cases, both under statute and at common law the trial judge has a discretion to exclude legally admissible evidence tendered by the prosecution. On the common law discretion, see *R* v *Sang* [1980] AC 402 where it was held that:

(a) a trial judge, as part of his or her duty to ensure that an accused receives a fair trial, always has a discretion to exclude evidence tendered by the prosecution if, in his or her opinion, its prejudicial effect outweighs its probative value; but

(b) save with regard to admissions and confessions and generally with regard to evidence obtained from the accused after the commission of the offence, the judge has no discretion to exclude relevant admissible evidence on the ground that it was obtained by improper or unfair means.

The remainder of this section of this chapter is concerned with (a), the 'fair trial' discretion. Concerning (b), the discretion to exclude prosecution evidence obtained by improper or unfair means, see **Chapter 10**.

At first sight, the test for exercising the 'fair trial' discretion may seem confusing: after all, all prosecution evidence, if relevant, will be likely to be prejudicial to the defence case, and therein lies its probative value. In a sense, therefore, the more prejudicial, the more probative it is likely to be. The test, however, requires us to envisage cases where the evidence is admissible in law, perhaps only technically, but is of minimal probative value, of little cogency, of dubious reliability, or such that there is a real risk that it will confuse the jury or prevent them, once they have heard it, from taking a dispassionate view of the other evidence in the case: see *per* Roskill J in *R* v *List* [1966] 1 WLR 9 at 12.

In *R* v *Sang* it was held that the 'fair trial' discretion is of general application and not to be confined to a closed list of specific types of otherwise admissible evidence.

It is difficult to raise a successful appeal against a judge's refusal to exercise the 'fair trial' discretion. This is because exercise of the discretion is essentially unpredictable, being a subjective matter in which much turns on the facts of the particular case. In *Selvey* v *DPP* [1970] AC 304, HL, Lord Guest said that it was inevitable, in the case of a discretion, that its exercise might be whimsical and depend upon the individual idiosyncrasies of the judge. To minimise this unpredictability, the appellate courts have from time to time, and in a number of different contexts, laid down guidelines for exercise of the discretion. The Court of Appeal will also interfere where there is no material upon which the trial judge could properly have arrived at his or her decision or where he or she has 'erred in principle'.

The 'fair trial' discretion can be used to exclude evidence tendered by the prosecution but not evidence tendered by any co-accused. In *Lobban* v *R* [1995] 2 All ER 602, the Privy Council approved the following description of this principle as described in Keane, *The Modern Law of Evidence*, 3rd edn:

> There is no discretion to exclude, at the request of one co-accused, evidence tendered by another. Thus although . . . there is a discretion to exclude similar fact evidence tendered by the prosecution, such evidence, when tendered by an accused to show the misconduct on another occasion of a co-accused is, if relevant to the defence of the accused, admissible whether or not it prejudices the co-accused. (See *per* Devlin J in *R* v *Miller* [1952] 2 All ER 667 (Winchester Assizes), approved in *R* v *Neale* (1977) 65 Cr App R 304, CA.) Similarly, there is no discretion to prevent an accused from cross-examining a co-accused about his previous convictions and bad character when, as a matter of law, he becomes entitled to do so pursuant to [s. 1(3)(iii)], Criminal Evidence Act 1898, i.e. where the co-accused has 'given evidence against' the accused, because, it is said, the accused, in seeking to defend himself, should not be fettered in any way. (See *Murdoch* v *Taylor* [1965] AC 574, HL.)

In *Lobban* v *R* itself it was held, on the basis of this principle, that the judge has no discretionary power, at the request of one co-accused, either (a) to exclude the exculpatory part of a 'mixed' statement (i.e. partly exculpatory and partly inculpatory — see **5.1.4.2**) on which another co-accused intends to rely, or (b) to edit out the exculpatory parts of such a statement. L and R were charged with three murders. R made a 'mixed' statement. The exculpatory part of the statement implicated L by name. The prosecution tendered R's statement, for the truth of its contents, against R. L argued that the trial judge should have used his discretion to edit R's statement to exclude the parts implicating L. The Privy Council held that no such discretion existed. The discretionary power applies only to evidence on which the prosecution proposes to rely; and although R's statement was tendered by the prosecution, it supported R's defence and could not be used by the prosecution as evidence against L. But see also *per* Evans LJ in *R* v *Thompson* [1995] 2 Cr App R 589, CA, at pp. 596–7.

In addition to the common-law discretion but of more practical importance (through more widespread usage), is the statutory discretion. The Police and Criminal Evidence Act 1984, s. 78, provides that:

> (1) *In any proceedings the court may refuse to allow evidence on which the prosecution proposes to rely to be given if it appears to the court that, having regard to all the circumstances, including the circumstances in which the evidence was obtained, the admission of the evidence would have such an adverse effect on the fairness of the proceedings that the court ought not to admit it.*
> (2) *Nothing in this section shall prejudice any rules of law requiring a court to exclude evidence.*
> (3) *This section shall not apply in the case of proceedings before a magistrates' court inquiring into an offence as examining justices.*

Note that this section applies to evidence on which the prosecution *proposes* to rely. Thus it cannot be relied on once the evidence has been given. In those circumstances the defence will have to rely on the common law discretion preserved by s. 82(3) of the 1984 Act. See *R* v *Sat-Bhambra* (1989) 88 Cr App R 55.

From its wording, it is clear that this section overlaps with the common-law discretion. One example of evidence which would have 'an adverse effect on the fairness of the proceedings' would be evidence the prejudicial effect of which outweighs its probative value.

Thus s. 78 is not concerned exclusively with police misconduct, but embraces circumstances which need not involve any improper conduct (whether on the part of the police or anyone else): see *R* v *Brine* [1992] Crim LR 122, CA.

However, s. 78 clearly goes beyond such cases; and *may* be relied upon when it is sought to exclude prosecution evidence obtained by illegal or improper means. In *R* v *Quinn* [1990] Crim LR 581 Lord Lane CJ said:

> The function of the judge is . . . *to protect the fairness of the proceedings*, and normally proceedings are fair if a jury hears *all* relevant evidence which either side wishes to place before it, but proceedings may become unfair if, for example, one side is allowed to adduce relevant evidence which, for one reason or another, the other side cannot properly challenge or meet, or where there has been an abuse of process, e.g. because evidence has been obtained in deliberate breach of procedures laid down in an official code of practice.

The effectiveness of s. 78 to exclude evidence obtained by improper means where those means have not affected the reliability of the evidence was put in doubt in *R* v *Chalkley and Jeffries* [1998] 2 All ER 155. But this decision is at odds with other appellate decisions. See Choo, A, and Nash, S, 'What's the matter with section 78?' [1999] Crim LR 929. Several speeches in *R* v *Looseley* [2001] 4 All ER 897 suggest a wider scope for s. 78; see especially Lord Hoffmann, p. 909.

A judge's exercise of the s. 78 discretion can only be challenged on appeal if it is perverse according to the principles of *Associated Provincial Picture Houses Ltd* v *Wednesbury Corp.* [1948] 1 KB 223, i.e. a decision which no reasonable trial judge could have reached, in which case the Court of Appeal will exercise the discretion itself: see *R* v *O'Leary* (1988) 87 Cr App R 387, CA at p. 391; *R* v *Christou* [1992] 1 QB 979, CA; *R* v *Dures* [1997] Crim LR 673, CA; and *R* v *Khan* [1997] Crim LR 508, CA.

The main importance of s. 78, the use to which it can be put in excluding confessions, evidence obtained by illegal, improper or unfair means, and identification evidence, is considered in **Chapters 10 and 12**.

2.9 Functions of Judge and Jury

The general rule is that legal questions are for the judge, factual questions for the jury.

2.9.1   QUESTIONS OF LAW

Apart from resolving questions of substantive law and directing the jury on this in the summing up, issues of law for the judge include:

(a)   whether a witness is competent to give evidence;

(b)   whether evidence is admissible;

(c)   the sufficiency of evidence (see below); and

(d)   in the summing-up, directing the jury on a variety of evidential points including, e.g. that law is for him or her and facts for them and that the burden of proof is on this or that party and must be satisfied to this or that standard of proof. As to the special directions that are called for in (i) cases involving corroboration and (ii) cases depending wholly or substantially on the correctness of identification(s) of the accused which the defence alleges to be mistaken, see **Chapter 12**.

In *R* v *Jackson* [1992] Crim LR 214, the Court of Appeal commended the following specimen direction of the Judicial Studies Board on the respective functions of judge and jury.

It is my job to tell you what the law is and how to apply it to the issues of fact that you have to decide and to remind you of the important evidence on these issues. As to the law, you must accept what I tell you. As to the facts, you alone are the judges. It is for you to decide what evidence you accept and what evidence you reject or of which you are unsure. If I appear to have a view of the evidence or of the facts with which you do not agree, reject my view. If I mention or emphasise evidence that you regard as unimportant disregard that evidence. If I do not mention what you regard as important, follow your own view and take that evidence into account.

Note that as in the case of other specimen directions, this one may require adaptation to meet the precise circumstances of the particular case.

In *R* v *O'Donnell* (1917) 12 Cr App R 219, the judge told the jury that the accused's story was 'remarkable', but the conviction was upheld. In *R* v *Canny* (1945) 30 Cr App R 143, however, where the judge kept on telling the jury that the defence was 'absurd', the conviction was quashed. See also *R* v *Winn-Pope* [1996] Crim LR 521, CA. In *R* v *Harris* [1986] Crim LR 123, the Court of Appeal held that judges should not make comments placing police witnesses in any special category or leading the jury to think that there will be adverse consequences for them if a verdict of not guilty is returned. See also *R* v *Culbertson* (1970) 54 Cr App R 311, *R* v *Gale* [1994] Crim LR 208, CA, and *Mears* v *R* [1993] 1 WLR 818, PC (where the comments were weighted against the accused). In *R* v *Iroegbu, The Times*, 2 August 1988, the Court of Appeal said that a judge should not express his own views about whether a witness has told the truth or not.

In *R* v *Donoghue* (1987) 86 Cr App R 267, the Court of Appeal held that it would be helpful if prosecuting counsel made a checklist of the directions on the law which they considered the trial judge ought to give and drew the attention of the judge to any failure on his part to give an essential direction *before* the jury retired. In *R* v *L, The Times*, 9 February 2001, the Court of Appeal said that in a criminal trial both prosecution and defence counsel have a duty to assist the judge by drawing attention to inadequate or inaccurate directions to the jury in the summing-up.

The Court of Appeal has frequently said that counsel have a duty to make submissions, whether or not invited to do so by the judge, about directions to be given in the summing-up where there is room for argument about the form they should take. See, e.g., *R* v *Higgins, The Times*, 11 August 1995.

Note that although a judge can direct a jury to acquit when there is no evidence which could justify a conviction, in *DPP* v *Stonehouse* [1978] AC 55, the House of Lords held that in the converse situation, i.e. where, on the facts, a reasonable jury properly directed on the law should convict, the judge must not direct the jury to convict, because the issues of fact are still for them.

2.9.2 PRELIMINARY FACTS AND THE *VOIR DIRE*

Preliminary facts (facts to be proved as a condition precedent to the admissibility of certain kinds of evidence) are decided by the judge in a hearing on the *voir dire* (or 'trial within a trial'). A trial within a trial is called a hearing on the *voir dire* because the witnesses give their evidence on a special form of oath known as the *voir dire*. (See further **Advocacy Manual**, **Chapter 22**.)

The jury will be asked to retire because it is almost impossible to discuss the admissibility of evidence in their presence without revealing to them the very nature of the evidence to which objection is made. Such evidence may be prejudicial to the accused, or indeed prosecution, but, in the event, ruled inadmissible. The modern practice therefore, is to ask the jury to retire whenever there is a risk of their being exposed to evidence which may be ruled inadmissible or which, in any event, is likely to prejudice the accused: see *R* v *Deakin* [1994] 4 All ER 769, CA. When the jury has returned, the judge should give no explanations of what has taken place to them (*Mitchell* v *R* [1998] AC 695, PC).

2.9.2.1 Example

The prosecution propose to adduce in evidence a confession made by the accused. The accused has told counsel for the defence that he only confessed to the police because at the time, his head, which the investigating officer was bringing into repeated and noisy contact with the wall of the police cell, was beginning to hurt. In these circumstances, before the start of the trial defence counsel would tell counsel for the prosecution that at the trial a defence submission will be made that the confession is inadmissible because it was obtained by oppression (see **10.1.2**, especially **10.1.2.1**). Counsel for the prosecution will then be duty bound to make no reference to the confession in his or her opening speech. When it gets to the stage when otherwise counsel for the prosecution would have called the officer in question to give evidence of the confession, he or she will instead request a hearing on the *voir dire*. The jury will not be told the precise nature and purpose of the application. The dialogue, for example, could take the following form.

> Prosecution counsel: Your honour, I understand that my learned friend wishes, at this stage, to make a representation on a question of law which need not concern the jury.

> Judge: Yes, I see. Members of the jury, it seems that a matter of law has arisen with which you need not be concerned. This would be a convenient time, therefore, for you to retire to your room and take a break.

> Defence counsel (after the jury have retired): Your honour, the prosecution wishes to adduce evidence of a confession made by the accused which the defence says is inadmissible because obtained by oppression . . .

Witnesses will then be called, examined and cross-examined before counsel make their respective submissions on the admissibility of the confession. If the judge decides that the confession is inadmissible, no more will be heard of it — the jury will return to court and be none the wiser. If the judge rules that the confession is admissible, once the jury return to court the prosecution will proceed by calling the officer to give evidence of the confession.

2.9.2.2 Competence of a witness in criminal cases

When a judge considers that there should be an investigation into a witness's competence under Youth Justice and Criminal Evidence Act 1999, s. 54, it should be conducted in open court in the presence of the accused but *not* the jury. The jury's function is to assess the witness's evidence after he or she has been found competent to give it. The exercise of determining competence is not a necessary aid to that function. Equally, the evidence of a psychologist or other expert witness on the competence of a witness should be heard on a *voir dire* in the absence of the jury: s. 54(5).

2.9.2.3 Magistrates

The function of the *voir dire* is to allow the arbiter of law to decide a point of law in the absence of the arbiter of fact. In the magistrates' court, of course, the magistrates decide both law and fact. Concerning the appropriateness of a *voir dire* in a magistrates' court, in *F* v *Chief Constable of Kent* [1982] Crim LR 682, the Divisional Court held that:

(a) magistrates may hear evidence on the preliminary facts and then decide on admissibility but, if they decide to admit the evidence in question, it need not be repeated because they have already heard it (whereas in the Crown Court, of course, the evidence would need to be repeated in the presence of the jury); and

(b) it is impossible to lay down any general rule as to when a question of admissibility should be decided or as to when the magistrates should give their decision on it, because every case is different.

This approach was adoped in *R* v *Epping and Ongar Justices, ex parte Manby* [1986] Crim LR 555, DC. The accused contested the admissibility of certain documentary evidence and wanted the question resolved as a preliminary issue. The magistrates refused and admitted the evidence as providing a prima facie case for the accused to deal with later, if he saw fit. It was held that the justices had not erred — within statutory constraints, they must determine their own procedure. In *Vel* v *Chief Constable of North Wales* [1987] Crim LR 496, the Divisional Court held that Police and Criminal Evidence Act 1984, s. 78, is *not* a statutory constraint for these purposes. Further guidance has been provided by *Halawa* v *Federation Against Copyright Theft* [1995] 1 Cr App R 21, DC. In that case it was held that:

(a) the duty of a magistrate on an application under s. 78 is either to deal with it when it arises or to leave the decision until the end of the hearing, the objective being to secure a trial that is fair and just to both sides;

(b) in some cases there will be a trial within a trial in which the accused is given the opportunity to exclude the evidence before he or she is required to give evidence on the main issues, but in most cases the better course will be for the whole of the prosecution case to be heard, including the disputed evidence, before any trial within a trial is held; and

(c) in order to decide, the court may ask the accused the extent of the issues to be covered by his or her evidence in the trial within a trial. A trial within a trial may be appropriate if the issues are limited, but not if it is likely to be protracted and to raise issues which will be re-examined when the trial itself resumes.

However, s. 76(2) of the 1984 Act, whereby the defence may represent to the court that a confession made by the accused should be excluded (see **10.1.2**), is a statutory constraint. In *R* v *Liverpool Juvenile Court, ex parte R* [1988] QB 1, DC, it was held that in these circumstances, the magistrates must hold a *voir dire*, in which the accused is entitled to give evidence, and must make a ruling on admissibility at or before the end of the prosecution case. An alternative contention based on s. 78 should also be examined in the same *voir dire* at the same time: *Halawa* v *Federation Against Copyright Theft*.

2.9.3 THE SUFFICIENCY OF EVIDENCE

Questions of sufficiency of evidence (i.e. whether a party has adduced sufficient evidence to justify a finding on a particular fact in that party's favour) are for the judge.

Where a party bears what is known as an evidential burden in relation to a particular fact in issue — see **3.1.2** — that party has to be able to show that there is *sufficient* evidence of that fact, i.e. such evidence as *could* result in a favourable finding by the tribunal of fact. If the evidence is insufficient, the matter cannot even be submitted to the jury but is withdrawn from them.

2.9.3.1 Example

The accused is charged with wounding with intent to do grievous bodily harm. His defence is self-defence. The accused will bear the evidential burden in relation to the issue of self-defence (see **3.3**). If the defence cannot point to sufficient evidence of self-defence, the judge will withdraw that issue from the jury and direct them that it is not an issue in the case. If the defence is able to point to sufficient evidence of self-defence to make that a live issue, the prosecution must rebut that defence beyond reasonable doubt before there can be a conviction.

2.9.3.2 No case to answer

The prosecution usually bears the evidential burden in respect of all the ingredients of the offence and therefore if it adduces insufficient evidence on any one of the ingredients, it will necessarily fail in the whole case and the judge will direct the jury to acquit. In a Crown Court trial, the question of sufficiency of evidence may be raised by the defence, after the prosecution has adduced its evidence, in what is known as a submission of no case to answer. The submission should be made in the absence of the jury and, if the trial proceeds, should not be referred to by the judge in his or her summing up: *R* v *Smith & Doe* (1987) 85 Cr App R 197, CA. If the judge rules in favour of the submission (a) on some but not all charges or (b) in respect of some accused but not others, the jury need only be told that the decision was taken for legal reasons, because any further explanation risks potential injustice: *Crosdale* v *R* [1995] 2 All ER 500, PC.

In *R* v *Galbraith* [1981] 1 WLR 1039, the Court of Appeal held that:

> (1) If there is no evidence that the crime alleged has been committed by the defendant there is no difficulty — the judge will stop the case. (2) The difficulty arises where there is some evidence but it is of a tenuous character, for example, because of inherent weakness or vagueness or because it is inconsistent with other evidence: (a) where the judge concludes that the prosecution evidence, taken at its highest is such that a jury properly directed could not properly convict on it, it is his duty on a submission being made to stop the case; (b) where, however, the prosecution evidence is such that its strength or weakness depends on the view to be taken of a witness's reliability or other matters which are generally speaking within the jury's province and where on one possible view of the facts there is evidence on which the jury could properly conclude that the defendant is guilty, then the judge should allow the matter to be tried by the jury.

See also *R* v *Cockley* (1984) 79 Cr App R 181, CA.

Under *Practice Direction* [1962] 1 WLR 227, DC, as a matter of practice justices should be guided by the following considerations:

> A submission that there is no case to answer may properly be made and upheld: (a) when there has been no evidence to prove an essential element in the alleged offence: (b) when the evidence adduced by the prosecution has been so discredited as a result of cross-examination or is so manifestly unreliable that no reasonable tribunal could safely convict on it.

For a useful case on the sufficiency of evidence, see *Chief Constable of Avon & Somerset* v *Jest* [1986] RTR 372, DC: the fact that a print from the accused's left thumb was found on the internal rearview mirror of a car was insufficient evidence of possession of the vehicle to found a case of taking and driving away.

In civil cases tried with a jury, the rule is that the judge has a discretion to rule on a submission of no case to answer without requiring the party who makes it to elect whether to call evidence: *Young* v *Rank* [1950] 2 KB 510.

See also *Payne v Harrison* [1961] 2 QB 403, CA.

2.9.4 SPECIAL CASES

In a number of special cases, questions of fact are decided, either wholly or in part, by the judge.

2.9.4.1 The meaning of words

In *Brutus v Cozens* [1973] AC 854, HL, the appellant, during the annual tennis tournament at Wimbledon, went on to court number two while a match was in progress, blew a whistle and threw leaflets around. When he blew the whistle, nine or ten others invaded the court with banners and placards. The appellant then sat down and had to be forcibly removed. Charged with using insulting behaviour whereby a breach of the peace was likely to be occasioned under the Public Order Act 1936, the magistrates dismissed the information on the grounds that the behaviour was not insulting. On appeal by case stated, the question was whether the decision was *legally* correct. The Divisional Court ruled against the appellant but the House of Lords allowed his appeal. Lord Reid held that although the proper construction of a statute was a question of law, the meaning of an ordinary word of the English language like 'insulting' was a question of fact. His Lordship envisaged two exceptional cases where the meaning of a word would be a question of law:

(a) where the context shows that the word is used in an unusual sense, in which case the judge must decide what that unusual sense is; and

(b) where, the tribunal of fact having decided that the words in question do apply to the facts proved, it is argued on appeal that their decision was perverse in the sense that no tribunal acquainted with the ordinary use of language could possibly have reached that decision.

See e.g. *R v Feely* [1973] QB 530, CA: the word 'dishonestly' used in the Theft Act 1968, s. 1(1) is an ordinary word in common use and therefore entirely a question of fact for the jury.

Subsequently, however, both the Court of Appeal and the House of Lords have reached decisions involving elaborate legal definition of ordinary words without reference to *Brutus v Cozens*. This has prompted one commentator to observe that *Brutus v Cozens*, after a mute inglorious career of 15 years or so, seems to have come to an ignominious end (see Professor D. W. Elliott [1989] Crim LR 323).

2.9.4.2 Defamation

In criminal proceedings for libel and also, as a result of the House of Lords decision in *Nevill v Fine Arts & General Insurance Co. Ltd* [1897] AC 68, in civil libel proceedings, it is for the judge to decide whether the document in question is capable of bearing the defamatory meaning alleged and for the jury to decide whether it does in fact bear that meaning and is, therefore, a libel.

2.9.4.3 Perjury

Under Perjury Act, 1911, s. 1(1), a person commits the offence of perjury if, while lawfully sworn as a witness or interpreter in a judicial proceeding, he or she wilfully makes a statement 'material' in that proceeding which he or she knows to be false or does not believe to be true. Section 11(6) of the same Act provides that: 'The question whether a statement on which perjury is assigned was material is a question of law to be determined by the court of trial'.

2.9.4.4 Foreign law

Questions of foreign law are issues of fact calling for evidence. Prior to 1920, foreign law, like other questions of fact, was decided by the jury. The Administration of Justice Act 1920, s. 15, provides that:

Where, for the purpose of disposing of any action or other matter which is being tried by a judge with a jury in any court in England or Wales, it is necessary to ascertain the law of any other country which is applicable to the facts of the case, any question as to the effect of the evidence given with respect to that law shall, instead of being submitted to the jury, be decided by the judge alone.

Section 15 applies only to criminal proceedings, but the position is similar in relation to civil proceedings in both the High Court and county courts: see Supreme Court Act 1981, s. 69(5), and County Courts Act 1984, s. 68.

2.9.4.5   Reasonableness

Subject to minor exceptions, questions of reasonableness are questions of fact for the jury. For one such exception, see *Herniman* v *Smith* [1938] AC 305, HL: in an action for malicious prosecution, it is for the jury to decide whether the prosecutor took reasonable care to inform himself or herself of the true state of the case and honestly believed in the charge, but for the judge, on the basis of the jury's findings, to decide whether those facts amount to 'reasonable and probable cause' for the prosecution.

Questions

OBJECTIVES

This chapter is designed to ensure that you have a sound understanding of:

(a)   the basic terminology of the law of evidence;

(b)   the facts that are open to proof or disproof under English law;

(c)   the distinction between the concepts of relevance, admissibility and weight;

(d)   the division of functions between the judge and jury; and

(e)   the discretion to exclude evidence (apart from evidence obtained by illegal or unfair means).

Question 1, part 1

Alan Smith has been charged with the theft of a bottle of claret from Walter's Wine Warehouse, Hackney. He intends to plead not guilty. The prosecution proposes to call, among others, Mrs Edwina Walter, the owner of the Warehouse, WPC Duncan, Mr Hughes and Inspector Jenkins.

The following are extracts from the witness statement made by Mrs Walter:

In late April 2001, I had an argument with a customer, Alan Smith, who claimed that I had short-changed him. I denied this. He became very angry and started swearing. He insisted that I was mistaken and said that I would live to regret it . . . Mr Smith has been back in the Warehouse many times since then and I suspect that he has been up to no good . . . My takings have been considerably lower than normal in the three months of May, June and July 2001. At about 1.20 p.m. on 7 August 2001, I saw Mr Smith enter the Warehouse. He was wearing a baggy brown coat. He went to the far end of the shop where we keep our best claret. He bent down behind some wine crates, out of my line of vision, then got up and hurriedly left the shop. Later that day, WPC Duncan showed me a bottle of claret priced £17.50 which I identified as having come from the Warehouse. She also asked me for a till roll to see if it showed the sale of any item priced £17.50. It did not.

WPC Duncan, in her witness statement, says:

I was passing the Warehouse at about 1.25 p.m. on 7 August when a man wearing a large brown trenchcoat emerged. He looked startled to see me and rushed off. I followed him. He kept looking over his shoulder and then ran off. I ran after him. He turned into Cambridge Passage but by the time I got to the Passage, he had disappeared. I inspected some dustbins there and inside one of them I found a bottle of claret bearing a small price sticker bearing the words 'Walter's Wine Warehouse', and a price, £17.50 . . . At 4.15 p.m. I arrested and cautioned Alan Smith. He was still wearing the trenchcoat. I subsequently discovered inside the coat there was a false pocket, inexpertly stitched by hand, and measuring some 12 inches by 8 inches.

The statement of Mr Hughes, a suitably qualified expert, is to the effect that the bottle found by WPC Duncan bears fingerprints matching those taken from Alan Smith.

The statement of Inspector Jenkins relates to three interviews with Alan Smith at the police station. The third interview concludes as follows:

Q.   Come on Al, don't waste any more of our time.

A.   OK. OK. My hands are up. It was me. I took the bloody wine. That's what you thugs want to hear isn't it. Now lay off.

Alan Smith proposes to testify that he was, at the time of the alleged offence, with Mr Evans, whom he intends to call, at the Slug and Lettuce public house, Islington. He will say that Mrs Walter is lying because he once caught her out short-changing him, and proposes to cross-examine her about that and about the fact that she is blind in one eye and short-sighted in the other. He will also say that he confessed to the crime because Inspector Jenkins, exasperated by his constant denials in all three interviews, had threatened to punch him where it would hurt: a confession seemed the only way to prevent this from happening.

(a)   What are the facts in issue in this case?

(b)   Of the facts which the parties are proposing to prove, which, if any, may be referred to as being:

(i)   collateral; and

(ii)   preliminary?

(c)   What direct (as opposed to circumstantial) evidence is there of the offence charged?

(d)   Of the evidence which the parties propose to adduce, which items, if any:

(i)   are properly classified as:

(1)   hearsay (whether or not admissible hearsay);

(2)   original evidence; and

(3)   circumstantial evidence; and

(ii)   will be ruled inadmissible because irrelevant?

(e)   What real evidence, if any, would you advise the parties to adduce?

(f)   Which items of evidence, if any, require a *voir dire* to determine their admissibility?

Question 1, part 2
Alan Smith was convicted of theft. The following are extracts from the summing-up of the trial judge:

At the end of the prosecution case, I rejected the defence submission that there was no case to answer as being entirely without foundation. So now it falls to you, members of the jury, to decide whether the accused is guilty or not . . . Another vital element that the prosecution must prove is dishonesty and we all know what that is, it's knavery, deceitfulness or fraud . . . And so we come to the testimony of Inspector Jenkins. Do you really think that he would jeopardise his long and distinguished career by threatening to beat up a suspect? Bear in mind, if you will, that that is the likely result if you decide to reject his account of how the confession came to be made . . . And what did you make of the evidence of Mr Evans? He contradicted himself more than once about the precise times at which the accused arrived at and left the public house. Did he not strike you as somewhat hesitant and unconvincing? I would not believe him but that is not to the point because this is not a matter for me but a question of fact entirely for you.

Draw up a list of the grounds on which Mr Smith may appeal.

Question 2

(a) Ian is charged with indecently assaulting John, a boy of 13. The prosecution is able to prove that Ian is a homosexual.

   Is this evidence relevant?

   Give reasons for your answer.

(b) Kevin is charged with the rape of Linda. The prosecution is able to prove that Kevin is a heterosexual.

   Is this evidence relevant?

   Give reasons for your answer.

(c) Michael is charged with burglary. The prosecution is able to prove that he has ten previous convictions for burglary.

Is this evidence relevant?

Give reasons for your answer.

THREE

BURDEN AND STANDARD OF PROOF AND PRESUMPTIONS

Which party has the obligation to prove which facts (the burden of proof)?

If a party bears such a burden, what degree of cogency or persuasiveness is required of the evidence adduced by that party before the burden is discharged (the standard of proof)?

Are the answers to the above two questions the same in civil and criminal cases?

What is the position at a trial within a trial?

When can the court treat a fact as having been proved notwithstanding that no evidence or insufficient evidence has been adduced to establish it (presumptions)?

3.1 Burden of Proof

The question for consideration here is simply this: which party has the obligation to prove which facts in issue? The answer is not quite so simple and calls for a distinction to be drawn between two different burdens, the legal and evidential.

3.1.1 LEGAL BURDEN

The legal burden is the obligation on a party to prove a fact in issue. Whether the burden has been discharged is decided at the end of the trial by the tribunal of fact.

The legal burden is also known as the burden of proof, the persuasive burden, the probative burden, the ultimate burden, the burden of proof on the pleadings (i.e. the statements of case), or the risk of non-persuasion.

3.1.2 EVIDENTIAL BURDEN

The term 'evidential burden' can be misleading because it is capable of suggesting that it is some sort of burden of *proof*. It is not. It is best seen as a rule of common sense, which says that for a particular issue to be a live one in a trial, there must be *some* evidence to support it.

3.2 Incidence of the Legal Burden

Which party bears the legal burden on which facts in issue?

3.2.1 CIVIL CASES

The general rule is that the legal burden on any fact in issue is borne by the party asserting and not denying: he who asserts must prove, not he who denies. For example,

C claims that he was injured by D's negligent driving. It will be for C to prove that D's driving fell below the standard of the reasonably prudent driver in a way that caused the injury, and not for D to show that he was not driving negligently. The incidence of the legal burden is usually clear from the statements of case. See *Wilsher* v *Essex Area Health Authority* [1988] AC 1074, HL.

3.2.1.1 Statute

The incidence of the legal burden may be fixed by statute. For example, if, in proceedings referred to in s. 139(1) of the Consumer Credit Act 1974, the debtor or any surety alleges that the credit bargain is extortionate, it is for the creditor to prove the contrary: s. 171(7), *ibid*. See *Coldunell Ltd* v *Gallon* [1986] QB 1184, CA; 1 WLR 994, HL.

3.2.1.2 Contract and insurance policy cases

In contract cases, which party bears the legal burden on a certain issue may be fixed by the express terms of the contract. Questions of construction have arisen in contracts of insurance and contracts for the carriage of goods but the authorities are not entirely clear. For example, if the defendant relies on an exemption clause in a contract, does he or she have to show that the facts come within it or does the claimant have to show that they do not? Examples from case law illustrate the problem. In *Hurst* v *Evans* [1917] 1 KB 352, a policy of insurance insured against loss of or damage to jewellery 'arising from any cause whatsoever . . . except breakage . . . and save and except loss by theft or dishonesty committed by . . . any servant . . . in the exclusive employment of the assured'. During a robbery, jewellery was taken and damaged. The defendant insurance company claimed that the loss was caused by the theft or dishonesty of a named servant in the exclusive employment of the plaintiff. At trial, the question arose as to whether the defendant had to prove the dishonesty or theft by the employee or whether the plaintiff had to negative the dishonesty. Lush J held that the burden lay on the plaintiff to show that the lost goods were covered by the policy, and that the loss was one against which the defendant had agreed to indemnify the plaintiff (i.e. that the loss was not committed by the dishonesty of his employee). To hold that the burden was on the defendant, on the facts of the case, would be to 'produce absurd results' (*per* Lush J). In reaching this decision the judge took into account pleading practice relating to marine insurance policies, but did not regard himself as bound by any authority from not expressing his own views on the question.

One of the cases mentioned by Lush J was *The Glendarroch* [1894] P 226. The plaintiffs sued for damage to goods shipped on *The Glendarroch*. No bill of lading had been signed, but the contract was treated as if it were covered by the terms of an ordinary bill of lading, which contained a number of exceptions to liability, including one relating to losses caused by perils of the sea. The defendant shippers claimed that the cargo was damaged as a result of perils of the sea, but the plaintiffs alleged that that peril only arose as a result of negligent navigation. The Court of Appeal held that a term should be implied (by necessary inference) into the bill of lading that the peril of the sea should not have been occasioned by negligence of the shippers. But on whom should the burden of proving negligence lie? Should the plaintiffs have to prove that the peril of the sea was negligently brought about, or should the defendants have to prove that they were not negligent? Lord Esher MR held that the term relating to negligence should be read as an exception to the list of exceptions, so that the term would read 'Except if the loss is by perils of the sea, unless or except that loss is the result of the negligence of the servants of the owner'. It was therefore for the plaintiffs to prove the contract and the non-delivery, the defendants to bring the case within the ordinary meaning of the exception relating to perils of the sea, but for the plaintiffs to make out the second exception relating to the negligence of the defendants. In reaching this decision, Lord Esher relied on the way pleadings relating to bills of lading had been treated over time.

In *Munro, Brice & Co.* v *War Risks Association Ltd* [1918] 2 KB 78, a marine insurance policy against loss by perils of the sea contained a clause excepting loss by capture, seizure, and consequences of hostilities. The insured ship left port and was never heard of again. Bailhache J found that the disappearance of the ship did bring it within perils of the sea, but the question arose as to whether the assured had to show that the loss was not caused by one of the excepted reasons. Reviewing a number of authorities, including *Hurst* v *Evans*, it was held that it was for the assured to show the loss at sea, but for the underwriters to show that the loss came within the exceptions.

It may often be difficult to decide on the allocation of the burden of proof in cases not covered directly by express contractual terms, statute or binding authority: the allocation will often depend on the individual circumstances of any case, and the application of policy (see **3.2.1.4** below).

3.2.1.3 Negative assertions

He who asserts must prove. This remains the case even if the assertion is negative: see *Abrath* v *North Eastern Railways Co.* (1883) 11 QBD 440, CA; affirmed (1886) 11 App Cas 247, HL; *Pickford* v *ICI* [1998] 3 All ER 462, HL.

Sometimes a party may try to avoid a legal burden by so drafting his statement of case as to make assertions of his own look like assertions of his opponent. Consider *Soward* v *Leggatt* (1856) 7 C & P 613.

(a) A landlord claimed that his tenant 'did not repair' the premises.

(b) The tenant claimed that he 'did well and sufficiently repair'.

(c) Abinger CB held that the landlord could as easily have pleaded that the defendant tenant 'allowed the house to become dilapidated'. The landlord was alleging that the defendant had broken the covenant and therefore had to prove it.

3.2.1.4 Policy

In many cases it is difficult to know whether facts in issue are essential to the case of one party or to that of his or her opponent. In these cases, the courts have tended to put the legal burden on the party who would be expected to find its discharge least difficult.

In *Joseph Constantine Steamship Line Ltd* v *Imperial Smelting Corpn Ltd* [1942] AC 154, HL, the issue was the incidence of the legal burden of proving fault when frustration is pleaded by way of defence to an action on a contract. Charterers of a ship claimed damages from the owners for failure to load. The defence was frustration of the contract by destruction of the ship by explosion. On the evidence, the cause of the explosion was unclear.

The charterers' submission: the owners cannot rely on frustration unless they, the owners, can show that the explosion was not caused by fault on their part (i.e. on the part of the owners).

The owners' counter-submission: we can rely on frustration unless the charterers can show that the explosion was caused by our fault.

It was held that when frustration is pleaded as a defence, the claimant must prove the defendant's fault.

Compare this decision with the following bailment cases.

Coldman v *Hill* [1919] 1 KB 443, CA: it is for the bailee to prove that loss or damage was not caused by his or her fault.

Brook's Wharf & Bull Wharf Ltd v *Goodman Brothers* [1937] 1 KB 534, CA: it is for the bailee to prove that loss or damage was not caused by his or her negligence.

Levison v *Patent Carpet Cleaning Co. Ltd* [1977] 3 WLR 90, CA: it is for the bailee to prove that loss or damage was not caused by his or her fundamental breach.

See also *Amos* v *Hughes* (1835) 1 Mood & R 464.

3.2.2 CRIMINAL CASES

3.2.2.1 The general rule

The general rule is that the prosecution has the burden of proving the guilt of the accused. The rule applies to both negative and positive assertions. See *R* v *Horn* (1912) 7 Cr App R 200 and *R* v *Donovan* [1934] 2 KB 498 (absence of consent on charges of rape or assault). The burden is also on the prosecution to disprove a defence of mistaken belief in consent: *R* v *Thomas* (1983) 77 Cr App R 63 at p. 65 and *R* v *Gardiner* [1994] Crim LR 455, CA.

In *Woolmington* v *DPP* [1935] AC 462, W was convicted of the murder of his wife by shooting. W's wife had left him, and W claimed that he had gone to where she lived intending to kill himself if she refused to come back to him. He said that it was as he was showing her the gun with which he meant to shoot himself that it went off, and that he did not know it was pointing at his wife. The trial judge directed the jury that once it was shown that someone died through the act of another, it was presumed to be murder, unless the person who caused the death could satisfy the jury that what happened was manslaughter, an accident, or justifiable. The House of Lords held this to be a misdirection, and quashed the conviction.

Lord Sankey LC said at p. 481:

> Throughout the web of the English criminal law one golden thread is always to be seen, that it is the duty of the prosecution to prove the prisoner's guilt subject to what I have already said as to the defence of insanity and subject also to any statutory exception . . . No matter what the charge or where the trial, the principle that the prosecution must prove the guilt of the prisoner is part of the common law of England and no attempt to whittle it down can be entertained.

3.2.2.2 Exceptions

Insanity

See *M'Naghten's Case* (1843) 10 Cl & F 200, HL. See also *R* v *Burns* (1973) 58 Cr App R 364, CA.

Express statutory exceptions

Express statutory exceptions have traditionally involved the use of phrases of the following kind:

'unless the contrary is proved',

'unless the accused proves', and

'the proof whereof shall lie on the accused'.

Criminal Justice Act 1988, s. 139, provides that:

> *(1) Subject to subsections (4) and (5) below, any person who has an article to which this section applies with him in a public place shall be guilty of an offence.*
> . . .
> *(4) It shall be a defence for a person charged with an offence under this section to prove that he had good reason or lawful authority for having the article with him in a public place.*

The Misuse of Drugs Act 1971 creates a number of offences. Section 28(2) of the Act provides that it is a defence for the accused to prove that he neither knew of nor suspected nor had reason to suspect the existence of some fact alleged by the prosecution and which it is necessary for the prosecution to prove to secure a conviction.

Another example is provided by the Prevention of Terrorism (Temporary Provisions) Act 1989, s. 10(1):

> *A person is guilty of an offence if he—*
> *(c)   enters into or is otherwise concerned in an arrangement whereby money or other property is or is to be made available for the benefit of . . . [a proscribed] organisation.*

Section 10(2) provides that:

> *. . . in proceedings against a person for an offence under subsection 1(c) above it is a defence to prove that he did not know and had no reasonable cause to suspect that the arrangement related to a proscribed organisation.*

By Article 6(2) of the European Convention on Human Rights:

> *Everyone charged with a criminal offence shall be presumed innocent until proved guilty according to law.*

The impact of this provision on reverse burdens in criminal trials was considered by the House of Lords in *R* v *DPP, ex parte Kebilene* [2000] 1 Cr App R 275 (see particularly the speech of Lord Hope at pp. 321–33). In *R* v *Lambert* [2001] 3 All ER 577 the House of Lords rejected the accepted interpretation of the Misuse of Drugs Act 1971, s. 28(2), and, relying on the Human Rights Act 1998, s. 3(1), held that the section imposed only an evidential burden on defendants. (For the distinction between legal and evidential burdens, see **3.3** below.) The effect of this decision is to raise doubts about other provisions that until now have been thought to impose a legal burden on defendants. See further *Lynch* v *DPP* [2001] EWHC Admin 882, where the Divisional Court considered the Criminal Justice Act 1988, s. 139 in the light of the Human Rights Act 1998 and confirmed that it imposed a legal burden on defendants. Cf *R* v *Carass, The Times*, 21 January 2002, interpreting the Insolvency Act 1986, s. 206(1)(a).

Implied statutory exceptions, i.e. statutes creating offences subject to exceptions, provisos etc.
Implied statutory exceptions involve the use of phrases of the following kind:

'. . . without lawful authority or excuse',

'. . . provided that', and

'. . . other than'.

Magistrates' Courts Act 1980, s. 101 (formerly Magistrates' Courts Act 1952, s. 81):

> *Where the defendant to an information or complaint relies for his defence on any exception, exemption, proviso, excuse or qualification, whether or not it accompanies the description of the offence or matter of complaint in the enactment creating the offence or on which the complaint is founded, the burden of proving the exception, exemption, proviso, excuse or qualification shall be on him: and this notwithstanding that the information or complaint contains an allegation negativing the exception, exemption, proviso, excuse or qualification.*

A commonly given example of an implied statutory exception is the offence of driving a vehicle on a road without being the holder of a current driving licence.

Sometimes this statutory provision occasions difficulty. Consider, for example, the following sections of the Factories Act 1961:

(a)   s. 155(1): it is an offence not to comply with s. 29(1); and

(b)   s. 29(1): any workplace 'shall, so far as is reasonably practicable be made and kept safe for any person working therein'.

Is the phrase 'so far as is reasonably practicable' an excuse or qualification? If so, the accused employer has to prove it was not reasonably practicable to keep the premises safe. If not, the prosecution has to prove it was reasonably practicable to keep the premises safe. See *Nimmo* v *Alexander Cowan & Sons Ltd* [1968] AC 107, a Scottish case, in which the House of Lords, by a majority, took the former view.

On its wording, s. 101 is confined to summary trials. For the position at trials on indictment, see *R* v *Edwards* [1975] QB 27. E had been convicted of selling intoxicating liquor without a justices' licence. On appeal it was argued that at trial the prosecution did not call evidence to show that there was no justices' licence in force and the burden was not on E to prove that he possessed one. Lawton LJ, giving the judgment of the Court of Appeal dismissing the appeal, reviewed a number of authorities and said, at pp. 39–40:

> In our judgment this line of authority establishes that over the centuries the common law, as a result of experience and the need to ensure that justice is done both to the community and to defendants, has evolved an exception to the fundamental rule of our criminal law that the prosecution must prove every element of the offence charged. This exception, like so much else in the common law, was hammered out on the anvil of pleading. It is limited to offences arising under enactments which prohibit the doing of an act save in specified circumstances or by persons of specified classes or with specified qualifications or with the licence or permission of specified authorities. Whenever the prosecution seeks to rely on this exception, the court must construe the enactment under which the charge is laid. If the true construction is that the enactment prohibits the doing of acts, subject to provisos, exemptions and the like, then the prosecution can rely upon the exception.

> In our judgment its application does not depend upon either the fact, or the presumption, that the defendant has peculiar knowledge enabling him to prove the positive of any negative averment. . . . Two consequences follow. . . . First, as it comes into operation upon an enactment being construed in a particular way, there is no need for the prosecution to prove a prima facie case of lack of excuse, qualification or the like; and secondly, what shifts is the onus: it is for the defendant to prove that he was entitled to do the prohibited act. . . . When the exception as we have adjudged it to be is applied to this case it was for the defendant to prove that he was the holder of a justices' licence, not the prosecution.

See also the following examples pre-dating *R* v *Edwards:*

R v *Scott* (1921) 86 JP 69 (selling cocaine without a licence);

R v *Oliver* [1944] KB 68 (dealing in sugar without a licence); and

R v *Ewens* [1967] 1 QB 322 (possessing drugs without a prescription).

The merits of the decision in *Edwards* are debatable. One good consequence of the decision is that the test is now the same in summary trials and trials on indictment — there is, after all, no good reason why there should be a difference. On the other hand, it is the view of some that the accused should never bear more than an evidential burden. If the accused merely bears the evidential burden, and discharges it, the judge will direct the jury that the prosecution bears the legal burden of disproving the particular defence in question and must satisfy the jury in that respect beyond resonable doubt. If the accused bears the legal burden, the judge directs the jury that it is for the accused to prove the defence on a balance of probabilities. Thus in a case like *R* v *Champ* (1981) 73 Cr App R 367, CA, where the only issue was guilty knowledge, the judge would be entitled to say to the jury: 'If you are unable to conclude that the defence case is more probable than not, you must convict.'.

Since *R* v *Edwards* there has been a further and important development, the decision of the House of Lords in *R* v *Hunt* [1987] AC 352 concerning the following statutory provisions.

(a) Misuse of Drugs Act 1971, s. 5, provides that subject to any regulations under s. 7, it is an offence for a person to have a controlled drug in his possession.

(b) A controlled drug is defined by the Act to include a preparation or other product containing morphine.

(c) The Misuse of Drug Regulations 1973 provide that s. 5 shall have no effect in relation to, *inter alia*, any preparation of morphine containing not more than 0.2% of morphine.

When the matter came before the House of Lords, Lord Griffiths, at p. 374, said:

> I would summarise the position thus far by saying that *Woolmington* did not lay down a rule that the burden of proving a statutory defence only lay on the defendant if the statute specifically so provided: that a statute can, on its true construction, place a burden of proof on the defendant although it does not do so expressly and that if a burden of proof is placed on the defendant it is the same burden whether the case be tried summarily or on indictment, namely a burden that has to be discharged on the balance of probabilities.
>
> The real difficulty in these cases lies in determining on whom Parliament intended to place the burden of proof when the statute has not expressly so provided. It presents particularly difficult problems of construction when what might be regarded as a matter of defence appears in a clause creating the offence rather than in some subsequent proviso from which it may more readily be inferred that it was intended to provide for a separate defence which a defendant must set up and prove if he wishes to avail himself of it. This difficulty was acutely demonstrated in *Nimmo v Alexander Cowan* ... their Lordships were in agreement that if the linguistic construction of the statute did not clearly indicate on whom the burden should lie the court should look to other considerations to determine the intention of Parliament, such as the mischief at which the Act was aimed and practical considerations affecting the burden of proof and, in particular, the ease or difficulty that the respective parties would encounter in discharging the burden. I regard this last consideration as one of great importance, for surely Parliament can never lightly be taken to have intended to impose an onerous duty on a defendant to prove his innocence in a criminal case, and a court should be very slow to draw any such inference from the language of a statute.

Considering the case of *R v Edwards*, Lord Griffiths said, at pp. 375–6:

> In *R v Edwards* [1975] QB 27, 39–40, the Court of Appeal expressed their conclusion in the form of an exception to what they said was the fundamental rule of our criminal law that the prosecution must prove every element of the offence charged. They said that the exception 'is limited to offences arising under enactments which prohibit the doing of an act save in specified circumstances or by persons of specified classes or with specified qualifications or with the licence or permission of specified authorities.' I have little doubt that the occasions upon which a statute will be construed as imposing a burden of proof upon a defendant which do not fall within this formulation are likely to be exceedingly rare. But I find it difficult to fit *Nimmo v Alexander Cowan & Sons Ltd* [1968] AC 107 into this formula, and I would prefer to adopt the formula as an excellent guide to construction rather than as an exception to a rule. In the final analysis each case must turn upon the construction of the particular legislation to determine whether the defence is an exception within the meaning of section 101 of the Act of 1980 which the Court of Appeal rightly decided reflects the rule for trials on indictment. With this one qualification I regard *R v Edwards* as rightly decided.

The matter being one of construction, it was held that in order to establish guilt in H's case the prosecution had to prove that the prohibited substance was in the possession of H. As it is an offence to have morphine in one form but not an offence to have morphine in another form the prosecution had to prove that the morphine was in the prohibited form, otherwise no offence was made out.

See also *R* v *Cross* (1990) 91 Cr App R 115, CA.

3.3   Incidence of the Evidential Burden

A party bearing the legal burden on a particular issue usually bears the evidential burden on that issue as well. Two important categories of exception are (a) presumptions and (b) (in criminal cases) certain defences. Presumptions are considered below. Concerning many criminal defences, the evidential burden of adducing sufficient evidence to leave the defence before the jury is on the accused and, if that burden is discharged, the legal burden of disproving the defence is on the prosecution. Statutory examples include Criminal Law Act 1967, s. 3(1) (reasonable force in the prevention of crime etc.) — see *R* v *Khan* [1995] Crim LR 78, CA; and the defences of privacy, consent and exempted age on charges of attempting to procure an act of gross indecency contrary to Sexual Offences Act 1956, s. 13 and Sexual Offences Act 1967, s. 1 — see *R* v *Spight* [1986] Crim LR 817, CA.

As to common-law examples, see:

Bratty v *Attorney-General for Northern Ireland* [1963] AC 386, HL (non-insane automatism);

Mancini v *DPP* [1942] AC 1, HL (provocation);

R v *Lobell* [1957] 1 QB 547, CCA (self-defence);

Kennedy v *HM Advocate* 1944 JC 171 (drunkenness);

R v *Gill* (1963) 47 Cr App R 166, CCA (duress); and

R v *Bennett* (1978) 68 Cr App R 168, CA (impossibility in cases of common law conspiracy).

Equally, even if the defence do not specifically raise one of these defences, if there is sufficient evidence of such a defence, whether adduced by the prosecution or the defence, then the legal burden to disprove the defence will be on the prosecution: see *per* Lord Tucker in *Bullard* v *R* [1957] AC 635, PC. See also *R* v *Acott* [1997] 1 All ER 706, HL. This remains the case even if the defence in question has been expressly disclaimed by the defence (*R* v *Kachikwu* (1968) 52 Cr App R 538, CA) or is inconsistent with the defence which the accused has in fact raised (*R* v *Newell* [1989] Crim LR 906).

Where the defence to a charge of murder is self-defence, but there is material in the case capable of amounting to the defence of provocation, on which the defence does not rely, the judge should leave the issue of provocation to the jury and it is for the prosecution to disprove it beyond reasonable doubt: see *R* v *Rossiter* [1994] 2 All ER 752. However, if, in such circumstances, the judge fails to direct the jury on provocation, that failure should no longer be used to found a successful appeal against conviction: see *R* v *Cox* [1995] Crim LR 741, CA, in which it was held that if it appears to counsel for either the prosecution or the defence that there is evidence on which the jury could find provocation, they should regard it as their duty to point it out to the trial judge before he or she sums up. The duty established in *R* v *Cox*, it is submitted, should be extended so as to apply to any defence (in relation to which there is sufficient evidence), and not just provocation.

There are dicta in *R* v *Johnson* [1961] 1 WLR 1478, CCA, that the accused bears an evidential burden in relation to a defence of alibi; but see *R* v *Preece* (1993) 96 Cr App R 264. What is clear, however, is that if the defence adduce evidence in support of an alibi, the prosecution bear the legal burden of disproof: *R* v *Helliwell* [1995] Crim LR

79, CA. The judge should direct the jury accordingly. The judge should also direct the jury, in accordance with the standard direction recommended by the Judicial Studies Board, that an alibi is sometimes invented to bolster a genuine defence. Such a direction should routinely be given, but a failure to give it does not automatically render a conviction unsafe. That depends upon the facts of each case and the strength of the evidence: *R* v *Lesley* [1996] 1 Cr App R 39, CA. However, it seems that such a direction is not required where lies play no part in the way in which the Crown puts its case and are not something which the jury have to take into account separate from their decision on the main issue of whether the prosecution witnesses are lying or whether the accused is: *R* v *Harron* [1996] 2 Cr App R 457, CA.

In *DPP* v *Morgan* [1976] AC 182, HL, a majority took the view that on a charge of rape in which there is a defence of belief in consent, that issue cannot be separated from the issue of intent, on which the prosecution bears both the evidential and legal burden, and therefore the accused does not bear the evidential burden in relation to his defence.

3.4 Burden of Proof in a Trial within a Trial

The burden of proving preliminary facts is borne by the party alleging their existence and seeking to admit the evidence in question: see *R* v *Yacoob* (1981) 72 Cr App R 313, CA (the competence of a prosecution witness).

3.5 Right to Begin

The incidence of the burden of proof affects the question of which party has the right to begin adducing evidence in court. In civil proceedings, the rule is that the claimant has the right to begin adducing evidence unless the defendant bears the evidential burden on every issue: see *Pontifex* v *Jolly* (1839) 9 C & P 202 and *Re Parry's Estate, Parry* v *Fraser* [1977] 1 All ER 309. In criminal cases in which there is a not guilty plea, the prosecution normally has the right to begin since the prosecution will almost always bear some evidential burden on some issue.

3.6 Standard of Proof

The standard of proof is the degree of cogency or persuasiveness required of the evidence adduced by a party in order to discharge a burden borne by him or her.

3.6.1 CRIMINAL CASES

3.6.1.1 Legal burden

Borne by the prosecution
The time-honoured formula, approved by the House of Lords in *Woolmington* v *DPP* [1935] AC 462, HL, is that 'the prosecution must prove the case beyond reasonable doubt'.

This standard of proof was described in *Miller* v *Minister of Pensions* [1947] 2 All ER 372 by Denning J at pp. 373–4 in the following terms:

> It need not reach certainty, but it must carry a high degree of probability. Proof beyond reasonable doubt does not mean proof beyond the shadow of doubt. The law would fail to protect the community if it admitted fanciful possibilities to deflect the course of justice. If the evidence is so strong against a man as to leave only a remote possibility in his favour which can be dismissed with the sentence 'of course it is possible, but not in the least probable', the case is proved beyond reasonable doubt, but nothing short of that will suffice.

For an equally acceptable alternative to 'beyond reasonable doubt,' see *R* v *Kritz* [1950] 1 KB 82, CCA and *R* v *Summers* [1952] 1 All ER 1059, CCA: the jury 'must be sure' or 'should be satisfied so that they feel sure'.

See also *R* v *Hepworth and Fearnley* [1955] 2 QB 600, CCA.

A 'reasonable doubt' should not be defined as 'the sort of doubt which might affect you in the conduct of everyday affairs' (*R* v *Gray* (1973) 58 Cr App R 177) or as 'one for which you could give reasons if asked' (*R* v *Stafford* (1968) 53 Cr App R 1, CA). Indeed in most cases judges should not attempt any gloss upon the meaning of the phrase. In exceptional cases in which the jury ask for help, guidance on how to direct the jury may be derived from *R* v *Ching* (1976) 63 Cr App R 7, CA:

> A reasonable doubt, it has been said, is a doubt to which you can give a reason as opposed to a mere fanciful sort of speculation such as 'Well, nothing in this world is certain, nothing in this world can be proved' . . . It is sometimes said the sort of matter which might influence you if you were to consider some business matter. A matter, for example, of a mortgage concerning your house, or something of that nature.

See also *Walters* v *R* [1969] 2 AC 26, PC:

> a reasonable doubt is that quality and kind of doubt which, when you are dealing with matters of importance in your own affairs, you allow to influence you one way or the other.

Borne by the accused
In *R* v *Carr-Briant* [1943] KB 607, CA, Humphreys J said at p. 612:

> . . . in any case where, either by statute or at common law, some matter is presumed against an accused person 'unless the contrary is proved', the jury should be directed that it is for them to decide whether the contrary is proved, that the burden of proof required is less than that required at the hands of the prosecution in proving the case beyond a reasonable doubt, and that the burden may be discharged by evidence satisfying the jury of the probability of that which the accused is called upon to establish.

3.6.1.2 Evidential burden
In *Jayasena* v *R* [1970] AC 618 Lord Devlin said:

> the prosecution in order to stop an issue from being withdrawn from the jury must adduce such evidence as would be sufficient, if believed and left uncontradicted, to justify as a possibility a finding by the jury in their favour.

As to cases in which the accused bears the evidential, but not the legal burden on an issue, see *Bratty* v *Attorney-General for Northern Ireland* [1963] AC 386, HL, *per* Lord Morris of Borth-y-Gest:

> where the accused bears the evidential burden alone, he must adduce such evidence as would, if believed and left uncontradicted, induce a reasonable doubt in the mind of the jury as to whether his version might not be true.

3.6.2 CIVIL CASES

3.6.2.1 Legal burden
The civil standard of proof was described by Denning J in *Miller* v *Minister of Pensions* [1947] 2 All ER 372 at p. 374 in the following terms:

> It must carry a reasonable degree of probability, but not so high as is required in a criminal case. If the evidence is such that the tribunal can say: 'We think it more probable than not', the burden is discharged, but, if the probabilities are equal, it is not.

In some exceptional cases, the criminal standard is used: see *Re Bramblevale Ltd* [1970] Ch 128, CA and *Dean* v *Dean* [1987] 1 FLR 517, CA (where an order is sought to commit a person to prison for a civil contempt).

Sometimes in a civil case allegations are made of misconduct so serious that it could have formed the basis of a criminal prosecution. In *Hornal* v *Neuberger Products Ltd* [1957] 1 QB 247, CA it was held that the civil, not the criminal, standard still applied. But there was a division of opinion about *how* that standard should be applied. Denning LJ said, at p. 258:

The more serious the allegation the higher the degree of probability that is required.

Morris LJ said, at p. 266:

. . . the very elements of gravity become a part of the whole range of circumstances which have to be weighed in the scale when deciding as to the balance of probabilities.

Thus Lord Denning appeared to support the existence of a range of standards within the civil standard as a whole. This idea was rejected by a majority of the House of Lords in *Re H and Others* [1996] AC 563, 586–7. The majority supported the opinion of Morris LJ in *Hornal* v *Neuberger Products Ltd*: the more serious the allegation, the less likely it is to be true and so the stronger should be the evidence before the court concludes that it is proved on the balance of probability. If there were a different standard in some civil cases it would be necessary to identify what it was and when it applied. Attempts to do so would risk causing confusion and uncertainty, and it was better to stick to 'the existing, established law on this subject'. Contrary observations were incorrect. It follows from this decision that earlier cases stipulating a higher standard, let alone the criminal standard, for proof of adultery should now be regarded as obsolete.

For the problems that can arise on interim applications, see *Attock Cement Co. Ltd* v *Romanian Bank for Foreign Trade* [1989] 1 All ER 1189, CA, concerning the standard of proof that applies when an action falls within RSC O. 11, r. 1 (see now CPR, sch. 1). The Master sees whether the facts in the claimant's written evidence bring the case within the rule and if so grants permission (unless the evidence is incredible). If the defendant applies to set aside permission to serve the claim form out of the jurisdiction and there is a disputed question of fact essential to determining whether the action falls within O. 11, r. 1, the claimant must establish 'a good arguable case', i.e. the court, before allowing service to stand, must reach a provisional or tentative conclusion on all the admissible material before it that the claimant is probably right.

3.6.3 STANDARD OF PROOF IN A TRIAL WITHIN A TRIAL

In civil cases the standard is on a balance of probabilities; in criminal cases where the prosecution bears the burden the standard is proof beyond reasonable doubt and where the accused bears the burden the standard is proof on a balance of probabilities: see *R* v *Ewing* [1983] QB 1039, CA, but contrast *R* v *Angeli* [1979] 1 WLR 26, CA. See also *R* v *Yacoob* (1981) 72 Cr App R 313, CA.

These cases must be distinguished from cases in which the judge, before allowing certain items of evidence to be admitted, must be satisfied by prima facie evidence. See *R* v *Robson* [1972] 1 WLR 651, CA: in order to admit tape recordings the judge must satisfy himself that a prima facie case of originality has been made out by evidence which defines and describes the provenance and history of the recordings up to the moment of production in court.

As to the use in criminal trials of tape recordings and transcripts of police interviews, see also *R* v *Rampling* [1987] Crim LR 823, CA; the Code of Practice for Tape Recording of Police Interviews; *Practice Note* [1989] 2 All ER 415, QBD; and *R* v *Emmerson* (1991) 92 Cr App R 284, CA.

The requirement in *Robson* appears not to apply in the case of photographs and video tapes, where all that is required is proof that such material relates to the events in question. See generally (1989) 139 *New Law Journal* 1079–82.

3.7 Presumptions

On the operation of a presumption, a fact may or must be taken to have been proved notwithstanding that no evidence or insufficient evidence has been adduced to establish that fact. Put simply, the presumption can assist a party who might be expected to bear the burden of proving a particular fact by imposing a requirement, sometimes a requirement of disproof, on the other party. Three types of presumption need to be distinguished:

(a) presumptions of fact;

(b) irrebuttable presumptions of law; and

(c) rebuttable presumptions of law.

3.7.1 PRESUMPTIONS OF FACT (OR PROVISIONAL PRESUMPTIONS)

Presumptions of fact are nothing more than frequently recurring examples of circumstantial evidence: see **2.3.5**.

Thus on the proof or admission of a primary (basic) fact, another fact *may* be presumed in the absence of sufficient evidence to the contrary.

3.7.1.1 Presumption of intention

That a person intends the natural consequences of his or her acts was at common law regarded as a presumption of fact (see *R* v *Steane* [1947] KB 997, CCA). The decision in *DPP* v *Smith* [1961] AC 290 that in some cases it constituted a presumption of law, was reversed by Criminal Justice Act 1967, s. 8, which provides that:

> *A court or jury, in determining whether a person has committed an offence—*
> *(a) shall not be bound in law to infer that he intended or foresaw a result of his actions by reason only of its being a natural and probable consequence of those actions; but*
> *(b) shall decide whether he did intend or foresee that result by reference to all the evidence, drawing such inferences from the evidence as appear proper in the circumstances.*

3.7.1.2 Presumption of guilty knowledge

On a charge of theft or handling, if it is proved that the accused was found in possession of goods which were recently stolen and the accused offers no explanation or the jury is satisfied that the explanation he gives is false, the jury *may* infer guilty knowledge: see *R* v *Aves* (1950) 34 Cr App R 159. See also *R* v *Cash* [1985] QB 801, CA. It is desirable in most cases to direct the jury that the burden of proof remains on the prosecution and that if, therefore, the explanation given by the accused leaves them in doubt as to whether he came by the property honestly, they should acquit: see *R* v *Aves* [1950] 2 All ER 330, applied in *R* v *Moulding* [1996] Crim LR 440, CA.

3.7.1.3 Presumption of continuance of life

If a person is proved to be alive on a certain date, it may be inferred, in the absence of contrary evidence, that he or she was alive on a subsequent date. The strength of this presumption depends upon the facts, including such matters as the person's age and state of health on the first date and the length of time that has since elapsed: see *per* Lush J in *R* v *Lumley* (1869) LR 1 CCR 196.

3.7.2 IRREBUTTABLE PRESUMPTIONS OF LAW (OR CONCLUSIVE PRESUMPTIONS)

Irrebuttable presumptions of law are simply rules of substantive law.

Thus on the proof or admission of primary (basic) facts, another fact *must* be presumed as a matter of law.

An example is Civil Evidence Act 1968, s. 13(1): see **13.2.1.2**.

3.7.3 REBUTTABLE PRESUMPTIONS OF LAW

Where this kind of presumption applies, on the proof or admission of primary (basic) facts, another fact *must* be presumed in the absence of sufficient evidence to the contrary.

Concerning disproof of the presumed fact, the party against whom the presumption operates bears *either* a legal burden (a 'persuasive' or 'compelling' presumption) *or* an evidential burden (an 'evidential' presumption). In the case of a persuasive presumption, once A has proved the primary fact (to bring into operation the presumption), the burden is on B to prove that the presumed fact does not exist. In the case of an evidential presumption the legal burden remains on A throughout. Once the primary fact is proved by A he will be held to have proved the presumed fact (by operation of the evidential presumption) unless B adduces *some* evidence to the contrary. If B does so, A will have to prove the existence of the disputed fact in the ordinary way.

3.7.3.1 Presumption of marriage

Formal validity
Formal validity of a marriage means compliance with the formal requirements of the *lex loci celebrationis*. For example, in a Church of England marriage in England, banns must be published and a common licence obtained. If not, the marriage may be rendered void.

This persuasive presumption arises on proof or admission of the primary facts that a marriage ceremony, whether English or foreign, was celebrated between persons who intended to marry. See *Piers* v *Piers* (1849) 2 HL Cas 331; and *Mahadervan* v *Mahadervan* [1964] P 233.

Essential validity
Essential validity of a marriage means compliance with requirements such as the parties' capacity to marry and the reality of their consent. For example, under English law the parties should not be related within the prohibited degrees and neither should be a party to another marriage. If they are, the marriage is void.

This presumption (possibly also persuasive) arises on proof or admission of the primary fact that a formally valid marriage ceremony was celebrated. See *Re Peete* [1952] 2 All ER 599; and *Taylor* v *Taylor* [1967] P 25.

Cohabitation
There is a presumption of marriage (possibly also persuasive) arising from a man and woman cohabiting with the repute of man and wife. See *Re Taylor* [1961] 1 WLR 9, CA.

3.7.3.2 Presumption of legitimacy
This persuasive presumption arises on proof or admission of the basic fact that the child in question was born or conceived during lawful wedlock.

Notice that the presumption arises on proof of *either* birth during wedlock (see *The Poulett Peerage Case* [1903] AC 395) or conception during wedlock (see *Maturin* v *Attorney-General* [1938] 2 All ER 214).

The presumption will still operate if there is a maintenance order against the husband (even if based on desertion), if proceedings for divorce or nullity have been commenced, or even if the parties are living apart. The presumption does not operate, however, where a decree of judicial separation is in force or there is a court separation order. In these circumstances, if the child is born more than nine months after the separation, there is, according to *Hetherington* v *Hetherington* [1887] 12 PD 112, a rebuttable presumption of illegitimacy.

Family Law Reform Act 1969, s. 26, provides that:

> *Any presumption of law as to the legitimacy or illegitimacy of any person may in any civil proceedings be rebutted by evidence which shows that it is more probable than not that the person is illegitimate or legitimate as the case may be and it shall not be necessary to prove that fact beyond reasonable doubt in order to rebut the presumption.*

The presumption of legitimacy should not be used as a make-weight in the scale of legitimacy. Thus even weak evidence against legitimacy must prevail if there is no other evidence to counterbalance it. If the evidence is so evenly balanced that the court is unable to reach a decision on it, the party seeking to rebut the presumption will fail. See *T(HH)* v *T(E)* [1971] 1 WLR 429.

Evidence of the mother's adultery will not suffice as evidence in rebuttal unless there is also evidence that there were no sexual relations between the husband and wife at the date of the child's conception: *R* v *Inhabitants of Mansfield* (1841) 1 QB 444.

3.7.3.3 Presumption of death

Sachs J in *Chard* v *Chard* [1956] P 259 at p. 272 said:

> That presumption in its modern shape takes effect (without examining its terms too exactly) substantially as follows. Where as regards 'A.B.' there is no acceptable affirmative evidence that he was alive at some time during a continuous period of seven years or more, then if it can be proved first, that there are persons who would be likely to have heard of him over that period, secondly that those persons have not heard of him, and thirdly that all due inquiries have been made appropriate to the circumstances, 'A.B.' will be presumed to have died at some time within that period.

This is *probably* an evidential presumption: see *Prudential Assurance Co.* v *Edmonds* (1877) 2 App Cas 487, HL.

This presumption establishes death but not, in the absence of additional evidence, that the deceased died on any particular date during the seven-year period: see *Re Phené's Trusts* [1870] 5 Ch App 139 at p. 144. Is the date of presumed death the date of the legal proceedings in which the presumption arises (view 1) or the date at the end of the seven-year period (view 2)? The authorities conflict. See *Lal Chand Marwari* v *Mahant Ramrup Gir* (1925) 42 TLR 159, PC; *Re Westbrook's Trusts* [1873] WN 167; and *Chipchase* v *Chipchase* [1939] P 391, DC.

Additional to the common-law presumption of death, there exist the following analogous and related statutory provisions.

(a) The proviso to Offences Against the Person Act 1861, s. 57, reads:

> *Provided that nothing in this section shall extend . . . to any person marrying a second time whose husband or wife shall have been continually absent from such person for the space of seven years then last past, and shall not have been known by such person to be living within that time.*

In *R* v *Curgerwen* (1865) LR 1 CCR 1 it was held that it is for the prosecution to prove that the accused did know that the first spouse was 'living within that time'.

(b) Matrimonial Causes Act 1973, s. 19(3), provides that:

> *. . . the fact that for a period of seven years or more the other party to the marriage has been continually absent from the petitioner and the petitioner has no reason*

> *to believe that the other party has been living within that time shall be evidence that the other party is dead until the contrary is proved.*

(c) Law of Property Act 1925, s. 184, provides that:

> *In all cases where, after the commencement of this Act, two or more persons have died in circumstances rendering it uncertain which of them survived the other or others, such deaths shall (subject to any order of the court), for all purposes affecting the title to property, be presumed to have occurred in order of seniority, and accordingly the younger shall be deemed to have survived the elder.*

In *Hickman* v *Peacey* [1945] AC 304 four persons, who had died in a house as the result of a bomb explosion, were taken to have died in order of their seniority.

3.7.3.4 Presumption of regularity (*omnia praesumuntur rite esse acta*)

On proof or admission that a person acted in a judicial, official or public capacity, it is presumed, in the absence of contrary evidence, that the act complied with any necessary formalities and that the person in question was properly appointed. This is an evidential persumption. See, for example:

R v *Cresswell* (1873) 1 QBD 446, CCR (a building where marriages had been celebrated was presumed to have been duly consecrated);

R v *Roberts* (1874) 14 Cox CC 101, CCR (a deputy county court judge, acting as such, was presumed to have been duly appointed); and

R v *Gordon* (1789) Leach 515 (a police officer, acting as such, was presumed to have been duly appointed).

There is also a presumption that mechanical and other instruments were in working order at the time of their use. See *Tingle Jacobs & Co.* v *Kennedy* [1964] 1 WLR 638 n (traffic lights) and *Nicholas* v *Penny* [1950] 2 KB 466 (speedometers).

The authorities are in conflict as to whether this presumption can be used by the prosecution to prove the existence of facts central to the offence charged. See *Gibbins* v *Skinner* [1951] 2 KB 279, DC; and *Scott* v *Baker* [1961] 1 QB 659, DC. The Privy Council, in *Dillon* v *R* [1982] AC 484 has answered this question in the negative.

3.7.3.5 *Res ipsa loquitur*

Erle CJ in *Scott* v *London & St Katherine Docks Co.* (1865) 3 H & C 596 said, at p. 601:

> There must be reasonable evidence of negligence. But where the thing is shown to be under the management of the defendant or his servants, and the accident is such as in the ordinary course of things does not happen if those who have the management use proper care, it affords reasonable evidence, in the absence of explanation by the defendants, that the accident arose from want of care.

What sort of presumption is this, a presumption of fact, an evidential presumption or a persuasive presumption? Although there were conflicting decisions in the past, the modern view is that *res ipsa loquitur* is 'no more than an exotic, although convenient, phrase to describe what is in essence no more than a common sense approach, not limited by technical rules, to the assessment of the effect of evidence in certain circumstances'. The claimant will establish a prima facie case of negligence by relying on the fact of the accident. If the defendant adduces no evidence, there will be nothing to rebut the inference of negligence, and the claimant will have proved his case. If the defendant does adduce evidence, it will have to be evaluated to see if it is still reasonable to infer negligence from the mere fact of the accident. But the burden of proof rests throughout on the claimant. See *Lloyde* v *West Midlands Gas Board* [1971] 2 All ER 1240, CA; *Ng Chun Pui* v *Lee Chuen Tat* [1988] RTR 298, PC; *Fryer* v *Pearson, The Times*, 4 April 2000, CA.

3.7.4   CONFLICTING PRESUMPTIONS

Where two presumptions apply to the facts of a case, the one leading to a conclusion which conflicts with that of the other, do they neutralise each other so that the court should then proceed on the basis that no presumption at all is involved?

Monckton v *Tarr* (1930) 23 BWCC 504, CA and the judgment of Coleridge LCJ in *R* v *Willshire* (1881) 6 QBD 366, CCR provide *some* authority to support an affirmative answer. But see also *Taylor* v *Taylor* [1967] P 25, which suggests that where two presumptions of equal strength conflict, the court may choose between the different conclusions to which they lead by a comparison of the likelihood of the two conflicting presumed facts, or even on the basis of policy considerations.

Questions

OBJECTIVES

By the conclusion of this chapter, you should be able:

(a)   to analyse the facts in issue in both civil and criminal cases and indicate who bears the legal burden of proof and who bears the evidential burden on each fact in issue;

(b)   to decide who has the right to begin adducing evidence in a trial;

(c)   to identify the standard of proof appropriate to a burden;

(d)   to understand and to use properly the terminology applicable to both burdens and standards of proof;

(e)   to classify presumptions;

(f)   to know when to apply a presumption to a given set of facts; and

(g)   to know the effect which a presumption has on the incidence of the legal and evidential burdens.

Question 1

The table below has been used to list a number of facts in issue and to identify the incidence of the legal and evidential burdens and the appropriate standard of proof for each.

Alan has been charged with possessing an offensive weapon, contrary to Prevention of Crime Act 1953, s. 1. He is alleged to have had a chisel with him in a public street. He was found with the chisel at 2 a.m. He does not deny this but says he is a sculptor and while he was at a party, inspiration had struck him for a sculpture and he was on his way to his studio. He adds that he always carries a chisel in case he is attacked.

Prevention of Crime Act 1953, s. 1(1), provides that:

> *Any person who without lawful authority or reasonable excuse, the proof whereof shall lie on him, has with him in any public place any offensive weapon shall be guilty of an offence.*

Section 1(4) of the Act defines an offensive weapon as:

> *any article made or adapted for use for causing injury to the person, or intended by the person having it with him for such use by him.*

Table

For each fact in issue, indicate:

Fact in issue	Who must discharge the evidential burden	Who must discharge the legal burden of proof	The standard of proof on the legal burden
Possession of chisel	Prosecution	Prosecution	Beyond reasonable doubt
Public place	Prosecution	Prosecution	Beyond reasonable doubt
Offensive nature	Prosecution	Prosecution	Beyond reasonable doubt
Reasonable excuse	Defence	Defence	Balance of probabilities

Fill in a table for each of the following problems.

(a) Arabian Ltd, the charterers of a ship, are suing Bulk Traffic Co., the owners of the ship, for breach of contract. The ship blew up and sank during its voyage. No one is able to determine the cause of the explosion.

Bulk Traffic alleges that the contract was frustrated by the explosion. Arabian Ltd says that any frustration was self-induced and does not afford a defence to its action.

Table

Fact in issue	Evidential burden	Legal burden	Standard of proof on legal burden

(b) Following a collision between his car and a lamp-post, Charles is accused of driving without due care and attention. He told the police officer who interviewed him at the hospital that he remembered nothing of the incident. Later, he told the police that his doctor told him that in all likelihood he simply blacked out (non-insane automatism).

Table

Fact in issue	Evidential burden	Legal burden	Standard of proof on legal burden

(c) Daphne is the sole beneficiary of a trust, established by her late uncle, Edward. Frank is the trustee and Daphne is suing him for misuse of the trust fund. She alleges that he has deliberately mixed money from the fund with his own in his bank account and has spent it. Frank denies these allegations.

Table

Fact in issue	Evidential burden	Legal burden	Standard of proof on legal burden

Question 2
Explain the burdens and standard of proof in the following case.

In an action by A for breach of contract for the carriage of a consignment of television sets by lorry from London to Manchester, the contract provided that B, a lorry owner, was not liable for loss caused by fire provided that the lorry owner's servants were not negligent. The lorry and its load were destroyed by fire in a service area on the motorway. B claims that he is not liable for the loss. A asserts that B was facing bankruptcy and that the lorry was deliberately set on fire so that B could claim on his insurance from the insurers of the lorry. Alternatively A asserts that the fire was caused by the carelessness of the lorry driver.

(Think how each party might draft its statement of case.)

Question 3
Michael is charged with an offence which reads:

A person who promotes or takes part in a competition or trial (other than a race or trial of speed) involving the use of motor vehicles on a public highway shall be guilty of an offence unless the competition or trial is authorised, and is conducted in accordance with conditions imposed by or under regulations under this section.

Michael admits that he took part in a trial involving the use of a vehicle on a public highway but says that:

(a) it was a race or trial of speed; and

(b) the vehicle was not a *motor* vehicle.

Who will bear the burden of proof on each of these issues?

What standard of proof will be required to discharge them?

Question 4

On 1 January 1994 Mr and Mrs Bush (aged 22 and 24 respectively), set off from Folkestone, England in their yacht, *Mermaid*, to cruise to Australia. On 16 August 1996 the *Mermaid* was discovered adrift in open seas off the island of Bali in the Indian Ocean. Mr and Mrs Bush were not aboard.

Neither set of parents has heard from the couple since they left Folkestone, although Mrs Bush sent her parents a picture postcard of Cape Town which was postmarked '1 April 1995'. Title to Mr and Mrs Bush's house is registered at the Land Registry in Mrs Bush's name alone. Mr Bush's parents now claim:

(a) that as neither Mr Bush junior nor his wife have been heard from, save for the postcard, since they left Folkestone, they should be given up as dead; and

(b) that their son and daughter-in-law made mutual wills in which all property went to whichever outlived the other; that their son's will bequeathed the house to his parents should he survive his wife; and that since their son probably outlived his wife, they should inherit the house.

Advise Mr and Mrs Bush senior whether there are any presumptions of fact or law which will assist or hamper them in establishing their claims.

Question 5

Create a rebuttable presumption which assists the prosecution in a statute which makes it an offence knowingly to sell solvents to people under 18 years old for abuse.

FOUR

WITNESSES: COMPETENCE, COMPELLABILITY, OATHS AND PROCEDURE

Which persons can be called to give evidence and which can be forced to do so (competence and compellability)?

When can witnesses give their evidence unsworn (that is, without having taken the oath or made an affirmation)?

Do parties have any property in the evidence of a witness?

Do parties have an unfettered choice as to which witnesses to call?

May parties call their witnesses in any order they choose?

Must all of party's witnesses be called before the close of his or her case?

May the judge call witnesses?

When do witness statements need to be exchanged?

What is the effect of such exchange and what are the consequences of a failure to serve witness statements?

May witnesses use live television links or pre-record evidence?

4.1 Competence and Compellability

A witness is competent if he or she can as a matter of law be called by a party to give evidence. A witness is compellable if, being competent, he or she can as a matter of law be compelled by the court to give evidence. A compellable witness will be in contempt of court, and therefore liable to imprisonment if, having been ordered to attend court, he or she refuses to do so or, attending court, he or she refuses to give sworn evidence or gives sworn evidence but refuses to answer some of the questions put (not being questions in respect of which the witness is entitled to claim privilege — see **Chapter 14**).

4.1.1 THE GENERAL RULE

The general rule has two limbs:

(a) all persons are competent; and

(b) all competent witnesses are compellable.

See *Hoskyn* v *Metropolitan Police Commissioner* [1979] AC 474, HL, at pp. 484 and 500.

4.1.2　THE EXCEPTIONS

As to the competence of witnesses in criminal cases, Youth Justice and Criminal Evidence Act 1999, s. 53(1), provides that:

> At every stage in criminal proceedings all persons are (whatever their age) competent to give evidence.

However, this general rule is subject to s. 53(3):

> A person is not competent to give evidence in criminal proceedings if it appears to the court that he is not a person who is able to—
> (a)　understand questions put to him as a witness, and
> (b)　give answers to them which can be understood.

The general nature of s. 53(1) regarding competence and the general rule that all competent witnesses are compellable are subject to a number of statutory and common law limitations.

4.1.2.1　The accused

For the prosecution

A person charged in criminal proceedings is *not* competent to give evidence in the proceedings for the prosecution (whether he is charged alone or with others): Youth Justice and Criminal Evidence Act 1999, s. 53(4).

Section 53(5) provides that a '*person charged in criminal proceedings*' does not include a person who is not, or no longer, liable to be convicted of any offence in the proceedings (whether as a result of pleading guilty or otherwise).

A co-accused may become competent for the prosecution:

(a)　on acquittal (e.g. on making a successful submission of no case to answer),

(b)　where a *nolle prosequi* is entered on the direction of the Attorney-General,

(c)　on pleading guilty, or

(d)　by making a successful application for a separate trial.

In *R* v *Pipe* (1966) 51 Cr App R 17, CA it was held that an accomplice against whom proceedings are pending but who is not being tried in the proceedings in question, should not be called by the prosecution unless they have given an undertaking that proceedings will be discontinued against that accomplice. It was held to be wholly irregular, therefore, in a prosecution for theft, to call for the prosecution the alleged receiver of the stolen goods, who had been charged and would face a separate trial on some later date, to give evidence for the prosecution against the alleged thief of the goods. However, the Court of Appeal said in *R* v *Turner* (1975) 61 Cr App R 67, CA, that the rule was one of practice and not law, i.e. a matter of discretion for the judge.

For the defence

An accused is competent but not compellable to give evidence in his or her own defence: competent by Youth Justice and Criminal Evidence Act 1999, s. 53(1); not compellable by Criminal Evidence Act 1898, s. 1(1), which provides that:

> A person charged in criminal proceedings shall not be called as a witness in the proceedings except upon his own application.

If the accused chooses to give evidence, he or she is open to cross-examination by both the prosecution and any co-accused, and what he or she says will be evidence for all purposes of the case. Thus although an accused cannot give evidence as a witness for the prosecution against a co-accused, the accused, appearing in his or her own defence may give evidence-in-chief against a co-accused and such evidence can also be elicited from the accused by the prosecution in cross-examination. In *R* v *Paul* [1920] 2 KB 183 the accused went into the witness box and all he said in chief was, in effect, that he was guilty. The Court of Criminal Appeal held that the prosecution was perfectly entitled to cross-examine him with a view to getting him to incriminate a co-accused.

Concerning the giving of evidence by the accused *for* a co-accused, this is also governed by Youth Justice and Criminal Evidence Act 1999, s. 53(1) and Criminal Evidence Act 1898, s. 1(1). Thus an accused is competent as a witness for a co-accused but not compellable. Of course if he has ceased to be a co-accused, he will, like any other witness, be both competent and compellable. In *R* v *Richardson* (1967) 51 Cr App R 381, where the accused had been jointly charged, one accused, D, succeeded in his application for a separate trial because of his bad health and another accused, E, then sought a witness summons to compel D to give evidence for him. Lawton J at first instance held that D was both competent and compellable because no longer on trial with E.

If an accused decides not to testify, it should be the invariable practice of counsel to record the decision, and to cause the accused to sign the record, giving a clear indication that he has by his own will decided not to testify bearing in mind the advice, if any, given to him by his counsel: *R* v *Bevan* (1994) 98 Cr App R 354, CA.

Concerning the inferences that may be drawn from an accused's failure to give evidence, see **Chapter 11**.

4.1.2.2 The spouse of the accused

On one view, the spouse of an accused in addition to being competent, should also be compellable for the prosecution. The arguments in favour of this view are that:

(a) all relevant evidence should be admissible (and there may be no other relevant evidence);

(b) there is a public interest in bringing all criminals to justice; and

(c) in some cases the spouse may actually wish to give evidence against the accused (for example, a wife who is the victim of a serious offence of violence committed by her husband).

The counter-arguments are that:

(a) in many cases where the spouse is unwilling to give evidence against the accused, it is harsh to compel him or her to do so;

(b) such compulsion is hardly conducive to marital harmony; and

(c) in many cases, the spouse is likely to be biased in favour of the accused.

The problem becomes even more confusing when one considers whether a spouse of an accused should, in addition to being competent, be compellable for a co-accused. The spouse of co-accused X may be the only person who can substantiate the defence of co-accused Y, but if co-accused Y calls the spouse of co-accused X then in cross-examination the prosecution may seek to elicit evidence incriminating co-accused X.

Police and Criminal Evidence Act 1984, s. 80, reflects a compromise. It provides that:

(2) In any proceedings the wife or husband of a person charged in the proceedings shall, subject to subsection (4) below, be compellable to give evidence on behalf of that person.

(2A) In any proceedings the wife or husband of a person charged in the proceedings shall, subject to subsection (4) below, be compellable—

(a) to give evidence on behalf of any other person charged in the proceedings but only in respect of any specified offence with which that other person is charged; or

(b) to give evidence for the prosecution but only in respect of any specified offence with which any person is charged in the proceedings.

(3) In relation to the wife or husband of a person charged in any proceedings, an offence is a specified offence for the purposes of subsection (2A) above if—

(a) it involves an assault on, or injury or threat of injury to, the wife or husband or a person who was at the material time under the age of 16;

(b) it is a sexual offence alleged to have been committed in respect of a person who was at the material time under that age; or

(c) it consists of attempting or conspiring to commit, or of aiding, abetting, counselling, procuring or inciting the commission of, an offence falling within paragraph (a) or (b) above.

(4) No person who is charged in any proceedings shall be compellable by virtue of subsection (2) or (2A) above to give evidence in the proceedings.

(4A) References in this section to a person charged in any proceedings do not include a person who is not, or is no longer, liable to be convicted of any offence in the proceedings (whether as a result of pleading guilty or for any other reason).

(5) In any proceedings a person who has been but is no longer married to the accused shall be compellable to give evidence as if that person and the accused had never been married.

(6) Where in any proceedings the age of any person at any time is material for the purposes of subsection (3) above, his age at the material time shall for the purposes of that provision be deemed to be or to have been that which appears to the court to be or to have been his age at that time.

(7) In subsection (3)(b) above 'sexual offence' means an offence under the Sexual Offences Act 1956, the Indecency with Children Act 1960, the Sexual Offences Act 1967, section 54 of the Criminal Law Act 1977 or the Protection of Children Act 1978.

Police and Criminal Evidence Act 1984, s. 80A provides that:

The failure of the wife or husband of a person charged in any proceedings to give evidence in the proceedings shall not be made the subject of any comment by the prosecution.

For the prosecution

A spouse is competent to give evidence against the accused or any co-accused (Youth Justice and Criminal Evidence Act 1999, s. 53(1)). The only exception is where both spouses are charged in the proceedings (Youth Justice and Criminal Evidence Act 1999, s. 53(4)).

A spouse is compellable to give evidence against the accused or any co-accused only in the circumstances specified in Police and Criminal Evidence Act 1984, s. 80(3)(a) to (c). The only exception is where both spouses are charged in the proceedings (s. 80(4)).

The drafting of the 1984 Act, s. 80, gives rise to an apparent problem. This stems from the use of the word 'involves' in s. 80(3)(a). The question arises whether the test is factual or legal, i.e. whether s. 80(3) refers to cases where factually the offence charged involves an assault, injury or threat of injury (for example, a charge of arson in a case where, on the facts, the spouse of the accused was put in fear) or cases where, as a matter of law, the offence charged involves an assault etc.

Prior to the amendment of s. 80 by the Youth Justice and Criminal Evidence Act 1999 an ambiguity also existed in respect of the multiple-count indictment. If an accused is charged on the same indictment with two or more different offences, the first of which does involve an assault etc. to the spouse, but the others of which do not, and the prosecution compels the spouse to give evidence on the first count, is he or she obliged to answer questions concerning the other counts? Section 80(2A)(a) and (b), in using the wording 'only in respect of any specified offence', suggest that the answer is 'no'.

For the accused

A spouse is competent for the accused (Youth Justice and Criminal Evidence Act 1999, s. 53(1)). A spouse is also compellable for the accused (Police and Criminal Evidence Act 1984, s. 80(2)) and the only exception is s. 80(4).

For a co-accused

A spouse is competent for any co-accused (Youth Justice and Criminal Evidence Act 1999, s. 53(1)).

A spouse is compellable for any co-accused only in the circumstances specified in Police and Criminal Evidence Act 1984, s. 80(3)(a) to (c). The only exception is s. 80(4).

Former spouse

Under s. 80(5) of the 1984 Act the test for compellability is whether at the time of the proceedings a person is 'no longer married to the accused'. The question, therefore, is whether there has been a divorce or the marriage has been annulled. If a marriage was void *ab initio* there never was a spouse. Thus in *R v Khan (Junaid)* (1987) 84 Cr App R 44, the Court of Appeal held that a woman with whom a man had gone through a bigamous ceremony of marriage was a competent *witness* against him for the prosecution. (This case was decided at a time when s. 80(5) governed competence as well as compellability.) On the other hand, parties who are married remain married where they are judicially separated, or are simply not cohabiting (whether by reason of an informal arrangement, a separation agreement or a non-cohabitation order).

An ex-spouse is competent and compellable to give evidence in any proceedings after s. 80(5) came into effect (1 January 1986) about any relevant matter (whether occurring before or after 1 January 1986): *R v Cruttenden* [1991] 3 All ER 242.

4.1.2.3 Children

In relation to children, it is necessary to distinguish between competence to give sworn evidence and competence to give unsworn evidence. Almost invariably adult witnesses must give sworn evidence; whereas, subject to the rules to be considered, a child will often give unsworn evidence. For the meaning of sworn evidence, see **4.2.1**.

Civil cases

Children Act 1989, s. 96 provides that:

> *(1)   Subsection (2) applies where a child who is called as a witness in any civil proceedings does not, in the opinion of the court, understand the nature of an oath.*
> *(2)   The child's evidence may be heard by the court if, in its opinion —*
> *(a)   he understands that it is his duty to speak the truth and;*
> *(b)   he has sufficient understanding to justify his evidence being heard.*

A 'child', for those purposes, is a person under the age of 18: s. 105.

On matters of procedure, and on the question whether a child does not understand the nature of an oath, the courts are likely to be guided by authorities drawn from criminal cases at a time when the position was similar to that laid down in s. 96. (For the current situation in criminal cases see below.) Thus the question being for the judge, he or she should put to the child preliminary questions so as to be able to form an opinion: *R v Surgenor* (1940) 27 Cr App R 175. Whether a child is sufficiently young to warrant examination to see whether he or she can give sworn evidence is a matter for the judge to decide on the particular facts of the case. However, in *R v Khan* (1981) 73 Cr App R 190, CA it was held that although much depends on the type of child before the court, as a general working rule inquiry is necessary in the case of a child under the age of 14.

The test to determine whether the child understands the nature and consequences of an oath was reviewed by the Court of Appeal in *R v Hayes* [1977] 1 WLR 238. The test laid down in *Hayes* was 'whether the child has a sufficient appreciation of the solemnity of the occasion and the added responsibility to tell the truth, which is involved in taking an oath over and above the duty to tell the truth which is an ordinary duty of normal social conduct'. If, in civil proceedings, a child fails this test, his or her evidence may be given unsworn if the conditions in s. 96(2) are satisfied. It seems likely that the 'duty to speak the truth' in s. 96(2)(a) will be interpreted to mean the duty to tell the truth which is an ordinary duty of normal social conduct.

Criminal cases

Prior to statutory amendment, in criminal cases the competence of a child to give *sworn* evidence was governed by *R v Hayes*; and the competence of a child to give *unsworn* evidence was governed by the Children and Young Persons Act 1933, s. 38(1), whereby a child of tender years could give unsworn evidence if, in the opinion of the court, he or she did not understand the nature of the oath but was of sufficient intelligence to justify the reception of his or her evidence and understood the duty of speaking the truth.

The position is now governed by Youth Justice and Criminal Evidence Act 1999, ss. 53, 55 and 56.

Regarding basic competence to give evidence, the evidence of children is on the same footing as witnesses of any other age: s. 53(1). Should a party or the court itself raise the issue of whether a child (or indeed an adult witness) is competent to give evidence, e.g. because the child is so young that it is questionable whether the child could understand the questions put or give answers which could be understood (s. 53(3)), it is for the party calling the witness to satisfy the court, on a balance of probabilities, that the child is competent: s. 54(2). Such determination takes place in the absence of the jury (s. 54(4)), but in the presence of the parties (s. 54(6)). Expert evidence may be received (s. 54(5)), and the court shall treat the witness as having the benefit of any directions ('special measures directions') under s. 19 of the 1999 Act given or proposed in relation to the witness (s. 54(4)).

Competence to give sworn evidence is governed by s. 55. Section 55(2) provides that:

> *(2) The witness may not be sworn for that purpose* [i.e. giving evidence on oath] *unless—*
> *(a) he has attained the age of 14, and*
> *(b) he has a sufficient appreciation of the solemnity of the occasion and of the particular responsibility to tell the truth which is involved in taking an oath.*

A child of 13 or under cannot therefore give sworn evidence. A witness, if able to give intelligible testimony, is presumed to have a sufficient appreciation of the matters mentioned in s. 55(2)(b) if no evidence is adduced tending to show the contrary (s. 55(3)).

If evidence is adduced, it is for the party seeking to have the witness sworn to prove (on a balance of probabilities) attainment of both the necessary age and sufficient appreciation of the matters mentioned (s. 55(4)).

A person is able to give 'intelligible testimony' for the purposes of s. 55(3) if he is able to understand questions put to him as a witness and give answers to them which can be understood (s. 55(8)). This is in the same terms as the test for determining that a witness is not competent to give evidence under s. 53(3).

Section 55 also provides that the determination of whether a witness may be sworn (which can be raised by a party or the court) takes place in the absence of the jury (s. 55(5)), but in the presence of the parties. Expert evidence can be received (s. 55(6)). A witness who is competent to give evidence (i.e. within the terms of s. 53) but is prevented by s. 55(2) from giving sworn evidence, must give his or her evidence unsworn (s. 56(2)), which shall accordingly be received by a court in criminal proceedings (s. 56(4)).

4.1.2.4 Persons of defective intellect

Older common law authorities which held that the test for competence in the case of a person of defective intellect is simply whether he or she understands the nature and sanction of the oath have now been overtaken, but only in criminal trials, by the general statutory provisions relating to competence laid down by Youth Justice and Criminal Evidence Act 1999, s. 53. A person of defective intellect will therefore not be competent, in common with other witnesses, if he or she is unable to understand questions put to him or her as a witness or unable to give answers to them which can be understood (s. 53(3)). Proceedings for the determination of competence are held in the absence of the jury, but in the presence of the parties, and expert evidence may be received on the question (s. 54(4), (5) and (6)).

Where a mentally handicapped person does give evidence, the jury may attach to his or her evidence such weight as they see fit. Clearly if the evidence is so tainted with insanity as to be unworthy of credit, the jury will properly disregard it: *R* v *Hill* (1851) 2 Den CC 254. Equally, however, a person suffering from a mental illness may be a reliable witness. In *R* v *Barratt* [1996] Crim LR 495, CA, the witness was suffering from fixed belief paranoia and held bizarre beliefs about certain aspects of her private life, but the court could see no reason to suppose that on matters not affected by her condition, her evidence was not as reliable as that of any other witness.

4.1.2.5 The Sovereign, heads of sovereign states and diplomats
There is doubt as to whether the Sovereign is even a competent witness; the Sovereign is certainly not a compellable witness. Heads of other sovereign states are competent, but not compellable.

Diplomats, consular officials and the like enjoy total or partial immunity from compellability pursuant to a wide variety of statutory provisions.

4.1.2.6 Bankers
Bankers' Books Evidence Act 1879, s. 6, provides that bankers shall not be compellable, in legal proceedings to which the bank is not a party, to produce any bankers' book the contents of which can be proved under the Act, or to appear as witnesses to prove the matters etc. therein recorded, unless by order of a judge made for special cause.

4.1.2.7 Judges
Judges or masters cannot be compelled to give evidence relating to their judicial function (as opposed to extraneous matters such as a crime committed in the face of the court). However, they are competent to do so, and if their evidence is vital, they should be able to be relied on not to invoke their non-compellability in order to avoid giving evidence: *Warren* v *Warren* [1996] 4 All ER 664, CA.

4.2   Oaths and Affirmations

4.2.1   SWORN EVIDENCE

Evidence given by a witness who has taken an oath or has made an affirmation is known as sworn evidence. The present law is governed by the Oaths Act 1978.

Section 1(1) provides for oaths in the case of Christians and Jews. Such an oath will be administered, without enquiry on the part of the judge, unless the witness objects or is physically incapable of taking the oath: s. 1(2). For those of other religious beliefs, the oath shall be administered 'in any lawful manner': s. 1(3). Whether the oath is administered in a lawful manner does not depend on the intricacies of the particular religion in question (e.g. for Muslims, strictly an oath should be taken on a copy of the Koran *in Arabic*) but on:

(a) whether the oath appears to the court to be binding on the conscience of the witness, and

(b) whether it is an oath which the witness himself considers to be binding on his conscience: *R* v *Kemble* [1990] 3 All ER 116, CA.

To prevent a person with no religious belief from taking an oath and later alleging that the oath was therefore of no effect, s. 4(2) of the 1978 Act provides that the fact that a person taking an oath has no religious belief does not prevent it from being binding on him.

Under s. 5, anyone objecting to the taking of an oath is allowed instead to make a solemn affirmation, which is of exactly the same force and effect as an oath; and under s. 5(2), such an affirmation may be required of any person where it is not reasonably practicable to administer an oath in the manner appropriate to his or her religious belief. Concerning perjury, there is no difference between oath and affirmation — in either case, a witness will be guilty of the offence if he or she wilfully makes a statement material to the proceedings knowing it to be false or not believing it to be true.

4.2.2 UNSWORN EVIDENCE

The effect of unsworn evidence upon the validity of the proceedings will depend upon the type of proceedings.

For criminal cases, Youth Justice and Criminal Evidence Act 1999, s. 56(5), provides that:

> *Where a person ('the witness') who is competent to give evidence in criminal proceedings gives evidence in such proceedings unsworn, no conviction, verdict or finding in those proceedings shall be taken to be unsafe for the purposes of sections 2(1), 13(1) and 16(1) of the Criminal Appeal Act 1968 (grounds for allowing appeals) by reason only that it appears to the Court of Appeal that the witness was a person falling within section 55(2) (and should accordingly have given his evidence on oath).*

For civil cases, the general rule is that evidence must be sworn: a judgment founded on unsworn evidence, therefore, will be set aside as a nullity. However, note that in claims which have been allocated to the small claims track (see the **Civil Litigation Manual**), the court need not take evidence on oath: CPR, r. 27.8(4).

(Youth Justice and Criminal Evidence Act 1999, s. 57, provides that in the case of a witness giving unsworn evidence in accordance with s. 56(2) or (3), he or she will commit an offence if, had the evidence been given on oath, he or she would have been guilty of perjury.)

4.3 Procedural Issues

4.3.1 DOES A PARTY TO LITIGATION HAVE ANY PROPERTY IN THE EVIDENCE OF A WITNESS?

The short answer is no.

In *Harmony Shipping Co. SA v Saudi Europe Line Ltd* [1979] 1 WLR 1380, CA a handwriting expert was approached by the plaintiffs to authenticate a certain document. His view was that it was a forgery. Later, the defendants asked him to advise on the same issue and, forgetting his previous involvement in the case, he expressed the same view as before. On discovering that the plaintiffs had already retained him, the expert said that he could not continue to advise the defendants. The defendants then issued a subpoena against him. The Court of Appeal held that he was compellable to give evidence for the defendants. Lord Denning MR held that even if there had been a contract between him and the plaintiffs binding him not to appear for the defendants, it would have been unenforceable as being contrary to public policy. Thus, although *communications* between the expert and the plaintiffs might well have been protected by legal professional privilege (see **14.2.2.1**), the plaintiffs had no property in the *evidence* of the expert.

However, once a witness in criminal proceedings has given evidence for the prosecution, he or she cannot be called to give evidence for the defence: *R v Kelly*, The Times, 27 July 1985, CA.

4.3.2 ARE THE PARTIES UNDER ANY OBLIGATION TO CALL COMPETENT WITNESSES OR DO THEY HAVE AN UNFETTERED CHOICE?

In civil proceedings the parties do not have an unfettered choice. CPR, r. 32.1, provides that:

> *(1) The court may control the evidence by giving directions as to—*
> *(a)   the issues on which it requires evidence;*
> *(b)   the nature of the evidence which it requires to decide those issues; and*
> *(c)   the way in which the evidence is to be placed before the court.*
> *(2)   The court may use its power under this rule to exclude evidence that would otherwise be admissible.*
> *(3)   The court may limit cross-examination.*

In criminal proceedings the accused may call such witnesses to support his or her case as he or she thinks fit (subject to the rules about compelling a co-accused). As to the prosecution, the relevant rules were summarised in *R* v *Russell-Jones* [1995] 3 All ER 239, CA:

(a)   the prosecution must bring to court all whose statements have been served as witnesses on whom they intend to rely, if the defence wants them to attend;

(b)   the prosecution have a discretion, which should be exercised in the interests of justice to promote a fair trial, to call or tender for cross-examination by the defence, any witnesses it requires to attend;

(c)   the prosecution should normally call all the witnesses who can give direct evidence of the primary facts of the case, even if there are inconsistencies between one witness and another unless for good reason the prosecutor regards the witness's evidence as unworthy of belief;

(d)   it is for the prosecution to decide which witnesses can give direct evidence of the primary facts;

(e)   the prosecutor is the primary judge of whether a witness is unworthy of belief; and

(f)   the prosecutor is not obliged to proffer a witness merely to give the defence material with which to attack the credit of other prosecution witnesses.

Concerning the discretion of the trial judge to direct the prosecution to call or tender a witness, see also *R* v *Brown* [1997] 1 Cr App R 112, CA.

4.3.3 ARE THERE ANY RULES AS TO THE ORDER IN WHICH COMPETENT WITNESSES SHOULD BE CALLED?

Parties are generally free to call the witnesses in the order of their choice. The only major restriction relates to the order of defence witnesses in criminal trials. Police and Criminal Evidence Act 1984, s. 79, provides that:

> *If at the trial of any person for an offence—*
> *(a)   the defence intends to call two or more witnesses to the facts of the case; and*
> *(b)   those witnesses include the accused*
> *the accused shall be called before the other witness or witnesses unless the court in its discretion otherwise directs.*

The court may 'otherwise direct', e.g., in the case of

(a)   a witness whose evidence relates to some formal or uncontroversial matter, or

(b)   a witness who can testify to some event which occurred before the time of the events about which the accused will testify (where it is thought that the 'story' will be more readily understood if told in chronological order).

See also *Bayerische Rückversicherung AG* v *Clarkson Puckle Overseas Ltd*, *The Times*, 23 January 1989: if the issues in a commercial action are such that professional experts will be asked to express an opinion on the professional competence of someone else in the same profession, the High Court has power to order that all the oral evidence as to the facts be given by both sides before the expert evidence of either side is given.

4.3.4   **MUST ALL OF A PARTY'S WITNESSES BE CALLED BEFORE THE CLOSE OF THE PARTY'S CASE?**

The general rule is that all of a party's evidence should be adduced before the close of the party's case. A party will not be allowed at some later stage to remedy defects in his case, or contradict the evidence of his opponent, by adducing evidence available to him from the start and foreseeably relevant to his case. See *R* v *Day* [1940] 1 All ER 402, CCA where a conviction of forgery was quashed because the judge had allowed the prosecution to call a handwriting expert after the close of its case. The necessity of such evidence should have been foreseeable at the outset.

However, the court will normally allow evidence in rebuttal to be called in order to make good a purely formal omission: see *Price* v *Humphries* [1958] 2 QB 353, DC, where the prosecutor failed to prove that the Director of Public Prosecutions had given leave to bring the proceedings.

Also, the judge has a discretion to allow a party to call evidence in rebuttal of a matter which has arisen *ex improviso*, i.e. which could not reasonably have been anticipated or foreseen. See *R* v *Scott* (1984) 79 Cr App R 49, CA and *R* v *Hutchinson* (1986) 82 Cr App R 51, CA.

The discretion of a trial judge to allow the prosecution to call further evidence after the close of its case is not confined to the above two exceptions. The judge has a wider discretion, the limits of which should not be precisely defined, but which should be exercised only rarely outside the two established exceptions (*R* v *Francis* [1991] 1 All ER 225, CA), especially when the evidence is tendered after the case for the accused has begun (*R* v *Munnery* [1992] Crim LR 215, CA). In *R* v *Francis*, evidence having been given that at a group identification the man standing at position number 20 was identified, the prosecution was allowed to recall the inspector in charge of the identification to say that it was the appellant who was standing at position number 20. Counsel for the prosecution was under the impression that the name of the person standing at that position was not in issue. For a rare example of prosecution evidence being admitted *after* the case for the accused has begun, see *James* v *South Glamorgan County Council* (1994) 99 Cr App R 321, DC.

Note also that it is the practice, in the case of evidence which did not form part of the evidence upon which an accused was committed for trial, but which is capable of forming part of the affirmative case for the prosecution, to give notice of that additional evidence to the defence *before* it is tendered: *R* v *Kane* (1977) 65 Cr App R 270, CA. The fact that the accused might then trim his evidence is not a reason for witholding the material until he testifies. The rationale for the principle is that an accused needs to know in advance the case against him if he is to have a proper opportunity of answering that case to the best of his ability. The accused is also entitled to such knowledge when deciding whether to testify. It is better in the interests of justice that an accused is not induced, by thinking he is safe to do so, to exaggerate, or to embroider, or to lie. To do so might be to ambush the accused: *R* v *Phillipson* (1990) 91 Cr App R 226. See also *R* v *Sansom* (1991) 92 Cr App R 115, CA.

4.3.5   **IS THE JUDGE ENTITLED TO CALL WITNESSES?**

In civil proceedings, the general rule was that the judge could call witnesses if he or she had the consent of all parties. See *Re Enoch & Zaretsky, Bock & Co.'s Arbitration* [1910] 1 KB 327, CA. This rule must now be read subject to the power of the court to control the evidence contained in CPR, r. 32.1(1). It is submitted that the powers to direct on the issues, nature and way in which evidence is to be placed before the court are wide enough to allow the judge to direct that a witness give evidence even without the consent of the parties.

In criminal proceedings in the Crown Court the judge, without the consent of either party, may call and examine any witness not called by the parties: see *R* v *Chapman* (1838) 8 C & P 558: and *R* v *Harris* [1927] 2 KB 587. Magistrates also have the power to call witnesses themselves, but as in the case of professional judges, it is a power to be exercised rarely: *R* v *Haringey Justices, ex parte DPP* [1996] 1 All ER 828, DC.

There is a sacrosanct rule that when the jury or justices have retired to consider their verdict, no witness may be called or re-called, even if the jury has requested it and the defence consents. This rule extends to material, other than evidence, designed to assist them, as when the jury ask for scales to conduct weighing experiments with exhibits: see *R* v *Stewart* (1989) 89 Cr App R 273, CA. However, a magnifying glass, a ruler or a tape-measure does not normally raise the possibility of experiments with exhibits and there can be no objection to their use in the jury room: *R* v *Maggs* (1990) 91 Cr App R 243, CA.

Where the jury ask for an object in order to re-enact a situation and draw conclusions from that rather than from the evidence, as when they ask for something like a knife to re-enact a struggle between the accused and the victim of the offence, the judge should try to steer them away from such an exercise: see *R* v *Crees* [1996] Crim LR 830, CA.

If a tape, of which there is an agreed transcript, is played in court and contains no inadmissible material, the judge may permit the jury to play it in their retiring room: *R* v *Tonge* [1993] Crim LR 876, CA. However, where the transcript alone has been used in court, although the jury may listen to the tape after retirement, it should be played in open court if there is any risk of the jury hearing inadmissible material: *R* v *Riaz* (1991) 94 Cr App R 339, CA. See also *R* v *Hagan* [1997] 1 Cr App R 464, CA.

If a silent film or video has been shown in court and the jury, after retirement, ask to see it again, they may do so, but it is better that they see it again in open court: *R* v *Imran* [1997] Crim LR 754, CA.

Concerning a video-recording used as a child's evidence, if the jury, after retirement, want to be reminded of *what* the witness said, the judge should remind them from the transcript or his or her own notes; but if they want to be reminded of *how* the witness spoke, the judge may allow the video to be replayed in open court. Either way, the judge should give an appropriate direction on the risk of giving the evidence disproportionate weight by reason of its repetition and should remind the jury, from his or her notes, of the cross-examination and re-examination of the complainant: see *R* v *Rawlings* [1995] 1 All ER 580, CA, and *R* v *McQuiston* [1998] 1 Cr App R 139, CA. See also *R* v *M* [1996] 2 Cr App R 56, CA and *R* v *B* [1996] Crim LR 499, CA. These cases were decided when Criminal Justice Act 1988, s. 32A(2), permitted video-recordings of a child's evidence: now see ss. 27 and 28 of Youth Justice and Criminal Evidence Act 1999 for the circumstances when video evidence is admissible. It is submitted that the approach outlined in the above cases will continue to be adopted.

4.3.6 EXCHANGE OF WITNESS STATEMENTS

In criminal cases the prosecution must always furnish the defence with a witness statement of any witness they propose to call at trial, but in general there is no equivalent duty on the defence. Concerning the special rules regarding expert witnesses, see **13.1.3.7**.

In civil proceedings, CPR, r. 32.2, provides that the general rule is that any fact which needs to be proved by the evidence of witnesses is to be proved, at trial, by their oral evidence, but that this is subject to any provision to the contrary contained in the Civil Procedure Rules or elsewhere or to any order of the court. One such provision to the contrary is to be found in r. 32.5, which makes provision for the witness statement of a witness to stand as his or her evidence-in-chief.

A witness statement, for these purposes, is a written statement signed by a person which contains the evidence which that person would be allowed to give orally (r. 32.4(1)). The statement, therefore, should not contain any material which is irrelevant, privileged, or otherwise inadmissible. Under CPR, r. 32.4(2), the court will order a party to serve on the other parties any witness statement of the oral evidence which the party serving the statement intends to rely on in relation to any issues of fact to be decided at the trial; and under r. 32.4(3) the court may give directions as to the order in which the statements are to be served. Normally the court will direct the simultaneous exchange of statements (see PD 28, para. 3.9 and PD 29, para. 4.10).

A witness statement should be dated; it must, if practicable, be in the intended witness's own words and should be expressed in the first person; and it must also indicate which of the statements in it are made from the witness's own knowledge and which are matters of information or belief (see r. 32.8 and PD 32, paras 17.2, 18.1 and 18.2). The statement is the equivalent of the oral evidence which the witness would, if called, give in evidence, and must include a statement of truth by the intended witness, i.e. a signed statement that he/she believes the facts in it are true (PD 32, para. 20.1 and r. 22.1(6)). Where a witness statement does not comply with CPR, Part 32 or PD 32 in relation to its form, the court may refuse to admit it as evidence (PD 32, para. 25.1).

Rule 32.5 provides as follows:

> (1) If—
>   (a) a party has served a witness statement; and
>   (b) he wishes to rely at trial on the evidence of the witness who made the statement,
> he must call the witness to give oral evidence unless the court orders otherwise or he puts the statement in as hearsay evidence.
>   (2) Where a witness is called to give oral evidence under paragraph (1), his witness statement shall stand as his evidence in chief unless the court orders otherwise.
>   (3) A witness giving oral evidence at trial may with the permission of the court—
>   (a) amplify his witness statement; and
>   (b) give evidence in relation to new matters which have arisen since the witness statement was served on the other parties.
>   (4) The court will give permission under paragraph (3) only if it considers that there is good reason not to confine the evidence of the witness to the contents of his witness statement.
>   (5) If a party who has served a witness statement does not—
>   (a) call the witness to give evidence at trial; or
>   (b) put the witness statement in as hearsay evidence,
> any other party may put the witness statement in as hearsay evidence.

As to r. 32.5(2), it is likely that the court, in deciding whether to order that the statement should *not* stand as the witness's evidence-in-chief, will have regard to such matters as the extent to which his or her evidence is likely to be controversial and to go to the heart of the dispute, and the extent to which his or her credibility will be in issue: see *Mercer* v *Chief Constable of the Lancashire Constabulary* [1991] 2 All ER 504, CA, a decision under an earlier version of the rules.

Under r. 32.9, provision is made for a party who is unable to obtain a witness statement to apply for permission to serve a witness summary instead. Rule 32.9 provides as follows:

> (1) A party who—
>   (a) is required to serve a witness statement for use at trial; but
>   (b) is unable to obtain one,
> may apply, without notice, for permission to serve a witness summary instead.
>   (2) A witness summary is a summary of—
>   (a) the evidence, if known, which would otherwise be included in a witness statement; or

(b)   if the evidence is not known, the matters about which the party serving the witness summary proposes to question the witness.

(3)   Unless the court orders otherwise, a witness summary must include the name and address of the intended witness.

(4)   Unless the court orders otherwise, a witness summary must be served within the period in which a witness statement would have had to be served.

(5)   Where a party serves a witness summary, so far as practicable, rules 32.4 (requirement to serve witness statements for use at trial), 32.5(3) (amplifying witness statements), and 32.8 (form of witness statement) shall apply to the summary.

Under r. 32.10, if a witness statement or witness summary is not served in respect of an intended witness within the time specified by the court, then the witness may not be called to give oral evidence unless the court gives permission.

4.3.7   SPECIAL MEASURES DIRECTIONS

Part II, Chapter I (ss. 16–33) Youth Justice and Criminal Evidence Act 1999 introduced the concept of 'special measures directions' in criminal proceedings, for witnesses who are vulnerable or intimidated.

4.3.7.1   Procedure

The question of whether a special measures direction should be made can be raised by a party applying to the court or by the court of its own motion (s. 19). Where the court determines that the witness is an eligible one under ss. 16 or 17 (see below), it then has to determine whether any one or combination of available special measures directions would be 'likely to improve the quality of evidence' given by the witness, and, if so, determine which one or combination would be likely to maximise so far as practicable the quality of such evidence, and give a direction providing for the appropriate measure or measures to apply (s. 19(2)(a) and (b)). The views of the witness and whether any such measure might 'tend to inhibit' effective testing of the evidence are factors to which the court must pay particular attention (s. 19(3)).

Section 20 provides that a special measures direction has binding effect until the proceedings for which it was made are determined or abandoned. Directions can be discharged or varied if it is in the interests of justice.

The court must state in open court its reasons for giving, varying, refusing or discharging a direction.

4.3.7.2   Eligibility

The eligibility of a witness other than the accused for assistance by a special measures direction is set out in ss. 16–17 of the 1999 Act.

Under s. 16, a witness is eligible if he or she is under 17 (at the time of the hearing); or the quality of his or her evidence is likely to be diminished by reason of mental disorder (within the meaning of the Mental Health Act 1983), or because he or she otherwise has a 'significant impairment of intelligence and social functioning'; or he or she has a physical disability or physical disorder.

Under s. 17, a witness is eligible if the court is satisfied that the quality of his or her evidence is likely to be diminished by reason of fear or distress in connection with testifying. Section 17(2) lists a number of factors to be taken into account in determining this, including the nature and circumstances of the offence, the witness's age, social, cultural and ethnic factors, and behaviour towards the witness on the part of the accused, his or her family or associates. Section 17(4) provides that a complainant in a sexual offence who is a witness is eligible, unless the witness has informed the court of his or her wish not to be so eligible.

4.3.7.3   Availability

Witnesses eligible by virtue of s. 16 can have the special measures directions available under ss. 23–30 (see below).

Witnesses eligible by virtue of s. 17 can have the special measures directions available under ss. 23–28.

In summary, the special measures directions available are as follows (reference should be made to the statutory provision for full details):

Section 23: allows for a witness to be prevented from seeing the accused by means of a screen or other arrangement.

Section 24: permits giving evidence by a live link.

Section 25: provides for the exclusion during the giving of the witness's evidence of any specified person (not including the accused, his or her legal representatives or interpreters/persons appointed to assist the witness). This direction only applies to cases relating to sexual offences or where there are reasonable grounds to believe that anyone (other than the accused) has sought, or will seek, to intimidate the witness in connection with testifying.

Section 26: allows for the wearing of wigs and gowns to be dispensed with during the giving of the witness's evidence.

Section 27: provides for a video-recording of an interview with the witness to be admitted as evidence-in-chief.

Section 28: where a direction under s. 27 has been made, the direction may also provide for any cross-examination or re-examination to be video recorded and admitted in evidence.

Section 29: provides for any examination of a witness to be conducted through an interpreter, or by a court approved 'intermediary' (whose job it is to communicate to the witness the questions put to him or her, and then communicate the witness's answers to the person asking the questions).

Section 30: allows the provision of such device as the court considers appropriate with a view to enabling questions and answers to be communicated despite any disability, disorder or impairment on the part of the witness.

Where a special measures direction has been made in accordance with which a witness makes a statement forming part of his or her evidence but not in direct oral testimony in court, that statement is treated as if it were made in direct oral testimony in court (s. 31(1) and (2)).

In jury trials where a special measures direction has been given, the judge must give such warning (if any) as he or she considers necessary to ensure that the direction given does not prejudice the accused (s. 32).

4.3.7.4 **Specific provisions for child witnesses**

Where the court, in making a determination for the purposes of s. 19(2), decides that a witness is a child witness (defined as one eligible under s. 16(1)(a), i.e. under 17), the court is required first to have regard to s. 21(3) to (7), and then s. 19(2). Section 21(3) provides that:

> *The primary rule in the case of a child witness is that the court must give a special measures direction in relation to the witness which complies with the following requirements—*
> *(a) it must provide for any relevant recording to be admitted under section 27 (video recorded evidence-in-chief); and*
> *(b) it must provide for any evidence given by the witness in the proceedings which is not given by means of a video recording (whether in chief or otherwise) to be given by means of a live link in accordance with section 24.*

This primary rule is subject to the special measure being available (s. 21(4)(a)); subject to s. 27(2) (where it is in the interests of justice not to admit such a recording) (s. 21(4)(b)), and does not apply where the court is satisfied that compliance would not be likely to maximise so far as possible the quality of the witness's evidence (this may be the case where some other special measures direction has that effect) (s. 21(4)(c)). Section 21(4)(c) does not apply where the child witness is 'in need of special protection' (defined as being where any of the offences falls within s. 35(3)(a) of the 1999 Act (sexual offences) or within (s. 35(3)(b)–(d)) (kidnapping, assaults etc.). In such a case, any special measures direction complying with s. 21(3)(a) must also provide for the direction available under s. 28 (video recorded cross-examination and re-examination) to apply in relation to any cross-examination of the witness otherwise than by the accused in person, and any subsequent re-examination (s. 21(6)). This requirement is subject to the special measure being available, and does not apply if the witness has informed the court that he or she does not want the special measure direction to apply to him or her.

The provisions available under s. 21 can be extended to those witnesses who were under 17 at the time of making the recording, but who are now over 17 (s. 22).

4.3.8 **LIVE TELEVISION LINKS**

In addition to a special measures direction permitting a live link under Youth Justice and Criminal Evidence Act 1999, s. 24, in the case of eligible witnesses (see **4.3.7.2** above), Criminal Justice Act 1988 provides, in certain circumstances, for the use of live television links in the case of witnesses who are outside the UK. Section 32(1) and (1A) provide that:

> *(1)   A person other than the accused may give evidence through a live television link in proceedings to which subsection (1A) below applies if:*
> *(a)   the witness is outside the United Kingdom; . . .*
> *(1A)   This subsection applies:*
> *(a)   to trials on indictment, appeals to the criminal division of the Court of Appeal and hearings of references under section 17 of the Criminal Appeal Act 1968; and*
> *(b)   to proceedings in youth courts and appeals to the Crown Court arising out of such proceedings.*

In civil cases the court may allow a witness to give evidence through a video link or by other means: CPR, r. 32.3.

Questions

OBJECTIVES

By the conclusion of this chapter, you should be able:

(a)   to identify when, during the course of a trial, the issue of competence is likely to arise;

(b)   to know the procedure for determining the competence of a witness;

(c)   to know whether any given witness is competent;

(d)   to know whether any given witness is compellable;

(e)   to know when a witness may give unsworn evidence; and

(f)   to understand the procedural issues relating to witnesses.

Question 1
(a)   In what circumstances may a person who is alleged to have jointly committed the offence with the accused be competent and compellable to give evidence for the prosecution against the accused?

(b) John is 11 and Bob is 18. Bob is severely mentally handicapped and has difficulties in communicating with people. It is alleged that both John and Bob were sexually abused by Graham. Both are very nervous of giving evidence, and they claim that Graham's brother, Joshua, has been rude and offensive to them each time he sees them. Describe any likely procedural steps that might be taken before either of them gives evidence at Graham's trial on indictment for indecent assault.

(c) What is the test for determining whether a child is capable of giving sworn evidence in civil proceedings?

Question 2

Ellen leaves her husband, Edgar, and goes to live with George and his 12-year-old son, Gary. Edgar and his brother, Harry, are jointly charged with assaulting Gary, seriously wounding George, and attempting to kidnap Ellen.

(a) Advise whether Ellen and Gary are competent and compellable witnesses for the prosecution in respect of these three offences.

(b) Edgar and Harry both wish to call Harry's wife, Hilda, to give evidence in their favour. Hilda is now estranged from Harry and is reluctant to testify for the defence. Can she be compelled to do so?

(c) Advise whether Harry can be called as a defence witness either on his own behalf or for Edgar.

FIVE

EXAMINATION, CROSS-EXAMINATION AND RE-EXAMINATION

What are the rules governing the questions that you ask of your witnesses (examination-in-chief and re-examination)?

May a witness refresh his or her memory by reference to notes made before the case came to court?

What can you do if a witness you call fails to prove a certain matter or proves the opposite (unfavourable and hostile witnesses)?

What are the rules governing the questions that you can ask of your opponent's witnesses (cross-examination)?

5.1 Examination-in-Chief

5.1.1 LEADING QUESTIONS

Leading questions are those which suggest the answer sought, sometimes by putting a matter in dispute in a way designed to elicit a reply of no more than 'yes' or 'no', or which are framed in such a way that they assume certain facts not yet established. (See *Advocacy Manual,* **18.3.3**.) Such questions are not generally permitted in examination-in-chief (but may be put in cross-examination). The rationale of this general rule is to prevent the witness from being led into giving only evidence advantageous to the party calling him or her, rather than a more spontaneous narrative, 'warts and all'. If evidence is elicited by leading questions, it remains admissible, but the weight to be attached to it may be reduced: *Moor* v *Moor* [1954] 1 WLR 927.

5.1.1.1 Examples
1. *A question suggesting the answer sought*

'And the weather, was it snowing that afternoon?'

This clearly suggests the answer that on the afternoon in question it was snowing (and not raining, sleeting, sunny etc).

2. *A question putting a matter in dispute in a way designed to elicit a reply of 'yes'*

Assuming the matter in dispute is whether a certain event took place before or after 2 p.m.: 'Well, that must have been after 2 p.m., must it not?'

3. *A question putting a matter in dispute in a way designed to elicit a reply of 'no'*

Assuming, again, the matter in dispute is whether a certain event took place before or after 2 p.m.: 'Well, that couldn't possibly have been before 2 p.m., could it?'

4.   *A question framed in such a way that it assumes certain facts not yet established*

To a witness who has not even mentioned the weather conditions on a particular day: 'So what precautions did you take against the ice and snow?'

5.1.1.2   Exceptions

The rule is relaxed in relation to introductory and undisputed matters. Leading questions may also be put to a witness whom the judge rules hostile (see **5.1.3**).

5.1.2   REFRESHING MEMORY

5.1.2.1   In court

A witness may refresh his or her memory in the witness box by reference to a document that the witness made or verified provided that:

(a)   the document was made or verified at the time of the events in question or so shortly thereafter that the facts were fresh in the witness's memory;

(b)   the document is produced in court for inspection; and

(c)   if the original is available, the document is, in cases where the witness has no recollection of the events in question, but simply gives evidence as to the accuracy of the contents of the document, that original.

The rule applies not only where 'present recollection is revived' (i.e. on sight of the document the witness's train of memory is triggered), but also in the case of 'past recollection recorded' (i.e. the witness, his or her memory being a perfect blank, swears to the accuracy of the statement made in the document): see *Maugham* v *Hubbard* (1828) 8 B & C 14, where an issue arose as to whether a sum of money had been paid. A witness was called to prove receipt, and on looking at a written acknowledgement initialled by himself said that on the basis of seeing his initials he was sure he had received the money, although he had no recollection of so doing. It was held that the witness had properly been allowed to refresh his memory from the document. See also *Topham* v *McGregor* (1844) 1 Car & Kir 320.

A witness may even be allowed to refresh his or her memory in re-examination: see *R* v *Sutton* [1991] Crim LR 836, CA.

As to 'making' or 'verification' (which can be visual or aural), in *R* v *Whalley* (1852) 3 Car & Kir 54 it was held that entries in a ship's log made by the mate and inspected by the captain could be used to refresh the memory of the captain. In *R* v *Kelsey* (1982) 74 Cr App R 213, CA, it was held that a note dictated to a police officer and read back to, and confirmed by, an eye-witness, could be used to refresh the memory of the eye-witness, on proof that the note used in court was the note that was dictated and read over. *Cf. R* v *Eleftheriou* [1993] Crim LR 947, CA.

'Contemporaneity', in the literal sense, is not a necessary requirement. The document should have been written or verified either at the time of the events in question or shortly thereafter so that the facts were fresh in the memory: see *R* v *Richardson* [1971] 2 QB 484, CA and *R* v *Simmonds* (1967) 51 Cr App R 316, CA.

The jury may see the document if this would assist them in estimating the witness's credibility: see *R* v *Bass* [1953] 1 QB 680, CA, below. It may also be used by them as an *aide memoire* in cases where the witness's evidence is long and involved (but not, it seems, where the document is an unsigned record of an accused's confession): see *R* v *Sekhon* (1987) 85 Cr App R 19, CA and *cf. R* v *Dillon* (1983) 85 Cr App R 29.

In *R* v *Bass* the Court of Appeal held that a jury should have been allowed to inspect the notebooks from which two police officers, who denied collaboration, had read identical accounts of an interview with the accused, because it might have assisted them in estimating the credibility of the officers. It was also held not to be improper for officers to refresh their memory from notes made in collaboration. (Note that generally, however, discussions should not take place between witnesses as to the evidence they will give: *R* v *Skinner* (1994) 99 Cr App R 212, CA. See also *R* v *Arif, The Times*, 22 June 1993.)

Where the original note made by the witness has been destroyed or lost, a document which the witness made later, and which was based on the note, can be used to refresh his or her memory, provided the document contains substantially what was in the note. Thus in *Attorney-General's Reference (No. 3 of 1979)* (1979) 69 Cr App R 411, a police officer was permitted to refresh his memory from a full note based on jottings taken during the course of an interview; and in *R* v *Mills* [1962] 1 WLR 1152, CA, an officer who had heard, and made a tape-recording of, a conversation between two co-accused, was allowed to refer to notes subsequently written up with the assistance of the tape, which was not itself put in evidence. See also *R* v *Cheng* (1976) 63 Cr App R 20, CA.

Copies are also allowed when the original has been lost or destroyed and the copy can be proved to be accurate either by the witness or by some third party: see *Topham* v *McGregor* (1844) 1 Car & Kir 320. However, where the original is in existence and the witness has no recollection of the events in question (i.e. a case of 'past recollection recorded'), the original must be produced: *Doe* d *Church & Phillips* v *Perkins* (1790) 3 TR 749.

The best summary of the effect of inspecting and cross-examining on a memory-refreshing document is that of Sir Jocelyn Simon P in *Senat* v *Senat* (1965) P 172 at p. 177:

> Where a document is used to refresh a witness's memory, cross-examining counsel may inspect that document in order to check it, without making it evidence. Moreover he may cross-examine upon it without making it evidence provided that his cross-examination does not go further than the parts which are used for refreshing the memory of the witness.

5.1.2.2 Example

A police officer, in the witness box, uses a notebook to refresh her memory about a car accident which she claims to have witnessed.

She says, 'The man I now know as Mr Adams was driving erratically and hit the car of the man I now know as Mr Browne'.

Appearing on behalf of Mr Adams, and before embarking on your cross-examination of the officer, you ask to inspect the notebook. On inspecting it, you see that what the officer has said is indeed written down. But you also notice that in the sentence before, she has written that immediately before the accident Mr Browne was driving on the wrong side of the road.

In these circumstances you *could* elect to confine your cross-examination to those parts of the document used by the officer to refresh her memory (e.g. 'Officer, the fact is that Mr Adams wasn't driving erratically at all, was he?'). However, if you were to go further than the parts which were used by the officer to refresh her memory (e.g. 'Officer, the fact is that immediately before the accident Mr Browne was driving on the wrong side of the road, wasn't he?'), you would 'make the document evidence' and thereby allow the tribunal of fact to examine the document upon which the cross-examination was based.

5.1.2.3 Making the document evidence

The meaning of 'making the document evidence' in the case, varies according to whether the proceedings are civil or criminal. In civil proceedings, under the Civil

Evidence Act 1995, s. 1, evidence shall not be excluded on the ground that it is hearsay. Section 6 of the Act provides that:

> *(4) Nothing in this Act affects any of the rules of law as to the circumstances in which, where a person called as a witness in civil proceedings is cross-examined on a document used by him to refresh his memory, that document may be made evidence in the proceedings.*
>
> *(5) Nothing in this section shall be construed as preventing a statement of any description referred to above from being admissible by virtue of section 1 as evidence of the matters stated.*

It is arguable that subsection (5) has no bearing on subsection (4) because whereas subsection (5) refers to 'a statement of any description referred to above', there is no reference to any 'statement' in subsection (4). However, it is assumed that the Parliamentary intention underlying these cumbersome provisions was to preserve the rule set out clearly in the statutory precursor to s. 6(4) and (5) (namely the Civil Evidence Act 1968, s. 3(2)), which is that where a memory-refreshing document is received in evidence by virtue of cross-examination on it, any statement made in that document by the person using it to refresh memory shall be admissible as evidence of any fact stated in it of which direct oral evidence by him or her would be admissible.

In criminal proceedings, however, the document can only be used as evidence of consistency or inconsistency affecting the credibility of the witness: see *R* v *Virgo* (1978) 67 Cr App R 323, CA; and *R* v *Britton* [1987] 1 WLR 539, CA.

5.1.2.4 Out of court

It is obviously wrong for several witnesses to be handed their statements before the trial in circumstances enabling them to compare with one another what they have said: *R* v *Richardson* [1971] 2 QB 484, CA. Likewise such statements should not be read to witnesses in each other's presence: *R* v *Skinner* (1994) 99 Cr App R 212, CA at p. 216. However, a witness may refresh memory from his or her own statement outside the court room and before giving evidence. The pre-conditions which apply in the case of memory-refreshing documents in court have no application. However, concerning inspection and cross-examination upon a document used to refresh the memory outside court, the rules are the same as those applying to the use of memory-refreshing documents in the witness-box: see *R* v *Richardson* [1971] 2 QB 484, CA, *R* v *Westwell* [1976] 2 All ER 812, CA, and *Owen* v *Edwards* (1984) 77 Cr App R 191, DC.

A witness may likewise refresh his memory from a document outside the court room after he or she has begun to give evidence: *R* v *Da Silva* [1990] 1 All ER 29. See *per* Stuart-Smith LJ at p. 33:

> In our judgment, therefore, it should be open to the judge, in the exercise of his discretion and in the interests of justice, to permit a witness who has begun to give evidence to refresh his memory from a statement made near to the time of events in question, even though it does not come within the definition of contemporaneous, provided he is satisfied (1) that the witness indicates that he cannot now recall the details of events because of the lapse of time since they took place, (2) that he made a statement much nearer the time of the events and that the contents of the statement represented his recollection at the time he made it, (3) that he had not read the statement before coming into the witness box and (4) that he wished to have an opportunity to read the statement before he continued to give evidence.

> We do not think that it matters whether the witness withdraws from the witness box and reads his statement, as he would do if he had had the opportunity before entering the witness box, or whether he reads it in the witness box. What is important is that, if the former course is adopted, no communication must be had with the witness, other than to see that he can read the statement in peace. Moreover, if either course is adopted, the statement must be removed from him when he comes to give his evidence and he should not be permitted to refer to it again, unlike a contemporaneous statement which may be used to refresh memory while giving evidence.

In this case the initiative came from the judge, but it is clear that it is no ground of objection if the judge thinks it is in the interests of justice that he intervene: see *R* v *Fotheringham* [1975] Crim LR 710 and *R* v *Tyagi, The Times*, 21 July 1986.

R v *Da Silva* has not laid down as a matter of law that a witness, once in the witness box, can only refresh his or her memory if all four criteria specified in that case are satisfied. The court has a real discretion whether to permit a witness to refresh his or her memory from a non-contemporaneous statement: see *R* v *South Ribble Magistrates' Court, ex parte Cochrane* [1996] 2 Cr App R 544, DC, where the witness did not satisfy criterion (3), because he had read his statement before giving his evidence, although he had not taken it in properly. The court could see no logical difference between a witness in that position and someone who has not read his or her statement at all.

5.1.3 UNFAVOURABLE AND HOSTILE WITNESSES

The general rule at common law is that the credit of a party's own witnesses may not be impeached by that party, whether by:

(a) asking leading questions, or

(b) asking about or calling evidence to prove prior inconsistent statements, prior discreditable conduct, bad character, previous convictions or bias.

An unfavourable witness is a witness who, called by a party to prove a certain matter, simply fails to do so or proves the opposite.

The best definition of a hostile witness is that he or she is one who, in the opinion of the judge, 'is not desirous of telling the truth to the court at the instance of the party calling him'. See J. F. Stephen, *A Digest of the Law of Evidence*, 12 edn, 1936, Art. 147.

Lord Goddard CJ in *R* v *Fraser* (1956) 40 Cr App R 160, CCA, said that if a party has in its possession a previous statement in flat contradiction of the witness's testimony, that party is entitled to treat the witness as hostile and should apply to the judge to treat the witness as such. It is submitted that the word 'entitled' was used *per incuriam*: the witness, for example, may display no hostile animus and be in a position to explain away the seemingly 'flat contradiction'. In *R* v *Maw* [1994] Crim LR 841, it was held that if a witness gives evidence contrary to an earlier statement (or fails to give the evidence expected), the party calling the witness and the judge should not immediately proceed to treat him or her as hostile, unless that is the only appropriate course because of the degree of hostility, but should consider first inviting the witness to refresh his or her memory from appropriate material.

Where a party to civil proceedings is called by his opponent, he or she is not to be treated automatically as a hostile witness — the matter remains to be decided by the judge: *Price* v *Manning* (1880) 42 ChD 372, CA. For the power to do this, see Evidence Act 1851, s. 2 (parties) and Evidence Amendment Act 1853, s. 1 (spouses of parties).

Normally, the application for leave to treat a witness as hostile will be made during examination-in-chief. However, in rare cases in which the witness only shows signs of hostility in re-examination, an application can be made at this later stage: *R* v *Powell* [1985] Crim LR 592, CA.

In deciding whether a witness is hostile, the witness should not normally be questioned in the absence of the jury: *R* v *Darby* [1989] Crim LR 817, CA. In criminal cases it would appear that the prosecution may call a person even if he/she has shown that he/she is likely to be a hostile witness, as when, before the trial, he or she retracts an earlier statement and/or makes a second statement (see *R* v *Mann* (1972) 56 Cr App R 750, CA, and *R* v *Vibert*, unreported, 21 October 1974, CA); but in cases in which the person refuses to assist the prosecution or court, or claims to be no longer able to remember anything, the judge has a discretion to hold a *voir dire* to decide whether he or she should be allowed to give evidence: *R* v *Honeyghon and Sayles* [1999] Crim LR 221,

CA. The defence are likely to object to the prosecution calling such a person on the basis that it is simply a device to allow the jury to become aware of previous statements made by him/her and inconsistent with the testimony he/she is likely to give: although the judge must direct the jury that the previous statements are not evidence of the facts contained in them, the jury may find difficulty in complying with such a direction. See also *R* v *Dat* [1998] Crim LR 488, CA.

If a witness is merely unfavourable, the general rule holds good. All that the party calling the witness can do is to call other witnesses, if available, to prove what the witness in question failed to prove: *Ewer* v *Ambrose* (1825) 3 B & C 746.

If the judge grants leave to treat a witness as hostile, the party calling the witness may, at common law, ask leading questions: see *R* v *Thompson* (1976) 64 Cr App R 96, CA. That party may also ask the witness about, and prove, previous inconsistent statements.

Criminal Procedure Act 1865, s. 3, provides that:

> *A party producing a witness shall not be allowed to impeach his credit by general evidence of bad character; but he may, in case the witness shall in the opinion of the judge prove adverse, contradict him by other evidence, or, by leave of the judge, prove that he has made at other times a statement inconsistent with his present testimony; but before such last-mentioned proof can be given the circumstances of the supposed statement, sufficient to designate the particular occasion, must be mentioned to the witness, and he must be asked whether or not he has made such statement.*

In *Greenough* v *Eccles* (1859) 5 CB (NS) 786, it was held that (i) 'adverse' means hostile and (ii) the phrase 'he may . . . by other evidence' means that the party calling a hostile witness can do the same as in the case of an unfavourable witness, i.e. call other witnesses to prove what the witness in question failed to prove.

If the witness, under cross-examination on the previous inconsistent statement, confirms its contents, then that will stand as his or her evidence and can be accepted by the tribunal of fact, subject to assessment of the witness's credibility: *R* v *Maw*. If the witness refuses to accept the truth of the previous statement, the effect of proving it under s. 3 of the 1865 Act varies according to whether the proceedings are civil or criminal.

In civil proceedings, under Civil Evidence Act 1995, s. 1, evidence shall not be excluded on the ground that it is hearsay. Section 6 of the 1995 Act provides that:

> *(3)   Where in the case of civil proceedings section 3, 4 or 5 of the Criminal Procedure Act 1865 applies, which make provision as to—*
> *(a)   how far a witness may be discredited by the party producing him . . .*
> *this Act does not authorise the adducing of evidence of a previous inconsistent or contradictory statement otherwise than in accordance with those sections.*
> *. . .*
> *(5)   Nothing in this section shall be construed as preventing a statement of any description referred to above from being admissible by virtue of section 1 as evidence of the matters stated.*

In criminal proceedings, however, a previous statement can only be treated as evidence of inconsistency going to the witness's credit: see *R* v *White* (1922) 17 Cr App R 60 and *R* v *Golder* [1960] 1 WLR 1169, CCA. Because the statement is only relevant to credit, the jury should not be given copies of it: *R* v *Darby* [1989] Crim LR 817, CA.

There is no inflexible rule to the effect that the judge should direct the jury that the evidence of a hostile witness should be treated as unreliable. The strength of the direction turns on the particular circumstances of each case. In *R* v *Thomas* [1985] Crim LR 445, CA, the accused was charged with the murder of his six-month-old son. The prosecution case was that it was a typical baby-battering case and that the last of the injuries inflicted was likely to have been caused by the same person who inflicted earlier injuries. The sister of the accused admitted to the police that she had handled the baby roughly. She was called by the accused but went back on her police statements. The defence were given leave to treat her as a hostile witness. She then admitted violence to the child on two or three occasions. The accused appealed against his conviction on the grounds that the trial judge had improperly directed the jury to disregard the evidence of his sister. It was held on appeal, substituting a verdict of manslaughter, that since the evidence given was to the accused's benefit, the judge should have invited the jury to consider whether her evidence did not cast doubt on the Crown case and should have told them that she would have every motive for denying violence, but very few for admitting it. See also *R* v *Pestano* [1981] Crim LR 397, CA and *R* v *Goodway* [1993] 4 All ER 894, CA, at p. 899.

However, the judge should give a warning about the dangers of a witness who has contradicted himself or herself; and it will not suffice to direct the jury to approach the evidence with great caution and reservation: *R* v *Maw*. In that case it was stressed that it is only if the jury consider that they can give any credence to the witness that they may then turn to consider which parts of his or her testimony, if any, they will accept.

Where a spouse is competent but not compellable for the prosecution, the judge should explain to him or her *before* he or she is sworn, the possibility of being treated as a hostile witness because once such a witness starts giving evidence, changes heart and attempts to shield the accused, it is too late to assert non-compellability: *R* v *Pitt* [1983] QB 25, CA.

5.1.4 PREVIOUS CONSISTENT STATEMENTS

5.1.4.1 The general rule

In both civil and criminal cases, a witness may not be asked in chief whether formerly the witness has made a statement consistent with his or her testimony. What is banned is proof of the prior statement as evidence of the witness's consistency (*cf.* the rule against hearsay whereby the prior statement is not admissible as evidence of the facts contained in it). This would appear to be the reason why truth drug evidence is inadmissible: *Fennell* v *Jerome Property Maintenance Ltd, The Times,* 26 November 1986.

For an example from a criminal case, see *R* v *Roberts* [1942] 1 All ER 187. The accused was charged with the murder of a girl by shooting her. At the trial he gave evidence that the gun went off accidentally while he was trying to make up a quarrel with the girl. Two days after the alleged offence, the accused had told his father that his defence would be one of accident. The trial judge held that proof of this conversation was not permissible, a view confirmed by the Court of Criminal Appeal. The conversation would have been inadmissible hearsay if tendered for the truth of the facts asserted, but it was equally inadmissible if tendered merely to bolster the credibility of the accused by showing his consistency.

For an example from a civil case, see *Corke* v *Corke* [1958] P 93, CA.

5.1.4.2 The exceptions

Civil Evidence Act 1995
In civil proceedings, the previous statements of a witness may be admitted, with the leave of the court, both as evidence of the facts contained in them, and also as evidence of consistency, under Civil Evidence Act 1995, s. 6(2). See further **Chapter 9**.

Memory-refreshing documents
See **5.1.2**.

Complaints in sexual cases
Oliver Wendell Holmes J regarded this exception as 'a perverted survival of the ancient requirement that a woman should make hue and cry as a preliminary to an appeal of rape': see *Commonwealth* v *Cleary* (1898) 172 Mass 175.

In cases of rape and other sexual offences, if the complainant made a voluntary complaint at the first opportunity reasonably afforded, then the person to whom the complaint was made may give evidence of what was said in order to show its consistency with the complainant's evidence and, in cases in which consent is in issue, to negative consent.

In *White* v *R* [1999] 1 Cr App R 153, the Privy Council has held that if the person to whom the complaint was made does not give evidence, the complainant's own evidence that she made a complaint cannot assist in either proving her consistency or negativing consent, because without independent confirmation, her own evidence that she complained takes the jury nowhere in deciding whether she is worthy of belief. Lord Hoffmann held that although it does not follow that evidence that the complainant spoke to someone after the incident is inadmissible, the complainant should not be allowed to say that she had told people 'what had happened', because the jury will be bound to infer that she had made statements in terms substantially the same as her evidence. It was said that it is important not to infringe the spirit of the rule against previous consistent statements by conveying indirectly to the jury that the complainant has given a previous account of the incident, in similar terms, with a view to inviting them to infer that her credibility is supported by the fact of the complaint. It was also held that where evidence is given of the bare fact that the complainant spoke to someone after the incident, it is incumbent on the judge to give the jury clear instructions that they are not entitled to treat the evidence as confirming the complainant's credibility.

The exception is now confined to sexual cases: *R* v *Jarvis and Jarvis* [1991] Crim LR 374, CA. See also *R* v *Wink* (1834) 6 C & P 397 and *R* v *Lillyman* [1896] 2 QB 167.

What is the first opportunity depends on the circumstances, including:

(a) the character of the complainant; and

(b) the relationship between the complainant, and

   (i) the person to whom the complaint was made, and

   (ii) the persons to whom the complaint might have been made but was not.

Thus victims often need time before they can bring themselves to tell what has been done to them, and whereas some find it impossible to complain to anyone except a parent or a member of their family, others feel it quite impossible to tell such a person: *R* v *Valentine* [1996] 2 Cr App R 213, CA.

A complaint will not necessarily be excluded because there has been a previous complaint: see *R* v *Lee* (1912) 7 Cr App R 31 and *R* v *Wilbourne* (1917) 12 Cr App R 280. However, it is not permissible to lead evidence that the same complaint has been made in substantially the same terms on several occasions soon after the offence, if that would be prejudicial because it might lead the jury to treat the contents of the complaints as evidence of the truth of their contents: *R* v *Valentine*.

In *R* v *Osborne* [1905] 1 KB 551, CCR, Ridley J said:

> . . . the mere fact that the statement is made in answer to a question in such cases is not of itself sufficient to make it inadmissible as a complaint. Questions of a suggestive or leading character will, indeed, have that effect but a question such as this, put by the mother or other person, 'What is the matter?' or 'Why are you crying?' will not do so. These are questions which a person in charge will be likely to put; on the other hand, if she were asked, 'Did So-and-So (naming the prisoner) assault you?' 'Did he do this and that to you?' then the result would be different.

In *R* v *Camelleri* [1922] 2 KB 122, the Court of Criminal Appeal held that the exception applies in the case of sexual offences against males as well as females.

Where the exception applies, evidence may be given not only of the fact that a complaint has been made but also of the details of what was actually said by way of complaint. The complaint, however, is not evidence of the facts contained in it but only goes to consistency, and failure to direct the jury on this may result in a successful appeal (*R v Islam* [1998] Crim LR 575, CA). If consent is not in issue and the complainant does not give evidence, the complaint is inadmissible because there is no evidence with which it can be consistent: see *R v Wallwork* (1958) 42 Cr App R 153. Likewise, if the terms of the complaint are not ostensibly consistent with the terms of the complainant's testimony, the introduction of the complaint has no legitimate purpose and should be excluded: *R v Wright and Ormerod* (1990) 90 Cr App R 91, CA. See also *Kilby v R* (1973) 129 CLR 460, High Court of Australia.

The exception applies in the case of written, as well as oral complaints, and will even cover a note not intended to be read by anyone but given to someone by mistake: see *R v B* [1997] Crim LR 220, CA.

Statements made on accusation

A statement made by an accused when taxed with incriminating facts is admissible as evidence of attitude and reaction.

In *R v Storey* (1968) 52 Cr App R 334, the prosecution led evidence that when a quantity of cannabis had been found in the accused's flat, she had explained that it belonged to a man who had brought it there against her will. The defence relied on this in a submission of no case to answer, but the judge overruled the submission on the basis that the statement was not evidence of the facts stated. Upholding the decision, Widgery LJ held that the statement came in not for its truth, but as evidence of the reaction of the accused, which formed part of the general picture to be considered by the jury.

In *R v Pearce* (1979) 69 Cr App R 365, it was held that the principle is not limited to a statement made on the first encounter with the police (or anyone else). However, the longer the time that has elapsed after the first encounter, the less the weight to be attached to the denial. If an accused produces a carefully written statement to the police with a view to it being made part of the prosecution evidence, the trial judge may rule it inadmissible: see *R v Newsome* (1980) 71 Cr App R 325.

In *R v Tooke* (1990) 90 Cr App R 417, CA, it was held that the statement must be relevant as well as spontaneous and it is a matter for the judge's discretion where the dividing line falls. A statement will not be relevant if it does not add anything to the evidence already before the jury about the accused's reaction (e.g. evidence of an earlier statement, in similar terms, made by the accused at the scene of the alleged crime).

Where the accused makes a 'mixed statement', i.e. one which is partly inculpatory and partly exculpatory, both parts of the statement are admissible, because it would obviously be unfair for the prosecution to exclude answers favourable to the accused while admitting those unfavourable to him or her: *R v Storey* (1968) 52 Cr App R 334. Should the judge then direct the jury that the inculpatory parts are evidence of the facts they state (by way of exception to the hearsay rule) but that the exculpatory parts are only evidence of the accused's attitude and reaction? No. In *R v Duncan* (1981) 73 Cr App R 359, D was convicted of murder, having strangled the victim. In interview with the police he confessed to the killing but was unable to explain his motive. He suggested that he must have lost his temper by the victim teasing him by dancing in front of him. At trial he gave no evidence and called no witnesses. The trial judge, having considered the matter, withdrew the issue of provocation from the jury on the basis that as D's statements were self-serving, they could not be evidence of the facts. D appealed on the ground that the judge's ruling was wrong. Lord Lane CJ said:

> Where a 'mixed' statement is under consideration . . . in a case where the defendant has not given evidence, it seems to us that the simplest, and, therefore, the method most likely to produce a just result, is for the jury to be told that the whole statement, both the incriminating parts and the excuses or explanations, must be considered

by them in deciding where the truth lies. It is, to say the least, not helpful to try to explain to the jury that the exculpatory parts of the statement are something less than evidence of the facts they state. Equally, where appropriate, as it usually will be, the judge may, and should, point out that the incriminating parts are likely to be true (otherwise why say them?), whereas the excuses do not have the same weight.

The Court held that in so far as the judge's ruling was based on the reasoning that exculpatory remarks were inadmissible as evidence of their truth, he was in error. However, on the facts there was no evidence of provocation and the appeal was dismissed.

See also, applying *R v Duncan*, *R v Hamand* (1985) 82 Cr App R 65, CA and *R v Sharp* [1988] 1 WLR 7, HL. In *R v Garrod* [1997] Crim LR 445, the Court of Appeal addressed the question of how to identify the kind of interview which contained enough in the nature of admissions to justify calling it 'mixed'. The Court, acknowledging that it is almost impossible to conceive of any series of answers which could not be regarded as containing some admissions of relevant fact, as well as a statement of innocence and a denial of guilt, held that a statement should only be regarded as mixed if it contained an admission of fact which was significant to any issue in the case, i.e. capable of adding some degree of weight to the prosecution case on an issue which was relevant to guilt.

The principle established in *Duncan* and endorsed by the House of Lords in *Sharp* applies whether the 'mixed statement' is a written statement or a record of questions and answers at an interview, as between which there is no sensible distinction on grounds of logic or policy: *R v Polin* [1991] Crim LR 293, CA.

According to Lord Steyn in *R v Aziz* [1995] 3 All ER 149, HL, the principle only applies where a mixed statement is tendered by the *prosecution*; if the statement is not tendered by the prosecution, it is not admissible for the defence as evidence of any excuse or explanation. However, where the prosecution tender a mixed statement but do not rely on it as proof of any part of their case against the accused, the accused may rely upon it for the truth of its contents, although if the accused then fails to give evidence, and there is no other evidence to support the statement, it is highly likely that the weight to be attached to the excuse or explanation contained in it will be minimal: see *Western v DPP* [1997] 1 Cr App R 474, DC.

Previous identification

Evidence is admissible of a former identification of the accused by a witness out of court. It may be given either by that witness or by some other person present at the identification and may include the words declaratory of the identification, e.g. 'That's him!'

In *R v Christie* [1914] AC 545, for example, where a boy gave unsworn evidence identifying the accused as the man who had indecently assaulted him, a majority of the House of Lords held that both the boy's mother and a policeman could give evidence of a former identification by the boy when, shortly after the offence, he had approached the accused and had said, 'That is the man'.

Moreover, it is, in general, improper to identify the accused for the first time when he is in the dock: *R v Cartwright* (1914) 10 Cr App R 219. An obvious exception to this is when the accused refuses to take part in an identification parade: *R v John* [1973] Crim LR 113, CA. See also *R v Eatough* [1989] Crim LR 289, CC, and *R v Thomas* [1994] Crim LR 128, CA. It has been said, however, that the usual practice in a magistrates' court is different from that in the Crown Court. In *Barnes v Chief Constable of Durham* [1997] 2 Cr App R 505, B was convicted of failing to provide a specimen. He gave no indication at any time after he was charged that identity was in issue, and did not request an identification parade. At the trial, B was identified in the dock by an officer who had last seen him some 33 months earlier. The Divisional Court held that on the facts this had not been unfair. It was said that dock identifications were customary in magistrates' courts, in relation to driving offences at least, and that if, in every case where the defendant did not distinctly admit driving there had to be a parade, the whole process of justice in a magistrates' court would be severely impaired.

Evidence of previous identification may be excluded under Police and Criminal Evidence Act 1984, s. 78, especially if there have been serious and substantial breaches of the Code of Practice on Identification: see generally **Chapter 12**. Another limitation on the adducing of evidence of previous identification arises out the fact that sometimes identification involves the use of police photographs. If the witness is shown in court a police photograph used by him to identify the accused, it is almost impossible for the jury not to be prejudiced by the fact that the accused was known to the police, i.e. previously convicted: *R* v *Varley* (1914) 10 Cr App R 125. See, e.g., *R* v *Dwyer* [1925] 2 KB 799 where the jury were shown photographs of the accused wearing on his breast a large ticket stamped with his prisoner number! *Cf. R* v *Kingsland* (1979) 14 Cr App R 8, but see also *R* v *Governor of Pentonville Prison, ex parte Voets* [1986] 1 WLR 470, DC.

Statements in rebuttal of allegations of recent fabrication

Where, in cross-examination, it is suggested that a witness has recently fabricated his or her evidence, evidence is admissible in rebuttal to show that on an earlier occasion the witness made a statement consistent with that testimony. For a civil example, see *Flanagan* v *Fahy* [1918] 2 IR 361. It was put to a witness, who testified that a certain will was a forgery, that he had invented his evidence because of the hostility which existed between him and the defendant. The witness was then allowed to call evidence to show that he had told someone else that it was a forgery before the cause of the hostility between him and the defendant had arisen.

For a criminal example, see *R* v *Oyesiku* (1971) 56 Cr App R 240, CA. In this case D was charged with assault occasioning actual bodily harm and assaulting a police officer in the execution of his duty. Whilst D was in custody, following his arrest, his wife went to his solicitors and made a written statement on her own about the incident, which she had witnessed. At trial she was cross-examined by counsel for the prosecution, who suggested that she had made up her evidence, to help her husband. The trial judge allowed re-examination to the effect that she had made a previous statement in writing and allowed her to look at her statement and say that it was consistent with what she had told the jury, but refused to let the document go before the jury. The Court of Appeal held that the judge was wrong to so refuse and quashed the conviction.

This exception only arises, however, where what is alleged is *fabrication* at some period in time at or before the trial. Thus merely to impeach the witness's evidence in cross-examination by general allegations of unreliability or untruthfulness will not suffice: *Fox* v *General Medical Council* [1960] 1 WLR 1017, PC. See also *R* v *Williams* [1998] Crim LR 494, CA, where the prosecution alleged that the defendant's story was fabricated from the outset, rather than a late invention.

In criminal cases, the statement in rebuttal is admitted merely to bolster the witness's credibility by negativing the allegation of invention or reconstruction: see *R* v *Y* [1995] Crim LR 155, CA. In civil cases, however, the statement is also admitted for the truth of its contents. Under Civil Evidence Act 1995, s. 1, in civil proceedings evidence shall not be excluded on the ground that it is hearsay. Section 6 of the 1995 Act provides:

> *(2) A party who has called or intends to call a person as a witness in civil proceedings may not in those proceedings adduce evidence of a previous statement made by that person, except*
> . . .
> *(b) for the purpose of rebutting a suggestion that his evidence has been fabricated.*
> . . .
> *(5) Nothing in this section shall be construed as preventing a statement of any description referred to above from being admissible by virtue of section 1 as evidence of the matters stated.*

Res gestae statements

Under the doctrine of *res gestae*, evidence is admissible of any act or statement so closely associated in time, place and circumstances with some matter in issue that it can be said to be a part of the same transaction. See *R* v *Fowkes*, *The Times*, 8 March 1856 (Assizes) and generally, **9.2.1.1**. In *Fowkes*, D was charged with murder. Evidence was admissible that on seeing a face at the window through which a shot was fired, the son of the victim had said 'There's Butcher' (a name by which D was known).

5.2 Cross-Examination

5.2.1 LIABILITY TO CROSS-EXAMINATION

Where a witness has been called by a party and taken the oath, then the other party has the right to cross-examine. Usually, at least in criminal trials, a witness is examined in chief before being cross-examined. But sometimes a witness will simply be tendered by the prosecution for cross-examination. This could happen, for example, where one police officer gives evidence of observations that he made with a second officer, and the second officer has made a witness statement that confirms the first officer's evidence in every detail. In those circumstances, the prosecution might call the second officer after the first had given evidence in full. He would be sworn, but prosecuting counsel would ask no further questions about the details of his observations. Instead, he would leave him to be cross-examined by counsel for the defence. In civil trials the written witness statement of a witness can stand as evidence-in-chief (by CPR, r. 32.5(2)), and in such a case there might, in the absence of additional evidence, be no examination-in-chief, and cross-examination would follow immediately after the witness had been sworn and had identified his statement and acknowledged its truth.

5.2.1.1 Cross-examination in person

Generally, a witness called by one party to the proceedings and liable to cross-examination, may be cross-examined by counsel for the other party or, if that party is not represented, by that other party in person. However, in criminal proceedings there are provisions enacted in the Youth Justice and Criminal Evidence Act 1999 which prevent cross-examination by the accused in person. Section 34 provides that:

> *No person charged with a sexual offence may in any criminal proceedings cross-examine in person a witness who is the complainant, either—*
> *(a) in connection with that offence, or*
> *(b) in connection with any other offence (of whatever nature) with which that person is charged in the proceedings.*

'Sexual offence' is defined in s. 62 of the 1999 Act, and includes rape, burglary with intent to rape, indecent assault and other offences.

In addition to this general prohibition for sexual offences, the 1999 Act also prohibits cross-examination by the accused in other circumstances. Section 35(1) prevents such cross-examination on specified offences in the case of a 'protected witness'. A 'protected witness' is either the complainant to or witness of the specified offence and is either a child or is liable to be cross-examined either on a video recording (under s. 27 — see special measures directions at **4.3.7**) made at a time when the witness was a child or in any other way at any such time. The specified offences to which s. 35(1) applies are listed in s. 35(3) and include a number of sexual offences, kidnapping, false imprisonment, any offence under Children and Young Persons Act 1933, s. 1, and any other offence which involves an assault on, or injury or threat of injury to any person.

In cases where neither s. 34 nor s. 35 of the 1999 Act operate so as to prevent cross-examination in person, the court may still prevent it under s. 36, if it appears to the court that the quality of the evidence given is likely to be diminished by the cross-examination, that it would be likely to be improved if a direction were given, and that it would not be contrary to the interests of justice to give a direction. Factors to be taken into account by the court in reaching its decision are listed in s. 35(3) and include views expressed by the witness, the nature of the likely questions and the behaviour of the accused both towards the witness and generally. 'Witness' does not include any other person who is charged with an offence in the proceedings: s. 36(4)(a).

In cases where cross-examination by the accused is prevented under s. 34, 35 or 36, s. 38 applies. The court must invite the accused to arrange for a legal representative to act for him for the purposes of cross-examining, and require the accused to notify the court whether such a person is to act. If the accused fails to arrange for a legal representative or, failing notification, it appears that there will be no such representative, the court must consider whether it is necessary in the interests of justice for the witness to be cross-examined by a legal representative appointed to represent the accused's interests. If so, the court must appoint a qualified legal representative, who 'shall not be responsible to the accused': s. 38(5).

Under s. 39, a judge is required to give such warning as necessary (if any) to the jury, in a case where cross-examination in person has been prevented, to ensure that the accused is not prejudiced by any inferences that might be drawn from the fact that he or she has been prevented from cross-examining, and, where there is a court-appointed legal representative acting, that that person was not acting as the accused's own legal representative.

5.2.2 THE OBJECT AND SCOPE OF CROSS-EXAMINATION

The object of cross-examination is to qualify, weaken or destroy your opponent's case and, if you can, to establish your own case.

The cross-examining party must put to his opponent's witnesses every part of his own case as to which those witnesses can speak — if not he will be treated as having accepted their version and in his closing speech will not be allowed to attack their version or to put forward explanations which he did not put to the witnesses. See *R* v *Bircham* [1977] Crim LR 430, CA and *Browne* v *Dunn* (1893) 6 R 67, HL. If it is proposed to invite the jury to disbelieve a particular witness on a matter, it does not follow that it is always necessary to put to him explicitly that he is lying, provided that the overall tenor of the cross-examination is designed to show that his account is incapable of belief: *R* v *Lovelock* [1997] Crim LR 821, CA.

In cases tried by lay justices, however, the rule (that evidence unchallenged in cross-examination cannot be attacked in a closing speech and must be accepted by the tribunal of fact) does not apply: *O'Connell* v *Adams* [1973] Crim LR 113.

If counsel omits to cross-examine on a particular point by reason of inadvertence, the judge has a discretion to allow the witness to be recalled: *R* v *Wilson* [1977] Crim LR 553, CA.

Evidence which is inadmissible in chief remains inadmissible in cross-examination: see *R* v *Treacy* [1944] 2 All ER 229, CCA (an inadmissible confession) and *R* v *Gillespie* (1967) 51 Cr App R 172, CA (inadmissible hearsay).

In *R* v *Windass* (1989) 89 Cr App R 258, the Court of Appeal held that highly damaging statements contained in a document written by one co-accused may be admissible against that co-accused, if accompanied by a proper warning to the jury as to their status, but it is improper for the prosecution, during cross-examination of another co-accused, to ask him to explain such damaging statements when they are *inadmissible* against that other co-accused. See also *R* v *Gray* [1998] Crim LR 570, CA, where it was held to be improper for the prosecution to cross-examine a defendant on the contents of a co-defendant's interview, where the effect was to use what the co-defendant had said in interview as though it were evidence so as to undermine the defendant's own account.

In *Re P* [1989] Crim LR 897, it was held to be improper to cross-examine an accused in a sexual case on a complaint which is otherwise inadmissible because not a 'recent' complaint (see **5.1.4.2**).

The rule obtains in favour of any co-accused of the maker of a confession: *R* v *Rice* [1963] 1 QB 857, CCA. However if co-D1's inadmissible confession statement is relevant to the defence of co-D2 and co-D1 gives evidence inconsistent with the statement, co-D2 can cross-examine him on it, provided that the judge makes clear to the jury that it is no evidence of co-D1's guilt: *R* v *Rowson* [1986] QB 174, CA; *Lui Mei Lin* v *R* [1989] 1 All ER 359, PC. See also *R* v *Myers* [1997] 4 All ER 314, HL.

Counsel may produce a document, the contents of which are inadmissible hearsay, hand it to a witness, ask the witness to read it to himself, and then ask him if the contents are true. If the witness says that the contents are true, then they become the witness's evidence and can be revealed: see *R* v *Cooper (Warwick)* (1985) 82 Cr App R 74, CA and *R* v *Cross* (1990) 91 Cr App R 115, CA.

Counsel should not add to costs and waste time by protracted and irrelevant cross-examination but should cross-examine with restraint and the courtesy and consider-ation which witnesses are entitled to expect in a court of law: see *Mechanical & General Inventions Co. Ltd* v *Austin* [1935] AC 346. See also CPR, r. 32.1(3), at **2.8.2.1**.

There are also a number of rules to be observed which are set out in the Code of Conduct of the Bar of England and Wales, including in particular, the following paragraphs of Part VII (Conduct of Work):

701   A barrister:
   (a)   must in all his professional activities be courteous and act promptly conscien-tiously diligently and with reasonable competence and take all reasonable and practicable steps to avoid unnecessary expense or waste of the Court's time . . .
   . . .

708   A barrister when conducting proceedings in Court:
   . . .
   (e)   must not adduce evidence obtained otherwise than from or through the client or devise facts which will assist in advancing the lay client's case;
   . . .
   (g)   must not make statements or ask questions which are merely scandalous or intended or calculated only to vilify insult or annoy either a witness or some other person;
   (h)   must if possible avoid the naming in open Court of third parties whose character would thereby be impugned;
   (i)   must not by assertion in a speech impugn a witness whom he has had an opportunity to cross-examine unless in cross-examination he has given the witness an opportunity to answer the allegation;
   (j)   must not suggest that a victim, witness or other person is guilty of crime, fraud or misconduct or make any defamatory aspersion on the conduct of any other person or attribute to another person the crime or conduct of which his lay client is accused unless such allegations go to a matter in issue (including the credibility of the witness) which is material to the lay client's case and appear to him to be supported by reasonable grounds.

5.2.3   CROSS-EXAMINATION ON WITNESS STATEMENTS

In civil proceedings, where a witness is called to give evidence at trial, he/she may be cross-examined on his/her witness statement (see **4.3.6**) whether or not the statement or any part of it was referred to during his/her evidence-in-chief: CPR, r. 32.11.

5.2.4   CROSS-EXAMINATION AS TO CREDIT

There are numerous different types of question which can be put, in cross-examin-ation, with a view to attacking the credit of the witnesses called for the other side. For example, you may ask questions to show that their testimony contains errors or omissions, inconsistencies, exaggerations or improbabilities. You may ask questions about their means of knowledge, their opportunity for observing what they purport to have observed, their reasons for remembering or believing something, their experience, and their powers of memory and perception. Subject to the Criminal Evidence Act 1898, s. 1(3), which governs cross-examination of the accused (see **7.3.4**), one can also ask questions on previous convictions, bias, corruption, lack of veracity and discreditable conduct.

The limits to cross-examination on the bad character of one's opponent's witnesses are best summarised by Sankey LJ in *Hobbs* v *CT Tinling & Co. Ltd* [1929] 2 KB 1, CA:

> questions on bad character are only proper when the answer would seriously impair the credibility of the witness and are improper if either:
> (a) they relate to matters so remote in time or of such a character that, if true, they could not seriously impair the credibility of the witness, or
> (b) there is a substantial disproportion between the importance of the implication against the witness's character and the importance of his evidence to the issue to be decided.

In *R* v *Edwards (John)* [1991] 1 WLR 207, CA, it was held that police officers may be cross-examined as to any relevant criminal offences or disciplinary charges found proved against them but may not be questioned about (i) complaints by members of the public about behaviour on other occasions not yet adjudicated upon by the Police Complaints Authority or (ii) discreditable conduct by other officers in the same squad. It was further held that where an officer, who has allegedly fabricated an admission in case B, has also given evidence of an admission in case A, where there was an acquittal by virtue of which his evidence is demonstrated to have been disbelieved, the jury in case B should be made aware of that fact.

However, where the acquittal in case A does not necessarily indicate that the jury disbelieved the officer, such cross-examination should not be allowed. See also *R* v *H* (1990) 90 Cr App R 440, CA; *R* v *Gale* [1994] Crim LR 208, CA; *R* v *Meads* [1996] Crim LR 519, CA.

Where officers have been under investigation for perjury and other misconduct in relation to similar cases which resulted in acquittals, and in consequence charges against other accused have been dropped and appeals against conviction have gone uncontested, this would seem to constitute grounds for impugning their credibility, even if no formal proceedings have been taken against them: see *R* v *Edwards (Maxine)* [1996] 2 Cr App R 345, CA, followed in *R* v *Whelan* [1997] Crim LR 353, CA and *cf. R* v *Guney* [1998] 2 Cr App R 242, CA, at p. 262.

5.2.4.1 Protection of complainants in proceedings for sexual offences

In addition to preventing an accused charged with a sexual offence from cross-examining the complainant in person (see **5.2.1.1**), the Youth Justice and Criminal Evidence Act 1999 provides restrictions on evidence being given or questions being asked about the complainant's sexual history.

Section 41 of the 1999 Act provides that:

> (1) If at a trial a person is charged with a sexual offence, then, except with the leave of the court—
> (a) no evidence may be adduced, and
> (b) no question may be asked in cross-examination,
> by or on behalf of any accused at the trial, about any sexual behaviour of the complainant.
> (2) The court may give leave in relation to any evidence or question only on an application made by or on behalf of an accused, and may not give such leave unless it is satisfied—
> (a) that subsection (3) or (5) applies, and
> (b) that a refusal of leave might have the result of rendering unsafe a conclusion of the jury or (as the case may be) the court on any relevant issue in the case.
> (3) This subsection applies if the evidence or question relates to a relevant issue in the case and either—

    (a) that issue is not an issue of consent; or

    (b) it is an issue of consent and the sexual behaviour of the complainant to which the evidence or question relates is alleged to have taken place at or about the same time as the event which is the subject matter of the charge against the accused; or

    (c) it is an issue of consent and the sexual behaviour of the complainant to which the evidence or question relates is alleged to have been, in any respect, so similar—

        (i) to any sexual behaviour of the complainant which (according to evidence adduced or to be adduced by or on behalf of the accused) took place as part of the event which is the subject matter of the charge against the accused, or

        (ii) to any other sexual behaviour of the complainant which (according to such evidence) took place at or about the same time as that event,
that the similarity cannot reasonably be explained as a coincidence.

. . .

    (5) This subsection applies if the evidence or question—

    (a) relates to any evidence adduced by the prosecution about any sexual behaviour of the complainant; and

    (b) in the opinion of the court, would go no further than is necessary to enable the evidence adduced by the prosecution to be rebutted or explained by or on behalf of the accused.

    (6) For the purposes of subsections (3) and (5) the evidence must relate to a specific instance (or specific instances) of alleged sexual behaviour on the part of the complainant (and accordingly nothing in those subsections is capable of applying in relation to the evidence or question to the extent that it does not so relate).

The provisions of the 1999 Act replace earlier restrictions imposed by Sexual Offences (Amendment) Act 1976, s. 2, and represent a more restrictive approach in allowing questions than the 1976 Act. The definition of 'sexual offence' contained in s. 62 of the 1999 Act is wider than the concept of 'rape offence' used in the now-repealed provisions of the 1976 Act. 'Sexual behaviour' is defined by s. 42(1)(c) of the 1999 Act:

'sexual behaviour' means any sexual behaviour or other sexual experience, whether or not involving any accused or other person, but excluding (except in section 41(3)(c)(i) and (5)(a)) anything alleged to have taken place as part of the event which is the subject matter of the charge against the accused . . .

Under the provisions of the 1976 Act, the prohibition related to 'sexual experience' with a person other than the defendant. This phrase had been given a wide interpretation (including the complainant's *boasts* about her sexual experience — see *R* v *Hinds* [1979] Crim LR 111), but had no application to sexual practices on the part of the complainant not involving another person. The wording of s. 42(1)(c) of the 1999 Act makes it clear ('whether or not involving') that the interpretation of 'sexual behaviour' is wider than the old law under the 1976 Act. But questions about a previous false complaint by the complainant are not questions about sexual behaviour (*R* v *MH* [2002] Crim LR 73, CA).

Under s. 41 of the 1999 Act, questions or evidence about sexual behaviour can only be asked or adduced with leave, and leave will only be given where s. 41(3) or (5) applies *and* refusing leave might result in rendering unsafe a conclusion by the court or jury on any 'relevant issue in the case' (defined in s. 42(1)(a) as any issue falling to be proved by the prosecution or defence in the trial of the accused). No question or evidence will be held to relate to a relevant issue if it appears to the court to be reasonable to assume that the purpose (or main purpose) for so asking or adducing is to establish or elicit material for impugning the credibility of the complainant as a witness (s. 41(4)). Section 41(3) applies if the issue (to which the evidence or questions relate) is not consent (s. 41(3)(a)), or, if it is consent, the requirements of either s. 41(3)(b) or (c) are satisfied. The phrase 'at or about the same time' contained in s. 41(3)(b) would cover, it is submitted, circumstances similar to those in *R* v *Viola* [1982] 1 WLR 1138, CA (sexual advances to two men shortly before the alleged rape and the presence of another man in the flat, after the alleged rape, who was all but naked). Section 41(3)(c) requires such a similarity in sexual behaviour between that about which it is proposed to ask questions or adduce evidence and that which took place as part of, or about the same time as, the event forming the subject matter of the charge, that it cannot reasonably be explained as coincidence, It is submitted that where consent is in issue, s. 41(3)(b) and (c), compared to the provisions of the 1976 Act, reduce the scope for asking questions and adducing evidence. (Note that 'issue of consent' is defined in s. 41(1)(b) as meaning *any issue whether the complainant in fact consented to the conduct constituting the offence with which the accused is charged (and accordingly does not include any issue as to the belief of the accused that the complainant so consented.*) A defendant charged with rape who accepts that the complainant in fact did not consent, but puts forward his mistaken belief in consent would therefore have to satisfy s. 41(3)(a) rather than (b) or (c)).

Section 41(5) relates to the rebuttal or explanation of evidence of any sexual behaviour adduced *by the prosecution.*

In *R* v *A* [2001] 3 All ER 1 the House of Lords, interpreting s. 41(3)(c) in the light of the Human Rights Act 1998, held that the evidence or questioning should be admitted if it is so relevant to the issue of consent that to exclude it would endanger the fairness of the trial guaranteed by Article 6 of the European Convention on Human Rights.

5.2.4.2 Previous inconsistent statements

If a witness, cross-examined about a previous oral or written statement which is inconsistent with his or her evidence, admits to having made the previous statement, no further proof of the statement is required. However if the witness does not make such an admission, and the statement is relevant to the issues in the case, then it may be proved. Proof of such previous inconsistent statements is governed by Criminal Procedure Act 1865, ss. 4 and 5. In *R* v *Derby Magistrates' Court, ex parte B* [1995] 3 WLR 681, HL, Lord Taylor CJ confirmed (at p. 533) that whereas s. 4 of the 1865 Act applies to both oral and written statements, s. 5 of the Act is confined to written statements.

> 4. *If a witness, upon cross-examination as to a former statement made by him relative to the subject-matter of the indictment or proceeding, and inconsistent with his present testimony, does not distinctly admit that he has made such statement, proof may be given that he did in fact make it; but before such proof can be given the circumstances of the supposed statement, sufficient to designate the particular occasion, must be mentioned to the witness, and he must be asked whether or not he has made such statement.*

> 5. *A witness may be cross-examined as to previous statements made by him in writing, or reduced into writing, relative to the subject-matter of the indictment or proceeding, without such writing being shown to him; but if it is intended to contradict such witness by the writing, his attention must, before such contradictory proof can be given, be called to those parts of the writing which are to be used for the purpose of so contradicting him: Provided always, that it shall be competent for the judge, at any time during the trial, to require the production of the writing for his inspection, and he may thereupon make such use of it for the purposes of the trial as he may think fit.*

The phrase 'relative to the subject-matter of the indictment or proceeding', which is used in both s. 4 and s. 5, means relevant to the facts in issue as opposed to some collateral matter (typically, e.g. a matter simply going to credit): *R* v *Funderburk* [1990] 2 All ER 482, CA. In that case, it was held that if the inconsistent statement is not 'relative to the subject matter of the indictment . . .', s. 4 does not apply — whether counsel may cross-examine on the statement at all is determined by the common law, the test being whether the inconsistency relates to the witness's likely standing, after cross-examination, with the tribunal trying him or listening to his evidence: *R* v *Sweet-Escott* (1971) 55 Cr App R 316. The importance of this distinction is that if the cross-examination is permitted *under the common-law rule*, and the witness denies the earlier statement, then because the issue goes to credit only (a collateral matter), the cross-examining party cannot proceed to proof of the making of the statement with a view to impeaching the witness's credit — see the rule of finality of answers to collateral questions, **5.2.4.3**. However, if the cross-examination falls within s. 4, it explicitly states that if the witness does not distinctly admit that he has made the statement, proof may be given that he did in fact make it.

Counsel cross-examining under s. 5, even if he does not intend to show the writing to the witness with a view to contradicting him, must have the document with him in court: *R* v *Anderson* (1930) 21 Cr App R 178.

Where a witness has been cross-examined on a previous inconsistent statement, then (i) the judge may allow the whole of the statement to go before the jury, but has a discretion to allow the jury to see only those parts of the statement on which the cross-examination was based; and (ii) the party calling the witness is *not* entitled, merely by reason of such cross-examination, to re-examine the witness on a previous statement consistent with the witness's testimony, and the consistent statement, if in written form, should not be put before the jury: *R* v *Beattie* (1989) 89 Cr App R 303, CA.

Example (W = witness; C = cross-examining counsel; J = judge)

W.   Her fingers were smeared with a red substance.

C.   Do you remember making a statement about this incident to the police on April 1st, 1990?

W.   Yes, I made such a statement.

C.   And in that statement did you refer to her fingers being smeared with a red substance?

W.   Yes, I think I did, but to be honest I can't remember now.

C.   Your honour, may the witness be shown the statement?

J.   Of course.

C.   I'm much obliged.

[The usher hands the statement to the witness.]

C.   Is that the statement that you made?

W.   Yes.

C.   And does it bear your signature?

W.   Yes.

C.   When you signed it you were doubtless aware of the declaration at the top of that document of the consequences of wilfully stating in it anything that you knew to be false or did not believe to be true?

W.   I guess so.

C.   Would you look at the first line of the second page, please.

[Counsel waits for a moment or two.]

Now that you have read that, do you still say that her fingers were smeared with a red substance?

W.   Yes.

C.   You made that statement some two hours after you saw her, didn't you?

W.   That's right.

C. While the matter was doubtless fresh in your mind?

W. Yeah, but I was a bit shook up.

C. In your statement you say, and I quote: 'She was dressed in black, black dress, black hat, even black tights. All black, except for her gloves. They were white, bright white.'. Why did you just tell the jury that you saw red-smeared fingers?

W. I dunno . . . I should have said red-smeared gloves.

C. But there's no mention of red-smeared anything in your statement. Can you explain that to the jury?

W. I must have forgot in all the excitement.

C. The truth is that she was wearing bright white gloves and there were no smears of any kind or any colour. That's the truth, isn't it?

W. I must have been very confused.

C. Your honour, may the witness's statement be shown to the jury at this stage?

In criminal proceedings, the prior statement only goes to the witness's credibility: see *R* v *Askew* [1981] Crim LR 398.

In civil proceedings, the prior statement comes in for the truth of its contents as well as to attack the witness's credibility. Under Civil Evidence Act 1995, s. 1, in civil proceedings evidence shall not be excluded on the ground that it is hearsay. Section 6 of the 1995 Act provides that:

> (3) Where in the case of civil proceedings section . . . 4 or 5 of the Criminal Procedure Act 1865 applies, which make provision as to
> . . .
> > (b) the proof of contradictory statements made by a witness, and
> > (c) cross-examination as to previous statements made in writing,
> this Act does not authorise the adducing of evidence of a previous inconsistent or contradictory statement otherwise than in accordance with those sections.
> . . .
> (5) Nothing in this section shall be construed as preventing a statement of any description referred to above from being admissible by virtue of section 1 as evidence of the matters stated.

5.2.4.3 The rule of finality of answers to collateral questions and four exceptions
The rule is that where a witness, during cross-examination, answers questions on collateral matters, the answers are conclusive: the cross-examining party cannot then proceed to impeach the credit of the witness by calling other witnesses to contradict that witness.

What are 'collateral matters'? In *Attorney-General* v *Hitchcock* (1847) 1 Exch 91, Pollock CB said:

> If the answer of a witness is a matter which you would be allowed on your own part to prove in evidence — if it had such a connection with the issues, that you would be allowed to give it in evidence — then it is a matter on which you may contradict him.

For example, in *R* v *Burke* (1858) 8 Cox CC 44, the denial by a witness giving evidence through an interpreter that he had spoken English to two people in the court building, was treated as a collateral issue. In *Rv Marsh* (1985) 83 Cr App R 165, by contrast, a witness's denial that he had threatened the accused was not treated as a collateral issue, part of the defence being that the accused believed that the witness had intended to attack him.

In *R* v *Funderburk* [1990] 2 All ER 482, the Court of Appeal accepted that where the disputed issue is a sexual one between two persons in private, the difference between questions going to credit and questions going to the issue is reduced to vanishing-point because sexual intercourse, whether or not consensual, usually takes place in private and leaves few visible traces of having occurred, so that the evidence is often limited to that of the parties and much is likely to turn on the balance of credibility between them. This principle, however, is not confined to sexual cases involving sexual intercourse. In *R* v *Nagrecha* [1997] 2 Cr App R 401, CA, N denied having indecently assaulted U. There were no witnesses to the alleged assault. U denied in cross-examination that she had made allegations of sexual impropriety against other men. It was held that evidence in rebuttal was admissible, because it went not merely to her credit, but to the central issue of whether or not there had been an indecent assault. These cases must now be read subject to s. 41 of the Youth Justice and Criminal Evidence Act 1999.

In *R* v *Busby* (1981) 75 Cr App R 79, CA, two officers were cross-examined with a view to showing that they had fabricated statements alleged to have been made by the accused and threatened a potential defence witness to stop him giving evidence. They denied these allegations. The Court of Appeal held that the trial judge had improperly prevented the defence from calling the witness to rebut the police denials because the evidence was relevant to an issue in the case, namely whether the police were 'prepared to go to improper lengths to secure a conviction'. The decision in *Busby* has provoked considerable judicial comment in subsequent cases. In *R* v *Funderburk* [1990] 2 All ER 482, CA, it was taken to have added a further exception to the rule of finality. In *R* v *Edwards* [1991] 1 WLR 207, however, Lord Lane CJ was of the opinion that the fact that the police were allegedly prepared to prevent a potential defence witness from testifying fell within the exception of bias or partiality (see below). However, in *Edwards* itself it was held that (i) although officers could be cross-examined about other cases which had resulted in acquittal in circumstances which tended to cast doubt on their reliability (e.g. that in those other cases interview notes were inaccurate or had been rewritten to include admissions which did not exist in the originals), (ii) such allegations, if denied, could not be proved by evidence in rebuttal. See also, applying *R* v *Edwards*, *R* v *Irish* [1995] Crim LR 145, CA.

See also *sed quaere R* v *S* [1992] Crim LR 307, CA, in which it seems to be suggested that whether the rule of finality applies may turn on whether the matter which the cross-examining party seeks to prove is a single and distinct fact and therefore easy to prove as opposed to a broad and complex issue which it would be difficult to prove.

Bias or partiality

If a witness under cross-examination denies being biased or partial in relation to the parties or the cause, evidence in rebuttal is admissible to prove such bias or partiality. See *Thomas* v *David* (1836) 7 C & P 350 (a witness's denial that she was the kept mistress of the party calling her) and *R* v *Philips* (1936) 26 Cr App R 17 (denial by the accused's daughters that they had been 'schooled' by their mother to give evidence against him, his defence being that they had been persuaded by their mother to give false evidence against him).

See also *R* v *Mendy* (1976) 64 C App R 4, CA.

Previous convictions

Criminal Procedure Act 1865, s. 6, provides that:

> *A witness may be questioned as to whether he has been convicted of any felony or misdemeanour, and upon being so questioned, if he either denies or does not admit the fact, or refuses to answer, it shall be lawful for the cross-examining party to prove such conviction.*

This rule is subject to the provisions of Rehabilitation of Offenders Act 1974. Section 4(1) of the 1974 Act forbids the questioning of a 'rehabilitated' person about 'spent' convictions. Under s. 7(3), evidence of such convictions may be admitted in civil proceedings if the judge is satisfied that justice cannot be done except by admitting it. The evidence may be admitted under s. 7(3) if relevant either to an issue in the case or to the credit of the witness, but the judge should weigh its relevance against its prejudicial effect and only admit it if satisfied that otherwise the parties would not have a fair trial or the witness's credit could not be fairly assessed: *Thomas* v *Commissioner of Police of the Metropolis* [1997] 1 All ER 747, CA.

Although s. 7(2)(a) says that s. 4(1) does not apply to criminal cases, in a Practice Direction issued by the Lord Chief Justice in June 1975 ((1975) 61 Cr App R 260) it is recommended that in criminal cases no reference to a spent conviction should be made if it can reasonably be avoided and no reference should be made in open court to a spent conviction without the authority of the judge, which authority should only be given if the interests of justice so require.

In *R* v *Evans* [1992] Crim LR 125, CA, on a charge of wounding, the defence being self-defence, it was held that the defence should have been allowed to cross-examine the victim on her previous spent convictions for dishonesty and violence because there was a 'head-on' collision between her evidence and that of the accused. A retrial was ordered.

Note also that if a witness, cross-examined under s. 6, accepts the fact of having been convicted, but claims his or her innocence, the cross-examining party may then be prevented from adducing evidence in rebuttal: see *R* v *Irish*.

Evidence of reputation for untruthfulness

Evidence is admissible that a witness called by one's opponent bears such a general reputation for untruthfulness that he is unworthy of belief.

The rules were summarised by Edmund Davies LJ in *R* v *Richardson* (1968) 52 Cr App R 317 as follows:

(a) witness X may be asked (a) whether he knows of witness Y's general reputation for untruthfulness and (b) whether, on that basis, he would believe witness Y;

(b) witness X may also give his individual opinion based on his personal knowledge, on whether witness Y is to be believed on his oath; but

(c) witness X, during examination-in-chief, may not give the particular facts, circumstances or incidents which formed the basis of the opinion given under either (i) or (ii), although he may be cross-examined on them.

Evidence of disability affecting reliability

Lord Pearce in *Toohey* v *Metropolitan Police Commissioner* [1965] AC 595, HL, said at p. 609:

Medical evidence is admissible to show that a witness suffers from some disease or defect or abnormality of mind that affects the reliability of his evidence. Such evidence is not confined to a general opinion of the unreliability of the witness but may give all the matters necessary to show, not only the foundation of and reasons for the diagnosis, but also the extent to which the credibility of the witness is affected.

For example, in *R* v *Eades* [1972] Crim LR 99, Assizes, Nield J allowed the prosecution to call a consultant psychiatrist to prove that the accused's account of how he had recovered his memory after an accident was not consistent with current medical knowledge. *Cf. R* v *Turner* [1975] QB 834, CA: psychiatric experts are not allowed to give evidence, on the issue of provocation, as to whether the accused's nature is such that, in the circumstances of the case, he could or could not have been provoked. See also *R* v *MacKenney* (1983) 76 Cr App R 271.

5.3   Re-Examination

After cross-examination a witness may be re-examined by the party calling him. Except with the leave of the judge, re-examination must be confined to the matters which arose on cross-examination: it is an exercise in repairing damage done. See *Prince* v *Samo* (1838) 7 A & E 627.

As in examination-in-chief, leading questions may not be asked in re-examination.

Questions

OBJECTIVES

By the conclusion of this chapter, you should be able to understand and apply the rules (and exceptions) relating to leading questions, refreshing memory, previous consistent or self-serving statements, unfavourable and hostile witnesses, cross-examination on documents, cross-examination as to credit, previous inconsistent statements and the finality of answers to collateral matters.

Question 1

Cecil is charged with the rape of Barbara at a party attended also by Dora, Edward and Francis. Cecil claims that Barbara consented to intercourse, being a prostitute of whom he is a regular client. Barbara, who has a conviction for soliciting, testifies that she was raped by Cecil. Among the prosecution witnesses to the circumstances immediately before and after the alleged rape are:

(a)   Dora, who has a spent conviction for theft;

(b)   Edward, who has a history of mental illness; and

(c)   Francis, an importer of obscene films.

Advise Cecil whether the complainant and other prosecution witnesses may be cross-examined about the respective facts mentioned, and whether, if denied, those facts may be proved by the defence.

Question 2

Read the following witness statements. Then read the trial manuscript and as you do so, identify any procedural and evidential errors that ocurred during the course of the hearing. Prepare skeleton arguments on any points of objection or other submissions that you would have made if appearing at this trial:

(a)   for the prosecution; *and*

(b)   for the defence.

STATEMENT OF WITNESS

Statement of:	Stephen WELHAM
Age of witness:	Over 18
Occupation of witness:	Financial Services Manager
Address and telephone number:	187 St John's Avenue, Friern Barnet

This statement, consisting of two pages, each signed by me, is true to the best of my knowledge and belief and I make it knowing that, if it is tendered in evidence, I shall be liable to prosecution if I have wilfully stated in it anything which I know to be false or do not believe to be true.

Dated the 7th day of September 2000

Signed: S. Welham

Signature witnessed by: J. Osborn

On Wednesday 6 September 2000 I was returning from work at about 8 p.m., and left the Underground at Highgate. It is a short walk round the corner to the bus stop for the bus home. I must have been thinking about work, because the next thing I knew a young fellow had stepped in front of me barring my path. He was in his early 20s, casually dressed with a waist-length dark cotton coat. He must have been about 5'10", and well-built. He asked if I had a fiver. I started to say it was none of his business, when I noticed another youth standing against the railings a couple of yards away looking on casually. The man in front pulled me forward with one hand. I tried to push him away, but suddenly felt a sharp pain in my shin, followed by a blow to the side of my face. I lost my balance and fell to the ground. He then ran off in the direction of Muswell Hill. The other man simply disappeared — he must have gone in the other direction.

I picked myself up and went back to the main road. I saw a police car waiting at the lights. I flagged it down and explained to the driver that I had just been attacked by two muggers, and that one of them had run off towards Muswell Hill. I was told to get into the car and the other officer asked for a description. We went down a side road and stopped alongside some parked cars. The officers jumped out, and when I looked out of the side window I saw them with the man who had hit me.

I have a 2 inch long bruise on my left shin and am rather tender where I was hit in front of my right ear.

Signed: S. Welham

Signature witnesed by: J. Osborn

STATEMENT OF WITNESS

Statement of:	John WOOD
Age of witness:	Over 18
Occupation of witness:	Joiner
Address and telephone number:	157 Granville Avenue, London N22

This statement consisting of one page, each signed by me, is true to the best of my knowledge and belief and I make it knowing that, if it is tendered in evidence, I shall be liable to prosecution if I have wilfully stated in it anything which I know to be false or do not believe to be true.

Dated the 7th day of September 2000

Signed: J. Wood

Signature witnessed by: J. Osborn

Yesterday evening Alan LYNCH and myself went out for a drink. We are both unemployed at the moment. When we got to Highgate we both realised we didn't have any money. We stood talking outside the pub for a couple of minutes, a bit fed up. A City gent came round the corner, and Alan bumped into him. Alan asked for a fiver; it was all a piece of fun. I saw a police car coming up Archway Road, so decided to make myself scarce.

Signed: J. Wood

Signature witnessed: J. Osborn

STATEMENT OF WITNESS

Statement of:	D. Sgt William CRANSTOUN
Age of witness:	Over 18
Occupation of witness:	Detective Sergeant
Address and telephone number:	Muswell Hill Police Station

This statement consisting of two pages, each signed by me, is true to the best of my knowledge and belief and I make it knowing that, if it is tendered in evidence, I shall be liable to prosecution if I have wilfully stated in it anything which I know to be false or do not believe to be true.

Dated the 7th day of September 2000

Signed: W. Cranstoun

Signature witnessed by: J. Osborn

On 6 September 2000 at 20.00 acting on information received I went with D.C. Henson and Stephen WELHAM towards Muswell Hill via Queen's Wood Road. I noticed a young man who I now know to be Alan LYNCH walking along the pavement. He looked over his shoulder and then ducked behind a parked car. I pulled up, and D.C. HENSON and I got out. I introduced myself. Stephen WELHAM called out 'He is the one'. I asked LYNCH where he was going. LYNCH replied, 'I am meeting some friends in Hornsey'. I asked him whereabouts, to which he replied, 'The Nightingale'. I asked, 'Where do you live?' Lynch said 'Lymington Avenue'. D. C. HENSON said 'Wood Green?' LYNCH said 'Yes'. I said, 'But that's in the opposite direction'. LYNCH replied, 'Yeah, but I've not come from home'. I said, 'Where have you come from?' LYNCH said, 'I don't have to answer these questions, do I?' D. C. HENSON said, 'Why did you try to hide from us?' LYNCH said, 'I was doing up my shoelace'. I said, 'Have you been near Highgate Underground station this evening?' LYNCH replied, 'What's it to you?' I said, 'I have reason to believe you assaulted this gentleman', indicating Stephen WELHAM, 'and I am arresting you on suspicion of assault'. I then cautioned him, to which he said, 'You've got the wrong man. You are making a big mistake'. LYNCH was then taken to the police station.

Later, I saw LYNCH at the police station with D. C. HENSON. I reminded LYNCH of the caution. D. C. HENSON said, 'The man in the car was punched and kicked this evening near Highgate tube a couple of minutes before we stopped you. He has positively identified you. You tried to hide from us when you saw our car. Do you want to tell us about it?' LYNCH looked into the corner of the room for a couple of minutes, then said, 'All right, I might have asked for money. It was a bit of a lark. It wasn't nothing serious. Give us a break'. I asked if he wanted to make a written statement, to which LYNCH replied, 'No. Nothing in writing'.

On 6 September 2000 at 22.15 LYNCH was charged, the charge was read over, and he was cautioned. LYNCH made no reply.

Acting on local knowledge, on 7 September in company with D. C. HENSON, I attended at 157 Granville Avenue N22 where I saw John WOOD. As a result of our conversation John WOOD made a statement under caution at Muswell Hill Police Station.

Signed: W. Cranstoun

Signature witnessed by: J. Osborne

D. C. Henson made a statement in the same terms, with necessary changes.

Alan Lynch of 298 Lymington Avenue, Wood Green, N22 will say:

I am aged 22 and live at home with my parents, a brother and a sister. I am a car mechanic, but lost my job four months ago for bad timekeeping. I have several previous convictions for petty offences going back a long time. My most recent conviction was for fighting outside a pub when I was 20. I was fined £75.

On Wednesday 6 September I was arrested by the police. I was on my way to meet some friends at the Nightingale pub in Hornsey. We had nothing planned. We often meet for a drink and a game of pool. I had been to see a friend's car in Mill Hill, and decided to get off the tube at Highgate and walk through the woods and then across to the pub. I would say it was about a 1.5-mile walk.

The bloke in Mill Hill is really a friend of a friend. I had agreed with Trevor Jones, one of my friends, to look over a car one of Trevor's friends was going to buy. The car was in Oakhampton Road but I didn't go into the house so don't know the full address. I had been given a tenner for doing it, so didn't want to say anything to the police.

As I was coming up to the woods my shoelace came undone. I stopped to do it up. Then a car pulled up, and next thing I knew there were two policemen asking me a lot of questions about where I was going, where I had been and where I lived. They accused me of thumping a bloke they had in the car, arrested me and took me to Muswell Hill Police Station.

When I was seen by the police at the station I did not admit I had hit anybody. I did not do it and I never said that I did to the police. I might have said that I had asked for money to look over the car, and that I hadn't done anything seriously wrong, but those comments were not about hitting anybody.

Trevor moved to Borehamwood a couple of years ago. I don't have his address, he just meets us every so often. I haven't seen him since I was arrested.

A. Lynch

POLICE V ALAN LYNCH
Trial Transcript

A Clerk: The next case is Alan Lynch, sir, number 16 in the list. (*Lynch is brought into the court and enters the dock.*)
Clerk: Are you Alan Lynch?
Lynch: Yes.
Clerk: Alan Lynch, you are charged with assault occasioning actual bodily harm contrary to section 47 of the Offences Against the Person Act 1861 in that you, on the 6th day of September 2000, did assault one Stephen Welham thereby occasioning unto him actual bodily harm. Do you plead guilty or not guilty?
Lynch: Not guilty.
Clerk: You may sit down.

B Prosecution Counsel: May it please you, sir, I appear on behalf of the prosecution and my learned friend Miss Lucy Davies appears for the defence. It is the prosecution's case that the defendant assaulted his victim outside the Three Tuns public house in Highgate, which as I am sure you are aware is somewhat notorious. However, this case is not one in which alcohol is a factor. It is more in the nature of a mugging. The prosecution's first witness is the victim, Mr Stephen Welham, who will tell you about the circumstances of the assault on his way home from work and the extent of his injuries. The second witness will be Mr John Wood, an identification witness. He will be followed by Detective Sergeant Cranstoun, the arresting officer. I should at this stage mention that the arrest occurred a matter of

C just a few minutes after the incident. The fourth witness will be Detective Constable Henson, who was also present at the time of the arrest. Without further ado, and with your permission, sir, I will call Stephen Welham.
Usher: Mr Welham, please hold the Testament in your right hand and read the words on the card.
Welham: I swear by Almighty God that the evidence I shall give shall be the truth, the whole truth and nothing but the truth.
Pros: Is your full name Stephen Welham and do you live at 187 St John's Avenue, Barnet?
Welham: Yes.

D Pros: Are you a financial services manager?
Welham: That's right.
Pros: And who is your employer?
Welham: Barclays International, in the City.

A Pros: How do you get to work?
Welham: I catch the bus on Colney Hatch Lane down to Highgate tube on Archway Road, then change from the Northern Line at Tottenham Court Road on to the Central Line to Bank.
Pros: And the reverse on the way home?
Welham: Yes.
Pros: Do you remember your journey home on Wednesday 6th September 2000?
Welham: I think so — I'm not sure of the date.
Pros: Was there an occasion when your usual routine was broken?
Welham: Yes, a couple of months ago I was threatened in the street by him (*points*

B *to defendant in the dock*).
Pros: Could you tell us where this happened?
Welham: I was leaving the Underground and walking round the corner to catch the bus. As I turned the corner I was confronted by the defendant.
Pros: What did he do?
Welham: He demanded money. Ten pounds, as I remember. Of course I refused. He had an accomplice with him. He grabbed me by the throat and started kicking me and punching — he was really wild. I managed to push him away and they ran off.
Pros: Could you tell us what your injuries were?
Welham: I had a large bruise on my shin and the side of my face became puffed up.

C Pros: Were you cut at all?
Welham: No.
Pros: How clearly did you see your attacker?
Welham: He was facing me the whole time. He was a young man in his early 20s wearing a dark cotton jacket. It was still light and I remember the lights in the Three Tuns were on. I had a good look at him.
Pros: What did you do after the attack?
Welham: I went back to the main road, where there was a police car. We went off towards Muswell Hill. We caught up with him and he was arrested.
Pros: When the police car stopped, what did you do?

D Welham: I remained in it until I was asked to move into the front passenger seat.
Pros: When the police officers left the car, did you see what they did?
Welham: They arrested the defendant.
Pros: Did anyone say anything at that stage?
Welham: Yes, the police asked the defendant a lot of questions.
Pros: Did anyone else say anything?
Welham: The defendant gave them his name, and . . .
Pros: I had better stop you there. Did anyone apart from the police officers and the defendant say anything?
Welham: No.

E Pros: Was anyone else present?
Welham: No. Only myself.
Pros: Did you say anything?
Welham: No. The policemen asked all the questions.
Pros: After the car stopped, did you identify anyone to the police officers?
Welham: Yes. When I looked out of the window I saw that they had caught my attacker, and I shouted something like 'That's him!'
Pros: Thank you Mr Welham. Please wait there in case there are any further questions.

F *Cross-examination*
Def: Mr Welham, at what time do you finish work of an evening?
Welham: About 6 p.m.
Def: Do you work overtime?
Welham: No. I am not in a grade that gets paid overtime.
Def: Do you ever work late?
Welham: Not normally. It depends on how much work we have on.
Def: How long does it take to get to Highgate from your office?
Welham: About 45 minutes.
Def: You seem unsure about the date of the alleged assault. How can you be sure it was the 6th September?

A Welham: I think I was working late that night.
Def: At what time did you arrive at Highgate?
Welham: About 8 p.m.
Def: That's after lighting-up time at that time of year?
Welham: I don't know.
Def: Do you remember if the street lights were on?
Welham: I didn't notice. It was quite light.
Def: Did you make a statement to the police after the incident?
Welham: Yes.
Def: Have you recently read that statement?

B Welham: Why?
Def: I put it to you that you read your statement this morning before coming into court.
Welham: Well, I did, I wanted to get the facts straight.
Def: Do you drink, Mr Welham?
Welham: A little. Sometimes.
Def: Did you have a drink that evening?
Welham: No.
Def: I put it to you that the reason you were late that evening was that you had had a drink or two before leaving for home.

C Welham: I have told you I was working late.
Def: You said you were confronted by your attacker, and after a brief exchange of words, he punched and kicked you, then ran off.
Welham: That's right.
Def: It would all have been over very quickly.
Welham: Yes, that must be right.
Def: He demanded ten pounds, Mr Welham?
Welham: Yes.
Def: But that is not right, is it?
Welham: Yes, I have already said he demanded money.

D Def: You said ten pounds.
Welham: He demanded ten pounds.
Def: I put it to you, Mr Welham, that the man you saw did not demand ten pounds.
Welham: He demanded ten pounds.
Def: I put it to you, Mr Welham, that the man you saw did not demand ten pounds.
Welham: Yes, he did.
Def: I put it to you that when you described the attack to the police you did not mention a demand for ten pounds.
Welham: I did.

E Def: It is true, is it not, that you told the police the day after the incident that the man who attacked you demanded five pounds not ten?
Welham: All right, it may have been five.
Def: May, or was, five pounds?
Welham: It was five pounds.
Def: After your attacker grabbed hold of you, would I be right in thinking you would have been watching his hands?
Welham: I don't recall — but I did get a good look at his face.
Def: It's only a natural reaction to look at what his hands were doing, isn't it?
Welham: I'm not sure.
Def: You have already told this court that you were repeatedly kicked and punched.

F Welham: That's right.
Def: The assault you mentioned to the police wasn't at all wild, was it?
Welham: I don't know what you mean.
Def: I am referring to the statement you made to the police after the attack. The account of the attack contained in your statement is rather different from what you have told the court today, isn't it?
Welham: Not so far as I remember.
Def: Sir, perhaps the witness could be shown his statement. Mr Welham do you recognise this statement?
Welham: Yes.
Def: And is it your signature at the bottom?

A Welham: Yes.

Def: And have you signed a declaration to say that the statement is true to the best of your knowledge and belief?

Welham: I did.

Def: Would you look at the second half of the first paragraph of the statement. (*Witness reads statement to himself.*)

Def: Do you now wish to tell the justices again about the nature of the attack?

Welham: No.

Def: Very well. About half-way down the first page, the ninth sentence begins, 'I tried to push him away'. Could you read that sentence?

B Welham: I tried to push him away, but suddenly felt a sharp pain in my shin, followed by a . . . This is rather underhand.

Def: Could you please continue.

Welham: Followed by a blow to the side of my face. It is rather immaterial how many times he hit me. The fact is he hit me, and nothing can take that away.

Def: Will you accept that at the time of the incident you said you were only kicked once and punched once?

Welham: Of course, I have to.

Def: Tell me, Mr Welham, have you yourself ever been in trouble?

Welham: What do you mean?

C Def: Trouble with the police?

Welham: Er . . . no.

Def: Is it not the case that you have a criminal record?

Welham: In a manner of speaking, but it was a long time ago.

Def: Is it true that you have a record for indecent exposure?

Welham: It was while I was a student. I was fined.

Chairman: Mr Welham, what was the date of that conviction?

Welham: It was when I was about 20. It must have been 1982, or thereabouts.

Def: Thank you, Mr Welham.

D *Re-examination*

Pros: Mr Welham, I have one or two further questions to ask you. You were working late on the evening in question.

Welham: Yes.

Pros: At about what time did you leave the office?

Welham: Let me see. It must have been about 7.15 p.m.

Pros: Did you stop off anywhere either before catching the Underground or *en route*?

Welham: No.

Pros: Can you remind the Court how long it took to get to Highgate?

E Welham: 45 minutes.

Pros: And the time of the attack?

Welham: 8 p.m.

Pros: You were asked a number of questions by the defence about the lighting conditions and the period over which you saw your attacker. How well did you see him?

Welham: Very well. We were face to face for some time, and I got a very good look at him.

Pros: Mr Welham, you have already described him as a man in his early twenties wearing a dark cotton jacket. How tall was he?

F Welham: About 5' 10".

Pros: At the time of the attack, did you notice anyone else present?

Welham: There was an accomplice lounging against the railings.

Pros: Thank you, Mr Welham. Unless you have any questions, sir.

Chairman: Mr Welham, you go home via Highgate every day?

Welham: Yes

Chairman: Then you will appreciate that Muswell Hill Road slopes very steeply down towards Muswell Hill?

Welham: It does.

Chairman: Which way were you facing when you were attacked?

A Welham: Towards Muswell Hill.

Chairman: So you were uphill of your attacker?

Welham: Yes.

Chairman: When you described your attacker as 5′ 10″ did you take into account that you were uphill of him, and that he would therefore appear shorter than if you were at the same level as him?

Welham: I hadn't really thought about it. My impression was that he was about 5′ 10″. Bearing in mind what you say, it may be that he was a little taller than that.

Chairman: I have no further questions.

Pros: Sir, may the witness be released?

B Def: I have no objection.

Chairman: Very well, thank you Mr Welham.

(*J. Wood is called and sworn*).

Pros: Are you John Wood of 157 Granville Avenue, London N22?

Wood: I am.

Pros: Are you an unemployed joiner?

Wood: No. I got a job.

Pros: Who are you employed by, Mr Wood?

Wood: I've been taken on by me uncle.

C Pros: Do you remember the events of the evening of 6th September 2000?

Wood: No.

Pros: Do you remember an arrangement to visit a public house in Highgate?

Wood: Nope.

Pros: Have you ever visited a public house called the Three Tuns in Highgate? It's located at the corner of Archway Road and Muswell Hill Road. Do you know the public house I am referring to?

Wood: I don't live in Highgate.

Pros: It's not very far from Wood Green. Have you ever been to Highgate?

Wood: I may have passed through.

D Pros: Have you every stopped off at the Three Tuns?

Wood: I can't remember.

Pros: Do you recognise anyone in court today?

Wood: No.

Pros: Mr Wood, please look around the room, and think carefully before answering. Is there anyone here that you know?

Wood: No.

Pros: I have no further questions of this witness.

Def: No cross-examination, sir.

E (*D. S. Cranstoun is called and sworn.*)

Pros: Are you Detective Sergeant William Cranstoun, attached to Muswell Hill Police Station?

Cranstoun: I am.

Pros: Were you on patrol with Detective Henson on the evening of 6th September 2000?

Cranstoun: I was.

(*At this point D. S. Cranstoun produces a notebook from his top pocket and starts flicking through it.*)

Cranstoun: Do you mind if I refer to my notes, your worship?

F Pros: If I may help, sir.

Chairman: Please do.

Pros: Could you help us, Sergeant, by telling the court when the notes were written up?

Cranstoun: Contemporaneously, while the events were fresh in my memory.

Pros: In the circumstances I would ask that the witness be permitted to refresh his memory.

Chairman: Yes, please continue.

Pros: I think you were given a description of a person who was alleged to have committed an assault?

A Cranstoun: Yes, I was driving towards Muswell Hill along Queen's Wood Road.

Pros: Why did you choose that route?

Cranstoun: The main road to Muswell Hill is very long with only one turning off for some distance that leads anywhere. I guessed that the suspect would leave Muswell Hill Road as soon as he could, so I did the same.

Pros: As you were driving, did you notice anything suspicious?

Cranstoun: I noticed a young man walking along the pavement. He looked over his shoulder and then ducked behind a parked car.

Pros: Why was he looking over his shoulder?

Cranstoun: He must have been looking to see if he was being followed.

B Pros: Then what did you do?

Cranstoun: I stopped the car and got out. Detective Constable Henson did likewise.

Pros: Did you speak to the gentleman in the street?

Cranstoun: Yes, sir.

Pros: What did you say?

Cranstoun: I introduced myself. Mr Welham called out, 'He is the one'. At that time I ascertained that the man we had stopped was the defendant, Alan Lynch.

Pros: What did you say?

Cranstoun: I asked the defendant where he was going. He replied, 'I am meeting some friends in Hornsey'. I asked him whereabouts, to which he replied, 'The

C Nightingale'.

Pros: Where is that?

Cranstoun: It is about 2 miles from there, cutting through the side roads, on the corner of Nightingale Road and Hornsey High Street.

Pros: What did you say after that?

Cranstoun: I asked, 'Where do you live?' The defendant said, 'Lymington Avenue'. Detective Constable Henson asked if that was in Wood Green. The defendant said, 'Yes'. I said, 'But that's in the opposite direction'. The defendant said, 'Yeah, but I've not come from home'. I said, 'Where have you come from?' The defendant said, 'I don't have to answer these questions, do I?' Detective Constable Henson said, 'Why

D did you try to hide from us?' The defendant said, 'I was doing up my shoelace'. I said 'Have you been near Highgate Underground station this evening?' The defendant replied, 'What's it to you?'

Pros: I think you then told the defendant that you were arresting him for the assault on Mr Welham, and gave him the caution.

Cranstoun: That is right.

Pros: Did the defendant say anything in reply to the caution?

Cranstoun: Yes. He said, 'You've got the wrong man. You are making a big mistake'.

Pros: Was the accused then taken to Muswell Hill Police Station?

Cranstoun: Yes, sir.

E Pros: Did you speak to the defendant at the station?

Cranstoun: Yes, together with Detective Constable Henson. I started by reminding Lynch of the caution.

Pros: Did Detective Constable Henson remind the accused of the facts of the incident?

Cranstoun: He did. The defendant looked into space for a while, then said, let me see, 'All right, I might have asked for money. It was a bit of a lark. It wasn't nothing serious. Give us a break'.

Pros: I think you then asked the defendant if he wanted to make a written statement.

F Cranstoun: But he refused.

Pros: I understand the defendant was then charged.

Cranstoun: Yes, sir.

Pros: At what time was that?

Cranstoun: 10.15 p.m., sir.

Pros: Did he make any reply?

Cranstoun: No. None.

Pros: Thank you Sergeant.

SIX

SIMILAR FACT EVIDENCE

To what extent can the misconduct of a party on previous occasions be adduced to prove commission of an offence or a civil wrong in the current action? Can evidence of a party's inclinations or dispositions or propensity to act in a particular way be admitted to prove a case against him or her?

6.1   General

6.1.1   GENERAL INTRODUCTION TO CHAPTERS 6 AND 7

This chapter and the next chapter are broadly examining aspects of the character of a party to litigation. While 'character' has a precise definition in the courts, this chapter and the next examine the various ways in which a tribunal of fact is presented with evidence that does not directly show commission of an offence (or civil wrong) by proving or disproving the events that are said to have occurred during it. Instead, these chapters deal with the proof of facts about a party's past that will in some way render it more or less likely that that party is guilty (or liable).

To take an example, where a defendant is charged with a wounding offence, one would normally expect to hear evidence:

(a)   of eye-witnesses who saw the defendant stab the victim (direct evidence); or

(b)   that a knife was used to stab the victim and other evidence of a knife being found at the scene with the defendant's fingerprints upon it (circumstantial evidence).

However, this chapter and the next, deal with the admission of evidence that does not relate to that event itself such as evidence that:

(a)   the defendant had a particular way of committing wounding offences that is very similar to the way in which the current victim was wounded (similar fact evidence); or

(b)   that the two parties had a history of attacking one another (whether or not with knives), as shown by a string of previous convictions (another form of similar fact evidence); or

(c)   that the defendant's testimony to the effect that he was nowhere near the incident or was acting in self-defence is not to be believed because he is a dishonest individual (character evidence covered in **Chapter 7**); or

(d)   that he has never committed an offence before and therefore is to be believed when he raises his defence (also in **Chapter 7**).

The general rule for evidence relating to the previous bad character or disposition (i.e. in both **Chapters 6** and **7**) is that such evidence is not admissible (see, for example,

Lord Makin's first proposition in the case of *Makin v Attorney-General of New South Wales* at **6.2.1** below and Criminal Procedure Act 1898, s. 1(3), at **7.3.4**). The courts have prevented tribunals of fact from taking bad character into consideration because there is a risk that the tribunal of fact will read too much into such evidence. What will be seen for both chapters is that such evidence is admitted but only in very limited circumstances.

It is therefore important to bear in mind in both chapters that you are considering exceptions to the general rule. The exceptions all derive from the requirements of justice. As will be seen in this chapter, similar fact evidence (of various types) is admitted because of its strong probative force in showing that the accused did commit the offence being tried (or some probative force in showing that a party to a civil action is liable in the current action). In relation to **Chapter 7** it will be seen that evidence of bad character will be admitted in criminal cases where the defendant in question has put his or her character in issue (essentially by attacking prosecution witnesses or co-defendants or by claiming to be of good character).

6.1.2 INTRODUCTORY COMMENTS ON 'SIMILAR FACT EVIDENCE'

The bulk of this chapter considers criminal cases. A similar, but less stringent, test applies in civil cases (see **6.7** below).

6.1.2.1 The meaning of 'similar fact evidence'

It should be remembered that 'similar fact evidence' is a misnomer. As will be seen during this chapter, evidence of misconduct that bears no similarity to the actions alleged but is being admitted because it has some other strong probative force will occasionally be admitted as 'similar fact evidence'.

6.1.2.2 A note of caution about the case law

It will be seen that it is necessary in every case concerning similar fact evidence to have a clear idea of the probative value of the evidence in question. This involves understanding exactly what part the similar fact evidence plays in proving the guilt of the defendant. Because the probative value of evidence varies from case to case, it is important to remember, while reading the chapter, that nearly all cases will turn on their particular facts. As such the case law is useful for determining broad principles rather than setting strict precedents. Other similar fact cases can be at best guidance as to the approach you ought to adopt or the arguments you should make.

6.1.2.3 Cases in which similar fact issues arise

Similar fact cases can arise in two different ways.

In some cases a defendant is charged with an offence but the similar facts that are to be proved occurred on other occasions and are not the subject matter of the trial. They may be offences committed (and even tried) on previous occasions or non-criminal acts that are not part of the commission of the current offence. However, as they are not the subject matter of the current trial, if the tribunal of law determines that they do not fall within similar fact evidence principles, any evidence of these other events will not be admitted and the tribunal of fact will not be aware of them.

The second way in which similar fact evidence questions arise is more complicated. It is possible that a defendant is tried for more than one offence at the same trial (see the **Criminal Litigation Manual** (**9.2**) for the rules concerning when this is or is not appropriate). Often the evidence in relation to one of the offences being tried (offence A) may constitute similar fact evidence to support the other offence (offence B). In such cases, the evidence will be before a jury whether or not it is similar fact evidence. Evidence of offence A will be admissible to prove offence A even if it is not admissible as similar fact evidence to prove offence B. In such cases the issue is not simply admissibility but how the jury should be directed by the trial judge to use or not use evidence of offence A in respect of offence B. There are a number of these 'multiple count' similar fact cases referred to in this chapter. Occasionally it is necessary to appreciate this difference to understand the principles the appellate courts were adopting in analysing the similar fact evidence.

6.2   Criminal Cases: The Principles

The starting point, but certainly not the finishing point, for this complex and controversial area of the law of evidence is the dictum of Lord Herschell LC giving the judgment of the Privy Council in *Makin* v *Attorney-General for New South Wales* [1894] AC 57, PC at p. 65:

> In their Lordships' opinion the principles which must govern the decision of the case are clear, though the application of them is by no means free from difficulty. It is undoubtedly not competent for the prosecution to adduce evidence tending to show that the accused has been guilty of criminal acts other than those covered by the indictment, for the purpose of leading to the conclusion that the accused is a person likely from his criminal conduct or character to have committed the offence for which he is being tried. [THE FIRST PROPOSITION.] On the other hand, the mere fact that the evidence adduced tends to show the commission of other crimes does not render it inadmissible if it be relevant to an issue before the jury, and it may be so relevant if it bears upon the question whether the acts alleged to constitute the crime charged in the indictment were designed or accidental, or to rebut a defence which would otherwise be open to the accused. [THE SECOND PROPOSITION.]
>
> Lord Herschell went on to observe that the statement of these general principles is easy, but it is obvious that it may often be very difficult to draw the line and to decide whether a particular piece of evidence is on the one side or the other.

The current expression of the test is to be found in the case of *R* v *P* [1991] 3 All ER 337 in which Lord Mackay stated that 'the essential feature of the evidence which is to be admitted is that its probative force in support of the allegation that an accused person committed a crime is sufficiently great to make it just to admit the evidence, notwithstanding that it is prejudicial in tending to show that the accused is guilty of another crime'. This statement does not differ from the approach enunciated by Lord Makin as it identifies the two aspects that must be weighed in the balance to determine admissibility:

(a)   strong probative value deriving from the particular facts of the case and issues in dispute, and

(b)   likely prejudicial effect of revealing evidence of the past/disposition of the accused.

This chapter will show that similar fact evidence is admitted for a number of differing reasons. However, what the evidence does have in common in all cases is that:

(a)   it is evidence that shows the defendant to have a particular disposition (whether or not it has led to a criminal conviction);

(b)   evidence of disposition will have a strong prejudicial effect (usually by leading the tribunal of fact to conclude that he or she committed the offence because he or she is 'that type of person');

(c)   prejudicial effect is such that such evidence would generally excluded from the courts (the prejudicial effect);

(d)   but such evidence has a particular relevance to the current case (going beyond mere evidence of propensity to offend); and

(e)   it is not only relevant but has such a strong probative force that the courts will exceptionally admit the evidence despite its prejudicial effect (the probative value).

6.2.1   LORD HERSCHELL'S FIRST PROPOSITION: THE GENERAL RULE OF EXCLUSION

The first proposition means that prosecution evidence which shows *only* that the accused is disposed to crime in general, or to commit certain types of crime in particular, is not admissible to prove that he is guilty of the crime charged. The reason for the first proposition is probably best explained in *DPP* v *Boardman* [1975] AC 421, HL by Lord Cross of Chelsea at p. 456:

> . . . the reason for this general rule is not that the law regards such evidence as inherently irrelevant but that it is believed that if it were generally admitted jurors would in many cases think that it was more relevant than it was, so that, as it is put, its prejudicial effect would outweigh its probative value.

A good example of the first proposition is *R* v *Fisher* [1910] 1 KB 149. Mr Fisher was charged with obtaining a pony and trap from B by false pretences. Evidence that on another occasion he had obtained a quantity of oats and fodder from C by falsehood was held to be inadmissible. Channell J acknowledged that evidence that Mr Fisher had made false statements on other occasions tended to show that he was a swindler, but held that such evidence would only be admissible if all the frauds were of a similar character, showing a systematic course of swindling by the same method.

A second and more recent example is *R* v *B (RA)* [1997] 2 Cr App R 88, CA. B was charged with indecently assaulting his two grandsons. His defence was a denial, and he suggested that the boys had been put up by their mother to invent the allegations. It was held that the trial judge had improperly admitted in evidence homosexual pornographic magazines found in B's possession, and his answers to police questions about his sexual proclivities: the evidence was not probative of anything except propensity.

A good illustration of the principle that mere relevance is not enough is found in the case of *Noor Mohamed* v *R* [1949] AC 182, PC, the appellant had been convicted of the murder of a woman, A, who was living with him as his wife. The prosecution had adduced evidence concerning the death of his first wife, G. The appellant was a goldsmith. Both G and A had died of poisoning by potassium cyanide, a substance used by goldsmiths. There was evidence in relation to both incidents as to the victim having been found suffering from poisoning and there was some evidence in each case of motive on the part of the appellant. In relation to G but not in relation to A there was also some evidence of a trick that had been played by the appellant to get G to take the poison. The Privy Council concluded that there were no grounds for the admission of the evidence as to G's death. There was no evidence as to how A came by the poison that killed her and the evidence of a previous trick could not fill this evidential gap.

The mere fact that the defendant appears to offend with great frequency will not overcome the general prohibition. In *R* v *Marshall* [1989] Crim LR 819, CA, the defendant was charged with five burglaries and convicted of four of them. In the course of the trial evidence of interviews in which the defendant admitted the commission of 87 burglary offences was admitted. The Court of Appeal held that the evidence should not have been admitted. In the absence of evidence of a system or some other evidence of something more than a mere disposition to commit offences in general the other offences were probative of nothing but highly prejudicial.

In *DPP* v *Boardman* [1975] AC 421, HL, Lord Hailsham expressed the view that under *Makin* v *Attorney-General for New South Wales* similar fact evidence should not be admitted if the only purpose is a chain of reasoning which leads from propensity to guilt. See also *R* v *Lunt* (1987) 85 Cr App R 241, CA (applied in *R* v *Shore* (1989) 89 Cr App R 32, CA) per Neill LJ at p. 244:

> evidence is admissible as 'similar fact' evidence if, but only if, it goes beyond showing a tendency to commit crimes of the kind charged and is positively probative in regard to the crime charged . . . In order to decide whether the evidence is positively probative . . . it is first necessary to identify the issue to which the evidence is

directed. Thus the evidence may be put forward, e.g. to support an identification (where unusual points of similarity of appearance or method can be relevant and positively probative) or to prove intention, or to rebut a possible defence of accident or innocent association. In these several examples the answer to the question of what is positively probative may vary. Once the issue has been identified the question will be: will the 'similar fact' evidence be positively probative, in the sense of assisting the jury to reach a conclusion on that issue on some ground other than the accused's bad character or disposition to commit the sort of crime with which he is charged? If the evidence of similar facts will not assist the jury to this end, it is irrelevant and inadmissible.

6.2.2 LORD HERSCHELL'S SECOND PROPOSITION: EXCEPTIONS TO THE GENERAL RULE OF EXCLUSION

The second proposition is also probably best explained in *DPP* v *Boardman* by Lord Cross at p. 456:

Circumstances, however, may arise in which such evidence is so very relevant that to exclude it would be an affront to common sense.

6.2.2.1 Examples: striking similarity cases

The simplest examples of the second proposition are the cases where the probative force of the evidence derives from striking similarities between the alleged offence and other criminal behaviour of the accused, including *Makin* v *Attorney-General for New South Wales* [1894] AC 57, PC, itself. In that case Makin and his wife were charged with the murder of an infant child whom they had taken in from its mother for informal adoption, upon the payment by her of a small sum of money which was insufficient for the child's support. When the mother subsequently tried to see the child, there was deceit and evasion by the Makins, and even an attempt to pass off a different child as the child in question. There was also evidence that the baby was received in good health one day in one set of premises, but that two days later the Makins had moved on, surreptitiously and without the baby, to other premises. A child's corpse, wearing the child's clothes, was then found secretly buried in the garden of the first set of premises. There was also evidence that other babies had also been received from their mothers on the payment of similarly inadequate sums of money, and that the remains of no less than 13 other children's corpses had been found in three different sets of premises, all occupied, at different times, by the Makins. The Privy Council held this evidence to be admissible on the grounds that the Crown, in seeking to prove deliberate killing, were entitled to rely on evidence which negatived the possibility that the child in question had died accidentally or from natural causes. (In fact, this was not the defence — the accused simply denied all connection with both the mother and the baby.) In other words, to find so many bodies of children in the back-yards of so many sets of premises all of which had been occupied by the accused, rendered quite ludicrously incredible any suggestion that this had nothing to do with the accused but must have been accidental or coincidental.

The same reasoning was employed in another 'similar fact' case, the famous 'brides in the bath' case, *R* v *Smith* (1915) 11 Cr App R 229, CCA. Smith was charged with the murder of B. Smith had purported to marry her (he was already married) and they had started living together. Both of them made mutual wills. Smith then purchased a bath and installed it in a room without a lock on the door. Although there had been no reason to presume B suffered from ill health, Smith took her to a doctor and described symptoms that were consistent with epilepsy. The same doctor was then sent for by Smith to find that B was dead in a bath. There was medical evidence that the position in which B was found in the bath was not consistent with an epileptic fit. After B's death Smith disappeared. Smith's defence was that the death had been a result of the unfortunate accident of an epileptic fit while B was bathing. The prosecution, in order to disprove such an explanation, called evidence that Smith had subsequently been through two ceremonies of marriage with other women, that both of them had died in baths while living with Smith and that he had on both occasions benefited financially from their deaths because of life assurance he had taken out in respect of them. The

Court upheld the admission of the evidence. If what had happened in this case had happened once only, an explanation based on accident might have been plausible. But when it happened three times, in remarkably similar circumstances and on each occasion to the benefit of the accused, it gave rise to a very strong inference that the events were so very coincidental that they must have been brought about by design and not by accident.

In *R v Sims* [1946] KB 531, CCA, it was held that if strikingly similar allegations are made by different persons about the behaviour of the accused on different occasions, each allegation may be admitted on the basis that whereas the jury might think that one man might be telling an untruth, three or four, unless conspiring together, are hardly likely to tell the same untruth.

In *R v Wilmot* (1989) 89 Cr App R 341, the Court of Appeal held that there are circumstances in which, where it is proved or admitted that a man has had sexual intercourse with a number of young women, the question whether it is proved that one of them did not consent may in part be answered by proving that another of the women did not consent, if the cirumstances bear a striking resemblance.

6.2.2.2 Examples: similar fact evidence without striking similarity

It is important to note that 'striking similarity' is by no means the only route to admissibility. Despite the observations of Lord Hailsham in *DPP v Boardman*, some authorities show that propensity evidence has been admitted for the purpose of Lord Hailsham's 'forbidden' line of reasoning. An example is *R v Ball* [1911] AC 47, HL. In that case a brother and sister were convicted of incest which had taken place in 1910. There was evidence that they had lived together as man and wife and shared the same bed. In order to show that intercourse had taken place in 1910, evidence was also admitted that intercourse had taken place between them on former occasions and that the brother was the father of the sister's child. The House of Lords held the evidence to have been properly admitted to prove the offence charged. The probative value derived from the following analysis: it would be passing odd if a brother and sister who had practised sexual intercourse in the past, then lived together as man and wife and shared the same bed, but did not have sexual intercourse. In this case, the evidence was being used to strengthen an inference to be drawn from the other evidence available in the case, including the evidence that they were sleeping in the same room at the time that the charge was brought against them. The similar fact evidence put a completely different complexion on what might otherwise have been innocent behaviour.

Where similar fact evidence is admitted by the courts to establish the propensity of a defendant to commit offences the courts have been careful to identify the use to which it is being put. In the case of *R v Straffen* [1952] 2 QB 911, CA, for example, evidence of the particular way in which the defendant had committed offences in the past was said to go to establish the identity of the offender in the case before the court. The defendant had been a patient at Broadmoor. He had been sent there following two murders of young girls. In each of those cases the murder was by manual strangulation, there had been no attempt on the murderer's part to hide the bodies and there had been no sexual assault or other motive for the killing. The conviction against which the appeal was brought concerned a murder that had occurred while the defendant had escaped from Broadmoor. The victim was a young girl who had been manually strangled. There had been no attempt to hide the body nor had there been any sexual assault or other motive for the murder. The Court of Appeal concluded that the evidence had been rightly admitted to rebut a defence reasonably available to the defendant namely that he had not been identified as the murderer.

It follows that in determining whether evidence of previous misconduct is admissible the courts will examine what is in issue. In doing so the courts will consider not only defences actually raised but also those reasonably available to the defendant. In *Noor Mohamed v R*, at the time that the evidence of G's death was admitted, the appellant had not alleged any defence (although subsequently both accident and suicide were alleged). The Privy Council recognised that there may be cases in which the prosecution evidence may make certain defences available and that the prosecution can lead evidence in anticipation of such defences.

A case similar to *Noor Mohamed* v *R* is *R* v *Armstrong* [1922] 2 KB 555, CA. In that case the defendant was alleged to have poisoned his wife with arsenic. His account for his possession of the arsenic was that it was to be used as a weed killer. To disprove this, the prosecution led evidence that the defendant had approximately eight months later administered poison to a business competitor. In that case the Court of Appeal upheld the conviction that resulted. The Court decided that the evidence was admissible to answer the question 'with what design did he . . . provide himself with that poison'. The evidence that he had subsequently used it to poison another person was something from which the jury could infer that he had not had the innocent purpose at the time that his wife died. The difference between the cases of *Noor Mohamed* and *Armstrong* is that in the former case the evidence was not sufficiently likely to assist the jury in determining that a potential defence was not true whereas in the latter case it was.

6.2.2.3 Examples: evidence of other criminal behaviour

For another example of Lord Herschell's second proposition where the evidence in question was *not* strikingly similar to the facts of the offence charged, yet nevertheless had sufficient probative force to be admitted to rebut a defence open to the accused, see *R* v *Anderson* [1988] QB 678, CA. In that case A was convicted of conspiracy to cause explosions. She said she knew nothing about any such conspiracy and explained false identification papers and over £1,000 found in her possession on the basis that she was involved in an attempt to smuggle escaped IRA prisoners out of the country: she was to escort them and pretend that they were on holiday in order to hoodwink immigration officers. It was held that the prosecution were entitled to cross-examine her about the fact that she was wanted by the police for 'an offence' (unspecified) in order to show the unlikelihood of choosing her as an escort. Her being wanted by the police would not have diminished the risk of detection, but would have doubled it. See also *R* v *Williams* (1987) 84 Cr App R 229, CA (*cf. R* v *Carrington* [1990] Crim LR 330, CA) and *R* v *Sokialiois* [1993] Crim LR 872, CA.

Similarly it has been held that when, on a charge of importing controlled drugs, the accused denies any knowledge of how the drugs came to be concealed in his luggage or in his vehicle, evidence showing that he is connected with the same kind of drugs inside the UK, for example evidence of finding such drugs in his home, is admissible because the jury are entitled to consider such a coincidence, which may go to rebut the defence raised: see *R* v *Willis*, 29 January 1979, unreported, CA. See also *R* v *Peters* [1995] 2 Cr App R 77, CA, where the drugs found in the UK were of a different kind. Nor is the principle confined to drug couriers, but may extend to others alleged to have been involved in the illegal importation. In *R* v *Yalman* [1998] 2 Cr App R 269, CA, Y met his father at an airport on his arrival in England. The father was carrying a suitcase containing heroin. The prosecution case was that it was a family organised importation, but Y said that he was unaware of the drugs. It was held, applying *R* v *Groves* [1998] Crim LR 200, CA, that once there was a prima facie case for Y to answer, then evidence that he had used heroin and that drugs paraphernalia had been found at his home, was admissible on the issue whether he was *knowingly* involved in the importation, as tending to rebut his assertion that his presence at the airport was entirely innocent. In cases of this kind, however, the jury should also be directed that if they consider that the evidence does not assist them on the issue of knowledge or involvement, then they should disregard it altogether: *R* v *Barner-Rasmussen* [1996] Crim LR 497, CA.

6.3 Criminal Cases: Applying the Principles

As will be seen from **6.2**, it is necessary, in determining the admissibility of evidence under the similar fact principles to have a clear idea of the probative value of the evidence and a clear appreciation of the prejudicial effect it must overcome.

This chapter will consider the approaches to this analysis that the courts have adopted in the past. It is worth noting however, that the prejudicial effect in similar fact cases is generally left unstated or, at best, implicit. However, any application to admit evidence as similar fact will have to convince a judge (or on appeal the higher courts) that the evidence was more probative than prejudicial. It will be necessary, therefore, for any practitioner to evaluate the prejudice of evidence and to be able to explain this clearly to the court.

6.3.1 PROBATIVE VALUE: RELEVANCE

The first step in analysing the probative value (and therefore the admissibility of the evidence) is to determine the relevance of the evidence (i.e. to determine what conclusion it is hoped that the tribunal of fact will draw from the evidence). See **2.5** for more detail on relevance.

It is then necessary to determine the cogency or weight of the evidence (i.e. the extent to which it *will* prove that conclusion). See **2.7** for more detail on weight.

The approach adopted in determining the relevance of depends on:

(a)   the evidence of similar facts;

(b)   the other evidence in the case;

(c)   the actual issues in dispute.

Therefore relevance is determined by a close analysis of the facts of the case and as a matter of logic or common sense. However, consider the following two problem areas.

6.3.1.1   The relevance of propensity

Similar fact evidence is not generally admissible merely to prove that the defendant is the sort of person who would commit particular offences (for example a homosexual and therefore likely to commit an offence of a homosexual nature). However, it is possible that in some cases a person has a disposition or proclivity that is so distinctive that it could be of assistance to a jury in determining whether or not he or she committed an offence of a similarly distinct nature. The difficulty has proved to be determining when proclivities are so distinctive and when they are not.

This problem has been particularly marked where the offences charged and the previous offences were sexual offences. In such cases, it appeared at one time that evidence of the sexual preferences or proclivities of a defendant could regularly be deemed relevant evidence in that they show 'an abnormal and perverted propensity which stamps the individual as clearly as if marked by a physical deformity' (*R* v *Sims* [1946] KB 561). This approach was supported by observations that certain sexual offences were crimes of a special category and that in the case of such crimes, evidence of a previous acts of that kind or of a propensity towards that form of sexual conduct would be admissible evidence (see also *Thompson* v *R* [1918] AC 221; *R* v *King* [1967] 2 QB 338). This led to an impression that evidence of a sexual proclivity could be admitted without any particularly probative link between that proclivity and the offences being tried.

However, this broad approach has been firmly rejected. In *DPP* v *Boardman* the House of Lords made it clear that the more stringent test enunciated by Lord Herschell in *Makin* applies as much to sexual offences as any other: sexual offences require the application of the same principles as are used in relation to any other offence. It will therefore be necessary to identify clearly, in each particular case, how the sexual proclivity in question is relevant in determining whether or not the defendant committed the offences charged.

6.3.1.2   The relevance of the actual or likely defence

Similar fact evidence may be admissible if it is relevant to rebut a defence, which, even if not raised, is fairly open to the accused. In *Noor Mohamed* v *R* (see **6.2.1**), for example, it was stated that the prosecution would have been entitled in principle to admit evidence that showed that the death of A was unlikely to have been as a result of an accident or a trick even without the defendant having raised such defences. See also *Harris* v *DPP* [1952] AC 694, HL.

The nature of the defence, whether actually raised or fairly open to the accused, is a significant factor in determining relevance. For example, in *R* v *Chandor* [1959] 1 QB 545, the defendant was charged with five counts of indecent assault against three boys. His defence to all of the counts was that none of them had ever happened at all. The Court of Appeal held that while evidence of a series of offences might be relevant to disprove other defences such as innocent association or intent or to establish the identity of the offender, such evidence could not be admitted to disprove the defendant's denial that there had been any meeting or occasion for an incident at all. See also *R* v *Flack* [1969] 1 WLR 937, CA. However, in *DPP* v *Boardman* [1975] AC 421, HL, Lord Hailsham said he failed to see the logical distinction between a case of innocent association and a case of complete denial. See also Lord Cross, who said that he failed to see the distinction, in the case of a sexual offence, between a defence that the meeting at which the offence is said to have been committed never took place and a defence that the meeting did take place but that no offence was committed in the course of it. In both cases, said Lord Cross, the accused would be saying that the accuser is lying. Subsequent case law, however, maintains the validity of exactly these distinctions for the purpose of analysing probative value.

In *R* v *Lewis* (1983) 76 Cr App R 33, CA, the accused was convicted of offences of indecency against the twin daughters of a woman with whom he had been living. Four incidents were involved. In the case of three of them, the defence was accident or innocent explanation. In the fourth case, the accused denied that the incident had occurred at all. Evidence was admitted to show that the accused was interested in and sympathised with the Paedophilic Society. On an application for leave to appeal, the Court of Appeal, declaring that *DPP* v *Boardman* was of no direct assistance, because that case concerned 'similar fact' evidence, held that the evidence of paedophilia was admissible on the incidents where the defence was accident or innocent association but inadmissible on the incident which was denied. They also held that the evidence would have an unduly prejudicial effect if its true impact and significance were not carefully explained to the jury, but the judge had done this, directing the jury that the evidence by itself could not prove the crimes but, if it was accepted that the first three incidents did occur, could be relevant in deciding whether those incidents were designed, as opposed to accidental or innocent.

6.3.1.3 The abandonment of categories of relevance

Although at one time it was thought that there were categories of relevance comprising a closed list of the cases (e.g. 'proof of system', 'proof of identity', 'rebuttal of accident', 'rebuttal of mistake' or 'rebuttal of innocent association') in which similar fact evidence is admissible, such a view has now been repudiated. See *R* v *Bond* [1906] 2 KB 389 and *DPP* v *Boardman*.

In *Harris* v *DPP* [1952] AC 694, HL, Viscount Simon held that it is erroneous to draw up a closed list because it can only provide instances of a principle of general application — what matters is the principle itself and its proper application to the particular circumstances of the charge in question.

6.3.2 PROBATIVE VALUE: COGENCY

Having determined the relevance of the evidence, it is necessary to assess the weight (or cogency) that may be attached to it to assess its probative value. This requires an analysis not just of the similar fact evidence itself but also of the other evidence in the case. The court, in determining admissibility, will examine whether it is in the interests of justice to admit the similar fact evidence. To do this, analysis of the evidence other than the similar fact evidence is necessary as well as analysis of the similar fact evidence itself.

6.3.2.1 The cogency of the other evidence in the case

Similar fact evidence would appear to be admissible in cases where the other prosecution evidence, i.e. the evidence connecting the accused with the offence charged, is so weak that a submission of no case to answer would succeed: see *Harris* v *DPP*. See also *R* v *Straffen* where there was little evidence to associate the defendant with the case other than the distinctive way in which the offences had been committed.

6.3.2.2 The cogency of the 'similar fact' evidence

There are two aspects to the cogency of the similar fact evidence:

(a) First, how cogent is the evidence that the 'similar fact' events actually occurred (i.e. how cogent is the evidence that the defendant has a particular disposition)? For example, did the defendant actually commit the offence in a particular way in the past?

(b) Secondly, how cogent is the evidence of those events (or that disposition) in proving the events alleged in the current case? To use the above example, even if it is accepted that the previous offence was committed by the defendant, how probative is it that the defendant committed the offence currently being tried?

This section of the chapter examines the first point above. Paragraphs **6.3.3** to **6.3.7** examine the second point.

It is no bar to the admission of similar fact evidence that the defence disputes the facts that it seeks to prove: see *R* v *Rance* (1975) 62 Cr App R 462, CA.

However, there must be sufficient evidence to justify, as a possibility, a finding by the tribunal of fact, that the accused was guilty of the misconduct alleged to have occurred on another occasion.

In *Harris* v *DPP* a police constable was indicted on eight counts of larceny, acquitted on the first seven, and convicted on the eighth. The evidence showed that the offences occurred in May, June and July of the same year and that on each occasion the thief had entered the same office in Bradford market by the same method and taken only some of the money found. On the eighth count, the accused was on duty in the market at the relevant time and found by detectives near the building shortly after an alarm bell had gone off, which could have warned the thief to hide the money in a nearby bin, where it was found. On the other seven counts, however, the only evidence linking Harris with the offences was that on the dates in question he was not on leave but was on solitary duty and could have been near the market. The trial judge failed to warn the jury that the evidence of the first seven counts could not, by itself, implicate Harris on the eighth. The House of Lords allowed the appeal on the grounds that there was no proof that Harris had been near the office or even in the market at the time of the first seven thefts.

Harris v *DPP* may be compared with *R* v *Mansfield* (1977) 65 Cr App R 241, CA, where the accused was indicted on three counts of starting hotel fires. The trial judge told the jury that if they felt sure that all three fires had been started by the same person, they could use the evidence on the first two counts when considering Mansfield's guilt in respect of the third, and Mansfield was convicted on all three. The Court of Appeal dismissed the appeal, distinguishing *Harris* v *DPP* because on the facts there was overwhelming evidence in relation to the first two fires that Mansfield was not only in the vicinity, but had ample opportunity of starting those fires, and in relation to each of them behaved afterwards in a manner arousing suspicion.

To make sense of the difficulties it is necessary to appreciate two matters of criminal evidence and procedure:

(a) That weak identification evidence will be admissible only if there is supporting evidence, which may be other identification evidence (see *R* v *Turnbull* [1977] QB 224 and see **12.3**).

(b) That there will be cases where the jury hears a number of identifications in respect of different offences because those offences are being tried together in a 'multiple count' case (see **6.1** and the ***Criminal Litigation Manual***) but they need to be given directions by the court as to the extent to which they can use evidence on count A to support the evidence on count B and vice versa.

The courts have had to determine whether the identifications in respect of each offence can be combined to establish that the defendant committed any of the offences (an approach adopted in *R* v *Downey* [1995] 1 Cr App R 547 and in *R* v *Barnes* [1995] 2 Cr App R 491, CA) or whether the jury should be satisfied that the defendant *had* committed one of the offences before that offence could show he was likely to have committed offences with similar features (the approach adopted in *R* v *McGranaghan* [1995] 1 Cr App R 559). The answer would appear to depend upon the exact nature of the dispute in the case. Where the jury is satisfied that the evidence shows that the same person committed all of the offences in question but there is no clear identification in any of them, the *Downey* and *Barnes* approach of combining the identifications could be adopted. Where there is weak identification in relation to offence A, the evidence that the defendant committed offence B is capable of supporting that identification only if the jury is satisfied that the defendant in fact committed offence B. These cases are dealt with in more detail at **6.3.5**.

6.3.3 PROBATIVE VALUE FROM STRIKING SIMILARITY

The leading authority in relation to crimes committed in a strikingly similar manner to other crimes committed by the accused is *DPP* v *Boardman* [1975] AC 421, HL. The headmaster of a boarding-school for boys in Cambridge was convicted on an indictment containing, *inter alia*, two counts: (i) buggery with one boy S, and (ii) inciting another boy H to commit buggery with him. There was no application for separate trials. The defence was that S and H were lying and that the alleged incidents had never occurred. The trial judge ruled that the evidence of S was admissible as evidence on the count concerning H, and vice versa, on the grounds that in each case the sexual conduct alleged by the boys against the headmaster was of an unusual kind in that it involved a request by a middle-aged man to an adolescent to play the active role in buggery. The other similarities in the evidence of S and H were said to be that (i) both were woken up at about midnight in the dormitory and spoken to in a low voice and (ii) similar words were used to induce their participation in the offence in the headmaster's sitting-room. Both the Court of Appeal and the House of Lords dismissed the appeal. In reaching their decision, the House of Lords stressed that the test of admissibility is probative value, which in the case before them derived from a striking similarity between the facts testified to by the several witnesses. This was described in a number of different ways.

Lord Morris of Borth-y-Gest at p. 441 said:

> . . . there may be cases where a judge, having both limbs of Lord Herschell's famous proposition in mind, considers that the interests of justice (of which the interests of fairness form so fundamental a component) make it proper that he should permit a jury when considering one fact or set of facts also to consider the evidence concerning another fact or set of facts if between the two there is such close or striking similarity or such an underlying unity that probative force could fairly be yielded.

Lord Wilberforce at p. 444, dealing with the probative force of admissible similar fact evidence, said:

> This probative force is derived, if at all, from the circumstances that the facts testified to by the several witnesses bear to each other such a striking similarity that they must, when judged by experience and common sense, either all be true, or have arisen from a cause common to the witnesses or from pure coincidence. The jury may, therefore, properly be asked to judge whether the right conclusion is that all are true, so that each story is supported by the other(s).

Lord Cross of Chelsea at p. 456 said:

Circumstances, however, may arise in which such evidence is so very relevant that to exclude it would be an affront to common sense. . . The question must always be whether the similar fact evidence taken together with the other evidence would do no more than raise or strengthen a suspicion that the accused committed the offence with which he is charged or would point so strongly to his guilt that only an ultra-cautious jury, if they accepted it as true, would acquit in face of it.

Lord Salmon at p. 462 said:

It has . . . never been doubted that if the crime charged is committed in a uniquely or strikingly similar manner to other crimes committed by the accused the manner in which the other crimes were committed may be evidence on which a jury could reasonably conclude that the accused was guilty of the crime charged. The similarity would have to be so unique or striking that common sense makes it inexplicable on the basis of coincidence.

Lord Hailsham at p. 453 said:

A mere succession of facts is not normally enough . . . There must be something more than mere repetition. The test is whether there is such an underlying unity between the offences as to make coincidence an affront to common sense.

For an illustration of the point made by Lord Hailsham, see *R* v *Wells* (1991) 92 Cr App R 24, CA. The accused's home was raided twice, resulting in two sets of charges for possession of cocaine with intent to supply. As to the similarities between the items recovered on each of the two raids, paperfolds, scales and cocaine in 1 and $\frac{1}{2}$ gramme units were found — but these are all commonplace for drug suppliers; the cutting agent Mannitol was found — the most common in use; and the percentage purity of cocaine was 21% on the first raid, 15–23% on the second raid — this was hardly striking. Compare *R* v *Mullen* [1992] Crim LR 735. See also *R* v *Beggs* (1990) 90 Cr App R 430, CA and *R* v *Bedford* (1991) 93 Cr App R 113, CA.

In *DPP* v *Boardman*, the House of Lords made it quite clear that there is no special rule for sexual cases. Lords Cross and Wilberforce also regarded the case, on its facts, as borderline, Lord Wilberforce confessing to some fear that if regarded as an example, it might be setting the standard of striking similarity too low. The subsequent case of *Reza* v *GMC* [1991] 2 All ER 796, PC, is difficult to square with both of these aspects of *Boardman*. It contains suggestions that there is a special rule for certain types of sexual offence against the young; and it tends to justify Lord Wilberforce's fear. Reza was charged by the GMC with making improper and indecent remarks and behaving improperly to receptionists employed by him. The Privy Council held that his conduct, in introducing the subject of sex at every turn was distinctly unusual and on that basis held that the evidence of the various complainants was mutually corroborative similar fact evidence. In rejecting a defence submission that the individual breaches of indecency were commonplace, Lord Lowry said, by way of example, that in a case of incest involving two daughters, even if the acts committed and the circumstances are commonplace, the fact of the accused's preoccupation with young girls as a means of gratifying his desires and the fact that those girls are his daughters are, by themselves, far from commonplace; and in the case of indecency offences against young boys, the fact that an accused has a perverted interest in young boys and gratifies his lust at their expense, however unremarkable his methods, is scarcely commonplace.

6.3.4   PROBATIVE VALUE WITHOUT STRIKING SIMILARITY

The test of striking similarity is not appropriate in every case; what the law requires is positive probative value (albeit that in some cases such probative value is derived from striking similarity).

In *R* v *P* [1991] 3 All ER 337, HL, an important decision of the House of Lords, it was made clear that in cases where the evidence sought to be adduced comes from another alleged victim or victims, striking similarity is *not* an essential element except in cases where the identity of the offender is in issue. The accused was convicted on two counts of rape and eight counts of incest. One of the rapes and four of the incest counts related to daughter B. The other rape count and the other four incest counts related to daughter S. The trial judge found the following to be strikingly similar: (a) the extreme discipline and almost dictatorial power exercised over the female children of the family; (b) the abortions undergone by each girl paid for by P; and (c) the apparent acquiescence of the mother in his sexual attentions to his daughters. The Court of Appeal held that these features (with the possible exception of (b)) did not relate to P's *modus operandi* and could not be described as unusual features such as to make the account of one girl more credible because they were mirrored in the statement of the other. As to (a), the discipline was applied to all the family, not just the girls. As to (b), P's financial commitment was limited, his wife was also involved and the fact that he might have arranged and paid for the abortion did not necessarily point to his being responsible for the pregnancy. As to (c), the acquiescence related principally to the eldest girl and might have been due to fear of P. Moreover, it would be unusual if a third party's reaction to offences could ever operate as a striking similarity. The Court of Appeal allowed the appeal, therefore, because, as it understood the law, there was a requirement of similarity going beyond what was described as 'the incestuous father's stock-in-trade', and that feature was lacking. However, leave to appeal to the House of Lords was granted and the following point was certified:

> Where a father/step-father is charged with sexually abusing a young daughter of the family, is evidence that he has also similarly abused other young children of the family admissible (assuming there to be no collusion) in support of such charge in the absence of any other 'striking similarities'?

The House of Lords held that the true test of admissibility is whether the evidence in question has a probative force sufficiently great to make it just to admit it, notwithstanding that it is prejudicial in tending to show that the accused is guilty of another crime. There was no requirement, as the Court of Appeal believed, of some feature of similarity going beyond the incestuous father's stock-in-trade. Lord Mackay LC, giving the judgment of the House, answered the certified question as follows:

> When a question of the kind raised in this case arises I consider that the judge must first decide whether there is material upon which the jury would be entitled to conclude that the evidence of one victim, about what occurred to that victim, is so related to the evidence given by another victim, about what happened to that other victim, that the evidence of the first victim provides strong enough support for the evidence of the second victim to make it just to admit it, notwithstanding the prejudicial effect of admitting the evidence. This relationship, from which support is derived, may take many forms and while these forms may include 'striking similarity' in the manner in which the crime is committed, consisting of unusual characteristics in its execution the necessary relationship is by no means confined to such circumstances. Relationships in time and circumstances other than these may well be important relationships in this connection. Where the identity of the perpetrator is in issue, and evidence of this kind is important in that connection, obviously something in the nature of what has been called in the course of the argument a signature or other special feature will be necessary. To transpose this requirement to other situations where the question is whether a crime has been committed, rather than who did commit it, is to impose an unnecessary and improper restriction upon the application of the principle.

For these reasons, the appeal was allowed and the conviction restored.

R v *P* has necessarily lowered the standard for admissibility from that laid down in *DPP* v *Boardman*. Thus in the subsequent case of *R* v *Roy* [1992] Crim LR 185, evidence of indecent assaults by a doctor on female patients was held to be mutually corroborative similar fact evidence notwithstanding that the conduct could quite fairly be described as the stock-in-trade of a doctor sexually abusing his professional position. See also *R* v *Simpson* (1994) 99 Cr App R 48, CA, a decision acknowledged to be borderline, where in the circumstances of the case, evidence of an indecent assault on one victim in 1990 was held to be similar fact evidence on a charge of raping another victim five years earlier. It is submitted, however, that *R* v *P* should not now be used to give a retrospective validity to the views of Lord Lowry in *Reza* v *GMC*, above. In a case of incest (or indecency against males), it would seem that more is required than that there were two (or more) young victims. See, for example, *R* v *Channing* [1994] Crim LR 924, a case of indecent assaults against boys in which the Court of Appeal detailed the common features of the complaints on the basis of which they were held to amount to mutually corroborative similar fact evidence.

Some examples

Examples of probative value without striking similarity include cases involving homosexual misconduct and incriminating articles. In some of these cases, the evidence has probative value in identifying the accused. In others, such as *R* v *Lewis* (1983) 76 Cr App R 33, CA, it has probative value in rebutting a defence of innocent association. It should be stressed, however, that this is not to return to the repudiated view that admissibility is restricted to evidence falling within a closed list of categories of relevance — the sole test is probative value; each case turns on its own facts; and all the examples which follow are nothing more than instances of a doctrine of general application.

Cases involving homosexual misconduct

In *Thompson* v *R* [1918] AC 221, the House of Lords held that evidence of the defendant's homosexual inclinations was admissible in relation to offences of gross indecency against young boys. The prosecution alleged that he had committed the acts of indecency on two boys on 16 December and then made an arrangement to meet them in the same place on 19 December. On that occasion a police officer was present and confronted the defendant when he approached the boys. The defendant sought to explain the meeting and his payment of money to the two boys as acts of charity on his part and denied that there had been any meeting on the 16th. However, upon his arrest, the defendant was found in possession of powder puffs. Also, when his lodgings were subsequently searched photographs of naked young boys in suggestive poses were found. The prosecution case was that the meeting of the 19th was for the same purposes as that of the 16th and therefore supported the allegations of the two boys as to what had happened on the earlier date. Both the powder puffs and the photographs were admitted at trial to disprove both the denial of the meeting on the 16th and the innocent explanation of the meeting on the 19th.

The House of Lords upheld the convictions. The powder puffs found on the defendant's person were admissible as items that were to be used in the intended commission of indecency offences on the 19th (that they would be was accepted by the House without comment). They would therefore support the prosecution case that there was to be a second meeting with the boys for the same purposes as on the 16th. The House of Lords found the photographs a little more difficult but nonetheless considered them to have been properly admitted. The photographs were, according to Lord Sumner (at p. 235), 'the hall-mark of a specialised and extraordinary class' of person. As such they were admissible to prove that the defendant's explanation of the purpose of the meeting on the 19th was likely to be untrue.

In *R* v *King* [1967] 2 QB 358, CA, K was convicted of various offences of gross indecency, attempted buggery and indecent assault, his defence, on some of the counts, being innocent association. For example, he admitted meeting two boys in a public lavatory and asking them to spend the night in his room, and he also admitted that one of them shared his bed, but he denied any offence. The Court of Appeal, relying upon *Thompson* v *R* [1918] AC 221, HL, held that evidence of K's homosexuality was admissible. It is *possible* to justify the decision reached on the following basis: whereas in the abstract mere evidence of homosexual propensity — without any striking similarities — lacks the requisite degree of probative force, in the light of the prosecution evidence and the defence raised (K denied the offence but admitted inviting the boy home and sleeping in the same bed with him), the evidence of homosexuality took on a probative force that in the abstract it lacked. In cases where the defence is innocent association, however, much may turn on the degree of admitted intimacy. See, for example, *R* v *Horwood* [1970] 1 QB 358, CA.

Both *R* v *King* and *R* v *Horwood* were decided before *DPP* v *Boardman*, but may well remain good law. *R* v *King*, 7 April 1982, unreported, CA, tends to support this view. As in the earlier case of *King*, in this case various sexual offences were alleged in respect of boys who visited the accused's flat, the defence was innocent association, and there was evidence of the accused's homosexuality. The Court of Appeal held that where a man with homosexual propensities actually encourages boys to come to his flat by providing them with inducements (on the facts, games and bicycles), evidence of his homosexual propensity is admissible to disprove his avowed *innocent* interest in the young.

The case of *Thompson* v *R* might be looked at in a similar light. The powder puffs were uncritically accepted as items that were to be used in furtherance of a relevant crime on the later occasion. As such (as will be seen below) they would be admissible (although it is highly questionable whether such items found on a man today would carry any such probative force). As to the evidence of possession of the photographs, cf *R* v *B (RA)* (see **6.2.1** above).

Incriminating articles

Evidence of the accused's possession of incriminating articles may show nothing more than the accused's criminal disposition, in which case it will be inadmissible pursuant to the first of Lord Herschell's propositions in *Makin* v *Attorney-General for New South Wales* (**6.2**): see *R* v *Taylor* (1924) 17 Cr App R 109, in which the Court of Appeal held that an article that would show a disposition to commit a particular type of offence generally was inadmissible in the absence of evidence that it had been used to commit the offence in question. In that case the defendant was accused of burglary. The prosecution sought to admit evidence of the finding of a jemmy at the defendant's house. The prosecution evidence was that the defendant was found running from the property, the door of which had been forced open. The jemmy was not on his person at the time of the arrest and there was no evidence that a jemmy had been used to force the door. Clearly the effect of such evidence could only have been to establish that he was the type of person who burgled buildings rather than to confirm that he had been involved in the burglary of the building in question.

However, evidence of the possession of incriminating articles may be admitted under the similar fact evidence doctrine to identify the accused as the offender where the articles in question could have been used, even if they are not proved to have been used, in committing the offence charged.

For example, in *R* v *Reading* [1966] 1 WLR 836, CCA, the accused were charged with robberies which involved the hijacking of lorries. Articles were found in their possession which *could* have been used in the hijacking, such as car number-plates, walkie-talkie radios and a police uniform. The Court of Criminal Appeal held that evidence of possession of these articles had been properly admitted in order to confirm the identification of the accused by witnesses and to rebut the defence of alibi and mistaken identity. See also and cf *R* v *Mustafa* (1976) 65 Cr App R 26, CA.

6.3.4.2 Background evidence

Evidence of misconduct may be admitted not to show that the accused is more likely to have committed the offence by reason of his disposition, but in order to establish a particular and essential part of the prosecution case.

An example used by the late Sir Rupert Cross and based upon the Canadian case of *R* v *Ducsharm* [1956] 1 DLR 732 is, in a case where an accused denies being in the neighbourhood where the crime was committed, evidence that he committed another crime in that area shortly before or after the time of the commission of the offence in question. See also *R* v *Straffen* [1952] 2 QB 911, CCA (see **6.2.2** for the facts of this case). In that case the murder was committed during a period between Straffen's escape from Broadmoor and his recapture four hours later. The reference to Broadmoor came in not to show disposition to commit the crime, but because reference to the time of his escape from that institution was the only way of proving his presence in the area at the relevant time.

In *R* v *Sukhpal Singh* [2001] EWCA Crim 2884 the decision of the trial judge to admit evidence of a previous unlawful wounding offence was approved by the Court of Appeal. The defendant was charged with blackmail and burglary offences. Some of the victims said that the offender had warned them he had stabbed someone a year before. Proof of a conviction for stabbing a year before therefore went to establish the identity of the offender.

In *R* v *Salisbury* (1831) 5 C & P 155 a postman, A, was charged with stealing a letter belonging to B and containing bank-notes. There was evidence that the accused (A) had also opened a letter, also containing bank-notes, belonging to C, and that A had put the notes from B's letter into C's letter, and taken notes from C's letter to the same amount, which notes were found in A's possession. Such evidence was admissible to establish a link in the chain of events relating to the offence charged. See also *R* v *Ellis* (1826) 6 B & C 145 and *R* v *Mackie* (1973) 57 Cr App R 463, CA.

Evidence, notwithstanding that it reveals the bad character of the accused, may be admitted on the basis that it is part of a continual background or history which is relevant to the offence charged and without the totality of which the account placed before the jury would be incomplete or incomprehensible: *per* Purchas LJ in *R* v *Pettman*, 2 May 1985, unreported, CA and applied in *R* v *Sidhu* (1994) 98 Cr App 59, CA.

An illustration of the principle of 'background evidence' is to be found in the case of *R* v *M and others* [2000] 1 All ER 148. One of the defendants, M, had been charged, along with a number of other members of his family, with a number of sexual offences on other members of the family. M had been charged with two rapes of his sister. The prosecution had led evidence that, a number of years before the offences against S, M had been forced to watch and then to participate in sexual offences against two other siblings. M was not charged with these earlier sexual offences. The prosecution did not seek to argue that the evidence fell within the similar facts doctrine as defined in *R* v *P* [1991] 3 All ER 337, HL. Rather the prosecution argument was that evidence of the previous events was necessary to allow the jury to understand the offences against S with which M had been charged. The prosecution case alleged that there had been long-term and systematic abuse within the family as a result of which M would feel able to commit the offences without any threat from other family members and also that S would not feel able to seek help from those family members. The judge directed the jury in more restricted terms, telling them that the evidence of this culture of abuse would assist them in understanding how M felt able to abuse his sibling 'secure in the knowledge that she would not seek out the protection of her own parents'. The Court of Appeal, adopting commentary by Professor Birch ([1995] Crim LR 651), stated that the background evidence could be admitted 'in order to put the jury in the general picture about the characters involved in the action and the run-up to the alleged offence'. In the opinion of the Court of Appeal, the evidence was admissible for purposes wider than those envisaged by the trial judge. The Court also noted, however, that such evidence may be excluded under Police and Criminal Evidence Act 1984, s. 78, if its admission had an adverse effect on the fairness of the proceedings (for s. 78 see **10.2**).

In *R* v *B* [1997] Crim LR 220, CA, a trial of a father for indecent acts against his daughter. The fact that the evidence showed the commission of an offence with which he was not charged was not of itself a ground for excluding it. Neither was the fact that it came exclusively from the complainant, with no independent supporting evidence. Sometimes such 'background' evidence will reveal the motive of the accused for committing the offence. In *R* v *Williams* (1986) 84 Cr App R 299, CA, W was charged with threatening to kill E intending that she would fear that his threat would be carried out. W had previously committed acts of violence against E, including an assault resulting in his conviction and imprisonment. The present offence occurred six weeks after his release. Evidence of this previous history was admissible to show (i) that W's threat stemmed from resentment because of his imprisonment and (ii) that W intended his threat to be taken seriously.

6.3.5   PROBATIVE VALUE AND IDENTIFICATION

This dictum, however, has since been interpreted by the Court of Appeal, in *R* v *John W* [1998] 2 Cr App R 289, in such a way as to restrict the requirement even further.

W was convicted of false imprisonment of and indecent assault on C in Aldershot (counts 1 and 2) and of false imprisonment of S in Farnham two weeks later (count 3). The issue in both cases was identity, but the evidence revealed no 'signature or other special feature'. W appealed, relying on *R* v *P*, on the basis that the trial judge had failed to make it clear that the evidence was not mutually admissible, i.e. that the evidence on counts 1 and 2 was not admissible on count 3, and vice versa.

Hooper J held that Lord Mackay's dictum did not mean that there is a special rule in identity cases requiring a signature or other special feature: the Lord Chancellor simply had in mind identification cases in which the *only* evidence of any substance against an accused on a particular count is evidence of a signature or other very striking similarity.

It is submitted that this is a strained and unconvincing interpretation and that it would have been simpler to have said that what the Lord Chancellor had said was *obiter*, and that there is simply no *requirement* for striking similarity at all. What the law requires is a sufficient degree of probative force which, in *any* given case, may or may not be derived from striking similarity. Where the prosecution assert that the probative force of the evidence does derive from its striking similarity, the court will only rule the evidence admissible if its probative force is sufficiently great to admit it notwithstanding its prejudicial effect. In some cases the evidence of striking similarity may be admitted to rebut a defence of mistaken identity, but equally, in others, it may be admitted to rebut other defences, such as accident, mistake or, in a sexual case, innocent association.

In the case of *R* v *John W* itself, the Court of Appeal held that the evidence on the two counts did not need to be strikingly similar or in the nature of a signature. The Court went on to identify the proper test, but stressing at the same time that it was only appropriate in a case of the kind before it:

> Evidence tending to show that a defendant has committed an offence charged in count A may be used to reach a verdict on count B and vice versa, if: the circumstances of both offences (as the jury would be entitled to find them) are such as to provide sufficient probative support for the conclusion that the defendant committed both offences, and it would therefore be fair for the evidence to be used in this way notwithstanding the prejudicial effect of so doing.

The Court of Appeal held that this test, when applied to the facts of the case before it, was satisfied: most (but not all) of the descriptions of the attacker fitted the appellant, the descriptions of some of the attacker's clothes fitted the clothes that the appellant was known to be wearing, the appellant lived near both attacks, having moved from Aldershot to Farnham in the period between the time of the two attacks, the attacks took place within a short time of each other and they bore certain similarities. It is, however, necessary also to identify how a jury should be told to use similar fact evidence to decide the identity of the offender.

There is some doubt as to the approach to apply where the issue in the case is the identity of the defendant. In *R* v *P* [1991] 3 All ER 337 Lord Mackay observed that the requirement of a signature or some other significant or unusual feature is confined to cases in which the identity of the offender is in issue. *R* v *McGranaghan* [1995] 1 Cr App R 559 establishes that in cases where identity is in issue, there has to be some evidence to make the jury *sure* that the accused is the offender, because the similar facts go to show that the same man committed both offences, not that the accused was that man. McG was convicted of three separate aggravated burglaries of homes and rapes or grossly indecent assaults on women in those homes. McG denied having anything to do with any of the offences. The Court of Appeal held that the similarities in the features of all the alleged offences rendered the evidence on one admissible in relation to the others, but allowed the appeal on the grounds that the jury should have been directed to consider first whether, disregarding the similarity of the facts, the other evidence in the case was sufficient to make them sure that the accused committed at least one of the offences. Only if they were so sure, was evidence of similarity then admissible to prove that the accused committed the second offence. Glidewell LJ said: 'An identification about which the jury are not sure cannot support another identification of which the jury are also not sure however similar the facts of the two offences may be.'

The sentence from the judgment of Glidewell LJ set out above has been qualified by *R v Barnes* [1995] 2 Cr App R 491, CA, in which *R v McGranaghan* was cited with approval, but distinguished. In *R v Barnes*, the accused was convicted of three offences involving indecent assaults on two females and the wounding of a third. In each case the complainant was approached from behind by a man who asked for the time, threatened her with a knife and asked her for a kiss. Evidence was admitted of three other similar incidents. It was common ground that the various incidents were sufficiently similar to be admitted for the purpose of showing that all the offences on the indictment and the other three offences relied upon by the Crown were committed by the same man. It was held that the identification evidence of the three victims could be used cumulatively in deciding whether that man was the accused.

In reaching this conclusion, the court relied upon *R v Downey* [1995] 1 Cr App R 547, CA, to draw a distinction between two different types of situation. In *R v McGranaghan*, which was regarded as an illustration of the first, the court was considering the propriety of using similar fact evidence to support a doubtful identification. The issue in this first situation is whether the jury, in deciding whether the accused committed offence A, can have regard to evidence that he also committed offence B. This involves proof not only of similarity, but also that the accused did in fact commit offence B. The second situation, of which *R v Barnes* itself is an illustration, is where there is evidence, other than evidence of visual identification, on the basis of which the jury can conclude that offences A and B were committed by the same man, but that evidence, by itself, falls short of proving that that man was the accused in either case. In this situation, if the jury is satisfied that the other evidence shows both offences to have been committed by the same man, the identification evidence of the victims can be used cumulatively in deciding whether that man was the accused. It was held that Glidewell LJ's dictum in *R v McGranaghan* (as quoted above) is appropriate to the first situation. If it sought to go further it was considered to have been obiter and to have gone too far. See also *R v Grant* [1996] 2 Cr App R 272, CA; and *R v John W* [1998] 2 Cr App R 289, CA, below.

The principle of *R v Downey* can also apply where two or more offences bear the hallmark of the same gang or group. In *R v Brown* [1997] Crim LR 502, CA, two sets of offences were alleged to have been committed by members of a gang. It was held that once the jury were satisfied, by reason of striking similarities between the two sets of offences, that the same gang had committed both of them, then the issues were whether the prosecution had established on all the admissible evidence that the accused in question was a member of the gang and, where the prosecution said that he was a member on both occasions, whether the totality of the evidence established that beyond reasonable doubt. See also, and *cf.*, *R v Lee* [1996] Crim LR 825, CA.

6.3.6 PROBATIVE VALUE OF SURROUNDING CIRCUMSTANCES

6.3.6.1 Other crimes
Evidence of the circumstances surrounding other crimes committed by the accused is admissible under the similar fact evidence doctrine if those circumstances have a sufficient degree of probative force derived from a striking similarity between those circumstances and the circumstances surrounding the commission of the offence charged.

In *R v Novac* (1976) 65 Cr App R 107, CA, the accused was convicted on an indictment containing a number of counts of buggery and gross indecency with boys, the allegation being that on a number of different occasions he had accosted boys in amusement arcades, offered them treats such as meals or money to play gambling machines, and then taken them to his home or the beach where the offences were allegedly committed. Quashing the conviction on the grounds that there was no unique or striking similarity between the offences, Bridge LJ held that it was surely a commonplace feature of such offences to take the boys home and commit the offences in bed. That the boys were all picked up in an amusement arcade, he thought more nearly approximated to a striking similarity, but that was held to be a similarity in the surrounding circumstances and not sufficiently proximate to the commission of the crime itself. However, on almost identical facts, in *R v Johannsen* (1977) 65 Cr App R 101, CA, a similar appeal was dismissed.

In *R v Scarrott* [1978] QB 1016, CA, Scarman LJ attempted to reconcile the cases:

> Plainly some matters, some circumstances may be so distant in time or place from the commission of an offence as not to be properly considered when deciding whether the subject-matter of similar fact evidence displays striking similarities with the offence charged. On the other hand, equally plainly, one cannot isolate, as a sort of laboratory specimen, the bare bones of a criminal offence from its surrounding circumstances and say that it is only within the confines of that specimen, microscopically considered, that admissibility is to be determined.

See also *R v Smith* (1915) 11 Cr App R 229, CCA. In *Lanford v GMC* [1989] 2 All ER 921, PC, a doctor was charged with using obscene and indecent language and behaving improperly to two female patients in the course of professional consultations and examinations. The argument advanced for the appellant was that the admitted similarity in what the doctor allegedly said to Mrs A and Mrs B respectively could not properly be relied on by the prosecution when there was no striking similarity in what he allegedly did to them. The argument was rejected: the evidence of each patient was that the contact was indecent and improper; the evidence of what the doctor said before and after his examination tended, if believed, to prove that the contact was indecent; and the evidence of what the doctor allegedly said in one case, provided a striking similarity was found between the two cases, was capable of corroborating the evidence of indecency in the other.

6.3.6.2 Other non-criminal behaviour

Evidence of non-criminal behaviour of the accused is admissible under the similar fact evidence doctrine if such behaviour has a sufficient degree of probative force to prove commission of the offence charged. This is often derived from a striking similarity between that behaviour and the circumstances surrounding the commission of the offence charged.

A case where there was sufficient probative force is *R v Barrington* [1981] 1 WLR 419, CA, where the accused was charged with indecently assaulting three girls. The prosecution alleged that the girls had been lured to the house of a co-accused as baby-sitters, had been shown pornographic photographs, had been asked to pose for photographs in the nude, and had then been indecently assaulted. Evidence was also admitted from three other girls concerning another incident. They had *not* been indecently assaulted, but they had been lured to the house on the same pretext, had been shown the photographs and had been asked to pose in the nude. The Court of Appeal held the evidence to have been properly admitted on the grounds that although it included no evidence of the commission of offences, it was logically probative of guilt because inexplicable on the basis of coincidence.

Cf. R v Rodley [1913] 3 KB 468, CCA, where R was charged with burglary with intent to ravish A. Evidence that an hour later R had entered another house — down the chimney! — and had had sexual intercourse with B with B's consent was held to be inadmissible to prove R's guilty intent. See also *R v Butler* (1987) 84 Cr App R 12, CA. The case of *R v Tricoglus* (1976) 65 Cr App R 16, CA, also concerns the extent to which the court should exclude evidence of the defendant's disposition to a particular form of conduct short of criminal behaviour. The defendant was charged with rape. Two complainants alleged that they had been raped by the driver of a Mini after they had accepted his unsolicited offers of lifts home. The circumstances and details of the rapes were almost identical including details of particular sexual preferences on the part of the assailant. Neither of the complainants could identify the accused and one of them, G, had to some extent inaccurately described the defendant's car. The prosecution therefore called two other witnesses, M and C. They also gave evidence of a Mini driver who insistently offered lifts in the same area. Neither had accepted the lifts. One had taken down a registration number that had almost completely corresponded with the defendant's. The court allowed the defendant's appeal against the admission of this evidence. The court held that the evidence of G was admissible similar fact evidence. However, the evidence of M and C was only such as to show a particular disposition on the part of the defendant to 'kerb crawl'. At the time of this trial kerb crawling was not an offence. The court said that the evidence of M and C amounted to no more than an allegation that the defendant had 'unpleasant social habits': it did not link the defendant with the commission of the rapes in question. The court went on to conclude that the wrongful admission of M and C's evidence had led to such prejudice against the defendant that, despite the other evidence in the case, the appeal ought to be allowed.

6.3.7 PROBATIVE VALUE: THE CURRENT PRINCIPLE

As has been seen already, *R* v *P* represents the current test to be applied in analysing the probative value of evidence. Although, there is some dispute as to whether or not *R* v *P* represents the test in all cases, it seems likely that the best interpretation of that case and the subsequent case law is that it does. Striking similarity is not a *requirement* in any type of case. It is simply one way in which evidence can have strong probative value when applying the *R* v *P* test. As has been noted at **6.3.4** above, any observations on striking similarity in that case would have been *obiter*.

Furthermore there has recently been the growth of cases where evidence of bad character is admitted as 'background evidence' (see **6.3.4.2**). This may or may not be seen as an application of the rule in *R* v *P*. The evidence has not been justified as 'so probative' that it is in the interest of justice to admit it. In fact in cases such as *R* v *M and others*, the court stated that background evidence was not admissible under similar fact doctrines. However, it is submitted that, as the admission of the evidence was to prevent the evidence before the jury from being 'incomplete and incomprehensible', this must be an aspect of probative value. The background evidence, taken with other admissible evidence, gives the totality of the evidence strong probative value where before there would have been none. However, as the end result is the same whether or not the cases are admitted under the mantle of 'similar fact evidence', it may be that it is of purely academic interest whether or not the evidence is technically defined as such.

The best view that can be taken of similar fact cases and the test to be applied is that the test laid down in *R* v *P*, therefore, applies to all evidence of previous bad character, disposition to commit offences or other propensity.

Two propositions may still be derived from *DPP* v *Boardman*:

(a) The admission of similar fact evidence is exceptional and requires a strong degree of probative force.

(b) Sufficient probative force *may* (but not necessarily *may only*) be gained where the evidence of disposition and as to the facts in issue display such a close or striking similarity or such an underlying unity that, if accepted, it would be inexplicable, in common sense, on grounds of coincidence.

6.4 Proving Similar Fact Evidence

6.4.1 'SIMILAR FACTS' SUBSEQUENT TO THE OFFENCE CHARGED

Evidence may be given of misconduct alleged to have occurred on another occasion either before or after the crime with which the accused is charged: see *R* v *Smith* (1915) 11 Cr App R 229, CCA and *R* v *Geering* (1849) 18 LJ MC 215.

6.4.2   CONVICTIONS

If the accused was convicted of an offence in respect of his conduct on some other occasion and evidence of that conduct is admissible under the similar fact evidence doctrine, are the prosecution also entitled to prove the fact of the conviction? The position is not clear, but *R* v *Shepherd* (1980) 71 Cr App R 120 suggests an answer in the negative. See also Police and Criminal Evidence Act 1984, s. 74(3) at **13.2.2.2**.

6.4.3   ACQUITTALS

Where a person has been tried for, and acquitted of an offence on some previous occasion, that does not necessarily mean that the evidence of the commission of *that* offence would not be admissible as similar fact evidence to prove the commission of some other offence at a later date: *R* v *Z* [2000] 3 All ER 385, HL. In *Z* the defendant had been tried on three previous occasions for rape and had been acquitted having run the defence of consent. He was then tried for a fourth rape in which he also ran the defence of consent. There were similarities between his conduct on all four occasions. The House of Lords held that, as the purpose of adducing the evidence was not to show that the defendant was guilty of the earlier offences but rather to show that he was guilty of the offence being tried, evidence of those earlier offences would be admitted. This would be the case insofar as the evidence in question did not place the defendant in double jeopardy, which he was not in the current case because the current prosecution was not based on the facts of the earlier offences but on new facts: the previous offences were only admissible as similar fact evidence. The House went on to observe that the evidence could still be excluded if its prejudicial effect outweighed its probative value or pursuant to Police and Criminal Evidence Act 1984, s. 78 (admission of the evidence was unfair in all the circumstances). For s. 78, see **Chapter 10** of this Manual and for double jeopardy see the *Criminal Litigation Manual*.

6.4.4   DISCRETION

There are numerous dicta to the effect that the trial judge does have a discretion to exclude otherwise admissible similar fact evidence if its prejudicial effect outweighs its probative value: see, e.g. *Noor Mohamed* v *R*, *Harris* v *DPP*, *DPP* v *Boardman*, and *R* v *Lunt*. However, given that under the modem law the true test of admissibility is whether the similar fact evidence is so very relevant or probative as to offset its obviously prejudicial effect, then it would seem that, generally speaking, there is little scope for the subsequent operation of such an exclusionary *discretion*. Note, however, that Police and Criminal Evidence Act 1984, s. 78, may apply to background evidence (*R* v *M and others* [2000] 1 All ER 148).

6.4.5   ALLEGATIONS OF COLLUSION

Where an accused is charged with two or more offences and the evidence of the two or more complainants is relied on as mutually corroborative similar fact evidence, but their evidence is tainted by deliberate conspiracy or collaboration, or has been innocently contaminated by knowledge of the account each intends to give as a result of discussions they have held (see *R* v *W* [1994] 2 All ER 872, CA) or media publicity (see *per* Lord Wilberforce in *DPP* v *Boardman* [1975] AC 421, HL, at p. 444), the question arises whether such collaboration or contamination goes to (a) the admissibility of the evidence (a question for the judge which may necessitate a *voir dire*) or (b) the credibility of the complainants and the quality and weight of their evidence (questions for the jury).

One might have supposed that in principle, since the probative value of such similar fact evidence stems from the fact that the various witnesses give *independent* accounts of separate incidents which are — to the degree necessary — similar or inter-related, if there is a real risk of collaboration or contamination (which provides another explanation for the degree of similarity or inter-relationship), the probative value of the evidence diminishes to such an extent, if it does not disappear altogether, that the evidence should *not* be admissible as similar fact evidence: see *R* v *Ryder* [1994] 2 All

ER 859, CA, applying *R v Ananthanarayanan* [1994] 2 All ER 847, CA. Such reasoning, however, was in large measure, if not entirely, rejected by the House of Lords in *R v H* [1995] 2 All ER 865.

R v H was a case of sexual offences against a daughter and a step-daughter. There was a risk that they had colluded. The House of Lords held that except in very rare cases, the question of collusion has no bearing on the admissibility of similar fact evidence but goes to the credibility of the evidence. The judge should not decide whether there is a risk of collusion because to do so would be to consider whether the evidence of the complainants is true or false and therefore whether the accused is guilty or not guilty, the very question for the jury to decide. Lord Mackay LC identified four situations.

(a) Where the defence seek to exclude similar fact evidence on the basis of deliberate collusion or innocent contamination, the judge should approach the question of admissibility on the basis that the similar facts alleged are true. Generally, therefore, collusion is not relevant at this stage.

(b) If the submission is such that the judge has difficulty in applying the test of admissibility laid down in *R v P*, it is *possible* that he may then be compelled to hold a *voir dire*. The situations in which collusion is relevant in considering admissibility will arise only in very exceptional cases (examples of which the Lord Chancellor could not envisage but did not rule out).

(c) If the similar fact evidence is admitted and evidence is then adduced which indicates that no reasonable jury could accept the evidence as free from collusion, the judge should direct the jury that it cannot be relied upon for any purpose adverse to the defence.

(d) Where this is not the case, but the question of collusion has been raised, the judge should clearly draw the importance of collusion to the attention of the jury and leave it to them to decide whether notwithstanding the evidence of collusion they are satisfied that the evidence can be relied on as free from collusion and direct them that if not so satisfied, they cannot use it for any purpose adverse to the defence.

As to (c), see also *R v Hunt* [1995] Crim LR 42, CA.

6.5 'Similar Fact' Evidence in Criminal Cases for the Defence

It is not normally permissible for one co-accused to give evidence showing the misconduct of another co-accused on some other occasion. However, such evidence may be admissible, notwithstanding that it prejudices the other co-accused, if it be relevant to the defence of the first co-accused.

These two principles derive from *R v Miller* [1952] 2 All ER 667, a case decided at Winchester Assizes by Devlin J. The co-accused were charged with offences in connection with the evasion of customs duties. The defence of one of them, B, was that he was not concerned in the illegal acts and that the offences were all committed by another of the co-accused, C, who had masqueraded as B and used B's office for their commission. In pursuance of that defence, therefore, he asked a prosecution witness whether or not the offences stopped when C was sent to prison and re-started only after his release. Devlin J held that the question was proper because relevant to the defence put forward and, if necessary, could be justified by calling evidence in support. *Cf. R v Neale* (1977) 65 Cr App R 304, CA, approving the decision in *R v Miller*. See also *Lowery v R* [1974] AC 85, *R v Bracewell* (1978) 68 Cr App R 44 and *R v Goddard* [1994] Crim LR 46, CA.

In *R v Douglass* (1989) 89 Cr App R 264, CA, D and P were charged with causing death by reckless driving. A van driven by P collided head-on with another car. D and P were allegedly vying together before the accident, D having pulled out into the centre of the

111

road several times to prevent P from overtaking. Their vehicles collided and this caused P's van to hit the oncoming car. P gave no evidence but his counsel, in cross-examination of P's girlfriend, elicited evidence that P had never drunk alcohol in the two years that she had known him. The prosecution suggested that D had been drinking before the accident. Evidence of P's previous convictions, which included offences involving drink, was ruled inadmissible. P was acquitted. D was convicted.

It was held that the fact that joint enterprise was not alleged was no basis for excluding evidence of character if it became relevant to the issue of guilt of one of the accused. The evidence elicited on behalf of P as to his lack of propensity to have driven as alleged became relevant to the issue of D's guilt. In such a case contradictory evidence as to propensity could be called by D. D should have been allowed to adduce evidence of P's criminal record.

6.6   Statutory Provisions in Criminal Cases

Theft Act 1968, s. 27(3) provides that:

> *Where a person is being proceeded against for handling stolen goods (but not for any offence other than handling stolen goods), then at any stage of the proceedings, if evidence has been given of his having or arranging to have in his possession the goods the subject of the charge, or of his undertaking or assisting in, or arranging to undertake or assist in, their retention, removal, disposal or realisation, the following evidence shall be admissible for the purpose of proving that he knew or believed the goods to be stolen goods:—*
>   *(a)   evidence that he has had in his possession, or has undertaken or assisted in the retention, removal, disposal or realisation of, stolen goods from any theft taking place not earlier than 12 months before the offence charged; and*
>   *(b)   (provided that seven days' notice in writing has been given to him of the intention to prove the conviction) evidence that he has within the five years preceding the date of the offence charged been convicted of theft or of handling stolen goods.*

In *R v Wilkins* [1975] 2 All ER 734, CA, it was held that evidence admissible under s. 27(3) is only relevant to those counts in which guilty knowledge is in issue.

In *R v Bradley* (1980) 70 Cr App R 200, CA (applied in *R v Wood* [1987] 1 WLR 799, CA) it was held that under sub-paragraph (a) the only evidence admissible is that which the sub-paragraph describes. However, according to *R v Fowler* (1987) 86 Cr App R 219, CA at p. 226, providing a description of the stolen goods appears to be unavoidable.

Sub-paragraph (b) has to be read in conjunction with Police and Criminal Evidence Act 1984, s. 73, which provides that the fact of a conviction may be proved by producing a certificate of conviction giving 'the substance and effect (omitting the formal parts) of the indictment and of the conviction'. In *R v Hacker* [1995] 1 All ER 45, the House of Lords held that this wording renders admissible, in addition to the fact, date and place of the conviction, a description of the stolen goods.

Note also that the judge has a discretion to exclude the evidence where its prejudicial effect is such as to make it virtually impossible for a jury thereafter to take a dispassionate view of the crucial facts of the case: see *R v List* [1966] 1 WLR 9, *R v Knott* [1973] Crim LR 36, CA and *R v Perry* [1984] Crim LR 680, CA. In *R v Rasini, The Times*, 20 March 1986, the Court of Appeal said that s. 27(3)(b) should only be used where the interests of justice so demand and not as a matter of course. *Cf. R v Hacker*, a trial for handling the bodyshell of an Escort RS Turbo motor car. The accused denied that the goods had been stolen and also denied guilty knowledge or belief. It was held that the judge was entitled, in his discretion, to admit evidence of a previous conviction of receiving a Ford RS Turbo motor car, because it was highly relevant to the issue of knowledge.

6.7 Civil Cases

In civil cases, the emphasis is not so much on prejudicial effect as on probative force, i.e. the relevance of the evidence to the facts in issue. For this reason, in civil cases, similar fact evidence tends to be much more readily admissible than in criminal cases: see *Hollingham* v *Head* (1858) 27 LJ CP 241 and *Joy* v *Phillips Mills & Co. Ltd* [1916] 1 KB 849, CA. A more recent example is *Sattin* v *National Union Bank* (1978) 122 SJ 367, CA, where the plaintiff claimed in respect of the loss by the bank of a diamond deposited with them as security for an overdraft. The defence of the bank was that they had used reasonable safeguards in securing the property deposited at the bank by their customers. The Court of Appeal held that the plaintiff was entitled to adduce evidence of another occasion when jewellery deposited with the bank had gone missing, because it was relevant to rebut the defence put forward.

In *Mood Music Publishing Co. Ltd* v *De Wolfe Ltd* [1976] Ch 119, CA, the plaintiffs were music publishers seeking damages for the infringement of their copyright on a piece of incidental television music called 'Sogno Nostalgico'. They alleged that the defendants, another music publishing company, had copied the plaintiffs' music in producing a piece of music of their own called 'Girl in the Dark'. The defendants argued that any similarity between the two pieces of music was coincidental. To prove that the defendants were likely to have copied 'Sogno Nostalgico', the plaintiffs produced three more musical scores owned by the defendants each of which appeared very similar to music owned by the plaintiffs. The Court of Appeal held that such evidence was admissible as logically probative to disprove the defence of coincidence. Whereas it was possible for there to be one case of coincidental similarity, it was very unlikely that there would be four coincidences. In explaining the difference between the approach to similar fact evidence in civil and criminal cases, Lord Denning MR said:

> The criminal courts have been very careful not to admit such evidence unless its probative value is so strong that it should be received in the interests of justice; and its admission will not operate unfairly to the accused . . . In civil cases the courts will admit evidence of similar facts if it is logically probative, that is, if it is logically relevant in determining the matter which is in issue: provided that it is not oppressive or unfair to the other side; and also that the other side has fair notice of it and is able to deal with it.

See also *Berger* v *Raymond Sun Ltd* [1984] 1 WLR 625.

Questions

OBJECTIVES

This chapter is designed to assist you:

(a) to understand the rationale for the admission of evidence of disposition and behaviour on other occasions to prove commission of the offence by the accused despite the general rule to the contrary; and

(b) to relate the rules discussed in this Chapter to the concepts of relevance, admissibility and weight discussed in **Chapter 2**.

Question 1

INSTRUCTIONS TO COUNSEL

Our client, Ms Dorothea Wise, is charged with four counts of theft from the offices of a firm for which she was contracted to clean typewriters on a regular basis. She stands to be tried later this month.

The prosecution case is that unattended handbags were stolen within a four-week period from four separate open plan offices in the same vicinity. On each occasion the staff had just received their pay and the thefts occurred when the staff were at lunch in the staff canteen. On the final occasion Ms Wise (who has bright red hair and on this occasion was wearing a leather jacket) was chased by one of the employees, a Victoria Giggs. Miss Giggs accused Ms Wise of stealing her handbag, which was in fact found to be in Ms Wise's possession at that time. Ms Wise claimed at the time that her handbag was very similar to that belonging to Miss Giggs and Ms Wise claimed that she must have picked up the wrong bag by mistake. Later a bag very similar to Miss Giggs's was found on the floor of her office and Ms Wise claimed that this belonged to her.

Office workers in the three other offices from which handbags were stolen made statements to the effect that they recalled seeing Ms Wise in the offices on pay days, but were unable to recall the exact time. In one of these three offices, Ms Wise had been questioned about a missing handbag which was found in her bucket of cleaning materials. Ms Wise's explanation, which was accepted at the time, was that the missing bag must have been knocked off the desk and fallen into her bucket.

Counsel is asked to the admissibility of the evidence of the first three counts in support of the fourth count. Counsel should be aware that Ms Wise has previously served a short term of imprisonment following a conviction for a series of thefts of credit cards, from the locker-room of the supermarket at which Ms Wise worked as a cashier, and which belonged to four of her fellow employees.

Question 2
Mark is charged with causing grievous bodily harm with intent contrary to the Offences Against the Person Act 1861, s. 18. The case is that on 23 December Mark was involved in a loud argument with a publican whom he hit with a billiard cue. Mark claims that it was an accident. The police have evidence that a few weeks earlier Mark had threatened the publican because he suspected that he was having an affair with Mark's former girlfriend. Advise the prosecution as to the admissibility of the evidence of the threats.

Question 3
David has been convicted of indecently assaulting Elaine. Elaine, a girl of 12, gave unsworn evidence that when she was exercising her puppy at dusk in a public park she was approached by a man who said that he had a puppy exactly like hers, and invited her to his home, which he said was two minutes away, to see it. On the way he talked obscenities to her and pulled her behind some bushes, where he committed an indecent assault on her. She was not confident in her identification of the accused as the man involved. Despite the objection of defence counsel, Fay, a girl of 15, was allowed to give sworn evidence of an almost identical approach to her, two days after the assault on Elaine, at dusk in a public park three miles away. She said she had run away when the man started talking obscenities and that no assault had been committed on her. She identified the accused confidently as the man. The defence bring out that Elaine and Fay attend the same school, though they hardly know each other, and that there have been rumours circulating there about a man molesting young girls. Should Fay's evidence have been admitted?

Question 4
Alan is charged on two counts of handling stolen goods. On count 1 he denies that the goods were ever in his possession; on count 2 he admits that the goods were in his possession but denies that he knew they were stolen. Two years ago Alan was convicted of theft arising out of shoplifting and the police found three stolen video cassettes in a lock-up garage of which Alan had the use. Advise the prosecution as to the use which may be made of this evidence.

SEVEN

CHARACTER EVIDENCE

May evidence be adduced to show the good character of a party or of his or her witnesses?

May you adduce evidence to show the bad character of your opponent or of his or her witnesses?

7.1 Civil Cases

Evidence of a person's good or bad character is admissible, in civil proceedings, if among the facts in issue in the case or of direct relevance to the facts in issue. A simple example is a defamation action in which the defendant's defence is justification. Evidence of the claimant's character is also admissible, if he succeeds, on the question of quantum of damages: see generally *Scott* v *Sampson* (1882) 8 QBD 491.

Evidence of a person's good or bad character, if not among, or of direct relevance to, the facts in issue and if not relevant to credit (see below) is generally excluded even though it may have some relevance to the facts in issue. See *Narracott* v *Narracott* (1864) 3 Sw & Tr 408: in a divorce case a husband, in disproof of a particular act of cruelty, cannot tender evidence of his general character for humanity. See also *Attorney-General* v *Bowman* (1791) 2 Bos & P 532.

Evidence of the character of a party to civil proceedings (or a witness called by him) may be adduced because of its relevance to his credibility. See generally **Chapter 5** and *Mechanical & General Inventions Co. Ltd* v *Austin* [1935] AC 346 and *Hobbs* v *CT Tinling & Co. Ltd* [1929] 2 KB 1, CA.

7.2 Criminal Cases: Character as a Fact in Issue

In criminal cases, evidence of a person's character is admissible if it is among the facts in issue in the case or of direct relevance to the facts in issue. The fact of an accused's previous conviction may also be a fact in issue when it is an essential ingredient of the offence with which he is charged: see, e.g., Firearms Act 1968, s. 21 or driving whilst disqualified.

7.3 Criminal Cases: Character Relevant to a Fact in Issue or to Credit

7.3.1 THE PROSECUTOR AND WITNESSES OTHER THAN THE ACCUSED

In the absence of authority to the contrary, it would appear that evidence of the character of the prosecutor or any witness other than the accused is admissible to the extent that it is relevant to the facts in issue in the case. Evidence of the character of such persons may also be adduced because of its relevance to their credibility. See generally **Chapter 5**.

7.3.2 THE ACCUSED: GOOD CHARACTER

The accused is allowed to call evidence of his good character provided that it is confined to evidence of his general reputation amongst those to whom he is known: evidence of a witness's opinion as to his good character and evidence of particular creditable acts is inadmissible: see *R* v *Rowton* (1865) Le & CA 520, CCR and *R* v *Redgrave* (1982) 74 Cr App R 10, CA.

For many years there had been confusion as to:

(a) whether a judge must direct the jury about evidence of the good character of the accused; and

(b) if so, whether the judge should direct the jury that good character is relevant only to the credibility of the accused (the first limb) or is also relevant to the issue of guilt or innocence, because it shows that the accused is less likely to have committed the offence(s) charged (the second limb).

However, a spate of conflicting decisions on both issues resulted in the Court of Appeal in *R* v *Vye* [1993] 1 WLR 471 laying down the following three principles.

(a) The judge should give a first limb direction (i.e. on credibility) (i) if the accused testifies and also (ii) if the accused does not testify but relies on exculpatory statements, i.e. pre-trial answers or statements made to the police or others. (It is clear from *R* v *Aziz* [1995] 3 All ER 149, HL, that 'pre-trial answers or statements' means 'mixed' statements, i.e. statements which are both inculpatory and exculpatory and which are therefore admissible as evidence of the truth of all the facts they contain. Thus an accused who does not give evidence but relies on *wholly* exculpatory pre-trial answers or statements, is *not* entitled to a first limb direction because such statements would not be admissible and there is therefore nothing for the jury to assess the credibility of. This was the case in *R* v *Garrod* [1997] Crim LR 445, CA, where the accused's interview with the police was treated as a wholly exculpatory statement notwithstanding that it contained some limited admissions of fact: see **5.1.4.2** under the heading 'Statements made on accusation'.)

(b) The judge should give a second limb direction (i.e. on relevance to a fact in issue) whether or not the accused has testified or made pre-trial answers or statements. It is for the judge to decide how to tailor the direction to the particular circumstances. Judges would probably wish to indicate, as is commonly done, that good character cannot amount to a defence.

(c) Where an accused of good character is jointly tried with an accused of bad character, the first and second principles still apply (rejecting the suggestion of Lord Lane CJ in *R* v *Gibson* (1991) 93 Cr App R 9, CA, that the judge may decide to say little if anything about the good character of the one accused). As to the accused of bad character, in some cases the judge may think it best to tell the jury that there has been no evidence about his character and that they must not speculate or treat the absence of information as evidence against him or her; in other cases the judge may think it best to say nothing about the absence of such information. The proper approach depends on the circumstances of the case, for example how great an issue was made of character during the evidence and speeches.

As to the meaning of 'good character' for these purposes, an accused may be treated as being of previous good character even if he or she has previous convictions. This may happen when the previous convictions relate to different types of offence which occurred a long time ago. In this situation, the judge may give *Vye* directions but qualify them by reference to the previous convictions: see *R* v *Aziz* [1995] 3 All ER 149, HL, *R* v *Timson* [1993] Crim LR 58, CA and *R* v *H* [1994] Crim LR 205, CA. But see also *R* v *Hickmet* [1996] Crim LR 588, CA, in which the accused's previous convictions were over 20 years old, where it was held that a propensity direction could have confused the jury.

Equally, an accused may be treated as *not* being of previous good character if, although he or she has no previous convictions, evidence is admitted of his or her previous dishonesty or criminal conduct. By way of example in *R v Sabahat* [2001] EWCA Crim 2588 the Court of Appeal held that a trial judge had not acted outside his discretion in refusing a good character for the appellant due to his having been cautioned for a dishonesty offence while allowing a co-defendant a good character despite previous convictions that included driving whilst disqualified.

In *R v Aziz*, Lord Steyn, accepting that this situation was one in which generalisations are hazardous, held that a judge has a residual discretion not to give *Vye* directions if he considers it an insult to common sense to give such directions, as when an accused with no previous convictions is shown beyond doubt to have been guilty of serious criminal behaviour similar to the offence charged and therefore any claim to good character would be spurious. However, it was also held that (a) this discretionary power is narrowly circumscribed and prima facie the directions *should* be given and (b) the judge will often be able to paint a fair and balanced picture for the jury by giving *Vye* directions suitably qualified by reference to the proven or possible misconduct. See also *R v Zoppola-Barraza* [1994] Crim LR 833, CA, where the accused, charged with drug smuggling, gave evidence of smuggling gold and jewels, and *R v Buzalek* [1991] Crim LR 115, CA.

Difficult problems also arise where an accused pleads guilty to only one or some of the counts on the indictment. If an accused pleads guilty to an offence which is an alternative to that on which he is being tried, and the facts are such that if he is convicted on the greater offence then the guilty plea on the lesser will have to be vacated, a good character direction should be given, but should be tailored to take into account the guilty plea: *R v Teasdale* [1993] 4 All ER 290. In *R v Challenger* [1994] Crim LR 202, CA, it was held that *Teasdale* was the exception to the general rule, the general rule being that if an accused pleads guilty to another count on the indictment, he or she ceases to be a person of good character and the full direction becomes inappropriate. If the jury are not told of the guilty plea, it would be misleading to direct them that the accused is of good character. However, in other circumstances a direction may become appropriate. For example, if the accused testifies, the jury are made aware of the guilty plea and defence counsel says to the jury that when assessing the accused's credibility, the guilty plea is in his or her favour and makes it more likely that he or she is telling the truth in claiming innocence on the remaining count(s), then the judge may remind the jury of that argument. See also *R v Shepherd* [1995] Crim LR 153, CA.

As to the first principle from *R v Vye*, it seems that the judge should direct the jury clearly that good character *is* relevant to credibility and it is a serious misdirection to direct them that they may put good character 'in the scales': *R v Boyson* [1991] Crim LR 274, CA. See also *R v Miah* [1997] Crim LR 351, CA, a decision which appears to cover both limbs of the direction. In that case the trial judge said to the jury that they were 'entitled' to take good character into account. It was held that there was no obligation on judges to use any particular form of words, but that it might be wise to select words other than those that had been used by the trial judge (because they suggested that the jury had a choice whether or not to take the evidence into account).

As to the third principle from *R v Vye*, in so far as it concerns the direction to be given about the accused of bad character, it relates to either:

(a) an accused in respect of whom no evidence of character is adduced, one way or the other; or

(b) an accused of bad character whose bad character is not revealed in evidence.

In *R v Cain* [1994] 2 All ER 398, CA, there were three co-accused and the evidence relating to the character of each was different. In the case of A, there was evidence of good character. In the case of B, there was no evidence either way. In the case of C, there was evidence of previous convictions. It was held that A was entitled to a full direction, that the judge had a discretion whether to say anything at all about B's character, and that the judge should have warned the jury that C's convictions were not relevant to his guilt but to his credibility.

7.3.3 THE ACCUSED — BAD CHARACTER: AT COMMON LAW

The general rule is that the prosecution may not adduce evidence of the accused's bad character nor cross-examine the accused or any defence witness with a view to eliciting such evidence. *At common law*, there are only two exceptions:

(a) where the evidence is admissible under the similar facts doctrine (see **Chapter 6**); and

(b) where the defence adduces evidences of the accused's good character.

See also *R* v *Butterwasser* [1948] 1 KB 4, CCA.

If the accused puts his character in issue by giving or calling evidence of his good character or cross-examining witnesses to that effect, then at common law the prosecution may call evidence of his bad character in rebuttal: *R* v *Rowton* (1865) Le & Ca 520, CCR, where it was also held that the evidence in rebuttal should be restricted in the same way as evidence of good character given by the defence, i.e. it should be confined to evidence of reputation. But see also *R* v *Waldman* (1934) 24 Cr App R 204, CCA: evidence in rebuttal may include evidence of the accused's previous convictions.

The evidence in rebuttal need not be confined to the character trait under consideration but may refer to any character trait of the accused. See *R* v *Winfield* (1939) 27 Cr App R 139, CCA. The defendant to a charge of indecent assault adduced evidence of his sexual morality. The Court of Appeal approved the admission of evidence relating to his previous convictions for dishonesty offences.

Of course the accused himself may choose to introduce evidence of his previous convictions to show that he pleaded guilty on the previous occasions and ought therefore to be believed now when he denies his guilt. In the case of convictions for offences of dishonesty, the judge must then direct the jury that the previous convictions are relevant to the defendant's credibility and that the jury *may* take such evidence into account: *R* v *Prince* [1990] Crim LR 49, CA.

7.3.4 THE ACCUSED — BAD CHARACTER: STATUTE

Where the accused gives evidence further rules apply. The general rule at common law that the prosecution may not adduce evidence of the accused's bad character applies equally to questions asked in cross-examination of the accused: see, e.g. *R* v *Weekes* (1983) 77 Cr App R 207, CA. However, the rule, in its application to cross-examination of the accused, is subject to the important statutory exceptions set out in Criminal Evidence Act 1898, s. 1:

> (2) *A person charged in criminal proceedings who is called as a witness in the proceedings may be asked any question in cross-examination notwithstanding that it would tend to criminate him as to any offence with which he is charged in the proceedings.*
>
> (3) *A person charged in criminal proceedings who is called as a witness in the proceedings shall not be asked, and if asked shall not be required to answer, any question tending to show that he has committed or been convicted of or been charged with any offence other than one with which he is then charged, or is of bad character, unless—*
>
> *(i) the proof that he has committed or been convicted of such other offence is admissible evidence to show that he is guilty of an offence with which he is then charged; or*

> *(ii)   he has personally or by his advocate asked questions of the witnesses for the prosecution with a view to establish his own good character, or has given evidence of his good character, or the nature or conduct of the defence is such as to involve imputations on the character of the prosecutor or the witnesses for the prosecution or the deceased victim of the alleged crime; or*
>
> *(iii)   he has given evidence against any other person charged in the same proceedings.*

Note: The text above sets out sections of the Act as amended by the Youth Justice and Criminal Evidence Act 1999. Before these amendments, what is now subsection (2) was proviso (e) and subsection (3) was proviso (f) to section 1. Minor amendments were also made to the wording of the subsections, but these have not altered the effect of the 1898 Act.

7.3.4.1   The relationship between subsections (2) and (3)

In *Jones* v *DPP* [1962] AC 635, HL, Jones was charged with murder of a young girl. At trial he alleged that when the girl disappeared he had been with a prostitute in London. In his evidence-in-chief he explained that his wife had been concerned about articles in the Sunday papers concurring the disappearance of the murdered girl and that he had therefore confessed to her where he had been. He gave details of the arguments that had ensued between them as a result of this confession.

However, when the police investigating the murder had questioned him, he had initially told them that he had been visiting his sister-in-law some distance away. She not only refused to confirm this but was also called as a prosecution witness. It was therefore necessary for Jones to explain during the course of the trial why he had originally lied. He said that he had previously been 'in trouble with the police' and that he had attempted to set up an alibi that he could substantiate with another witness (in contrast to the unknown prostitute). Jones' barrister had asked prosecution witnesses about this 'trouble' in the past and Jones had mentioned 'trouble' in his evidence-in-chief but that word had not been expanded upon before the jury. The defence gave no indication of the nature of the trouble.

When the prosecution came to cross-examine Jones, leave was obtained from the judge to ask particular questions of him. Jones was asked about the previous occasion when he had been in trouble. The questioning related to the alibi that he had raised on that occasion and the conversation that had gone on between him and his wife. The conversation on the previous occasion and the conversation alleged in relation to the murder alibi were almost identical in content. The prosecution sought to establish that, given the similarity of the two conversations, the conversation in relation to the murder must have been a fabrication and therefore the alibi to which it related must be untrue.

Although neither the prosecution nor defence led any evidence on the details of it, the previous instance of 'trouble' related to the rape of a Girl Guide for which Jones had been convicted. The only reference at the murder trial to the rape concerned the alibi that Jones had raised in relation to it and the conversation alleged to have taken place between him and his wife on that occasion.

The defendant appealed, arguing that he had been improperly cross-examined on the details of the alibi he had alleged on the previous occasion as this was not permissible under s. 1(3) of the 1898 Act. The questions tended to show that he had 'committed or been convicted of or been charged with' an offence other than that with which he was charged, namely the previous rape incident. Such questions, it was argued, did not fall within any of the three categories of exception set out in (i) to (iii) of subsection (3).

The House of Lords, by a majority, rejected this argument on the grounds that the words 'tending to show' should be taken to mean tending to reveal for the first time. In determining whether this was so in any given case, it was necessary not to look at the question or questions complained of in isolation but to look at the trial as a whole to get the overall picture. In this case the defendant had already referred to the 'trouble' that he had been in. The questions put by the prosecution were no more specific about the nature of the 'trouble' than the defendant had been. For this reason the prosecution evidence had not revealed anything to the jury that the defendant had not revealed already. Therefore, s. 1(3) did not apply to the case.

It was also noted that:

(a) Subsection (2) permits questions which tend *directly* to incriminate the accused (i.e. questions relating to evidence as to the facts of the offence or offences for which he or she is currently being tried). As such subsection (2) confirms that the mere fact that it is the defendant, as opposed to some other person, who is giving evidence, does not exempt him or her from cross-examination about the issues in the case (i.e. his or her guilt and his or her defence).

(b) Subsection (3) generally prohibits questions that would *indirectly* incriminate the defendant. Such indirect incrimination would result from questions revealing that the accused has previous convictions or is of general bad character or disposed to commit offences or that he or she ought not to be believed on oath. Such evidence would only be admissible if it falls within one of the three categories set out by paragraphs (i) to (iii) (which will be examined in more detail below).

7.3.4.2   Subsection (3): the prohibition

'Any question tending to show' means 'tending to show for the first time'. Thus if the prosecution has already adduced evidence of the accused's misconduct on other occasions under the similar facts doctrine, or the accused himself has given evidence of his previous misconduct or convictions, then the accused may be cross-examined on the matter: see *R* v *Anderson* [1988] QB 678, CA and *R* v *Ellis* [1910] 2 KB 746, CCA.

In *Stirland* v *DPP* [1944] AC 315, the House of Lords held that 'charged with any offence' means 'accused before a criminal court', and not merely suspected or accused without a criminal prosecution. The defendant was charged with forgery. He had alleged that he was of good character and had not been charged with any offence before. He was then cross-examined by the prosecution as to why he had left a previous job. It was put to him that he had left that job after being questioned about a forged signature. The House of Lords concluded that he ought not to have been asked such questions as no criminal proceedings had been commenced against him.

In *R* v *Dunkley* [1927] 1 KB 323, CCA, it was held that evidence of 'bad character' is not confined to evidence of general reputation, but covers both reputation and disposition. More recently, in *R* v *Carter* [1997] Crim LR 505, it was held that the accused had been improperly cross-examined about his discreditable behaviour in relation to a civil claim. The Court of Appeal held that character encompasses disposition as well as reputation, and that the prohibition on questions includes cross-examination which tends to show the accused to be of bad character as well as that which tends to show that he has a criminal record.

Where cross-examination on offences is permitted under s. 1(3) because the accused has lost his shield, the accused may be asked about an offence whether it was committed before or after commission of the offence with which he is charged: see *R* v *Wood* [1920] 2 KB 179, CCA and *R* v *Coltress* (1978) 68 Cr App R 193, CA.

In *Maxwell* v *DPP* [1935] AC 309, HL, it was held that where the shield is lost, cross-examination is still subject to the requirement of relevance; questions about a previous acquittal will usually be inadmissible because irrelevant both to the charge and the credibility of the accused.

7.3.4.3   Section 1(3)(i)

If evidence of the accused's commission of another offence is admissible under the similar fact evidence doctrine because of its probative value in relation to the accused's guilt, the accused can be cross-examined about such matters under s. 1(3)(i). Such cross-examination is relevant to the issue of the accused's guilt.

However the questions that s. 1(3)(i) permits are not co-extensive with those prohibited under the prohibition. Thus s. 1(3)(i) cannot be used to cross-examine an accused about a charge in respect of which he has been acquitted: *R* v *Cokar* [1960] 2 QB 207, CCA.

It seems that the accused can be cross-examined under s. 1(3)(i) even if the similar fact evidence has *not* been proved as a part of the prosecution case: see *Jones* v *DPP* [1962] AC 635, HL and *R* v *Coombes* (1960) 45 Cr App R 36 and *cf. R* v *Anderson* [1988] QB 678, CA.

7.3.4.4 **Section 1(3)(ii): attempts to establish good character**
The accused will lose his shield if he puts his good character in issue either (i) by cross examination of the prosecution witnesses or (ii) by giving evidence about it himself or also, presumably, (iii) by calling defence witnesses to give evidence about it. However, the shield is not lost when a defence witness *volunteers* a statement as to the good character of the accused which he has not been asked to make: *R* v *Redd* [1923] 1 KB 104.

Whether or not the defendant's good character is in issue is a question of fact for the judge in each case. Consider the following examples in which the courts have concluded that the defendant's good character has been put in issue (and cross-examination under s. 1(3)(ii) was therefore appropriate):

R v *Ferguson* (1909) 2 Cr App R 250: a religious man who had attended church services for a number of years.

R v *Baker* (1912) 7 Cr App R 252: earning an honest living for a number of years.

R v *Coulman* [1927] 20 Cr App R 106: a married man with a family and in regular work.

R v *Samuel* (1956) 40 Cr App R 8, CCA: in which the defendant was charged with theft of a camera that he had found at a museum. He was found in possession of the camera five weeks after it had gone missing. The defendant gave evidence that he had on two previous occasions returned valuable property to its owner. Cross-examination as to his previous convictions was held by the Court of Appeal to have been justified as the defendant had put his good character in issue. Such evidence would be useful to the jury in determining whether his assertion that he was the type of person who returned lost items was worthy of belief.

On the other side of the line, consider the following cases:

R v *Lee* [1976] 1 WLR 71, CA: a defence conducted in such a way as to involve imputations on the character of persons other than prosecution witnesses (or the deceased victim of the alleged crime), because 'it is not implicit in an accusation of dishonesty that the accuser himself is an honest man'.

R v *Beecham* [1921] 3 KB 464: the defendant was led into making assertions of good character by prosecution counsel in cross-examination.

R v *Hamilton* [1969] Crim LR 486, CA: the wearing of a regimental blazer!

R v *Robinson* [2001] Crim LR 478: a defendant had not put his character in issue by (a) giving evidence that he was a successful businessman where to do so was relevant to explain his presence near the scene of the crime; (b) asserting that he did not want to give the name of a friend as a witness for fear of his (the defendant's) reputation: this was not an assertion of innocence or respectability; (c) taking the oath and holding onto the bible during testimony; or (d) any of these facts taken together.

See also *Malindi* v *R* [1967] AC 439 and *R* v *Stronach* [1988] Crim LR 48.

Once an accused puts his character in issue, he puts his whole character in, character for these purposes being indivisible. See *Stirland* v *DPP* [1944] AC 315, HL, *per* Viscount Simon at p. 324:

He cannot assert his good character in certain respects without exposing himself to inquiry as to the rest of his record.

In *R* v *Marsh* [1994] Crim LR 52, CA, M was charged with inflicting grievous bodily harm while playing in a rugby match. He wished to adduce evidence that he had no previous convictions. It was held that this would entitle the prosecution to cross-examine M on his disciplinary record of violent play on the rugby field.

In *R* v *Wright* [2000] Crim LR 851, W was cross-examined as to his dismissal from is employment for racist behaviour. W was on trial for a racially aggravated offence and had asserted that he had never entertained racist ideas. His conviction was upheld.

The primary purpose of cross-examination under this part of s. 1(3)(ii) is, apparently, to show that the accused should not be believed on his oath: see *R* v *Richardson* [1969] 1 QB 299, CA and *cf. Maxwell* v *DPP* [1935] AC 309, HL.

7.3.4.5 Section 1(3)(ii): imputations on the character of prosecution witnesses

This part of the sub-paragraph operates on a tit-for-tat principle: where the defence makes an attack on the character of the prosecutor, a prosecution witness, or the deceased victim of the alleged crime, e.g. by imputing misconduct or bad character, the accused renders himself liable to cross-examination on his own bad character and previous convictions: see *R* v *Biggin* [1920] KB 213. The rationale of the tit-for-tat principle is that where a defendant has put the credibility of a prosecution witness in issue, it is appropriate for the jury to hear evidence of the character of the defendant so that they can decide which account is more credible.

This remains the case even if the Crown do not dispute the truth of what is alleged: *R* v *Wainwright* [1998] Crim LR 665, CA.

Prosecution witness

A 'prosecution witness', for these purposes, includes not only a person giving oral evidence for the prosecution at the trial, but also the maker of a deposition or a statement adduced by the prosecution under an exception to the rule against hearsay: see *R* v *Miller* [1997] 2 Cr App R 178. In that case, which involved an imputation on the character of someone who did not testify through fear, and whose deposition from the committal proceedings was admitted under the Criminal Justice Act 1988, s. 23 (see **9.2.2.1**), it was held that any other construction would be a charter for interference with witnesses: it would mean that a witness discouraged from attending trial could be attacked with impunity by or on behalf of an accused with a criminal record.

Discretion

Although the 1898 Act allows the prosecution to cross-examine the defendant when it finds that an imputation has been cast upon the prosecution witness under s. 1(3)(ii), it was confirmed in *Selvey* v *DPP* [1970] AC 304 that the trial judge retains a discretion to refuse to permit cross-examination. This discretion is unfettered and its exercise is dependent on the circumstances of the case and the overriding judicial duty to ensure a fair trial.

It will therefore be necessary, in analysing a case falling under s. 1(3)(ii), to consider two issues:

(a) was an imputation cast; and

(b) if so, should the court nonetheless exercise its discretion to prevent the cross-examination of the accused.

The courts have issued some guidance as to the exercise of this discretion in cases such as *R* v *Britzmann* [1983] 1 WLR 350, CA, although as that case shows, there has been a tendency to conflate the two issues.

Imputations

Where the court concludes that imputations have been cast upon a prosecution witness and cross-examination of the defendant is appropriate, this is commonly referred to as 'losing the shield' (the shield being that provided by the wording of s. 1(3) preventing questions about other offences etc.).

Note that this part of s. 1(3)(ii) is triggered by 'the nature or conduct of the defence'. It seems that evidence given by an accused when being cross-examined by the prosecution should *generally* be treated as part of the prosecution case and that in any event the shield should not be lost if the accused was trapped into making the imputation by the form of the question put: see *R v Jones* (1909) 3 Cr App R 67. However, the shield may be lost during cross-examination if the imputation was voluntary and gratuitous: *R v Courtney* [1995] Crim LR 63, CA.

As a matter of practice, prosecuting counsel will indicate in advance his or her intention to rely on s. 1(3)(ii). The practice is also for the judge to caution the defence if they are 'sailing close to the wind' and the shield is about to be lost. Such a warning, however, although desirable in many cases, is not mandatory: *R v Stanton* [1994] Crim LR 834, CA. In cases in which the shield is lost under s. 1(3)(ii), but prosecuting counsel fails to apply for leave to cross-examine, the trial judge may properly initiate discussion about invoking the provision: see *R v Chinn* [1996] Crim LR 729, CA.

The shield will be lost even if the imputation is a necessary part of the defence. In these circumstances, however, the judge has a *discretion* to refuse to permit cross-examination. The shield was lost in *R v Hudson* [1912] 2 KB 464, CCA, where the accused claimed that a prosecution witness had committed the offence.

The shield was also lost in *R v Bishop* [1975] QB 274, CA, in which the accused claimed that he had had a homosexual relationship with a prosecution witness.

In the leading case of *Selvey v DPP* [1970] AC 304, HL, it was held that:

(a)   the words of the statute should be given their ordinary natural meaning;

(b)   (approving *R v Hudson*) s. 1(3)(ii) permits cross-examination not only (i) when imputations are cast on prosecution witnesses to show their unreliability independently of the evidence given by them, but also (ii) when the casting of such imputations is necessary to enable the accused to establish his defence.

The accused will not lose the shield if he merely asserts his innocence or denies his guilt, albeit in emphatic terms.

Bearing in mind that each case falls to be decided on its exact facts and circumstances and the exact language used (*R v Levy* (1966) 50 Cr App R 238 at 241), consider the following examples.

In *R v Rouse* [1904] 1 KB 184, CCR, it was alleged that the evidence of the prosecution witness was 'a lie' and the witness 'a liar'. This was treated as an emphatic denial of guilt. See also *R v St Louis* (1984) 79 Cr App R 53 and *R v Wignall* [1993] Crim LR 62.

In *R v Rappolt* (1911) 6 Cr App R 156, CCA, it was alleged that the prosecution witness was 'such a horrible liar that his brother would not speak to him'. This was held to be an imputation. See also *R v Owen* (1986) 83 Cr App R 100, CA.

In *R v Lasseur* [1991] Crim LR 53, CA, it was put to an accomplice who had turned Queen's evidence that he was lying and that he was implicating the accused so that he would get a lenient sentence. This was also held to be an imputation.

In rape cases, the accused may allege consent without thereby placing himself in danger of cross-examination on his bad character: see *R v Sheean* (1908) 21 Cox CC 56 and *R v Turner* [1944] KB 463.

Most allegations of misconduct or impropriety will expose the accused to cross-examination. Consider the following examples of imputations:

(a) *R* v *Wright* (1910) 5 Cr App R 131 in which it was alleged that a confession was obtained by bribes;

(b) *R* v *Jones* (1923) 17 Cr App R 117 in which it was alleged that the accused was deliberately held on four remands in order to manufacture a confession; and

(c) *R* v *Cook* [1959] 2 QB 340 in which it was alleged that an admission was extorted by threatening to charge the accused's wife.

But see also *R* v *Westfall* (1912) 7 Cr App R 176 (an allegation that the prosecutor was a habitual drunkard did not amount to an imputation on character). See also *R* v *MacLean* [1978] Crim LR 430 (an allegation that a man was drunk and swearing did not amount to an imputation on character); and *R* v *Stanton* [1994] Crim LR 834, CA.

One area of particular complexity concerns cases in which the defence challenge the evidence of police officers about alleged confession statements. In the case of *R* v *Nelson* (1978) 68 Cr App R 12, the prosecution called evidence that the defendant had confessed to the arson with which he was charged. Counsel for the defendant cross-examined the police witness in question, putting it to him that there had never been any conversation at all between the police officer and the defendant. The Court of Appeal held that cross-examination of the defendant should not have been allowed. The cross-examination of the police witness was not an imputation because it did not seek to establish that he was unreliable independently of his testimony in this case. In other words, the cross-examination did not seek to establish that the witness was not generally worthy of belief and as a result of that not worthy of belief in relation to this particular testimony. The Court considered that only if the cross-examination were of this sort would there be an imputation under s. 1(3)(ii). The denial had been no more than an emphatic denial of Nelson's involvement.

In *R* v *McGee* (1980) 70 Cr App R 247, CA, the defendant was alleged by a police witness to have admitted being present at a stabbing but to have implicated his co-accused as the person who stabbed the victim. At trial the police witness was cross-examined as to the detail of the alleged confession. It was put to him that the accused had not implicated his co-accused, that he had not even been present when a stabbing occurred and that blood found on his person was there because he had attempted to prevent the victim from stabbing his co-accused. It was also alleged that the police had omitted reference to another person who might have committed the offence, that the accused had been refused access to a solicitor and that he had been refused an identity parade when he had requested one. The accused gave evidence to this effect as well. It was of significance to the defence case that there had been more than one police witness and that they had compiled their police notebooks some time after the case. The prosecution were permitted to cross-examine the accused as to his previous convictions and the Court of Appeal held that this had been correct. The Court concluded that an aspect of the challenge to the prosecution case (although never expressly raised) was that the police officers had put their heads together to fabricate a case against the defendants. It was held that, having regard to the nature and conduct of the defence as a whole, imputations had been cast to show the unreliability of the witnesses independently of their testimony. See also *R* v *Tanner* (1977) 66 Cr App R 56, CA.

The subtlety of the differences in such cases led the Court of Appeal, in the case of *R* v *Britzmann* [1983] 1 WLR 350, to recognise that for defence counsel to challenge the evidence of police witnesses was 'like walking through a legal minefield'. In that case, two defendants were charged with burglary. Police officers gave evidence that they had confessed to involvement in the robbery during detailed interviews that the police officers recorded in their notebooks. They also gave evidence that the two co-defendants then held a conversation in the cells that was overheard by police officers. The conversation supported an inference that both defendants were guilty.

Britzmann's case was that there had been no interview with police officers and that he had no such conversation with his co-accused. He was cross-examined as to his previous convictions. The Court of Appeal upheld the conviction that resulted. On the facts of the case there could be no possibility of mistake. This was so even though Britzmann, in giving evidence, had used the word 'mistaken' and cross-examination on his behalf stopped at the suggestion that there had been no such conversations. Questioning the approach adopted in *Nelson*, it was held that the line of defence run by Britzmann must have had the effect of alleging that the police officers were giving false evidence.

A mere denial of a conversation in circumstances where this could not be accepted as a mistake or misinterpretation would amount to an imputation on the person alleging that the conversation had taken place. No distinction could be drawn between a defence so conducted as to make specific allegations of fabrication and one in which such allegations arose by way of necessary and reasonable implication. The Court also held that there is no requirement that an imputation must relate to an allegation independent of challenge or denial of the witness's evidence. The Court laid down the following guidelines:

(a) Exercise the discretion if the accused merely denies, however emphatically or offensively, an incident or the contents of a short interview (as opposed to a long period of detailed observation or a long conversation).

(b) Allow the cross-examination where there is no chance of mistake, misunderstanding or confusion and the jury will have to decide whether the prosecution witness has fabricated evidence. In the case of an accused making wild allegations, allowance should be made for the strain of being in the witness box and the exaggerated use of language resulting from that or from lack of education or mental stability. Allowance should also be made for an accused led into making allegations during cross-examination.

(c) Disallow the cross-examination where the evidence against the accused is overwhelming.

The purpose of cross-examination under section 1(3)(ii)
Evidence obtained by cross-examination under s. 1(3)(iii) goes to credit only. Its sole purpose is to show that the accused should not be believed on his oath: see *R v Jenkins* (1945) 31 Cr App R 1 and *R v Cook* [1959] 2 QB 340.

A judicial failure to tell the jury that the cross-examination goes only to credit and not to the question of guilt furnishes a good ground of appeal: *R v Inder* (1977) 67 Cr App R 143, CA. In every case therefore, the judge, in the summing-up, should tell the jury that the questioning goes only to credit and that they should not consider that it shows a propensity to commit the offence they are considering: *R v McLeod* [1994] 3 All ER 254, CA.

In *Maxwell v DPP* [1935] AC 309, HL, Viscount Sankey LC said that the trial judge, in the exercise of his discretion, should disallow the cross-examination 'if there is any risk of the jury being misled into thinking that it goes not to credibility but to the probability of (the accused) having committed the offence with which he is charged'. See also *R v Watts* [1983] 3 All ER 101, CA, *R v Braithwaite*, 24 November 1983, CA (unreported) and *R v Showers* [1996] Crim LR 739, CA.

However, mere similarity of previous offences to those being charged does not mean that the trial judge ought, necessarily, to exercise the discretion. See, for example, *Selvey v DPP* [1970] AC 304, HL, *R v Burke* (1985) 82 Cr App R 156, CA, *R v Powell* [1985] 1 WLR 1364, CA and *R v Lasseur* [1991] Crim LR 53, CA.

In *R v Powell*, P, the appellant, was convicted of knowingly living on the earnings of prostitution. P alleged that the police had fabricated evidence upon which the prosecution was based. He also put his own character in issue, and thus came within both limbs of s. 1(3)(ii). The trial judge then allowed cross-examination on his previous convictions, which were for allowing his premises to be used for the purposes of prostitution. On appeal, it was argued that the judge should not have permitted the cross-examination because the jury would have had the greatest difficulty in relating the evidence strictly to the issue of credibility, but would have concluded that P had a propensity to commit offences relating to prostitution. Dismissing the appeal, Lord Lane CJ held that Viscount Sankey's dictum in *Maxwell* v *DPP* could not be interpreted as meaning that convictions for the same or kindred offences can never be admitted. The accused had lost his shield under both parts of s. 1(3)(ii), but had either ground stood alone, the cross-examination should have been allowed. Lord Lane CJ said (at p. 1370):

> . . . if there is a deliberate attack being made upon the conduct of a prosecution witness calculated to discredit him wholly, if there is a real issue about the conduct of an important witness which the jury will have to settle in order to reach their verdict, the judge is entitled to let the jury know the previous convictions of the man who is making the attack. The fact that the defendant's convictions are not for offences of dishonesty, the fact that they are for offences bearing a close resemblance to the offences charged, are matters for the judge to take into consideration when exercising his discretion, but they certainly do not oblige the judge to disallow the proposed cross-examination.

Similarly, in *R* v *McLeod* [1994] 3 All ER 254, CA, it was held that the mere fact that the offences are of a similar type to that charged, or because of their number and type have the incidental effect of suggesting a tendency or disposition to commit the offence charged, does not make them improper. See also *R* v *Wheeler* [1995] Crim LR 312, CA, a case of assault occasioning actual bodily harm in which it was alleged that W had deliberately head-butted a police officer, the defence being that W, having been assaulted by the police, was not in control of his body at the relevant time. It was held that the judge had not erred in exercising his discretion to permit cross-examination of W on four previous convictions for assault occasioning actual bodily harm.

Limits on cross-examination

Given that the sole purpose of cross-examination under this part of s. 1(3)(ii) is to attack the accused's credibility as a witness, does it follow that cross-examination, where allowed, should not extend to the factual details of the offences in question? Should it, rather, be limited to the fact of the previous conviction alone?

R v *France* [1979] Crim LR 48, CA provides some support for confining the cross-examination in this way, but *cf. R* v *Duncalf* [1979] 1 WLR 918, CA. In *R* v *Khan* [1991] Crim LR 51, CA, at K's trial for affray and assault, including assault on the police, his defence involved an imputation on the character of the prosecution's witnesses. Anticipating a loss of shield, his counsel elicited in chief a previous conviction for assault on the police. K was then cross-examined at length about the detailed facts of the previous incident. It was held, allowing the appeal, but referring to neither *R* v *France* nor *R* v *Duncalf*, that evidence of previous convictions must only relate to the issue of credibility and therefore 'any evidence which is introduced, no matter in what manner, which tends to go beyond that and into the territory of disposition is inadmissible'.

In *R* v *McLeod* the Court of Appeal held that this dictum went too far. It is undesirable that there should be prolonged or extensive cross-examination in relation to previous offences, because it would divert the jury from the principal issue in the case, the guilt of the accused on the instant offence and not the details of earlier ones. Thus unless the earlier offences were admissible as similar fact evidence, prosecuting counsel should not seek to probe or emphasise similarities between the underlying facts of previous offences and the instant one. In *R* v *Davison-Jenkins* [1997] Crim LR 816, CA, in which the accused, charged with shoplifting cosmetics, was treated as having put her character in issue, it was held that she had been improperly cross-examined on the detail of her previous convictions, one of which was for shoplifting clothes and cosmetics. It was also held, however, that since the cross-examination was only designed to impugn her credibility, that could have been achieved by not referring to her two previous shoplifting convictions at all, but by referring instead to her three previous convictions for other forms of dishonesty.

In *R* v *McLeod* it was also held that similarities of defences which had been rejected by juries on previous occasions, and whether or not the accused pleaded guilty or was disbelieved having given evidence on oath, could be legitimate matters for questions. Those matters did not show a disposition to commit the offence in question but they were clearly relevant to credibility. It was further held that underlying facts that showed particularly bad character over and above the bare facts of the case were not necessarily to be excluded; but that the judge should be careful to balance the gravity of the attack on the prosecution with the degree of prejudice to the accused which would result from disclosure of the facts in question. The court observed that details of sexual offences against children were likely to be regarded by a jury as particularly prejudicial to an accused and that this might well be the reason why, in *R* v *Watts*, the court thought the questions impermissible. See also *R* v *Barsoum* [1994] Crim LR 194, CA.

Cross-examination under section 1(3)(ii) by a co-defendant

Nothing in the wording of s. 1(3)(ii) prohibits the cross-examination from being conducted by counsel for a co-accused. With the leave of the judge, co-defendant 1 may cross-examine co-defendant 2 if co-defendant 2 has cast imputations on the character of a prosecution witness: *R* v *Lovett* [1973] 1 WLR 241, CA.

If an accused, charged in one indictment with two offences and convicted of one but acquitted of the other, faces a subsequent trial at which the prosecution cross-examines him under s. 1(3)(ii) on the previous conviction, then in appropriate circumstances the defence may be allowed to re-examine him on the acquittal. See e.g. *R* v *Doosti* [1985] 82 Cr App R 181, CA in which at the subsequent trial, evidence of the acquittal was likely to throw doubt on the reliability of a prosecution witness, and *cf. R* v *Henri* [1990] Crim LR 51, CA.

7.3.4.6   **Section 1(3)(iii): evidence against a co-accused**
The rationale of this sub-paragraph is that if one co-accused gives evidence against another, that other should be entitled to treat the first as if he were a witness appearing for the prosecution and, accordingly, liable to cross-examination on his character. The jury will be assisted, in deciding which of two conflicting defence cases to believe, by evidence as to the relative credibility of each defendant.

The leading case on s. 1(3)(iii) is *Murdoch* v *Taylor* [1965] AC 574, HL, from which the following eight propositions derive.

(a)   'Evidence against' means evidence which supports the prosecution case in 'a material respect' or which undermines the defence of the co-accused.

(b)   One test is to ask whether the evidence would be included in a summary of the evidence in the case which, if accepted, would lead to the conviction of the co-accused.

(c)   Evidence which only contradicts something which a co-accused has said without further advancing the prosecution case in any significant degree is not 'evidence against'.

(d)   'Evidence against' may be given either in examination-in-chief or in cross-examination.

(e)   Section 1(3)(iii) is not confined to cases where the 'evidence against' is given with hostile intent. The intention or state of mind of the person giving the 'evidence against' is irrelevant. What is material is the effect of the evidence on the minds of the jury. The test is objective, not subjective.

(f) The purpose of cross-examination is to show that the person giving 'evidence against' is not to be believed on his oath.

(g) Subject to (h), where cross-examination is permissible, the judge has no discretion to prevent it: an accused, in seeking to defend himself, should not be fettered in any way. In *R* v *Corelli* [2001] Crim LR 913 the Court of Appeal, following *Murdoch* v *Taylor*, held that the trial judge has no discretion to disallow cross-examination on spent convictions under s. 1(3)(iii).

(h) The prosecution may cross-examine under s. 1(3)(iii) but the court does have a discretion to prevent it as part of its function to exclude any prosecution evidence the prejudicial effect of which outweighs its probative value.

Section 1(3)(iii) has no application where an accused gives evidence to the same effect as the Crown on a factual matter on which there is no issue between the Crown and the co-accused, because such an accused is supporting the Crown in a respect which is not contentious and therefore not in 'a material respect': *R* v *Crawford* [1998] 1 Cr App R 338, CA.

On the meaning of 'undermining the defence of the co-accused' see *R* v *Bruce* [1975] 1 WLR 1252, CA. In that case eight co-accused were charged with robbery. One of them, M, admitted a plan to rob but denied being a party to the actual robbery. Another, B, denied that there was a plan to rob. The trial judge ruled that B had given evidence against M and allowed M to cross-examine B about his previous convictions. The Court of Appeal, however, held that B had not given evidence against M because, despite the contradiction of M, the evidence was more in his favour than against him because it gave to M a different and possibly better defence. Stephenson LJ said that evidence which undermines a co-accused's defence is only evidence against that co-accused if it makes his acquittal less likely.

The Court of Appeal was faced with a similar situation in reverse in *R* v *Hatton* (1976) 64 Cr App R 88, a case concerning a plan to steal scrap metal. There it was the co-defendant who was allowed to cross-examine who alleged that there was no plan. The appellant had accepted that there was a plan but alleged that it was not a dishonest one. The Court of Appeal distinguished the case from *R* v *Bruce* on the grounds that the evidence had not provided a better defence, but had assisted the prosecution by confirming an essential element of the case (the plan). To the extent that it undermined both the co-defendant's case (no plan) and the prosecution's case (dishonesty) the overall effect was to undermine the co-defendant's case more.

It is possible to undermine the defence of a co-accused even if, although pleading not guilty, he gives evidence in which he appears to be confessing to the offence charged. He remains in the jury's charge and even if he only has a scintilla of a defence (because the jury may miraculously and inexplicably come to his rescue) there is still the possibility of undermining it and the judge has no discretion in the matter: see *R* v *Mir* [1989] Crim LR 894, CA.

In *R* v *Varley* [1982] 2 All ER 519, CA, two defendants, D and A, were tried for robbery. D's case was that both he and A had taken part but his involvement was because of duress exerted on him by A. The defence of A was that he was not there at all and therefore D's evidence was untrue. D was granted leave to cross-examine A under s. 1(3)(iii) and A was convicted. In the course of the judgment of the Court of Appeal it was held that a mere denial of participation in a joint venture is not of itself sufficient to rank as evidence against a co-accused. Where one accused asserts a view of the joint venture which is directly contradicted by the other, such contradiction may be evidence against the co-accused. In *Varley* this had clearly occurred. The denial of involvement by A directly contradicted D's contention that A had forced him to participate in the robbery and therefore deprived him of his defence.

The Court of Appeal also noted that for s. 1(3)(iii) to apply, a denial of participation in a joint venture 'must' lead to the conclusion that if one did not participate then it must have been the other who did. An illustration of this proposition is to be found in the earlier case of *R* v *Davis* [1975] 1 WLR 345, where two accused were charged with theft. The circumstances were such that one, the other or both of them must have committed the offence, and D denied the theft. The Court of Appeal in that case held that cross-examination of D under s. 1(3)(iii) was proper because although, on the face of it, he had merely denied the offence, in the circumstances that necessarily meant that the other accused had committed the offence.

In *R* v *Crawford* [1998] 1 Cr App R 338, CA, the victim of a robbery alleged that she had been alone in the lavatories of a restaurant with three other women, all of whom had committed the offence. The three were C, her co-accused A, and a third woman, L. C's evidence was to the effect that A and L were in the lavatories at the material time, but that she was not. A's evidence, which was put to C during cross-examination, was that C and L had committed the robbery while she, A, had been an innocent bystander. It was held that the trial judge had properly allowed A to cross-examine C on her previous convictions, because if the jury accepted C's evidence that only A and L were in the lavatories at the material time, that was very damaging to the credibility of A and made it much less likely that A was simply a passive bystander. It was submitted on appeal that this outcome was in conflict with the proposition in *R* v *Varley* to the effect that for s. 1(3)(iii) to apply, a mere denial of participation in a joint venture 'must' lead to the conclusion that if the accused did not participate, then it must have been the co-accused who did: this was not a case where it was either C or A who had committed the offence, and if it was not C therefore it must have been A. Rejecting this submission, the Court of Appeal held that insofar as the proposition from *R* v *Varley* had been cast in mandatory terms, it went too far: the word 'may' was more appropriate. See also, and *cf.*, *R* v *Kirkpatrick* [1998] Crim LR 63, CA.

In appropriate circumstances, cross-examination on previous convictions under s. 1(3)(iii) may go beyond the fact of the conviction and elicit the facts underlying the previous conviction. See *R* v *Reid* [1989] Crim LR 719, CA, in which the co-accused, charged with robbery, was cross-examined on a previous conviction for robbery. There was a real issue of credibility arising from consideration of the detailed circumstances of both robberies. The evidence went to two questions. First, did the co-accused seek to run the same lying defence when charged with robbery (leaving before the robbery occurred)? The second and more directly relevant question was did that lying defence involve the co-accused seeking falsely to incriminate others?

7.4   Inadmissible Evidence of Previous Convictions

There are two further restrictions on the admissibility of evidence of previous convictions over and above the common-law and statutory restrictions already considered.

(a)   As to the first, the Rehabilitation of Offenders Act 1974, see **5.2.4.3**. In *R* v *Nye* (1982) 75 Cr App R 247 the Court of Appeal held that the Act does not confer on an accused who is a rehabilitated person the right to put himself forward as being of good character. If the defence wish to refer to the accused as being 'of good character without relevant convictions', they should apply to the trial judge at the outset of the trial. The judge's ruling is an exercise of discretion. See also *R* v *Bailey* [1989] Crim LR 723, CA, and *R* v *O'Shea* [1993] Crim LR 951, CA.

(b)   The second, Children and Young Persons Act 1963, s. 16(2), provides that:

In any proceedings for an offence committed or alleged to have been committed by a person of or over 21, any offence of which he was found guilty while under the age of 14 shall be disregarded for the purposes of any evidence relating to his previous convictions; and he shall not be asked, and if asked shall not be required to answer, any question relating to such an offence, notwithstanding that the question would otherwise be admissible under section 1 of the Criminal Evidence Act 1898.

Questions

OBJECTIVES

This chapter is designed to ensure that you:

(a) understand the reasons for the prohibition of cross-examination of the accused as to character;

(b) understand the nature of the exceptions contained in s. 1(3)(i), (ii) and (iii) of the Criminal Evidence Act 1898;

(c) understand the distinction between character relevant to a fact in issue and character relevant to credit; and

(d) develop a sense of the tactical use of character evidence.

Question 1

Henry, James and Albert are jointly charged with burglary of a shop. They each have a number of previous convictions for the same offence. The only evidence which connects them with the crime is that of Sam, who claims to have driven their get-away car and has now turned Queen's evidence.

(a) Henry gives no evidence but his counsel puts to Sam in cross-examination that he has 14 previous convictions for offences involving dishonesty and Sam admits this to be true. Can the prosecution lead evidence of Henry's previous convictions?

(b) James says in evidence that Sam is a liar. Can the prosecution cross-examine James on his previous convictions?

(c) Albert says in evidence that Henry, James and Sam invited him to help with the break-in but he refused and did not take part. Can Henry's counsel cross-examine Albert on his previous convictions?

(d) Assuming Henry's counsel does not cross-examine Albert on his previous convictions, can the prosecution cross-examine Albert on them?

Question 2

Philip is charged with theft of Anita's company car.

Scenario 1: Philip's counsel cross-examines Anita and puts to her that she had given Philip permission to borrow the car, that her employer saw him using it and that she made up the theft to save her job. Anita denies this.

Scenario 2: Philip's counsel cross-examines a police officer and suggests that Philip is a man of good character and excellent reputation which the officer is then unable to dispute.

(a) May the prosecution cross-examine Philip, if he gives evidence, as to his previous convictions for taking a motor vehicle without consent and causing death by reckless driving, which the officer has now discovered?

(b) Would it make any difference if the conviction for taking a motor vehicle related to an offence committed on a date subsequent to that of the offence now charged?

(c) Assuming that the previous taking a motor vehicle offence can be put to Philip in cross-examination, may he also be asked in detail about the manner in which it was committed?

(d) If it came to light that Philip had been dismissed from his previous employment for abusing a colleague's company car privileges, could this matter be adduced in court in any way?

(e) If Philip elects not to give evidence, what, if anything, can the prosecution do in the light of the cross-examination by Philip's counsel?

Question 3

Oliver, Peter and Quentin are jointly charged with the theft of equipment from their employer. All three plead not guilty. In evidence, Oliver denies his guilt and says that he has worked for the employer for 11 years in a position of trust, that he feels loyalty and gratitude to the employer for giving him a job which has allowed him to go straight, and would not have done anything to injure the company. Peter testifies that he knew of Oliver and Quentin's plans to steal the equipment but he took no part in it. Quentin claims in his evidence that a policeman who testified that he had confessed to the offence was being 'terminologically inexact'.

All three accused have previous convictions, although Oliver's are spent. May these convictions be put to them in cross-examination?

EIGHT

HEARSAY: THE EXCLUSIONARY RULE

A central principle of the English judicial system is that a witness will attend court to give testimony as to what he or she has personally observed. To what extent will the courts depart from this principle by admitting as evidence statements made (whether orally, in writing or by conduct) outside of the witness box? It will be seen in this chapter that the answer to this question largely depends on the purpose to be achieved by admitting evidence of these out of court statements.

8.1 An Attempt at Definition

A primary difficulty is to define hearsay accurately. This was acknowledged by Lord Reid in *Myers* v *DPP* [1965] AC 1001, HL: 'it is difficult to make any general statement about the law of hearsay which is entirely accurate'.

The rule against hearsay is usually cast in the following terms:

> any statement other than one made by a witness while giving testimony in the proceedings in question is inadmissible as evidence of the facts stated.

8.1.1 THE SCOPE OF THE RULE

It is worth analysing the rule in a little more detail.

(a) The term '*statement*' includes:

    (i) any statement, whether oral, written, by gesture, on oath or unsworn;

    (ii) both those made with the intention of communicating (such as a letter) and those made without any such intention (such as the contents of a private diary).

(b) The phrase '*other than by a witness while giving testimony in the proceedings in question*' means *any* statement not made under oath in the proceedings in question and therefore:

    (i) clearly applies to statements made by persons other than the witness in question

    (ii) in relation to statements made by other persons, the rule applies even if that person is a witness in the current proceedings but was not giving testimony when making the statement in question (see *R* v *Rothwell* (1994) 99 Cr App R 388, CA);

(iii) the rule also applies to statements made by a witness when he or she was not giving evidence in the current proceedings (and therefore applies to previous consistent statements: see **Chapter 5**);

(iv) the phrase 'out of court', which is commonly used to reflect this aspect of the rule is a useful 'short-hand' but is potentially misleading in that a statement made by a witness under oath in *other* court proceedings *is* covered by the rule. 'Out of court' means outside of the court trying the current case.

(c) The phrase '*inadmissible as evidence of the facts stated*' means that statements are hearsay only if the purpose in tendering the evidence (i.e. its relevance to the proceedings) depends on the truth of the statement. If the truth of the statement matters, it is hearsay. If the truth does not matter but it is tendered for some other reason, the statement is *original* evidence. It is this concept that causes many difficulties in applying the rule and this will be considered in more detail later (see **8.4**).

Note that the rule applies to statements whether they are admitted through examination or cross-examination: see *R* v *Gillespie* (1967) 51 Cr App R 172, CA. The rule also applies to statements made in documents that are admitted in evidence (although documentary hearsay is subject to a number of exceptions: see **Chapter 9**).

As to the use of interpreters in the interrogation of suspects, see *R* v *Attard* (1958) 43 Cr App R 90: the translated answers, if admissible, can be given in evidence by the interpreter but not the police.

8.1.2   ATTEMPTS AT EVASION OF THE RULE

Two devices used by counsel to try to evade the rule are improper. The first is to ask not what was actually said in a conversation but what that conversation was about. The second is to ask about what was done but not said, using questions to which the answer can only be either 'yes' or 'no', with a view to enabling the tribunal of fact to infer what was said. See *Glinski* v *McIver* [1962] AC 726, HL. For example, assuming that Mr B makes an out-of-court statement to Mr A that 'X killed Y' (inadmissible hearsay), consider the impropriety of the following series of questions put by counsel for the prosecution to A during the course of his examination-in-chief at X's trial for the murder of Y:

Q.   You say that you came across Mr B. What happened then?
A.   We held a conversation. He said that . . .
Q.   Sorry to interrupt, Mr A. I don't want you to tell the court what Mr B said but, if you can, to answer this question 'yes' or 'no': as a result of that conversation with Mr B, did you do anything?
A.   Yes.
Q.   What was that?
A.   Well of course I instantly used my citizen's rights and arrested X.

The rule will also operate to prevent a witness from stating as a fact a conclusion that a witness has reached on the basis of the truth of out of court statements (i.e. on the basis of what would be hearsay evidence). For example in *R* v *Rothwell* (1994) 99 Cr App R 388, CA, a police officer observed persons passing packages and money back and forth. At trial he sought to give evidence that he had observed drug deals taking place. He said that he knew the transactions were drug deals because he knew the persons involved to be drug users. The basis of this knowledge was his involvement in the investigation of drugs offences and initiating prosecutions in the Newcastle area. He would therefore only have known such details as a result of having been told by other people that the defendants were drug dealers. He did not have first-hand knowledge of any fact that could lead to the conclusion that the defendants were drug users. The Court of Appeal therefore held that, in the absence of evidence that he had seen the persons in question using drugs or had observed other signs of drug use such as needle marks on their arms, he could not give evidence that the defendants were drug users and therefore that the transactions he saw were drug deals.

8.2   Rationale

The primary purpose of the rule of exclusion is to ensure that witnesses give evidence as to facts that are within their own knowledge rather than something they have heard from another source.

A number of reasons may be advanced to justify the exclusion of hearsay evidence, none of which, taken alone, is entirely convincing.

(a) To admit hearsay is often to admit superfluous material and raise side-issues, both of which result in an undue protraction of the trial. However, the material sought to be admitted in cases like *Sparks v R* [1964] AC 964, *Myers v DPP* [1965] AC 1001, and *R v Turner* (1975) 61 Cr App R 67 was highly relevant to the central issues in those cases and cannot fairly be described as 'superfluous'.

(b) Juries find it difficult to evaluate hearsay properly. This is surely open to debate. Compared to the other intellectual feats demanded of them by the law of evidence, juries might find it quite easy, if properly directed, to evaluate hearsay properly.

(c) To admit hearsay is to increase the opportunities for fraud or the deliberate manufacture of evidence. However, statements made at the time of, or shortly after, the events in question are often likely to be much more reliable than statements made months or years later. By the time of the trial, the witnesses may have forgotten, be ill or be dead.

(d) To admit hearsay is to enable a party to achieve a tactical advantage of surprise. The answer to this objection, to the extent that it is valid, is to introduce a notice requirement.

(e) Hearsay statements are only occasionally made on oath and usually not in the solemn and serious circumstances which surround the giving of evidence in court.

(f) The tribunal of fact has no opportunity to observe the speaker's demeanour, inflection, tone of voice etc.

(g) The opponent has no opportunity to cross-examine the speaker to probe his or her veracity, sincerity, powers of perception, means of knowledge etc. This objection, together with those set out in (e) and (f), loses force where the speaker can still be called as a witness: in these circumstances, although neither on oath nor open to observation or cross-examination at the time when the statement was made, the witness can repeat the statement in court on oath and then be cross-examined on it.

(h) There is a danger of mistake resulting from repetition, especially in the case of multiple oral hearsay.

(i) Hearsay is not the best evidence and admitting it encourages the substitution of weaker evidence for stronger evidence. This argument hardly holds water if hearsay is the only available evidence on the fact in issue.

For a fuller examination of arguments for and against the hearsay rule, see generally Law Commission Consultation Paper No. 138, *Evidence in Criminal Proceedings: The Hearsay Rule and Related Topics*, 1995, and the Law Commission Report No. 216, *The Hearsay Rule in Civil Proceedings*, Cm 2321, 1993.

8.3 Identifying Hearsay: Some Examples

In the case of oral statements, consider the following examples (and note the potential for injustice).

In *Sparks* v *R* [1964] AC 964, PC, the defendant was tried for indecent assault of a four year old girl. Soon after the incident the girl had said to her mother, when questioned as to the description of the assailant: 'It was a coloured boy'. The girl did not give evidence at trial. Sparks was white and at trial sought to lead evidence from the girl's mother that this comment had been made to establish that he could not have been the assailant. The Privy Council had no hesitation in concluding that this evidence was hearsay evidence.

Although not fully expounded by the Board, the reasoning would have been as follows:

* The statement was: 'It was a coloured boy'.

* The statement was not made by the girl in testimony at the trial: it was made out of court.

* The defence wanted to rely on the statement for its truth (i.e. its purpose was to show that the culprit was 'coloured' to establish that the defendant could not have committed the offence).

* It was therefore hearsay.

(Note that the girl did not give evidence. Had she done so this statement may have been admissible as a recent complaint in a sexual case: see **5.1.4.2**.)

In *R* v *Turner* (1975) 61 Cr App R 67, CA (applied in *R* v *Callan* [1994] Crim LR 198, CA), it was held that evidence that a third party, not called as a witness, had admitted that he had committed the robbery with which the accused was charged, was inadmissible. Milmo J stated:

> The idea, which may be gaining prevalence in some quarters, that in a criminal trial the defence is entitled to adduce hearsay evidence to establish facts which if proved would be relevant and would assist the defence, is wholly erroneous.

Where, however, the prosecution do not seek to admit a confession made by an accused, because there have been breaches of the Codes of Practice (see **Chapter 10**), a co-accused may elicit evidence of the confession, by way of exception to the hearsay rule, provided that it is relevant to his defence or undermines the prosecution case against him: see *R* v *Myers* [1997] 4 All ER 314, HL.

The potential for injustice also exists in relation to hearsay statements contained in documents. The leading case is *Myers* v *DPP* [1965] AC 1001, HL. The accused was convicted of a conspiracy concerning stolen cars. It was alleged that the conspiracy involved buying wrecked cars together with their logbooks, stealing cars nearly identical to the wrecked ones, disguising the stolen ones so that they corresponded with the logbooks of the wrecked ones, and then selling the stolen cars as the wrecked ones. In order to show that the cars sold were the stolen ones, the prosecution called an employee of a car manufacturer to produce microfilm of cards completed by other employees and showing that the numbers stamped on the cylinder blocks of the cars sold were identical to those on the cylinder blocks of the cars stolen. The Court of Criminal Appeal upheld the conviction because of the probability that the information in the records was correct. However, the House of Lords held that the records were inadmissible hearsay and should not have been admitted: the records were statements by unidentifiable workmen that the cars they saw bore certain cylinder-block numbers and the witness called was unable to give any direct evidence that the numbers in the records were the numbers on the cars. The majority of their lordships went on to hold that they were not prepared to create a new exception to the hearsay rule, because any addition to the categories of admissible hearsay was for Parliament and not the judiciary. No matter, therefore, how cogent or reliable the evidence may be, unless an exception to the hearsay rule applies, it is inadmissible. However, the House unanimously dismissed the appeal against conviction on the grounds of no substantial miscarriage of justice.

Parliament's response to the majority view was the Criminal Evidence Act 1965, the effect of which is now achieved by Criminal Justice Act 1988, ss. 23 and 24. See **9.2.2**.

In *Patel* v *Comptroller of Customs* [1966] AC 356, PC, bags of coriander seed inscribed with the words 'produce of Morocco' were held to be inadmissible to establish their country of origin. See also *R* v *Brown* [1991] Crim LR 835, CA.

In *Jones* v *Metcalfe* [1967] 1 WLR 1286, DC, a case which should now be read subject to Criminal Justice Act 1988, s. 24 (see **9.2.2.1**), the accused was convicted of driving without due care and attention, the police alleging that his lorry collided with a car. A witness called for the prosecution said that he saw the collision and gave the lorry's number to a police officer. A police officer gave evidence that, as a result of information received, he had interviewed the accused who had admitted that he drove his lorry, bearing the registration number in question, at the time and place of the incident, but who had denied being involved in any collision. The Divisional Court set the conviction aside on the grounds that there was no evidence that the accused's lorry was the one involved in the accident. What the witness had said to the police was inadmissible hearsay and it was improper, therefore, to infer what he had said. There was simply no admissible evidence of the number of the lorry involved in the collision. This decision was applied, albeit with the utmost reluctance, in *R* v *McLean* (1968) 52 Cr App R 80, CA, which concerned a dictated note of the registration number of a vehicle.

In the case of statements made by signs or gestures, consider *R* v *Gibson* (1887) 18 QBD 539, CCR. That case concerned a statement made partly orally and partly by a gesture or sign. The accused was convicted of unlawful wounding. The prosecutor gave evidence that immediately after a stone had been thrown at him, he heard an unidentified woman say, 'The man who threw the stone went in there', and saw her pointing towards the accused's house. On appeal, the conviction was quashed. In *Chandrasekera* v *R* [1937] AC 220, PC, the appellant was tried for the murder of a woman by slitting her throat. The nature of the injury was such that the woman was unable to speak. She therefore had to communicate by gestures. She made signs indicating that it was the appellant who had cut her throat. The Privy Council regarded this conduct as hearsay (but admissible under a Ceylon statutory exception).

8.4   Identifying Hearsay Evidence

8.4.1   HEARSAY EVIDENCE AGAINST ORIGINAL EVIDENCE

As will be noted from the rule stated above (**8.1**) and the examples given (see **8.3**), it is necessary to have a clear idea as to why the statement in question is to be adduced as evidence at all (i.e. its purpose). If the statement is to be admitted to prove that what was said was true, it will be hearsay evidence and inadmissible unless it falls within one of the exceptions to the rule set out in **Chapter 9**. If, however, the statement is to be adduced to prove a fact *other* than the truth of what was said in the statement, it is original evidence and may be admissible if that fact other than the truth of the statement is relevant.

For example, if a witness says that he saw the defendant on the High Street on Monday morning:

(a)   If the statement is used to prove that the defendant was on the High Street on Monday morning, this statement has to be true to prove those facts and the statement would therefore be admissible.

(b) If the statement is used to prove that the witness knows of the existence of the defendant, the statement does not have to be true (the defendant does not have to have been on the High Street) to achieve that purpose, so the statement would be original evidence.

It is useful, in determining whether or not the evidence will be admissible, to adopt a methodical approach:

(a) First, it is necessary to determine exactly what the *statement* is. Is the statement merely something that will be given in oral testimony without involving any repetition of what has been said outside of the court? If so, it will not be hearsay or original evidence it will be testimony. There would be no difficulty, in the example above, with the witness saying in the witness box that he had seen the defendant on the High Street on Monday. If, however, the statement was originally made somewhere else but is being repeated in the witness box, or is contained in a letter, or is something that the witness can only know on the basis of having been told by someone else, then one must go on to consider whether or not it is being tendered for the truth of its contents. To do this it is necessary to:

(b) Identify the *relevance* (i.e. the purpose) of the statement as evidence. A statement may have a bearing on a number of issues in a case. It is therefore necessary to determine for which purpose (or purposes) the statement might be admitted. What is it hoped that the statement in question will prove? (For example, whether the defendant was on the High Street or that the witness knows the defendant.)

(c) Having determined this relevance/purpose, it is necessary to determine whether, to achieve that purpose, the words narrated in the statement have to be *true* or whether the purpose will be achieved by simply showing that the statement was made (whether or not what was actually said was correct or true or accurate). If the statement has to be true to achieve its purpose, it will be hearsay evidence. If, to achieve its relevant purpose, the statement simply has to be made, the statement will be original evidence and not subject to a rule of exclusion.

In *Ratten v R* [1972] AC 378, PC, Lord Wilberforce said at p. 387:

The mere fact that evidence of a witness includes evidence as to words spoken by another person who is not called, is no objection to its admissibility. Words spoken are facts just as much as any other action by a human being. If the speaking of the words is a relevant fact, a witness may give evidence that they were spoken. A question of hearsay only arises when the words spoken are relied on 'testimonially', i.e. as establishing some fact narrated by the words.

Therefore, if the statement is relevant to establish the fact of *something* having been said (whether or not true), the statement will be original evidence. It is worth bearing in mind that, as a matter of substantive law, the speaking of words, whether or not true or intended to be true can have legal consequences (e.g. misrepresentations, offences involving the making of threats). In other cases the making of statements, true or not, can be common or even necessary features of establishing a fact in issue (e.g. a threat being made to a defendant as evidence to establish the defence of duress). In all such cases the relevant purpose of the out of court statement is not to show that what was said was true but to show that it was said.

The relevant purpose (other than proving the truth of the facts contained in the statement) may therefore be, for instance:

(a) simply to show that the statement was made, e.g. in a contract case in which the formation of the contract is disputed, to show that an offer was made and accepted or its terms; or where there has been an allegation that a witness has recently fabricated his testimony, to prove that the same thing was said on previous occasions (see **5.1.4.2**);

(b)   to show the state of mind or knowledge of the maker of the statement, e.g. to show that the victim of a crime was in a state of emotion or fear because of an existing or impending emergency;

(c)   to show the state of mind of the person who heard the statement, e.g. a case of misrepresentation in which the plaintiff gives evidence of a statement made to him by the defendant to show that he was misled by the defendant, i.e. to show what the plaintiff, on hearing the statement, thought or believed.

To identify the relevant purpose, it is clearly necessary to understand exactly what must be established to make a case. This will turn on the substantive law in any case. As it is not necessary, in a contract action to establish that an offer to sell goods was genuine, it is not necessary to prove that the maker of the offer to sell goods meant to sell the goods. Therefore it does not matter whether the statement 'I will sell you the goods' was true or not. All that must be established is that an offer was made (i.e. the words were in fact spoken). Therefore the statement (including the exact words used) will be admissible, original evidence.

Consider the following examples.

In *R* v *Chapman* [1969] 2 QB 436, CA, the evidence of a police officer that a doctor had *not* objected, on the grounds of prejudice to the proper care or treatment of the patient, to the provision of a breath specimen, was admissible, on a charge of driving with excess alcohol, to establish the fact that the doctor had not objected where doing so would have afforded a defence.

In *Woodhouse* v *Hall* (1980) 72 Cr App R 39, DC, the defendant was charged with 'acting in the management of a brothel'. The prosecution case was that the massage parlour she ran was in fact a brothel. To prove this fact, police officers were called to give evidence that they had visited the parlour in the guise of customers and that, while being massaged by the defendant's employees, these employees had offered them sexual services. The evidence of these offers being made was held not to constitute hearsay evidence. The relevant fact was whether any offers of sexual services were made, not whether the offers were true (i.e. intended to be acted upon or made willingly by the employees).

For cases where the statement is original evidence because the fact of the statement shows the maker's state of mind, consider the following:

In *Ratten* v *R* [1972] AC 378, PC, R was convicted of the murder of his wife by shooting her with a gun. His defence was that the gun had gone off accidentally. The prosecution called as a witness a telephone operator who gave evidence that at a certain time, which could be shown by other evidence to be shortly before the time of the killing, she had received a telephone call, from the address of the accused, made by a woman who, in an hysterical and sobbing voice, had said, 'Get me the police, please'. The accused denied that this call had been made. The Privy Council held that this evidence was not hearsay but admissible because relevant to two issues in the case: first it was relevant, irrespective of what was actually said, to show that, contrary to the accused's evidence, a call had been made by a woman who could only have been the victim; secondly, the evidence that the voice was hysterical and had asked for the police was relevant because it allowed the jury to infer that the woman, at that time, was in a state of emotion or fear because of an existing or impending emergency, which would have tended to rebut the defence that the gun went off accidentally. The words used 'Get me the police, please' had not been admissible at trial to establish that the caller actually wanted the police or wanted the police because a crime was being committed. Instead the fact of the words having been used, together with the hysterical nature of the voice, had the purpose of showing that the caller was in a state of distress and fear.

In *R* v *Gilfoyle* [1996] 1 Cr App R 302, the accused's wife was found dead in circumstances which, in view of suicide notes produced by the appellant, suggested that she had taken her own life. At the trial, the suicide notes were admitted as evidence of the wife's suicidal frame of mind. However, evidence from three of the wife's friends, of what she had said to them about the suicide notes, was not admitted. The statements attributed to the wife by these three witnesses were to the effect that she had been asked by her husband to write the suicide notes for a project at work (he was an auxiliary nurse) and that this had worried and frightened her. On appeal it was held that the evidence of the three friends, although inadmissible to prove the truth of the fact that the accused had asked his wife to write the suicide notes (unless admissible under an exception to the hearsay rule), was admissible because relevant to the wife's state of mind: the statements tended to prove that she was not depressed or worried to the point of suicide when she wrote the notes, but rather wrote them in the belief that to do so would be to assist the accused in his project at work.

Cf. R v *Harry* (1988) 86 Cr App R 105, CA, where evidence of telephone calls made to P's flat asking for a man called Sacha, P's nickname, and enquiring whether drugs were for sale, was held to be inadmissible to prove that P was running a drug-dealing business from the flat. A similar approach was adopted in *R* v *Blastland* [1986] AC 41, HL, and in *R* v *Kearley* [1992] 2 All ER 345, HL below, cases that show the difficulty of reconciling this form of original evidence with implied hearsay (see **8.4.2**).

For a case concerning the state of mind of a person hearing the statement consider *Subramaniam* v *Public Prosecutor* [1956] 1 WLR 965, PC. Evidence of what terrorists had said to the accused, after they had captured him, should have been admitted in order to show whether they might reasonably have induced in him an apprehension of immediate death if he failed to comply with their wishes, which was of direct relevance to the issue of duress.

An out-of-court statement may be admitted as original evidence if tendered not for the truth of its contents, but for its falsity. In such cases the purpose is not to prove the words narrated in the statement but to prove that the statement was made. Alongside further evidence showing that the statement was not true, a tribunal of fact can conclude that the statement was, in fact, a lie. In *Attorney-General* v *Good* (1825) M'Cle & Yo 286, for example, evidence of a wife's demonstrably untrue statement that her husband was away from home was admissible in order to show the husband's intention to defraud his creditors. Similarly, in *R* v *Dyer* [1997] Crim LR 442, CA, the prosecution relied on the contents of a log compiled by Greek customs officers on the basis of information supplied by the accused, not for their truth, but for their falsity, to illustrate the dishonest plan on the part of the accused. See also *Mawaz Khan* v *R* [1967] 1 AC 454, PC. That case was a prosecution of two co-defendants for murder. In addition to various items of circumstantial evidence, the prosecution sought to prove statements made by each co-defendant individually in which they alleged that they were, at the time of the murder, at a particular club. The prosecution also called other witnesses who contradicted this alibi evidence. The trial judge then told the jury that the alibi statements could be used in determining whether or not the co-defendants had fabricated an alibi and had therefore co-operated after the murder. This direction to the jury formed the foundation of an appeal to the Privy Council on the basis that the evidence should not have been left to the jury as evidence against each co-accused because it was hearsay. The Board concluded that this was not the case. The purpose of adducing the evidence was not to prove that the matters stated were true (i.e. not to show that the two co-defendants *were* at the club). The statements were admissible as original evidence. What was relevant was that the statements were made at all (to show that the co-defendants *said* that they were at the club). Proof of that fact alongside the witnesses who effectively said that they were not there would lead the jury to conclude that the statements were false. From this fact the jury could infer not only that each defendant had lied, but that they had co-operated in doing so. See also the case of *R* v *Binham* [1991] Crim LR 774, CA. As to lies generally, see also **11.2.1**.

8.4.2   IMPLIED ASSERTIONS

Does the hearsay rule apply to implied assertions, i.e. statements or conduct resting on some assumption of fact which can be inferred by the court? Until recently, the English authorities were not entirely clear.

The authorities suggesting that the rule does *not* apply to implied assertions include *Ratten* v *R* (**8.4.1**), where the Privy Council had stated that the request for the police was not admitted to prove that the caller wanted the police but to prove that she was in a state of distress. However, in showing the distress, some probative force must derive from the fact that it was the police rather than anyone else that the caller was asking for. Otherwise, it would have been possible to have proven the distress by simply admitting evidence (a) that a call was made (but not including the detail of it) and (b) that the voice was hysterical. By approving of the admission of the words used, the Privy Council were (however implicitly) endorsing the view that what was implied in the words used was not capable of being hearsay. Similarly in *Woodhouse* v *Hall* (**8.4.1**), while the Divisional Court in that case concluded that it was enough that offers were made (irrespective of whether or not seriously intended) for the offence in question to be committed, it was arguably necessary to establish that the offer was a genuine one and therefore to imply into the statement that the offer was genuine for it to have a relevant purpose.

In *Manchester Brewery Co. Ltd* v *Coombs* the defence wanted to prove that beer supplied by the plaintiff company was of poor quality and therefore wanted to call witnesses to give evidence of complaints about the beer which had been received from customers. Farwell J was of the opinion that such evidence could be called because evidence could certainly be given of facts from which the poor quality of the beer could be inferred, for instance evidence of the fact that a customer ordered beer, tasted it but did not finish it and then either left it or threw it away.

Authorities to suggest that the hearsay rule *does* operate to exclude implied assertions include, in the case of oral statements, *Teper* v *R* [1952] AC 480, PC and *R* v *Harry* (**8.4.1**) and, in the case of written statements, *Wright* v *Doe d Tatham* (1837) 7 A & E 313.

In *Teper* v *R* the accused was charged with arson of a shop belonging to his wife. The defence being alibi, the prosecution sought to prove his presence in the area by calling a policeman to give evidence that nearly half an hour after the fire had started, he had heard a woman bystander, who was not identified, shout to a passing motorist, who bore some resemblance to the accused, 'Your place burning down and you going away from the fire'. Of course that statement was never intended by the woman to be an express assertion that the accused was present at the place in question, although it clearly conveyed that fact by implication. The Privy Council held that the policeman's evidence had been improperly admitted because it was inadmissible hearsay, and quashed Teper's conviction.

Wright v *Doe d Tatham* concerned the validity of the will of a man named Marsden. Evidence had been adduced by the party contesting the validity of the will that Marsden did not have the mental capacity to make a valid will. To prove Marsden's sanity the party seeking to rely on the will sought to tender evidence of letters that had been written by third parties. The Court of Exchequer held that the letters were inadmissible for this purpose. In the judgment of Parke B, it was stated that the purpose of the letters was to show by their content and tone that the writers believed Marsden to be sane. If the letters had stated this fact expressly ('Marsden is sane') they would not have been admissible, as they would have been hearsay. They were therefore equally inadmissible as implied assertions of Marsden's sanity.

The question appears to have been settled by the House of Lords in *R* v *Kearley*. K's flat was raided by the police who found drugs there, but not in sufficient quantities to raise the inference that he was a dealer. After the search, the police remained there for several hours and intercepted ten telephone calls in which the caller asked to speak to K and asked for drugs. Later, while the police were still on the premises, seven persons arrived at the flat, some with money, also asking for K and asking to be supplied with drugs. At the relevant times, K was either not present or not within earshot. K denied a charge of possession with intent to supply. At the trial, the prosecution were allowed to call the police officers who had intercepted the calls or received the visitors at the flat to give evidence of the conversations they had had with the callers or visitors. The Court of Appeal dismissed the appeal against conviction but certified the following question as raising a point of law of general public importance:

Whether evidence may be adduced at a trial of words spoken (namely a request for drugs to be supplied by K), not spoken in the presence or hearing of the defendant, by a person not called as a witness, for the purpose not of establishing the truth of any fact narrated by the words, but of inviting the jury to draw an inference from the fact that the words were spoken (namely that K was a supplier of drugs).

The House of Lords, by a majority of three to two, held that evidence of such a request was irrelevant because it could only be evidence of the state of mind of the person making the request, which was not a relevant issue at the trial — the issue at the trial was whether or not K intended to supply drugs, and in so far as evidence of a request was relevant to that issue (as an implied assertion that K was a supplier of drugs), it was inadmissible hearsay in the same way that an express out-of-court assertion to the same effect would be inadmissible hearsay, and it made no difference that there was a large number of such requests all made at the same place on the same day. Accordingly, the appeal was allowed.

In reaching this decision, the majority applied *R v Blastland* [1986] AC 41 and *Wright v Doe d Tatham* (above) and cited with approval *R v Harry* (**8.4.1**). *Woodhouse v Hall* (**8.4.1**) was distinguished on the basis that in order to establish that premises are being used as a brothel, it is sufficient to prove that at the premises more than one woman *offers* herself as a participant in physical acts of indecency for the sexual gratification of men; and the evidence of the conversations in that case provided direct evidence of these offers — it was original and not hearsay evidence. *Ratten v R* (**8.4.1**) was distinguished on the basis that:

(a) the fact that a call was made from the premises at all at the relevant time was directly in issue;

(b) the fact that it was made by a woman who was both frightened and hysterical was relevant to the accused's defence of accident; and

(c) in so far as the evidence was admitted for the truth of the inference that the victim was under attack from her husband, that could only have been justified by treating the contents of the call as part of the *res gestae*.

8.4.3 NEGATIVE HEARSAY

In principle, it is clear that the hearsay rule should apply not only to positive statements (e.g. 'The goods in question were repossessed') but also to negative statements, i.e. statements concerning the non-existence as opposed to the existence of certain facts (e.g. 'The goods in question were not repossessed'). Proving a negative by direct rather than hearsay evidence, however, can sometimes be a notoriously difficult matter, and some authorities indicate that the non-existence of a fact may be proved by evidence of the absence of a recording of that fact in a record in which, having regard to its compilation and custody, one might have expected that fact, had it existed, to have been recorded.

In the case of *R v Patel* [1981] 3 All ER 94, CA, the defendant was charged with assisting the entry of an illegal immigrant contrary to the Immigration Act. To prove this charge, the prosecution sought to call a chief immigration officer to give evidence that if the name of the alleged illegal immigrant, A, was not on a Home Office record but that he was in the country, he was an illegal immigrant. This immigration officer had no involvement in compiling the Home Office record. The Court of Appeal held that the record was therefore a hearsay document. However, the court went on to hold (*obiter*) that the absence of an entry corresponding to A could have established that he was an illegal immigrant if:

(a) an officer responsible for the compiling of the record had given evidence that a particular method was adopted for making entries in the record and for storing the records, and

(b) that officer had also given evidence that, as a result of such a process, the absence of an entry for a particular person meant that that person was an illegal immigrant.

This dictum was applied in *R* v *Shone* (1983) 76 Cr App R 72, CA, where the accused was charged with handling stolen goods, three vehicle springs. The springs bore numbers which enabled them to be identified as having been supplied by a manufacturer to a particular company, from which it was alleged that they had been stolen. Their arrival at the company was recorded on stock record cards, and in order to prove that the goods must have been stolen from the company the prosecution called two employees from the company, who were responsible for these records, to give evidence that the cards were marked to show when parts were sold and used and that the cards in relation to the springs bore no such marks. On appeal against conviction, it was argued that this evidence was inadmissible hearsay. Applying the dictum from *R* v *Patel*, the Court of Appeal dismissed the appeal on the grounds that the witnesses, in giving evidence of the method of compilation and the significance of the absence of marks on the cards, had not given hearsay evidence, but direct evidence from which the jury were entitled to infer, if they saw fit, that the springs were not sold or used, and therefore must have been stolen.

A case which extended the notion of negative hearsay is *R* v *Muir* (1984) 79 Cr App R 153, CA. The defendant was alleged to have stolen a video recorder from a hire company but alleged in his defence that two men had repossessed it. To disprove this the prosecution called the district manager of the hire company who gave evidence that repossession would be effected either by the local showroom or by the company's head office. His evidence was that if the local showroom had repossessed the recorder, the process was such that he would have been informed. He also gave evidence that he had checked at the Head Office and had been told that they had not repossessed it. It was the second conclusion in relation to Head Office that was challenged on appeal. It was only possible for him to accurately conclude that Head Office had not repossessed the recorder if what he had been told when he rang Head Office was true. That would constitute a hearsay statement. The proper course, the defendant argued, was to call the person who had compiled the Head Office records to give evidence of the absence of any record of repossession along the lines identified in *Patel* and *Shone*.

The Court of Appeal rejected this argument on the grounds that the district manager had full knowledge of the repossession transaction and 'was the best person to give the relevant evidence'. It would appear that the court placed some reliance on the fact that the district manager said during re-examination that if the recorder had not been repossessed by Head Office he personally would have continued in his efforts to repossess it and that he was 100% certain that he would have been told of the repossession if it had occurred in any way. However, it is difficult to see how either of these conclusions could meaningfully have been reached by the district manager without him relying on the truth of what he had been told by some other person.

8.4.4   STATEMENTS PRODUCED BY CALCULATORS AND OTHER ELECTRONIC OR MECHANICAL DEVICES

Where a computer or other electronic or mechanical device is used as a calculator, that is, as a tool which does not contribute its own knowledge but merely does a calculation, albeit a sophisticated one, which could have been done manually, the resulting print-out, reading or other information produced by the device is not hearsay but admissible as a variety of real evidence.

The proof and relevance of such evidence, however, depends upon the testimony of the person or persons in charge of the computer or other device, such as the computer programmer and operator.

In *R* v *Wood* (1982) 76 Cr App R 23, CA, the prosecution sought to prove that certain metal was part of a stolen consignment. To that end the prosecution adduced evidence of an analysis of the chemical composition of the metal. During the analysis a computer was programmed to carry out the relevant calculations and was operated by the chemist responsible for the analysis. The Court of Appeal held that the computer printout showing the results of these calculations was not hearsay because the computer was being used to do a sophisticated calculation which could have been done manually. The printout, therefore, was merely a piece of real evidence, the actual proof and relevance of which depended on the testimony of the computer operator (the chemist) and the computer programmer. In the course of his judgment, Lord Lane CJ gave another example, a speak-your-weight machine. Evidence by a witness of what he or she had heard from such a machine would not be hearsay although the witness might have to be cross-examined about whether he or she had kept a foot on the ground, and the accuracy of the machine might have to be investigated. However, such evidence, in the absence of any printout or other physical recording to bring to court, could not be categorised as real evidence.

Similarly, in *Castle* v *Cross* [1984] 1 WLR 1372, DC, the print-out of an Intoximeter 3000 breath-test machine, recording that it did not have a sufficient sample to perform an analysis, was admissible on a charge of failure to provide a specimen of breath when required to do so.

In *R* v *Spiby* (1990) 91 Cr App R 186, the Court of Appeal held that the print-out from a computerised machine used to monitor telephone calls and record such information as the numbers from which and to which the calls were made and the duration of the calls, is not hearsay but real evidence. Compare *R* v *Neville* [1991] Crim LR 288, CA. See also *Garner* v *DPP* (1990) 90 Cr App R 178, DC. In *R* v *Governor of Brixton Prison, ex parte Levin* [1997] 3 WLR 117, HL, the issue was whether L had used a computer terminal to gain unauthorised access to the computerised fund transfer service of a bank and to make fraudulent transfers of funds from accounts of clients of the bank to accounts which he controlled. Each request for transfer was processed automatically and a record of the transaction was copied to the computer's historical records. The House of Lords held that printouts of screen displays of these records were admissible to prove the transfers of funds they recorded. Lord Hoffmann said: 'They do not assert that such transfers took place. They record the transfers . . . The evidential status of the printouts is no different from that of a photocopy of a forged cheque'.

The principle under discussion is probably the best way to approach the case of *Taylor* v *Chief Constable of Cheshire* [1986] 1 WLR 1479, DC. In that case a youth was charged with theft of a packet of batteries from W.H. Smith. Unknown to him, a video recording was made of his actions. The recording was shown to the police who identified the person they saw on the screen as the accused. The recording was returned to W.H. Smith for safe keeping, where it was then accidentally erased from the video cassette. The magistrates held that police officers were entitled to give evidence as to what they had seen on the video. On appeal by way of case stated, it was argued that although the video recording itself would have been admissible evidence, the evidence of the officers was inadmissible hearsay because they had not witnessed the actual theft personally or directly but were merely repeating to the court the out-of-court 'statements' of the video. Dismissing the appeal, Ralph Gibson LJ held that evidence of what the witnesses saw on the video was no different in principle from evidence from witnesses who saw the events in question in direct vision from the particular position of the video camera. However, two cautionary notes were struck. First, it was said that where the recording is not available, a court should hesitate and consider very carefully whether or not they are sure of guilt on the basis of such evidence. Secondly, because identification was in issue, the weight and reliability of the evidence fell to be assessed by reference to the usual criteria laid down in the form of guidelines in the case of *R* v *Turnbull* [1977] QB 224 (**12.5**). Those criteria, said McNeill J, would have to be applied not only in relation to the camera itself, but also in relation to the witnesses who watched the video recording.

8.4.5 IDENTIFICATION CASES

The common theme of most of the following cases is that identification was in issue and in many of them there appears to have been evasion (or a 'side-stepping') of the hearsay rule. Consider first the following clear statement of principle in *Sparks* v *R* [1964] AC 964, PC, *per* Lord Morris of Borth-y-Gest at p. 981: 'There is no rule which permits the giving of hearsay evidence merely because it relates to identity'.

This statement has been side-stepped in two types of cases.

8.4.5.1 Identifications of other persons

In *R* v *Burke* (1847) 2 Cox CC 295, in which the victim of the crime identified the accused as the criminal shortly after the offence, but by the time of the trial was unable to do so, the prosecution were allowed to call a policeman to give evidence of the out-of-court identification. The same situation also arose in *R* v *Osbourne and Virtue* [1973] QB 678, CA. In that case a woman gave evidence that she could not remember having picked out anyone at an identification parade, which had taken place some seven months before the trial. A police officer in charge of that parade was then allowed to give evidence that in fact she had picked out the accused. The Court of Appeal upheld the admission of the evidence. No hearsay point was referred to, nor was there any reference to *Sparks* v *R* or the earlier cases on the identification of cars by their registration numbers, such as *Jones* v *Metcalfe* (see **8.3**). In the course of his judgment, Lawton LJ said: 'It would be wrong, in the judgment of this court, to set up artificial rules of evidence which hinder the administration of justice'. See also *R* v *McCay* [1990] 1 WLR 645, CA.

In *R* v *Percy Smith* [1976] Crim LR 511, CA, a sketch made by a police officer at the direction of a witness was admitted in evidence; and in *R* v *Okorudu* [1982] Crim LR 747, a photofit made by a witness was admitted in evidence.

The difficulty of reconciling cases such as *Sparks* v *R* with cases such as *R* v *Percy Smith* and *R* v *Okorudu* has now been side-stepped. In *R* v *Cook* [1987] QB 417, CA it was held that a photofit and a sketch made by a police officer are, like photographs taken when a suspect is actually committing an offence, in a class of evidence of their own to which neither the rule against hearsay nor the rule against the admission of an earlier consistent statement applies. *R* v *Cook* was applied in *R* v *Constantinou* (1990) 91 Cr App R 74, CA.

8.4.5.2 Self-identification

A statement of self-identification, 'I am X', is clearly hearsay. It is tendered to prove its contents (that the maker was X). In principle such a statement might be admitted as a confession (and therefore an exception to the rule of exclusion: see **Chapter 11**). However, where this is not possible, it would appear to be possible to admit the detail of statements said in self-identification as original evidence. In *R* v *Ward* [2001] Crim LR 316, CA, a police witness sought to give evidence of an encounter with a person at the scene of a crime. In response to questions the person said he was Michael Ward and gave a date of birth and address. The officer could not identify the person in question at trial as the defendant, Ward. However, the date of birth and the address both corresponded with those of Ward. The Court of Appeal concluded that the details were not hearsay statements. Rather it was the fact of the statements having been made that was relevant. By combining the fact of those statements with independent evidence as to the date of birth and address of the defendant it was possible to show that the maker of the statements was in fact Ward because he had stated facts that not any member of the public would know. The relevance of the statements about date of birth and address were relevant (and therefore admissible original evidence) to show that the maker knew some personal details of Ward and therefore might have been him.

Another way in which hearsay presents problems concerns the presence of a person's name on an item (such as an item of clothing with a name tag or a book with a name written on the inside cover). Can such an item be used to prove that a person was in a particular place at a particular time?

A case that has caused some difficulty on this point is *R* v *Rice* [1963] 1 QB 857, CCA. On trial for conspiracies in relation to the sale of stolen cars, it was part of the prosecution case that two of the co-defendants, Rice and Hoather, had flown to

Manchester. To establish this, they sought to adduce in evidence an airline ticket bearing the names 'Rice' and 'Moore'. An airline representative produced the ticket and testified that the ticket had been kept in a place where tickets that had been used for air flights were located.

The Court rejected the defence argument that the ticket should not have been admitted due to its hearsay nature. It was recognised that the document would be hearsay if it was produced to establish that the person who made the booking was called Rice. In effect the ticket was making the statement 'I was issued to Rice' and was documentary hearsay for that purpose.

However, the Court went on to hold that the ticket was nonetheless admissible evidence as to who took the flight. Winn J, at p. 871 said:

> The relevance of that ticket in logic and its legal admissibility as a piece of real evidence both stem from the same root, viz., the balance of probability recognised by common sense and common knowledge that an air ticket which has been used on a flight and which had a name upon it has more likely than not been used by a man of that name or by one of two men whose names are upon it.

That reasoning was questioned by the House of Lords in *Myers* v *DPP*. It is worth looking more closely at Winn J's statement to understand why. Common sense recognises that a name on a used ticket is likely to be that of the person who took the flight where that name belongs to the person who booked the ticket. The conclusion is reached by combining two factual conclusions ((a) and (b) below) with a generalisation (c):

(a)   The ticket was booked by Rice.

(b)   The ticket was used.

(c)   A used ticket is likely to have been used by the person who booked it.

However, conclusion (a) is the implied hearsay statement the Court had ruled inadmissible.

Contrast this with the case of *R* v *Lydon* (1987) 85 Cr App R 221, CA. Sean Lydon, charged with robbery, ran a defence of alibi. On the verge of the road on the route taken by the getaway car, about a mile from the place of the robbery, the police found a gun and, nearby, two pieces of rolled paper containing the written messages, 'Sean rules' and 'Sean rules 85'. There was ink on the gun barrel and it was of similar appearance and composition to that on the bits of paper. The Court of Appeal held that this evidence had been properly admitted: if the jury concluded that the gun had been used in the robbery and that the gun was linked to the bits of paper, then the words 'Sean' on the bits of paper would be consistent with the allegation that Sean Lydon had committed the robbery. In reaching this conclusion, the Court questioned the reasoning adopted in *Rice*. In *Lydon* the words contained in the statement were not admitted for their truth (it did not matter whether Sean did rule). The evidence simply showed that someone had alleged Sean did rule. The jury could conclude that a person named Sean was making such statements from the fact of their being made rather than from the truth of their contents.

It is worth contrasting the reasoning in *Rice* with that adopted in *R* v *Van Vreden* (1973) 57 Cr App R 818. In that case two defendants were being prosecuted in relation to the dishonest use of a credit card. The prosecution case was that the two (male) defendants were using a credit card that had been issued to a female in South Africa. To prove this a representative of the credit card company was called to give evidence. He explained that the system used in the South African subsidiary was the same as that used in the UK and that he had obtained a document from the South African subsidiary which was the approved application form for the card used by the defendants. This form contained two relevant statements. The first statement was by the person who filled out the form to the effect that the applicant was a woman. The second statement was the entry upon the form when the application was approved identifying the number of the card that this applicant had received. The number assigned was that recorded on the credit card the defendants had used. The Court of Appeal held that the form was clearly a hearsay document.

In *R* v *McIntosh* [1992] Crim LR 651, CA, calculations as to the purchase and sale prices of 12 ounces of an unnamed commodity were found concealed in the chimney of a house where M had been living. Although not in M's handwriting, the calculations were held to be admissible as circumstantial evidence tending to connect him with drug-related offences. *McIntosh* was applied in *Roberts* v *DPP* [1994] Crim LR 926, DC. R was charged with assisting in the management of a brothel and running a massage parlour without a licence. It was held that documents found at his offices and home, which included repair and gas bills and other accounts relating to the premises in use as a brothel and massage parlour, were admissible as circumstantial evidence linking him with those premises.

Cf. R v *Horne* [1992] Crim LR 304, CA.

Questions

OBJECTIVES

The aim of this chapter is to ensure that you have a thorough grasp of:

(a) what constitutes hearsay;

(b) the difference between hearsay and original evidence;

(c) the difference between hearsay and real evidence (including statements produced by mechanical and other devices); and

(d) the particular problems associated with implied assertions and the non-existence of facts (or negative hearsay).

Question 1

(a) Peter is charged with indecently assaulting Ruth, a 14-year-old girl. The prosecution case is that Peter fondled her breast while standing at a bus stop. Peter instructs his solicitor as follows:

I was standing at a bus stop awaiting a number 17 bus at about 9 p.m. one evening. There were two other people there. One of them was an elderly lady. The other was teenage girl. I heard the elderly lady shout out 'This child tried to pick my pocket. Catch the thief!' The girl looked as though she was about to escape so I caught hold of her from behind. She cried out 'Stop touching me up, you dirty old man'.

Unfortunately while all this was happening, a bus arrived and for some reason the old lady got onto it. She was probably frightened.

The police arrived soon afterwards and I told them what had happened. However Ruth said 'He grabbed me to fondle me. He is making this all up. There was no woman here'.

The police arrested me and charged me with indecent assault. I was released on bail. On my way home I noticed a wallet lying on the pavement at the bus stop. In it there was some cash and a bus pass. The bus pass identified the owner as 'Dorothy Owen' and gave the date of birth as 12 March 1929. The picture resembled the woman I had seen.

It is true that I have a previous conviction for indecent exposure arising out of some high spirited antics after a football match. Unfortunately I have also recently lost my job. Some female colleagues said that I had made indecent suggestions to them while working there.

(i) Discuss the evidential matters raised in these instructions (there are some revision points here).

(ii) What are the likely consequences (if any) if Peter chooses to give evidence of his version of events?

(b) The following is an extract from a prosecution witness statement concerning a fight between Tina and Carol, who have been charged with affray. The statement was made by a prosecution witness, Vicky.

I know both Tina and Carol and have done for some time. We work together in a shoe shop. A couple of years ago, Carol started going out with a bloke named Danny.

Last May I met Carol to do some shopping before we went to work. Carol said she had had a row with Danny and that he had stormed out. He had come back the following day and they had made up.

As we were having lunch someone who appeared to be a friend of Carol's came and spoke to us. She said that she had been in the local pub the previous evening and she had seen Danny who was with a girl with dark hair about 5′ 5″ tall. They had been chatting away in a very friendly manner. At one stage she had overheard the girl say, 'She won't find out if you don't tell her. We can go to my Dad's allotment'. Danny and the girl had then left. Danny had his arm around the girl.

I instantly knew that the girl was Tina. She is about 5′ 5″, has black hair and her dad owns an allotment. I was due to work the afternoon shift. Carol must have known too because she said 'That bitch, Tina. She is going to get it for this!'

When we got to work, Tina was there and Carol went straight over to her and said 'What do you think you are doing you dirty slag?' Tina replied 'What are you talking about?' Carol said 'You know. If you don't leave Danny alone, I will sort you out'. Carol and I then turned away to go and get changed for work. As we were leaving I heard Tina say 'Don't you think you can mess with me. Don't blame me if you can't keep your bloke.' I then heard a loud smacking sound and Carol fell over. Some of the other staff members and customers came over to hold Tina back. The manager and I took Carol upstairs. The manager gave her first aid while I went to call an ambulance.

Identify any hearsay statements or original evidence in the statement, and give reasons.

Question 2
Robert Smith is being prosecuted for causing death by reckless driving and for failing to stop after an accident in Kensington, London. Robert says that on the night in question he was driving his car (registration number NFC 62P) in Bristol. Immediately after the accident, Mary saw a car disappearing and memorised the number, which she quickly wrote down with lipstick on the back of her hand. Later she showed her hand to a police officer, who wrote down the number in his notebook. Mary cannot remember the number any more but says she wrote the correct number on her hand, while the police officer says that he saw 'NFC 62P' written on her hand. May the *police officer* be called to give evidence to this effect?

Question 3
Duncan Jones, a director of a public company, is charged with conspiracy to defraud. It is alleged that at a meeting of directors on 7 September 2001, Duncan and others agreed to produce and publish false accounts in order to deceive investors and

creditors. Duncan's defence is that on 7 September 2001 he could not have been at the meeting because he was in France. Duncan wants to know whether a used ticket, which he has in his possession, for a journey from Calais to Ramsgate dated 8 September 2001, and bearing the name 'Jones', is admissible, *at common law*, in support of his defence.

Question 4
Edward has been charged with selling food unfit for human consumption. May Fred give evidence for the prosecution that while visiting Edward's restaurant he saw a number of customers leave their food unfinished and, clutching their stomachs, rush to the lavatories?

NINE

HEARSAY EXCEPTIONS

When is hearsay admissible?

9.1 General Points

Whereas hearsay is generally not admissible, such a statement which falls within any of the hearsay exceptions considered in this chapter is admissible as evidence of the truth of the facts it contains.

There are many common law and statutory hearsay exceptions and it is not easy to draw up useful general classifications but probably the most significant is between criminal and civil cases. This is because the most important statutory exceptions tend to be restricted either to criminal cases or civil cases (and most of the common law exceptions no longer apply in civil cases).

The position in criminal cases is covered by a wide range of common law and statutory exceptions. However, whilst there is a much greater variety of hearsay exceptions in criminal cases their scope is much narrower than the scope of the exception created for civil cases by Civil Evidence Act 1995 — see below at **9.3**. Moreover the courts have set their face against the creation of new common-law (judge-made) exceptions to the hearsay rule: see *Myers* v *DPP* [1965] AC 1001, HL. The overall effect is that hearsay is much less likely to be admissible in criminal cases than in civil cases.

9.2 Hearsay Exceptions Applicable in Criminal Cases

9.2.1 COMMON-LAW EXCEPTIONS

9.2.1.1 *Res gestae*
The phrase '*res gestae*' (or 'part of the *res gestae*') has been used to describe an out-of-court statement which relates to and is closely associated in time and place with a relevant state of affairs or 'event' as it arises or occurs. The broad theory is that such statements should generally be admitted since the 'events' in question are likely to monopolise the thoughts of the maker of the statement to an extent where the chances of concoction (arguably the main risk with hearsay statements) can be safely discounted: see *R* v *Callender* [1998] Crim LR 337. The formation of more specific principles of admissibility has depended upon the type of 'event' which the statement relates to. There are essentially four main categories of statement which fall under the umbrella heading *res gestae*.

Category 1: Statements relating to a specific event (usually a crime)
The 'usual' examples of this aspect of *res gestae* are cases where the victim of a murderous assault makes a statement identifying the assailant shortly after the assault (the victim subsequently dies from his or her wounds and cannot testify). The leading case now is *R* v *Andrews* [1987] AC 281. The facts were that X was attacked and mortally wounded by two men. Several minutes after the attack X told police

officers that Andrews was one of his attackers. The police officers gave evidence to this effect. The House of Lords held that although the police officers' evidence was clearly hearsay, it was admissible under this exception. For similar facts with a similar result see *R v Turnbull* (1985) 80 Cr App R 104. For a recent illustration see *R v Carnall* [1995] Crim LR 944 where there was a one-hour gap between the murderous assault and the making of the statement. At p. 300 in *Andrews*, Lord Ackner stated the general test of admissibility:

1.   The primary question which the judge must ask himself is — can the possibility of concoction or distortion be disregarded?

2.   To answer that question the judge must first consider the circumstances in which the particular statement was made, in order to satisfy himself that the event was so unusual or startling or dramatic as to dominate the thoughts of the victim, so that his utterance was an instinctive reaction to that event, thus giving no real opportunity for reasoned reflection. In such a situation the judge would be entitled to conclude that the involvement or the pressure of the event would exclude the possibility of concoction or distortion, providing that the statement was made in conditions of approximate but not exact contemporaneity.

3.   In order for the statement to be sufficiently 'spontaneous' it must be so closely associated with the event which has excited the statement, that it can be fairly stated that the mind of the declarant was still dominated by the event. Thus the judge must be satisfied that the event, which provided the trigger mechanism for the statement, was still operative. The fact that the statement was made in answer to a question is but one factor to consider under this heading.

4.   Quite apart from the time factor, there may be special features in the case, which relate to the possibility of concoction or distortion. In the instant appeal the defence relied on evidence to support the contention that the deceased had a motive of his own to fabricate or concoct, namely a malice which resided in him against . . . the appellant . . . The judge must be satisfied that the circumstances were such that having regard to the special feature of malice, there was no possibility of any concoction or distortion to the advantage of the maker or the disadvantage of the accused.

5.   As to the possibility of error in the facts narrated in the statement, if only the ordinary fallibility of human recollection is relied on, this goes to the weight to be attached to and not the admissibility of the statement . . . However . . . there may be special features that may give rise to the possibility of error [e.g. when the declarant had drunk to excess or suffered from defective eyesight]. In such circumstances the trial judge must consider whether he can exclude the possibility of error.

It is necessary to *prove* that the declarant's thoughts were dominated by the event (see point 2 in the *Andrews* test above). It is therefore unlikely that it will be possible to rely on this exception when it is not possible to establish who made the statement in question (i.e. the declarant's identity is unknown). In *Teper v R* [1952] AC 480 the Privy Council held that testimony by a police officer that, as he approached the scene of crime, he heard an unknown person identify the accused (allegedly fleeing the scene) was inadmissible.

The test of admissibility stated in *R v Andrews* assumes the declarant to be the victim of the offence. However, there is no reason in principle why it should not also be satisfied where the declarant is not the victim — see *obiter dicta* in *Ratten v R* [1972] AC 378, PC. In *R v Glover* [1991] Crim LR 48 the maker of the statement was Glover himself. In the course of an alleged assault he exclaimed (unfortunately for him as it turned out — the issue at trial being identity) 'I am David Glover . . . we will not think twice of shooting you and your kids'. It was held that this hearsay statement was admissible under the *res gestae* exception (it would also seem to be admissible under the confessions exception — see **Chapter 10**). Although, often, the declarant will be dead at the time of the trial, this need not be so: see *R v Nye* (1977) 66 Cr App R 252 (assault) and *Edwards v DPP* [1992] Crim LR 576 (theft).

However, the exception should not generally be relied upon simply as a matter of convenience where the maker of the statement is available as a witness. See *Tobi* v *Nicholas* (1988) 86 Cr App R 323 where a statement (by X, the driver of a coach), made roughly 20 minutes after an accident (involving the coach and, allegedly, a car driven by the accused) was held inadmissible under this *res gestae* exception (because X was available as a witness).

Category 2: Statements relating to the maker's state of mind or emotion

There is sometimes a dispute about whether such statements are truly categorised as hearsay as opposed to original evidence. See *Thomas* v *Connell* (1838) 4 M & W 267 where it was held that X's statement that he was insolvent was original evidence of his state of mind (i.e. he *impliedly* asserted that he knew he was insolvent). But in *R* v *Blastland* [1986] AC 41, the House of Lords made it clear that courts should scrutinise the argument that such statements are not hearsay with great care. An *express assertion* of a state of mind or emotion does seem to be properly classified as hearsay. For it to be admissible hearsay under this exception the state of mind of the declarant must, of course, be a relevant issue in the case in question.

On the assumption that the statement in question is hearsay, what is the scope of this second category of res gestae?

The statement is admissible to prove the mental/emotional state of the maker of the statement at the time when the statement was made — i.e. the statement should be in the present tense, e.g. a statement by X that he is in fear. The statement is not admissible to prove the *cause* of the mental/emotional state.

Statements of current intention are sometimes proved to support the inference that the intention was acted upon: see *R* v *Buckley* (1873) 13 Cox CC 293; *R* v *Moghal* (1977) 65 Cr App R 56; but in *R* v *Wainwright* (1875) 13 Cox CC 171 and *R* v *Thomson* [1912] 3 KB 19 it was doubted whether the exception should be relied upon in this way. *R* v *Callender* [1998] Crim LR 337 tends to confirm that the exception should not be used for this purpose.

Category 3: Statements relating to the maker's physical state

The statement must be approximately contemporaneous with the 'occurrence' of the physical state. See *Aveson* v *Kinnaird* (1805) 6 East 188 (where X's statement to a friend that she was very poorly was held admissible under this head of *res gestae* as evidence that X was indeed very poorly at the time she made the statement) and *R* v *Black* (1922) 16 Cr App R 118.

The statement can prove the existence of the physical state but not its cause. See *Gilbey* v *GWR* (1910) 102 LT 202, and *R* v *Gloster* (1888) 16 Cox CC 471.

Category 4: Statements relating to the maker's performance of an act

The statement must be approximately contemporaneous with the act, and, the maker of the statement and the performer of the act must be the same person. See *Peacock* v *Harris* (1836) 5 Ad & El 449 and *Howe* v *Malkin* (1878) 40 LT 196.

The act should, in itself, be relevant to an issue before the court (i.e. the act should not be simply an excuse for admitting the statement). See *R* v *Bliss* (1837) 7 A & E 550, *cf. R* v *McCay* [1990] 1 WLR 645, CA.

In *Skinner* v *Shew & Co.* [1894] 2 Ch 581, the exception was relied upon to prove a letter terminating contractual negotiations which explained the reason for termination. Another example would be a case where, to avoid creditors, a man flees to a foreign country and explains why he does so. See *Rawson* v *Haigh* (1824) 2 Bing 99.

9.2.1.2   **Statements by persons since deceased (persons who are dead at the time of the trial)**
This heading embraces several distinct exceptions each with its own set of rules. The feature which is common to all is that the maker of the statement (M) is dead (a fact

which needs to be proved as a pre-condition of reliance on these exceptions). Clearly there is no question of calling M as a witness! There is no general common law exception relating to statements by persons since deceased. If the statement by the person since deceased was made in documentary form it may well be admissible under Criminal Justice Act 1988, s. 23 or s. 24 (see below at **9.2.2.1**). However, if the statement was made orally, in criminal cases reliance must still be placed on the following exceptions.

Dying declarations

A dying person's statement of the cause of his or her death is admissible in trials for that person's murder or manslaughter if, when the statement was made, M had a settled, hopeless expectation of impending death: *R* v *Perry* [1909] 2 KB 697. *The exception is very narrow — it does not apply to all deathbed statements* — only those relating to the causes of M's death in trials for M's murder or manslaughter. The rationale seems to be that M will know that he has little to gain from lying when making such a statement. The main difficulty in relying on the exception will be to establish M's state of mind: again see *R* v *Perry*. The statement will only be admitted if M would have been able to give direct oral evidence of the facts (if alive), see *R* v *Pike* (1829) 3 C & P 598. It seems that if the statement is incomplete it may not be admitted: *Waugh* v *R* [1950] AC 203. For a recent application of the exception see *Nembhard* v *R* (1982) 74 Cr App R 144, PC. In this case a policeman was shot outside his house. His wife heard the shots and ran out to him. He said that he was going to die and named his attacker (N). The Privy Council held that the policemen's statement to his wife was admissible to show that N was the murderer.

Statements in the course of duty

Statements about acts made by the person who performed them in the course of duty are generally admitted (on M's death) to prove the performance of the act in question: see *Price* v *Torrington* (1703) 1 Salk 285 a breach of contract case relating to the supply of beer where entries in a ledger countersigned by a deceased deliveryman were properly received as evidence of the supply of beer. The statement should be contemporaneous with the act and the act in question should be M's. In *The Henry Coxon* (1878) 3 PD 156 a ship's log was not admitted because it was made two days after the acts in question and it referred to acts other than M's. The exception does not apply to a record of opinions see *R* v *McGuire* (1985) 81 Cr App R 323. The practical value of this exception has been greatly diminished by Criminal Justice Act 1988, s. 23 and s. 24, since most statements falling within the exception will be in documentary form.

Statements against proprietary or pecuniary interest

Statements against the proprietary or pecuniary interest of M are generally admitted (on M's death). The exception does *not* extend to statements which tend to incriminate M unless they are also against his proprietary or pecuniary interests: see the *Sussex Peerage Case* (1844) 11 Cl & F 85 and *B* v *Attorney-General* [1965] P 278. M must have known the facts on which the statement was based and that it was against his proprietary or pecuniary interests: see *Ward* v *Pitt & Co.* [1913] 2 KB 130. But it does not matter how significant the interest in question. Thus it seems any statement conceding indebtedness or the satisfaction of a debt owed to M would suffice. Where this exception applies it can be used to admit facts which were incidental to the statement against interest. Thus in *Higham* v *Ridgway* (1808) 10 East 109 a midwife's statement recording a payment for assisting at the birth of a child on a particular day was received as evidence of the date of birth of the child. However incidental matters are only admissible insofar as they are necessary to explain the nature of the statement against interest: see *R* v *Rogers* [1995] 1 Cr App R 374. R was charged *inter alia* with possession of heroin. A third party, X, stated, shortly before he (X) died, that he (X) was the owner of the heroin in question and that several guys were after him for the money for the heroin. It was held that X's statement was inadmissible. It did not fall under this exception because:

(a) as to the ownership of the heroin, this did not explain the indebtedness; and

(b) as to the indebtedness, it was not a true statement of indebtedness (there were several reasons why guys could be after him for the money).

9.2.1.3 Evidence given in former proceedings

At common law statements made by witnesses in former proceedings are generally inadmissible (despite their being made on oath). However, such statements are admissible if they were subject to cross-examination by the party against whom the statement is to be proved (X) so long as the witness is dead or unable to attend or give evidence or is kept out of the way by X. See *R* v *Thomson* [1982] QB 647 where a prosecution witness testified in the first trial but was unfit for the retrial. It was held that a transcript of the witness's evidence was admissible at retrial. This exception is likely to be of diminishing importance as the evidence will probably be recorded in documentary form and should therefore be admissible under Criminal Justice Act 1988 (see **9.2.2.1**).

9.2.1.4 Public documents (including published works and records)

This common law exception also applies in civil cases. It is specially preserved by Civil Evidence Act 1995, s. 7. The scope of this exception is narrow. For a document to qualify as a public document the facts recorded in it must be of public interest and concern and the person recording the facts must be under a public duty to do so and to satisfy himself of the truth of the facts. In *R* v *Halpin* [1975] QB 907, it was held that the exception applied to extracts from documents which had to be filed at the Companies Registry. However this exception would not generally apply to the 'internal' records of a company. Examples of public documents are given in s. 7 of the 1995 Act.

(**Note**: There are two very narrow exceptions relating to statements about reputation and family tradition which are of minimal relevance in criminal cases but which have been preserved in civil cases: see Civil Evidence Act 1995, s. 7(3).)

9.2.2 STATUTORY EXCEPTIONS

9.2.2.1 Criminal Justice Act 1988, sections 23 and 24

These sections create the most important statutory exceptions in criminal cases. However, they only apply to documentary hearsay (that is, the statement which is to be proved must be made in or contained in a document).

The words 'statement' and 'document' which appear frequently in ss. 23 and 24 are defined for the purposes of the Act in sch. 5 para. 2 (as amended by Civil Evidence Act 1995). 'Statement' means any representation of fact, however made. 'Document' means anything in which information of any description is recorded.

Even if the requirements of s. 23 and s. 24 are satisfied the court is given a specific discretion to exclude the statement in question by s. 25. Moreover by virtue of s. 26 if the document in question is prepared for the purposes of either pending or contemplated criminal proceedings or a criminal investigation it cannot be admitted under s. 23 or s. 24 without the leave of the court (see below at **9.2.2.2**).

Criminal Justice Act 1988, section 23

> *(1) Subject—*
> *(a) to subsection (4) below; and*
> *(b) to paragraph 1A of Schedule 2 to the Criminal Appeal Act 1968 (evidence given orally at original trial to be given orally at retrial),*
> *a statement made by a person in a document shall be admissible in criminal proceedings as evidence of any fact of which direct oral evidence by him would be admissible if—*
> *(i) the requirements of one of the paragraphs of subsection (2) below are satisfied; or*
> *(ii) the requirements of subsection (3) below are satisfied.*
> *(2) The requirements mentioned in subsection (1)(i) above are—*

> *(a) that the person who made the statement is dead or by reason of his bodily or mental condition unfit to attend as a witness;*
> *(b) that—*
> > *(i) the person who made the statement is outside the United Kingdom; and*
> > *(ii) it is not reasonably practicable to secure his attendance; or*
> *(c) that all reasonable steps have been taken to find the person who made the statement, but that he cannot be found.*
>
> *(3) The requirements mentioned in subsection (1)(ii) above are—*
> *(a) that the statement was made to a police officer or some other person charged with the duty of investigating offences or charging offenders; and*
> *(b) that the person who made it does not give oral evidence through fear or because he is kept out of the way.*
>
> *(4) Subsection 1 above does not render admissible a confession made by an accused person that would not be admissible under section 76 of the Police and Criminal Evidence Act 1984.*
>
> *(5) This section shall not apply to proceedings before a magistrates' court inquiring into an offence as examining justices.*

Commentary

The following is a preliminary guide to s. 23. In cases of doubt reference should be made to the exact wording of the section. Before a hearsay statement in a document can be admitted at trial under s. 23 three main questions must be answered in the affirmative:

(a) Was the hearsay statement *made* in a document? The document in question should be in such form as, 'I saw X punch Y', or 'I heard a gunshot at 11 p.m.' or 'Fred hit me', i.e. the 'eye-witness' (or, to be more exact, the person who claims any form of direct perception of the facts) should be the creator or author of the document. (But remember that a tape is a document so that an eye-witness who knowingly records his own statement of fact on a tape thereby makes a statement in a document.) Also the concept of agency would apply, e.g. if the eye-witness acknowledges (e.g. by signing) a document which is written at his dictation by another person. There may be circumstances in which it is not possible for the person dictating the statement to sign it. In *R v McGillivray* (1993) 97 Cr App R 232, the deceased victim of an arson attack could not sign a statement he dictated to a police officer because he was heavily bandaged. Nonetheless the statement could be admitted because there was evidence that the police officer taking the statement had noted the evidence and read it back to the victim, who had confirmed that what was recorded was accurate. That confirmation constituted acknowledgement notwithstanding the absence of a signature.

(b) Could the eye-witness/author have given direct oral evidence of the *facts* contained in the statement? If, for example, he would not have been a competent witness or the facts are themselves inadmissible, s. 23 will not overcome the problem.

(c) Does the eye-witness/author not give evidence for one of the reasons specified in s. 23? The reason must be proved by admissible evidence (beyond reasonable doubt for the prosecution and on the balance of probabilities for the defence). The s. 23 reasons for not giving evidence are:

   (i) He is dead or unfit (by reason of his bodily or mental condition) (s. 23(2)(a)). As to mental unfitness, see *R v Setz-Dempsey* [1994] Crim LR 123 in which the mental condition of the witness in question was an inability to recall events or give a coherent account of them under stress. The witness in question had made a statement to the police and had in fact attended at trial to give evidence and had been sworn. However, he could not recall the events in question during his examination in chief even though he was shown his statement to allow him to refresh his memory. The judge therefore allowed that statement to be admitted under s. 23(2)(a). The defence contended that the 'mental condition' must have the effect of preventing the witness attending to give evidence at all. The Court of Appeal rejected this argument, stating that s. 23(2)(a) also covered inability to give meaningful testimony when actually in court. Equally, where a witness was physically able to attend court to give evidence but that the stress of doing so presented a modest risk of potentially serious, permanent physical consequences, such a witness could properly be found to be unfit to attend: *R* v *Millett*, 21 July 2000, unreported.

(ii) (1) He is outside the UK *and* (2) it is not reasonably practicable to secure his attendance (s. 23(2)(b)).

So far as the first requirement is concerned, in *R* v *Jiminez-Paez* [1993] Crim LR 596, the Court of Appeal held that a consular official resident in the United Kingdom but diplomatically immune from being compelled to give evidence was not 'outside the United Kingdom' for the purposes of this section.

It is necessary for there to be evidence that it was not reasonably practicable to secure the attendance of the witness in question. In *R* v *Bray* (1988) 88 Cr App R 354 the maker of the statement, K, was an employee of a bank from which the defendant was alleged to have stolen a large sum of money. Only K could establish that the money had in fact been in the bank. Unfortunately at the time of trial the bank had sent K to Korea on business without informing the prosecution. Nevertheless the trial judge admitted K's statement. The Court of Appeal allowed the defendant's appeal. No evidence had been adduced by the prosecution that it was not reasonably practicable to secure the attendance of K.

It was also stated that reasonable practicability did not apply just in relation to the day upon which the witness was expected to attend. The question is whether, looking at the case as a whole, it would have been reasonably practicable to secure the attendance of the witness at all.

However the fact that it may be possible to secure the attendance of the witness on some later date does not mean that a trial judge must adjourn the case rather than admit the statement under s. 23. In *R* v *French* (1993) 97 Cr App R 421, the Court of Appeal stated that the date at which reasonable practicability ought to be considered was the date of the application to admit the statement (i.e. when the trial was due to go ahead). Judges should not, in such cases, be expected to look to the future to determine when attendance would be reasonably practicable.

In *R* v *Maloney* [1994] Crim LR 525, CA, it was stated that 'reasonably practicable' did not mean 'physically possible'. The reasonableness requirement meant that what was and was not practicable ought to be examined in the light of what would normally be expected of that party (having regard to his or her means and resources). In that case the police had attempted to secure the attendance of Greek naval cadets but had been informed that they were either at sea, on leave or at naval college and that a formal application would have to be made to secure their attendance. The judge had been satisfied that reasonable steps had been taken in the case and the Court of Appeal confirmed his decision. It was also noted in *French* that the words are 'reasonably practicable to secure' the attendance of the witness rather than 'reasonably practicable to attend'. In the case of a witness outside of the jurisdiction, although it might be reasonably practicable for the witness to attend, should he or she wish to do so, the fact that he or she does not so desire may render it not reasonably practicable to secure the attendance.

In *R* v *Hurst* [1995] 1 Cr App R 82, the Court of Appeal recognised that circumstances may occur at short notice which render it impractical to secure the attendance of the witness on the day when he is required to testify and when practicable arrangements have already been made for him to attend. However, if it were shown that no steps whatever had been taken to secure the attendance of the witness, the court could not be satisfied that it was not reasonably practical to secure his attendance. In *R* v *Castillo* [1996] 1 Cr App R 438, the Court of Appeal stated that the judge must consider the following general factors:

(a)   the importance of the evidence the witness could give;

(b)   the expense and inconvenience of securing attendance; and

(c)   the weight to be given to the reasons put forward for non-attendance.

In *R* v *Radak* [1999] 1 Cr App R 187 the Court of Appeal accepted that the witness's refusal to attend was sufficient to satisfy this condition.

(iii)   All reasonable steps have been taken to find him but he cannot be found (s. 23(2)(c)).

(iv)   Through fear or because he is kept out of the way (s. 23(3)) (this remarkably vague reason only applies when the statement was made to a police officer or some other person charged with the duty of investigating offences or charging offenders).

Section 23(3) 'does not give oral evidence through fear' has already spawned a considerable amount of case law.

In *R* v *Acton Justices, ex parte McMullen* (1990) 92 Cr App R 98, the Divisional Court rejected the argument that X's fear should be based on reasonable grounds but went on to say that the fear should be a consequence of the commission of the material offence or of something said or done subsequently in relation to that offence and the possibility of X testifying as to it. However, in *R* v *Martin* [1996] Crim LR 589 the Court of Appeal held that the words 'through fear' should not be treated as being qualified in any way (X claimed to have been put in fear by the presence of a silent stranger who loitered outside X's house). In *R* v *H* [2001] All ER (D) 150, CA, it was stated that fear should be judged at the stage the witness was due to give evidence, not on some early stage (such as when the incident causing fear arose).

X's out-of-court oral statement of his or her fear is admissible at common law under the *res gestae* exception (category 2): see above at **9.2.1.1** and *Neill* v *North Antrim Magistrates' Court* [1992] 1 WLR 1221. In *R* v *Belmarsh Magistrates' Court, ex parte Gilligan* [1998] 1 Cr App R 14, the Divisional Court suggested that a *written* statement by the witness claiming fear would not be sufficient. But the Court of Appeal in *R* v *Rutherford* [1998] Crim LR 490 seems to have accepted a written statement as sufficient evidence of fear (which would seem to be more in accordance with principle). Section 23(3) can be relied upon even where X has started to give oral evidence before 'drying up' through fear. In *R* v *Ashford Justices, ex parte Hilden* (1993) 96 Cr App R 92, the Divisional Court held that, in such a case, s. 23(3) would still apply. This was confirmed by the Court of Appeal in *R* v *Waters* [1997] Crim LR 823. It seems from the Court of Appeal's decision in *R* v *Wood and Fitzsimmons* [1998] Crim LR 213 that if X is present he may be cross-examined (in the absence of the jury) as to whether he really is in fear.

In *R* v *Holt* (1996) *The Times*, 31 October 1996, the Court of Appeal encouraged prosecutors to make wider use of s. 23(3) in cases where the victims of serious assaults were frightened to testify against the alleged assailant (the accused).

Where s. 23(3) is relied upon by the prosecution in a trial on indictment the judge should not indicate to the jury why X has not given evidence since this would prejudice the defendant: see *R* v *Churchill* [1993] Crim LR 285. See also *R* v *Jennings* [1995] Crim LR 810.

Even if these conditions are satisfied the court may still exclude the statement under s. 25 or s. 26. (See **9.2.2.2**, below.)

Criminal Justice Act 1988, section 24

(1)   Subject—

(a)   to subsections (3) and (4) below; and

(b)   to paragraph 1A of Schedule 2 to the Criminal Appeal Act 1968,

a statement in a document shall be admissible in criminal proceedings as evidence of any fact of which direct oral evidence would be admissible, if the following conditions are satisfied—

(i)   the document was created or received by a person in the course of a trade, business, profession or other occupation, or as the holder of a paid or unpaid office; and

(ii)   the information contained in the document was supplied by a person (whether or not the maker of the statement) who had, or may reasonably be supposed to have had, personal knowledge of the matters dealt with.

(2)   Subsection (1) above applies whether the information contained in the document was supplied directly or indirectly but, if it was supplied indirectly, only if each person through whom it was supplied received it—

(a)   in the course of a trade, business, profession or other occupation; or

(b)   as the holder of a paid or unpaid office.

(3)   Subsection (1) above does not render admissible a confession made by an accused person that would not be admissible under section 76 of the Police and Criminal Evidence Act 1984.

(4)   A statement prepared otherwise than in accordance with section 3 of the Criminal Justice (International Cooperation) Act 1990 or an order under paragraph 6 of Schedule 13 to this Act or under section 30 or 31 below for the purposes—

(a)   of pending or contemplated criminal proceedings; or

(b)   of a criminal investigation.

shall not be admissible by virtue of subsection (1) above unless—

(i)   the requirements of one of the paragraphs of subsection (2) of section 23 above are satisfied; or

(ii)   the requirements of subsection (3) of that section are satisfied; or

(iii)   the person who made the statement cannot reasonably be expected (having regard to the time which has elapsed since he made the statement and to all the circumstances) to have any recollection of the matters dealt with in the statement.

(5)   This section shall not apply to proceedings before a magistrates' court inquiring into an offence as examining justices.

Commentary

The following is a preliminary guide to s. 24. In cases of doubt reference should be made to the exact wording of the section. In general s. 24 lets in (subject to s. 25 or s. 26) any stage of hearsay if:

(a)   the document containing the statement which is to be proved was either *created* by a person in the course of a trade, business etc. (see s. 24(1)(c)(i)) or *received* by such person;

and

(b)   any intermediaries between the eye-witness and the creator of the document were acting in the course of a trade, business etc.;

and

(c)   it is a reasonable inference that the person claiming to be the eye-witness did indeed have personal knowledge of the facts in question (s. 24(1)(c)(ii)).

The key to s. 24 is the requirement that the creator or receiver of the document to be proved (and any intermediaries) are acting in the course of trade etc. In deciding whether this requirement is satisfied the court can draw inferences from the documents themselves and from the method or route by which the documents are produced: see *R* v *Foxley* [1995] 2 Cr App R 523.

There is no *general* requirement under s. 24 to show why the eye-witness does not give evidence (*cf.* s. 23).

However, if the document was prepared for the purposes of either pending or contemplated criminal proceedings *or* a criminal investigation then it must be shown so far as the maker of the statement is concerned either that one of the s. 23 reasons for the maker of the document not giving evidence exists *or* that he cannot reasonably be expected to have any recollection of the matters dealt with in the statement. (This reason is added by s. 24(4)(b)(iii).)

As to the meaning of the phrase 'maker of the statement' under s. 24(4), there is conflicting authority as to who this is. In *R* v *Carrington* (1994) 99 Cr App R 376, CA and in *Brown* v *Secretary of State for Social Security*, *The Times*, 7 December 1994, DC, it was taken to mean the person who created the document. However, in *R* v *Derodra* [2000] 1 Cr App R 41, CA, the maker of the statement was held to be the person who was the source of the information contained in the document. In that case the s. 24 document was a police computer record that had been compiled by a police officer on the basis of information supplied by a civilian. The civilian could not be found but the officer was available to give evidence at the trial. The Court of Appeal held that the document was properly admitted.

It would appear that the approach adopted in *Brown* accords with a literal interpretation of s. 24 while the approach adopted by *Derodra* accords with the purpose that the Act was clearly trying to achieve. The Court in *Derodra* drew some assistance from the fact that the police officer who created the document in that case was just someone who acted as a 'conduit pipe' for the information that originated with the civilian and ended up in the s. 24 document. For all evidential purposes it was the person who was the source of the information who mattered. The court drew assistance from factors that might lead to exclusion under ss. 25 and 26 (see **9.2.2.2**) such as the difficulties presented by the unavailability of the 'maker of the statement' to give evidence. It was considered relevant that if the 'maker of the statement' was merely someone who recorded information rather than the person who claimed to have the information itself then the lack of availability of the maker to be challenged or questioned on that information would be of far less significance.

Clearly, in addition to satisfying the tests laid down in s. 24(4), a document prepared as part of a criminal investigation or in contemplation of criminal proceedings will require leave under s. 26. As to the meaning of 'prepared for the purposes of criminal proceedings etc.' see *R* v *Bedi* (1992) 95 Cr App R 21. The fact that it is quite likely that a document will be used in criminal proceedings does *not* necessarily mean that it will be taken as prepared for such purposes. However most documents created by a police officer after the crime has been committed will fall into this category. In *R* v *Hogan* [1997] Crim LR 349 the Court of Appeal held that s. 24(4) applied to a custody record and property sheet (relating to the confiscation of a suspect's property). The court went on to hold that, even though s. 24(4) applied, the custody record etc. was still admissible under s. 24 because by virtue of s. 24(4)(b)(iii) the person who made the statement (the compiler of the custody record etc.) could not reasonably have been expected to have any recollection of the matters dealt with in the statement (the record had been compiled 16 months before it was produced in evidence).

In theory, it would be possible to convert a document created by X otherwise than in the course of trade etc. into a document which is nonetheless admissible (in principle) under s. 24 by the simple expedient of sending or giving it to a person, Y, who *is* acting in the course of trade etc. In such a case it may be argued that Y receives the document in the course of trade etc. But if, for example, Y receives the document unexpectedly, i.e. it is not a regular 'trade' communication, it is equally arguable that Y does not receive the document in the course of trade etc. Moreover, if X's purpose in creating and sending the document is to ensure that it becomes admissible under s. 24 it would be a document prepared for the purposes of criminal proceedings etc. and the requirements of s. 24(4) would need to be satisfied as regards X.

9.2.2.2 Provisions ancillary to sections 23 and 24

Criminal Justice Act 1988, sections 25 and 26

25.—*(1)   If, having regard to all the circumstances—*
  (a)   the Crown Court—
    (i)   on a trial on indictment;
    (ii)   on an appeal from a magistrates' court;
    (iii)   on the hearing of an application under section 6 of the Criminal Justice Act 1987 (applications for dismissal of charges of fraud transferred from magistrates' court to Crown Court); or
  (b)   the criminal division of the Court of Appeal; or
  (c)   a magistrates' court on a trial of an information,
is of the opinion that in the interests of justice a statement which is admissible by virtue of section 23 or 24 above nevertheless ought not to be admitted, it may direct that the statement shall not be admitted.

  (2)   Without prejudice to the generality of subsection (1) above, it shall be the duty of the court to have regard—
  (a)   to the nature and source of the document containing the statement and to whether or not, having regard to its nature and source and to any other circumstances that appear to the court to be relevant, it is likely that the document is authentic;
  (b)   to the extent to which the statement appears to supply evidence which would otherwise not be readily available;
  (c)   to the relevance of the evidence that it appears to supply to any issue which is likely to have to be determined in the proceedings; and
  (d)   to any risk, having regard in particular to whether it is likely to be possible to controvert the statement if the person making it does not attend to give oral evidence in the proceedings, that its admission or exclusion will result in unfairness to the accused or, if there is more than one, to any of them.

26.   *Where a statement which is admissible in criminal proceedings by virtue of section 23 or 24 above appears to the court to have been prepared, otherwise than in accordance with section 3 of the Criminal Justice (International Cooperation) Act 1990 or an order under paragraph 6 of Schedule 13 to this Act or under section 30 or 31 below, for the purposes—*
  (a)   of pending or contemplated criminal proceedings; or
  (b)   of a criminal investigation,
the statement shall not be given in evidence in any criminal proceedings without the leave of the court, and the court shall not give leave unless it is of the opinion that the statement ought to be admitted in the interests of justice; and in considering whether its admission would be in the interests of justice, it shall be the duty of the court to have regard—
  (i)   to the contents of the statement;
  (ii)   to any risk, having regard in particular to whether it is likely to be possible to controvert the statement if the person making it does not attend to give oral evidence in the proceedings, that its admission or exclusion will result in unfairness to the accused or, if there is more than one, to any of them; and
  (iii)   to any other circumstances that appear to the court to be relevant.

Commentary
The difference between s. 25 and s. 26 was explained in *R* v *Cole* [1990] 2 All ER 108:

By s. 25 if, having regard to all the circumstances, the court is of the opinion that a statement, admissible by virtue of ss. 23 or 24, in the interests of justice ought not to be admitted, it may direct that it be not admitted. In short, the court must be made to hold the opinion that the statement ought not to be admitted. By contrast, under s. 26, when a statement is admissible by virtue of ss. 23 and 24 and was prepared for the purposes of criminal proceedings, the statement shall not be given in evidence unless the court is of the opinion that the statement ought to be admitted in the interests of justice. The court is not to admit the statement unless made to hold the opinion that it ought to be admitted.

The following points about the courts' approach to ss. 25 and 26 have emerged:

(a) Where there are multiple defendants it may be difficult to determine where the 'interests of justice' lie. In *R* v *Duffy* [1999] 1 Cr App R 307, CA, two defendants, D and H, were charged with murder and robbery of an elderly man. D alleged she had not been involved in the attack and had attempted to dissuade H from killing the victim. This account was supported by a police interview of the victim's son admissible under s. 23. However, counsel for H objected to the interview under s. 26 as it would be unfair to H to admit evidence implicating him in the attack that would not then be subject to cross-examination. The trial judge declined to allow the interview evidence to be admitted and D appealed. The Court of Appeal upheld the appeal. When considering the operation of s. 26, the affect of the evidence on H was only one of the factors that the court should consider. In doing so, a distinction had to be drawn between the prejudicial impact of the evidence on H's defence and any unfairness to him. In this case admission would not be unfair to H even if it undermined and therefore prejudiced his defence. Although he could not cross-examine the maker of the statement, it would still have been possible for him to controvert the statement by giving evidence himself (which he chose not to do). In contrast, it was unfair to D for the interview not to be admitted because it deprived her of support for her defence.

(b) The fact that it will be difficult to controvert the statement without the testimony of the accused is not in itself a reason for refusing leave (or exercising the discretion to exclude): see *R* v *Cole* (supra) and *R* v *Gokal* [1997] 2 Cr App R 266.

(c) An important factor is the quality of the evidence contained in the statement, i.e. how credible and complete is it? See *Scott* v *R* [1989] AC 1242 *per* Lord Griffiths (approved in *R* v *Cole*) and *R* v *Patel* (1993) 97 Cr App R 294 where the Court of Appeal upheld a trial judge's decision to refuse leave under s. 26 where the statement by an alibi witness, X (who was outside the UK etc.), was nothing more than an assertion that X could confirm the alibi. See also *R* v *Irish* [1994] Crim LR 922. In *R* v *Fairfax* [1995] Crim LR 949 the Court of Appeal, when upholding leave to admit identification evidence in a written statement, stressed the clarity and precision of the evidence. In *Neill* v *North Antrim Magistrates' Court* [1992] 1 WLR 1221, the House of Lords suggested that where identification evidence forms the principal element in the prosecution case the court should, in general, be reluctant to admit it under s. 23 or s. 24.

(d) The courts have taken conflicting approaches in respect of the importance of the evidence in the s. 23 or s. 24 statement in the context of the case. Some courts have indicated a reluctance to grant leave unless there is other evidence relating to the issues referred to in the statement: see *R* v *Cole* and *R* v *French* (1993) 97 Cr App R 421. However, it is now clear that there is no automatic rule to this effect and the Court of Appeal has approved the admission of s. 23 statements even when they are of central importance to the case: see *R* v *Grafton* [1995] Crim LR 61, *R* v *Fairfax* [1995] Crim LR 949 and *R* v *Dragic* [1996] 2 Cr App R 232. However, the courts are likely to seek guidance from the Commission and European Court of Human Rights decisions on the extent to which hearsay exceptions run counter to Article 6(3)(d) of the European Convention for the Protection of Human Rights and Fundamental Freedoms (which provides for the accused's right to cross-examine the witnesses against him). In *R* v *Thomas* [1998] Crim LR 887 the Court of Appeal referred with approval to decisions by the Commission which placed some reliance on the fact that the statement in question was not the only evidence on the point at issue. Also, in *R v Radak* [1999] 1 Cr App R 187, the Court of Appeal, in holding that a s. 23 statement should have been excluded under s. 26, seems to have been influenced *to an extent* by the fact that the statement was an essential link in the prosecution case.

Note: A judge who decides to admit a s. 23 or s. 24 statement must direct the jury that the evidence has not been tested in cross-examination: see *R v Cole*, *R v Kennedy* [1994] Crim LR 50 and *R v Curry*, *The Times*, 23 March 1998. Again the Commission and European Court of Human Rights cases on Article 6(3)(d) may be relevant. The Commission has approved a direction to the jury (in respect of a s. 23 statement) that they should attach *much less weight* to statements which had not been tested by cross-examination. However, it is arguable that this goes too far in terms of usurping the jury's role in weighing *admissible* evidence and at the time of writing this does not represent the usual direction on s. 23 statements which is still that which was stated in *Cole*.

Criminal Justice Act 1988, section 27

Where a statement contained in a document is admissible as evidence in criminal proceedings, it may be proved—
(a)   by the production of that document; or
(b)   (whether or not that document is still in existence) by the production of a copy of that document, or of the material part of it,
authenticated in such manner as the court may approve; and it is immaterial for the purposes of this subsection how many removes there are between a copy and the original.

Note: If both the original and copies are destroyed, oral evidence as to the contents of the document may be admissible at common law: see *R v Nazeer* [1998] Crim LR 750.

Criminal Justice Act 1988, section 28

(1)   Nothing in this part of this Act shall prejudice—
(a)   the admissibility of a statement not made by a person while giving oral evidence in court which is admissible otherwise than by virtue of this part of this Act; or
(b)   any power of a court to exclude at its discretion a statement admissible by virtue of this part of this Act.
(2)   Schedule 2 to this Act shall have effect for the purpose of supplementing this part of this Act.

SCHEDULE 2 Documentary Evidence — Supplementary

1.   Where a statement is admitted as evidence in criminal proceedings by virtue of part II of this Act—
(a)   any evidence which, if the person making the statement had been called as a witness, would have ben admissible as relevant to his credibility as a witness shall be admissible for that purpose in those proceedings;
(b)   evidence may, with the leave of the court, be given of any matter which, if that person had been called as a witness, could have been put to him in cross-examination as relevant to his credibility as a witness but of which evidence could not have been adduced by the cross-examining party; and
(c)   evidence tending to prove that that person, whether before or after making the statement, made (whether orally or not) some other statement which is inconsistent with it shall be admissible for the purpose of showing that he has contradicted himself.

2.   A statement which is given in evidence by virtue of part II of this Act shall not be capable of corroborating evidence given by the person making it.

3. In estimating the weight, if any, to be attached to such a statement regard shall be had to all the circumstances from which any inference can reasonably be drawn as to its accuracy or otherwise.

4. Without prejudice to the generality of any enactment conferring power to make them—
- *(a) Crown Court Rules;*
- *(b) Criminal Appeal Rules; and*
- *(c) rules under section 144 of the Magistrates' Courts Act 1980,*

may make such provision as appears to the authority making any of them to be necessary or expedient for the purposes of part II of this Act.

5. Expressions used in part II of this Act and in part I of the Civil Evidence Act 1968 are to be construed in part II of this Act in accordance with section 10 of that Act.

6. In part II of this Act 'confession' has the meaning assigned to it by section 82 of the Police and Criminal Evidence Act 1984.

Commentary

Where the accused, in reliance on para. 1 (above), attacks the character of a witness whose statement is admitted pursuant to s. 23 or 24, the accused may lose the shield under Criminal Evidence Act 1898, s. 1(3) — see *R* v *Miller* [1997] 2 Cr App R 178 and **7.3.4** (above). The opportunity of attaching the credibility of the 'absent' witness is, however, an important factor in ensuring that admitting witness statements pursuant to s. 23 does not conflict with Article 6 of the Convention (the right to a fair trial): see *R* v *Thomas* [1998] Crim LR 887.

Criminal Justice Act 1988, sections 30 and 31 and Criminal Justice (International Cooperation) Act 1990, section 3

These sections are referred to in Criminal Justice Act 1988. ss. 24(4) and 26. They deal with a variety of specific forms of documentary evidence. The Criminal Justice Act 1988, s. 30, deals with evidence in expert reports (see **13.1.4.2**) and s. 31 deals with glossaries. The Criminal Justice (International Cooperation) Act 1990, s. 3, is concerned with letters of request to foreign authorities.

Criminal Appeal Act 1968, schedule 2, paragraph 1A

(See Criminal Justice Act 1988, ss. 23(1)(b) and 24(1)(b).) This makes separate provision for documentary evidence at re-trials ordered by the Court of Appeal.

9.2.2.3 Bankers' Books Evidence Act 1879, sections 3 and 4

(This statutory exception also applies in civil cases.)

Bankers' Books Evidence Act 1879, s. 3, provides that:

a copy of any entry in a banker's book shall in all legal proceedings be received as prima facie evidence of such entry, and of the matters, transactions, and accounts therein recorded.

Section 4 adds that the book in question must have been one of the ordinary books of the bank, that the entry was made in the usual and ordinary course of business and that the book is in the custody or control of the bank. Important considerations are what is meant by 'bank' and what is meant by 'bankers' book'. As originally enacted the definitions restricted the utility of the exception given the development of the banking system (especially in recent years). The Banking Act 1987 amended the 1879 Act to provide that 'bank' refers to an institution authorised under Banking Act 1987 or a municipal bank within the meaning of that Act, a trustee savings bank, the National Savings Bank and the Post Office in the exercise of its powers to provide banking services.

'Bankers' books' include ledgers, day books, cash books, account books and other records used in the ordinary business of the bank, whether these records are in written form or are kept on microfilm, magnetic tape or any other form of mechanical or electronic data retrieval mechanism.

Even these extended definitions cause some problems. In *Williams* v *Williams* [1988] QB 161 it was held that paying-in slips and paid cheques were not entries in bankers' books for the purposes of the 1879 Act. This case actually related to another aspect of the Act, namely, the very wide powers given in s. 7 for the court to order that a party to legal proceedings be at liberty to inspect and take copies of bankers' books for the purposes of such proceedings.

9.2.2.4 Written statements and depositions in committal proceedings: Magistrates' Courts Act 1980, ss. 5A–5F

5A.—*(1)   Evidence falling within subsection (2) below, and only that evidence, shall be admissible by a magistrates' court inquiring into an offence as examining justices.*
(2)   Evidence falls within this subsection if it—
(a)   is tendered by or on behalf of the prosecutor, and
(b)   falls within subsection (3) below.
(3)   The following evidence falls within this subsection—
(a)   written statements complying with section 5B below;
. . .
(c)   depositions complying with section 5C below;
(d)   . . .
(e)   statements complying with section 5D below;
(f)   documents falling within section 5E below.
(4)   In this section 'document' means anything in which information of any description is recorded.

5B.—*(1)   For the purposes of section 5A above a written statement complies with this section if—*
. . .
(2)   . . .
(a)   the statement purports to be signed by the person who made it;
(b)   the statement contains a declaration by that person to the effect that it is true to the best of his knowledge and belief and that he made the statement knowing that, if it were tendered in evidence, he would be liable to prosecution if he wilfully stated in it anything which he knew to be false or did not believe to be true;
(c)   before the statement is tendered in evidence a copy of the statement is given, by or on behalf of the prosecutor, to each of the other parties to the proceedings.

5C.—*(1)   For the purposes of section 5A above a deposition complies with this section if—*
(a)   a copy of it is sent to the prosecutor under section 97A(9) below,
(b)   the condition falling within subsection (2) below is met, . . .
(2)   The condition falling within this subsection is that before the magistrates' court begins to inquire into the offence concerned as examining justices a copy of the deposition is given, by or on behalf of the prosecutor, to each of the other parties to the proceedings.

5D.—*(1)   For the purposes of section 5A above a statement complies with this section if the conditions falling within subsections (2) to (4) below are met.*
(2)   The condition falling within this subsection is that, before the committal proceedings begin, the prosecutor notifies the magistrates' court and each of the other parties to the proceedings that he believes—
(a)   that the statement might by virtue of section 23 or 24 of the Criminal Justice Act 1988 (statements in certain documents) be admissible as evidence if the case came to trial, and
(b)   that the statement would not be admissible as evidence otherwise than by virtue of section 23 or 24 of that Act if the case came to trial.
(3)   The condition falling within this subsection is that—

    (a) *the prosecutor's belief is based on information available to him at the time he makes the notification,*

    (b) *he has reasonable grounds for his belief, and*

    (c) *he gives the reasons for his belief when he makes the notification.*

  (4) *The condition falling within this subsection is that when the court or a party is notified as mentioned in subsection (2) above a copy of the statement is given, by or on behalf of the prosecutor, to the court or the party concerned.*

5E.—(1) *The following documents fall within this section—*

    (a) *any document which by virtue of any enactment is evidence in proceedings before a magistrates' court inquiring into an offence as examining justices;*

    (b) *any document which by virtue of any enactment is admissible, or may be used, or is to be admitted or received, in or as evidence in such proceedings;*

    (c) *any document which by virtue of any enactment may be considered in such proceedings;*

    (d) *any document whose production constitutes proof in such proceedings by virtue of any enactment;*

    (e) *any document by the production of which evidence may be given in such proceedings by virtue of any enactment.*

Commentary

One of the more important changes introduced by Criminal Procedure and Investigations Act 1996 related to the form of committal proceedings. These are now always based on written evidence produced by the prosecution (so long as the investigation did not *precede* 1 April 1997). Sections 5A to 5F bring this change into effect. Section 5C is a major innovation. It allows for evidence to be given by way of a deposition taken pursuant to Magistrates' Courts Act 1980, s. 97A (*in advance of the committal*) from a person who is likely to be able to make a written statement for the prosecution containing material evidence *but who will not do so voluntarily.* If a magistrate is satisfied of these very broad conditions, then a summons and, if necessary, a warrant, can be issued to secure that person's attendance. The procedure does not require a court to be convened for the deposition to be taken. Moreover, neither the accused nor his or her legal advisers need be present, nor even notified that the deposition is being taken.

Section 5D allows examining justices to rely on first-hand hearsay which *might* be admissible at trial by virtue of Criminal Justice Act 1988, s. 23 or 24 (see **9.2.2.1**). The prosecutor need not prove that the conditions laid down in s. 23 or 24 are satisfied, but must notify the examining justices of *his belief* that the statement will be admissible under s. 23 or 24. Such belief must be based on reasonable grounds.

(**Note**: Sections 5A to 5F have no direct effect on the admissibility of documentary evidence *at trial* (i.e. they are only applicable to committals). However, by virtue of Criminal Procedure and Investigations Act 1996, sch. 2, paras 1 and 2, the documentary evidence admissible at the committal under ss. 5A–5C, i.e. witness statements and depositions, is rendered *potentially* admissible at trial. These provisions are set out in full below.)

SCHEDULE 2 Statements and depositions

1.—(1) *Sub-paragraph (2) applies if—*

    (a) *a written statement has been admitted in evidence in proceedings before a magistrates' court inquiring into an offence as examining justices,*

    (b) *in those proceedings a person has been committed for trial,*

    (c) *for the purposes of section 5A of the Magistrates' Courts Act 1980 the statement complied with section 5B of that Act prior to the committal for trial,*

    (d) *the statement purports to be signed by a justice of the peace, and*

    (e) *sub-paragraph (3) does not prevent sub-paragraph (2) applying.*

  (2) *Where this sub-paragraph applies the statement may without further proof be read as evidence on the trial of the accused, whether for the offence for which he was*

committed for trial or for any other offence arising out of the same transaction or set of circumstances.

   (3) Sub-paragraph (2) does not apply if—

      (a) it is proved that the statement was not signed by the justice by whom it purports to have been signed,

      (b) the court of trial at its discretion orders that sub-paragraph (2) shall not apply, or

      (c) a party to the proceedings objects to sub-paragraph (2) applying.

   (4) If a party to the proceedings objects to sub-paragraph (2) applying the court of trial may order that the objection shall have no effect if the court considers it to be in the interests of justice so to order.

   2.—*(1) Sub-paragraph (2) applies if—*

      (a) in pursuance of section 97A of the Magistrates' Courts Act 1980 (summons or warrant to have evidence taken as a deposition etc.) a person has had his evidence taken as a deposition for the purposes of proceedings before a magistrates' court inquiring into an offence as examining justices,

      (b) the deposition has been admitted in evidence in those proceedings,

      (c) in those proceedings a person has been committed for trial,

      (d) for the purposes of section 5A of the Magistrates' Courts Act 1980 the deposition complied with section 5C of that Act prior to the committal for trial,

      (e) the deposition purports to be signed by the justice before whom it purports to have been taken, and

      (f) sub-paragraph (3) does not prevent sub-paragraph (2) applying.

   (2) Where this sub-paragraph applies the deposition may without further proof be read as evidence on the trial of the accused, whether for the offence for which he was committed for trial or for any other offence arising out of the same transaction or set of circumstances.

   (3) Sub-paragraph (2) does not apply if—

      (a) it is proved that the deposition was not signed by the justice by whom it purports to have been signed,

      (b) the court of trial at its discretion orders that sub-paragraph (2) shall not apply, or

      (c) a party to the proceedings objects to sub-paragraph (2) applying.

   (4) If a party to the proceedings objects to sub-paragraph (2) applying the court of trial may order that the objection shall have no effect if the court considers it to be in the interests of justice so to order.

Commentary

The effect of these provisions is that witness statements and depositions admitted in committal proceedings (under ss. 5A–5C) are *potentially* admissible in a subsequent trial of the accused for the offence for which he was committed or a related offence. However, paras 1(3) and 2(3) give the accused the opportunity to object to the admissibility of such statements/depositions (the objection must be given in writing to the prosecutor and the Crown Court within 14 days of committal (Magistrates' Court Rules, r. 8). The fact that an objection is made does not necessarily preclude admissibility. Paragraphs 1(4) and 2(4) expressly provide that the court may override the objection if it considers it to be in the interests of justice. To this extent ss. 5A–5C create very broad exceptions to the hearsay rule not just for committals but for trial also (however it seems likely that courts will be reluctant to override defence objections to the documentary evidence described in ss. 5A–5C particularly in the light of statements made in Parliament when Criminal Procedure and Investigations Act 1996 was enacted).

9.2.2.5   **Miscellaneous statutory exceptions depending on the consent of the defence or prosecution**

Criminal Justice Act 1967, section 9 (as amended by Children and Young Persons Act 1969)

   (1) In any criminal proceedings, other than committal proceedings, a written statement by any person shall, if such of the conditions mentioned in the next

following subsection as are applicable are satisfied, be admissible as evidence to the like extent as oral evidence to the like effect by that person.

(2) The said conditions are—

(a) the statement purports to be signed by the person who made it;

(b) the statement contains a declaration by that person to the effect that it is true to the best of his knowledge and belief and that he made the statement knowing that, if it were tendered in evidence, he would be liable to prosecution, if he wilfully stated in it anything which he knew to be false or did not believe to be true;

(c) before the hearing at which the statement is tendered in evidence, a copy of the statement is served, by or on behalf of the party proposing to tender it, on each of the other parties to the proceedings; and

(d) none of the other parties or their solicitors, within seven days from the service of the copy of the statement, serves a notice on the party so proposing objecting to the statement being tendered in evidence under this section:

Provided that the conditions mentioned in paragraphs (c) and (d) of this subsection shall not apply if the parties agree before or during the hearing that the statement shall be so tendered.

(3) The following provisions shall also have effect in relation to any written statement tendered in evidence under this section, that is to say—

(a) if the statement is made by a person under the age of 18, it shall give his age;

(b) if it is made by a person who cannot read it, it shall be read to him before he signs it and shall be accompanied by a declaration by the person who so read the statement to the effect that it was so read; and

(c) if it refers to any other document as an exhibit, the copy served on any other party to the proceedings under paragraph (c) of the last foregoing subsection shall be accompanied by a copy of that document or by such information as may be necessary in order to enable the party on whom it is served to inspect that document or a copy thereof.

(3A) In the case of a statement which indicates in pursuance of subsection (3)(a) of this subsection that the person making it has not attained the age of 14, subsection (2)(b) of this section shall have effect as if for the words from 'made' onwards there were substituted the word 'understands the importance of telling the truth in it'.

Theft Act 1968, section 27(4)

Statutory declarations relating to goods in transmission (whether by post or otherwise) e.g. that a particular parcel did not arrive.

9.3 Hearsay Exceptions in Civil Cases

9.3.1 CIVIL EVIDENCE ACT 1995

The Civil Evidence Act 1995 creates a massive exception to the hearsay rule in civil proceedings. Section 11 of the Act defines civil proceedings as civil proceedings, before any tribunal, in relation to which the strict rules of evidence apply, whether as a matter of law or by agreement of the parties. The Act also preserves certain common law and statutory exceptions. Because of their importance the main provisions of the 1995 Act are set out here in full. The Civil Evidence Act 1968, Part I (which previously governed the use of hearsay evidence in most types of of civil case), is repealed by Civil Evidence Act 1995 (by virtue of s. 15(2) and sch. 2). The 1995 Act therefore creates a complete code as regards hearsay in civil cases (except for hearsay *already* admissible by virtue of any provision apart from the 1995 Act — see s. 1(3) and (4) and, generally, **9.3.2**).

1.—(1) In civil proceedings evidence shall not be excluded on the ground that it is hearsay.

(2) In this Act—

(a) 'hearsay' means a statement made otherwise than by a person while giving oral evidence in the proceedings which is tendered as evidence of the matters stated; and

(b) references to hearsay include hearsay of whatever degree.

(3) Nothing in this Act affects the admissibility of evidence admissible apart from this section.

(4) The provisions of sections 2 to 6 (safeguards and supplementary provisions relating to hearsay evidence) do not apply in relation to hearsay evidence admissible apart from this section, notwithstanding that it may also be admissible by virtue of this section.

2.—*(1) A party proposing to adduce hearsay evidence in civil proceedings shall, subject to the following provisions of this section, give to the other party or parties to the proceedings—*

    (a) such notice (if any) of that fact, and

    (b) on request, such particulars of or relating to the evidence,

as is reasonable and practicable in the circumstances for the purpose of enabling him or them to deal with any matters arising from its being hearsay.

    (2) Provision may be made by rules of court—

    (a) specifying classes of proceedings or evidence in relation to which sub-section (1) does not apply, and

    (b) as to the manner in which (including the time within which) the duties imposed by that subsection are to be complied with in the cases where it does apply.

    (3) Subsection (1) may also be excluded by agreement of the parties; and compliance with the duty to give notice may in any case be waived by the person to whom notice is required to be given.

    (4) A failure to comply with subsection (1), or with rules under subsection (2)(b), does not affect the admissibility of the evidence but may be taken into account by the court—

    (a) in considering the exercise of its powers with respect to the course of proceedings and costs, and

    (b) as a matter adversely affecting the weight to be given to the evidence in accordance with section 4.

3. *Rules of court may provide that where a party to civil proceedings adduces hearsay evidence of a statement made by a person and does not call that person as a witness, any other party to the proceedings may, with the leave of the court, call that person as a witness and cross-examine him on the statement as if he had been called by the first-mentioned party and as if the hearsay statement were his evidence-in-chief.*

4.—*(1) In estimating the weight (if any) to be given to hearsay evidence in civil proceedings the court shall have regard to any circumstances from which any inference can reasonably be drawn as to the reliability or otherwise of the evidence.*

    (2) Regard may be had, in particular, to the following—

    (a) whether it would have been reasonable and practicable for the party by whom the evidence was adduced to have produced the maker of the original statement as a witness;

    (b) whether the original statement was made contemporaneously with the occurrence or existence of the matters stated;

    (c) whether the evidence involves multiple hearsay;

    (d) whether any person involved had any motive to conceal or misrepresent matters;

    (e) whether the original statement was an edited account, or was made in collaboration with another or for a particular purpose;

    (f) whether the circumstances in which the evidence is adduced as hearsay are such as to suggest an attempt to prevent proper evaluation of its weight.

5.—*(1) Hearsay evidence shall not be admitted in civil proceedings if or to the extent that it is shown to consist of, or to be proved by means of, a statement made by a person who at the time he made the statement was not competent as a witness.*

For this purpose 'not competent as a witness' means suffering from such mental or physical infirmity, or lack of understanding, as would render a person incompetent as a witness in civil proceedings; but a child shall be treated as competent as a witness if he satisfies the requirements of section 96(2)(a) and (b) of the Children Act 1989 (conditions for reception of unsworn evidence of child).

(2) Where in civil proceedings hearsay evidence is adduced and the maker of the original statement, or of any statement relied upon to prove another statement, is not called as a witness—

(a) evidence which if he had been so called would be admissible for the purpose of attacking or supporting his credibility as a witness is admissible for that purpose in the proceedings; and

(b) evidence tending to prove that, whether before or after he made the statement, he made any other statement inconsistent with it is admissible for the purpose of showing that he had contradicted himself.

Provided that evidence may not be given of any matter of which, if he had been called as a witness and had denied that matter in cross-examination, evidence could not have been adduced by the cross-examining party.

6.—*(1) Subject as follows, the provisions of this Act as to hearsay evidence in civil proceedings apply equally (but with any necessary modifications) in relation to a previous statement made by a person called as a witness in the proceedings.*

(2) A party who has called or intends to call a person as a witness in civil proceedings may not in those proceedings adduce evidence of a previous statement made by that person, except—

(a) with the leave of the court, or

(b) for the purpose of rebutting a suggestion that his evidence has been fabricated.

This shall not be construed as preventing a witness statement (that is, a written statement of oral evidence which a party to the proceedings intends to lead) from being adopted by a witness in giving evidence or treated as his evidence.

(3) Where in the case of civil proceedings section 3, 4 or 5 of the Criminal Procedure Act 1865 applies, which make provision as to—

(a) how far a witness may be discredited by the party producing him,

(b) the proof of contradictory statements made by a witness, and

(c) cross-examination as to previous statements in writing,

this Act does not authorise the adducing of evidence of a previous inconsistent or contradictory statement otherwise than in accordance with those sections.

This is without prejudice to any provision made by rules of court under section 3 above (power to call witness for cross-examination on hearsay statement).

(4) Nothing in this Act affects any of the rules of law as to the circumstances in which, where a person called as a witness in civil proceedings is cross-examined on a document used by him to refresh his memory, that document may be made evidence in the proceedings.

(5) Nothing in this section shall be construed as preventing a statement of any description referred to above from being admissible by virtue of section 1 as evidence of the matters stated.

7.—*(1) The common law rule effectively preserved by section 9(1) and (2)(a) of the Civil Evidence Act 1968 (admissibility of admissions adverse to a party) is superseded by the provisions of this Act.*

(2) The common law rules effectively preserved by section 9(1) and (2)(b) to (d) of the Civil Evidence Act 1968, that is, any rule of law whereby in civil proceedings—

(a) published works dealing with matters of a public nature (for example, histories, scientific works, dictionaries and maps) are admissible as evidence of facts of a public nature stated in them,

(b) public documents (for example, public registers, and returns made under public authority with respect to matters of public interest) are admissible as evidence of facts stated in them, or

(c) records (for example, the records of certain courts, treaties, Crown grants, pardons and commissions) are admissible as evidence of facts stated in them,

shall continue to have effect.

(3) The common law rules effectively preserved by section 9(3) and (4) of the Civil Evidence Act 1968, that is, any rule of law whereby in civil proceedings—

(a) evidence of a person's reputation is admissible for the purpose of proving his good or bad character, or

(b) evidence of reputation or family tradition is admissible—

(i) for the purpose of proving or disproving pedigree or the existence of a marriage, or

(ii) for the purpose of proving or disproving the existence of any public or general right or of identifying any person or thing,

shall continue to have effect in so far as they authorise the court to treat such evidence as proving or disproving that matter.

Where any such rule applies, reputation or family tradition shall be treated for the purposes of this Act as a fact and not as a statement or multiplicity of statements about the matter in question.

(4) The words in which a rule of law mentioned in this section is described are intended only to identify the rule and shall not be construed as altering it in any way.

8.—(1) Where a statement contained in a document is admissible as evidence in civil proceedings, it may be proved—

(a) by the production of that document, or

(b) whether or not that document is still in existence, by the production of a copy of that document or of the material part of it,

authenticated in such manner as the court may approve.

(2) It is immaterial for this purpose how many removes there are between a copy and the original.

9.—(1) A document which is shown to form part of the records of a business or public authority may be received in evidence in civil proceedings without further proof.

(2) A document shall be taken to form part of the records of a business or public authority if there is produced to the court a certificate to that effect signed by an officer of the business or authority to which the records belong.

For this purpose—

(a) a document purporting to be a certificate signed by an officer of a business or public authority shall be deemed to have been duly given by such an officer and signed by him; and

(b) a certificate shall be treated as signed by a person if it purports to bear a facsimile of his signature.

(3) The absence of an entry in the records of a business or public authority may be proved in civil proceedings by affidavit of an officer of the business or authority to which the records belong.

(4) In this section—

'records' means records in whatever form;

'business' includes any activity regularly carried on over a period of time, whether for profit or not, by any body (whether corporate or not) or by an individual;

'officer' includes any person occupying a responsible position in relation to the relevant activities of the business or public authority or in relation to its records; and

'public authority' includes any public or statutory undertaking, any government department and any person holding office under Her Majesty.

(5) The court may, having regard to the circumstances of the case, direct that all or any of the above provisions of this section do not apply in relation to a particular document or record, or description of documents or records.

10.—(1) The actuarial tables (together with explanatory notes) for use in personal injury and fatal accident cases issued from time to time by the Government Actuary's Department are admissible in evidence for the purpose of assessing, in an action for personal injury, the sum to be awarded as general damages for future pecuniary loss.

(2) They may be proved by the production of a copy published by Her Majesty's Stationery Office.

(3) For the purposes of this section—

(a) 'personal injury' includes any disease and any impairment of a person's physical or mental condition; and

(b) 'action for personal injury' includes an action brought by virtue of the Law Reform (Miscellaneous Provisions) Act 1934 or the Fatal Accidents Act 1976.

11. In this Act 'civil proceedings' means civil proceedings, before any tribunal, in relation to which the strict rules of evidence apply, whether as a matter of law or by agreement of the parties.

References to 'the court' and 'rules of court' shall be construed accordingly.

12.—(1) Any power to make rules of court regulating the practice or procedure of the court in relation to civil proceedings includes power to make such provision as may be necessary or expedient for carrying into effect the provisions of this Act.

(2) Any rules of court made for the purposes of this Act as it applies in relation to proceedings in the High Court apply, except in so far as their operation is excluded by agreement, to arbitration proceedings to which this Act applies, subject to such modifications as may be appropriate.

Any question arising as to what modifications are appropriate shall be determined, in default of agreement, by the arbitrator or umpire, as the case may be.

13. In this Act—

'civil proceedings' has the meaning given by section 11 and 'court' and 'rules of court' shall be construed in accordance with that section;

'document' means anything in which information of any description is recorded, and 'copy', in relation to a document, means anything onto which information recorded in the document has been copied, by whatever means and whether directly or indirectly;

'hearsay' shall be construed in accordance with section 1(2);

'oral evidence' includes evidence which, by reason of a defect of speech or hearing, a person called as a witness gives in writing or by signs;

'the original statement', in relation to hearsay evidence, means the underlying statement (if any) by—

(a) in the case of evidence of fact, a person having personal knowledge of that fact, or

(b) in the case of evidence of opinion, the person whose opinion it is; and

'statement' means any representation of fact or opinion, however made.

Commentary

In general the provisions of the Act are self-explanatory. Clearly the Act has had a major impact. In summary, the main effect is that by virtue of s. 1, in civil proceedings, a hearsay statement (whether oral or documentary and at whatever stage of hearsay) *will* be admissible unless it falls to be excluded under a distinct exclusionary rule. Thus the Act prevents the hearsay nature of evidence being the reason it cannot be admitted. This does not mean that *all* hearsay evidence is admissible. If the evidence is inadmissible because of some other rule of evidence (such as privilege (see **Chapter 14**) or the lack of competence of the witness (see s. 5(1) of the Act)) this Act will not render such evidence admissible.

Even though hearsay evidence is now generally admissible it is still necessary to determine whether the evidence is hearsay or original evidence and whether it would be admissible under some other provision (see **9.3.2**) in any event, because:

(a) there are notice requirements under s. 2 for all hearsay evidence admissible under the 1995 Act and sanctions for failure to comply with these requirements; and

(b) for some hearsay evidence leave is still required before it will be admissible under the 1995 Act (s. 6).

The requirement of leave

Hearsay evidence is admissible without leave in all cases except those in which the maker of the statement in question has been or will be called to give evidence (s. 6(2)).

Where such a witness has been or will be called, a previous hearsay statement can be adduced only if *either* the court grants leave to do so (s. 6(2)(a)) *or* the statement in question is adduced to rebut a suggestion that the testimony of the witness is fabricated (see **5.1.4.2**).

The requirement of notice

A party proposing to adduce hearsay evidence shall give such notice (if any) as is reasonable and practicable to the other party (s. 2). However, failure to give such notice will not prevent the evidence being admitted. The party failing to comply with the notice requirements of s. 2 may suffer other sanctions:

(a) under s. 2(4)(a) the court may exercise its powers against the defaulting party by adjourning the case and requiring the defaulting party to pay the costs wasted as a result; and

(b) under ss. 2(4)(b) and 4(2)(f) the court may attach less weight to the hearsay evidence.

The notice procedure

The detailed rules on the notice procedure are contained in CPR, rr. 33.2 and 33.3:

33.1 INTRODUCTORY

In this Part—

(a) 'hearsay' means a statement made, otherwise than by a person while giving oral evidence in proceedings, which is tendered as evidence of the matters stated; and

(b) references to hearsay include hearsay of whatever degree.

33.2 NOTICE OF INTENTION TO RELY ON HEARSAY EVIDENCE

(1) Where a party intends to rely on hearsay evidence at trial and either—

(a) that evidence is to be given by a witness giving oral evidence; or

(b) that evidence is contained in a witness statement of a person who is not being called to give oral evidence;

that party complies with section 2(1)(a) of the Civil Evidence Act 1995 by serving a witness statement on the other parties in accordance with the court's order.

(2) Where paragraph (1)(b) applies, the party intending to rely on the hearsay evidence must, when lie serves the witness statement—

(a) inform the other parties that the witness is not being called to give oral evidence; and

(b) give the reason why the witness will not be called.

(3) In all other cases where a party intends to rely on hearsay evidence at trial, that party complies with section 2(1)(a) of the Civil Evidence Act 1995 by serving a notice on the other parties which—

(a) identifies the hearsay evidence;

(b) states that the party serving the notice proposes to rely on the hearsay evidence at trial; and

(c) gives the reason why the witness will not be called.

(4) The party proposing to rely on the hearsay evidence must—

(a) serve the notice no later than the latest date for serving witness statements; and

(b) if the hearsay evidence is to be in a document, supply a copy to any party who requests him to do so.

33.3 CIRCUMSTANCES IN WHICH NOTICE OF INTENTION TO RELY ON HEARSAY EVIDENCE IS NOT REQUIRED

Section 2(1) of the Civil Evidence Act 1995 (duty to give notice of intention to rely on hearsay evidence) does not apply—

(a) to evidence at hearings other than trials;

(b) to a statement which a party to a probate action wishes to put in evidence and which is alleged to have been made by the person whose estate is the subject of the proceedings; or

(c) where the requirement is excluded by a practice direction.

There are, therefore, broadly three types of hearsay statement that require differing degrees of notification:

(a) Hearsay contained in a witness' statement: the notice is given when the witness statement is served through the normal procedure;

(b)   Hearsay contained in a statement of a person who will not be called as a witness at trial: notice has been given when *both*:

   (i)   the person's witness statement is served, *and*

   (ii)   other parties have been notified that the person will not be called as a witness and why that is so.

(c)   Where the hearsay is not contained in any witness statement (e.g. hearsay in a document that will be produced at trial): in such circumstances it will not be possible to give notice by service of a witness statement so, in such circumstances, it is necessary to serve a notice:

   (i)   identifying the hearsay evidence, and

   (ii)   stating that the hearsay will be relied upon, and

   (iii)   identifying why the maker of the hearsay statement will not be called to give evidence.

Proof of a hearsay statement

It is important not to overlook the fact that it is always necessary to prove hearsay statements.

Where the hearsay statement is oral this will be achieved by proving that the words were spoken (whether by a witness at trial or through an admissible hearsay document). However the statement cannot be proved by a person who is not a competent witness (s. 5(1)).

However, where the hearsay is contained in a document, it is not adequate merely to hand the document to the court (*per* Staughton LJ in *Ventouris v Mountain (No. 2)* [1992] 1 WLR 817). At common law there are rules as to how a document may be 'proved' and the reference in s. 8(1)(a) to 'production' must be read accordingly. A witness must attend court to identify the document and to verify its authenticity by oral testimony.

What if the document is available but there is no person available who can verify the document? May hearsay evidence be used to prove the document? This was the problem faced in *Ventouris v Mountain (No. 2)*, a case concerning the similar provisions under the Civil Evidence Act 1968. There the document in question was a tape recording of conversations between G and a number of divers who had been hired to blow up a boat for insurance purposes. The defendants, who were the insurers of the boat, wished to adduce this evidence to exempt them from having to make an insurance payment to the plaintiff. G was not available to give evidence. However, he had told an English solicitor what the tape recordings concerned. The Court of Appeal was satisfied that the solicitor would have been able to prove the tapes by repeating what G had told him about the tapes. That this logic would apply to proof of a document by another document is strengthened by s. 1(2)(b), which allows hearsay 'of whatever degree' to be admitted. Clearly a fact stated in a letter by C referred to in a document written by B which was mentioned in a letter written by A would be admissible upon formal proof of A's letter.

Section 8 states that a copy of a document (or even a copy of a copy) shall be admissible as evidence even if the original document is in existence. However the copy must be 'authenticated', i.e., the court must be satisfied that it is an accurate copy.

Sections 9 and 10 make particular provision for the admissibility of particular documents without this process of formal proof. Section 9 concerns any document forming part of the records of businesses or public authorities. A document falling within that section will be admissible if a signed certificate is produced. Section 9(3) allows for the proof of negative hearsay (see **8.4.3**) by affidavit. The meaning of the word 'record' had caused great difficulty to the courts under the precursor to the 1995 Act. Section 9(4) states that records can be in any form.

Section 10 provides for the admissibility of Ogden tables in personal injury cases.

Attacking or supporting the credibility of the hearsay statement

Clearly if it is sought to establish a fact by way of a hearsay statement under the 1995 Act rather than by oral testimony, the party wishing to contest the evidence contained in it will be at a disadvantage because the maker cannot be cross-examined. To prevent parties from hiding a weak case behind hearsay statements, the Act makes provision for rules to require the maker of a hearsay statement to attend at trial to be cross-examined (see s. 3). Although it is the party contesting the evidence who wishes the witness to be called, the rules treat the witness in question as though he or she had been called by the person relying on the evidence. The rules are contained in CPR, r. 33.4.

> *33.4   POWER TO CALL WITNESS FOR CROSS-EXAMINATION ON HEARSAY EVIDENCE*
> *(1)   Where a party—*
> *(a)   proposes to rely on hearsay evidence; and*
> *(b)   does not propose to call the person who made the original statement to give oral evidence,*
> *the court may, on the application of any other party, permit that party to call the maker of the statement to be cross-examined on the contents of the statement.*
> *(2)   An application for permission to cross-examine under this rule must be made not more than 14 days after the day on which a notice of intention to rely on the hearsay evidence was served on the applicant.*

Where the maker of the statement is not produced as a witness, the court may attach less weight to the hearsay statement if it would have been reasonable and practical for this to have occurred (s. 4(2)(a)).

Where the witness does not attend for cross-examination the Act makes provision for challenging the credibility of the evidence. By s. 5(2) the hearsay evidence can be challenged by evidence in the same way that a witness attending to give evidence may be challenged. In other words the Act allows the operation of the normal rules on cross-examination of witnesses (see **5.2.4**). Section 5(2) of the Act allows two forms of evidence to be adduced by the challenging party:

(a)   evidence undermining the credibility of the witness;

(b)   evidence of statements inconsistent with the hearsay statement.

Given that the Act has not changed the rules of evidence except in relation to hearsay evidence, all other restrictions as to what may or may not be adduced in evidence (as set out at **5.2.4**) still apply. Note in particular that evidence cannot be adduced if it would offend the rule of finality (see **5.2.4.3**).

Section 5(2)(a) states that evidence 'for the purpose of attacking or supporting his credibility . . . is admissible for that purpose' and s. 5(2)(b) states that evidence is 'admissible for the purpose of showing that he had contradicted himself'. Therefore such evidence as is admitted under s. 5 will only go to the issue of credibility rather than to prove the truth of its contents.

For the notice requirements where a person wishes to challenge the credibility of a hearsay statement, see CPR, r. 33.5.

> *33.5   CREDIBILITY*
> *(1)   Where a party—*
> *(a)   proposes to rely on hearsay evidence; but*
> *(b)   does not propose to call the person who made the original statement to give oral evidence; and*

(c)   another party wishes to call evidence to attack the credibility of the person who made the statement,

the party who so wishes must give notice of his intention to the party who proposes to give the hearsay statement in evidence.

(2)   A party must give notice under paragraph (1) not more than 14 days after the day on which a hearsay notice relating to the hearsay evidence was served on him.

Hearsay statement by a witness at the trial

Unlike Criminal Justice Act 1988, s. 23, there is no requirement that a witness must be unavailable to give evidence before a hearsay statement may be admitted. Section 6(2) of the Act deals with cases in which the witness has been or will be called to give evidence but the party calling him or her wishes to use previous hearsay statements made by the witness. In such a situation the hearsay statement is not admissible unless either the court grants leave (s. 6(2)(a)) *or* the statement is adduced to disprove an allegation of fabrication (s. 6(2)(b)).

Section 6(3) also preserves the rules relating to cross-examination of the witness in relation to previous inconsistent statements (see **5.2.4.2**) and s. 6(4) preserves the rules relating to the use of memory refreshing documents as evidence (see **5.1.2**).

Insofar as any of these items of evidence would normally go only to the issue of the credibility of the witness in question, s. 6(5) makes it clear that when adduced in a civil trial they are also admissible to prove the truth of the matters they state.

Assessing the weight of a hearsay statement

Section 4 sets out the considerations to which the court may have regard in deciding what, if any, weight ought to be attached to a hearsay statement admissible under the 1995 Act. Note the relationship between parts of s. 4 and other sections of the Act:

(a)   **The lack of oral testimony**   Section 4(2)(a) allows the court to take into account the practicability of calling the maker of the statement as a witness. This must be examined alongside ss. 3 and 5 which make provision for securing the attendance of the maker to be cross-examined and for undermining his or her credibility where he or she does not attend.

(b)   **Ambush hearsay evidence**   Section 4(2)(f) allows the court to take into account anything to suggest that the party producing the statement may have sought to prevent its proper evaluation. This must be looked at alongside s. 2(4)(b) which allows the court to attach less weight to a hearsay statement where the party producing it has not given such notice as was reasonable and practicable.

Section 4(2)(d) refers to 'any person' with a motive to conceal or misrepresent. In the case of multiple hearsay, therefore, the court should consider whether any person repeating the hearsay statement may have had such a motive and therefore may have misrepresented the facts in question.

Preservation of common law rules

Section 7 of the Act preserves particular common law exceptions to the rule against hearsay, but not the exception in the case of informal admissions. Informal admissions are now admissible by virtue of s. 1 of the Act, and are subject to the general provisions of the Act, including those relating to notice and weight.

9.3.2   HEARSAY ADMISSIBLE UNDER OTHER PROVISIONS

9.3.2.1   Children Act 1989; Child Support Act 1991

The Children (Admissibility of Hearsay Evidence) Order 1993 (made under Children Act 1989, s. 96 and effective on 5 April 1993) provides that in civil proceedings before the High Court or a county court and in family proceedings and civil proceedings under Child Support Act 1991 in a magistrates' court, evidence may be given in connection with the upbringing, maintenance or welfare of a child notwithstanding that the evidence in question would otherwise be inadmissible because of the 'hearsay rule' in the law of evidence.

See, as to the effect of this Order and the question of compellability of the child who has made the statement, *R* v *B County Council, ex parte P* [1991] 2 All ER 65.

9.3.2.2 Implied statutory exceptions

In cases involving public interest petitions to wind up a company pursuant to s. 124A of the Insolvency Act 1986 and applications to disqualify company directors under s. 8 of the Insolvency Act, the court can place reliance upon hearsay evidence in reports prepared by Department of Trade inspectors pursuant to powers contained in Companies Act 1985, part XIV. Since the Secretary of State can take into consideration such reports in deciding to initiate the proceedings, it is implicit in the statutory powers that the courts can take account of such material in determining the outcome of such proceedings: see *Re Rex Williams Leisure plc* [1994] 4 All ER 27.

9.3.2.3 Miscellaneous

As pointed out at **9.2**, certain exceptions applicable in criminal cases, e.g. public records (see **9.2.1.4**) and Bankers' Books Evidence Act 1879 (see **9.2.2.3**) are also applicable in civil cases. The application of these exceptions in civil cases is not affected by the CEA 1995.

Questions

OBJECTIVES

This chapter is designed to ensure that you can:

(a) demonstrate a sound understanding of the principles underlying the exceptions to the hearsay rule (other than the special provision relating to confessions which will be dealt with in **Chapter 10** of this Manual);

(b) identify the circumstances in which the exceptions may apply;

(c) identify which preliminary facts need to be proved and (when applicable) which procedural steps need to be taken; and

(d) raise and/or counter an objection to hearsay evidence.

Question 1

Arthur is charged with murdering his ex-lover Edith in June 1996. He has pleaded not guilty and has given notice of an alibi defence.

(a) Advise the prosecution whether it will be possible to adduce the following items of evidence:

(i) Testimony by a police officer that as he was approaching the place where Edith was found dying from stab wounds he heard an unknown person shout, 'Hello Arthur, where are you rushing off to?'.

(ii) Testimony by a doctor that just before she died Edith said, 'I have a terrible pain in my back where Arthur stabbed me'.

(iii) Testimony by Oliver, a friend of Edith's, that several days before she was stabbed she told him that Arthur had threatened to kill her.

(b) Advise Arthur whether he can adduce evidence of a deathbed confession by Judas that he (not Arthur) had murdered Edith.

Question 2

(a) Alvin is being prosecuted for causing death by dangerous driving. The prosecution case is that Alvin ran down Bert as he was crossing the road at a pelican crossing when the lights were on red to traffic. The prosecution alleges that Alvin was driving at excessive speed for the conditions (it was dark and raining), and that he failed to keep a proper look out.

Alvin's case is that he was driving at a reasonable speed and that Bert ran across the road in front of his car when the crossing lights were on green to traffic.

PC Trotter was on the scene soon after the accident and spoke to Charles who stated that the crossing lights were on red to traffic at the time of the accident and that another witness had told him (Charles) that Alvin was driving too fast. PC Trotter noted down Charles' statement. Unfortunately shortly after the accident Charles died of natural causes. It has not been possible to locate any other eye-witnesses.

Although he did not sustain any head injury Bert died in hospital several days after the accident. Whilst he was being taken to the hospital he told an ambulanceman that he had waited until the crossing lights changed in his favour before starting to walk across the road.

The prosecution proposes to call PC Trotter to prove the note and to call the ambulanceman to give evidence. Leaving aside any tactical considerations, prepare an objection to this evidence and, in each case, prepare an argument to support the overruling of the objection.

(b) Assume that the case described above was the subject of a civil action brought by Bert's dependants. Advise them whether at the trial of the civil action they may rely on the evidence of PC Trotter (and his note) and the ambulanceman and if so which, if any, procedural requirements should be complied with.

TEN

CONFESSIONS AND ILLEGALLY OR IMPROPERLY OBTAINED EVIDENCE (OTHER THAN CONFESSIONS) IN CRIMINAL CASES

When is a confession, made by an accused person prior to a criminal trial, admissible in the trial to prove that the accused is guilty of the offence?

In a criminal trial when, if at all, may the prosecution adduce evidence obtained improperly or illegally?

10.1 Confessions

10.1.1 INTRODUCTION

The position in relation to the admissibility of a confession by an accused is governed by Police and Criminal Evidence Act 1984.

10.1.1.1 Definition of confession

The Police and Criminal Evidence Act 1984, s. 82(1) provides that:

> 'Confession' includes any statement wholly or partly adverse to the person who made it, whether made to a person in authority or not and whether made in words or otherwise.

This statutory definition is very wide (the only significant limit was noted in *R v Sat-Bhambra* (1988) 88 Cr App R 44, where the Court of Appeal restricted the definition of 'confessions' to statements which were adverse *when made*. Statements which were favourable when made, but which later proved to be adverse, e.g. false alibis, are not, it seems, confessions). It is important to stress that there is no requirement in the definition that the confession should be in any particular form. Moreover, the statutory definition confirms the rule stated by the House of Lords in *R v Sharp* [1988] 1 WLR 7, that, if an out of court statement by the accused is partly adverse and partly exculpatory, both the exculpatory parts and the adverse parts are to be taken together as one 'confession'. The whole statement should then be left to the jury. As to where a statement can properly be said to be mixed in this way see *R v Garrod* [1997] Crim LR 445 and *Western v DPP* [1997] 1 Cr App R 474. Very often an entire interview between a police officer and a suspect will be proved by the prosecution as a confession so long as some of the accused's answers were incriminating. It seems that a video re-enactment of a crime by an accused also qualifies as a confession: see *Li Shu-Ling v R* [1989] AC 270.

10.1.1.2 Confessions generally admissible (albeit hearsay)

An accused's confession was generally admissible, albeit hearsay, at common law and this general rule is adopted and put into statutory form by the 1984 Act, s. 76(1), which provides:

> *In any proceedings a confession made by an accused person may be given in evidence against him in so far as it is relevant to any matter in issue in the proceedings and is not excluded by the court in pursuance of this section.*

10.1.1.3 The confession should be based on known facts

The confession must generally be based on facts which are known to the accused who makes it. See *R* v *Hulbert* (1979) 69 Cr App R 243. In this case H, charged with handling stolen goods, confessed *inter alia* that the person from whom she bought the goods told her that they were stolen. It was held that this confession was inadmissible to prove that the goods *were* stolen (albeit admissible to show that H thought they were stolen). See also *Attorney-General's Reference (No. 4 of 1979)* [1981] 1 WLR 667, and *Comptroller of Customs* v *Western Lectric Co. Ltd* [1966] AC 367, PC. However, this does not mean that a confession must always consist of fact not opinion. If the opinion would be admissible under the opinion evidence rules (see **Chapter 13**), the fact that it is expressed in a confession will not alter the position as to admissibility: see *R* v *Chatwood* [1980] 1 WLR 874.

10.1.1.4 The confession is only admissible against the accused who made it

Although a confession made with the authority of the accused will be admissible against him or her (see *Kirkstall Brewery Co.* v *Furness Railway Co.* (1874) LR 9 QB 468), a confession by one accused is generally no evidence against a co-accused because accused X is not the agent of accused Y for the purpose of making confessions. This, of course, leads to difficulties where in joint trials the confession of accused X contains statements which are adverse to accused Y. The problem arises because the confession of X is admissible against X but not against Y (i.e. it is a case of multiple admissibility (see **2.5.1**)). X is entitled to have the confession proved in its entirety (including the parts incriminating Y). See generally *R* v *Pearce* (1979) 69 Cr App R 365 and *R* v *Rogers* [1971] Crim LR 413. Clearly the judge must direct the jury that X's confession is no evidence against Y, but is a direction sufficient? In *R* v *Silcot* [1987] Crim LR 765 it was suggested that a judge had a discretion to allow editing of the confession to remove references to Y. However, in *Lobban* v *R* [1995] 2 All ER 602, the Privy Council held that, because the discretion to exclude evidence whose probative value is outweighed by its prejudicial effect applies only to prosecution evidence, the judge does not have a discretion to allow editing (because X's confession is for these purposes defence evidence). It would seem that if X has no objection to the editing, the reasoning in *Lobban* would not apply. Another option may be to apply for separate trials of X and Y, though it is generally in the interests of justice not to allow separate trials: see *R* v *Gunewardene* [1951] 2 KB 600 and *R* v *Lake* (1977) 64 Cr App R 172.

In *R* v *Gray* [1998] Crim LR 570, the Court of Appeal held that, where X has made a confession implicating Y (and X and Y are tried together), it is not legitimate for counsel prosecuting to ask Y in cross-examination to explain the part of the confession in which X had implicated Y. Although the jury could hear X's whole confession (including the part implicating Y), since the part of the confession was not evidence against Y it should not be put to him in cross-examination because this might be seen as giving to X's confession a status it did not merit and did not have.

One apparent exception to this principle (that X's confession is only admissible against X) is that the statements of accused X, *made in pursuance of a common purpose*, are evidence against accused Y. Thus, if X, *in the course of committing an offence in concert with Y*, makes statements which incriminate both X and Y, the statements are admissible against both X and Y. Thus in *R* v *Devonport* [1996] 1 Cr App R 221 the Court of Appeal held that a note of the proposed division of the proceeds of a conspiracy was prima facie prepared in furtherance of the conspiracy and so admissible against the defendants named in it, even though they had had no part in making the note and did not know of its existence. The principle is not limited to cases of conspiracy — it applies to any offence which is alleged to have been committed by the accused acting in concert: see *R* v *Gray* [1995] 2 Cr App R 100 and *R* v *Murray* [1997] 2 Cr App R 136. Also, according to the Court of Appeal in *R* v *Devonport* [1996] 1 Cr App R 221, it is sufficient if the statement is in fact made in the commission of the offence even though it was not actually necessary to make the statement in order to commit the offence: see also *R* v *Jones* [1997] 2 Cr App R 119.

The common purpose must be proved independently (i.e. by evidence other than the statement). However, it may be possible to prove the statement conditionally so that the judge can decide at the end of the case whether there is independent proof and, hence, whether X's statement is admissible against Y. See *R* v *Donat* (1985) 82 Cr App R 173 and *R* v *Governor of Pentonville Prison, ex parte Osman* [1989] 3 All ER 701, QBD.

10.1.1.5 Statutory restrictions on admissibility — introduction

The general rule admitting confessions (see **10.1.1.2**) is (and always has been) subject to exception, for example, where the confession was obtained by threats or violence on the part of the interrogator. Accordingly, s. 76(1) is subject to s. 76(2) (see **10.1.2**) which provides grounds on which such confessions *will* be excluded. Moreover the confession *may* be excluded by virtue of the discretions provided for in s. 78(1) and s. 82(3) which apply to prosecution evidence generally (including confessions — see *R* v *Mason* [1988] 1 WLR 139). (See **10.1.3**.)

The main barrier to the admissibility of confessions is s. 76(2) for the reason that it operates as a matter of law whereas the other barrier (ss. 78 and 82(3)) operates as a matter of discretion.

10.1.1.6 The Codes of Practice

The Codes of Practice provided for under Police and Criminal Evidence Act 1984, s. 66, have become a very important factor in relation to this topic. Section 67(11) provides that the court *shall* take account of the codes in determining any question (to which the codes might be relevant) arising in any proceedings. The codes are expressed as applying to police officers, however, s. 67(9) provides that:

> *persons other than police officers who are charged with the duty of investigating offences or charging offenders shall in the discharge of that duty have regard to any relevant provision of [the] Codes.*

In *R* v *Seelig & Spens* (1992) 94 Cr App R 17, the Court of Appeal accepted a narrow interpretation of the words 'charged with the duty of investigating offences' when upholding a decision, on the facts, that Department of Trade inspectors were not persons who were 'charged with the duty of investigating offences' (as to investigations by the SFO see *R* v *Director of Serious Fraud Office, ex parte Smith* [1992] 3 All ER 456). However, in *R* v *Twaites* (1991) 92 Cr App R 106, *R* v *Bayliss* (1994) 98 Cr App R 235 and *R* v *Okafor* (1994) 99 Cr App R 97 the Court of Appeal seems to accept a wider interpretation which is capable of applying to a variety of persons whose employment duties include the investigation of offences (e.g. a bookmaker's own investigators, store detectives and customs officers, respectively).

The codes which are important in the context of confessions are those relating to the detention, treatment and questioning of suspects (Code C) and the tape recording of interviews (Code E). Codes C and E are set out at **10.3** and **10.4**.

The broad effect of Code E (as amended) is to require that, except in terrorist or official secrets cases, interviews in police stations in respect of indictable offences *shall* be tape-recorded. The Code then goes on to provide detailed rules relating to the recording. See also Practice Direction (1989) 89 Cr App R 132. The general effect of the Practice Direction is that even though an interview is tape-recorded, it will normally be proved at trial in the form of a transcript. However, in *R* v *Riaz; R* v *Burke* [1992] Crim LR 366, the Court of Appeal held that, even after the jury retired, the jury was entitled to hear the tape of the interview which had been proved in the first instance by transcript. As the Court of Appeal said, the evidence was the tape itself — the transcript is merely a convenient means of presenting it. See also *R* v *Aitken* (1992) 94 Cr App R 85.

Many of the provisions of Code C only apply to 'interviews'. An interview for these purposes is defined in para. 11.1A of Code C. See also *R* v *Weekes* (1993) 97 Cr App R 222, *R* v *Ward* (1994) 98 Cr App R 337 and *R* v *Miller* [1998] Crim LR 209 (in which the Court of Appeal held that one question could constitute an interview).

10.1.2   **THE FIRST BARRIER TO ADMISSIBILITY — POLICE AND CRIMINAL EVIDENCE ACT 1984, SECTION 76(2) AND (3)**

By s. 76:

> (2) *If, in any proceedings where the prosecution proposes to give in evidence a confession made by an accused person, it is represented to the court that the confession was or may have been obtained—*
>   *(a) by oppression of the person who made it; or*
>   *(b) in consequence of anything said or done which was likely, in the circumstances existing at the time, to render unreliable any confession which might be made by him in consequence thereof*
> *the court shall not allow the confession to be given in evidence against him except insofar as the prosecution proves to the court beyond reasonable doubt that the confession (notwithstanding that it may be true) was not obtained as aforesaid.*
> (3) *In any proceedings where the prosecution proposes to give in evidence a confession made by an accused person, the court may of its own motion require the prosecution, as a condition of allowing it to do so, to prove that the confession was not obtained as mentioned in subsection (2) above.*

10.1.2.1 Preliminary and procedural points

(a)   Section 76(2) comes into operation where *the prosecution* proposes to give in evidence a confession and representations about s. 76(2) are made or the court raises the issue of its own motion (s. 76(3)). In *R* v *Sat-Bhambra* (1988) 88 Cr App R 55, the court stated:

> If a defendant wishes under section 76 to exclude a confession, the time to make his submission to that effect is before the confession is put in evidence and not afterwards.

> *Cf. R* v *Liverpool Juvenile Court, ex parte R* [1988] QB 1, DC. In *Sat-Bhambra* the Court of Appeal held that, once a confession had been ruled admissible on the *voir dire*, the trial judge has no power under s. 76 or s. 78 of the Police and Criminal Evidence Act 1984 to reconsider his or her decision if the evidence given at the trial convinces the judge that he or she was wrong. However, the judge may exercise his or her discretion to exclude the confession under s. 82(3), and direct the jury to disregard it.

(b)   Section 76(2) is only directed at the prosecution. This means that, in a trial involving co-accused X and Y, even though the prosecution chooses not to rely on X's confession due to the possible effect of s. 76(2), Y can prove X's confession against X as part of Y's case: see *R* v *Campbell* [1993] Crim LR 448 and *R* v *Myers* [1997] 4 All ER 314, HL. It seems that the only restriction is that X's confession must have been made voluntarily. In *R* v *Corelli* [2001] Crim LR 913 the Court of Appeal held that the observations in *R* v *Myers* about the worthlessness of an involuntary confession related only to the question whether it was possible to adduce evidence of such a confession by a co-defendant from someone other than that co-defendant. An involuntary confession can still be put to the co-defendant himself by another defendant in cross-examination. But where this happens, the jury should be warned that the only relevance of the cross-examination on that matter is to the credibility of the maker of the confession, and the judge should explain why the prosecution was not allowed to refer to the confession.

(c) Once the admissibility issue is raised it seems it *must* be determined on the *voir dire* (see *R v Oxford City Justices, ex parte Berry* [1988] QB 507). In jury trials the *voir dire* will be in the absence of the jury (*R v Hendry* [1988] Crim LR 766). A *voir dire* is not required if the sole issue is whether the confession was in fact made. Since this is a matter of fact (and not law) the jury should decide it: see *Ajodha v The State* [1982] AC 204 and *R v Fleming* (1987) 86 Cr App R 32. However, the fact that the accused denies making the confession will not necessarily prevent the defence calling upon the prosecution to discharge its burden of proof under s. 76(2) as to the circumstances in which any confession was obtained: see *R v Keenan* [1990] 2 QB 54.

(d) The defence may choose as a tactical device to allow the prosecution to prove a confession and then challenge the circumstances in which it was obtained in the presence of the jury. However, it would not then be possible to get the confession ruled inadmissible under s. 76(2) because in this case the prosecution will already have relied on the confession, i.e. it will not be a case 'where the prosecution proposes to give in evidence a confession' (which is a precondition for the application of s. 76(2)) see *R v Sat Bhambra* (1988) 88 Cr App R 55.

(e) Evidence given by the accused on the *voir dire* is generally inadmissible in the trial proper and the accused should not be asked whether the confession is true.

In *Wong Kam-Ming v R* [1980] AC 247, W gave evidence at trial and was cross-examined in detail as to statements made in the *voir dire* which were inconsistent with his testimony. The Privy Council held that the confession having been excluded at the *voir dire*, it was not open to the prosecution to conduct such cross-examination. This case was applied in *R v Brophy* [1982] AC 476. Although these cases preceded the 1984 Act it is likely that the law remains the same.

(f) Proving the confession — documentary or oral evidence. For tape-recorded confessions, see **10.1.1.6** above. A confession which is not taped may be proved as documentary evidence if the accused has acknowledged a documentary record of the confession but not otherwise. See *R v Todd* (1980) 72 Cr App R 299 and *R v Dillon* (1983) 85 Cr App R 29.

(g) Section 76 does not apply in committal proceedings, i.e. the examining magistrates must accept the accused's confession as admissible under s. 76(1) (see Criminal Procedure and Investigations Act 1996, sch. 1, para. 25).

10.1.2.2 Oppression (section 76(2)(a))
By s. 76(8):

> *In this section 'oppression' includes torture, inhuman or degrading treatment, and the use or threat of violence (whether or not amounting to torture).*

For more specific guidance see *R v Fulling* [1987] QB 426 *per* Lord Lane CJ at p. 432 (emphasis added):

> 'Oppression' in s. 76(2)(a) should be given its ordinary dictionary meaning. The *Oxford English Dictionary* as its third definition of the word runs as follows: 'Exercise of authority or power in a burdensome, harsh, or wrongful manner; unjust or cruel treatment of subjects, inferiors etc., the imposition of unreasonable or unjust burdens.' One of the quotations given under that paragraph runs as follows: 'There is not a word in our language which expresses more detestable wickedness than oppression'. . . *We find it hard to envisage any circumstances in which such oppression would not entail some impropriety on the part of the interrogator.*

In *Fulling* the accused was suspected of making a bogus insurance claim. The police suspected that she had been put up to it by X, a man with whom she was infatuated (and with whom she had been living). She claimed that she only confessed after the police had informed her that X had been having an affair with another woman throughout the time that she and X had been living together and that 'the other woman' was being held in the next cell. The police denied acting in this way. On appeal (the confession having been admitted at trial) the Court of Appeal held that even if the accused's account was correct, there was no oppression under s. 76(2)(a).

In relation to oppressive questioning techniques see *R* v *Seelig* [1991] 4 All ER 429, *R* v *Paris* (1992) 97 Cr App R 99 and *Burut* v *Public Prosecutor* [1995] 4 All ER 300 and *cf. R* v *L* [1994] Crim LR 839. In *Seelig* the trial judge in deciding whether questioning had been oppressive by DTI inspectors investigating the Guinness affair, took into account the fact that the person being questioned was 'an experienced merchant banker' who was 'intelligent and sophisticated'. In *Paris* the court took into account the fact that M was on the borderline of mental handicap. The manner of questioning adopted by the police in that case was both hostile and intimidating, and would have been deemed oppressive even with a suspect of normal intelligence.

10.1.2.3 Unreliability (section 76(2)(b))

This element is so widely drafted that it leaves a good deal of latitude to the court. However, some useful guidelines in the context of a police interview are to be found in *R* v *Barry* (1992) 95 Cr App R 384:

> Where a defendant alleges that his confession was unreliable within s. 76(2) of the Police and Criminal Evidence Act 1984, the correct approach is first, to identify the thing said or done, which requires the trial judge to take into account everything said and done by the police. The second step is to ask whether what was said and done was likely in the circumstances to render unreliable a confession made in consequence. The test is objective taking into account all the circumstances. The last step is to ask whether the prosecution have proved beyond reasonable doubt that the confession was not obtained in consequence of the thing said and done, which is a question of fact to be approached in a common sense way.

There must be things said and done by a person other than the accused. In *R* v *Goldenberg* (1988) 88 Cr App R 285, G's admissions were alleged by the defence to be (a) an attempt to get bail and (b) undermined by the fact that he was a heroin addict suffering from withdrawal symptoms who wanted to gain release as soon as possible in order to feed his addiction. The Court of Appeal decided that in seeking to exclude a confession under Police and Criminal Evidence Act 1984, s. 76(2)(b), the words 'anything said or done' in the subsection did not extend to include anything said or done by the person making the confession, but were limited to something external to him or her and to something which was likely to have some influence on him or her.

However, in assessing the effect of things said or done, any mental, physical or personality abnormalities of the accused may be relevant. In *R* v *Everett* [1988] Crim LR 826, E aged 42 with a mental age of 8 had been discovered in a compromising position with a 5-year-old. On the way to, and at, the police station, he admitted to having indecently assaulted the child. The Court of Appeal held that the suspect's mental condition at the time of the confession should have been taken into account. The test was objective, and not what the police officers thought. The confession ought to have been excluded. The Court of Appeal in *R* v *Walker* [1998] Crim LR 211 emphasised that nothing limits the form of mental or psychological conviction or disorder on which a defendant can rely to show the unreliability of a confession. But see also the more restricted approach adopted in *R* v *O'Brien*, *The Times*, 16 February 2000.

Breaches of Code C (even breaches by omission) can amount to 'things done'. In *R* v *Delaney* (1988) 88 Cr App R 338, D confessed at the end of an one and a half hour interview which had not been recorded in accordance with the Code. The court held that the breach was significant, and sufficient to exclude the confession. However, the mere fact that there has been a breach of the Code does not mean that the confession has to be excluded. See also *R* v *Chung* (1991) 92 Cr App R 314 and *R* v *Stephen Perry*, 28 April 2000, unreported.

It was confirmed in *R* v *Fulling* [1987] QB 426 that, even though something was said which may have caused the confession to be made, the court must also consider the likelihood of unreliability.

Section 76(2)(a) and (b), by use of the phrases 'by oppression' and 'in consequence of anything said or done', make clear the need for a causal link. In *R* v *Rennie* [1982] 1 WLR 64, Lord Lane CJ held that a judge should approach this concept as would a jury, and apply his or her common sense. See *R* v *Tyrer* (1989) 90 Cr App R 446 and *R* v *Crampton* (1991) 92 Cr App R 369 approving the *dicta* in *Rennie* and *R* v *Barry* (1992) 95 Cr App R 384.

The words 'any confession' are to be understood as referring to any such confession as the accused has made (*R* v *Bow Street Magistrates' Court, ex parte Proulx* [2001] 1 All ER 57).

10.1.3 THE DISCRETION(S) TO EXCLUDE

Police and Criminal Evidence Act 1984, s. 78 provides that:

> *(1) In any proceedings the court may refuse to allow evidence on which the prosecution proposes to rely to be given if it appears to the court that, having regard to all the circumstances, including the circumstances in which the evidence was obtained, the admission of the evidence would have such an adverse effect on the fairness of the proceedings that the court ought not to admit it.*
> *(2) Nothing in this section shall prejudice any rule of law requiring a court to exclude evidence.*
> *(3) This section shall not apply to proceedings before a magistrates' court inquiring into an offence as examining justices.*

Police and Criminal Evidence Act 1984, s. 82(3) provides that:

> *Nothing in this part of this Act shall prejudice any power of a court to exclude evidence (whether by preventing questions from being put or otherwise) at its discretion.*

Section 82(3) preserves any common law discretion to exclude evidence which existed prior to Police and Criminal Evidence Act 1984.

10.1.3.1 Section 78 and the *voir dire*

In the Crown Court a *voir dire* is necessary to determine whether a confession should be excluded under s. 78: see *R* v *Manji* [1990] Crim LR 512. In *Halawa* v *Federation Against Copyright Theft* [1995] 1 Cr App R 21, the Divisional Court suggested that, in a magistrates' court, the matter is entirely at the court's discretion but that if the issues can easily be confined or if the confession is a key aspect of the prosecution case then the accused could generally be heard as on a *voir dire*. Section 78 has no application when magistrates are acting as examining justices, i.e. in committal proceedings (see Criminal Procedure and Investigations Act 1996, sch. 1, para. 26).

10.1.3.2 Tricks/subterfuge depriving a suspect of rights under the 1984 Act and Code C

The discretion to exclude a confession is likely to be exercised when the confession has been obtained by *deliberate impropriety or bad faith* which has resulted in the accused's deprivation of rights to be questioned fairly. In *R* v *Mason* [1988] 1 WLR 139 the accused was arrested on suspicion of committing arson. The police allowed him to see his solicitor but told them both that the accused's fingerprints had been found on a piece of glass at the scene of the crime. This was untrue. The accused in these circumstances made a confession to the police. The confession was admitted against the accused at his trial but, on appeal, the Court of Appeal had no hesitation in saying that the confession should have been excluded under s. 78. However, it is not always easy to say which cases will fall clearly into this category. There is an important distinction between cases where there is evidence on which to base an arrest and cases where there is not (often reflected by whether the accused is in custody). See *R* v *Jelen* (1989) 90 Cr App R 456; *R* v *Christou* (1992) 95 Cr App R 264, *R* v *Bryce* (1992) 95 Cr App R 320 and *R* v *Edwards* [1997] Crim LR 348. In *Christou*, Lord Taylor CJ said:

It is true that the provisions of the Code are very largely concerned with those who are in custody, but not exclusively so . . . [T]he Code will also apply where a suspect, not in detention, is being questioned about an offence by a police officer acting as a police officer for the purpose of obtaining evidence . . . It would be wrong for police officers to adopt or use an undercover pose or disguise to enable themselves to ask questions about an offence uninhibited by the requirements of the Code and with the effect of circumventing it.

This important dictum by Lord Taylor CJ highlights a fairly acute difficulty for plain clothes police officers. If they already have grounds to suspect that a person has committed an offence and wish to question that person about his or her involvement in the offence (i.e. in order to obtain a confession), they should reveal their identity, caution the suspect (see Code C para. 10.1) and proceed to question in accordance with Code C (see Code C para. 11.1A).

Where there has been use of intrusive surveillance devices, Article 8 of the European Convention on Human Rights is relevant. This provides:

1. *Everyone has the right to respect for his private and family life, his home and his correspondence.*
2. *There shall be no interference by a public authority with the exercise of this right except such as is in accordance with the law and is necessary in a democratic society in the interests of national security, public safety or the economic well-being of the country, for the prevention of disorder or crime, for the protection of health or morals, or for the protection of the rights or freedoms of others.*

In *Khan* v *UK* [2000] Crim LR 684, the European Court had to consider whether there had been a breach of a defendant's right to a fair trial under Article 6(1) of the Convention by virtue of a breach of his rights under Article 8. The Court held that the defendant's rights under Article 8 had been violated because UK domestic law did not at that time regulate the use of intrusive surveillance devices. The interference with those rights by use of a covert listening device had accordingly not been 'in accordance with the law' as required by Article 8(2). But the Court held by a majority that a violation of Article 6(1) had not been established. Relying on earlier decisions, the Court said that it would not decide as a matter of principle that unlawfully obtained evidence should always be excluded. In this case the defendant had had ample opportunity to challenge the authenticity of the recording and, under s. 78(1), its use at his trial. See also *PG and JH* v *UK*, *The Times*, 19 October 2001, where the European Court emphasised again that a breach of Article 8 will not automatically involve also a breach of Article 6.

The use of intrusive surveillance devices is now regulated by the Police Act 1997, Part III, and by a code of practice issued under s. 101 of the Act.

10.1.3.3 The effect of breaches of Code C
In *R* v *Delaney* (1988) 88 Cr App R 338, 341 Lord Lane said: 'It is no part of the duty of the court to rule a statement inadmissible simply in order to punish the police for failure to observe the codes of practice'. However, in *R* v *Canale* [1990] 2 All ER 187 Lord Lane suggested that flagrant and cynical breaches of the Code would normally lead to exclusion of confessions under s. 78.

Moreover subsequent cases show that failure to observe the Code (even if not deliberate) can lead to exclusion of confessions under s. 78. In *R* v *Keenan* [1989] 3 All ER 598, the Court of Appeal quashed a conviction on the grounds that evidence obtained at a police interview had not been recorded contemporaneously, in breach of Code C. Hodgson J stated 'if the breaches are significant and substantial we think it makes good sense to exclude'.

In *R* v *Aspinall* [1999] Crim LR 741, the court stressed that fundamental breaches will lead to exclusion, as when an appropriate adult has not been made available to a mentally disordered defendant at a police interview.

In *R* v *Kirk* [1999] 4 All ER 698, the Court of Appeal held that where the police have arrested a suspect for one offence, and then propose to question him further about a different or more serious offence, they must first either charge him with the more serious offence or at least ensure that he is aware of the true nature of the investigation. Evidence obtained in breach of this principle may well be excluded under s. 78.

R v *Walsh* (1990) 91 Cr App R 161, 163 *per* Saville J, 'Although bad faith may make substantial or significant that which might not otherwise be so, the contrary does not follow. Breaches which are in themselves significant and substantial are not rendered otherwise by the good faith of the officers concerned'.

10.1.3.4 Confessions obtained after an unjustified refusal of access to legal advice
Police and Criminal Evidence Act 1984, s. 58 provides that:

(1)   A person arrested and held in custody in a police station or other premises shall be entitled, if he so requests, to consult a solicitor privately at any time.

(2)   Subject to subsection (3) below, a request under subsection (1) above and the time at which it was made shall be recorded in the custody record.

(3)   Such a request need not be recorded in the custody record of a person who makes it at a time while he is at a court after being charged with an offence.

(4)   If a person makes such a request, he must be permitted to consult a solicitor as soon as is practicable except to the extent that delay is permitted by this section.

(5)   In any case he must be permitted to consult a solicitor within 36 hours from the relevant time, as defined in section 41(2) above.

(6)   Delay in compliance with a request is only permitted—

(a)   in the case of a person who is in police detention for a serious arrestable offence; and

(b)   if an officer of at least the rank of superintendent authorises it.

(7)   An officer may give an authorisation under subsection (6) above orally or in writing but, if he gives it orally, he shall confirm it in writing as soon as is practicable.

(8)   An officer may only authorise delay where he has reasonable grounds for believing that the exercise of the right conferred by subsection (1) above at the time when the person detained desires to exercise it—

(a)   will lead to interference with or harm to evidence connected with a serious arrestable offence or interference with or physical injury to other persons; or

(b)   will lead to the alerting of other persons suspected of having committed such an offence but not yet arrested for it; or

(c)   will hinder the recovery of any property obtained as a result of such an offence.

(9)   If delay is authorised—

(a)   the detained person shall be told the reason for it; and

(b)   the reason shall be noted on his custody record.

(10)   The duties imposed by subsection (9) above shall be performed as soon as is practicable.

(11)   There may be no further delay in permitting the exercise of the right conferred by subsection (1) above once the reason for authorising delay ceases to subsist.

(12)   The reference in subsection (1) above to a person arrested includes a reference to a person who has been detained under the terrorism provisions.

(13)   In the application of this section to a person who has been arrested or detained under the terrorism provisions—

(a)   subsection (5) above shall have effect as if for the words from 'within' onwards there were substituted the words 'before the end of the period beyond which he may no longer be detained without the authority of the Secretary of State';

(b)   subsection (6)(a) above shall have effect as if for the words 'for a serious arrestable offence' there were substituted the words 'under the terrorism provisions'; and

(c)   subsection (8) above shall have effect as if at the end there were added 'or

(d)   will lead to interference with the gathering of information about the commission, preparation or instigation of acts of terrorism; or

(e)   by alerting any person, will make it more difficult—

(i)   to prevent an act of terrorism; or

(ii) to secure the apprehension, prosecution or conviction of any person in connection with the commission, preparation or instigation of an act of terrorism.'

(14) If an officer of appropriate rank has reasonable grounds for believing that, unless he gives a direction under subsection (15) below, the exercise by a person arrested or detained under the terrorism provisions of the right conferred by subsection (1) above will have any of the consequences specified in subsection (8) above (as it has effect by virtue of subsection (13) above), he may give a direction under that subsection.

(15) A direction under this subsection is a direction that a person desiring to exercise the right conferred by subsection (1) above may only consult a solicitor in the sight and hearing of a qualified officer of the uniformed branch of the force of which the officer giving the direction is a member.

(16) An officer is qualified for the purpose of subsection (15) above if—

(a) he is of at least the rank of inspector; and

(b) in the opinion of the officer giving the direction he has no connection with the case.

(17) An officer is of appropriate rank to give a direction under subsection (15) above if he is of at least the rank of Commander or Assistant Chief Constable.

(18) A direction under subsection (15) above shall cease to have effect once the reason for giving it ceases to subsist.

(See also Code C, para. 6.)

A 'serious arrestable offence' is defined in s. 116. By s. 116(2) the following arrestable offences are always serious:

(a) Offences specified in Part I of sch. 5. These cover common law and statutory offences and include treason, murder, manslaughter, kidnapping, rape and some other sexual offences, and offences under the Customs and Excise Management Act 1979, s. 170 (evading the prohibition on importing indecent or obscene articles).

(b) Offences specified in Part II of sch. 5 (various statutory offences).

(c) Certain offences mentioned in the Drug Trafficking Act 1994.

By s. 116(3), any other arrestable offence is serious only if its commission has led to any of the consequences specified in s. 116(6), or is intended or likely to lead to any of those consequences.

By s. 116(4), an arrestable offence which consists of making a threat is serious if carrying out the threat would be likely to lead to any of the consequences specified in s. 116(6).

The consequences specified in s. 116(6) are:

(a) serious harm to the security of the State or to public order;

(b) serious interference with the administration of justice or with the investigation of offences or of a particular offence;

(c) the death of any person;

(d) serious injury to any person;

(e) substantial financial gain to any person; and

(f) serious financial loss to any person.

By s. 116(7), loss is serious if, having regard to all the circumstances, it is serious for the person who suffers it. By s. 116(8), 'injury' includes any disease and any impairment of a person's physical or mental condition.

Scope of the rules and consequences of breach

To justify a refusal of access under s. 58(8), the police should be in a position to show that the solicitor might, wittingly or unwittingly, alert the accused's confederates and create the risks referred to in s. 58(8)(a)–(c). In *R* v *Samuel* [1988] QB 615, it was held that a person detained by the police to investigate a serious arrestable offence, had a fundamental right under s. 58(1) of the Police and Criminal Evidence Act 1984 to consult a solicitor. Access to a solicitor should not be denied or delayed on the grounds that the solicitor may advise the detainee not to answer questions.

Deliberate flouting of the rules will *normally* lead to exclusion under s. 78. However, in *R* v *Parris* (1989) 89 Cr App R 68, the Court of Appeal stated that 'the mere fact that there has been a breach of the Codes of Practice does not of itself mean that evidence has to be rejected'. Every case will be determined on its own particular facts. But if a breach was not deliberate and the accused was not prejudiced by the absence of his or her solicitor then the court is entitled to decline to exclude under s. 78. In *R* v *Alladice* (1988) 87 Cr App R 380, the Court of Appeal held that although the defendant was denied access to a solicitor under s. 58 of the 1984 Act (albeit by officers genuinely misconstruing the section) the trial judge was not obliged to rule the confession inadmissible. The defendant had told the police that he was able to cope with the interviews and matters would not have been improved by having a solicitor. His appeal against conviction was dismissed. See also *R* v *Dunford* (1990) 91 Cr App R 150.

Miscellaneous points about section 58

See *R* v *Beycan* [1990] Crim LR 185 (consent to being interviewed in the absence of a solicitor must be freely given).

R v *Chief Constable of Avon & Somerset, ex parte Robinson* [1989] 2 All ER 15 (chief constable entitled to regulate access by solicitors' clerks — see now Code C, para. 6.12).

In *R* v *Dunn* (1990) 91 Cr App R 150, there had been serious breaches of the Codes: no contemporaneous notes had been made of the disputed conversation, and the reason for the failure was not recorded in the officer's notebook. However, the accused had a legal representative (solicitor's clerk) present throughout the alleged conversation and therefore the admission of the evidence did not have an adverse effect on the fairness of the proceedings. The presence of the clerk was likely to have deterred any fabrication.

10.1.4 THE INCIDENTAL EFFECTS OF EXCLUDING A CONFESSION

Police and Criminal Evidence Act 1984, s. 76(4), (5) and (6) provides that:

> *(4) The fact that a confession is wholly or partly excluded in pursuance of this section shall not affect the admissibility in evidence—*
> *(a) of any facts discovered as a result of the confession: or*
> *(b) where the confession is relevant as showing that the accused speaks, writes or expresses himself in a particular way, of so much of the confession as is necessary to show that he does so.*
> *(5) Evidence that a fact to which this subsection applies was discovered as a result of a statement made by an accused person shall not be admissible unless evidence of how it was discovered is given by him or on his behalf.*
> *(6) Subsection (5) above applies—*
> *(a) to any fact discovered as a result of a confession which is wholly excluded in pursuance of this section: and*
> *(b) to any fact discovered as a result of a confession which is partly so excluded, if the fact is discovered as a result of the excluded part of the confession.*

Note:

(a) Although s. 76(4) refers to exclusion under s. 76 the same must apply to discretionary exclusion under s. 78.

(b)   These subsections have no effect in committal proceedings.

The effect of s. 76(4) to (5) is that when a confession is excluded under s. 76(2) any *facts* discovered as a result of the confession are admissible (s. 76(4)(a)) but it cannot be proved that the facts were discovered as a result of something said by the accused (s. 76(5)). Section 76(5) cannot be avoided by reference to a video re-enactment by the accused of the crime: see *Lam Chi-ming* v *R* [1991] 3 All ER 172, where video recordings showing the accused going to the waterfront and indicating where the murder weapon had been thrown were held to be as inadmissible as the oral confessions which had been extracted by police brutality.

Example: A, who is charged with the theft of some gold coins, confesses (as a result of oppression) and in his confession informs the police that the coins are buried at a particular spot in Epping Forest. This is confirmed by a police search. Assuming that the confession is excluded under s. 76(2), the prosecution may nevertheless prove that the coins were found buried in Epping Forest (s. 76(4)(a)) but *not* that this resulted from something said by the accused (s. 76(5)). It hardly needs saying that the effect of s. 76(5) in such a case is that the evidential impact against A of the discovery of the coins is nil (unless, of couse, the coins can be linked to A *factually*, e.g. by the presence of his fingerprints).

R v *Voisin* [1918] 1 KB 531 provides an illustration of the potential application of s. 76(4)(b). V was charged with the murder of a woman. Part of the body was found in a parcel with a hand-written note bearing the legend 'Blodie Belgiam'. V was not cautioned, but asked by the police to write the words 'Bloody Belgian'. V did this and misspelt them in precisely the same fashion as the writer of the note.

The fact that a confession is excluded under s. 76 or s. 78 does not mean that a subsequent confession will also be excluded. This depends on whether the factors which led to exclusion of the earlier confession have ceased to operate when the subsequent confession is made: see *R* v *Neil* [1994] Crim LR 441 and *R* v *Nelson* [1998] 2 Cr App R 399.

If incriminating documents are wrongfully seized, the documents are liable to be excluded. See *R* v *Barker* [1941] 2 KB 381 and **10.2** below.

10.2   Illegally or Improperly Obtained Evidence other than Confessions

There is no rule of law to the effect that evidence (other than confessions) must be excluded simply because it has been obtained illegally or improperly — see *Kuruma* v *R* [1955] AC 197. However this leaves open the question whether and to what extent a court may, at its discretion, exclude evidence other than confessions.

Again see Police and Criminal Evidence Act 1984, ss. 78 and 82(3) in **10.1.3**.

In *R* v *Sang* [1980] AC 402 the House of Lords seemed to suggest that *at common law* a court did not have a discretion to exclude illegally or improperly obtained evidence (*other than confessions and evidence analogous to confessions*) unless its probative value was outweighed by its prejudicial effect (see **2.8.2.2**). For an example of evidence analogous to a confession see *R* v *Payne* [1963] 1 WLR 637. In this case the accused was induced into providing a specimen of blood by the pretence that it was required to determine whether he was ill. In fact the reason for obtaining the specimen was to show that the accused was unfit to drive because he had been drinking alcohol. The Court of Appeal had no doubt that the evidence should have been excluded. See also *R* v *Nathaniel* [1995] 2 Cr App R 565 and the special rules for the taking of body samples and the consequences of breach in **Chapter 12** at **12.5.2.7**.

The effect of *R* v *Sang* is therefore that s. 82(3) (which preserves the common law position), would have no effect on, for example, an illegal search which produces relevant evidence unless the evidence can be equated with a confession or its probative value is outweighed by its prejudicial effect.

However, s. 78, which applies to *all* prosecution evidence, makes specific reference to 'the circumstances in which the evidence was obtained'. The courts have held that under s. 78 (as opposed to common law), evidence other than confessions may be excluded at the court's discretion by reason of the fact that it has been obtained illegally or improperly even though its probative value is not outweighed by its prejudicial effect. In *R v Quinn* [1990] Crim LR 581, Lord Lane stated, in interpreting s. 78 in the context of a case involving identification evidence, 'Proceedings may become unfair . . . where there has been an abuse of process, for example, because evidence has been obtained in deliberate breach of procedures laid down in an official code of practice'. In *R v Nathaniel* [1995] 2 Cr App R 565, Lord Taylor CJ took a similar view regarding breaches of the rules on body samples, see **12.5.2.7**.

In *Matto v DPP* [1987] Crim LR 641, the court quashed the defendant's conviction for drink driving after officers acted *mala fides* in requesting a breath specimen on private property. See also *R v Wright* [1994] Crim LR 55 (illegal search).

There are still occasional *dicta* that courts should only exclude non-confession evidence if its *quality* is such as to render its use at trial unfair: see e.g. *R v Chalkley* [1998] 2 All ER 155. However, these fly in the face of cases such as *Quinn*, *Nathaniel* and *Matto* (supra). See Choo, A, and Nash, S, 'What's the matter with section 78?' [1999] Crim LR 929. Several speeches in *R v Looseley* [2001] 4 All ER 897 suggest a wider scope for s. 78; see especially Lord Hoffmann, p. 909.

Evidence obtained by police undercover operations can give rise to problems if it is claimed that the evidence has been obtained by 'entrapment'. Entrapment arises where the State, through its agents, lures citizens into committing illegal acts and then prosecutes them (*R v Looseley* [2001] 4 All ER 897, 899). In *R v Smurthwaite* [1994] 1 All ER 892 the Court of Appeal acknowledged that entrapment did not of itself require a judge to exclude evidence. But the Court laid down the following guidelines for judges considering the exercise of their discretion under s. 78 in such cases:

> In exercising his discretion whether to admit the evidence of an undercover officer, some, but not an exhaustive list, of the factors that the judge may take into account are as follows: Was the officer acting as an *agent provocateur* in the sense that he was enticing the defendant to commit an offence he would not otherwise have committed? What was the nature of any entrapment? Does the evidence consist of admissions to a completed offence, or does it consist of the actual commission of an offence? How active or passive was the officer's role in obtaining the evidence? Is there an unassailable record of what occurred, or is it strongly corroborated? In *Christou and Wright* (1992) 95 Cr App R 264, this Court held that discussions between suspects and undercover officers, not overtly acting as police officers, were not within the ambit of the Codes under the 1984 Act. However, officers should not use their undercover pose to question suspects so as to circumvent the Code. In *Bryce* (1992) 95 Cr App R 320, the Court held that the undercover officer had done just that. Accordingly, a further consideration for the judge in deciding whether to admit an undercover officer's evidence, is whether he has abused his role to ask questions which ought properly to have been asked as a police officer and in accordance with the Codes.

An alternative remedy for entrapment is a stay of proceedings, and this should normally be preferred to exclusion of evidence under s. 78 (*R v Looseley* [2001] 4 All ER 987). In *Looseley*, the House of Lords identified some relevant factors where an application is made to stay proceedings on the basis of entrapment. These can be summarised as follows:

(a) Did the undercover officer behave like an ordinary member of the public, or did he offer extraordinary inducements?

(b)　In the case of some regulatory offences, the law could not be effective unless enforcement officers are able to make random tests. But normally it will be improper for police to provide people not suspected of being engaged in any criminal activity with the opportunity to commit crimes.

(c)　The justification of entrapment will depend partly on the nature of the offence being investigated. The fact that the offence is a serious one is not by itself sufficient. But where it is difficult to obtain evidence because of the nature of the offence, entrapment methods are likely to be justified. Examples are consensual offences, such as dealing in drugs; offences with no immediate victim, such as bribery; and offences which victims are reluctant to report.

(d)　Whether there has been entrapment cannot be determined simply by asking whether the defendant was given the opportunity to commit the offence, of which he freely availed himself. Nor is it possible to determine the existence of entrapment by a mechanical application of a distinction between 'active' and 'passive' conduct on the part of the undercover officer. But the greater the inducement held out by the police, and the more forceful or persistent their overtures, the more likely it is that a court will find entrapment.

10.3　PACE Code C: Code of Practice for the Detention, Treatment and Questioning of Persons by Police Officers

Commencement — Transitional Arrangements
This code applies to people in police detention after
midnight on 9 April 1995, notwithstanding that their
period of detention may have commenced before that time.

1.　General

1.1　All persons in custody must be dealt with expeditiously, and released as soon as the need for detention has ceased to apply.

1.1A　A custody officer is required to perform the functions specified in this code as soon as is practicable. A custody officer shall not be in breach of this code in the event of delay provided that the delay is justifiable and that every reasonable step is taken to prevent unnecessary delay. The custody record shall indicate where a delay has occurred and the reason why. [See Note 1H]

1.2　This code of practice must be readily available at all police stations for consultation by police officers, detained persons and members of the public.

1.3　The notes for guidance included are not provisions of this code, but are guidance to police officers and others about its application and interpretation. Provisions in the annexes to this code are provisions of this code.

1.4　If an officer has any suspicion, or is told in good faith, that a person of any age may be mentally disordered or mentally handicapped, or mentally incapable of understanding the significance of questions put to him or his replies, then that person shall be treated as a mentally disordered or mentally handicapped person for the purposes of this code. [See Note 1G]

1.5　If anyone appears to be under the age of 17 then he shall be treated as a juvenile for the purposes of this code in the absence of clear evidence to show that he is older.

1.6　If a person appears to be blind or seriously visually handicapped, deaf, unable to read, unable to speak or has difficulty orally because of a speech impediment, he should be treated as such for the purposes of this code in the absence of clear evidence to the contrary.

1.7　In this code 'the appropriate adult' means:
　　(a)　in the case of a juvenile:
　　　(i)　his parent or guardian (or, if he is in care, the care authority or voluntary organisation. The term 'in care' is used in this code to cover all cases in which a juvenile is 'looked after' by a local authority under the terms of the Children Act 1989);
　　　(ii)　a social worker; or
　　　(iii)　failing either of the above, another responsible adult aged 18 or over who is not a police officer or employed by the police.
　　(b)　in the case of a person who is mentally disordered or mentally handicapped:
　　　(i)　a relative, guardian or other person responsible for his care or custody;

      (ii)   someone who has experience of dealing with mentally disordered or mentally handicapped persons but is not a police officer or employed by the police (such as an approved social worker as defined by the Mental Health Act 1983 or a specialist social worker); or

      (iii)   failing either of the above, some other responsible adult aged 18 or over who is not a police officer or employed by the police.

[See Note 1E]

1.8   Whenever this code requires a person to be given certain information he does not have to be given it if he is incapable at the time of understanding what is said to him or is violent or likely to become violent or is in urgent need of medical attention, but he must be given it as soon as practicable.

1.9   Any reference to a custody officer in this code includes an officer who is performing the functions of a custody officer.

1.10   Subject to paragraph 1.12, this code applies to people who are in custody at police stations in England and Wales whether or not they have been arrested for an offence and to those who have been removed to a police station as a place of safety under section 135 and 136 of the Mental Health Act 1983. Section 15 (reviews and extensions of detention) however applies solely to people in police detention, for example those who have been brought to a police station under arrest for an offence or have been arrested at a police station for an offence after attending there voluntarily.

1.11   Persons in police detention include persons taken to a police station after being arrested under section 14 of the Prevention of Terrorism (Temporary Provisions) Act 1989 or under paragraph 6 of schedule 5 to that Act by an examining officer who is a constable.

1.12   This code does not apply to the following groups of people in custody:

      (i)   people who have been arrested by officers from a police force in Scotland exercising their powers of detention under section 137(2) of the Criminal Justice and Public Order Act 1994 (Cross Border powers of arrest etc.);

      (ii)   people arrested under section 3(5) of the Asylum and Immigration Appeals Act 1993 for the purpose of having their fingerprints taken;

      (iii)   people who have been served a notice advising them of their detention under powers contained in the Immigration Act 1971;

      (iv)   convicted or remanded prisoners held in police cells on behalf of the prison Service under the Imprisonment (Temporary Provisions) Act 1980);

but the provisions on conditions of detention and treatment in sections 8 and 9 of this code must be considered as the minimum standards of treatment for such detainees.

Notes for Guidance

1A   Although certain sections of this code (e.g., section 9 — treatment of detained persons) apply specifically to persons in custody at police stations, those there voluntarily to assist with an investigation should be treated with no less consideration (e.g., offered refreshments at appropriate times) and enjoy an absolute right to obtain legal advice or communicate with anyone outside the police station.

1B   This code does not affect the principle that all citizens have a duty to help police officers to prevent crime and discover offenders. This is a civic rather than a legal duty; but when a police officer is trying to discover whether, or by whom, an offence has been committed he is entitled to question any person from whom he thinks useful information can be obtained, subject to the restrictions imposed by this code. A person's declaration that he is unwilling to reply does not alter this entitlement.

1C   A person, including a parent or guardian, should not be an appropriate adult if he is suspected of involvement in the offence in question, is the victim, is a witness, is involved in the investigation or has received admissions prior to attending to act as the appropriate adult. If the parent of a juvenile is estranged from the juvenile, he should not be asked to act as the appropriate adult if the juvenile expressly and specifically objects to his presence.

1D   If a juvenile admits an offence to or in the presence of a social worker other than during the time that the social worker is acting as the appropriate adult for that juvenile, another social worker should be the appropriate adult in the interest of fairness.

1E   In the case of people who are mentally disordered or mentally handicapped, it may in certain circumstances be more satisfactory for all concerned if the appropriate adult is someone who has experience or training in their care rather than a relative lacking such qualifications. But if the person himself prefers a relative to a better qualified stranger or objects to a particular person as the appropriate adult, his wishes should if practicable be respected.

1EE   A person should always be given an opportunity, when an appropriate adult is called to the police station, to consult privately with a solicitor in the absence of the appropriate adult if they wish to do so.

1F   A solicitor or lay visitor who is present at the police station in that capacity may not act as the appropriate adult.

1G   The generic term 'mental disorder' is used throughout this code. 'Mental disorder' is defined in section 1(2) of the Mental Helath Act 1983 as 'mental illness, arrested or incomplete development of mind, psychopathic disorder and any other disorder or disability of mind'. It should be noted that 'mental disorder' is different from 'mental handicap' although the two are dealt with similarly throughout this code. Where the custody officer has any doubt as to the mental state or capacity of a person detained an appropriate adult should be called.

1H   Paragraph 1.1A is intended to cover the kinds of delays which may occur in the processing of detained persons because, for example, a large number of suspects are brought into the police station simultaneously to be placed in custody, or interview rooms are all being used, or where there are difficulties in contacting an appropriate adult, solicitor or interpreter.

1I   It is important that the custody officer reminds the appropriate adult and the detained person of the right to legal advice and records any reasons for waiving it in accordance with section 6 of this code.

2.   Custody records

2.1   A separate custody record must be opened as soon as practicable for each person who is brought to a police station under arrest or is arrested at the police station having attended there voluntarily. All information which has to be recorded under this code must be recorded as soon as practicable in the custody record unless otherwise specified. Any audio or video recording made in the custody area is not part of the custody record.

2.2   In the case of any action requiring the authority of an officer of a specified rank, his name and rank must be noted in the custody record. The recording of names does not apply to officers dealing with persons detained under the Prevention of Terrorism (Temporary Provisions) Act 1989. Instead the record shall state the warrant or other identification number and duty station of such officers.

2.3   The custody officer is responsible for the accuracy and completeness of the custody record and for ensuring that the record or a copy of the record accompanies a detained person if he is transferred to another police station. The record shall show the time of and reason for transfer and the time a person is released from detention.

2.4   A solicitor or appropriate adult must be permitted to consult the custody record of a person detained as soon as practicable after their arrival at the police station. When a person leaves police detention or is taken before a court, he or his legal representative or his appropriate adult shall be supplied on request with a copy of the custody record as soon as practicable. This entitlement lasts for 12 months after his release.

2.5   The person who has been detained, the appropriate adult, or the legal representative shall be permitted to inspect the original custody record after the person has left police detention provided they give reasonable notice of their request. A note of any such inspection shall be made in the custody record.

2.6   All entries in custody records must be timed and signed by the maker. In the case of a record entered on a computer this shall be timed and contain the operator's identification. Warrant or other identification numbers shall be used rather than names in the case of detention under the Prevention of Terrorism (Temporary Provisions) Act 1989.

2.7   The fact and time of any refusal by a person to sign a custody record when asked to do so in accordance with the provisions of this code must itself be recorded.

3.   Initial action

(a)   Detained persons: normal procedure

3.1   When a person is brought to a police station under arrest or is arrested at the police station having attended there voluntarily the custody officer must tell him clearly of the following rights and of the fact that they are continuing rights which may be exercised at any stage during the period in custody.
    (i)   the right to have someone informed of his arrest in accordance with section 5 below;
    (ii)   the right to consult privately with a solicitor in accordance with section 6 below, and the fact that independent legal advice is available free of charge; and
    (iii)   the right to consult this and the other codes of practice.
[See Note 3E]

3.2   In addition the custody officer must give the person a written notice setting out the above three rights, the right to a copy of the custody record in accordance with paragraph 2.4 above and the caution in the terms prescribed in section 10 below. The notice must also explain the arrangements for obtaining legal advice. The custody officer must also give the person an additional written notice briefly setting out his entitlements while in custody. [See Notes 3A and 3B] The custody officer shall ask the person to sign the custody record to acknowledge receipt of these notices and any refusal to sign must be recorded on the custody record.

3.3   A citizen of an independent Commonwealth country or a national of a foreign country (including the Republic of Ireland) must be informed as soon as practicable of his rights of communication with his High Commission, Embassy or Consulate (see Section 7).

3.4   The custody officer shall note on the custody record any comment the person may make in relation to the arresting officer's account but shall not invite comment. If the custody officer authorises a person's detention he must inform him of the grounds as soon as practicable and in any case before that person is then questioned about any offence. The custody officer shall note any comment the person may make in respect of the decision to detain him but, again, shall not invite comment. The custody officer shall not put specific questions to the person regarding his involvement in any offence, nor in respect of any comments he may make in response to the arresting officer's account or the decision to place him in detention. Such an exchange is likely to constitute an interview as defined by paragraph 11.1A and would require the associated safeguards included in section 11. [See also paragraph 11.13 in respect of unsolicited comments.]

3.5   The custody officer shall ask the detained person whether at this time he would like legal advice (see paragraph 6.5). The person shall be asked to sign the custody record to confirm his decision. The custody officer is responsible for ensuring that in confirming any decision the person signs in the correct place.

3.5A   If video cameras are installed in the custody area, notices which indicate that cameras are in use shall be prominently displayed. Any request by a detained person or other person to have video cameras switched off shall be refused.

(b)   Detained persons: special groups

3.6   If the person appears to be deaf or there is doubt about his hearing or speaking ability or ability to understand English, and the custody officer cannot establish effective communication, the custody officer must as soon as practicable call an interpreter, and ask him to provide the information required above. [See Section 13]

3.7   If the person is a juvenile, the custody officer must, if it is practicable, ascertain the identity of a person responsible for his welfare. That person may be his parent or guardian (or, if he is in care, the care authority or voluntary organisation) or any other person who has, for the time being, assumed responsibility for his welfare. That person must be informed as soon as practicable that the juvenile has been arrested, why he has been arrested and where he is detained. This right is in addition to the juvenile's right in section 5 of the code not to be held incommunicado. [See Note 3C]

3.8   In the case of a juvenile who is known to be subject to a supervision order, reasonable steps must also be taken to notify the person supervising him.

3.9   If the person is a juvenile, is mentally handicapped or appears to be suffering from a mental disorder, then the custody officer must, as soon as practicable, inform the appropriate adult (who in the case of a juvenile may or may not be a person responsible for his welfare, in accordance with paragraph 3.7 above) of the grounds for his detention and his whereabouts, and ask the adult to come to the police station to see the person.

3.10   It is imperative that a mentally disordered or mentally handicapped person who has been detained under section 136 of the Mental Health Act 1983 should be assessed as soon as possible. If that assessment is to take place at the police station, an approved social worker and a registered medical practitioner should be called to the police station as soon as possible in order to interview and examine the person. Once the person has been interviewed and examined and suitable arrangements have been made for his treatment or care, he can no longer be detained under section 136. The person should not be released until he has been seen by both the approved social worker and the registered medical practitioner.

3.11   If the appropriate adult is already at the police station, then the provisions of paragraphs 3.1 to 3.5 above must be complied with in his presence. If the appropriate adult is not at the police station when the provisions of paragraphs 3.1 to 3.5 above are complied with, then these provisions must be complied with again in the presence of the appropriate adult once that person arrives.

3.12   The person should be advised by the custody officer that the appropriate adult (where applicable) is there to assist and advise him and that he can consult privately with the appropriate adult at any time.

3.13   If, having been informed of the right to legal advice under paragraph 3.11 above, either the appropriate adult or the person detained wishes legal advice to be taken, then the provisions of section 6 of this code apply. [See Note 3G]

3.14   If the person is blind or seriously visually handicapped or is unable to read, the custody officer should ensure that his solicitor, relative, the appropriate adult or some other person likely to take an interest in him (and not involved in the investigation) is available to help in checking any documentation. Where this code requires written consent or signification, then the person who is assisting may be asked to sign instead if the detained person so wishes. [See Note 3F]

(c)   Persons attending a police station voluntarily

3.15   Any person attending a police station voluntarily for the purpose of assisting with an investigation may leave at will unless placed under arrest. If it is decided that he should not be allowed to do so then he must be informed at once that he is under arrest and brought before the custody officer, who is responsible for ensuring that he is notified of his rights in the same way as other detained persons. If he is not placed under arrest but is cautioned in accordance with section 10 below, the officer who gives the caution must at the same time inform him that he is not under arrest, that he is not obliged to remain at the police station but that if he remains at the police station he may obtain free legal advice if he wishes. The officer shall point out that the right to legal advice includes the right to speak with a solicitor on the telephone and ask him if he wishes to do so.

3.16   If a person who is attending the police station voluntarily (in accordance with paragraph 3.15) asks about his entitlement to legal advice, he should be given a copy of the notice explaining the arrangements for obtaining legal advice. [See paragraph 3.2].

(d)   Documentation

3.17   The grounds for a person's detention shall be recorded, in his presence if practicable.

3.18   Action taken under paragraphs 3.6 to 3.14 shall be recorded.

Notes for Guidance

3A   The notice of entitlements is intended to provide detained persons with brief details of their entitlements over and above the statutory rights which are set out in the notice of rights. The notice of entitlements should list the entitlements contained in this code, including visits and contact with outside parties (including special provisions for Commonwealth citizens and foreign nationals), reasonable standards of physical comfort, adequate food and drink, access to toilets and washing facilities, clothing, medical attention, and exercise where practicable. It should also mention the provisions relating to the conduct of interviews, the circumstances in which an appropriate adult should be available to assist the detained person and his statutory rights to make representation whenever the period of his detention is reviewed.

3B   In addition to the notices in English, translations should be available in Welsh, the main ethnic minority languages and the principal European languages whenever they are likely to be helpful.

3C   If the juvenile is in the care of a local authority or voluntary organisation but is living with his parents or other adults responsible for his welfare then, although there is no legal obligation on the police to inform them, they as well as the authority or organisation should normally be contacted unless suspected of involvement in the offence concerned. Even if a juvenile in care is not living with his parents, consideration should be given to informing them as well.

3D   Most local authority Social Services Departments can supply a list of interpreters who have the necessary skills and experience to interpret for the deaf at police interviews. The local Community Relations Council may be able to provide similar information in cases where the person concerned does not understand English.
[See Section 13]

3E   The right to consult the codes of practice under paragraph 3.1 above does not entitle the person concerned to delay unreasonably any necessary investigative or administrative action while he does so. Procedures requiring the provision of breath, blood or urine specimens under the terms of the Road Traffic Act 1988 need not be delayed.

3F   Blind or seriously visually handicapped persons may be unwilling to sign police documents. The alternative of their representative signing on their behalf seeks to protect the interests of both police and suspects.

3G   The purpose of paragraph 3.13 is to protect the rights of a juvenile, mentally disordered or mentally handicapped person who may not understand the significance of what is being said to him. If such a person wishes to exercise the right to legal advice the appropriate action should be taken straightaway and not delayed until the appropriate adult arrives.

4. Detained persons' property

(a) Action

4.1 The custody officer is responsible for:
  (a) ascertaining:
    (i) what property a detained person has with him when he comes to the police station (whether on arrest, re-detention on answering to bail, commitment to prison custody on the order or sentence of a court, on lodgement at the police station with a view to his production in court from such custody, on arrival at a police station on transfer from detention at another station or from hospital or on detention under section 135 or 136 of the Mental Health Act 1983);
    (ii) what property he might have acquired for an unlawful or harmful purpose while in custody.
  (b) the safekeeping of any property which is taken from him and which remains at the police station.
To these ends the custody officer may search him or authorise his being searched to the extent that he considers necessary (provided that a search of intimate parts of the body or involving the removal of more than outer clothing may only be made in accordance with **Annex A** to this code). A search may only be carried out by an officer of the same sex as the person searched. [See Note 4A]

4.2 A detained person may retain clothing and personal effects at his own risk unless the custody officer considers that he may use them to cause harm to himself or others, interfere with evidence, damage property or effect an escape or they are needed as evidence. In this event the custody officer may withhold such articles as he considers necessary. If he does so he must tell the person why.

4.3 Personal effects are those items which a person may lawfully need or use or refer to while in detention but do not include cash and other items of value.

(b) Documentation

4.4 The custody officer is responsible for recording all property brought to the police station that a detained person had with him, or had taken from him on arrest. The detained person shall be allowed to check and sign the record of property as correct. Any refusal to sign should be recorded.

4.5 If a detained person is not allowed to keep any article of clothing or personal effects the reason must be recorded.

Notes for Guidance

*4A Section 54(1) of PACE and paragraph 4.1 require a detained person to be searched where it is clear that the custody officer will have continuing duties in relation to that person or where that person's behaviour or offence makes an inventory appropriate. They do not require **every** detained person to be searched. Where, for example, it is clear that a person will only be detained for a short period and is not to be placed in a cell, the custody officer may decide not to search him. In such a case the custody record will be endorsed 'not searched', paragraph 4.4 will not apply, and the person will be invited to sign the entry. Where the person detained refuses to sign, the custody officer will be obliged to ascertain what property he has on him in accordance with paragraph 4.1.*

4B Paragraph 4.4 does not require the custody officer to record on the custody record property in the possession of the person on arrest, if by virtue of its nature, quantity or size, it is not practicable to remove it to the police station.

4C Paragraph 4.4 above is not to be taken as requiring that items of clothing worn by the person be recorded unless withheld by the custody officer in accordance with paragraph 4.2.

5. Right not to be held incommunicado

(a) Action

5.1 Any person arrested and held in custody at a police station or other premises may on request have one person known to him or who is likely to take an interest in his welfare informed at public expense as soon as practicable of his whereabouts. If the person cannot be contacted the person who has made the request may choose up to two alternatives. If they too cannot be contacted the person in charge of detention or of the investigation has discretion to allow further attempts until the information has been conveyed. [See Notes 5C and 5D]

5.2 The exercise of the above right in respect of each of the persons nominated may be delayed only in accordance with **Annex B** to this code.

5.3 The above right may be exercised on each occasion that a person is taken to another police station.

5.4 The person may receive visits at the custody officer's discretion. [See Note 5B]

5.5 Where an enquiry as to the whereabouts of the person is made by a friend, relative or person with an interest in his welfare, this information shall be given, if he agrees and if **Annex B** does not apply. [See Note 5D]

5.6 Subject to the following condition, the person should be supplied with writing materials on request and allowed to speak on the telephone for a reasonable time to one person [See Notes 5A and 5E]. Where an officer of the rank of Inspector or above considers that the sending of a letter or the making of a telephone call may result in:

(a) any of the consequences set out in the first and second paragraph of **Annex B** and the person is detained in connection with an arrestable or a serious arrestable offence, for which purpose, any reference to a serious arrestable offence in Annex B includes an arrestable offence; or

(b) either of the consequences set out in paragraph 8 of **Annex B** and the person is detained under the Prevention of Terrorism (Temporary Provisions) Act 1989,

that officer can deny or delay the exercise of either or both these privileges. However, nothing in this section permits the restriction or denial of the rights set out in sections 5.1 and 6.1.

5.7 Before any letter or message is sent, or telephone call made, the person shall be informed that what he says in any letter, call or message (other than in the case of a communication to a solicitor) may be read or listened to as appropriate and may be given in evidence. A telephone call may be terminated if it is being abused. The costs can be at public expense at the discretion of the custody officer.

(b) Documentation

5.8 A record must be kept of:

(a) any request made under this section and the action taken on it;

(b) any letters, messages or telephone calls made or received or visits received; and

(c) any refusal on the part of the person to have information about himself or his whereabouts given to an outside enquirer. The person must be asked to countersign the record accordingly and any refusal to sign should be recorded.

Notes for Guidance

5A An interpreter may make a telephone call or write a letter on a person's behalf.

5B In the exercise of his discretion the custody officer should allow visits where possible in the light of the availability of sufficient manpower to supervise a visit and any possible hindrance to the investigation.

5C If the person does not know of anyone to contact for advice or support or cannot contact a friend or relative, the custody officer should bear in mind any local voluntary bodies or other organisations who might be able to offer help in such cases. But if it is specifically legal advice that is wanted, then paragraph 6.1 below will apply.

5D In some circumstances it may not be appropriate to use the telephone to disclose information under paragraphs 5.1 and 5.5 above.

5E The telephone call at paragraph 5.6 is in addition to any communication under paragraphs 5.1 and 6.1.

6. Right to legal advice

(a) Action

6.1 Subject to the provisos in Annex B all people in police detention must be informed that they may at any time consult and communicate privately, whether in person, in writing or by telephone with a solicitor, and that independent legal advice is available free of charge from the duty solicitor. [See paragraph 3.1 and Note 6B and Note 6J]

6.2 [Not Used]

6.3 A poster advertising the right to have legal advice must be prominently displayed in the charging area of every police station. [See Note 6H]

6.4 No police officer shall at any time do or say anything with the intention of dissuading a person in detention from obtaining legal advice.

6.5 The exercise of the right of access to legal advice may be delayed only in accordance with **Annex B** to this code. Whenever legal advice is requested (and unless **Annex B** applies) the custody officer must act without delay to secure the provision of such advice to the person concerned. If, on being informed or reminded of the right to legal advice, the person declines to speak to a solicitor in person, the officer shall point out that the right to legal advice includes the right to speak with a solicitor on the telephone and ask him if he wishes to do so. If the person continues to waive his right to legal advice the officer shall ask him the reasons for doing so, and any reasons shall be recorded on the custody record or the interview record as appropriate. Reminders of the right to legal advice must be given in accordance with paragraphs 3.5, 11.2, 15.3, 16.4 and 16.5 of this code and paragraphs 2.15(ii) and 5.2 of Code D. Once it is clear that a person neither wishes to speak to a solicitor in person nor by telephone he should cease to be asked his reasons. [See Note 6K]

6.6   A person who wants legal advice may not be interviewed or continue to be interviewed until he has received it unless:

 (a)   **Annex B** applies; or

 (b)   an officer of the rank of superintendent or above has reasonable grounds for believing that:

  (i)   delay will involve an immediate risk of harm to persons or serious loss of, or damage to, property; or

  (ii)   where a solicitor, including a duty solicitor, has been contacted and has agreed to attend, awaiting his arrival would cause unreasonable delay to the process of investigation; or

 (c)   The solicitor nominated by the person, or selected by him from a list:

  (i)   cannot be contacted; or

  (ii)   has previously indicated that he does not wish to be contacted; or

  (iii)   having been contacted, has declined to attend;

and the person has been advised of the Duty Solicitor Scheme (where one is in operation) but has declined to ask for the duty solicitor, or the duty solicitor is unavailable. (In these circumstances the interview may be started or continued without further delay provided that an officer of the rank of Inspector or above has given agreement for the interview to proceed in those circumstances — See Note 6B).

 (d)   the person who wanted legal advice changes his mind.

In these circumstances the interview may be started or continued without further delay provided that the person has given his agreement in writing or on tape to being interviewed without receiving legal advice and that an officer of the rank of Inspector or above, having inquired into the person's reasons for his change of mind, has given authority for the interview to proceed. Confirmation of the person's agreement, his change of mind, his reasons where given and the name of the authorising officer shall be recorded in the taped or written interview record at the beginning or recommencement of interview. [See Note 6I]

6.7   Where 6.6(b)(i) applies, once sufficient information to avert the risk has been obtained, questioning must cease until the person has received legal advice or 6.6(a), (b)(ii), (c) or (d) apply.

6.8   Where a person has been permitted to consult a solicitor and the solicitor is available (i.e., present at the station or on his way to the station or easily contactable by telephone) at the time the interview begins or is in progress, he must be allowed to have his solicitor present while he is interviewed.

6.9   The solicitor may only be required to leave the interview if his conduct is such that the investigating officer is unable properly to put questions to the suspect. [See Notes 6D and 6E]

6.10   If the investigating officer considers that a solicitor is acting in such a way, he will stop the interview and consult an officer not below the rank of superintendent, if one is readily available, and otherwise an officer not below the rank of inspector who is not connected with the investigation. After speaking to the solicitor, the officer who has been consulted will decide whether or not the interview should continue in the presence of that solicitor. If he decides that it should not, the suspect will be given the opportunity to consult another solicitor before the interview continues and that solicitor will be given an opportunity to be present at the interview.

6.11   The removal of a solicitor from an interview is a serious step and, if it occurs, the officer of superintendent rank or above who took the decision will consider whether the incident should be reported to the Law Society. If the decision to remove the solicitor has been taken by an officer below the rank of superintendent, the facts must be reported to an officer of superintendent rank or above who will similarly consider whether a report to the Law Society would be appropriate. Where the solicitor concerned is a duty solicitor, the report should be both to the Law Society and to the Legal Aid Board.

6.12   In Codes of Practice issued under the Police and Criminal Evidence Act 1984, 'solicitor' means a solicitor who holds a current practising certificate, a trainee solicitor, a duty solicitor representative or an accredited representative included on the register of representatives maintained by the Legal Aid Board. If a solicitor wishes to send a non-accredited or probationary representative to provide advice on his behalf, then that person shall be admitted to the police station for this purpose unless an officer of the rank of inspector or above considers that such a visit will hinder the investigation of crime and directs otherwise. (Hindering the investigation of a crime does not include giving proper legal advice to a detained person in accordance with Note 6D.) Once admitted to the police station, the provisions of paragraphs 6.6 to 6.10 apply.

6.13   In exercising his discretion under pargraph 6.12, the officer should take into account in particular whether the identity and status of the non-accredited or probationary representative have been [satisfactorily] established; whether he is of suitable character to provide legal advice (a person with a criminal record is unlikely to be suitable unless the conviction was for a minor offence and is not of recent date); and any other matters in any written letter of authorisation provided by the solicitor on whose behalf the clerk or legal executive is attending the police station. [See Note 6F]

6.14 If the inspector refuses access to a non-accredited or probationary representative or a decision is taken that such a person should not be permitted to remain at an interview, he must forthwith notify a solicitor on whose behalf the non-accredited or probationary representative was to have acted or was acting, and give him an opportunity to make alternative arrangements. The detained person must also be informed and the custody record noted.

6.15 If a solicitor arrives at the station to see a particular person, that person must (unless **Annex B** applies) be informed of the solicitor's arrival whether or not he is being interviewed and asked whether he would like to see him. This applies even if the person concerned has already declined legal advice or having requested it, subsequently agreed to be interviewed without having received advice. The solicitor's attendance and the detained person's decision must be noted in the custody record.

(b) Documentation

6.16 Any request for legal advice and the action taken on it shall be recorded.

6.17 If a person has asked for legal advice and an interview is begun in the absence of a solicitor or his representative (or the solicitor or his representative has been required to leave an interview), a record shall be made in the interview record.

Notes for Guidance

6A In considering whether paragraph 6.6(b) applies, the officer should where practicable ask the solicitor for an estimate of the time that he is likely to take in coming to the station, and relate this information to the time for which detention is permitted, the time of day (i.e., whether the period of rest required by paragraph 12.2 is imminent) and the requirements of other investigations in progress. If the solicitor says that he is on his way to the station or that he will set off immediately, it will not normally be appropriate to begin an interview before he arrives. If it appears that it will be necessary to begin an interview before the solicitor's arrival he should be given an indication of how long police would be able to wait before paragraph 6.6(b) applies so that he has an opportunity to make arrangements for legal advice to be provided by someone else.

6B A person who asks for legal advice should be given an opportunity to consult a specific solicitor or another solicitor from that solicitor's firm or the duty solicitor. If advice is not available by these means, or he does not wish to consult the duty solicitor, the person should be given an opportunity to choose a solicitor from a list of those willing to provide legal advice. If this solicitor is unavailable, he may choose up two alternatives. If these attempts to secure legal advice are unsuccessful, the custody officer has discretion to allow further attempts until a solicitor has been contacted and agrees to provide legal advice. Apart from carrying out his duties under Note 6B, a police officer must not advise the suspect about any particular firm of solicitors.

6C [Not Used]

6D A detained person has a right to free legal advice and to be represented by a solicitor. The solicitor's only role in the police station is to protect and advance the legal rights of his client. On occasions this may require the solicitor to give advice which has the effect of his client avoiding giving evidence which strengthens a prosecution case. The solicitor may intervene in order to seek clarification or to challenge an improper question to his client or the manner in which it is put, or to advise his client not to reply to particular questions, or if he wishes to give his client further legal advice. Paragraph 6.9 will only apply if the solicitor's approach or conduct prevents or unreasonably obstructs proper questions being put to the suspect or his response being recorded. Examples of unacceptable conduct include answering questions on a suspect's behalf or providing written replies for him to quote.

6E In a case where an officer takes the decision to exclude a solicitor, he must be in a position to satisfy the court that the decision was properly made. In order to do this he may need to witness what is happening himself.

6F If an officer of at least the rank of inspector considers that a particular solicitor or firm of solicitors is persistently sending non-accredited or probationary representatives who are unsuited to provide legal advice, he should inform an officer of at least the rank of superintendent, who may wish to take the matter up with the Law Society.

*6G Subject to the constraints of **Annex B**, a solicitor may advise more than one client in an investigation if he wishes. Any question of a conflict of interest is for the solicitor under his professional code of conduct. If, however, waiting for a solicitor to give advice to one client may* *lead to unreasonable delay to the interview with another, the provisions of paragraph 6.6(b) may apply.*

6H In addition to the poster in English advertising the right to legal advice, a poster or posters containing translations into Welsh, the main ethnic minority languages and the principal European languages should be displayed wherever they are likely to be helpful and it is practicable to do so.

6I Paragraph 6.6(d) requires the authorisation of an officer of the rank of Inspector or above, to the continuation of an interview, where a person who wanted legal advice changes his mind. It is permissable for such authorisation to be given over the telephone, if the authorising officer is able to satisfy himself as to the reason for the person's change of mind and is satisfied that it is proper to continue the interview in those circumstances.

6J Where a person chooses to speak to a solicitor on the telephone, he should be allowed to do so in private unless this is impractical because of the design and layout of the custody area or the location of telephones.

6K A person is not obliged to give reasons for declining legal advice and should not be pressed if he does not wish to do so.

7. Citizens of independent Commonwealth countries or foreign nationals

(a) Action

7.1 Any citizen of an independent Commonwealth country or a national of a foreign country (including the Republic of Ireland) may communicate at any time with his High Commission, Embassy or Consulate. He must be informed of this right as soon as practicable. He must also be informed as soon as practicable of his right, upon request to have his High Commission, Embassy or Consulate told of his whereabouts and the grounds for his detention. Such a request should be acted upon as soon as practicable.

7.2 If a person is detained who is a citizen of an independent Commonwealth or foreign country with which a bilateral consular convention or agreement is in force requiring notification of arrest, the appropriate High Commission, Embassy or Consulate shall be informed as soon as practicable, subject to paragraph 7.4 below. The countries to which this applies as an 1 January 1995 are listed in **Annex F**.

7.3 Consular officers may visit one of their nationals who is in police detention to talk to him and, if required, to arrange for legal advice. Such visits shall take place out of the hearing of a police officer.

7.4 Notwithstanding the provisions of consular conventions, where the person is a political refugee (whether for reasons of race, nationality, political opinion or religion) or is seeking political asylum, a consular officer shall not be informed of the arrest of one of his nationals or given access to or information about him except at the person's express request.

(b) Documentation

7.5 A record shall be made when a person is informed of his rights under this section and of any communications with a High Commission, Embassy or Consulate.

Note for Guidance

*7A The exercise of the rights in this section may not be interfered with even though **Annex B** applies.*

8. Conditions of Detention

(a) Action

8.1 So far as is practicable, not more than one person shall be detained in each cell.

8.2 Cells in use must be adequately heated, cleaned and ventilated. They must be adequately lit, subject to such dimming as is compatible with safety and security to allow people detained overnight to sleep. No additional restraints shall be used within a locked cell unless absolutely necessary, and then only suitable handcuffs. In the case of a mentally handicapped or mentally disordered person, particular care must be taken when deciding whether to use handcuffs. [See **Annex E** paragraph 13]

8.3 Blankets, mattresses, pillows and other bedding supplied should be of a reasonable standard and in a clean and sanitary condition. [See Note 8B]

8.4 Access to toilet and washing facilities must be provided.

8.5 If it is necessary to remove a person's clothes for the purposes of investigation, for hygiene or health reasons or for cleaning, replacement clothing of a reasonable standard of comfort and cleanliness shall be provided. A person may not be interviewed unless adequate clothing has been offered to him.

8.6   At least two light meals and one main meal shall be offered in any period of 24 hours. [See Note 8C] Drinks should be provided at mealtimes and upon reasonable request between mealtimes. Whenever necessary, advice shall be sought from the police surgeon on medical or dietary matters. As far as practicable, meals provided shall offer a varied diet and meet any special dietary needs or religious beliefs that the person may have; he may also have meals supplied by his family or friends at his or their own expense. [See Note 8B]

8.7   Brief outdoor exercise shall be offered daily if practicable.

8.8   A juvenile shall not be placed in a police cell unless no other secure accommodation is available and the custody officer considers that it is not practicable to supervise him if he is not placed in a cell or the custody officer considers that a cell provides more comfortable accommodation than other secure accommodation in the police station. He may not be placed in a cell with a detained adult.

8.9   Reasonable force may be used if necessary for the following purposes:
      (i)   to secure compliance with reasonable instructions, including instructions given in pursuance of the provisions of a code of practice; or
      (ii)   to prevent escape, injury, damage to property or the destruction of evidence.

8.10   People detained shall be visited every hour, and those who are drunk, at least every half hour. A person who is drunk shall be roused and spoken to on each visit. [See Note 8A] Should the custody officer feel in any way concerned about the person's condition, for example because he fails to respond adequately when roused, then the officer shall arrange for medical treatment in accordance with paragraph 9.2 of this code.

(b)   Documentation

8.11   A record must be kept of replacement clothing and meals offered.

8.12   If a juvenile is placed in a cell, the reason must be recorded.

Notes for Guidance

8A   Whenever possible juveniles and other persons at risk should be visited more frequently.

8B   The provisions in paragraphs 8.3 and 8.6 respectively regarding bedding and a varied diet are of particular importance in the case of a person detained under the Prevention of Terrorism (Temporary Provisions) Act 1989, immigration detainees and others who are likely to be detained for an extended period.

8C   Meals should so far as practicable be offered at recognised meal times.

9.   Treatment of Detained Persons

(a)   General

9.1   If a complaint is made by or on behalf of a detained person about his treatment since his arrest, or it comes to the notice of any officer that he may have been treated improperly, a report must be made as soon as practicable to an officer of the rank of inspector or above who is not connected with the investigation. If the matter concerns a possible assault or the possibility of the unnecessary or unreasonable use of force then the police surgeon must also be called as soon as practicable.

(b) Medical Treatment

9.2   The custody officer must immediately call the police surgeon (or, in urgent cases, — for example, where a person does not show signs of sensibility or awareness, — must send the person to hospital or call the nearest available medical practitioner) if a person brought to a police station or already detained there:
      (a)   appears to be suffering from physical illness or a mental disorder; or
      (b)   is injured; or
      (c)   [Not Used]
      (d)   fails to respond normally to questions or conversation (other than through drunkenness alone); or
      (e)   otherwise appears to need medical attention.
This applies even if the person makes no request for medical attention and whether or not he has recently had medical treatment elsewhere (unless brought to the police station direct from hospital). It is not intended that the contents of this paragraph should delay the transfer of a person to a place of safety under section 136 of the Mental Health Act 1983 where that is applicable. Where an assessment under that Act is to take place at the police station, the custody officer has discretion not to call the police surgeon so long as he believes that the assessment by a registered medical practitioner can be undertaken without undue delay. [See Note 9A]

9.3   If it appears to the custody officer, or he is told, that a person brought to the police station under arrest may be suffering from an infectious disease of any significance he must take steps to isolate the person and his property until he has obtained medical directions as to where the person should be taken, whether fumigation should take place and what precautions should be taken by officers who have been or will be in contact with him.

9.4   If a detained person requests a medical examination the police surgeon must be called as soon as practicable. He may in addition be examined by a medical practitioner of his own choice at his own expense.

9.5   If a person is required to take or apply any medication in compliance with medical directions, but prescribed before the person's detention, the custody officer should consult the police surgeon prior to the use of the medication. The custody officer is responsible for the safekeeping of any medication and for ensuring that the person is given the opportunity to take or apply medication which the police surgeon has approved. However no police officer may administer medicines which are also controlled drugs subject to the Misuse of Drugs Act 1971 for this purpose. A person may administer a controlled drug to himself only under the personal supervision of the police surgeon. The requirement for personal supervision will have been satisfied if the custody officer consults the police surgeon (this may be done by telephone) and both the police surgeon and the custody officer are satisfied that, in all the circumstances, self administration of the controlled drug will not expose the detained person, police officers or anyone to the risk of harm or injury. If so satisfied, the police surgeon may authorise the custody officer to permit the detained person to administer the controlled drug. If the custody officer is in any doubt, the police surgeon should be asked to attend. Such consultation should be noted in the custody record.

9.6   If a detained person has in his possession or claims to need medication relating to a heart condition, diabetes, epilepsy or a condition of comparable potential seriousness then, even though paragraph 9.2 may not apply, the advice of the police surgeon must be obtained.

(c)   Documentation

9.7   A record must be made of any arrangements made for an examination by a police surgeon under paragraph 9.1 above and of any complaint reported under that paragraph together with any relevant remarks by the custody officer.

9.8   A record must be kept of any request for a medical examination under paragraph 9.4, of the arrangements for any examination made, and of any medical directions to the police.

9.9   Subject to the requirements of section 4 above the custody record shall include not only a record of all medication that a detained person has in his possession on arrival at the police station but also a note of any such medication he claims he needs but does not have with him.

Notes for Guidance

9A   The need to call a police surgeon need not apply to minor ailments or injuries which do not need attention. However, all such ailments or injuries must be recorded in the custody record and any doubt must be resolved in favour of calling the police surgeon.

9B   It is important to remember that a person who appears to be drunk or behaving abnormally may be suffering from illness or the effects of drugs or may have sustained injury (particularly head injury) which is not apparent, and that someone needing or addicted to certain drugs may experience harmful effects within a short time of being deprived of their supply. Police should therefore always call the police surgeon when in any doubt, and act with all due speed.

9C   If a medical practitioner does not record his clinical findings in the custody record, the record must show where they are recorded.

10.   Cautions

(a)   When a caution must be given

10.1   A person whom there are grounds to suspect of an offence must be cautioned before any questions about it (or further questions if it is his answers to previous questions which provide the grounds for suspicion) are put to him regarding his involvement or suspected involvement in that offence if his answers or his silence (i.e., failure or refusal to answer a question or to answer satisfactorily) may be given in evidence to a court in a prosecution. He therefore need not be cautioned if questions are put for other purposes, for example, solely to establish his identity or his ownership of any vehicle or to obtain information in accordance with any relevant statutory requirement (see paragraph 10.5C) or in furtherance of the proper and effective conduct of a search (for example to determine the need to search in the exercise of powers of stop and search or to seek co-operation while carrying out a search), or to seek verification of a written record in accordance with paragraph 11.13.

10.2   Whenever a person who is not under arrest is initially cautioned or is reminded that he is under caution (see paragraph 10.5) he must at the same time be told that he is not under arrest and is not obliged to remain with the officer (see paragraph 3.15).

10.3   A person must be cautioned upon arrest for an offence unless:
   (a)   it is impracticable to do so by reason of his condition or behaviour at the time; or
   (b)   he has already been cautioned immediately prior to arrest in accordance with paragraph 10.1 above.

(b)   Action: general

10.4   The caution shall be in the following terms:

> You do not have to say anything. But it may harm your defence if you do not mention when questioned something which you later rely on in court. Anything you do say may be given in evidence.

Minor deviations do not constitute a breach of this requirement provided that the sense of the caution is preserved. [See Note 10C]

10.5   When there is a break in questioning under caution the interviewing officer must ensure that the person being questioned is aware that he remains under caution. If there is any doubt the caution should be given again in full when the interview resumes. [See Note 10A]

Special warnings under sections 36 and 37 of the Criminal Justice and Public Order Act 1994

10.5A   When a suspect who is interviewed after arrest fails or refuses to answer certain questions, or to answer them satisfactorily, after due warning, a court or jury may draw such inferences as appear proper under sections 36 and 37 of the Criminal Justice and Public Order Act 1994. This applies when:
   (a)   a suspect is arrested by a constable and there is found on his person, or in or on his clothing or footwear, or otherwise in his possession, or in the place where he was arrested, any objects, marks or substances, or marks on such objects, and the person fails or refuses to account for the objects, marks or substances found; or
   (b)   an arrested person was found by a constable at a place at or about the time the offence for which he was arrested, is alleged to have been committed, and the person fails or refuses to account for his presence at that place.

10.5B   For an inference to be drawn from a suspect's failure or refusal to answer a question about one of these matters or to answer it satisfactorily, the interviewing officer must first tell him in ordinary language:
   (a)   what offence he is investigating;
   (b)   what fact he is asking the suspect to account for;
   (c)   that he believes this fact may be due to the suspect's taking part in the commission of the offence in question;
   (d)   that a court may draw a proper inference if he fails or refuses to account for the fact about which he is being questioned;
   (e)   that a record is being made of the interview and that it may be given in evidence if he is brought to trial.

10.5C   Where, despite the fact that a person has been cautioned, failure to co-operate may have an effect on his immediate treatment, he should be informed of any relevant consequences and that they are not affected by the caution. Examples are when his refusal to provide his name and address when charged may render him liable to detention, or when his refusal to provide particulars and information in accordance with a statutory requirement, for example, under the Road Traffic Act 1988, may amount to an offence or may make him liable to arrest.

(c)   Juveniles, the mentally disordered and the mentally handicapped

10.6   If a juvenile or a person who is mentally disordered or mentally handicapped is cautioned in the absence of the appropriate adult, the caution must be repeated in the adult's presence.

(d)   Documentation

10.7   A record shall be made when a caution is given under this section, either in the officer's pocket book or in the inteview record as appropriate.

Notes for guidance

10A   In considering whether or not to caution again after a break, the officer should bear in mind that he may have to satisfy a court that the person understood that he was still under caution when the interview resumed.

10B   [Not Used]

10C   If it appears that a person does not understand what the caution means, the officer who has given it should go on to explain it in his own words.

10D   [Not Used]

11.   Interviews: general

(a)   Action

11.1A   An interview is the questioning of a person regarding his involvement or suspected involvement in a criminal offence or offences which, by virtue of paragraph 10.1 of Code C, is required to be carried out under caution. Procedures undertaken under section 7 of the Road Traffic Act 1988 do not constitute interviewing for the purpose of this code.

11.1   Following a decision to arrest a suspect he must not be interviewed about the relevant offence except at a police station (or other authorised place of detention) unless the consequent delay would be likely:

(a)   to lead to interference with or harm to evidence connected with an offence or interference with or physical harm to other persons; or

(b)   to lead to the alerting of other persons suspected of having committed an offence but not yet arrested for it; or

(c)   to hinder the recovery of property obtained in consequence of the commission of an offence.

Interviewing in any of these circumstances should cease once the relevant risk has been averted or the necessary questions have been put in order to attempt to avert that risk.

11.2   Immediately prior to the commencement or re-commencement of any interview at a police station or other authorised place of detention, the interviewing officer shall remind the suspect of his entitlement to free legal advice and the interview can be delayed for him to obtain legal advice (unless the exceptions in paragraph 6.6 or **Annex C** apply). It is the responsibility of the interviewing officer to ensure that all such reminders are noted in the record of interview.

11.2A   At the beginning of an interview carried out in a police station, the interviewing officer, after cautioning the suspect, shall put to him any significant statement or silence which occurred before his arrival at the police station, and shall ask him whether he confirms or denies that earlier statement or silence and whether he wishes to add anything. A 'significant' statement or silence is one which appears capable of being used in evidence against the suspect, in particular a direct admission of guilt, or failure or refusal to answer a question or to answer it satisfactorily, which might give rise to an inference under part III of the Criminal Justice and Public Order Act 1994.

11.3   No police officer may try to obtain answers to questions or to elicit a statement by the use of oppression. Except as provided for in paragraph 10.5C, no police officer shall indicate, except in answer to a direct question, what action will be taken on the part of the police if the person being interviewed answers questions, makes a statement or refuses to do either. If the person asks the officer directly what action will be taken in the event of his answering questions, making a statement or refusing to do either, then the officer may inform the person what action the police propose to take in that event provided that action is itself proper and warranted.

11.4   As soon as a police officer who is making enquiries of any person about an offence believes that a prosecution should be brought against him and that there is sufficient evidence for it to succeed, he should ask the person if he has anything further to say. If the person indicates that he has nothing more to say the officer shall without delay cease to question him about that offence. This should not, however, be taken to prevent officers in revenue cases or acting under the confiscation provisions of the Criminal Justice Act 1988 or the Drug Trafficking Offences Act 1986 from inviting suspects to complete a formal question and answer record after the interview is concluded.

(b)   Interview records

11.5   (a)   An accurate record must be made of each interview with a person suspected of an offence, whether or not the interview takes place at a police station.

(b)   The record must state the place of the interview, the time it begins and ends, the time the record is made (if different), any breaks in the interview and the names of all those present; and must be made on the forms provided for this purpose or in the officer's pocket-book or in accordance with the code of practice for the tape-recording of police interviews with suspects.

(c)   The record must be made during the course of the interview, unless in the investigating officer's view this would not be practicable or would interfere with the conduct of the interview, and must constitute either a verbatim record of what has been said or, failing this, an account of the interview which adequately and accurately summarises it.

11.6   The requirement to record the names of all those present at an interview does not apply to police officers interviewing persons detained under the Prevention of Terrorism (Temporary

Provisions) Act 1989. Instead the record shall state the warrant or other identification number and duty station of such officers.

11.7 If an interview record is not made during the course of the interview it must be made as soon as practicable after its completion.

11.8 Written interview records must be timed and signed by the maker.

11.9 If an interview record is not completed in the course of the interview the reason must be recorded in the officer's pocket book.

11.10 Unless it is impracticable the person interviewed shall be given the opportunity to read the interview record and to sign it as correct or to indicate the respects in which he considers it inaccurate. If the interview is tape-recorded the arrangements set out in the relevant code of practice apply. If the person concerned cannot read or refuses to read the record or to sign it, the senior police officer present shall read it over to him and ask him whether he would like to sign it as correct (or make his mark) or to indicate the respects in which he considers it inaccurate. The police officer shall then certify on the interview record itself what has occurred. [See Note 11D]

11.11 If the appropriate adult or the person's solicitor is present during the interview, he should also be given an opportunity to read and sign the interview record (or any written statement taken down by a police officer).

11.12 Any refusal by a person to sign an interview record when asked to do so in accordance with the provisions of this code must itself be recorded.

11.13 A written record should also be made of any comments made by a suspected person, including unsolicited comments, which are outside the context of an interview but which might be relevant to the offence. Any such record must be timed and signed by the maker. Where practicable the person shall be given the opportunity to read that record and to sign it as correct or to indicate the respects in which he considers it inaccurate. Any refusal to sign should be recorded. [See Note 11D]

(c) Juveniles, the mentally disordered and the mentally handicapped

11.14 A juvenile or a person who is mentally disordered or mentally handicapped, whether suspected or not, must not be interviewed or asked to provide or sign a written statement in the absence of the appropriate adult unless paragraph 11.1 or **Annex C** applies.

11.15 Juveniles may only be interviewed at their places of education in exceptional circumstances and then only where the principal or his nominee agrees. Every effort should be made to notify both the parent(s) or other person responsible for the juvenile's welfare and the appropriate adult (if this is a different person) that the police want to interview the juvenile and reasonable time should be allowed to enable the appropriate adult to be present at the interview. Where awaiting the appropriate adult would cause unreasonable delay and unless the interviewee is suspected of an offence against the educational establishment, the principal or his nominee can act as the appropriate adult for the purposes of the interview.

11.16 Where the appropriate adult is present at an interview, he should be informed that he is not expected to act simply as an observer; and also that the purposes of his presence are, first, to advise the person being questioned and to observe whether or not the interview is being conducted properly and fairly, and, secondly, to facilitate communication with the person being interviewed.

Notes for guidance

11A   [Not Used]

11B   It is important to bear in mind that, although juveniles or persons who are mentally disordered or mentally handicapped are often capable of providing reliable evidence, they may, without knowing or wishing to do so, be particularly prone in certain circumstances to provide information which is unreliable, misleading or self-incriminating. Special care should therefore always be exercised in questioning such a person, and the appropriate adult should be involved, if there is any doubt about a person's age, mental state or capacity. Because of the risk of unreliable evidence it is also important to obtain corroboration of any facts admitted whenever possible.

11C   It is preferable that a juvenile is not arrested at his place of education unless this is unavoidable. Where a juvenile is arrested at his place of education, the principal or his nominee must be informed.

11D   When a suspect agrees to read records of interviews and of other comments and to sign them as correct, he should be asked to endorse the record with words such as 'I agree that this is a correct record of what was said' and add his signature. Where the suspect does not agree with the record, the officer should record the details of any disagreement and then ask the suspect to read these details and then sign them to the effect that they accurately reflect his disagreement. Any refusal to sign when asked to do so shall be recorded.

12. Interviews in police stations

(a) Action

12.1   If a police officer wishes to interview, or conduct enquiries which require the presence of a detained person the custody officer is responsible for deciding whether to deliver him into his custody.

12.2   In any period of 24 hours a detained person must be allowed a continuous period of at least 8 hours for rest, free from questioning, travel or any interruption by police officers in connection with the investigation concerned. This period should normally be at night. The period of rest may not be interrupted or delayed, except at the request of the person, his appropriate adult or his legal representative, unless there are reasonable grounds for believing that it would:
    (i)   involve a risk of harm to persons or serious loss of, or damage to, property;
    (ii)   delay unnecessarily the person's release from custody; or
    (iii) otherwise prejudice the outcome of the investigation.
If a person is arrested at a police station after going there voluntarily, the period of 24 hours runs from the time of his arrest and not the time of arrival at the police station. Any action which is required to be taken in accordance with section 8 of this code, or in accordance with medical advice or at the request of the detained person, his appropriate adult or his legal representative, does not constitute an interruption to the rest period such that a fresh period must be allowed.

12.3   A detained person may not be supplied with intoxicating liquor except on medical directions. No person who is unfit through drink or drugs to the extent that he is unable to appreciate the significance of questions put to him and his answers may be questioned about an alleged offence in that condition except in accordance with **Annex C**. [See Note 12B]

12.4   As far as practicable interviews shall take place in interview rooms which must be adequately heated, lit and ventilated.

12.5   Persons being questioned or making statements shall not be required to stand.

12.6   Before the commencement of an interview each interviewing officer shall identify himself and any other officers present by name and rank to the person being interviewed, except in the case of persons detained under the Prevention of Terrorism (Temporary Provisions) Act 1989 when each officer shall identify himself by his warrant or other identification number and rank rather than his name.

12.7   Breaks from interviewing shall be made at recognised meal times. Short breaks for refreshment shall also be provided at intervals of approximately two hours, subject to the interviewing officer's discretion to delay a break if there are reasonable grounds for believing that it would:
    (i)   involve a risk of harm to persons or serious loss of, or damage to, property;
    (ii)   delay unnecessarily the person's release from custody; or
    (iii) otherwise prejudice the outcome of the investigation.

[See Note 12C]

12.8   If in the course of the interview a complaint is made by the person being questioned or on his behalf concerning the provisions of this code then the interviewing officer shall:
    (i)   record it in the interview record; and
    (ii)   inform the custody officer, who is then responsible for dealing with it in accordance with section 9 of this code.

(b) Documentation

12.9   A record must be made of the times at which a detained person is not in the custody of the custody officer, and why; and of the reason for any refusal to deliver him out of that custody.

12.10   A record must be made of any intoxicating liquor supplied to a detained person, in accordance with paragraph 12.3 above.

12.11   Any decision to delay a break in an interview must be recorded, with grounds, in the interview record.

12.12   All written statements made at police stations under caution shall be written on the forms provided for the purpose.

12.13   All written statements made under caution shall be taken in accordance with **Annex D** to this code.

Notes for Guidance

12A   If the interview has been contemporaneously recorded and the record signed by the person interviewed in accordance with paragraph 11.10 above, or has been tape recorded, it is normally unnecessary to ask for a written statement. Statements under caution should normally be taken in these circumstances only at the person's express wish. An officer may, however, ask him whether or not he wants to make such a statement.

12B   The police surgeon can give advice about whether or not a person is fit to be interviewed in accordance with paragraph 12.3 above.

12C   Meal breaks should normally last at least 45 minutes and shorter breaks after two hours should last at least 15 minutes. If the interviewing officer delays a break in accordance with paragraph 12.7 of this code and prolongs the interview, a longer break should then be provided. If there is a short interview, and a subsequent short interview is contemplated, the length of the break may be reduced if there are reasonable grounds to believe that this is necessary to avoid any of the consequences in paragraph 12.7 (i) to (iii).

13. Interpreters

(a)   General

13.1   Information on obtaining the services of a suitably qualified interpreter for the deaf or for persons who do not understand English is given in Note for Guidance 3D.

(b)   Foreign languages

13.2   Except in accordance with paragraph 11.1 or unless Annex C applies, a person must not be interviewed in the absence of a person capable of acting as interpreter if:
    (a)   he has difficulty in understanding English;
    (b)   the interviewing officer cannot himself speak the person's own language; and
    (c)   the person wishes an interpreter to be present.

13.3   The interviewing officer shall ensure that the interpreter makes a note of the interview at the time in the language of the person being interviewed for use in the event of his being called to give evidence, and certifies its accuracy. He shall allow sufficient time for the interpreter to make a note of each question and answer after each has been put or given and interpreted. The person shall be given an opportunity to read it or have it read to him and sign it as correct or to indicate the respects in which he considers it inaccurate. If the interview is tape-recorded the arrangements set out in the relevant code of practice apply.

13.4   In the case of a person making a statement in a language other than English:
    (a)   the interpreter shall take down the statement in the language in which it is made;
    (b)   the person making the statement shall be invited to sign it; and
    (c)   an official English translation shall be made in due course.

(c)   Deaf people and people with a speech handicap

13.5   If a person appears to be deaf or there is doubt about his hearing or speaking ability, he must not be interviewed in the absence of an interpreter unless he agrees in writing to be interviewed without one or paragraph 11.1 or **Annex C** applies.

13.6   An interpreter should also be called if a juvenile is interviewed and the parent or guardian present as the appropriate adult appears to be deaf or there is doubt about his hearing or speaking ability, unless he agrees in writing that the interview should proceed without one or paragraph 11.1 or **Annex C** applies.

13.7   The interviewing officer shall ensure that the interpreter is given an opportunity to read the record of the interview and to certify its accuracy in the event of his being called to give evidence.

(d)   Additional rules for detained persons

13.8   All reasonable attempts should be made to make clear to the detained person that interpreters will be provided at public expense.

13.9   Where paragraph 6.1 applies and the person concerned cannot communicate with the solicitor, whether because of language, hearing or speech difficulties, an interpreter must be called. The interpreter may not be a police officer when interpretation is needed for the purposes of obtaining legal advice. In all other cases a police officer may only interpret if he first obtains the detained person's (or the appropriate adult's) agreement in writing or if the interview is tape-recorded in accordance with Code E.

13.10   When a person is charged with an offence who appears to be deaf or there is doubt about his hearing or speaking ability or ability to understand English, and the custody officer cannot establish effective communication, arrangements must be made for an interpreter to explain as soon as practicable the offence concerned and any other information given by the custody officer.

(e) Documentation

13.11   Action taken to call an interpreter under this section and any agreement to be interviewed in the absence of an interpreter must be recorded.

Note for Guidance

13A   If the interpreter is needed as a prosecution witness at the person's trial, a second interpreter must act as the court interpreter.

14.   Questioning: special restrictions

14.1   If a person has been arrested by one police force on behalf of another and the lawful period of detention in respect of that offence has not yet commenced in accordance with section 41 of the Police and Criminal Evidence Act 1984 no questions may be put to him about the offence while he is in transit between the forces except in order to clarify any voluntary statement made by him.

14.2   If a person is in police detention at a hospital he may not be questioned without the agreement of a responsible doctor. [See Note 14A]

Note for Guidance

14A   If questioning takes place at a hospital under paragraph 14.2 (or on the way to or from a hospital) the period concerned counts towards the total period of detention permitted.

15.   Reviews and extensions of detention

(a) Action

15.1   The review officer is responsible under section 40 of the Police and Criminal Evidence Act 1984 (or, in terrorist cases, under Schedule 3 to the Prevention of Terrorism (Temporary Provisions) Act 1989) for determining whether or not a person's detention continues to be necessary. In reaching a decision he shall provide an opportunity to the detained person himself to make representations (unless he is unfit to do so because of his condition or behaviour) or to his solicitor or the appropriate adult if available at the time. Other persons having an interest in the person's welfare may make representations at the review officer's discretion.

15.2   The same persons may make representations to the officer determining whether further detention should be authorised under section 42 of the Act or under Schedule 3 to the 1989 Act. [See Note 15A]

15.2A   After hearing any representations, the review officer or officer determining whether further detention should be authorised shall note any comment the person may make if the decision is to keep him in detention. The officer shall not put specific questions to the suspect regarding his involvement in any offence, nor in respect of any comments he may make in response to the decision to keep him in detention. Such an exchange is likely to constitute an interview as defined by paragraph 11.1A and would require the associated safeguards included in section 11. [See also paragraph 11.13]

(b) Documentation

15.3   Before conducting a review the review officer must ensure that the detained person is reminded of his entitlement to free legal advice (see paragraph 6.5). It is the responsibility of the review officer to ensure that all such reminders are noted in the custody record.

15.4   The grounds for and extent of any delay in conducting a review shall be recorded.

15.5   Any written representations shall be retained.

15.6   A record shall be made as soon as practicable of the outcome of each review and application for a warrant of further detention or its extension.

Notes for Guidance

15A   If the detained person is likely to be asleep at the latest time when a review of detention or an authorisation of continued detention may take place, the appropriate officer should bring it forward so that the detained person may make representations without being woken up.

15B   An application for a warrant of further detention or its extension should be made between 10am and 9pm, and if possible during normal court hours. It will not be practicable to arrange for a court to sit specially outside the hours of 10am to 9pm. If it appears possible that a special sitting may be needed (either at a weekend, Bank/Public Holiday or on a weekday outside normal court hours but between 10am and 9pm) then the clerk to the justices should be given notice and informed of this possibility, while the court is sitting if possible.

15C   If in the circumstances the only practicable way of conducting a review is over the telephone then this is permissible, provided that the requirements of section 40 of the Police and

Criminal Evidence Act 1984 or of Schedule 3 to the Prevention of Terrorism (Temporary Provisions) Act 1989 are observed. However, a review to decide whether to authorise a person's continued detention under section 42 of the 1984 Act must be done in person rather than over the telephone.

16. Charging of detained persons

(a) Action

16.1   When an officer considers that there is sufficient evidence to prosecute a detained person, and that there is sufficient evidence for a prosecution to succeed, and that the person has said all that he wishes to say about the offence, he should without delay (and subject to the following qualification) bring him before the custody officer who shall then be responsible for considering whether or not he should be charged. When a person is detained in respect of more than one offence it is permissible to delay bringing him before the custody officer until the above conditions are satisfied in respect of all the offences (but see paragraph 11.4). Any resulting action should be taken in the presence of the appropriate adult if the person is a juvenile or mentally disordered or mentally handicapped.

16.2   When a detained person is charged with or informed that he may be prosecuted for an offence he shall be cautioned in the terms:

> You do not have to say anything. But it may harm your defence if you do not mention now something which you later rely on in court. Anything you do say may be given in evidence.

16.3   At the time a person is charged he shall be given a written notice showing particulars of the offence with which he is charged and including the name of the officer in the case (in terrorist cases, the officer's warrant or other identification number instead), his police station and the reference number for the case. So far as possible the particulars of the charge shall be stated in simple terms, but they shall also show the precise offence in law with which he is charged. The notice shall begin with the following words:

> You are charged with the offence(s) shown below. You do not have to say anything. But it may harm your defence if you do not mention now something which you later rely on in court. Anything you do say may be given in evidence.

If the person is a juvenile or is mentally disordered or mentally handicapped the notice shall be given to the appropriate adult.

16.4   If at any time after a person has been charged with or informed he may be prosecuted for an offence, a police officer wishes to bring to the notice of the person any written statement made by another person or the content of an interview with another person, he shall hand to that person a true copy of any such written statement or bring to his attention the content of the interview record, but shall say or do nothing to invite any reply or comment save to warn him that he does not have to say anything but that anything he does say may be given in evidence and to remind him of his right to legal advice in accordance with paragraph 6.5 above. If the person cannot read then the officer may read it to him. If the person is a juvenile or mentally disordered or mentally handicapped the copy shall also be given to, or the interview record brought to the attention of, the appropriate adult.

16.5   Questions relating to an offence may not be put to a person after he has been charged with that offence, or informed that he may be prosecuted for it, unless they are necessary for the purpose of preventing or minimising harm or loss to some other person or to the public or for clearing up an ambiguity in a previous answer or statement, or where it is in the interests of justice that the person should have put to him and have an opportunity to comment on information concerning the offence which has come to light since he was charged or informed that he might be prosecuted. Before any such questions are put to him, he shall be warned that he does not have to say anything but that anything he does say may be given in evidence and reminded of his right to legal advice in accordance with paragraph 6.5 above. [See Note 16A]

16.6   Where a juvenile is charged with an offence and the custody officer authorises his continued detention he must try to make arrangements for the juvenile to be taken into the care of a local authority to be detained pending appearance in court unless he certifies that it is impracticable to do so, or, in the case of a juvenile of at least 12 years of age, no secure accommodation is available and there is a risk to the public of serious harm from that juvenile, in accordance with section 38(6) of the Police and Criminal Evidence Act 1984, as amended by Section 59 of the Criminal Justice Act 1991 and section 24 of the Criminal Justice and Public Order Act 1994. [See Note 16B]

(b) Documentation

16.7   A record shall be made of anything a detained person says when charged.

16.8   Any questions put after charge and answers given relating to the offence shall be contemporaneously recorded in full on the forms provided and the record signed by that person or, if he refuses, by the interviewing officer and any third parties present. If the questions are tape-recorded the arrangements set out in Code E apply.

16.9   If it is not practicable to make arrangements for the transfer of a juvenile into local authority care in accordance with paragraph 16.6 above the custody officer must record the reasons and make out a certificate to be produced before the court together with the juvenile.

Notes for Guidance

16A   The service of the Notice of Intended Prosecution under sections 1 and 2 of the Road Traffic Offenders Act 1988 does not amount to informing a person that he may be prosecuted for an offence and so does not preclude further questioning in relation to that offence.

16B   Except as provided for in 16.6 above, neither a juvenile's behviour nor the nature of the offence with which he is charged provides grounds for the custody officer to decide that it is impracticable to seek to arrange for his transfer to the care of the local authority. Similarly, the lack of secure local authority accommodation shall not make it impracticable for the custody officer to transfer him. The availability of secure accommodation is only a factor in relation to a juvenile aged 12 or over when the local authority accommodation would not be adequate to protect the public from serious harm from the juvenile. The obligation to transfer a juvenile to local authority accommodation applies as much to a juvenile charged during the daytime as it does to a juvenile to be held overnight, subject to a requirement to bring the juvenile before a court under section 46 of the Police and Criminal Evidence Act 1984.

ANNEX A
INTIMATE AND STRIP SEARCHES (see paragraph 4.1)

A.   INTIMATE SEARCH

1.   An 'intimate search' is a search which consists of the physical examination of a person's body orifices other than the mouth.

(a)   Action

2.   Body orifices may be searched only if an officer of the rank of superintendent or above has reasonable grounds for believing:
   (a)   that an article which could cause physical injury to a detained person or others at the police station has been concealed; or
   (b)   that the person has concealed a Class A drug which he intended to supply to another or to export; and
   (c)   that in either case an intimate search is the only practicable means of removing it.
The reasons why an intimate search is considered necessary shall be explained to the person before the search takes place.

3.   An intimate search may only be carried out by a registered medical practitioner or registered nurse, unless an officer of at least the rank of superintendent considers that this is not practicable and the search is to take place under sub-paragraph 1(a) above.

4.   An intimate search under sub-paragraph 1(a) above may take place only at a hospital, surgery, other medical premises or police station. A search under sub-paragraph 1(b) may take place only at a hospital, surgery or other medical premises.

5.   An intimate search at a police station of a juvenile or a mentally disordered or mentally handicapped person may take place only in the presence of the appropriate adult of the same sex (unless the person specifically requests the presence of a particular adult of the opposite sex who is readily available). In the case of a juvenile the search may take place in the absence of the appropriate adult only if the juvenile signifies in the presence of the appropriate adult that he prefers the search to be done in his absence and the appropriate adult agrees. A record should be made of the juvenile's decision and signed by the appropriate adult.

6.   Where an intimate search under sub-paragraph 2(a) above is carried out by a police officer, the officer must be of the same sex as the person searched. Subject to paragraph 5 above, no person of the opposite sex who is not a medical practitioner or nurse shall be present, nor shall anyone whose presence is unnecessary but a minimum of two people, other than the person searched, must be present during the search. The search shall be conducted with proper regard to the sensitivity and vulnerability of the person in these circumstances.

(b)   Documentation

7.   In the case of an intimate search the custody officer shall as soon as practicable record which parts of the person's body were searched, who carried out the search, who was present, the reasons for the search and its result.

8.   If an intimate search is carried out by a police officer, the reason why it is impracticable for a suitably qualified person to conduct it must be recorded.

B.   STRIP SEARCH

9.   A strip search is a search involving the removal of more than outer clothing.

(a)   Action

10.   A strip search may take place only if it is considered necessary to remove an article which a person would not be allowed to keep, and the officer reasonably considers that the person might have concealed such an article. Strip searches shall not be routinely carried out where there is no reason to consider that articles have been concealed.

The conduct of strip searches

11.   The following procedures shall be observed when strip searches are conducted:
    (a)   a police officer carrying out a strip search must be of the same sex as the person searched;
    (b)   the search shall take place in an area where the person being searched cannot be seen by anyone who does not need to be present, nor by a member of the opposite sex (except an appropriate adult who has been specifically requested by the person being searched);
    (c)   except in cases of urgency, where there is a risk of serious harm to the person detained or to others, whenever a strip search involves exposure of intimate parts of the body, there must be at least two people present other than the person searched, and if the search is of a juvenile or a mentally disordered or mentally handicapped person, one of the people must be the appropriate adult. Except in urgent cases as above, a search of a juvenile may take place in the absence of the appropriate adult only if the juvenile signifies in the presence of the appropriate adult that he prefers the search to be done in his absence and the appropriate adult agrees. A record shall be made of the juvenile's decision and signed by the appropriate adult. The presence of more than two people, other than an appropriate adult, shall be permitted only in the most exceptional circumstances
    (d)   the search shall be conducted with proper regard to the sensitivity and vulnerability of the person in these circumstances and every reasonable effort shall be made to secure the person's co-operation and minimise embarrassment. People who are searched should not normally be required to have all their clothes removed at the same time, for example, a man shall be allowed to put on his shirt before removing his trousers, and a woman shall be allowed to put on her blouse and upper garments before further clothing is removed;
    (e)   where necessary to assist the search, the person may be required to hold his or her arms in the air or to stand with his or her legs apart and to bend forward so that a visual examination may be made of the genital and anal areas provided that no physical contact is made with any body orifice;
    (f)   if, during a search, articles are found, the person shall be asked to hand them over. If articles are found within any body orifice other than the mouth, and the person refuses to hand them over, their removal would constitute an intimate search, which must be carried out in accordance with the provisions of part A of this Annex;
    (g)   a strip search shall be conducted as quickly as possible, and the person searched allowed to dress as soon as the procedure is complete.

(b)   Documentation

12.   A record shall be made on the custody record of a strip search including the reason it was considered necessary to undertake it, those present and any result.

ANNEX B
DELAY IN NOTIFYING ARREST OR ALLOWING ACCESS TO
LEGAL ADVICE

A.   Persons detained under the Police and Criminal Evidence Act 1984

(a)   Action

1.   The rights set out in sections 5 or 6 of the code or both may be delayed if the person is in police detention in connection with a serious arrestable offence, has not yet been charged with an offence and an officer of the rank of superintendent or above has reasonable grounds for believing that the exercise of either right:
    (i)   will lead to interference with or harm to evidence connected with a serious arrestable offence or interference with or physical injury to other persons; or
    (ii)   will lead to the alerting of other persons suspected of having committed such an offence but not yet arrested for it; or
    (iii)   will hinder the recovery of property obtained as a result of such an offence.
[See Note B3]

2. These rights may also be delayed where the serious arrestable offence is either:

(i) a drug trafficking offence and the officer has reasonable grounds for believing that the detained person has benefited from drug trafficking, and that the recovery of the value of that person's proceeds of drug trafficking will be hindered by the exercise of either right or;

(ii) an offence to which part VI of the Criminal Justice Act 1988 (covering confiscation orders) applies and the officer has reasonable grounds for believing that the detained person has benefited from the offence, and that the recovery of the value of the property obtained by that person from or in connection with the offence or if the pecuniary advantage derived by him from or in connection with it will be hindered by the exercise of either right.

3. Access to a solicitor may not be delayed on the grounds that he might advise the person not to answer any questions or that the solicitor was initially asked to attend the police station by someone else, provided that the person himself then wishes to see the solicitor. In the latter case the detained person must be told that the solicitor has come to the police station at another person's request, and must be asked to sign the custody record to signify whether or not he wishes to see the solicitor.

4. These rights may be delayed only for as long as is necessary and, subject to paragraph 9 below, in no case beyond 36 hours after the relevant time as defined in section 41 of the Police and Criminal Evidence Act 1984. If the above grounds cease to apply within this time, the person must as soon as practicable be asked if he wishes to exercise either right, the custody record must be noted accordingly, and action must be taken in accordance with the relevant section of the code.

5. A detained person must be permitted to consult a solicitor for a reasonable time before any court hearing.

(b) Documentation

6. The grounds for action under this Annex shall be recorded and the person informed of them as soon as practicable.

7. Any reply given by a person under paragraphs 4 or 9 must be recorded and the person asked to endorse the record in relation to whether he wishes to receive legal advice at this point.

B. Persons detained under the Prevention of Terrorism (Temporary Provisions) Act 1989

(a) Action

8. The rights set out in sections 5 or 6 of this code or both may be delayed if paragraph 1 above applies or if an officer of the rank of superintendent or above has reasonable grounds for believing that the exercise of either right:

(a) will lead to interference with the gathering of information about the commission, preparation or instigation of acts of terrorism; or

(b) by alerting any person, will make it more difficult to prevent an act of terrorism or to secure the apprehension, prosecution or conviction of any person in connection with the commission, preparation or instigation of an act of terrorism.

9. These rights may be delayed only for as long as is necessary and in no case beyond 48 hours from the time of arrest. If the above grounds cease to apply within this time, the person must as soon as practicable be asked if he wishes to exercise either right, the custody record must be noted accordingly, and action must be taken in accordance with the relevant section of this code.

10. Paragraphs 3 and 5 above apply.

(b) Documentation

11. Paragraphs 6 and 7 above apply.

Notes for Guidance

*B1 Even if **Annex B** applies in the case of a juvenile, or a person who is mentally disordered or mentally handicapped, action to inform the appropriate adult (and the person responsible for a juvenile's welfare, if that is a different person) must nevertheless be taken in accordance with paragraph 3.7 and 3.9 of this code.*

B2 In the case of Commonwealth citizens and foreign nationals see Note 7A.

B3 Police detention is defined in section 118(2) of the Police and Criminal Evidence Act 1984.

B4 The effect of paragraph 1 above is that the officer may authorise delaying access to a specific solicitor only if he has reasonable grounds to believe that that specific solicitor will, inadvertently or otherwise, pass on a message from the detained person or act in some other way which will lead to any of the three results in paragraph 1 coming about. In these circumstances the officer should offer the detained person access to a solicitor (who is not the specific solicitor referred to above) on the Duty Solicitor Scheme.

B5   The fact that the grounds for delaying notification of arrest under paragraph 1 above may be satisfied does not automatically mean that the grounds for delaying access to legal advice will also be satisfied.

ANNEX C
VULNERABLE SUSPECTS: URGENT INTERVIEWS AT
POLICE STATIONS

1.   When an interview is to take place in a police station or other authorised place of detention if, and only if, an officer of the rank of superintendent or above considers that delay will lead to the consequences set out in paragraph 11.1 (a) to (c) of this Code:

   (a)   a person heavily under the influence of drink or drugs may be interviewed in that state; or

   (b)   a juvenile or a person who is mentally disordered or mentally handicapped may be interviewed in the absence of the appropriate adult; or

   (c)   a person who has difficulty in understanding English or who has a hearing disability may be interviewed in the absence of an interpreter.

2.   Questioning in these circumstances may not continue once sufficient information to avert the immediate risk has been obtained.

3.   A record shall be made of the grounds for any decision to interview a person under paragraph 1 above.

Note for Guidance

C1   The special groups referred to in this Annex are all particularly vulnerable. The provisions of the annex, which override safeguards designed to protect them and to minimise the risk of interviews producing unreliable evidence, should be applied only in exceptional cases of need.

ANNEX D
WRITTEN STATEMENTS UNDER CAUTION (see paragraph 12.13)

(a)   Written by a person under caution

1.   A person shall always be invited to write down himself what he wants to say.

2.   Where the person wishes to write it himself, he shall be asked to write out and sign before writing what he wants to say, the following:

   I make this statement of my own free will. I understand that I do not have to say anything but that it may harm my defence if I do not mention when questioned something which I later rely on in court. This statement may be given in evidence.

3.   Any person writing his own statement shall be allowed to do so without any prompting except that a police officer may indicate to him which matters are material or question any ambiguity in the statement.

(b)   Written by a police officer

4.   If a person says that he would like someone to write it for him, a police officer shall write the statement, but, before starting, he must ask him to sign, or make his mark, to the following:

   I, ..., wish to make a statement. I want someone to write down what I say. I understand that I need not say anything but that it may harm my defence if I do not mention when questioned something which I later rely on in court. This statement may be given in evidence.

5.   Where a police officer writes the statement, he must take down the exact words spoken by the person making it and he must not edit or paraphrase it. Any questions that are necessary (e.g., to make it more intelligible) and the answers given must be recorded contemporaneously on the statement form.

6.   When the writing of a statement by a police officer is finished the person making it shall be asked to read it and to make any corrections, alterations or additions he wishes. When he has finished reading it he shall be asked to write and sign or make his mark on the following certificate at the end of the statement:

   I have read the above statement, and I have been able to correct, alter or add anything I wish. This statement is true. I have made it of my own free will.

7.   If the person making the statement cannot read, or refuses to read it, or to write the above mentioned certificate at the end of it or to sign it, the senior police officer present shall read it over to him whether he would like to correct, alter or add anything and to put his signature or make his mark at the end. The police officer shall then certify on the statement itself what has occurred.

ANNEX E
SUMMARY OF PROVISIONS RELATING TO MENTALLY DISORDERED
AND MENTALLY HANDICAPPED PERSONS

1.   If an officer has any suspicion or is told in good faith that a person of any age, whether or not in custody, may be suffering from mental disorder or mentally handicapped, or cannot understand the significance of questions put to him or his replies, then he shall be treated as a mentally disordered or mentally handicapped person. [See paragraph 1.4]

2.   In the case of a person who is mentally disordered or mentally handicapped, 'the appropriate adult' means:
 (a)   a relative, guardian or some other person responsible for his care or custody;
 (b)   someone who has experience of dealing with mentally disordered or mentally handicapped persons but is not a police officer or employed by the police; or
 (c)   failing either of the above, some other responsible adult aged 18 or over who is not a police officer or employed by the police.
[See paragraph 1.7(b)]

3.   If the custody officer authorises the detention of a person who is mentally handicapped or appears to be suffering from a mental disorder he must as soon as practicable inform the appropriate adult of the grounds for the person's detention and his whereabouts, and ask the adult to come to the police station to see the person. If the appropriate adult is already at the police station when information is given as required in paragraphs 3.1 to 3.5 the information must be given to the detained person in the appropriate adult's presence. If the appropriate adult is not at the police station when the provisions of 3.1 to 3.5 are complied with then these provisions must be complied with again in the presence of the appropriate adult once that person arrives. [See paragraphs 3.9 and 3.11]

4.   If the appropriate adult, having been informed of the right to legal advice, considers that legal advice should be taken, the provisions of section 6 of the code apply as if the mentally disordered or mentally handicapped person has requested access to legal advice. [See paragraph 3.13 and Note E2]

5.   If a person brought to a police station appears to be suffering from mental disorder or is incoherent other than through drunkenness alone, or if a detained person subsequently appears to be mentally disordered, the custody officer must immediately call the police surgeon or, in urgent cases, send the person to hospital or call the nearest available medical practitioner. It is not intended that these provisions should delay the transfer of a person to a place of safety under section 136 of the Mental Health Act 1983 where that is applicable. Where an assessment under that Act is to take place at the police station, the custody officer has discretion not to call the police surgeon so long as he believes that the assessment by a registered medical practitioner can be undertaken without undue delay. [See paragraph 9.2]

6.   It is imperative that a mentally disordered or mentally handicapped person who has been detained under section 136 of the Mental Health Act 1983 should be assessed as soon as possible. If that assessment is to take place at the police station, an approved social worker and a registered medical practitioner should be called to the police station as soon as possible in order to interview and examine the person. Once the person has been interviewed and examined and suitable arrangements have been made for his treatment or care, he can no longer be detained under section 136.   The person should not be released until he has been seen by both the approved social worker and the registered medical practitioner. [See paragraph 3.10]

7.   If a mentally disordered or mentally handicapped person is cautioned in the absence of the appropriate adult, the caution must be repeated in the adult's presence. [See paragraph 10.6]

8.   A mentally disordered or mentally handicapped person must not be interviewed or asked to provide or sign a written statement in the absence of the appropriate adult unless the provisions of paragraph 11.1 or **Annex C** of this code apply. Questioning in these circumstances may not continue in the absence of the appropriate adult once sufficient information to avert the risk has been obtained. A record shall be made of the grounds for any decision to begin an interview in these circumstances. [See paragraphs 11.1 and 11.14 and **Annex C**]

9.   Where the appropriate adult is present at an interview, he should be informed that he is not expected to act simply as an observer; and also that the purposes of his presence are, first, to advise the person being interviewed and to observe whether or not the interview is being conducted properly and fairly, and, secondly to facilitate communication with the person being interviewed. [See paragraph 11.16]

10.   If the detention of a mentally disordered or mentally handicapped person is reviewed by a review officer or a superintendent, the appropriate adult must, if available at the time be given

opportunity to make representations to the officer about the need for continuing detention. [See paragraph 15.1 and 15.2]

11.   If the custody officer charges a mentally disordered or mentally handicapped person with an offence or takes such other action as is appropriate when there is sufficient evidence for a prosecution this must be done in the presence of the appropriate adult. The written notice embodying any charge must be given to the appropriate adult. [See paragraphs 16.1 to 16.3]

12.   An intimate or strip search of a mentally disordered or mentally handicapped person may take place only in the presence of the appropriate adult of the same sex, unless the person specifically requests the presence of a particular adult of the opposite sex. A strip search may take place in the absence of an appropriate adult only in cases of urgency where there is a risk of serious harm to the person detained or to others. [See **Annex A**, paragraphs 5 and 11(c)]

13.   Particular care must be taken when deciding whether to use handcuffs to restrain a mentally disordered or mentally handicapped person in a locked cell. [See paragraph 8.2]

Notes for guidance

E1   In the case of mentally disordered or mentally handicapped people, it may in certain circumstances be more satisfactory for all concerned if the appropriate adult is someone who has experience or training in their care rather than a relative lacking such qualifications. But if the person himself prefers a relative to a better qualified stranger or objects to a particular person as the appropriate adult, his wishes should if practicable be respected. [See Note 1E]

E2   The purpose of the provision at paragraph 3.13 is to protect the rights of a mentally disordered or mentally handicapped person who does not understand the significance of what is being said to him. If the person wishes to exercise the right to legal advice, the appropriate action should be taken and not delayed until the appropriate adult arrives. [See Note 3G] A mentally disordered or mentally handicapped person should always be given an opportunity, when an appropriate adult is called to the police station, to consult privately with a solicitor in the absence of the appropriate adult if he wishes to do so. [See Note 1EE].

E3   It is important to bear in mind that although persons who are mentally disordered or mentally handicapped are often capable of providing reliable evidence, they may, without knowing or wishing to do so, be particularly prone in certain circumstances to provide information which is unreliable, misleading or self-incriminating. Special care should therefore always be exercised in questioning such a person, and the appropriate adult involved, if there is any doubt about a person's mental state or capacity. Because of the risk of unreliable evidence, it is important to obtain corroboration of any facts admitted whenever possible. [See Note 11B]

*E4   Because of the risks referred to in Note E3, which the presence of the appropriate adult is intended to minimise, officers of superintendent rank or above should exercise their discretion to authorise the commencement of an interview in the adult's absence only in exceptional cases, where it is necessary to avert an immediate risk of serious harm. [See **Annex C**, sub-paragraph 1(1) and Note C1]*

ANNEX F
COUNTRIES WITH WHICH BILATERAL CONSULAR CONVENTIONS OR AGREEMENTS REQUIRING NOTIFICATION OF THE ARREST AND DETENTION OF THEIR NATIONALS ARE IN FORCE AS AT 1 JANUARY 1995

Armenia	Kyrgyzstan
Austria	Macedonia
Azerbaijan	Mexico
Belarus	Moldova
Belgium	Mongolia
Bosnia-Hercegovina	Norway
Bulgaria	Poland
China*	Romania
Croatia	Russia
Cuba	Slovak Republic
Czech Republic	Slovenia
Denmark	Spain
Egypt	Sweden
France	Tajikistan
Georgia	Turkmenistan
German Federal Republic	Ukraine
Greece	USA

Hungary   Uzbekistan
Kazakhstan   Yugoslavia

*Police are required to inform Chinese officials of arrest/detention in the Manchester consular district only. This comprises Derbyshire, Durham, Greater Manchester, Lancashire, Merseyside, North, South and West Yorkshire, and Tyne and Wear.

10.4 PACE Code E: Code of Practice on Tape Recording of Interviews with Suspects

Commencement — Transitional Arrangements

This code applies to interviews carried out after midnight on 9 April 1995, notwithstanding that the interview may have commenced before that time.

1. General

1.1   This code of practice must be readily available for consultation by police officers, detained persons and members of the public at every police station to which an order made under section 60(1)(b) of the Police and Criminal Evidence Act 1984 applies.

1.2   The notes for guidance included are not provisions of this code. They form guidance to police officers and others about its application and interpretation.

1.3   Nothing in this code shall be taken as detracting in any way from the requirements of the Code of Practice for the Detention, Treatment and Questioning of Persons by Police Officers (Code C). [See *Note 1A*].

1.4   This code does not apply to those groups of people listed in paragraph 1.12 of Code C.

1.5   In this code the term 'appropriate adult' has the same meaning as in paragraph 1.7 of Code C; and the term 'solicitor' has the same meaning as in paragraph 6.12 of Code C.

Note for Guidance

1A   As in Code C, references to custody officers include those carrying out the functions of a custody officer.

2. Recording and the sealing of master tapes

2.1   Tape recording of interviews shall be carried out openly to instil confidence in its reliability as an impartial and accurate record of the interview. [See *Note 2A*].

2.2   One tape, referred to in this code as the master tape, will be sealed before it leaves the presence of the suspect. A second tape will be used as a working copy. The master tape is either one of the two tapes used in a twin deck machine or the only tape used in a single deck machine. The working copy is either the second tape used in a twin deck machine or a copy of the master tape made by a single deck machine. [See *Notes 2B and 2C*].

Notes for Guidance

2A   Police Officers will wish to arrange that, as far as possible, tape recording arrangements are unobtrusive. It must be clear to the suspect, however, that there is no opportunity to interfere with the tape recording equipment or the tapes.

2B   The purpose of sealing the master tape before it leaves the presence of the suspect is to establish his confidence that the integrity of the tape is preserved. Where a single deck machine is used the working copy of the master tape must be made in the presence of the suspect and without the master tape having left his sight. The working copy shall be used for making further copies where the need arises. The recorder will normally be capable of recording voices and have a time coding or other security device.

2C   Throughout this code any reference to 'tapes' shall be construed as 'tape', as appropriate, where a single deck machine is used.

3. Interviews to be tape recorded

3.1   Subject to paragraph 3.2 below, tape recording shall be used at police stations for any interview:
   (a)   with a person who has been cautioned in accordance with section 10 of Code C in respect of an indictable offence (including an offence triable either way) [see *Notes 3A and 3B*];
   (b)   which takes place as a result of a police officer exceptionally putting further questions to a suspect about an offence described in sub-paragraph (a) above after he has been charged with, or informed he may be prosecuted for, that offence [see *Note 3C*]; or

(c)   in which a police officer wishes to bring to the notice of a person, after he has been charged with, or informed he may be prosecuted for an offence described in sub-paragraph (a) above, any written statement made by another person, or the content of an interview with another person [see *Note 3D*].

3.2   Tape recording is not required in respect of the following:
(a)   an interview with a person arrested under section 14(1)(a) or Schedule 5 paragraph 6 of the Prevention of Terrorism (Temporary Provisions) Act 1989 or an interview with a person being questioned in respect of an offence where there are reasonable grounds for suspecting that it is connected to terrorism or was committed in furtherance of the objectives of an organisation engaged in terrorism. This sub-paragraph applies only where the terrorism is connected with the affairs of Northern Ireland or is terrorism of any other description except terrorism connected solely with the affairs of the United Kingdom or any part of the United Kingdom other than Northern Ireland, 'Terrorism' has the meaning given by section 20(1) of the Prevention of Terrorism (Temporary Provisions) Act 1989 [see *Notes 3E, 3F, 3G* and *3H*];
(b)   an interview with a person suspected on reasonable grounds of an offence under section 1 of the Official Secrets Act 1911 [see *Note 3H*].

3.3   The custody officer may authorise the interviewing officer not to tape record the interview:
(a)   where it is not reasonably practicable to do so because of failure of the equipment or the non-availability of a suitable interview room or recorder and the authorising officer considers on reasonable grounds that the interview should not be delayed until the failure has been rectified or a suitable room or recorder becomes available [see *Note 3J*]; or
(b)   where it is clear from the outset that no prosecution will ensue.
In such cases the interview shall be recorded in writing and in accordance with section 11 of Code C. In all cases the custody officer shall make a note in specific terms of the reasons for not tape recording. [See *Note 3K*].

3.4   Where an interview takes place with a person voluntarily attending the police station and the police officer has grounds to believe that person has become a suspect (i.e. the point at which he should be cautioned in accordance with paragraph 10.1 of Code C) the continuation of the interview shall be tape recorded, unless the custody officer gives authority in accordance with the provisions of paragraph 3.3 above for the continuation of the interview not to be recorded.

3.5   The whole of each interview shall be tape recorded, including the taking and reading back of any statement.

Notes for Guidance

3A   Nothing in this code is intended to preclude tape recording at police discretion of interviews at police stations with people cautioned in respect of offences not covered by paragraph 3.1, or responses made by interviewees after they have been charged with, or informed they may be prosecuted for, an offence, provided that this code is complied with.

3B   Attention is drawn to the restrictions in paragraph 12.3 of Code C on the questioning of people unfit through drink or drugs to the extent that they are unable to appreciate the significance of questions put to them or of their answers.

3C   Circumstances in which a suspect may be questioned about an offence after being charged with it are set out in paragraph 16.5 of Code C.

3D   Procedures to be followed when a person's attention is drawn after charge to a statement made by another person are set out in paragraph 16.4 of Code C. One method of bringing the content of an interview with another person to the notice of a suspect may be to play him a tape recording of that interview.

3E   Section 14(1)(a) of the Prevention of Terrorism (Temporary Provisions) Act 1989, permits the arrest without warrant of a person reasonably suspected to be guilty of an offence under section 2, 8, 9, 10 or 11 of the Act.

3F   Section 20(1) of the Prevention of Terrorism (Temporary Provisions) Act 1989 says 'terrorism means the use of violence for political ends, and includes any use of violence for the purpose of putting the public or any section of the public in fear'.

3G   It should be noted that the provisions of paragraph 3.2 apply only to those suspected of offences connected with terrorism connected with Northern Ireland, or with terrorism of any other description other than terrorism connected solely with the affairs of the United Kingdom or any part of the United Kingdom other than Northern Ireland, or offences committed in furtherance of such terrorism. Any interviews with those suspected of offences connected with terrorism of any other description or in furtherance of the objectives of an organisation engaged in such terrorism should be carried out in compliance with the rest of this code.

3H   When it only becomes clear during the course of an interview which is being tape recorded that the interviewee may have committed an offence to which paragraph 3.2 applies the interviewing officer should turn off the tape recorder.

3J   Where practicable, priority should be given to tape recording interviews with people who are suspected of more serious offences.

3K   A decision not to tape record an interview for any reason may be the subject of comment in court. The authorising officer should therefore be prepared to justify his decision in each case.

4.   The interview

(a)   Commencement of interviews

4.1   When the suspect is brought into the interview room the police officer shall without delay, but in the sight of the suspect, load the tape recorder with clean tapes and set it to record. The tapes must be unwrapped or otherwise opened in the presence of the suspect. [See *Note 4A*].

4.2   The police officer shall then tell the suspect formally about the tape recording. He shall say:
   (a)   that the interview is being tape recorded;
   (b)   his name and rank and the name and rank of any other police officer present except in the case of enquiries linked to the investigation of terrorism where warrant or other identification numbers shall be stated rather than names;
   (c)   the name of the suspect and any other party present (e.g. a solicitor);
   (d)   the date, time of commencement and place of the interview; and
   (e)   that the suspect will be given a notice about what will happen to the tapes.
[See *Note 4B*].

4.3   The police officer shall then caution the suspect in the following terms:

   'You do not have to say anything. But it may harm your defence if you do not mention when questioned something which you later rely on in court. Anything you do say may be given in evidence.'

Minor deviations do not constitute a breach of this requirement provided that the sense of the caution is preserved. [See *Note 4C*].

4.3A   The police officer shall remind the suspect of his right to free and independent legal advice and that he can speak to a solicitor on the telephone in accordance with paragraph 6.5 of Code C.

4.3B   The police officer shall then put to the suspect any significant statement or silence (i.e. failure or refusal to answer a question or to answer it satisfactorily) which occurred before the start of the tape-recorded interview, and shall ask him whether he confirms or denies that earlier statement or silence or whether he wishes to add anything. A 'significant' statement or silence means one which appears capable of being used in evidence against the suspect, in particular a direct admission of guilt, or failure or refusal to answer a question or to answer it satisfactorily, which might give rise to an inference under Part III of the Criminal Justice and Public Order Act 1994.

Special warnings under sections 36 and 37 of the Criminal Justice and Public Order Act 1994
4.3C   When a suspect who is interviewed after arrest fails or refuses to answer certain questions, or to answer them satisfactorily, after due warning, a court or jury may draw a proper inference from this silence under sections 36 and 37 of the Criminal Justice and Public Order Act 1994. This applies when:
   (a)   a suspect is arrested by a constable and there is found on his person, or in or on his clothing or footwear, or otherwise in his possession, or in the place where he was arrested, any objects, marks or substances, or marks on such objects, and the person fails or refuses to account for the objects, marks or substances found; or
   (b)   an arrested person was found by a constable at a place at or about the time the offence for which he was arrested, is alleged to have been committed, and the person fails or refuses to account for his presence at that place.

4.3D   For an inference to be drawn from a suspect's failure or refusal to answer a question about one of these matters or to answer it satisfactorily, the interviewing officer must first tell him in ordinary language:
   (a)   what offence he is investigating;
   (b)   what fact he is asking the suspect to account for;
   (c)   that he believes this fact may be due to the suspect's taking part in the commission of the offence in question;
   (d)   that a court may draw a proper inference from his silence if he fails or refuses to account for the fact about which he is being questioned;

(e) that a record is being made of the interview and may be given in evidence if he is brought to trial.

4.3E Where, despite the fact that a person has been cautioned, failure to cooperate may have an effect on his immediate treatment, he should be informed of any relevant consequences and that they are not affected by the caution. Examples are when his refusal to provide his name and address when charged may render him liable to detention, or when his refusal to provide particulars and information in accordance with a statutory requirement, for example, under the Road Traffic Act 1988, may amount to an offence or may make him liable to arrest.

(b) Interviews with the deaf

4.4 If the suspect is deaf or there is doubt about his hearing ability, the police officer shall take a contemporaneous note of the interview in accordance with the requirements of Code C, as well as tape record it in accordance with the provisions of this code. [See *Notes 4E and 4F*].

(c) Objections and complaints by the suspect

4.5 If the suspect raises objections to the interview being tape recorded either at the outset or during the interview or during a break in the interview, the police officer shall explain the fact that the interview is being tape recorded and that the provisions of this code require that the suspect's objections shall be recorded on tape. When any objections have been recorded on tape or the suspect has refused to have his objections recorded, the police officer may turn off the recorder. In this eventuality he shall say that he is turning off the recorder and give his reasons for doing so and then turn it off. The police officer shall then make a written record of the interview in accordance with section 11 of Code C. If, however, the police officer reasonably considers that he may proceed to put questions to the suspect with the tape recorder still on, he may do so. [See *Note 4G*].

4.6 If in the course of an interview a complaint is made by the person being questioned, or on his behalf, concerning the provisions of this code or of Code C, then the officer shall act in accordance with paragraph 12.8 of Code C. [See *Notes 4H and 4J*].

4.7 If the suspect indicates that he wishes to tell the police officer about matters not directly connected with the offence of which he is suspected and that he is unwilling for these matters to be recorded on tape, he shall be given the opportunity to tell the police officer about these matters after the conclusion of the formal interview.

(d) Changing tapes

4.8 When the recorder indicates that the tapes have only a short time left to run, the police officer shall tell the suspect that the tapes are coming to an end and round off that part of the interview. If the police officer wishes to continue the interview but does not already have a second set of tapes, he shall obtain a set. The suspect shall not be left unattended in the interview room. The police officer will remove the tapes from the tape recorder and insert the new tapes which shall be unwrapped or otherwise opened in the suspect's presence. The tape recorder shall then be set to record on the new tapes. Care must be taken, particularly when a number of sets of tapes have been used, to ensure that there is no confusion between the tapes. This may be done by marking the tapes with an identification number immediately they are removed from the tape recorder.

(e) Taking a break during interview

4.9 When a break is to be taken during the course of an interview and the interview room is to be vacated by the suspect, the fact that a break is to be taken, the reason for it and the time shall be recorded on tape. The tapes shall then be removed from the tape recorder and the procedures for the conclusion of an interview set out in paragraph 4.14 below followed.

4.10 When a break is to be a short one and both the suspect and a police officer are to remain in the interview room the fact that a break is to be taken, the reasons for it and the time shall be recorded on tape. The tape recorder may be turned off; there is, however, no need to remove the tapes and when the interview is recommenced the tape recording shall be continued on the same tapes. The time at which the interview recommences shall be recorded on tape.

4.11 When there is a break in questioning under caution the interviewing officer must ensure that the person being questioned is aware that he remains under caution and of his right to legal advice. If there is any doubt the caution must be given again in full when the interview resumes. [See *Notes 4K and 4L*].

(f) Failure of recording equipment

4.12 If there is a failure of equipment which can be rectified quickly, for example by inserting new tapes, the appropriate procedures set out in paragraph 4.8 shall be followed, and when the recording is resumed the officer shall explain what has happened and record the time the interview recommences. If, however, it will not be possible to continue recording on that particular tape recorder and no replacement recorder or recorder in another interview room is readily available, the interview may continue without being tape recorded. In such circumstances the procedures in paragraph 3.3 above for seeking the authority of the custody officer will be followed. [See *Note 4M*].

(g) Removing tapes from the recorder

4.13   Where tapes are removed from the recorder in the course of an interview, they shall be retained and the procedures set out in paragraph 4.15 below followed.

(h) Conclusion of interview.

4.14   At the conclusion of the interview, the suspect shall be offered the opportunity to clarify anything he has said and to add anything he may wish.

4.15   At the conclusion of the interview, including the taking and reading back of any written statement, the time shall be recorded and the tape recorder switched off. The master tape shall be sealed with a master tape label and treated as an exhibit in accordance with the force standing orders. The police officer shall sign the label and ask the suspect and any third party present to sign it also. If the suspect or third party refuses to sign the label, an officer of at least the rank of inspector, or if one is not available the custody officer, shall be called into the interview room and asked to sign it. In the case of enquiries linked to the investigation of terrorism, an officer who signs the label shall use his warrant or other identification number.

4.16   The suspect shall be handed a notice which explains the use which will be made of the tape recording and the arrangements for access to it and that a copy of the tape shall be supplied as soon as practicable if the person is charged or informed that he will be prosecuted.

Notes for Guidance

4A   The police officer should attempt to estimate the likely length of the interview and ensure that the appropriate number of clean tapes and labels with which to seal the master copies are available in the interview room.

4B   It will be helpful for the purpose of voice identification if the officer asks the suspect and any other people present to identify themselves.

4C   If it appears that a person does not understand what the caution means, the officer who has given it should go on to explain it in his own words.

4D   [Not Used]

4E   This provision is intended to give the deaf equivalent rights of first hand access to the full interview record as other suspects.

4F   The provisions of paragraphs 13.2, 13.5 and 13.9 of Code C on interpreters for the deaf or for interviews with suspects who have difficulty in understanding English continue to apply. In a tape recorded interview there is no requirement on the interviewing officer to ensure that the interpreter makes a separate note of interview as prescribed in section 13 of Code C.

4G   The officer should bear in mind that a decision to continue recording against the wishes of the suspect may be the subject of comment in court.

4H   Where the custody officer is called immediately to deal with the complaint, wherever possible the tape recorder should be left to run until the custody officer has entered the interview room and spoken to the person being interviewed. Continuation or termination of the interview should be at the discretion of the interviewing officer pending action by an inspector under paragraph 9.1 of Code C.

4I   [Not Used]

4J   Where the complaint is about a matter not connected with this code of practice or Code C, the decision to continue with the interview is at the discretion of the interviewing officer. Where the interviewing officer decides to continue with the interview the person being interviewed shall be told that the complaint will be brought to the attention of the custody officer at the conclusion of the interview. When the interview is concluded the interviewing officer must, as soon as practicable, inform the custody officer of the existence and nature of the complaint made.

4K   In considering whether to caution again after a break, the officer should bear in mind that he may have to satisfy a court that the person understood that he was still under caution when the interview resumed.

4L   The officer should bear in mind that it may be necessary to show to the court that nothing occurred during a break in an interview or between interviews which influenced the suspect's recorded evidence. The officer should consider, therefore, after a break in an interview or at the beginning of a subsequent interview summarising on tape the reason for the break and confirming this with the suspect.

4M   If one of the tapes breaks during the interview it should be sealed as a master tape in the presence of the suspect and the interview resumed where it left off. The unbroken tape should be copied and the original sealed as a master tape in the suspect's presence, if necessary after the interview. If equipment for copying the unbroken tape is not readily available, both tapes should be sealed in the suspect's presence and the interview begun again. If the tape breaks when a single deck machine is being used and the machine is one where a broken tape cannot be copied on available equipment, the tape should be sealed as a master tape in the suspect's presence and the interview begun again.

5.   After the interview

5.1   The police officer shall make a note in his notebook of the fact that the interview has taken place and has been recorded on tape, its time, duration and date and the identification number of the master tape.

5.2   Where no proceedings follow in respect of the person whose interview was recorded the tapes must nevertheless be kept securely in accordance with paragraph 6.1 and *Note 6A*.

Note for Guidance

5A   Any written record of a tape recorded interview shall be made in accordance with national guidelines approved by the Secretary of State.

6.   Tape security

6.1   The officer in charge of each police station at which interviews with suspects are recorded shall make arrangements for master tapes to be kept securely and their movements accounted for on the same basis as other material which may be used for evidential purposes, in accordance with force standing orders. [See *Note 6A*].

6.2   A police officer has no authority to break the seal on a master tape which is required for criminal proceedings. If it is necessary to gain access to the master tape, the police officer shall arrange for its seal to be broken in the presence of a representative of the Crown Prosecution Service. The defendant or his legal adviser shall be informed and given a reasonable opportunity to be present. If the defendant or his legal representative is present he shall be invited to reseal and sign the master tape. If either refuses or neither is present this shall be done by the representative of the Crown Prosecution Service. [See *Notes 6B and 6C*].

6.3   Where no criminal proceedings result it is the responsibility of the chief officer of police to establish arrangements for the breaking of the seal on the master tape, where this becomes necessary.

Notes for Guidance

6A   This section is concerned with the security of the master tape which will have been sealed at the conclusion of the interview. Care should, however, be taken of working copies of tapes since their loss or destruction may lead unnecessarily to the need to have access to master tapes.

6B   If the tape has been delivered to the crown court for their keeping after committal for trial the crown prosecutor will apply to the chief clerk of the crown court centre for the release of the tape for unsealing by the crown prosecutor.

6C   Reference to the Crown Prosecution Service or to the crown prosecutor in this part of the code shall be taken to include any other body or person with a statutory responsibility for prosecution for whom the police conduct any tape recorded interviews.

Questions

OBJECTIVES

This chapter is designed to ensure that you can:

(a)   demonstrate a sound understanding of the principles governing the admissibility of confessions (with particular reference to Police and Criminal Evidence Act 1984, ss. 76 and 78);

(b)   apply the principles to specific factual situations;

(c) describe the procedural requirements when the admissibility of a confession is challenged;

(d) demonstrate a sound understanding of the basis upon which a judge might exclude evidence *other than* confessions on the ground that it is illegally or improperly obtained (including any procedural requirements); and

(e) raise and/or counter an objection to the admissibility of confessions and illegally or improperly obtained evidence.

Question 1

Smith and Jones are indicted for robbery and attempted murder. The case arises from an armed robbery during which a security guard was shot and seriously wounded. Both men are denying the offences and have put forward alibis. Assuming that they are tried jointly consider the admissibility of the evidence obtained in the following circumstances.

(a) Smith made a taped confession after he was subjected to a series of violent assaults by a police officer (who has since been disciplined and has left the force). As a result of detailed information given in the confession the police went to a derelict farmhouse where they found a suitcase containing most of the money stolen in the robbery and a sawn-off shotgun which was used in the robbery. Smith's fingerprints are discovered both on the suitcase and on the sawn-off shotgun.

(b) Jones made a taped confession shortly after a police officer had informed him that Smith had been having an affair with his (Jones's) wife. Although he asserted that he had accompanied Smith on the robbery he claimed that he had only done so because he was frightened of Smith and that he had not been involved in the planning of the robbery nor in the shooting. Shortly before this confession was made the police had conducted an illegal search of Jones's country mansion and had discovered there several shotguns which were of a similar type to that used in the robbery and maps and plans in Jones's handwriting of the area where the robbery occurred.

Question 2

DI Alladice was investigating a gang believed to be involved in smuggling cannabis from Holland to the UK. Without obtaining proper authorisation, he planted a listening device in a flat rented by Ben, a suspected member of the gang. The listening device recorded a conversation between Ben and an unknown visitor, in which Ben said, 'There's a load of cannabis coming into Harwich tomorrow. Charlie is using the Volvo for the job. He'll drop the stuff off with Dave in Birmingham.' The following day Alladice kept watch at the ferry terminal at Harwich. He arrested Charlie as Charlie disembarked in a Volvo car from the ferry. The car was searched, and bags of cannabis were found concealed in the doors. There were no fingerprints on the bags.

At the police station Charlie was cautioned. He asked for his solicitor, Mr Grabbit, but was told that he could not see him, as any delay would lead to the alerting of Charlie's accomplices. He was then interviewed for several hours by Alladice. Charlie denied all knowledge of the cannabis or the gang. At one stage he said to Alladice, 'I've never had anything to do with drugs in my life.' At last Alladice said, 'Look son, do yourself some good. We've bugged your house and we've got cast iron evidence against you. You're going to go down, but just remember that the judge will make it easier for you if you co-operate.' Charlie then said, 'All right. I agreed to bring the cannabis in and take it to Dave, but only because Ben threatened to beat me up if I didn't.' Charlie's flat was later searched, and three ecstasy tablets were found in a bathroom cabinet.

Charlie agreed to deliver the Volvo to Dave under covert police surveillance. Alladice replaced the cannabis in the car and also hid a revolver under the back seat, instructing Charlie to tell Dave that Ben thought he would need it to protect the consignment of cannabis. Charlie followed these instructions. Alladice arrested Dave after Dave had taken possession of the cannabis and the revolver.

Ben, Charlie and Dave have been charged with conspiracy to evade the prohibition on the importation of a controlled drug, and Dave is also charged with unlawful possession of a firearm.

Advise the prosecution on the evidential matters arising.

Question 3

Steve and Dave were arrested on suspicion of committing a burglary. Steve and Dave were taken to the local police station where they were interviewed separately.

Steve claims that he asked to see his solicitor but that his request was refused on the ground that waiting for his solicitor would cause unreasonable delay to the investigation. He further claims that it was only when the police told him that Dave had confessed (and had implicated Steve) that he decided to confess. Steve then made a taped statement in which he admitted his part in the burglary but claimed that it had been master-minded by Dave. In fact Dave had not made any confession and he maintained his silence throughout his interrogation. Both men now stand jointly charged with burglary. During the trial a *voir dire* is held to determine the admissibility of Steve's confession.

On the assumption that the trial judge accepts in substance Steve's account of what took place during his interrogation, prepare an argument to support the exclusion of his confession:

(i)   under Police and Criminal Evidence Act 1984, s. 76(2), and

(ii) under Police and Criminal Evidence Act 1984, s. 78.

If Steve's confession is admitted, explain the position regarding those parts of Steve's confession in which Dave is implicated.

ELEVEN

CIRCUMSTANTIAL EVIDENCE OF A PARTY'S EVASIVE CONDUCT

11.1 Civil Cases

Generally speaking in civil cases there has been no difficulty about this category of evidence. A party's conduct has been treated in the same way as other items of circumstantial evidence, i.e. so long as it has relevance it is admissible; the strength of the inference to be drawn is simply a matter of weight. Thus in *Moriarty* v *London, Chatham and Dover Railway* (1870) LR 5 QB 314 it was held that evidence of a plaintiff's conduct in inducing witnesses to commit perjury was admissible (and cogent) circumstantial evidence of the weakness and falsity of his case. Also in *Bessela* v *Stern* (1877) 2 CPD 265 the defendant's silence in the face of the plaintiff's direct assertion of breach of promise of marriage was held to be admissible circumstantial evidence of the truth of the plaintiff's assertion. On the other hand in *Wiedmann* v *Walpole* [1891] 2 QB 534 it was held that a failure to answer an accusatory letter was not admissible as circumstantial evidence of the truth of the accusation. There are any number of reasons for failing to answer such letters. A failure to call evidence may support an adverse inference — see *British Railways* v *Herrington* [1972] AC 877. In *Francisco* v *Diedrick*, *The Times*, 3 April 1998, it was held that where a plaintiff had shown a prima facie case against a defendant, the defendant's failure to testify meant that the prima facie case had become a very strong case.

11.2 Criminal Cases

In criminal cases the courts have generally been much more circumspect about this category of evidence. This has been for a variety of reasons, some of which are concerned with the reliability of such evidence, whilst others are overtly concerned with public policy issues affecting the accused's right to silence. The result has been a mixture of rules relating either to the way the judge should direct the jury or to the circumstances in which it is legitimate to draw any inference at all.

11.2.1 THE ACCUSED'S LIES

It has generally been accepted that lies told by the accused may support an inference that the accused had a sense of guilt and sought to conceal it. However, the accused who lies might also be affected by a variety of other powerful motives, e.g. fear or shame. Accordingly, the courts have required judges to direct the jury very carefully about the evidential use of the accused's lies. In *R* v *Lucas* [1981] QB 720, Lord Lane CJ said (at p. 724):

> To be capable of amounting to corroboration the lie told out of court must first of all be deliberate. Secondly it must relate to a material issue. Thirdly the motive for the lie must be realisation of guilt and a fear of the truth. The jury should in appropriate cases be reminded that people sometimes lie, for example, in an attempt to bolster up a just cause, or out of shame or out of a wish to conceal disgraceful behaviour

from their family. Fourthly the statement must be clearly shown to be a lie by evidence other than that of the accomplice who is to be corroborated, that is to say by admission or by evidence from an independent witness . . . As a matter of good sense it is difficult to see why, subject to the same safeguards, lies proved to have been told in court by a defendant should not equally be capable of providing corroboration.

In *R* v *Burge* [1996] 1 Cr App R 163 it was said that the lie must be admitted by the defendant, or the jury must find it proved beyond reasonable doubt, before it can be taken into account; and, the jury must be warned that the mere fact that the defendant has lied is not in itself evidence of guilt because defendants may lie for innocent reasons. A lie can support the prosecution case only if the jury is sure that the defendant did not lie for an innocent reason. The Court also said that a direction on these lines is usually required in four cases:

(a) Where the defence raised an alibi.

(b) Where the judge considered it desirable or necessary to suggest that the jury should look for support for one piece of evidence from other evidence in the case and among that other evidence drew attention to lies told or allegedly told by the defendant.

(c) Where the prosecution sought to show that something said either in or out of the court in relation to a separate and distinct issue was a lie, and to rely on that lie as evidence of guilt in relation to the charge which was sought to be proved.

(d) Where although the prosecution had not adopted the approach referred to in (c) above the judge reasonably envisaged that there was a real danger that the jury might do so.

Kennedy LJ went on to say that the trial judge should consider with counsel (before closing speeches) whether a *Lucas* direction is required and that the Court of Appeal is unlikely to be persuaded in cases allegedly falling within item (d) above that there was a real danger that the jury would treat a particular lie as evidence of guilt if defence counsel had not alerted the trial judge to that danger and asked the judge to give a *Lucas* direction. The Court of Appeal relied upon this dictum by Kennedy LJ in *R* v *McGuiness* [1999] Crim LR 318 when observing that the fact that defence counsel (at McGuiness's trial) had not raised the question whether a *Lucas* direction was required suggested that the relevant lie was not a large feature in the case and the absence of a *Lucas* direction did not make the conviction unsafe.

A direction is not required if rejection by the jury of the defendant's evidence would leave them no choice but to convict. Thus in *R* v *Patrick* [1999] 6 Archbold News 4 the Court of Appeal held that a *Lucas* direction is unnecessary where the only basis for rejecting an alibi is the jury's acceptance of identification evidence from prosecution witnesses. See also *R* v *Harron* [1996] 2 Cr App R 457.

11.2.2   **INFERENCES FROM THE ACCUSED'S FAILURE TO TESTIFY: CRIMINAL JUSTICE AND PUBLIC ORDER ACT 1994, SECTION 35**

Until s. 35 came into effect, an accused's failure to testify could not be commented on by the prosecution (Criminal Evidence Act 1898, s. 1(b)) and there were strict limitations on the nature and extent of the trial judge's direction to the jury about it.

In the leading authority *prior to s. 35*, *R* v *Martinez-Tobon* [1994] 2 All ER 90, Lord Taylor CJ, in approving the old Judicial Studies Board model direction, confirmed that, although the judge could comment on the accused's failure to give evidence, the essentials of the direction were that (i) the accused has a right not to give evidence and (ii) *it must not be assumed that the accused is guilty because he/she has not gone into the witness-box.* Indeed the model direction stated, in terms, that failing to give evidence did *nothing* to establish [the accused's] guilt, i.e. it was of no evidential effect.

The position is now governed by *s. 35*, as amended by s. 35 of the Crime and Disorder Act 1998, which provides:

(1)   At the trial of any person for an offence, subsections (2) and (3) below apply unless—

(a)   the accused's guilt is not in issue; or

(b)   it appears to the court that the physical or mental condition of the accused makes it undesirable for him to give evidence;

but subsection (2) below does not apply if, at the conclusion of the evidence for the prosecution, his legal representative informs the court that the accused will give evidence or, where he is unrepresented, the court ascertains from him that he will give evidence.

(2)   Where this subsection applies, the court shall, at the conclusion of the evidence for the prosecution, satisfy itself (in the case of proceedings on indictment, in the presence of the jury) that the accused is aware that the stage has been reached at which evidence can be given for the defence and that he can, if he wishes, give evidence and that if he chooses not to give evidence, or having been sworn, without good cause refuses to answer any question, it will be permissible for the court or jury to draw such inferences as appear proper from his failure to give evidence or his refusal, without good cause, to answer any question.

(3)   Where this subsection applies, the court or jury, in determining whether the accused is guilty of the offence charged, may draw such inferences as appear proper from the failure of the accused to give evidence or his refusal without good cause, to answer any question.

(4)   This section does not render the accused compellable to give evidence on his own behalf, and he shall accordingly not be guilty of contempt of court by reason of a failure to do so.

(5)   For the purposes of this section a person who, having been sworn, refuses to answer any question shall be taken to do so without good cause unless —

(a)   he is entitled to refuse to answer the question by virtue of any enactment, whenever passed or made, or on the ground of privilege; or

(b)   the court in the exercise of its general discretion excuses him from answering it.

(6)   Where the age of any person is material for the purposes of subsection (1) above, his age shall for those purposes be taken to that which appears to the court to be his age.

(7)   This section applies —

(a)   in relation to proceedings on indictment for an offence, only if the person charged with the offence is arraigned on or after the commencement of this section;

(b)   in relation to proceedings in a magistrates' court, only if the time when the court begins to receive evidence in the proceedings falls after the commencement of this section.

The Criminal Evidence Act 1898, s. 1(b) (prohibiting prosecution comment), is repealed by Criminal Justice and Public Order Act 1994, s. 167(3) and sch. 11.

Section 35 clearly changes the position of the accused who fails to testify. Rather than the accused's failure to testify having no evidential effect, the tribunal of fact may now draw such inferences as appear proper (see s. 35(3)).

An accused who testifies but refuses to answer a question does so *without* good cause unless:

(a)   he is statutorily entitled not to answer on the ground of privilege; or

(b)   the judge in his or her discretion excuses the accused from answering

(see *R* v *Ackinclose* [1996] Crim LR 747).

11.2.2.1   Evidential effect of a failure to testify

The evidential effect of failure to testify has been considered by the House of Lords in *Murray* v *DPP* [1994] 1 WLR 1. This case related to Northern Ireland legislation introduced in 1988 which had virtually the same wording as s. 35.

The first point is that the provision can only help to prove the case beyond reasonable doubt once the prosecution has raised a prima facie case (i.e. it cannot help the prosecution raise a prima facie case). This should follow from general principles because the prosecution must generally raise a prima facie case *before* the accused testifies; it was nevertheless reassuring that in *Murray* Lord Mustill clearly asserted this to be the effect of the statutory words. Thus the accused's failure to testify cannot assist the prosecution to make out a prima facie case but it can help to *confirm* that the accused is guilty.

The crucial question is, how might the accused's failure to testify help to confirm that the accused is guilty? Lord Mustill said:

> [Once a prima facie case is raised] the fact finder wants to see whether in relation to each evidential ingredient of the offence the direct evidence which it is at least possible to believe, should in the event be believed, and whether inferences that might be drawn from such evidence should actually be drawn. Usually the most important of the events for which the fact finder is keeping his judgment in suspense will be the evidence of the accused himself . . . If in such circumstances the defendant does not go on oath to say that the witnesses [for the prosecution] are untruthful or unreliable or that an inference which appears on its face to be plausible is in reality unsound for reasons within his personal knowledge, the fact finder may suspect that the defendant does not tell his story because he has no story to tell or none which will stand up to scrutiny; *and this suspicion may be sufficient to convert a possible prosecution case into one which is actually proved.* (Emphasis added.)

However, Lord Mustill went on to say that the accused's failure to testify will not always help the prosecution to prove the case.

> Everything depends on the nature of the issue, the weight of the evidence adduced by the prosecution upon it and on the extent to which the accused should in the nature of things be able to give his own account of the particular matter in question.

It appears that restrictions on comment by the judge or prosecution about an accused's failure to call *other witnesses* are unaffected by s. 35, see e.g., *R* v *Gallagher* [1974] 1 WLR 1204 and Police and Criminal Evidence Act 1984, s. 80(8).

11.2.2.2 Procedure

The procedure to be adopted in relation to s. 35 has been clarified in a *Practice Note* by Lord Taylor CJ [1995] 2 All ER 499:

If the accused is legally represented
If the accused is legally represented and at the conclusion of the evidence for the prosecution the accused's legal representative *either* does not inform the court that the accused will give evidence *or* informs the court that the accused will not give evidence, the judge should in the presence of the jury inquire of the representative in these terms:

> 'Have you advised your client that the stage has now been reached at which he may give evidence and, if he chooses not to do so or, having been sworn, without good cause refuses to answer any question, the jury may draw such inferences as appear proper from his failure to do so?'

If the representative replies to the judge that the accused has been so advised, then the case shall proceed. If counsel replies that the accused has not been so advised then the judge shall direct the representative to advise his client of the consequences set out here and should adjourn briefly for this purpose before proceeding further.

If the accused is not legally represented
If the accused is not represented the judge shall at the conclusion of the evidence for the prosecution and in the presence of the jury say to the accused:

'You have heard the evidence against you. Now is the time for you to make your defence. You may give evidence on oath, and be cross-examined like any other witness. If you do not give evidence or, having been sworn, without good cause refuse to answer any question the jury may draw such inferences as appear proper. That means they may hold it against you. You may also call any witness or witnesses whom you have arranged to attend court. Afterwards you may also, if you wish, address the jury by arguing your case from the dock. But you cannot at that stage give evidence. Do you now intend to give evidence?'

(**Note**: For the procedure for the judge to determine the accused's fitness to testify under s. 35(1)(b) see *R* v *A* [1997] Crim LR 883.)

11.2.2.3   How should the judge direct the jury?

In *R* v *Cowan* [1996] 1 Cr App R 1, the Court of Appeal, in allowing C's appeal against conviction, rejected the argument that s. 35 watered down the burden of proof: the prosecution had to establish a prima facie case before the section applied — silence cannot be the only factor on which to base a conviction. The judge had failed to highlight this point when directing the jury. Lord Taylor CJ stated that the following direction was a sound guide but that it may be necessary to adapt it to the particular circumstances of an individual case:

> The defendant has not given evidence. That is his right. But as he has been told, the law is that you may draw such inferences as appear proper from his failure to do so. Failure to give evidence on its own cannot prove guilt but, depending on the circumstances, you may hold his failure against him when deciding whether he is guilty.

> [There is evidence before you on the basis of which the defendant's advocate invites you not to hold it against the defendant that he has not given evidence before you, namely . . ... If you think that because of this evidence you should not hold it against the defendant that he has not given evidence, do not do so. But if the evidence he relies on presents no adequate explanation for his absence from the witness box then you may hold his failure to give evidence against him. You do not have to do so.] (The words in brackets are to be used only where there is evidence.)

> What proper inferences can you draw from the defendant's decision not to give evidence before you? If you conclude that there is a case for him to answer, you may think that the defendant would have gone into the witness box to give you an explanation for or an answer to the case against him.

> If the only sensible explanation for his decision not to give evidence is that he has no answer to the case against him, or none that could have stood up to cross-examination, then it would be open to you to hold against him his failure to give evidence. It is for you to decide whether it is fair to do so.

Lord Taylor added that it would be open to a judge to advise a jury against drawing an adverse inference if either there was some evidential basis for doing so or some exceptional factors in the case making that a fair course to take.

The Court of Appeal, in *R* v *Birchall* [1999] Crim LR 311, emphasised the need to follow *Cowan* directions carefully and held that the requirement that the jury had to be satisfied that the prosecution has established a case to answer was an essential precondition to their drawing any inference from a defendant's failure to testify under s. 35. The judge's failure to direct the jury *specifically* on this point meant that the conviction was unsafe. See also *R* v *El Hannachi* [1998] 2 Cr App R 226.

11.2.3   INFERENCES FROM THE ACCUSED'S SILENCE OUT OF COURT: CRIMINAL JUSTICE AND PUBLIC ORDER ACT 1994 (SECTIONS 34, 36 AND 37)

The position at common law was that, in general, inferences could not be drawn from the accused's silence in the face of accusations or questioning occurring out of court.

The only exceptions recognised at common law were situations where the accused had not been cautioned *and* it could be said that the suspect was on equal terms with the accuser; see *Parkes* v *R* [1976] 1 WLR 1251. For these purposes it is relatively clear from the authorities that an accuser is *not* on equal terms if he or she is a police officer or a person charged with the duty of investigating offences; see *Hall* v *R* [1971] 1 WLR 298, the only caveat here is based on an obiter dictum in *R* v *Chandler* [1976] 1 WLR 585, to the effect that a suspect is put on equal terms with the police by the presence of his or her solicitor (but in such cases one would normally expect the caution to have been given so that the common law cases would not apply; for the rules about cautioning see Code C, para. 10 in **Chapter 10**). If the accuser is on equal terms, e.g. the victim of the alleged offence, it does not matter that the accusation is made in the presence of the police, i.e. a proper inference can still be drawn; see *R* v *Christie* [1914] AC 545; *R* v *Horne* [1990] Crim LR 188.

11.2.3.1 Section 34

The position must now be considered first in the light of Criminal Justice and Public Order Act 1994, s. 34 (as amended by the Youth Justice and Criminal Evidence Act 1999), which provides:

(1)   Where, in any proceedings against a person for an offence, evidence is given that the accused—

(a)   at any time before he was charged with the offence, on being questioned under caution by a constable trying to discover whether or by whom the offence had been committed, failed to mention any fact relied on in his defence in those proceedings; or

(b)   on being charged with the offence or officially informed that he might be prosecuted for it, failed to mention any such fact,

being a fact which in the circumstances existing at the time the accused could reasonably have been expected to mention when so questioned, charged or informed, as the case may be, subsection (2) below applies.

(2)   Where this subsection applies . . .

(c)   the court, in determining whether there is a case to answer; and

(d)   the court or jury, in determining whether the accused is guilty of the offence charged,

may draw such inferences from the failure as appear proper.

(2A)   Where the accused was at an authorised place of detention at the time of the failure, subsections (1) and (2) above do not apply if he had not been allowed an opportunity to consult a solicitor prior to being questioned, charged or informed as mentioned in subsection (1) above.

(3)   Subject to any directions by the court, evidence tending to establish the failure may be given before or after evidence tending to establish the fact which the accused is alleged to have failed to mention.

(4)   This section applies in relation to questioning by persons (other than constables) charged with the duty of investigating offences or charging offenders as it applies in relation to questioning by constables; and in subsection (1) above 'officially informed' means informed by a constable or any such person.

(5)   This section does not —

(a)   prejudice the admissibility in evidence of the silence or other reaction of the accused in the face of anything said in his presence relating to the conduct in respect of which he is charged in so far as evidence thereof would be admissible apart from this section; or,

(b)   preclude the drawing of any inference from any such silence or other reaction of the accused which could properly be drawn apart from this section.

(6)   This section does not apply in relation to a failure to mention a fact if the failure occurred before the commencement of this section.

Commentary

Obviously s. 34 made it necessary to amend the caution. The new caution is in the following terms:

You do not have to say anything. But it may harm your defence if you do not mention when questioned something which you later rely on in court. Anything you do say may be given in evidence.

Section 34 makes it *possible* for the court to draw inferences from the accused's failure to mention when questioned under caution or charged (officially informed etc.), a fact which the accused later relies on in his/her defence (if he/she could reasonably have been expected to mention that fact at that time).

Although s. 34(2) expressly states that the inference can help the court 'in determining whether there is a case to answer', it is certainly arguable that s. 34 may not have this effect. Section 34 only applies to a failure to mention facts which are *relied on in the accused's defence*. The normal time for an accused to state his or her defence is *after* the prosecution case is closed (i.e. after the prosecution have raised a prima facie case). Although s. 34(3) states that the prosecution can prove the failure to mention the fact *before* the accused calls evidence of the fact in question, can the accused be said to have *relied* on the fact before opening his or her case? This question raises other questions: Does merely cross-examining a prosecution witness about a fact amount to reliance on that fact? In *R v Moshaid* [1998] Crim LR 420, the defendant gave a 'no comment' interview. At trial he gave no evidence and called no witnesses. The Court of Appeal held that the trial judge should not have commented adversely on his silence at interview because the defendant had not failed to mention 'any fact relied on in his defence at trial'. A case like *Moshaid* is likely to be rare.

In *R v Bowers* [1998] Crim LR 817, the Court of Appeal stated *obiter* that the accused could be said to rely on facts in his defence if the facts were put to a prosecution witness in cross-examination and accepted by the witness as true. Since prosecution witnesses will not usually do this, the Court of Appeal appear to be envisaging a very limited possibility of the accused relying on facts during cross-examination of prosecution witnesses.

However, in *R v Hart*, 23 April 1998, unreported, the Court of Appeal suggested *obiter* that the accused may be said to rely on facts in his defence 'where the defence has involved putting a positive case on behalf of the accused'. This seems to imply that simply putting facts to prosecution witnesses in cross examination might involve a reliance on those facts by the accused for the purposes of s. 34. This clearly goes further than *Bowers*. At the time of writing a clear answer to this important question has not been given.

The importance of showing the accused had positively relied on the fact in question was indicated by the Court of Appeal in *R v Nickolson* [1999] Crim LR 61 where the Court held that the accused could not be said to have relied on a fact in his defence simply by putting forward at trial an innocent explanation of potentially incriminating facts which he had not been asked about in interview. *Nickolson* also shows that the facts the accused have failed to mention must be facts which he/she could reasonably have been expected to mention. If the accused has not been asked about a particular topic it would often not be reasonable to expect him/her to volunteer information about that topic. It may be possible to avoid the application of s. 34 by use of a prepared statement at police interviews. See *R v Ali* (2001) 151 NLJ 1321.

In *R v Condron* [1997] 1 Cr App R 185, the Court of Appeal held that a judge was entitled to leave it open to the jury to draw an adverse inference for the accused's failure to answer questions, notwithstanding that the solicitor had advised it.

The Crown's case had relied on police surveillance of exchanges between the defendants, their co-accused and third parties. Before interview they were cautioned. Their solicitor did not consider the defendants fit for interview because they were suffering from heroin withdrawal. A police doctor found that the defendants were fit for interview. The defendants remained silent during interview on the advice of their solicitor, but at trial they gave explanations for the exchanges observed by the police.

The European Court of Human Rights recently considered this case. In *Condron & Condron v UK* [2000] Crim LR 677, the Court stated that as a matter of fairness, the jury should have been directed that it could only draw an adverse inference if satisfied that the applicant's silence at police interview could only sensibly be attributed to their having no answer or none that would stand up to cross-examination. A direction to this effect was more than merely desirable and as a result the initial judge's direction was seen as incompatible with the applicants' exercise of their right to silence at the police station. The court therefore decided that the applicants did not receive a fair trial within the meaning of Article 6 of the Convention.

The Court of Appeal in *R v Argent* [1997] Crim LR 346 stressed that the jury, when considering why an accused failed to answer questions, should consider matters such as the time of day, the defendant's age, experience, mental capacity, state of health, sobriety, tiredness, knowledge and personality; and any legal advice given. These are issues upon which a judge might and usually should give appropriate directions, but which he or she should ordinarily leave the jury to decide. This, of course, puts the solicitor who attends an interview under some difficulty, especially as the Law Society guidelines suggest that to remain silent is appropriate advice when the police have made less than full disclosure of the evidence available. However in *Argent* the Court of Appeal held on this point:

> . . . the jury is not concerned with the correctness of the solicitor's advice, nor with whether it complies with the Law Society's guidelines, but with the reasonableness of the appellant's conduct in all the circumstances which the jury have found to exist. Although the advice given is a circumstance to be considered by the jury, neither the Law Society by its guidance, nor the solicitor by his advice can preclude consideration by the jury of the issue which Parliament has left to the jury to determine.

See also *R v Roble* [1997] Crim LR 449 where the Court of Appeal held that the fact that the accused had been advised by his solicitor not to answer questions was not in itself likely to be regarded as a sufficient reason for not mentioning facts relevant to the defence. The accused would generally need to indicate the reason for that advice (which might involve calling the solicitor) because that was relevant when the jury were assessing the reasonableness of his conduct in remaining silent. The approach taken on the need to *explain* the legal advice obviously raised issues as to the waiver of professional privilege. These were fully considered by the Court of Appeal in *R v Bowden* [1999] 4 All ER 43. Lord Bingham CJ observed:

> If, at trial, the defendant or his solicitor gave evidence not merely of the defendant's refusal to answer pre-trial questions on legal advice but also of the grounds on which such advice was given or if, as here, the defence elicited evidence at trial of a statement made by a defendant or his solicitor pre-trial of the grounds on which legal advice was given to answer no questions, the defendant voluntarily withdrew the veil of privilege and having done so could not resist questioning directed to the nature of that advice and the factual premises on which it had been based.

In giving a s. 34 direction the judge must identify the fact on which the defendant relies and then direct the jury that:

(a) it is for them to decide whether in the circumstances it was something that the defendant could reasonably have been expected to mention; and, if they think it was, that they are not obliged to draw any inferences, but have a discretion to do so;

(b) a suspect is not bound to answer police questions;

(c) an inference from silence cannot by itself prove guilt;

(d) they must be satisfied that the prosecution has established a case to answer before drawing any adverse inferences from silence;

(e) they can draw an adverse inference only if satisfied that the defendant was silent because he had no answer, or none that would stand up to investigation.

See *R* v *Gill* [2001] 1 Cr App R 160, *R* v *Betts and Hall* [2001] 2 Cr App R 257.

A restriction on the use of s. 34 appears in the case of *R* v *Mountford* [1999] Crim LR 575, which held that where a fact is so central to a defence that its rejection by the jury will inevitably lead to a finding of guilt, a s. 34 direction is unnecessary, and should not be given. See also *Gill* above. But see *R* v *Gowland-Wynn, The Times*, 7 December 2001, where the Court of Appeal refused to follow these decisions.

Where s. 34 does not apply, the judge should specifically direct the jury that adverse inferences should not be drawn from the accused's silence: see *R* v *McGarry* [1999] 1 Cr App R 377.

11.2.3.2 Sections 36 and 37 (as amended by Youth Justice and Criminal Evidence Act 1999)

36.—*(1) Where—*
   (a) a person is arrested by a constable, and there is—
     (i) on his person; or
     (ii) in or on his clothing or footwear; or
     (iii) otherwise in his possession; or
     (iv) in any place in which he is at the time of his arrest,
any object, substance or mark, or there is any mark on any such object; and
   (b) that or another constable investigating the case reasonably believes that the presence of the object, substance or mark may be attributable to the participation of the person arrested in the commission of an offence specified by the constable; and
   (c) the constable informs the person arrested that he so believes, and requests him to account for the presence of the object, substance or mark; and
   (d) the person fails or refuses to do so,
then if, in any proceedings against the person for the offence so specified, evidence of those matters is given, subsection (2) below applies.
   (2) Where this subsection applies —
   (a) a magistrates' court, inquiring into the offence as examining justices;
   (b) a judge, in deciding whether to grant an application made by the accused under —
     (i) section 6 of the Criminal Justice Act 1987 (application for dismissal of charge of serious fraud in respect of which notice of transfer has been given under section 4 of that Act); or
     (ii) paragraph 5 of Schedule 6 to the Criminal Justice Act 1991 (application for dismissal of charge of violent or sexual offence involving child in respect of which notice of transfer has been given under section 53 of that Act);
   (c) the court, in determining whether there is a case to answer; and
   (d) the court or jury, in determining whether the accused is guilty of the offence charged,
may draw such inferences from the failure or refusal as appear proper.
   (3) Subsections (1) and (2) above apply to the condition of clothing or footwear as they apply to a substance or mark thereon.
   (4) Subsections (1) and (2) above do not apply unless the accused was told in ordinary language by the constable when making the request mentioned in subsection (1)(c) above what the effect of this section would be if he failed or refused to comply with the request.
   (4A) Where the accused was at an authorised place of detention at the time of the failure or refusal, subsections (1) and (2) above do not apply if he had not been allowed an opportunity to consult a solicitor prior to the request being made.
   (5) This section applies in relation to officers of customs and excise as it applies in relation to constables.
   (6) This section does not preclude the drawing of any inference from a failure or refusal of the accused to account for the presence of an object, substance or mark or from the condition of clothing or footwear which could properly be drawn apart from this section.
   (7) This section does not apply in relation to a failure or refusal which occurred before the commencement of this section.

Commentary

In summary, s. 36 makes it *possible*, in the circumstances stated, for a court to draw inferences from an accused's silence when challenged about the presence, at the time of arrest, of objects, substances etc. which are found:

(a) in or on the accused's clothing,

(b) on the accused's person,

(c) in the place where the accused was arrested.

37.—*(1) Where—*

    (a) a person arrested by a constable was found by him at a place at or about the time the offence for which he was arrested is alleged to have been committed; and

    (b) that or another constable investigating the offence reasonably believes that the presence of the person at that place and at that time may be attributable to his participation in the commission of the offence; and

    (c) the constable informs the person that he so believes, and requests him to account for that presence; and

    (d) the person fails or refuses to do so,

then if, in any proceedings against the person for the offence, evidence of those matters is given, subsection (2) below applies.

(2) Where this subsection applies —

    (a) a magistrates' court, inquiring into the offence as examining justices;

    (b) a judge, in deciding whether to grant an application made by the accused under —

        (i) section 6 of the Criminal Justice Act 1987 (application for dismissal of charge of serious fraud in respect of which notice of transfer has been given under section 4 of that Act); or

        (ii) paragraph 5 of Schedule 6 to the Criminal Justice Act 1991 (application for dismissal of charge of violent or sexual offence involving child in respect of which notice of transfer has been given under section 53 of that Act);

    (c) the court, in determining whether there is a case to answer; and

    (d) the court or jury, in determining whether the accused is guilty of the offence charged,

may draw such inferences from the failure or refusal as appear proper.

(3) Subsections (1) and (2) do not apply unless the accused was told in ordinary language by the constable when making the request mentioned in subsection (1)(c) above what the effect of this section would be if he failed or refused to comply with the request.

(3A) Where the accused was at an authorised place of detention at the time of the failure or refusal, subsections (1) and (2) do not apply if he had not been allowed an opportunity to consult a solicitor prior to the request being made.

(4) This section applies in relation to officers of customs and excise as it applies in relation to constables.

(5) This section does not preclude the drawing of any inference from a failure or refusal of the accused to account for his presence at a place which could properly be drawn apart from this section.

(6) This section does not apply in relation to a failure or refusal which occurred before the commencement of this section.

Commentary

In summary, s. 37 makes it *possible* in the circumstances stated for a court to draw inferences from an accused's failure or refusal to account for being present at a particular place at or about the time the offence for which he/she was arrested is alleged to have been committed. Note that Youth Justice and Criminal Evidence Act 1999, s. 58, has amended ss. 34 and 36 to 38 of the 1994 Act by providing that inferences from silence are not permissible where a suspect has not been allowed an opportunity to obtain legal advice. See also *R v Gayle* [1999] Crim LR 502, where the Court of Appeal held that s. 34 does not apply to silence at an interview that was in breach of Code C.

11.2.4 GENERAL POINTS ABOUT SECTIONS 34 TO 37

Various interpretation points are dealt with in Criminal Justice and Public Order Act 1994, s. 38:

> **38.**—*(1) In sections 34, 35, 36 and 37 of this Act—*
> *'legal representative' means an authorised advocate or authorised litigator, as defined by section 119(1) of the Courts and Legal Services Act 1990, and*
> *'place' includes any building or part of a building, any vehicle, vessel aircraft or hovercraft and any other place whatsoever.*
> *(2) In sections 34(2), 35(3), 36(2) and 37(2), references to an offence charged include references to any other offence of which the accused could lawfully be convicted on that charge.*
> *(2A) In each of sections 34(2A), 36(4A) and 37(3A) 'authorised place of detention' means—*
> > *(a) a police station; or*
> > *(b) any other place prescribed for the purposes of that provision by order made by the Secretary of State.*
> *(3) A person shall not have the proceedings against him transferred to the Crown Court for trial, have a case to answer or be convicted of an offence solely on an inference drawn from such a failure or refusal as is mentioned in section 34(2), 35(3), 36(2) or 37(2).*
> *(4) A judge shall not refuse to grant such an application as is mentioned in section 34(2)(b), 36(2)(b) and 37(2)(b) solely on an inference drawn from such a failure as is mentioned in section 34(2), 36(2) or 37(2).*
> *(5) Nothing in sections 34, 35, 36 or 37 prejudices the operation of a provision of any enactment which provides (in whatever words) that any answer or evidence given by a person in specified circumstances shall not be admissible in evidence against him or some other person in any proceedings or class of proceedings (however described, and whether civil or criminal).*
> *In this subsection, the reference to giving evidence is a reference to giving evidence in any manner, whether by furnishing information making discovery, producing documents or otherwise.*
> *(6) Nothing in sections 34, 35, 36 or 37 prejudices any power of a court, in any proceedings, to exclude evidence (whether by preventing questions being put or otherwise) at its discretion.*

11.2.5 REFUSING TO GIVE BODY SAMPLES

There are strict rules about the way in which a person can be called upon to provide body samples (see **Chapter 12** and **12.3.2.5** in particular). An intimate sample can only be obtained by consent; however, Police and Criminal Evidence Act 1984, s. 62(10) provides that where the appropriate consent to the taking of an intimate sample from a person was refused without good cause, in any proceedings against that person for an offence (a) the court, in determining (i) whether to commit that person for trial; or (ii) whether there is a case to answer; and (b) the court or jury, in determining whether that person is guilty of the offence charged, may draw such inferences from the refusal as appear proper.

As to a refusal to allow a non-intimate sample to be taken, see s. 63 of the 1984 Act, and *R* v *Smith* (1985) 81 Cr App R 286. (Note, in certain circumstances, a non-intimate sample can be taken without consent see **Chapter 12** and **12.5.2.7**.)

11.2.6 FAILING TO PROVIDE ADVANCE DISCLOSURE OF THE DEFENCE CASE

The Criminal Procedure and Investigations Act 1996 makes provision for defence disclosure (compulsory or voluntary) under ss. 5 and 6 respectively. Section 11 goes on to provide what consequences may ensue if the accused fails to make disclosure in accordance with s. 5 or 6.

> **11.**—*(1) This section applies where section 5 applies and the accused—*
> > *(a) fails to give a defence statement under that section,*

(b) gives a defence statement under that section but does so after the end of the period which, by virtue of section 12, is the relevant period for section 5,

(c) sets out inconsistent defences in a defence statement given under section 5,

(d) at his trial puts forward a defence which is different from any defence set out in a defence statement given under section 5,

(e) at his trial adduces evidence in support of an alibi without having given particulars of the alibi in a defence statement given under section 5, or

(f) at his trial calls a witness to give evidence in support of an alibi without having complied with subsection (7)(a) or (b) of section 5 as regards the witness in giving a defence statement under that section.

(2) This section also applies where section 6 applies, the accused gives a defence statement under that section, and the accused—

(a) gives the statement after the end of the period which, by virtue of section 12, is the relevant period for section 6,

(b) sets out inconsistent defences in the statement,

(c) at his trial puts forward a defence which is different from any defence set out in the statement,

(d) at his trial adduces evidence in support of an alibi without having given particulars of the alibi in the statement, or

(e) at his trial calls a witness to give evidence in support of an alibi without having complied with subsection (7)(a) or (b) of section 5 (as applied by section 6) as regards the witness in giving the statement.

(3) Where this section applies—

(a) the court or, with the leave of the court, any other party may make such comment as appears appropriate;

(b) the court or jury may draw such inferences as appear proper in deciding whether the accused is guilty of the offence concerned.

(4) Where the accused puts forward a defence which is different from any defence set out in a defence statement given under section 5 or 6, in doing anything under subsection (3) or in deciding whether to do anything under it the court shall have regard—

(a) to the extent of the difference in the defences, and

(b) to whether there is any justification for it.

(5) A person shall not be convicted of an offence solely on an inference drawn under subsection (3).

(6) Any reference in this section to evidence in support of an alibi shall be construed in accordance with section 5.

Questions

OBJECTIVES

By the conclusion of this chapter you should be able:

(a) to identify the general circumstances in which a party's evasive conduct can be put before the tribunal of fact as supporting an inference which is adverse to the party in question;

(b) as regards lies by the accused, to recognise which factors affect the probative value of the lies as circumstantial evidence against the accused and say how a judge should direct the jury on such evidence;

(c) as regards silence by the accused (including a failure to make a defence statement), to recognise which factors affect (i) the probative value of such evidence and (ii) the public policy aspects of permitting such evidence to support any inference against the accused and state when silence can support an adverse inference against the accused.

(d) as regards a refusal to give body samples, to recognise that there are rules about the taking of such samples and state the evidential effect of a refusal without good cause to consent to the taking of such samples.

Question 1

Joe was charged jointly with Arthur with theft from a newsagents' shop. At trial Joe and Arthur ran cut throat defences, each man suggesting that the other had committed the theft. When first questioned by the police about the offence Joe had claimed that he had been ill on the date of the theft and had spent the day at home in bed. However, when the police proved this to be false, he claimed that he had spent the day fishing (he explained his false account to the police by saying that he had told his employer that he was ill). When Joe gave evidence he gave details of his alibi which he had not previously mentioned to the police. However, his testimony was evasive and contradictory and Arthur's counsel was allowed to cross-examine Joe on his previous convictions for theft. Although, in cross-examination of prosecution witnesses and of Joe, Arthur had sought to suggest that Joe was, alone, guilty of the offence, Arthur decided not to testify. Moreover when interviewed by the police he had answered every question by saying 'No comment' (his solicitor had been present throughout the interviews in question).

Consider how the judge should deal with this case when summing up to the jury.

Question 2

Alan, aged 30, is charged with having unlawful sexual intercourse with Martha, aged 15. The alleged offence came to light in the following circumstances. Martha's mother found Martha in bed with a naked man who promptly leapt out of the bedroom window and ran off. Martha's mother then telephoned the police. About two minutes after the phone call a police officer arrested Alan (who was naked) approximately a half mile away from Martha's house. The officer then asked Alan to explain his presence in that place in that condition (naked). Alan refused to do this. Meanwhile Martha told her mother that she had met Alan at a fun fair two weeks previously and that he had been the man in bed with her when her mother came into her bedroom. When interviewed by the police Alan claimed that, although he knew Martha, he had not met her at the fun fair. The police have now discovered that Martha's friend Louise can confirm that Martha met Alan at the fun fair.

Consider what, if any, inferences of guilt may be drawn from Alan's conduct.

TWELVE

SUSPECT WITNESSES, CARE WARNINGS AND IDENTIFICATION EVIDENCE

12.1   General Introduction

In English law the general rule is that a court's decision can properly be based upon the evidence of a single witness. There is usually no legal requirement as to the amount of evidence which should be produced, nor any principle governing the proper weight to attach to that evidence.

This chapter is concerned with situations where that general rule is not applied or is modified, so that there is a requirement either to produce additional evidence or to alert the fact-finders about the danger of relying on a single source of evidence. This type of requirement occurs in situations where the usual sources or types of evidence are thought to have a greater than normal risk of unreliability — to be suspect. This unreliability may arise deliberately (for example, the witness is lying) or through error (circumstances make it difficult for the witness's evidence to be accurate). Of course, these risks can occur in any sort of case, civil or criminal, but the law of evidence has recognised a number of situations where the risk is predictable and requires a predetermined response by the court. Ultimately, the problem is one for the fact-finders to deal with; in civil cases, the fact-finder is a trained lawyer and should be aware of the risks, but in criminal cases the fact-finders are typically non-lawyers and will need alerting to the risks. Thus, the problem is visible mainly in criminal cases and this chapter will reflect that. One should also note that these risks are usually concerned with the evidence produced by the prosecution to establish the guilt of the accused.

12.2   Discretionary Care Warnings

Hypothetically, decisions on whether to warn fact-finders to take care when considering the reliability of a particular witness's evidence could be taken on either one of two bases. First, a case-by-case basis, depending on the view taken by the trial judge of whether the reliability of a specific witness was suspect. Secondly, a class basis where a decision is taken that every witness in a particular category would be presumed suspect and require a warning from the trial judge (for example, an accomplice testifying for the prosecution).

Until 1994, the 'class' basis prevailed. Examples included

(a)   an accomplice giving evidence for the prosecution;

(b)   the complainant in a sexual case;

(c)   children; and

(d)   other witnesses thought to be of dubious veracity (for example, inmates from a secure mental institution, and prisoners).

The rationales for these classes varied between them and, by the 1980s, were largely discredited. The Criminal Justice Act 1988, s. 34 (as amended by Criminal Justice Act 1991 and Criminal Justice and Public Order Act 1994) removed the obligation to give a care warning about accepting the uncorroborated evidence of a child. Henceforth, a warning could be given about the truthfulness of a child's evidence but it would depend upon the view taken by the judge in the particular trial. It is now discretionary and determined on a case-by-case basis. In 1994, the Criminal Justice and Public Order Act, s. 32, removed the obligation on judges to warn the jury to be cautious before relying upon the testimony of a witness who was either an accomplice testifying for the prosecution or a complainant in a sexual case (usually known as a 'care' warning). Again, the result is that whether to give a care warning about any witness and, if so, the content of the warning, is left to the discretion of the judge in each trial.

In *R* v *Makanjuola* [1995] 1 WLR 1348, Lord Taylor CJ summarised the new position in eight points. In view of their importance, they are set out here in full:

1.   Section 32(1) abrogated the requirement to give a corroboration direction in respect of an alleged accomplice or a complainant of a sexual offence, simply because a witness falls into one of those categories.

2.   It is a matter for the judge's discretion what, if any, warning he considers appropriate in respect of such a witness as indeed in respect of any other witness in whatever type of case. Whether he chooses to give a warning and in what terms will depend on the circumstances of the case, the issues raised and the content and quality of the witness's evidence.

3.   In some cases it might be appropriate for the judge to warn the jury to exercise caution before acting upon the unsupported evidence of a witness. This will not be so simply because the witness is a complainant of a sexual offence, nor will it necessarily be so because a witness is alleged to be an accomplice. There will need to be an evidential basis for suggesting that the evidence of the witness may be unreliable. An evidential basis does not include mere suggestion by cross-examining counsel.

4.   If any question arises as to whether the judge should give a special warning in respect of a witness, it is desirable that the question be resolved by discussion with counsel in the absence of the jury before final speeches.

5.   Where the judge does decide to give some warning in respect of a witness, it will be appropriate to do so as part of the judge's review of the evidence and his comments as to how the jury should evaluate it rather than as a set-piece legal direction.

6.   Where some warning is required it will be for the judge to decide the strength and terms of the warning. It does not have to be invested with the whole florid regime of the old corroboration rules.

7.   It follows that we emphatically disagree with the tentative submission made by the editors of *Archbold, Criminal Pleading, Evidence and Practice*, vol. 1 in the passage at paragraph 16.36. Attempts to reimpose the straitjacket of the old corroboration rules are strongly to be deprecated.

8.   Finally, this court will be disinclined to interfere with a trial judge's exercise of his discretion save in a case where that exercise is unreasonable in the *Wednesbury* sense: *Associated Provincial Picture Houses* v *Wednesbury Corporation* [1948] 1 KB 223.

The crucial factor is that the trial judge always has a discretion whether to warn or not. He or she has to decide (a) if any warning is appropriate and if so, (b) what form that warning should take. The decision will depend on the issues raised in the trial, the circumstances of the case and the judge's view of the content and quality of the witness's evidence; see *R* v *L* [1999] Crim LR 489. The importance of the witness's evidence to the outcome of the case may be an important consideration in deciding what sort of warning, if any, to give (see *R* v *Warwick Muncaster* [1999] Crim LR 409). Note that, although class (d) above (other witnesses of dubious veracity) was not specifically dealt with by s. 32 of the 1994 Act, it was treated in the same way by Lord Taylor CJ in *Makanjuola*.

12.3 Supporting Evidence

If the judge does give a warning, he or she will also tell the jury to look for any evidence which may support the reliability of the suspect witness. In the past, such evidence was very strictly defined (see *R* v *Baskerville* [1916] 2 KB 658 per Lord Reading CJ — it 'must be independent testimony which affects the accused by connecting or tending to connect him with the crime'). Supporting evidence now is a broader concept; according to Lord Widgery CJ in *R* v *Turnbull* [1977] QB 224 (a case turning on a challenged identification):

> This may be corroboration in the sense that lawyers use that word; but it need not be so if its effect is to make the jury sure that there has been no mistaken identification.

For example, a decision by the accused not to testify at trial could constitute supporting evidence, if it occurs in a situation where the judge decides that an inference could be drawn (*cf.* s. 35, Criminal Justice and Public Order Act 1994). Conversely, it has been said that evidence of a 'recent complaint' in a sexual offence trial (evidence that the victim complained at an early opportunity) is relevant only to the victim's veracity. It may help the jury to decide whether the victim has told the truth in the witness box but the jury should be told that it is not evidence which supports the victim's account. See *R* v *Islam* [1999] 1 Cr App R 22; *R* v *Churchill* [1999] Crim LR 664. If there is evidence which a jury might think offers support but which in law cannot do so, the judge should tell the jury this if and when they are given a care warning (see, for example, *R* v *B(MT)* [2000] Crim LR 181, where the accused had not mentioned something at interview but the circumstances were such that no inference could be drawn from his silence, under s. 34 of the 1994 Act).

12.4 Categories of Case where some Form of Corroboration is Required

12.4.1 THE HISTORY

Statute law has identified certain situations where the risks of fabrication or error could be foreseen and usually has responded to them by requiring a second source of evidence to confirm (or 'corroborate') the first witness. In the absence of a second source, the case would fail. Some such situations survive today (see **12.4.2**). There are other situations where judges have decided that it would not be proper to convict in the absence of supporting evidence. In these situations, a submission of no case is likely to succeed and the judge will withdraw the case from the jury (see **12.4.3**).

12.4.2 WHERE CORROBORATION IS REQUIRED AS A MATTER OF STATUTE LAW

12.4.2.1 Perjury

A person cannot be convicted of the offence of perjury 'solely upon the evidence of one witness as to the falsity of any statement alleged to be false': Perjury Act 1911, s. 13. The accused may make a formal admission that the statement is false, in which case no further evidence is needed on this issue (remember that these categories were created to *protect* the accused). But, in the absence of such admission, the jury must be directed by the judge to look for evidence which supports that given by the main (prosecution) witness; if they can find none, they should acquit the accused. See *R* v *Rider* (1986) 83 Cr App R 207.

12.4.2.2 Speeding

A person cannot be convicted of speeding solely on the opinion evidence of one witness as to the speed of the vehicle: Road Traffic Regulation Act 1984, s. 89. Expert evidence derived from, for example, the length of skid marks on the road could offer the necessary support. If, as is common now, evidence of the vehicle's speed comes from a reading on a speedometer or radar gun, this will not be classed as opinion evidence and s. 89 will not apply.

12.4.2.3 Attempts

Where a defendant is charged with attempting to commit either of the two preceding offences (i.e. perjury or speeding), the same requirement for corroboration applies to the trial for the attempt as it would in a trial for the completed offence. See Criminal Attempts Act 1981, s. 2(2)(g).

12.4.2.4 Inferences from silence

In certain circumstances, the jury can properly draw inferences from the accused's silence (see, for example, Criminal Justice and Public Order Act 1994, ss. 34(2), 35(3), 36(2) and 37(2)). However, the accused cannot be convicted solely upon such inference (see s. 38(3) of the 1994 Act). If this was the only damning evidence that the prosecution produced at trial, which is highly unlikely, a submission of no case would succeed.

12.4.3 OTHER CASES WHERE A SUBMISSION OF NO CASE WILL SUCCEED IN THE ABSENCE OF SUPPORTING EVIDENCE

12.4.3.1 Poor quality identification evidence

Where the prosecution case depends substantially on *poor quality* (fleeting glimpse) identification evidence which the defence alleges is mistaken, the judge should withdraw the case from the jury unless there is evidence to support the reliability of the identification. See *R* v *Turnbull* [1977] QB 224. Typically, this would be tested on a submission of no case to answer at the close of the prosecution's case. See further **12.5** below.

12.4.3.2 Confessions by the mentally handicapped

Concern about the reliability of such confessions is reflected in Police and Criminal Evidence Act 1984, s. 77. This requires the trial judge to warn the jury of the special need for caution where the prosecution evidence is wholly or substantially a confession by a defendant suffering from mental handicap. Section 77 provides:

> *(1) Without prejudice to the general duty of the court at a trial on indictment to direct the jury on any matter on which it appears to the court appropriate to do so, where at such a trial—*
>
> *(a) the case against the accused depends wholly or substantially on a confession by him; and*
>
> *(b) the court is satisfied—*
>
> *(i) that he is mentally handicapped; and*
>
> *(ii) that the confession was not made in the presence of an independent person,*
>
> *the court shall warn the jury that there is special need for caution before convicting the accused in reliance on the confession, and shall explain that the need arises because of the circumstances mentioned in pararaphs (a) and (b) above.*
>
> *(2) In any case where at the summary trial of a person for an offence it appears to the court that a warning under subsection (1) above would be required if the trial were on indictment, the court shall treat the case as one in which there is a special need for caution before convicting the accused on his confession.*
>
> *(3) In this section—*
>
> *'independent person' does not include a police officer or a person employed for, or engaged on, police purposes;*

> *'mentally handicapped,' in relation to a person, means that he is in a state of arrested or incomplete development of mind which includes significant impairment of intelligence and social functioning.*

The judge will give the warning in the course of summing-up the case to the jury at the end of the trial. However, case law since 1984 has recognised that a submission of no case may be made successfully in such cases, at the close of the prosecution evidence. Where the prosecution case depends wholly upon confession evidence, and the accused suffers from a significant degree of mental handicap, and (in the opinion of the judge) the confession evidence is unconvincing to a point where the jury, properly directed by the judge, could not properly convict in reliance on that evidence, then the judge should withdraw the case from the jury. See, for example, *R* v *Mackenzie* (1993) 96 Cr App R 98. In effect, this is simply the application of a standard test for upholding submissions of no case: see *R* v *Galbraith* [1981] 1 WLR 1039.

12.5   Identification Evidence

12.5.1   THE NEED FOR SPECIAL CAUTION

Intuitively, most people consider that identification evidence is very reliable and accurate. Indeed, identification witnesses themselves often think so and come into the witness box convinced that they have identified the criminal correctly. That there are dangers in over-reliance on such evidence has been plain since at least the early 20th Century and the case of *Adolf Beck*. Beck was twice convicted wrongly (in 1896 and 1904) of offences of fraud. In the 1870s, when Beck claimed to have been in South America, a 'John Smith' was convicted in England of several frauds. Each offence alleged that Smith had become intimate with a woman, persuaded her to put valuable jewellery into his possession, and then disappeared. In 1895, several more women were called as witnesses at a new trial. The offences seemed identical. Each woman identified the accused, this time Adolf Beck. The prosecution even called two police officers to testify that Adolf Beck and John Smith were the same man. Beck was convicted and sentenced to seven years' imprisonment. After his release, the offences started again. In 1904, Beck was again convicted on the word of several women, each of whom claimed to have been intimate with him. Whilst Beck was held in custody, awaiting sentence, John Smith was caught committing another offence. Smith's appearance matched the descriptions given by the women, which included the fact that their seducer was circumcised. Prison records from the 1870s indicated that 'John Smith' was circumcised. Beck was not circumcised. Beck was released, pardoned and received a substantial sum in compensation. Following this case, the Court of Criminal Appeal was set up and the first set of general instructions on the conduct of identification parades was issued.

However, miscarriages of justice continued to occur in cases based upon identification evidence. As Lord Devlin has pointed out:

> In 1912 a man on a charge of murder was identified by no less than 17 witnesses, but fortunately was able to establish an irrefutable alibi. In 1928 Oscar Slater, after he had spent 19 years in prison . . . had his conviction for murder quashed; he had been identified by 14 witnesses. Nevertheless, cases continued to be left to the jury as if they raised only a simple issue between the identifier and the accused as to which was telling the truth . . . In 1974 two shattering cases of mistaken identity came to light within four weeks of each other. (Patrick Devlin, *The Judge*, 1981)

In May 1974, Lord Devlin was invited to chair a committee to investigate the law and procedure on identification and his committee's report (*Report to the Secretary of State for the Home Department of the Departmental Committee on Evidence of Identification in Criminal Cases*) was published in April 1976. It made several recommendations for changes to the gathering of identification evidence and its treatment in the courtroom, all of which were to be effected by statute. However, as Lord Devlin has observed:

The Court of Appeal decided to forestall legislation by giving in July 1976 . . . a comprehensive judgment laying down a new approach . . .

That judgment was given in *R* v *Turnbull* [1977] QB 224 by Lord Widgery CJ. The 'new approach' is as follows (see pp. 228–230 of the report):

(1)   First, whenever the case against an accused depends wholly or substantially on the correctness of one or more identifications of the accused which the defence alleges to be mistaken, the judge should warn the jury of the special need for caution before convicting the accused in reliance on the correctness of the identification or identifications. In addition he should instruct them as to the reason for the need for such a warning and should make some reference to the possibility that a mistaken witness can be a convincing one and that a number of such witnesses can all be mistaken. Provided this is done in clear terms the judge need not use any particular form of words.

(2)   Secondly, the judge should direct the jury to examine closely the circumstances in which the identification by each witness came to be made. How long did the witness have the accused under observation? At what distance? In what light? Was the observation impeded in any way, as for example by passing traffic or a press of people? Had the witness ever seen the accused before? How often? If only occasionally, had he any special reason for remembering the accused? How long elapsed between the original observation and the subsequent identification to the police?

(3)   Was there any material discrepancy between the description of the accused given to the police by the witness when first seen by them and his actual appearance?

(4)   If in any case, whether it is being dealt with summarily or on indictment, the prosecution have reason to believe that there is such a material discrepancy they should supply the accused or his legal advisers with particulars of the description the police were first given. In all cases if the accused asks to be given particulars of such descriptions, the prosecution should supply them. Finally, he should remind the jury of any specific weakness which had appeared in the identification evidence.

(5)   Recognition may be more reliable than identification of a stranger; but even when the witness is purporting to recognise someone whom he knows, the jury should be reminded that mistakes in recognition of close relatives and friends are sometimes made.

(6)   When the quality (of the identifying evidence) is good, as for example when the identification is made after a long period of observation, or in satisfactory conditions by a relative, a neighbour, a close friend, a workmate and the like, the jury can safely be left to assess the value of the identifying evidence even though there is no other evidence to support it: provided always, however, that an adequate warning has been given about the special need for caution.

(7)   When, in the judgment of the trial judge, the quality of the identifying evidence is poor, as for example when it depends solely on a fleeting glance or on a longer observation made in difficult conditions, the situation is very different. The judge should then withdraw the case from the jury and direct an acquittal unless there is other evidence which goes to support the correctness of the identification. This may be corroboration in the sense lawyers use that word; but it need not be so if its effect is to make the jury sure that there has been no mistaken identification.

(8)   The trial judge should identify to the jury the evidence which he adjudges is capable of supporting the evidence of identification. If there is any evidence or circumstances which the jury might think was supporting when it did not have this quality, the judge should say so.

(9)   Care should be taken by the judge when directing the jury about the support for an identification which may be derived from the fact that they have rejected an alibi.

False alibis may be put forward for many reasons . . . It is only when the jury is satisfied that the sole reason for the fabrication was to deceive them and there is no other explanation for its being put forward can fabrication provide any support for identification evidence. The jury should be reminded that proving the accused has told lies about where he was at the material time does not by itself prove that he was where the identifying witness says he was.

Points to note

(a) A failure to observe the *Turnbull* guidelines will often lead to a successful appeal: see *R* v *Hunjan* (1979) 68 Cr App R 99. Indeed, the Privy Council said, in *Reid* v *R* (1990) 90 Cr App R 121, that they had:

> no hesitation in concluding that a significant failure to follow the identification guidelines as laid down in *Turnbull* . . . will cause a conviction to be quashed because it will have resulted in a substantial miscarriage of justice . . . If convictions are to be allowed upon uncorroborated identification evidence there must be strict insistence upon a judge giving a clear warning of the danger of a mistaken identification which the jury must consider before arriving at their verdict. It is only in the most exceptional circumstances that a conviction based on uncorroborated identification evidence will be sustained in the absence of such a warning.

See also *Scott* v *R* [1989] AC 1242. An example of 'exceptional circumstances' justifying the dismissal of an appeal in the absence of a *Turnbull* warning, may be found in *Freemantle* v *R* [1994] 3 All ER 225. Here, the Privy Council said that if the identification evidence was of exceptionally good quality, this would be an exceptional circumstance. Amongst the factors which the Privy Council thought showed the exceptionally good quality of the identification evidence, was a dialogue between the accused, Freemantle, and one of the eye-witnesses, Campbell. Campbell shouted to the man he saw, 'Freemantle me see you'; the man's reply was regarded as an implied acknowledgement of the accuracy of that identification.

Identification evidence given by police officers has no special status. Typically, officers receive training in observation and they might be thought to possess greater ability to identify people than is possessed by ordinary members of the public. However, in *Reid*, their Lordships stated that:

> . . . experience has undoubtedly shown that police identification can be just as unreliable and is not therefore to be excepted from the now well established need for the appropriate warnings.

This remains the position, even where the police witness claims to have recognised the accused at the scene of crime, having known him previously: see *R* v *Bowden* [1993] Crim LR 379.

(b) Regarding 'supporting evidence':

A defendant's lying alibi can 'support' but a careful direction is required: *R* v *Keane* (1977) 65 Cr App R 247. See also **11.2.1**.

In the absence of other sources of evidence to support a poor quality identification (e.g. D's fingerprints on the murder weapon), the judge should consider whether several identification witnesses may support each other. If they have each been hampered in their observation (e.g. passengers on a night bus passing an incident on the street), the judge may have to withdraw the case from the jury and direct an acquittal. If they have observed in satisfactory conditions (e.g. several spectators at a sunny day-time football match observe an assault by a fellow spectator), then their evidence may be presented to the jury as capable of supporting each other's identification evidence. In that situation, the judge should also direct the jury that several honest witnesses can all be mistaken. See *R* v *Weeder* (1980) 71 Cr App R 228; also *R* v *Breslin* (1985) 80 Cr App R 226.

Supporting evidence, for these purposes, need not amount to '*Baskerville*' corroboration. The risk in relation to *Turnbull* identification evidence is of mistake (rather than invention) — this risk may be countered by evidence which is not independent.

(c) The form of a *Turnbull* warning:

When a trial judge directs a jury about identification evidence, in the summing-up, there is no set form of words that is needed for the *Turnbull* warning. In *Mills* v *R* [1995] 1 WLR 511, the Privy Council stated that *Turnbull* was not a statute and did not require the incantation of a formula. A judge has:

> a broad discretion to express himself in his own way when he directs a jury on identification. All that is required . . . is that he should comply with the sense and spirit of the guidance in . . . *Turnbull* . . .

Where the defendant admits to being present at the scene of the crime but denies that he was the offender, this may not involve an issue of identification at all. See (d) below for cases which restrict the circumstances in which a *Turnbull* direction is required.

(d) Regarding the limits of the requirement to give a *Turnbull* warning:

A *Turnbull* warning is not always necessary, even though the defendant denies being the offender. If there is no possibility of the witness being mistaken about the identity of the offender, there is no need for a *Turnbull* warning.

One example is when the only person who could be the offender is the defendant. In *R* v *Slater* [1995] 1 Cr App R 584, the offence took place in a nightclub and the accused accepted that he had been there. The accused was 6′ 6″ tall and the Court of Appeal noted that there was no evidence to suggest that anyone remotely similar in height to the accused was present in the nightclub where the offence took place; no *Turnbull* warning was needed. Conversely, in *R* v *Thornton* [1995] 1 Cr App R 578, the offence took place at a wedding reception. The accused accepted that he was at the reception. There were a number of people present who were dressed similarly to the accused (black leather jacket, black trousers) and several people were allegedly involved in the offence. The Court of Appeal thought that a mistaken identification was clearly possible; a *Turnbull* warning should have been given.

Another example of a situation where a *Turnbull* warning is not automatically needed is where the defence allege that the 'identification' witness is lying. Where the defence allege that the identification has been fabricated by the prosecution witness(es), the sole issue would seem to be the veracity of the witness(es). In *R* v *Courtnell* [1990] Crim LR 115, the Court of Appeal accepted that point but noted that if there was evidence that might support the contention of mistaken identification, the judge should direct the jury accordingly, even though the defence had not raised that issue at the trial. In *Courtnell*, there was no such evidence and the judge had not erred in omitting a *Turnbull* direction. Similarly, in *R* v *Cape* [1996] 1 Cr App R 191, the defendants were alleged to have been involved in a fight in a pub. The pub landlord, who knew the men, testified that they were so involved. The defendants admitted being in the pub at the time but denied involvement; they suggested the landlord was lying and motivated by a grudge. The issue for the jury was simply whether they accepted the evidence of the landlord as truthful; that did not call for a *Turnbull* warning. In *Beckford* v *R* (1993) 97 Cr App R 409, the Privy Council reiterated the need to consider carefully all of the issues before the jury. Beckford and two co-accused were tried for murder. The sole witness to the crime identified all three men as being present. At trial, the accused ran alibi defences and alleged that the witness was lying because either (i) he was a compulsive and inveterate liar or (ii) he was susceptible to mental aberrations (having previously been a patient in a mental hospital). The Privy Council considered that there were two questions for the jury to consider:

(1) Is the witness honest? This was at the heart of the defence case. If the jury found he was not honest, they would disregard his evidence.

If the jury found him to be an honest witness, they would need to consider (and be directed on) a second question.

(2) Could the witness be mistaken? If this was a possibility, on the evidence, it would require a *Turnbull* direction from the judge. The direction should then be given even if the defence did not rely on the possibility of mistake.

Another example of a situation in which the possibility of mistaken identification can be discounted is *R* v *Beckles and Montague* [1999] Crim LR 148. Here, the victim alleged that he had been lured to a fourth-floor flat by a woman. Once there, he had been robbed by two men and held prisoner. After some three hours there, the victim left the flat by a window. He alleged that he had been thrown out of it by the three accused. They admitted being in the flat but suggested that the victim had jumped from the window of his own choice. There was evidence that the victim had been drinking. The Court of Appeal held that this was not a 'fleeting glance' case, the issue was more the veracity of the victim rather than the accuracy of his evidence and so a *Turnbull* warning was not needed.

Where the prosecution try to prove that a defendant was present at a particular place by calling witnesses who will say that they saw a man driving a car, and they can identify the car, then a full *Turnbull* warning is not needed. The prosecution need to rely upon other evidence to prove that the defendant was driving the car at the material time. This was the view taken by the Court of Appeal in *R* v *Browning* (1991) 94 Cr App R 109. The explanation for the distinction between identification of a person and of a car was said to be that, whereas people may change their appearance frequently (e.g. facial expression or bodily posture), cars do not change their shape, colour or size (unless of course they are altered deliberately). Nevertheless, a jury should still be directed as to any difficulties regarding observation of the car (e.g. if the witness was a driver who got a fleeting glance of the car whilst being overtaken).

Where an eye-witness gives evidence only of *description* (for example, clothing or general characteristics), an identification parade is not required. This is not identification evidence and Code D, para. 2.15 (see **12.6**) is inapplicable. In *R* v *Gayle* [1999] 2 Cr App R 130, the Court of Appeal noted that there is a special need for caution when considering identification evidence because of the possibility that an honest witness may be mistaken. However, the danger of an honest witness being mistaken about distinctive clothing, or the general description of a person he or she has seen (e.g. short or tall, black or white, direction of movement) is minimal. What the jury need to concentrate upon is the honesty of the witness.

(e) Regarding cases where the identification evidence is poor:

At the conclusion of the prosecution evidence in a trial, the defence may make a submission of no case to answer (see **2.9.3.2**). Generally, such submissions are governed by the principles set out in *R* v *Galbraith* [1981] 1 WLR 1039 but in cases where evidence of identification is disputed, the submission will be based upon *Turnbull*. Where there is no identification evidence at all, the judge's decision is simple. Where there is identification evidence but it is of poor quality and is unsupported by other evidence, again the judge should withdraw the case from the jury. First, the judge should assume the identification evidence to be honest (i.e. he or she does not need to form a view about the credibility of the prosecution witness). Then if he or she considers that the identification evidence has a base which is so slender that it is unreliable and thus not sufficient to found a conviction, he or she should uphold the submission and order the defendant's acquittal on the charge. See *Daley* v *R* [1993] 4 All ER 86.

According to *R* v *Akaidere* [1990] Crim LR 808, a judge should not tell a jury that the poor identification evidence would have been withdrawn if there was no supporting evidence. The reason for this embargo is that, whilst it is for the judge to decide if there is evidence *capable* of supporting the identification, it is a question of fact for the jury to decide whether it does support it. The jury might be inappropriately influenced in their decision if they knew of the judge's view.

12.5.2 THE ADMISSIBILITY QUESTION(S)

12.5.2.1 General points

Quite apart from the risks which attach to identification evidence in general (to which the *Turnbull* direction relates) questions arise as to the ways in which identification evidence should be (a) gathered and (b) presented in court. Some forms of identification evidence, e.g. dock identifications, are thought to carry such a risk of prejudice to the accused that the courts have frequently excluded such evidence (exclusion has been at the court's discretion either at common law or, now, under Police and Criminal Evidence Act 1984, s. 78). In general the courts have sought to ensure that identification evidence is gathered in 'controlled circumstances' and to this end a code of practice (Code D) has been laid down by virtue of s. 66 of the 1984 Act (see Code D at **12.6**). Recent Court of Appeal decisions illustrate that non-compliance with the Code may be an important factor in deciding whether to exclude the evidence. Some aspects of the admissibility of identification evidence have already been dealt with in **Chapters 5** and **8** of this Manual.

12.5.2.2 Cases where the link between the accused and the crime is based upon an eye-witness — dock identification, identity parades, confrontations, etc.

(See Code of Practice D, para. 2 and annexes A to D at **12.6**.)

(a) In-court eye-witness identification (usually called dock identification):

R v *Howick* [1970] Crim LR 403: dock identification should not generally be allowed. The reason for this ban is the lack of probative value of a dock identification. It is easy for a witness to 'identify' the alleged criminal when he or she is standing rather obviously in the dock and the exercise adds little or nothing to a previous act of identification. In the absence of a previous identification by that witness, to allow a dock identification would flout the basic principles that govern the production of identification evidence (through an identification parade, for example).

A dock identification may be permissible when defendant refuses to attend a parade (*R* v *John* [1973] Crim LR 113, CA) or renders a parade impracticable, e.g. by changing his appearance (*R* v *Mutch* [1973] 1 All ER 178, CA).

There is no logic in making a distinction between a dock identification in a Crown Court and in a magistrates' court. However, in road traffic offences it is usually necessary to prove that the defendant was the driver of the car at the time of the offence. Generally, there is no dispute that the accused was the driver but a failure to call any evidence on that issue is likely to result in an acquittal. In summary trials for road traffic offences, the custom has evolved where a witness (usually a police officer) is asked, 'Do you see the driver in court?' Because of the sheer number of such offences which are tried by magistrates, if there had to be an identification parade in every case where the accused did not expressly admit that he or she was the driver, 'the whole process of justice in a magistrates' court would be severely impaired' (*Barnes* v *Chief Constable of Durham* [1997] 2 Cr App R 505). Thus, it seems that in this type of case the onus is on the accused to raise the issue of disputed identification before the trial starts, and seek an identification parade.

(b) Out of court eye-witness identification.

The obvious way to avoid the prejudice of a dock identification is to make prior reference to an out of court identification made in less prejudicial circumstances. Code D lays down a regime for ensuring this, so far as is possible; see, in particular, Code D, para. 2. All the forms of out of court identification mentioned below would seem to be admissible either as prior consistent statements (under the principle in *R* v *Christie*) or under the rules in *R* v *Osbourne and Virtue* [1973] QB 678. See also *R* v *Rogers* [1993] Crim LR 386 confirming the admissibility of a street identification.

(i) Where the *identity* of the *suspect* is *known* to the police *and* he or she is *available*, four forms of identification procedure may be used to confirm or refute identification. If the suspect does not dispute identification by a witness, no identification procedure is necessary unless the officer in charge of the investigation considers it would be useful (para. 2.14). If identification is disputed, an identification procedure shall be held if practicable unless, in all the circumstances, it would serve no useful purpose in determining the suspect's involvement in the offence (paras 2.14 and 2.15). There will be no such useful purpose where it is not disputed that the suspect is already well-known to the eye-witness, or there is no reasonable possibility of the witness making an identification.

If an identification procedure is to be used, the officer in charge of the case will consult with the identification officer as to the suitability and practicability of holding either a video identification or an identification parade. (An identification officer is the officer responsible for the arrangement and conduct of identification procedures, usually an inspector; para. 2.13.) A video identification will normally be more suitable if it can be done sooner than a parade (para. 2.16). The officer in charge of the case will then offer the chosen procedure to the suspect (para. 2.16). A group identification may be offered to the suspect instead, if the officer in charge of the investigation considers it to be more satisfactory to do so (para. 2.17). The suspect may refuse the offered procedure and then make representations as to why a different procedure should be used. The identification officer shall then offer an alternative procedure if one is suitable and practicable. If the suspect refuses or fails to take part in any practicable identification procedure, arrangements may be made for covert video identification or covert group identification (para. 2.19). As a last resort, if none of the other procedures are practicable, a confrontation may be arranged.

In a *video identification*, the witness is shown images of a suspect, together with images of at least eight other people who resemble the suspect. The images may be moving or still (see Annex A). An *identification parade* puts the suspect into a line-up of at least eight other people who resemble the suspect as far as possible (see Annex B). *Group identification* is less formal — the suspect is put into an informal group of people, perhaps walking through a shopping centre or a queue at a bus station (see Annex C). *Confrontation* involves a direct confrontation between witness and suspect. This will usually take place in a police station and the witness shall be asked, 'Is this the person?' (see Annex D).

(ii) Where the *identity* of the *suspect* is *known* to the police *but* he or she is *not available*, the identification officer may arrange a video identification. The suspect will be unavailable if they are not immediately available to participate in a procedure and will not become available within a reasonably short time. Failure or refusal to participate may be treated as not being available. See para. 2.12.

(iii)   Where the *identity* of the *suspect* is *not known* to the *police* then clearly the steps outlined above cannot be taken. To discover the identity of the suspect an eye-witness may be taken to a particular neighbourhood (usually shortly after the alleged offence) to make (if possible) a street identification. Alternatively, a witness may be asked to look through police photographs, at least 12 at a time (para. 2.26 and see Annex E).

Finally, note that compliance or non-compliance with Code D does not determine whether the identification evidence is admissible or not. It is simply a factor to be considered if an application is made to exclude the evidence by operation of s. 78 of the 1984 Act (see **10.1.3**).

(c)   Effect of breaches of the Code.

The court may well exclude evidence obtained as a result of a breach of Code D, pursuant to s. 78 of the 1984 Act, see:

R v *Leckie* [1983] Crim LR 543 (non-compliance with confrontation rules).

R v *Gall* (1990) 90 Cr App R 64 and *R* v *Conway* [1990] Crim LR 402 (non-compliance with identification parade rules). In *R* v *Quinn* [1995] 1 Cr App R 480, although the Court of Appeal fell short of saying that the identification evidence should have been excluded, it held that the trial judge should have directed the jury specifically about breaches of the identification parade rules.

R v *Nagah* (1991) 92 Cr App R 344 (confrontation inappropriate where parade requested by defendant and practicable). See also *R* v *Allen* [1995] Crim LR 643.

However, breaches of Code D do not automatically lead to the exclusion of the identification evidence, see *R* v *Grannell* (1990) 90 Cr App R 149; *R* v *Quinn* [1990] Crim LR 581; *R* v *Penny* [1992] Crim LR 184. For example, in *R* v *Forbes* [2001] AC 473, the House of Lords held that the evidence of two street identifications by the eye-witness had been rightly allowed in at the trial, notwithstanding the breach of what is now Code D, para. 2.14.

If an eye-witness makes an identification after a parade has ended, the suspect and his or her solicitor should be informed and the police should consider whether to give the witness a second opportunity at a parade (Code D, Annex B, para. 20). Where two witnesses were put into the same room after taking part in a parade, and only one had identified the suspect, but later the second made a statement doing so, neither witness's evidence had to be excluded. See *R* v *Willoughby* [1999] 2 Cr App R 82, where the Court of Appeal held that merely 'firming-up' a tentative identification at a parade does not come within the ambit of what is now para. 20. As to the witness who had not previously identified the suspect, the Court observed that even if para. 20 is breached, so long as the breach is relatively minor and innocent (e.g. no coaching has occurred), then the trial judge may decide not to exclude that evidence under s. 78 of the 1984 Act.

12.5.2.3   Cases where the link between the accused and the crime is based upon security film/photographs etc.
Kajala v *Noble* (1982) 75 Cr App R 149, DC and *R* v *Dodson* [1984] 1 WLR 971 are authorities for the proposition that the jury can look at the film etc. and form their own view as to whether the person shown in the film etc. is the accused. According to *R* v *Blenkinsop* [1995] 1 Cr App R 7 a full *Turnbull* warning would not be appropriate in such cases. However, it may be preferable to call a witness who knows the accused and recognises him on the film (in which case a *Turnbull* warning would generally be appropriate).

R v *Fowden* [1982] Crim LR 588, *R* v *Grimer* [1982] Crim LR 674, *Taylor* v *Chief Constable of Cheshire* [1987] 1 All ER 225 and *R* v *Caldwell* (1994) 99 Cr App R 73 deal with the situation where witnesses who know the accused (usually police officers) are called upon to identify him as the person caught on film etc. The propositions which emerge from these cases are that:

(a) Attempts should be made not to reveal to the jury that the witness knows the accused through previous encounters in the course of investigations into other criminal offences.

(b) A *Turnbull* warning should be given.

(c) Where there are several witnesses they should not be allowed to view the film etc. together but should be asked to view the film individually and state whether they recognise the person on the film (see also Code D, Annex A).

In *R* v *Stockwell* (1993) 97 Cr App R 260, the Court of Appeal accepted that the opinion evidence of a facial-mapping expert is admissible, particularly in cases where there was a possibility that the person caught on the film was disguised. In *R* v *Clarke* [1995] 2 Cr App R 425, the Court of Appeal held that evidence of facial mapping by way of video superimposition (of police photographs of the accused upon photographs of the offender taken by a security camera) was admissible as a species of real evidence to which no special rules applied.

In *R* v *Clare* [1995] 2 Cr App R 333, the Court of Appeal accepted that a police officer, who had viewed a security video of a crowd disturbance at a football match over 40 times (having the facility to stop the video and examine it in slow motion), had thereby become an expert on that video so as to justify calling him to give evidence interpreting the video and the role and identification of the person caught on the video. In *R* v *Thomas*, 22 November 1999, unreported, the Court of Appeal held that there was no obligation on the prosecution to put the accused on an identification parade before people on whom neither the police nor the Crown ever intended to rely as identification witnesses. Before T was put on trial for four bank robberies, a police officer studied CCTV videos and single frame shots of the robberies 'repeatedly'. The Court of Appeal said that the officer had 'acquired special knowledge that the [trial] court did not possess'; in effect, he had become an 'expert' and there was no purpose in seeing if he could pick out T on a parade.

In *R* v *McNamara* [1996] Crim LR 750 the Court of Appeal held that where a jury requested a view of the accused to compare with a man on a video, no inference could properly be drawn if the accused chose to absent himself from the dock.

Where a crime has been seen by an eye-witness as well as being recorded on a surveillance video, the witness may be allowed to view the video and to amend his/her witness statement in the light of what he/she sees on it: see *R* v *Roberts*, *The Times*, 2 May 1998.

12.5.2.4 Cases where the link between the accused and the crime is made by recognition of voice
An alleged recording of an accused's voice should be heard by the jury but expert evidence on it should also be presented: see *R* v *Bentum* (1989) 153 JP 538; *R* v *Robb* (1991) 93 Cr App R 161.

In *R* v *Deenik* [1992] Crim LR 578, a witness testified to recognising the accused's voice (as that of the person who had committed the offence) on overhearing the accused being interviewed. It was held that it was not necessary to exclude the evidence merely because the accused was unaware that the witness was listening to the interview. The Court of Appeal has said that where a witness identifies a suspect by hearing his or her voice, Code D has no application and there is no obligation to hold a voice identification parade (cf. Annex B, para. 18). What the judge should do is to direct the jury using a suitably adapted form of *Turnbull* warning. Research suggests that identification by voice is less reliable than visual identification, so that the warning should be in stronger terms. See further *R* v *Hersey* [1998] Crim LR 281; *R* v *Gummerson and Steadman* [1999] Crim LR 680; *R* v *Roberts* [2000] Crim LR 183.

12.5.2.5 **Cases where the link between the accused and the crime is made by fingerprints or DNA profiles**

The problems here are primarily concerned with how the accused's fingerprint or body sample can *properly* be obtained from the accused. The governing statutory provisions in this regard are to be found in the Police and Criminal Evidence Act 1984, ss. 61–65 (as amended) and supplemented by Code D, para. 3 (fingerprints) and para. 5 (body samples).

12.5.2.6 **Fingerprints**

The Police and Criminal Evidence Act 1984 provides:

61.—(1) Except as provided by this section no person's fingerprints may be taken without the appropriate consent.

(2) Consent to the taking of a person's fingerprints must be in writing if it is given at a time when he is at a police station.

(3) The fingerprints of a person detained at a police station may be taken without the appropriate consent—

(a) if an officer of at least the rank of superintendent authorises them to be taken; or

(b) if—

(i) he has been charged with a recordable offence or informed that he will be reported for such an offence; and

(ii) he has not had his fingerprints taken in the course of the investigation of the offence by the police.

(4) An officer may only give an authorisation under subsection (3)(a) above if he has reasonable grounds—

(a) for suspecting the involvement of the person whose fingerprints are to be taken in a criminal offence; and

(b) for believing that his fingerprints will tend to confirm or disprove his involvement.

(5) An officer may give an authorisation under subsection (3)(a) above orally or in writing but, if he gives it orally, he shall confirm it in writing as soon as is practicable.

(6) Any person's fingerprints may be taken without the appropriate consent if he has been convicted of a recordable offence.

(7) In a case where by virtue of subsection (3) or (6) above a person's fingerprints are taken without the appropriate consent—

(a) he shall be told the reason before his fingerprints are taken; and

(b) the reason shall be recorded as soon as is practicable after the fingerprints are taken.

(7A) If a person's fingerprints are taken at a police station, whether with or without the appropriate consent—

(a) before the fingerprints are taken, an officer shall inform him that they may be the subject of a speculative search; and

(b) the fact that the person has been informed of this possibility shall be recorded as soon as is practicable after the fingerprints have been taken.

(8) If he is detained at a police station when the fingerprints are taken, the reason for taking them and, in the case falling within subsection 7A above, the fact referred to in paragraph (b) of that subsection shall be recorded on his custody record.

(9) Nothing in this section—

(a) affects any power conferred by paragraph 18(2) of schedule 2 to the immigration Act 1971; or

(b) except as provided in section 15(10) of, and paragraph 7(6) of Schedule 5 to, the Prevention of Terrorism (Temporary Provisions) Act 1989, applies to a person arrested or detained under the terrorism provisions.

Notes: The definition of 'recordable offence', to be found in the National Police Records (Recordable Offences) Regulations 1985 (SI 1985 No. 1941), includes *all* offences punishable by imprisonment.

Other definitions of importance here are in **s. 65** of the 1984 Act (the definitions section):

'fingerprints' include palm prints;

'appropriate consent' means—

(a)   in relation to a person who has attained the age of 17 years, the consent of that person;

(b)   in relation to a person who has not attained that age but has attained the age of 14 years, the consent of that person and his parent or guardian; and

(c)   in relation to a person who has not attained the age of 14 years, the consent of his parent or guardian.

12.5.2.7   Body samples (DNA profiles)

The governing provisions, i.e., Police and Criminal Evidence Act 1984, ss. 62 and 63, as amended by Criminal Justice and Public Order Act 1994, are set out below. Section 62 deals with intimate samples and s. 63 deals with non-intimate samples.

'*Intimate sample*' means (a) a sample of blood, semen or any other tissue fluid, urine or pubic hair; (b) a dental impression; (c) a swab taken from a person's body orifice other than the mouth; ('intimate search' means a search which consists of the physical examination of a person's body orifices other than the mouth).

'*Non-intimate sample*' means (a) a sample of hair other than pubic hair; (b) a sample taken from a nail or from under a nail; (c) a swab taken from any part of a person's body including the mouth but not any other body orifice; (d) saliva; (e) a footprint or a similar impression of any part of a person's body other than a part of his hand.

Section 62 of the 1984 Act provides:

(1)   An intimate sample may be taken from a person in police detention only—

(a)   If a police officer of at least the rank of superintendent authorises it to be taken; and

(b)   if the appropriate consent is given.

(1A)   An intimate sample may be taken from a person who is not in police detention but from whom, in the course of the investigation of an offence, two or more non-intimate samples suitable for the same means of analysis have been taken which have proved insufficient —

(a)   if an officer of at least the rank of superintendent authorises it to be taken; and

(b)   if the appropriate consent is given.

(2)   An officer may only give an authorisation under subsection (1) or (1A) above if he has reasonable grounds—

(a)   for suspecting the involvement of the person from whom the sample is to be taken in a recordable offence; and

(b)   for believing that the same will tend to confirm or disprove his involvement.

[(3)–(9) contain various procedural rules about the taking of intimate samples.]

(10)   Where the appropriate consent to the taking of an intimate sample from a person was refused without good cause, in any proceedings against that person for an offence—

(a)   the court, in determining whether . . . there is a case to answer; and (b) the court or jury, in determining whether that person is guilty of the offence charged, may draw such inferences from the refusal as appear proper.

For the definition of 'recordable offence' see the note following s. 61 above.

Section 63 of the 1984 Act provides:

(1)   Except as provided by this section, a non-intimate sample may not be taken from a person without the appropriate consent.

(2)   Consent to the taking of a non-intimate sample must be given in writing.

(3)   A non-intimate sample may be taken from a person without the appropriate consent if—

(a)   he is in police detention or is being held in custody by the police on the authority of a court; and

(b)   an officer of at least the rank of superintendent authorises it to be taken without the appropriate consent.

(3A)   A non-intimate sample may be taken from a person (whether or not he falls within subsection 3(a) above) without the appropriate consent if—

(a)   he has been charged with a recordable offence or informed that he will be reported for such an offence; and

(b)   either he has not had a non-intimate sample taken from him in the course of the investigation of the offence by the police or he has had a non-intimate sample taken from him but either it was not suitable for the same means of analysis or, though so suitable, the sample proved insufficient.

(3B)   A non-intimate sample may be taken from a person without the appropriate consent if he has been convicted of a recordable offence.

(3C)   A non-intimate sample may also be taken from a person without the appropriate consent if he is a person to whom section 2 of the Criminal Evidence (Amendment) Act 1997 applies (persons detained following acquittal on grounds of insanity or finding of unfitness to plead).

(4)   An officer may only give an authorisation under subsection (3) above if he has reasonable grounds—

(a)   for suspecting the involvement of the person from whom the sample is to be taken in a recordable offence; and

(b)   for believing that the sample will tend to confirm or disprove his involvement.

[(5)–(9) contain various procedural rules about the taking of non-intimate samples. See also Code D, para. 5 at **12.6**.]

(9A)   Subsection (3B) above shall not apply to any person convicted before 10th April 1995 unless he is a person to whom section 1 of the Criminal Evidence (Amendment) Act 1997 applies (persons imprisoned or detained by virtue of pre-existing conviction for sexual offence etc.).

Notes: Section 63 (especially s. 63(3A) and (3B)) brings the position with regard to obtaining *non-intimate* samples into line with the position relating to obtaining fingerprints (see above). Thus a *non-intimate* sample can be taken from a person for the first time without the appropriate consent in a variety of circumstances, e.g., whenever the person has been convicted of a recordable offence (s. 63(3B)). Even where a non-intimate sample cannot be taken without the appropriate consent, the refusal to consent may at common law form the basis for an inference of guilt (see **11.2.5**). Section 63(3C) and s. 63(9A) were inserted by the Criminal Evidence (Amendment) Act 1997.

Section 64 of the 1984 Act makes provision for the destruction of samples where suspects are eventually cleared of any offence — see Code D, paras 5.8 and 5.8A at **12.6**.

Regarding the effect of breaches of these statutory rules, see *R v Nathaniel* [1995] 2 Cr App R 565, in which it was held that the trial judge should have applied s. 78 to exclude evidence obtained from a blood sample which should have been destroyed. Lord Taylor CJ said:

> To allow that blood sample to be used in evidence . . . when the sample had been retained in breach of statutory duty and in breach of undertakings to the accused must . . . have had an adverse effect on the fairness of the proceedings.

Subsequently, the House of Lords has drawn a distinction between, on the one hand, trying to use a DNA profile in evidence when it should have been destroyed (as was the case in *Nathaniel*) and using such a profile as part of a criminal investigation. The position is governed by different parts of s. 64 — s. 64(3B)(a) and (b), respectively. In *R v B (Attorney-General's Reference (No. 3 of 1999))* [2001] 1 Cr App R 475, the House of Lords considered the use of a DNA profile from a man acquitted of burglary. It had been placed on the national DNA database but, contrary to s. 64(3B)(b), was not removed following his acquittal. Subsequently, the profile provided a match with DNA extracted from a rape victim. The man was arrested and one of his hairs was removed legally, without his consent. The hair provided another DNA match. At the trial, the prosecution did not rely upon the first DNA profile. The man was convicted and appealed. The House of Lords held that the 1984 Act did not stipulate a consequence for a breach of s. 64(3B)(b) and that subsection did not legislate that evidence obtained as a result of the prohibited investigation was inadmissible. Section 64(3B)(b) had to be read in conjunction with s. 78 of the 1984 Act. Section 64(3B)(b) prohibited a sample liable to destruction from being used for the purposes of any investigation of other offences, but it would not have prohibited evidence resulting from such an investigation from being used in subsequent criminal proceedings. The House also considered Article 8 of the European Convention on Human Rights and concluded that its interpretation of s. 64(3B) did not contravene the Convention.

12.5.2.8 Adducing evidence of DNA profiles

In *R* v *Doheny; R* v *Adams* [1997] 1 Cr App R 369, the Court of Appeal laid down the following guidelines as regards the adducing (in court) of DNA evidence:

1. The scientist should adduce the evidence of the DNA comparisons between the crime stain and the defendant's sample together with his calculations of the random occurrence ratio.

2. Whenever DNA evidence is to be adduced the Crown should serve on the defence details as to how the calculations have been carried out which are sufficient to enable the defence to scrutinise the basis of the calculations.

3. The Forensic Science Service should make available to a defence expert, if requested, the databases upon which the calculations have been based.

4. Any issue of expert evidence should be identified and, if possible, resolved before trial. This area should be explored by the court in the pre-trial review.

5. In giving evidence the expert will explain to the jury the nature of the matching DNA characteristics between the DNA in the crime stain and the DNA in the defendant's blood sample.

6. The expert will, on the basis of empirical statistical data, give the jury the random occurence ratio — the frequency with which the matching DNA characteristics are likely to be found in the population at large.

7. Provided that the expert has the necessary data, it may then be appropriate for him to indicate how many people with the matching characteristics are likely to be found in the United Kingdom or a more limited relevant sub-group, for instance the caucasian, sexually active males in the Manchester area.

8. It is then for the jury to decide, having regard to all the relevant evidence, whether they are sure that it was the defendant who left the crime stain, or whether it is possible that it was left by someone else with the same matching DNA characteristics.

9. The expert should not be asked his opinion on the likelihood that it was the defendant who left the crime stain, nor when giving evidence should he use terminology which may lead the jury to believe that he is expressing such an opinion.

10. It is appropriate for an expert to expound a statistical approach to evaluating the likelihood that the defendant left the crime stain, since unnecessary theory and complexity deflect the jury from their proper task.

11. In the summing-up careful directions are required in respect of any issues of expert evidence and guidance should be given to avoid confusion caused by areas of expert evidence where no real issue exists.

12. The judge should explain to the jury the relevance of the random occurrence ratio in arriving at their verdict and draw attention to the extraneous evidence which provides the context which gives that ratio its significance, and to that which conflicts with the conclusion that the defendant was responsible for the crime stain.

13. In relation to the random occurrence ratio, a direction along the following lines may be appropriate, tailored to the facts of the particular case: 'Members of the jury, if you accept the scientific evidence called by the Crown this indicates that there are probably only four or five white males in the United Kingdom from whom that semen stain could have come. The defendant is one of them. If that is the position, the decision you have to reach, on all the evidence, is whether you are sure that it was the defendant who left that stain or whether it is possible that it was one of that other small group of men who share the same DNA characteristics.'

12.6 PACE Code D: Code of Practice for the Identification of Persons by Police Officers

Commencement — Transitional Arrangements
This code has effect in relation to any identification
procedure carried out after midnight on 9 April 1995.
Paragraph 2 and Annexes A to E have been inserted by the Police
and Criminal Evidence Act (Codes of Practice) (Temporary Modifications
to Code D) Order 2002. The Order came into force 1 April 2002
and will be in force for two years from that date.

1. General

1.1 This code of practice must be readily available at all police stations for consultation by police officers, detained persons and members of the public.

1.2 The notes for guidance included are not provisions of this code, but are guidance to police officers and others about its application and interpretation. Provisions in the Annexes to the code are provisions of this code.

1.3 If an officer has any suspicion, or is told in good faith, that a person of any age may be suffering from mental disorder or mentally handicapped, or mentally incapable of understanding the significance of questions put to him or his replies, then that person shall be treated as a mentally disordered or mentally handicapped person for the purposes of this code.

1.4 If anyone appears to be under the age of 17 then he shall be treated as a juvenile for the purposes of this code in the absence of clear evidence to show that he is older.

1.5 If a person appears to be blind or seriously visually handicapped, deaf, unable to read, unable to speak or has difficulty orally because of a speech impediment, he should be treated as such for the purposes of this code in the absence of clear evidence to the contrary.

1.6 In this code the term 'appropriate adult' has the same meaning as in paragraph 1.7 of Code C, and the term 'solicitor' has the same meaning as in paragraph 6.12 of Code C.

1.7 Any reference to a custody officer in this code includes an officer who is performing the functions of a custody officer. Any reference to a solicitor in this code includes a clerk or legal executive except in Annex D, paragraph 7.

1.8 Where a record is made under this code of any action requiring the authority of an officer of a specified rank, his name (except in the case of enquiries linked to the investigation of terrorism, in which case the officer's warrant or other identification number should be given) and rank must be included in the record.

1.9 All records must be timed and signed by the maker. Warrant or other identification numbers should be used rather than names in the case of detention under the Prevention of Terrorism (Temporary Provision) Act 1989.

1.10 In the case of a detained person records are to be made in his custody record unless otherwise specified.

1.11 In the case of any procedure requiring a suspect's consent, the consent of a person who is mentally disordered or mentally handicapped is only valid if given in the presence of the appropriate adult; and in the case of a juvenile the consent of his parent or guardian is required as well as his own (unless he is under 14, in which case the consent of his parent or guardian is sufficient in its own right). [See Note 1E]

1.12   In the case of a person who is blind or seriously visually handicapped or unable to read, the custody officer should ensure that his solicitor, relative, the appropriate adult or some other person likely to take an interest in him (and not involved in the investigation) is available to help in checking any documentation. Where this code requires written consent or signification, then the person who is assisting may be asked to sign instead if the detained person so wishes. [See Note 1F]

1.13   In the case of any procedure requiring information to be given to or sought from a suspect, it must be given or sought in the presence of the appropriate adult if the suspect is mentally disordered, mentally handicapped or a juvenile. If the appropriate adult is not present when the information is first given or sought, the procedure must be repeated in his presence when he arrives. If the suspect appears to be deaf or there is doubt about his hearing or speaking ability or ability to understand English, and the officer cannot establish effective communication, the information must be given or sought through an interpreter.

1.14   Any procedure in this code involving the participation of a person (whether as a suspect or a witness) who is mentally disordered, mentally handicapped or a juvenile must take place in the presence of the appropriate adult; but the adult must not be allowed to prompt any identification of a suspect by a witness.

1.15   Subject to paragraph 1.16 below, nothing in this code affects any procedure under:
   (i)   Sections 4 to 11 of the Road Traffic Act 1988 or sections 15 and 16 of the Road Traffic Offenders Act 1988;
   (ii)   paragraph 18 of Schedule 2 to the Immigration Act 1971; or
   (iii)   the Prevention of Terrorism (Temporary Provisions) Act 1989; section 15(9), paragraph 8(5) of Schedule 2, and paragraph 7(5) of Schedule 5.

1.16   Notwithstanding paragraph 1.15, the provisions of section 3 below on the taking of fingerprints, and of section 5 below on the taking of body samples, do apply to people detained under section 14 of, or paragraph 6 of Schedule 5 to, the Prevention of Terrorism (Temporary Provisions) Act 1989. (In the case of fingerprints, section 61 of PACE is modified by section 15(10) of, and paragraph 7(6) of Schedule 5 to, the 1989 Act.) In the case of samples, sections 62 and 63 of PACE are modified by section 15(11) of and paragraph 7(6A) of Schedule 5 to the 1989 Act. The effect of both of these modifications is to allow fingerprints and samples to be taken in terrorist cases to help determine whether a person is or has been involved in terrorism, as well as where there are reasonable grounds for suspecting that person's involvement in a particular offence. There is, however, no statutory requirement (and, therefore, no requirement under paragraph 3.4 below) to destroy fingerprints or body samples taken in terrorist cases, no requirement to tell the people from whom these were taken that they will be destroyed, and no statutory requirement to offer such people an opportunity to witness the destruction of their fingerprints.

1.17   In this code, references to photographs, negatives and copies include reference to images stored or reproduced through any medium.

Notes for Guidance

1A   A person, including a parent or guardian, should not be the appropriate adult if he is suspected of involvement in the offence, is the victim, is a witness, is involved in the investigation or has received admissions prior to attending to act as the appropriate adult. If the parent of a juvenile is estranged from the juvenile, he should not be asked to act as the appropriate adult if the juvenile expressly and specifically objects to his presence.

1B   If a juvenile admits an offence to or in the presence of a social worker other than during the time that the social worker is acting as the appropriate adult for that juvenile, another social worker should be the appropriate adult in the interest of fariness.

1C   In the case of people who are mentally disordered or mentally handicapped, it may in certain circumstances be more satisfactory for all concerned if the appropriate adult is someone who has experience or training in their care rather than a relative lacking such qualifications. But if the person himself prefers a relative to a better-qualified stranger, or objects to a particular person as the appropriate adult, his wishes should if practicable be respected.

1D   A solicitor or lay visitor who is present at the station in that capacity may not act as the appropriate adult.

1E   For the purposes of paragraph 1.11 above, the consent required to be given by a parent or guardian may be given, in the case of a juvenile in the care of a local authority or voluntary organisation, by that authority or organisation.

1F   Persons who are blind, seriously visually handicapped or unable to read may be unwilling to sign police documents. The alternative of their representative signing on their behalf seeks to protect the interests of both police and suspects.

1G   Further guidance about fingerprints and body samples is given in Home Office circular 27/1989.

1H   The generic term 'mental disorder' is used throughout this code. 'Mental disorder' is defined in section 1(2) of the Mental Health Act 1983 as 'mental illness, arrested or incomplete development of mind, psychopathic disorder and any other disorder or disability of mind'. It should be noted that 'mental disorder' is different from 'mental handicap' although the two are dealt with similarly throughout this code. Where the custody officer has any doubt as to the mental state or capacity of a person detained an appropriate adult should be called.

2.   Identification by witnesses

Introduction
2.1   Identification by witnesses arises, for example, if the offender is seen committing the crime and a witness is given an opportunity to identify the suspect in a video identification, identification parade, or similar procedure. The procedures are designed to test the ability of the witness to identify the person they saw on a previous occasion and to provide safeguards against mistaken identification. Persons other than police officers, including 'approved persons' (see paragraph 2.13), who are charged with the duty of investigating offences or charging offenders must, in the discharge of that duty, have regard to any relevant provision of this and any other Code.

Identification by witnesses
2.2   A record shall be made of the description of the suspect as first given by a potential witness. This must be done before the witness takes part in the forms of identification under paragraphs 2.3 to 2.11 of this Code. The record may be made or kept in any form provided that details of the description as first given by the witness can accurately be produced from it in a written form which can be provided to the suspect or the suspect's solicitor in accordance with this Code. A copy shall be provided to the suspect or the suspect's solicitor before any procedures under paragraphs 2.3 to 2.11 of this Code are carried out [see *Note 2E*].

(a)   Cases where the suspect is known and available

2.3   In a case which involves disputed identification evidence, and where the identity of the suspect is known to the police and he is available, (see paragraph 2.12) the following identification procedures may be used:

Video identification
2.4   A video identification is where the witness is shown images of a known suspect together with images of other people who resemble the suspect.

2.5   Video identifications must be carried out in accordance with Annex A.

Identification parade
2.6   An identification parade is where the witness sees the suspect in a line of other people who resemble the suspect.

2.7   Identification parades must be carried out in accordance with Annex B.

Group identification
2.8   A group identification is where the witness sees the suspect in an informal group of people.

2.9   Group identifications must be carried out in accordance with Annex C.

Confrontation
2.10   A confrontation is where the suspect is directly confronted by the witness. This procedure may be used when it is not possible to arrange a video identification, identification parade, or group identification.

2.11   Confrontations must be carried out in accordance with Annex D.

2.12   References in this section to a suspect being 'known' means there is sufficient information known to the police to justify the arrest of a particular person for suspected involvement in the offence. A suspect being 'available' means that they are immediately available to take part in the procedure or will become available within a reasonably short time. A known suspect who fails or refuses to take part in any identification procedure which it is practicable to arrange, or takes steps to prevent themselves from being seen by a witness in such a procedure, may be treated as not being available for the purposes of this section.

Arranging identification procedures
2.13   Except as provided for in paragraph 2.23 below, the arrangements for, and conduct of these types of identification procedures shall be the responsibility of an officer not below the rank

of inspector who is not involved with the investigation ('the identification officer') other than for the purposes of these procedures. Unless otherwise specified, the identification officer may allow an 'approved person' to make arrangements for, and to conduct any of the identification procedures in paragraphs 2.3 to 2.11. Approved persons are engaged to carry out specified duties or procedures as allowed under this Code and:

   (i) appointed by the Chief Officer of any police force and under the control and direction of that Chief Officer; and

   (ii) employed by the police authority maintaining that force.

No officer or any other person involved with the investigation of the case against the suspect beyond the extent required by these procedures may take any part in these procedures or act as the identification officer. This does not prevent the identification officer from consulting the officer in charge of the investigation in order to determine which procedure to use.

Circumstances in which an identification procedure must be held

2.14 Whenever a suspect disputes an identification made or purported to have been made by a witness, an identification procedure shall be held if practicable unless paragraph 2.15 applies. Such a procedure may also be held if the officer in charge of the investigation considers that it would be useful. When an identification procedure is required to be held, in the interests of fairness to suspects and witnesses, it must be held as soon as practicable.

2.15 An identification procedure need not be held if, in all the circumstances, it would serve no useful purpose in proving or disproving whether the suspect was involved in committing the offence. Examples would be where it is not in dispute that the suspect is already well known to the witness who saw the suspect commit the crime or where there is no reasonable possibility that a witness would be able to make an identification.

Selecting an identification procedure

2.16 If, as a consequence of paragraph 2.14, it is proposed to hold an identification procedure, the suspect shall initially be offered either a video identification or an identification parade unless paragraph 2.18 applies. The officer in charge of the case may choose freely between these two options to decide which is to be offered. The identification officer and the officer in charge of the investigation shall consult each other to determine which of these two options is the most suitable and practicable in the particular case. An identification parade may not be practicable because of factors relating to the witnesses such as their number, state of health, availability and travelling requirements. A video identification would normally be more suitable if, in a particular case, it could be arranged and completed sooner than an identification parade (see paragraph 2.14).

2.17 A suspect who refuses the identification procedure which is first offered shall be asked to state their reason for refusing and may obtain advice from their solicitor and appropriate adult if present. The suspect, solicitor and appropriate adult shall be allowed to make representations as to why another procedure should be used. A record shall be made of the reasons for the suspect's refusal and of any representations made. After considering any reasons given and representations made the identification officer shall, if appropriate, arrange for the suspect to be offered an alternative which the officer considers is suitable and practicable in that particular case. If the officer decides that it is not suitable and practicable to offer an alternative identification procedure, the reasons for that decision shall be recorded.

2.18 A group identification may initially be offered where the officer in charge of the investigation considers that in the particular circumstances it is more satisfactory than a video identification or an identification parade and the identification officer considers it is practicable to arrange.

2.19 If the suspect refuses or fails to take part in a video identification, an identification parade or a group identification, or refuses or fails to take part in the only practicable options from that list, the identification officer has discretion to make arrangements for a covert video identification or a covert group identification. In making arrangements for a covert video identification or other arrangements to test the ability of the witness to identify the person they saw on a previous occasion, the identification officer has discretion to use any suitable images of the suspect, whether moving or still, which are available or can be obtained.

2.20 If none of the options referred to above are practicable, the identification officer may arrange for the suspect to be confronted by the witness. A confrontation does not require the suspect's consent.

Notice to suspect

2.21 Unless paragraph 2.24 applies, before a video identification, an identification parade or group identification is arranged the following shall be explained to the suspect:

   (i) the purposes of the video identification or identification parade or group identification;

    (ii)   the suspect's entitlement to free legal advice;

    (iii) the procedures for holding it (including the suspect's right to have a solicitor or friend present);

    (iv) that the suspect does not have to take part in a video identification, identification parade or group identification;

    (v)   whether, for the purposes of the video identification procedure, images of the suspect have previously been obtained (see paragraph 2.24) and if so, that they may co-operate in providing further suitable images which shall be used in place of those previously taken;

    (vi) where appropriate the special arrangements for juveniles;

    (vii) where appropriate the special arrangements for mentally disordered or otherwise mentally vulnerable people;

    (viii) that if the suspect does not consent to, and take part in, a video identification, identification parade or group identification, their refusal may be given in evidence in any subsequent trial and police may proceed covertly without their consent or make other arrangements to test whether a witness can identify them (see paragraph 2.19);

    (ix) that if the suspect should significantly alter their appearance between being offered an identification procedure and any attempt to hold an identification procedure, this may be given in evidence if the case comes to trial, and the identification officer may then consider other forms of identification [see paragraph 2.19 and *Note 2C*];

    (x)   that a video or photograph may be taken of the suspect when they attend for any identification procedure;

    (xi) whether the witness has been shown photographs, a computerised or artist's composite likeness or similar likeness or picture by the police during the investigation before the identity of the suspect became known [see *Note 2B*];

    (xii) that if the suspect changes their appearance before a identification parade it may not be practicable to arrange one on the day in question or subsequently and, because of the change of appearance, the identification officer may then consider alternative methods of identification [see *Note 2C*];

    (xiii) that the suspect or their solicitor will be provided with details of the description of the suspect as first given by any witnesses who are to attend the video identification, identification parade, group identification or confrontation.

2.22   This information must also be contained in a written notice which must be handed to the suspect. The suspect must be given a reasonable opportunity to read the notice, after which they shall be asked to sign a second copy of the notice to indicate whether or not they are willing to co-operate with the making of a video or take part in the identification parade or group identification. The signed copy shall be retained by the identification officer.

2.23   The duties of the identification officer under paragraphs 2.21 and 2.22 may be performed by the custody officer or any other officer not involved in the investigation of the case against the suspect if:

    (a) it is proposed to hold an identification procedure at a later date (for example if the suspect is to be bailed to attend an identification parade); and

    (b) an inspector is not available to act as the identification officer (see paragraph 2.13) before the suspect leaves the station where they are detained.

The officer concerned shall inform the identification officer of the action taken and give them the signed copy of the notice [see *Note 2C*].

2.24   If the identification officer and the officer in charge of the investigation have reasonable grounds to suspect that if the suspect was given the information and notice in accordance with paragraphs 2.21 and 2.22, they would thereafter take steps to avoid being seen by a witness in any identification procedure which it would otherwise be practicable to arrange, the identification officer has discretion to arrange for images of the suspect to be obtained for use in a video identification procedure before the information and notice in paragraphs 2.21 and 2.22 is given. If images of the suspect are obtained in these circumstances, the suspect may, for the purposes of a video identification procedure, co-operate in providing suitable images which shall be used in place of those previously taken (see paragraph 2.21(v)).

(b)   Cases where the suspect is known but is not available

2.25   Where a known suspect is not available or has ceased to be available for any reason (see paragraph 2.12), the identification officer has discretion to make arrangements for a video identification to be conducted. This must be done in accordance with the provisions applicable to covert video identification (see paragraph 2.19 and Annex A). However, any requirements of this section and Annex A for information in any form to be given to or sought from a suspect or for the suspect to be given an opportunity to view images before they are shown to a witness shall not apply if, at the time the requirement arises, the suspect is not available. For each such requirement, the record of the video identification shall indicate the reason why the suspect was not available [see paragraph 2.31 and *Note 2D*].

(c)   Cases where the identity of the suspect is not known

2.26   A witness may be taken to a particular neighbourhood or place to see whether they can identify the person whom they saw on the relevant occasion. Although the number, age, sex, race and general description and style of clothing of other people present at the location and the way in which any identification is made cannot be controlled, the principles applicable to the formal procedures under paragraphs 2.3 to 2.11 shall be followed so far as is practicable in the circumstances. For example:

(a)   Before asking the witness to make an identification, where practicable, a record shall be made of any description given by the witness of the suspect.

(b)   Care should be taken not to direct the witness's attention to any individual unless, having regard to all the circumstances, this cannot be avoided. However, this does not prevent a witness being asked to look carefully at the people who are around at the time or to look towards a group or in a particular direction if this appears to be necessary to ensure that the witness does not overlook a possible suspect simply because the witness is looking in the opposite direction and also to enable the witness to make comparisons between any suspect and others who are in the area at the time [see *Note 2F*].

(c)   Where there is more than one witness, every effort should be made to keep them separate and where practicable, witnesses should be taken to see whether they can identify a person independently.

(d)   Once there is sufficient information to justify the arrest of a particular individual for suspected involvement in the offence, for example after a witness makes a positive identification, formal identification procedures must be adopted for any other witnesses in relation to that individual.

(e)   The officer or approved person accompanying the witness shall make a record in their pocket book of the action taken as soon as practicable and in as much detail as possible. The record should include: the date, time and place of the relevant occasion the witness claims to have previously seen the suspect; where any identification was made; how it was made and the conditions at the time (for example, the distance the witness was from the suspect, the weather and light); if the witness's attention was drawn to the suspect; the reason for this; and anything said by the witness or the suspect about the identification or the conduct of the procedure.

2.27   A witness must not be shown photographs, computerised or artist's composite likenesses or similar likenesses or pictures if the identity of the suspect is known to the police and the suspect is available to take part in a video identification, an identification parade or a group identification. If the identity of the suspect is not known, the showing of such pictures to a witness must be done in accordance with Annex E (see paragraphs 2.12, 2.21(xi) and 2.25).

(d)   Documentation

2.28   A record shall be made of the video identification, identification parade, group identification or confrontation on forms provided for the purpose.

2.29   If the identification officer considers that it is not practicable to hold a video identification or identification parade when either are requested by the suspect, the reasons shall be recorded and explained to the suspect.

2.30   A record shall be made of a person's failure or refusal to co-operate in a video identification, identification parade or group identification and, if applicable, of the grounds for obtaining images in accordance with paragraph 2.24.

(e)   Showing films and photographs of incidents and information released to the media

2.31   Nothing in this Code inhibits the showing of videos or photographs to the public at large through the national or local media, or to police officers for the purposes of recognition and tracing suspects. However, when such material is shown to potential witnesses (including police officers) [see *Note 2A*] for the purpose of obtaining identification evidence, it shall be shown on an individual basis so as to avoid any possibility of collusion, and the showing shall, as far as possible, follow the principles for video identification if the suspect is known (see paragraphs 2.12, 2.23 and Annex A) or identification by photographs if the suspect is not known (see paragraphs 2.12, 2.27 and Annex E) as appropriate.

2.32   Where a broadcast or publication is made, as in paragraph 2.31, a copy of the relevant material released by the police to the media for the purposes of recognising or tracing the suspect shall be kept and the suspect or their solicitor shall be allowed to view such material before any procedures under paragraphs 2.3 to 2.11 of this Code are carried out (see paragraph 2.12 and *Note 2E*) provided it is practicable to do so and would not unreasonably delay the investigation. Each witness who is involved in the procedure shall be asked after they have taken part whether they have seen any broadcast or published films or photographs relating to the offence or seen any description of any person suspected of the offence and their replies shall be recorded. This paragraph does not affect any separate requirement under the Criminal Procedure and Investigations Act 1996 to retain material in connection with criminal investigations.

(f) Destruction and retention of photographs and images taken or used in identification procedures

2.33   Section 64A of the Police and Criminal Evidence Act 1984 provides powers to take photographs and images of suspects detained at police stations and allows the photographs and images so taken to be used or disclosed only for purposes related to the prevention or detection of crime, the investigation of offences or the conduct of prosecutions by or on behalf of police or other law enforcement and prosecuting authorities inside and outside the United Kingdom. After being so used or disclosed, they may be retained but must not be used or disclosed except for these purposes. Section 64A, therefore, allows photographs and images of suspects detained at police stations to be taken and used for the purposes of the identification procedures in paragraphs 2.3 to 2.11.

2.34   Subject to paragraph 2.36 the photographs and images (and the negatives and all copies thereof) of suspects who have not been detained which are taken for the purposes of, or in connection with, the identification procedures in paragraphs 2.3 to 2.11 must be destroyed unless the suspect:

(a)   is charged with, or informed they may be prosecuted for, a recordable offence;

(b)   is prosecuted for a recordable offence;

(c)   is cautioned for a recordable offence or given a warning or reprimand in accordance with the Crime and Disorder Act 1998 for a recordable offence; or

(d)   gives informed consent in writing for the photograph or image to be retained for purposes described in paragraph 2.33.

2.35   When paragraph 2.34 requires the destruction of any photograph or image the person must be given an opportunity to witness the destruction or to have a certificate confirming the destruction provided that they so request within five days of being informed that the destruction is required.

2.36   Nothing in paragraph 2.34 affects any separate requirement under the Criminal Procedure and Investigations Act 1996 to retain material in connection with criminal investigations.

Notes for Guidance

2A   Except for the provisions of Annex E paragraph 1, a police officer who is a witness for the purposes of this part of the Code is subject to the same principles and procedures as a civilian witness.

2B   Where a witness attending an identification parade has previously been shown photographs, computerised or artist's composite likenesses, or similar likenesses or pictures, it is the responsibility of the officer in charge of the investigation to make the identification officer aware that this is the case.

2C   The purpose of paragraph 2.23 is to avoid or reduce delay in arranging identification procedures by enabling the required information and warnings (see sub-paragraphs 2.21(ix) and 2.21(xii)) to be given at the earliest opportunity.

2D   Paragraph 2.25 would apply where a known suspect deliberately makes him or herself 'unavailable' in order to delay or frustrate arrangements being made for obtaining identification evidence. It enables any suitable images of the suspect (moving or still) which are available or can be obtained to be used in a video identification.

2E   Where it is proposed to show photographs to a witness in accordance with Annex E it is the responsibility of the officer in charge of the investigation to confirm to the officer responsible for supervising and directing the showing that the first description of the suspect given by that witness has been recorded. If this description has not been recorded, the procedure under Annex E must be postponed (see Annex F paragraph 2).

2F   The admissibility and value of identification evidence obtained when carrying out the procedure under paragraph 2.26 may be compromised if:

(a)   before a person is identified, the witness's attention is specifically drawn to that person;

or

(b)   the identity of the suspect has become known before the procedure takes place.

3.   Identification by fingerprints

(a)   Action

3.1   A person's fingerprints may be taken only with his consent or if paragraph 3.2 applies. If he is at a police station consent must be in writing. In either case the person must be informed of the reason before they are taken and that they will be destroyed as soon as practicable if paragraph 3.4 applies. He must be told that he may witness their destruction if he asks to do so within five days of being cleared or informed that he will not be prosecuted.

3.2 Powers to take fingerprints without consent from any person over the age of ten years are provided by sections 27 and 61 of the Police and Criminal Evidence Act 1984. These provide that fingerprints may be taken without consent:

(a) from a person detained at a police station if an officer of at least the rank of superintendent has reasonable grounds for suspecting that the fingerprints will tend to confirm or disprove his involvment in a criminal offence and the officer authorises the fingerprints to be taken;

(b) from a person detained at a police station who has been charged with a recordable offence or informed that he will be reported for such an offence and he has not previously had his fingerprints taken in relation to that offence;

(c) from a person convicted of a recordable offence. Section 27 of the Police and Criminal Evidence Act 1984 provides power to require such a person to attend a police station for the purposes of having his fingerprints taken if he has not been in police detention for the offence nor had his fingerprints taken in the course of the investigation of the offence or since conviction. Reasonable force may be used if necessary to take a person's fingerprints without his consent.

3.2A A person whose fingerprints are to be taken with or without consent shall be informed beforehand that his prints may be subject of a speculative search against other fingerprints. [See Note 3B]

3.3 [Not Used]

3.4 The fingerprints of a person and all copies of them taken in that case must be destroyed as soon as practicable if:
(a) he is prosecuted for the offence concerned and cleared; or
(b) he is not prosecuted (unless he admits the offence and is cautioned for it).
An opportunity of witnessing the destruction must be given to him if he wishes and if, in accordance with paragraph 3.1, he applies within five days of being cleared or informed that he will not be prosecuted.

3.5 When fingerprints are destroyed, access to relevant computer data shall be made imposs- ible as soon as it is practicable to do so.

3.6 References to fingerprints include palm prints.

(b) Documentation

3.7 A record must be made as soon as possible of the reason for taking a person's fingerprints without consent and of their destruction. If force is used a record shall be made of the circumstances and those present.

3.8 A record shall be made when a person has been informed under the terms of paragraph 3.2A that his fingerprints may be subject of a speculative search.

Notes for Guidance

3A References to recordable offences in this code relate to those offences for which convictions may be recorded in national police records. (See section 27(4) of the Police and Criminal Evidence Act 1984.) The recordable offences to which this code applies at the time when the code was prepared, are any offences which carry a sentence of imprisonment on conviction (irrespective of the period, or the age of the offender or actual sentence passed) and non-imprisonable offences under section 1 of the Street Offences Act 1959 (loitering or soliciting for purposes of prostitution), section 43 of the Telecommunications Act 1984 (improper use of public telecommunications system), section 25 of the Road Traffic Act 1988 (tampering with motor vehicles), section 1 of the Malicious Communications Act 1988 (sending letters etc. with intent to cause distress or anxiety) and section 139(1) of the Criminal Justice Act 1988 (having article with a blade or point in a public place).

3B A speculative search means that a check may be made against other fingerprints contained in records held by or on behalf of the police or held in connection with or as a result of an investigation of an offence.

4. Photographs

(a) Action

4.1 The photograph of a person who has been arrested may be taken at a police station only with his written consent or if paragraph 4.2 applies. In either case he must be informed of the reason for taking it and that the photograph will be destroyed if paragraph 4.4 applies. He must be told that if he should significantly alter his appearance between the taking of the photograph and any attempt to hold an identification procedure this may be given in evidence if the case comes to trial. He must be told that he may witness the destruction of the photograph or be provided with a certificate confirming its destruction if he applies within five days of being cleared or informed that he will not be prosecuted.

4.2　The photograph of a person who has been arrested may be taken without consent if:

(i)　he is arrested at the same time as other persons, or at a time when it is likely that other persons will be arrested, and a photograph is necessary to establish who was arrested, at what time and at what place;

(ii)　he has been charged with, or reported for a recordable offence and has not yet been released or brought before a court [see Note 3A]; or

(iii)　he is convicted of such an offence and his photograph is not already on record as a result of (i) or (ii). There is no power of arrest to take a photograph in pursuance of this provision which applies only where the person is in custody as a result of the exercise of another power (e.g., arrest for fingerprinting under section 27 of the Police and Criminal Evidence Act 1984).

(iv)　an officer of at least the rank of superintendent authorises it, having reasonable grounds for suspecting the involvement of the person in a criminal offence and where there is identification evidence in relation to that offence.

4.3　Force may not be used to take a photograph.

4.4　Where a person's photograph has been taken in accordance with this section, the photograph, negatives and all copies taken in that particular case must be destroyed if:

(a)　he is prosecuted for the offence and cleared unless he has a previous conviction for a recordable offence; or

(b)　he has been charged but not prosecuted (unless he admits the offence and is cautioned for it or he has a previous conviction for a recordable offence).

An opportunity of witnessing the destruction or a certificate confirming the destruction must be given to him if he so requests, provided that, in accordance with paragraph 4.1, he applies within five days of being cleared or informed that he will not be prosecuted. [See Note 4B]

(b)　Documentation

4.5　A record must be made as soon as possible of the reason for taking a person's photograph under this section without consent and of the destruction of any photographs.

Notes for Guidance

4A　The admissibility and value of identification evidence may be compromised if a potential witness in an identification procedure views any photographs of the suspect otherwise than in accordance with the provisions of this code.

4B　This paragraph is not intended to require the destruction of copies of a police gazette in cases where, for example, a remand prisoner has escaped from custody, or a person in custody is suspected of having committed offences in other force areas, and a photograph of the person concerned is circulated in a police gazette for information.

5.　Identification by body samples and impressions

(a)　Action

Intimate samples
5.1　Intimate samples may be taken from a person in police detention only:

(i)　if an officer of the rank of superintendent or above has reasonable grounds to believe that such an impression or sample will tend to confirm or disprove the suspect's involvement in a recordable offence and gives authorisation for a sample to be taken; and

(ii)　with the suspect's written consent.

5.1A　Where two or more non-intimate samples have been taken from a person in the course of an investigation of an offence and the samples have proved unsuitable or insufficient for a particular form of analysis and that person is not in police detention, an intimate sample may be taken from him if a police officer of at least the rank of superintendent authorises it to be taken, and the person concerned gives his written consent. [See Note 5B and Note 5E]

5.2　Before a person is asked to provide an intimate sample he must be warned that if he refuses without good cause, his refusal may harm his case if it comes to trial. [See Note 5A] If he is in police detention and not legally represented, he must also be reminded of his entitlement to have free legal advice (see paragraph 6.5 of Code C) and the reminder must be noted in the custody record. If paragraph 5.1A above applies and the person is attending a police station voluntarily, the officer shall explain the entitlement to free legal advice as provided for in accordance with paragraph 3.15 of Code C.

5.3　Except for samples of urine or saliva, intimate samples may be taken only by a registered medical or dental practitioner as appropriate.

Non-intimate samples

5.4   A non-intimate sample may be taken from a detained person only with his written consent or if paragraph 5.5 applies.

5.5   A non-intimate sample may be taken from a person without consent in accordance with the provisions of section 63 of the Police and Criminal Evidence Act 1984, as amended by section 55 of the Criminal Justice and Public Order Act 1994. The principal circumstances provided for are as follows:

(i)   if an officer of the rank of superintendent or above has reasonable grounds to believe that the sample will tend to confirm or disprove the person's involvement in a recordable offence and gives authorisation for a sample to be taken; or

(ii)   where the person has been charged with a recordable offence or informed that he will be reported for such an offence; and he has not had a non-intimate sample taken from him in the course of the investigation or if he has had a sample taken from him, it has proved unsuitable or insufficient for the same form of analysis [See Note 5B]; or

(iii)   if the person has been convicted of a recordable offence after the date on which this code comes into effect. Section 63A of the Police and Criminal Evidence Act 1984, as amended by section 56 of the Criminal Justice and Public Order Act 1994, describes the circumstances in which a constable may require a person convicted of a recordable offence to attend a police station in order that a non-intimate sample may be taken.

5.6   Where paragraph 5.5 applies, reasonable force may be used if necessary to take non-intimate samples.

(b)   Destruction

5.7   [Not Used]

5.8   Except in accordance with paragraph 5.8A below, where a sample or impression has been taken in accordance with this section it must be destroyed as soon as practicable if:
(a)   the suspect is prosecuted for the offence concerned and cleared; or
(b)   he is not prosecuted (unless he admits the offence and is cautioned for it).

5.8A   In accordance with section 64 of the Police and Criminal Evidence Act 1984 as amended by section 57 of the Criminal Justice and Public Order Act 1994 samples need not be destroyed if they were taken for the purpose of an investigation of an offence for which someone has been convicted, and from whom a sample was also taken. [See Note 5F]

(c)   Documentation

5.9   A record must be made as soon as practicable of the reasons for taking a sample or impression and of its destruction. If force is used a record shall be made of the circumstances and those present. If written consent is given to the taking of a sample or impression, the fact must be recorded in writing.

5.10   A record must be made of the giving of a warning required by paragraph 5.2 above. A record shall be made of the fact that a person has been informed under the terms of paragraph 5.11A below that samples may be subject of a speculative search.

(d)   General

5.11   The terms intimate and non-intimate samples are defined in section 65 of the Police and Criminal Evidence Act 1984, as amended by section 58 of the Criminal Justice and Public Order Act 1994, as follows:
(a)   'intimate sample' means a dental impression or a sample of blood, semen or any other tissue fluid, urine, or pubic hair, or a swab taken from a person's body orifice other than the mouth;
(b)   'non-intimate sample' means:
(i)   a sample of hair (other than pubic hair) which includes hair plucked with the root [See Note 5C];
(ii)   a sample taken from a nail or from under a nail;
(iii)   a swab taken from any part of a person's body including the mouth but not any other body orifice;
(iv)   saliva;
(v)   a footprint or similar impression of any part of a person's body other than a part of his hand.

5.11A   A person from whom an intimate or non-intimate sample is to be taken shall be informed beforehand that any sample taken may be the subject of a speculative search. [See Note 5D]

5.11B   The suspect must be informed, before an intimate or non-intimate sample is taken, of the grounds on which the relevant authority has been given, including where appropriate the nature of the suspected offence.

5.12   Where clothing needs to be removed in circumstances likely to cause embarrassment to the person, no person of the opposite sex who is not a medical practitioner or nurse shall be present, (unless in the case of a juvenile, that juvenile specifically requests the presence of a particular adult of the opposite sex who is readily available) nor shall anyone whose presence is unnecessary. However, in the case of a juvenile this is subject to the overriding proviso that such a removal of clothing may take place in the absence of the appropriate adult only if the juvenile signifies in the presence of the appropriate adult that he prefers the search to be done in his absence and the appropriate adult agrees.

Notes for Guidance

5A   In warning a person who is asked to provide an intimate sample in accordance with paragraph 5.2, the following form of words may be used:

You do not have to [provide this sample] [allow this swab or impression to be taken], but I must warn you that if you refuse without good cause, your refusal may harm your case if it comes to trial.

5B   An insufficient sample is one which is not sufficient either in quantity or quality for the purpose of enabling information to be provided for the purpose of a particular form of analysis such as DNA analysis. An unsuitable sample is one which, by its nature, is not suitable for a particular form of analysis.

5C   Where hair samples are taken for the purpose of DNA analysis (rather than for other purposes such as making a visual match) the suspect should be permitted a reasonable choice as to what part of the body he wishes the hairs to be taken from. When hairs are plucked they should be plucked individually unless the suspect prefers otherwise and no more should be plucked than the person taking them reasonably considers necessary for a sufficient sample.

5D   A speculative search means that a check may be made against other samples and information derived from other samples contained in records or held by or on behalf of the police or held in connection with or as a result of an investigation of an offence.

5E   Nothing in paragraph 5.1A prevents intimate samples being taken for elimination purposes with the consent of the person concerned but the provisions of paragraph 1.11, relating to the role of the appropriate adult, should be applied.

5F   The provisions for the retention of samples in 5.8A allow for all samples in a case to be available for any subsequent miscarriage of justice investigation. But such samples — and the information derived from them — may not be used in the investigation of any offence or in evidence against the person who would otherwise be entitled to their destruction.

ANNEX A
VIDEO IDENTIFICATION

(a)   General

1.   The arrangements for obtaining and ensuring the availability of a suitable set of images to be used in a video identification must be the responsibility of an identification officer or investigation officers who have no direct involvement with the relevant case.

2.   The set of images must include the suspect and at least eight other people who so far as possible resemble the suspect in age, height, general appearance and position in life. Only one suspect shall appear in any set unless there are two suspects of roughly similar appearance in which case they may be shown together with at least twelve other people.

3.   The images used to conduct a video identification shall, as far as possible, show the suspect and other people in the same positions or carrying out the same sequence of movements. They shall also show the suspect and other people under identical conditions unless the identification officer reasonably believes:
     (a)   that because of the suspect's failure or refusal to co-operate or other reasons, it is not practicable for the conditions to be identical; and
     (b)   that any difference in the conditions would not direct a witness's attention to any individual image.

4.   The reasons why identical conditions are not practicable shall be recorded on forms provided for the purpose.

5.   Provision must be made for each person shown to be identified by number.

6.   If police officers are shown, any numerals or other identifying badges must be concealed. If a prison inmate is shown, either as a suspect or not, then either all or none of the people shown should be in prison clothing.

7. The suspect or their solicitor, friend, or appropriate adult must be given a reasonable opportunity to see the complete set of images before it is shown to any witness. If the suspect has a reasonable objection to the set of images or any of the participants the suspect shall be asked to state the reasons for the objection. Steps shall, if practicable, be taken to remove the grounds for objection. If this is not practicable the suspect and/or their representative shall be told why their objections cannot be met and the objection, the reason given for it and why it cannot be met shall be recorded on forms provided for the purpose.

8. Before the images are shown in accordance with paragraph 7 the suspect or their solicitor shall be provided with details of the first description of the suspect by any witnesses who are to attend the video identification. Where a broadcast or publication is made, as in paragraph 2.31, the suspect or their solicitor must also be allowed to view any material released to the media by the police for the purpose of recognising or tracing the suspect provided it is practicable to do so and would not unreasonably delay the investigation.

9. The suspect's solicitor, where practicable, shall be given reasonable notification of the time and place that it is intended to conduct the video identification in order that a representative may attend on behalf of the suspect. If a solicitor has not been instructed then this information shall be given to the suspect. The suspect may not be present when the images are shown to the witness(es). In the absence of a person representing the suspect the viewing itself shall be recorded on video. No unauthorised people may be present.

(b)   Conducting the video identification

10. The identification officer is responsible for making the appropriate arrangements to ensure that, before they see the set of images, witnesses are not able to communicate with each other about the case or overhear a witness who has already seen the material. There must be no discussion with the witness about the composition of the set of images and they must not be told whether a previous witness has made any identification.

11. Only one witness may see the set of images at a time. Immediately before the images are shown the witness shall be told that the person they saw on an earlier relevant occasion may or may not appear in the images they are shown and that if they cannot make a positive identification they should say so. The witness shall be advised that at any point they may ask to see a particular part of the set of images or to have a particular image frozen for them to study. Furthermore, it should be pointed out to the witness that there is no limit on how many times they can view the whole set of images or any part of them. However, they should be asked not to make any decision as to whether the person they saw is on the set of images until they have seen the whole set at least twice.

12. Once the witness has seen the whole set of images at least twice and has indicated that they do not want to view the images or any part of them again, the witness shall be asked to say whether the individual they saw in person on an earlier occasion has been shown and, if so, to identify him or her by number of the image. The witness will then be shown that image to confirm the identification (see paragraph 17).

13. Care must be taken not to direct the witness's attention to any one individual image or to give any indication to the suspect's identity. Where a witness has previously made an identification by photographs, or a computerised or artist's composite likeness or similar likeness, the witness must not be reminded of such a photograph or composite likeness once a suspect is available for identification by other means in accordance with this Code. Neither must the witness be reminded of any description of the suspect.

14. After the procedure each witness shall be asked whether they have seen any broadcast or published films or photographs or any descriptions of suspects relating to the offence and their reply shall be recorded.

(c)   Image security and destruction

15. Arrangements shall be made for all relevant material containing sets of images used for specific identification procedures to be kept securely and their movements accounted for. In particular, no-one involved in the investigation against the suspect shall be permitted to view the material prior to it being shown to any witness.

16. Paragraph 2.33 of this Code (Destruction and retention of photographs and images taken or used in identification procedures) shall apply to a set of images obtained in respect of a detained suspect and paragraph 2.34 shall apply in respect of a suspect who has not been detained.

(d)   Documentation

17. A record must be made of all those participating in or seeing the set of images whose names are known to the police.

18.   A record of the conduct of the video identification must be made on forms provided for the purpose. This shall include anything said by the witness about any identifications or the conduct of the procedure and any reasons why it was not practicable to comply with any of the provisions of this Code governing the conduct of video identifications.

ANNEX B
IDENTIFICATION PARADES

(a)   General

1.   A suspect must be given a reasonable opportunity to have a solicitor or friend present, and the suspect shall be asked to indicate on a second copy of the notice whether or not they wish to do so.

2.   An identification parade may take place either in a normal room or in one equipped with a screen permitting witnesses to see members of the identification parade without being seen. The procedures for the composition and conduct of the identification parade are the same in both cases, subject to paragraph 8 below (except that an identification parade involving a screen may take place only when the suspect's solicitor, friend or appropriate adult is present or the identification parade is recorded on video).

3.   Before the identification parade takes place the suspect or their solicitor shall be provided with details of the first description of the suspect by any witnesses who are to attend the identification parade. Where a broadcast or publication is made as in paragraph 2.31, the suspect or their solicitor should also be allowed to view any material released to the media by the police for the purpose of recognising or tracing the suspect, provided it is practicable to do so and would not unreasonably delay the investigation.

(b)   Identification parades involving prison inmates

4.   If a prison inmate is required for identification, and there are no security problems about the person leaving the establishment, they may be asked to participate in an identification parade or video identification.

5.   An identification parade may be held in a Prison Department establishment but shall be conducted as far as practicable under normal identification parade rules. Members of the public shall make up the identification parade unless there are serious security or control objections to their admission to the establishment. In such cases, or if a group or video identification is arranged within the establishment, other inmates may participate. If an inmate is the suspect they shall not be required to wear prison clothing for the identification parade unless the other people taking part are other inmates in similar clothing or are members of the public who are prepared to wear prison clothing for the occasion.

(c)   Conduct of the identification parade

6.   Immediately before the identification parade the suspect must be reminded of the procedures governing its conduct and cautioned in the terms of paragraph 10.4 of Code C.

7.   All unauthorised people must be excluded from the place where the identification parade is held.

8.   Once the identification parade has been formed everything afterwards in respect of it shall take place in the presence and hearing of the suspect and of any interpreter, solicitor, friend or appropriate adult who is present (unless the identification parade involves a screen, in which case everything said to or by any witness at the place where the identification parade is held must be said in the hearing and presence of the suspect's solicitor, friend or appropriate adult or be recorded on video).

9.   The identification parade shall consist of at least eight people (in addition to the suspect) who so far as possible resemble the suspect in age, height, general appearance and position in life. One suspect only shall be included in an identification parade unless there are two suspects of roughly similar appearance, in which case they may be paraded together with at least twelve other people. In no circumstances shall more than two suspects be included in one identification parade and where there are separate identification parades they shall be made up of different people.

10.   Where the suspect has an unusual physical feature, for example, a facial scar or tattoo or distinctive hairstyle or hair colour which cannot be replicated on other members of the identification parade steps may be taken to conceal the location of that feature on the suspect and the other members of the identification parade if the suspect and their solicitor or appropriate adult agree. For example by use of a plaster or a hat, so that all members of the identification parade resemble each other in general appearance.

11.   Where all members of a similar group are possible suspects separate identification parades shall be held for each member of the group unless there are two suspects of similar appearance when they may appear on the same identification parade with at least twelve other members of the group who are not suspects. Where police officers in uniform form an identification parade any numerals or other identifying badges shall be concealed.

12.   When the suspect is brought to the place where the identification parade is to be held they shall be asked whether they have any objection to the arrangements for the identification parade or to any of the other participants in it and to state the reasons for the objection. The suspect may obtain advice from their solicitor or friend, if present, before the identification parade proceeds. If the suspect has a reasonable objection to the arrangements or any of the participants steps shall, where practicable, be taken to remove the grounds for objection. Where it is not practicable to do so, the suspect shall be told why their objections cannot be met and the objection, the reason given for it and why it cannot be met shall be recorded on forms provided for the purpose.

13.   The suspect may select their own position in the line, but may not otherwise interfere with the order of the people forming the line. Where there is more than one witness the suspect must be told, after each witness has left the room, that they can if they wish change position in the line. Each position in the line must be clearly numbered, whether by means of a numeral laid on the floor in front of each identification parade member or by other means.

14.   Appropriate arrangements must be made to ensure that, before witnesses attend the identification parade, they are not able to:
    (i)   communicate with each other about the case or overhear a witness who has already seen the identification parade;
    (ii)   see any member of the identification parade;
    (iii) see or be reminded of any photograph or description of the suspect or be given any other indication to the suspect's identity; or
    (iv)   see the suspect either before or after the identification parade.

15.   The person conducting a witness to an identification parade must not discuss with them the composition of the identification parade and, in particular, must not disclose whether a previous witness has made any identification.

16.   Witnesses shall be brought in one at a time. Immediately before the witness inspects the identification parade the witness shall be told that the person they saw on an earlier relevant occasion specified by the identification officer or approved person (see paragraph 2.13) conducting the procedure may or may not be on the identification parade and that if they cannot make a positive identification they should say so. The witness must also be told that they should not make any decision as to whether the person they saw is on the identification parade until they have looked at each member of the identification parade at least twice.

17.   When the identification officer or approved person (see paragraph 2.13) conducting the procedure is satisfied that the witness has properly looked at each member of the identification parade, they shall ask the witness whether the person they saw on an earlier relevant occasion is on the identification parade and, if so, to indicate the number of the person concerned (see paragraph 28).

18.   If the witness wishes to hear any identification parade member speak, adopt any specified posture or see an identification parade member move, the witness shall first be asked whether they can identify any person(s) on the identification parade on the basis of appearance only. When the request is to hear members of the identification parade speak, the witness shall be reminded that the participants in the identification parade have been chosen on the basis of physical appearance only. Members of the identification parade may then be asked to comply with the witness's request to hear them speak, to see them move or to adopt any specified posture.

19.   If the witness requests that the person they have indicated remove anything used for the purposes of paragraph 10 to conceal the location of an unusual physical feature, that person may be asked to remove it.

20.   If the witness makes an identification after the identification parade has ended the suspect and, if present, their solicitor, interpreter or friend shall be informed. Where this occurs consideration should be given to allowing the witness a second opportunity to identify the suspect.

21.   After the procedure each witness shall be asked whether they have seen any broadcast or published films or photographs or any descriptions of suspects relating to the offence and their reply shall be recorded.

22.   When the last witness has left the suspect shall be asked whether they wish to make any comments on the conduct of the identification parade.

(d)   Documentation

23.   A video recording must normally be taken of the identification parade. Where that is impracticable a colour photograph must be taken. A copy of the video recording or photograph shall be supplied on request to the suspect or their solicitor within a reasonable time.

24.   Paragraph 2.33 or 2.34, as appropriate, (Destruction and retention of photographs and images taken or used in identification procedures) shall apply to any photograph or video taken in accordance with paragraph 23 above.

25.   If the identification officer or approved person (see paragraph 2.13) asks any person to leave an identification parade because they are interfering with its conduct the circumstances shall be recorded.

26.   A record must be made of all those present at an identification parade whose names are known to the police.

27.   If prison inmates make up an identification parade the circumstances must be recorded.

28.   A record of the conduct of any identification parade must be made on forms provided for the purpose. This shall include anything said by the witness or the suspect about any identifications or the conduct of the procedure, and any reasons why it was not practicable to comply with any of the provisions of this Code.

ANNEX C
GROUP IDENTIFICATION

(a)   General

1.   The purpose of the provisions of this Annex is to ensure that, as far as possible, group identifications follow the principles and procedures for identification parades so that the conditions are fair to the suspect in the way they test the witness's ability to make an identification.

2.   Group identifications may take place either with the suspect's consent and co-operation or covertly without their consent.

3.   The location of the group identification is a matter for the identification officer, although the officer may take into account any representations made by the suspect, appropriate adult, their solicitor or friend.

4.   The place where the group identification is held should be one where other people are either passing by or waiting around informally, in groups such that the suspect is able to join them and be capable of being seen by the witness at the same time as others in the group. Examples include people leaving an escalator, pedestrians walking through a shopping centre, passengers on railway and bus stations, waiting in queues or groups or where people are standing or sitting in groups in other public places.

5.   If the group identification is to be held covertly the choice of locations will be limited by the places where the suspect can be found and the number of other people present at that time. In these cases suitable locations might be along regular routes travelled by the suspect, including buses or trains or public places frequented by the suspect.

6.   Although the number, age, sex, race and general description and style of clothing of other people present at the location cannot be controlled by the identification officer, in selecting the location the officer must consider the general appearance and numbers of people likely to be present. In particular, the officer must reasonably expect that over the period the witness observes the group they will be able to see, from time to time, a number of others (in addition to the suspect) whose appearance is broadly similar to that of the suspect.

7.   A group identification need not be held if the identification officer believes that because of the unusual appearance of the suspect none of the locations which it would be practicable to use satisfy the requirements of paragraph 5 necessary to make the identification fair.

8.   Immediately after a group identification procedure has taken place (with or without the suspect's consent) a colour photograph or a video should be taken of the general scene, where this is practicable, so as to give a general impression of the scene and the number of people present. Alternatively, if it is practicable, the group identification may be video recorded.

9.   If it is not practicable to take the photograph or video in accordance with paragraph 8 a photograph or film of the scene should be taken later at a time determined by the identification officer if the officer considers that it is practicable to do so.

10. An identification carried out in accordance with this Code remains a group identification notwithstanding that at the time of being seen by the witness the suspect was on his or her own rather than in a group.

11. Before the group identification takes place the suspect or their solicitor should be provided with details of the first description of the suspect by any witnesses who are to attend the identification. Where a broadcast or publication is made, as in paragraph 2.31, the suspect or their solicitor should also be allowed to view any material released by the police to the media for the purposes of recognising or tracing the suspect provided that it is practicable to do so and would not unreasonably delay the investigation.

12. After the procedure each witness shall be asked whether they have seen any broadcast or published films or photographs or any descriptions of suspects relating to the offence and their reply shall be recorded.

(b) Identification with the consent of the suspect

13. A suspect must be given a reasonable opportunity to have a solicitor or friend present. The suspect shall be asked to indicate on a second copy of the notice whether or not they wish to do so.

14. The witness, the person carrying out the procedure and suspect's solicitor, appropriate adult, friend or any interpreter for the witness may be concealed from the sight of the individuals in the group which they are observing if the person carrying out the procedure considers that this facilitates the conduct of the identification.

15. The person conducting a witness to a group identification must not discuss with the witness the forthcoming group identification and, in particular, must not disclose whether a previous witness has made any identification.

16. Anything said to or by the witness during the procedure regarding the identification should be said in the presence and hearing of those present at the procedure.

17. Appropriate arrangements must be made to ensure that, before witnesses attend the identification parade, they are not able to:
   (i)   communicate with each other about the case or overhear a witness who has already been given an opportunity to see the suspect in the group;
   (ii)   see the suspect; or
   (iii)   see or be reminded of any photographs or description of the suspect or be given any other indication of the suspect's identity.

18. Witnesses shall be brought to the place where they are to observe the group one at a time. Immediately before the witness is asked to look at the group the person conducting the procedure shall tell the witness that the person they saw may or may not be in the group and that if they cannot make a positive identification they should say so. The witness shall then be asked to observe the group in which the suspect is to appear. The way in which the witness should do this will depend on whether the group is moving or stationary.

Moving group
19. When the group in which the suspect is to appear is moving, for example leaving an escalator, the provisions of paragraphs 20 to 24 below should be followed.

20. If two or more suspects consent to a group identification each should be the subject of separate identification procedures. These may however be conducted consecutively on the same occasion.

21. The person conducting the procedure shall tell the witness to observe the group and ask the witness to point out any person they think they saw on the earlier relevant occasion.

22. Once the witness has been informed in accordance with paragraph 21 the suspect should be allowed to take whatever position in the group that they wish.

23. When the witness points out a person in accordance with paragraph 21 the witness shall, if it is practicable, be asked to take a closer look at the person to confirm the identification. If this is not practicable, or the witness is unable to confirm the identification, the witness shall be asked how sure they are that the person they have indicated is the relevant person.

24. The witness should continue to observe the group for the period which the person conducting the procedure reasonably believes is necessary in the circumstances for the witness to be able to make comparisons between the suspect and other individuals of broadly similar appearance to the suspect in accordance with paragraph 5.

Stationary groups
25. When the group in which the suspect is to appear is stationary, for example people waiting in a queue, the provisions of paragraphs 26 to 29 below should be followed.

26.   If two or more suspects consent to a group identification each should be the subject of separate identification procedures unless they are of broadly similar appearance when they may appear in the same group. Where separate group identifications are held the groups must be made up of different persons.

27.   The suspect may take whatever position in the group that they wish. Where there is more than one witness the suspect must be told, out of the sight and hearing of any witness, that they can, if they wish, change their position in the group.

28.   The witness shall be asked to pass along or amongst the group and to look at each person in the group at least twice, taking as much care and time as is possible according to the circumstances, before making an identification. Once the witness has done this they shall be asked whether the person they saw on an earlier relevant occasion is in the group and to indicate any such person by whatever means the person conducting the procedure considers appropriate in the circumstances. If this is not practicable the witness shall be asked to point out any person they think they saw on the earlier relevant occasion.

29.   When the witness makes an indication in accordance with paragraph 28 arrangements shall be made, if it is practicable, for the witness to take a closer look at the person to confirm the identification. If this is not practicable, or the witness is unable to confirm the identification, the witness shall be asked how sure they are that the person they have indicated is the relevant person.

All cases
30.   If the suspect unreasonably delays joining the group, or having joined the group, deliberately conceals themselves from the sight of the witness, this may be treated as a refusal to co-operate in a group identification.

31.   If the witness identifies a person other than the suspect that person should be informed what has happened and asked if they are prepared to give their name and address. There is no obligation upon any member of the public to give these details. There shall be no duty to record any details of any other member of the public present in the group or at the place where the procedure is conducted.

32.   When the group identification has been completed the suspect shall be asked whether they wish to make any comments on the conduct of the procedure.

33.   If the suspect has not been previously informed they shall be told of any identifications made by the witnesses.

(c)   Identification without suspect's consent

34.   Group identifications held covertly without the suspect's consent should, so far as is practicable, follow the rules for conduct of group identification by consent.

35.   A suspect has no right to have a solicitor, appropriate adult or friend present as the identification will, of necessity, take place without the knowledge of the suspect.

36.   Any number of suspects may be identified at the same time.

(d)   Identifications in police stations

37.   Group identifications should only take place in police stations for reasons of safety, security or because it is impracticable to hold them elsewhere.

38.   The group identification may take place either in a room equipped with a screen permitting witnesses to see members of the group without being seen, or anywhere else in the police station that the identification officer considers appropriate.

39.   Any of the additional safeguards applicable to identification parades should be followed if the identification officer considers it is practicable to do so in the circumstances.

(e)   Identifications involving prison inmates

40.   A group identification involving a prison inmate may only be arranged in the prison or at a police station.

41.   Where a group identification takes place involving a prison inmate, whether in a prison or in a police station, the arrangements should follow those in paragraphs 37 to 39 of this Annex. If a group identification takes place within a prison other inmates may participate. If an inmate is the suspect they should not be required to wear prison clothing for the group identification unless the other persons taking part are wearing the same clothing.

(f)   Documentation

42.   Where a photograph or video is taken in accordance with paragraph 8 or 9 above a copy of the photograph or video shall be supplied on request to the suspect or their solicitor within a reasonable time.

43.   Paragraph 2.33 or 2.34 of this Code, as appropriate, (Destruction and retention of photographs and images taken or used in identification procedures) shall apply where the photograph or film taken in accordance with paragraph 8 or 9 above includes the suspect.

44.   A record of the conduct of any group identification must be made on forms provided for the purpose. This shall include anything said by the witness or the suspect about any identifications or the conduct of the procedure and any reasons why it was not practicable to comply with any of the provisions of this Code governing the conduct of group identifications.

ANNEX D
CONFRONTATION BY A WITNESS

1.   Before the confrontation takes place the witness must be told that the person they saw may or may not be the person they are to confront and that if he or she is not that person then the witness should say so.

2.   Before the confrontation takes place the suspect or their solicitor shall be provided with details of the first description of the suspect given by any witness who is to attend the confrontation. Where a broadcast or publication is made, as in paragraph 2.31, the suspect or their solicitor should also be allowed to view any material released by the police to the media for the purposes of recognising or tracing the suspect provided that it is practicable to do so and would not unreasonably delay the investigation.

3.   Force may not be used to make the face of the suspect visible to the witness.

4.   Confrontation must take place in the presence of the suspect's solicitor, interpreter or friend unless this would cause unreasonable delay.

5.   The suspect shall be confronted independently by each witness, who shall be asked 'Is this the person?'. If the witness identifies the person but is unable to confirm the identification they shall be asked how sure they are that the person is the person they saw on the earlier relevant occasion.

6.   The confrontation should normally take place in the police station, either in a normal room or in one equipped with a screen permitting a witness to see the suspect without being seen. In both cases the procedures are the same except that a room equipped with a screen may be used only when the suspect's solicitor, friend or appropriate adult is present or the confrontation is recorded on video.

7.   After the procedure each witness shall be asked whether they have seen any broadcast or published films or photographs or any descriptions of suspects relating to the offence and their reply shall be recorded.

ANNEX E
SHOWING OF PHOTOGRAPHS

(a)   Action

1.   An officer of the rank of sergeant or above shall be responsible for supervising and directing the showing of photographs. The actual showing may be done by a constable or an approved person (see paragraph 2.13).

2.   The supervising officer must confirm that the first description of the suspect given by the witness has been recorded before the witness is shown the photographs. If the supervising officer is unable to confirm that the description has been recorded the officer shall postpone the showing.

3.   Only one witness shall be shown photographs at any one time. Each witness shall be given as much privacy as practicable and shall not be allowed to communicate with any other witness in the case.

4.   The witness shall be shown not less than twelve photographs at a time, which shall, as far as possible, all be of a similar type.

5.   When the witness is shown the photographs they shall be told that the photograph of the person they saw may or may not be amongst them and that if they cannot make a positive identification they should say so. The witness shall also be told that they should not make a decision until they have viewed at least twelve photographs. The witness shall not be prompted or guided in any way but shall be left to make any selection without help.

6.   If a witness makes a positive identification from photographs then, unless the person identified is otherwise eliminated from enquiries or is not available, other witnesses shall not be shown photographs. But both they and the witness who has made the identification shall be

asked to attend a video identification, an identification parade or group identification unless there is no dispute about the identification of the suspect.

7.   If the witness makes a selection but is unable to confirm the identification the person showing the photographs shall ask the witness how sure they are that the photograph they have indicated is the person that they saw on the earlier relevant occasion.

8.   Where the use of a computerised or artist's composite likeness or similar likeness has led to there being a known suspect who can be asked to participate in video identification, appear on an identification parade or participate in a group identification, that likeness shall not be shown to other potential witnesses.

9.   Where a witness attending a video identification, an identification parade or group identification has previously been shown photographs or computerised or artist's composite likeness or similar likeness (and it is the responsibility of the officer in charge of the investigation to make the identification officer aware that this is the case), then the suspect and their solicitor must be informed of this fact before the video identification, identification parade or group identification takes place.

10.   None of the photographs shown shall be destroyed, whether or not an identification is made, since they may be required for production in court. The photographs shall be numbered and a separate photograph taken of the frame or part of the album from which the witness made an identification as an aid to reconstituting it.

(b)   Documentation

11.   Whether or not an identification is made, a record shall be kept of the showing of photographs on forms provided for the purpose. This shall include anything said by the witness about any identification or the conduct of the procedure, any reasons why it was not practicable to comply with any of the provisions of this Code governing the showing of photographs and the name and rank of the supervising officer.

12.   The supervising officer shall inspect and sign the record as soon as practicable.

Questions

OBJECTIVES

This chapter is designed to ensure that, as regards corroboration, you are able to:

(a)   identify when corroboration or a corroboration warning or a general warning to exercise caution is required/desirable;

(b)   demonstrate an understanding of the legal definition of corroboration.

This chapter is designed to ensure that, as regards identification, you are able to:

(a)   identify the circumstances in which a judge might withdraw from the jury a case based on identification evidence;

(b)   identify the circumstances in which a *Turnbull* warning should be given and display knowledge of the usual terms and content of such a warning;

(c)   display a sound understanding of the basis upon which a judge might exclude an item of identification evidence (including an understanding of the key points of the Code of Practice on Identification issued pursuant to PACE 1984, s. 66); and

(d)   raise and/or counter an objection to identification evidence (including knowledge of appropriate procedural matters).

Question 1

Sam was tried for and convicted of a robbery at a supermarket. His co-accused Delilah pleaded guilty and gave prosecution evidence against Sam. In addition to her evidence of his participation in the robbery the following facts emerged at the trial. On the day after the robbery Sam had gone on holiday without telling his family or neighbours and without leaving a forwarding address. Delilah had told the police that the proceeds of the robbery were hidden in a lock-up garage and the police confirmed that this was so. The eye-witnesses to the robbery made a good identification of Delilah but were unable to identify the other robber (who had worn a mask) except to say that he was 'huge' (Sam certainly fell into this category).

How should the judge have directed the jury? Should the judge have given a *Turnbull* warning?

Question 2

Mark was tried and convicted on a charge of unlawfully wounding John (contrary to Offences against the Person Act 1861, s. 20). The assault occurred when a fight broke out outside a public house at closing time. John was the only eye-witness called by the prosecution. He was a regular at the pub but his assailant was a stranger. Mark's defence throughout the trial was mistaken identity. John had identified Mark as his assailant shortly after the alleged assault when the police took him to the local bus station where Mark was waiting. He was suffering from a hand injury which was consistent with his being involved in a fight but he explained that he had fallen over when he was running to try to catch a bus. He claimed that he had spent the evening at the cinema but he could not remember the name of the film or the price he had paid to get in.

The police officers who took John to the bus station gave evidence at trial of his confident identification of Mark on that occasion. However, John (whose general confidence had deteriorated since the assault), when called as a witness, was unable to state whom he identified at the bus station. Mark had requested an identity parade but the police decided it was impracticable to hold one.

In summing up on the identification issue the trial judge said:

> The defendant says that John has identified the wrong man. He says that he went to the cinema on that evening and that he had nothing to do with the events outside the pub. Of course, you should look with great care at the circumstances in which the identification was made. John did not know the defendant and he only had a short time to observe his attacker. Against this it is only fair to point out that only a short time had elapsed between the attack and John's clear identification of the defendant at the bus station. We have also heard how the defendant could remember nothing about the film he had just seen and there was the injury to his hand. Of course in the end, members of the jury, it is a matter for you to decide having heard the evidence of the prosecution witnesses and the defendant.

(a) Draft an argument in support of an appeal against conviction on behalf of Mark. You should also prepare a counter-argument on behalf of the prosecution.

(b) If Mark had admitted being present at the time of the assault but claimed that he had nonetheless been misidentified by John, would it have been unnecessary for the judge to give any *Turnbull* warning?

THIRTEEN

OPINION EVIDENCE AND JUDGMENTS AS EVIDENCE OF THE FACTS ON WHICH THEY ARE BASED

When may a party call a witness to give evidence of opinion (as opposed to evidence of fact)?

May a party adduce evidence of an earlier judgment or verdict to prove the facts on which that judgment or verdict was based (assuming such facts are relevant to the instant proceedings)?

13.1 Opinion Evidence

13.1.1 THE GENERAL RULE

Both in civil and criminal cases the opinions of witnesses are not, in general, admissible. Witnesses should normally be confined to stating the facts. The basic rationale of this exclusionary rule is that it is the task of the *court* (tribunals of fact and law) to form any opinions which need to be formed in any particular case (obviously the court must form some opinions in *every* case). There is a risk either that the court might be unduly influenced by the opinion of a person who will not necessarily share the court's impartiality, or that the court will be unaware of the factual basis (or lack of it) on which the opinion is founded. Alternatively, it may be thought that, when the court is perfectly capable of forming an opinion on the matter in issue, allowing a witness to state his opinion would waste the court's time.

The following cases, in which opinion evidence has been excluded, are merely intended to give a general impression of the impact of the rule in criminal and civil cases.

R v *Chard* (1971) 56 Cr App R 268
(murder case — expert witness not allowed to state opinion that in the light of the accused's personality he lacked the intent to commit murder. Intent is a matter for the jury, and, in the absence of any question of abnormality, does not call for expert evidence);

R v *Stamford* [1972] 2 QB 391; *R* v *Anderson* [1972] 1 QB 304
(both obscenity cases — expert witness not allowed to state opinion as to whether a particular article/publication had a tendency to deprave or corrupt);

R v *S* [2000] All ER (D) 2380
(psychiatric evidence was not admissible simply to show that, in the opinion of the doctor, the accused was especially timid, suggestible or vulnerable to threats. If the evidence had been that the accused suffered from some mental illness or recognised

psychiatric condition and that such people might be more susceptible to threats or pressure, then it might have been admissible);

R v *MacKenney* (1983) 76 Cr App R 271; *R* v *Turner* [1975] QB 834, CA
(murder cases — expert witness not allowed to state opinion as to whether another witness was telling the truth — the credibility of witnesses is a matter for the tribunal of fact);

R v *Gilfoyle* [2001] 2 Cr App R 57, CA
(evidence of a 'psychological autopsy' of the dead victim of an alleged crime was not expert evidence of a kind that could be placed before a court);

R v *Edwards* [2001] EWCA Crim 2185; (2001) 9 Archbold News 1, CA
(evidence about the practice of drug users from a police officer and from someone who had worked with addicts was held valueless and therefore inadmissible; in both cases the witnesses relied on accounts given by unidentified drug users, which were unsupported by any scientific material);

(**Note**: as to the admissibility of expert evidence that a child is or is not telling the truth about sexual abuse see *Re N (a minor)* [1996] 4 All ER 225 and *Re M and R (Minors)* [1996] 4 All ER 239.)

R v *Wood* [1990] Crim LR 264
(murder case — defence of unsuccessful suicide pact — likelihood of D's participation, psychiatric evidence inadmissible);

Haynes v *Doman* [1899] 2 Ch 13
(reasonableness of restraint of trade — affidavits from traders expressing opinions on the reasonableness of the clause in question inadmissible);

Rabin v *Gerson Berger Association Ltd* [1986] 1 WLR 526
(effect of trust deed — opinion evidence of barrister who had drafted the deed inadmissible);

North Cheshire & Manchester Brewery Co. Ltd v *Manchester Brewery Co. Ltd* [1899] AC 83
(passing-off action — witness not allowed to state opinion as to whether defendant company intended to pass itself off as plaintiff company).

Any textual description of the rule against opinion evidence, even if it is supported with examples, fails to give a true impression of the impact of the rule upon the questioning of witnesses. An objection to a particular question is often made (and sustained) on the basis that the witness is being invited to state opinion. Sometimes the question itself is really nothing more than comment on the witness's evidence.

The general rule excluding opinion evidence is subject to two important exceptions. These arise in cases where the court lacks the witness's competence to form an opinion on a particular issue whether through lack of the necessary direct knowledge or through lack of the necessary expertise.

13.1.2   EYE-WITNESS OPINIONS OR OPINIONS AS SHORTHAND FOR FACTS

Statements of opinion by an eye-witness (E) to the facts in issue are often in essence a convenient way of stating several facts. Thus an assertion by E that the defendant was drunk is a convenient way of stating the various facts which E saw (heard or smelt) which led him to form that opinion. See *R* v *Davies* [1962] 1 WLR 1111. Such a statement will generally be admissible as long as a proper appraisal of the facts does not call for any special expertise (see below).

In a case concerning a road accident it will often be necessary to consider the speed at which the vehicles involved were travelling — again E will be allowed to state his opinion on this issue.

A very important issue in many cases is the *identification* of persons, animals, places or things. Statements of identification might seem to be factual but they are, technically speaking, statements of opinion. Clearly it is often necessary for the courts to have regard to such statements and they would generally be admissible under this exception. See *Fryer* v *Gathercole* (1849) 4 Exch 262 (but special rules apply to the identification of an accused — see **Chapter 12**). If it is necessary to identify handwriting (as it often is — especially in relation to signatures) it may be possible to call the alleged writer or a person who saw the alleged writer doing the writing or a person who is well acquainted with the writing in question. However, if it is not possible to prove the document in this way and comparison between different samples of handwriting is necessary, the court should seek assistance from a handwriting expert (see below).

In civil cases this exception has been put into statutory form — Civil Evidence Act 1972, s. 3(2):

> It is hereby declared that where a person is called as a witness in any civil proceedings, a statement of opinion by him on any relevant matter on which he is not qualified to give expert evidence, if made as a way of conveying relevant facts personally perceived by him, is admissible evidence of what he perceived.

13.1.3 EXPERT OPINIONS

13.1.3.1 General points

There are many situations in which the issues the court is required to determine are so far removed from the court's experience that it needs to obtain the opinions of experts to help it determine the issue in question. See generally *Folkes* v *Chadd* (1782) 3 Doug KB 157. When such need arises the opinion of an expert *is* admissible. (If an issue does call for expert evidence, the evidence of a non-expert should not be admitted; see *R* v *Inch* (1989) 91 Cr App R 51.) The amount of expert evidence which can be used in civil cases is affected by CPR, r. 35.7(1) which provides:

> Where two or more parties wish to submit expert evidence on a particular issue, the court may direct that the evidence on that issue is to be given by one expert only. Unless the parties agree on the expert under this rule, the court may select an expert from a list submitted by the parties, or direct how the expert should be selected. Once selected, each instructing party may give instructions to the expert, sending a copy to the other instructing parties.

It is not possible to list all the matters in respect of which expert evidence is required; some matters (e.g. medical and scientific) obviously call for the opinions of experts. However, the line between matters which do call for expert evidence and matters which do not is often extremely fine (especially in relation to psychiatric evidence) and the courts consider the question most carefully. In *R* v *Turner* [1975] QB 834, CA at p. 841 Lawton LJ put the point very effectively in this way:

> The fact that an expert witness has impressive scientific qualifications does not by that fact alone make his opinion on matters of human nature and behaviour *within the limits of normality* any more helpful than that of the jurors themselves; but there is a danger that they may think it does. (Emphasis added.)

But this sometimes begs the question, 'What is normality?'. In *R* v *Masih* [1986] Crim LR 395 the Court of Appeal kept faith with Lawton LJ in deciding that psychiatric evidence in respect of an accused who had an intelligence quotient of 72 (2 points *above* the subnormal level) was inadmissible — see further M. Beaumont, 'Psychiatric evidence: over-rationalising the abnormal' [1988] Crim LR 290.

Note: There are particular difficulties in criminal cases when there *is* evidence of *abnormality* but the central issue in the case turns on the application of an objective test. By definition the 'reasonable man' cannot be assumed to be abnormal. Insofar as an expert's evidence would *only* be relevant if such an assumption could be made then it would appear to be inadmissible. See *R* v *Howe* [1987] AC 417 and *R* v *Hurst* [1995] 1 Cr App R 82 (as regards duress, but *cf. R* v *Bowen* [1996] 2 Cr App R 157) and *R* v *Coles* [1995] 1 Cr App R 157 (as regards *Caldwell* recklessness).

The Privy Council in *Luc Thiet Thuan* v *R* [1996] 2 All ER 1033 adopted this approach in relation to the defence of provocation.

However in *R* v *Campbell* [1997] 1 Cr App R 199 the Court of Appeal refused to follow this Privy Council decision in that it ran counter to relatively recent Court of Appeal decisions (e.g. *R* v *Humphries* [1995] 4 All ER 1008) enlarging to a limited extent the scope of the defence of provocation. Lord Bingham CJ observed (p. 207E) that if (in the context of the provocation defence) the concept of the reasonable man were accepted without any qualification, successful pleas of provocation would be rare indeed, since it is not altogether easy to imagine circumstances in which a reasonable man would strike a fatal blow with the necessary mental intention, whatever the provocation. See also *R* v *Smith (Morgan James)* [1999] 1 Cr App R 256.

The following list is intended to give a general guide to the sort of questions which have been held to call for expert evidence (and should be compared with the cases *excluding* opinion given in **13.1.1**).

R v *Holmes* [1953] 1 WLR 686
(whether an accused (A) is suffering from a disease of the mind within the M'Naghten rules);

R v *Bailey* (1977) 66 Cr App R 31
(whether A is suffering from diminished responsibility — but note the distinction drawn between diminished responsibility and other forms of incapacity, e.g. drunkenness in *R* v *Tandy* [1989] 1 All ER 267);

R v *Smith* [1979] 1 WLR 1445
(whether A, who had put forward a defence of non-insane automatism, was sleep-walking);

Toohey v *Metropolitan Police Commissioner* [1965] AC 595, HL; *cf. R* v *MacKenney* (1983) 76 Cr App R 271
(whether a witness is suffering from a mental disability such as to render him incapable of giving reliable evidence — but expert evidence will not be admitted on the question whether a witness who has a normal capacity for reliability is actually giving reliable evidence — this is always a matter for the tribunal of fact; see *R* v *MacKenney*);

R v *Tilley* [1961] 1 WLR 1309
(whether two samples of handwriting were written by the same person);

Pugsley v *Hunter* [1973] 1 WLR 578
(as to the effect on the level of blood alcohol of 'spiked' drinks);

Lowery v *R* [1974] AC 85 but *cf. R* v *Turner* [1975] QB 834, CA
(as to the relative likelihood of one accused having committed a sadistic murder rather than another);

DPP v *A & BC Chewing Gum Ltd* [1968] 1 QB 159 but *cf. R* v *Stamford* [1972] 2 QB 391 and *R* v *Anderson* [1972] 1 QB 304
(as to the psychological effect *on children* of cards depicting, in graphic detail, the horrors of war and, thus, whether the cards had a tendency to deprave or corrupt);

R v *Skirving* [1985] QB 819
(as to the various ways of using cocaine and the adverse effects thereof and, thus, whether an article describing these matters had a tendency to deprave or corrupt);

R v *Oakley* (1979) 70 Cr App R 7
(as to the probable circumstances and causes of a fatal accident);

R v *Toner* (1991) 93 Cr App R 382
(as to the possible effects of a *medical condition* on a person's mental processes and ability to form an intent);

R v *Silcott, Braithwaite and Raghip, The Times*, 9 December 1991
(as to the reliability of a confession made by a person who was abnormally susceptible to suggestion);

R v *Stockwell* (1993) 97 Cr App R 260
((evidence of facial mapping expert) as to whether the face on a video taken by a security camera was that of the accused).

This list has been drawn exclusively from criminal cases but this does not mean that expert evidence is less common in civil cases, indeed, in general, it is probably encountered more frequently in civil cases (and there are many rules of civil procedure which relate to expert evidence — see below and in the ***Civil Litigation Manual***).

13.1.3.2 The ultimate issue rule

The rule that an expert should not be asked to state his opinon on the ultimate issue in a case has been noticed more in its breach than in its observance even in criminal cases see *R* v *Holmes* [1953] 1 WLR 686. See also *R* v *Theodosi* [1993] RTR 179, CA; *R* v *Stockwell* (1993) 97 Cr App R 260. It has been abolished in civil cases by Civil Evidence Act 1972, s. 3(1) and (3):

> *(1) Subject to any rules of court made in pursuance of this Act, where a person is called as a witness in any civil proceedings, his opinion on any relevant matter on which he is qualified to give expert evidence shall be admissible in evidence.*
> . . .
> *(3) In this section 'relevant matter' includes an issue in the proceedings in question.*

13.1.3.3 Who is an expert?

Where a matter does call for expert evidence only a suitably qualified expert can give it. Indeed the starting-point in examining in chief an expert witness is to establish his or her expertise. But this does not necessarily mean that there must be formal qualifications — see e.g. *R* v *Silverlock* [1894] 2 QB 766 — solicitor who had for many years studied handwriting as a hobby (handwriting expert); *Ajami* v *Comptroller of Customs* [1954] 1 WLR 1405 — banker with 24 years' experience of Nigerian banking law (foreign law expert). (Matters of *foreign* law are generally treated as calling for expert evidence: obviously matters of English law are for the judge to determine.) However, it will not be easy to satisfy a judge that a witness is an expert in a field if he lacks formal qualifications.

13.1.3.4 The 'status' of expert evidence

In *R* v *Lanfear* [1968] 2 QB 77 Lord Diplock stated that expert evidence should be treated like the evidence of any other witness and it would be a misdirection to the jury that they must accept it.

However, in *R* v *Anderson* [1972] 1 QB 304 it was held that it would equally be a misdirection to tell a jury that it could disregard expert evidence which had been given by only one witness and which, if accepted, dictated one answer. See also, to the same effect, *R* v *Bailey* (1977) 66 Cr App R 31.

13.1.3.5 Nature and content of expert evidence

An expert's opinion will be based upon much more than the facts of the particular case he is considering. It will be based on the expert's experience and any information that he has obtained from extraneous sources such as textbooks, articles and journals. Such information (often referred to as secondary facts) is not treated as hearsay but simply as part of the basis for the expert opinion. Obviously the facts of the particular case on which the opinion is given (the primary facts) should be proved by admissible evidence (whether or not by the expert). For example, an expert valuer of antiques may give opinion evidence of the value of certain Chinese vases. His opinion may be based on his own knowledge of previous sale prices of similar vases; it may also be based on secondary facts — reports of sales at foreign auction rooms, or books published for the antiques trade specialist. However, if his valuation is based on the 'primary facts' that these vases date from the era of the Ming dynasty in China and are in excellent condition, these primary facts must be proved, either by this witness testifying as to what he observed when looking at the vases (maker's marks, absence of cracks, chips, etc.) or by other witnesses who have examined the vases. See generally *English Exporters (London) Ltd* v *Eldonwall Ltd* [1973] Ch 415 and *H* v *Schering Chemicals Ltd* [1983] 1 WLR 143 *cf. R* v *Bradshaw* (1986) Cr App R 79 — 'as a concession to the defence' a psychiatrist was allowed to base his opinion as to the accused's mental state upon statements made out of court by the accused (i.e. hearsay).

In *R* v *Jackson* [1996] 2 Cr App R 420 the Court of Appeal held that although strictly speaking an expert witness should not give an opinion based on scientific tests which had been made by assistants (in the expert's absence), maximum use should be made of written statements and formal admissions in proving such tests where there is no real issue as to whether the tests were properly carried out.

A good example of the difference between primary and secondary facts is *R* v *Abadom* (1983) 76 Cr App R 48. A was charged with robbery. A forensic expert gave opinion evidence that glass found on A's shoes came from a window which had been broken during the robbery. Samples of glass from both locations had the same refractive index. The expert stated that according to statistics produced by the Home Office Research Establishment the chances of the glass being from two distinct sources were minimal. A was convicted and appealed on the grounds that the HORE statistics were hearsay. The Court of Appeal held that the statistics were secondary facts supporting the expert's opinion. So long as the primary facts (i.e. that the glass compared was (a) the glass on A's shoes and (b) the glass from the robbery scene) were proved by admissible evidence the expert could (indeed should) state why he arrived at his opinion on those facts.

Secondary facts are essentially parasitic in that they cannot be stated in the absence of an expert's opinion. Thus in *Dawson* v *Lunn* [1986] RTR 234 the Divisional Court held that a defendant on a drink-driving charge could not make reference to a medical journal to support his defence. The defendant was not a medical expert.

13.1.3.6 Advance notice of expert evidence in civil cases

Civil Evidence Act 1972, s. 2(3), made provision for rules of court to be made in relation to advance notice of expert evidence in civil cases. By CPR, r. 35.13, a party who fails to disclose an expert's report may not use the report at the trial or call the expert to give evidence orally unless the court gives permission.

A party should be sure that he wishes to use the expert's report as part of his case *before* disclosing it to the other side because CPR, r. 35.11 provides that any party to whom such a report is disclosed can put it in evidence. In general an expert's advice which is sought by a party for the purposes of pending or contemplated litigation would be protected from disclosure (at any stage of the proceedings) by legal professional privilege (see **Chapter 14** of this Manual) but r. 35.11 makes it clear that the privilege cannot be relied on once the report has been disclosed under the advance notice procedure. Even where a party does rely on privilege in respect of an expert's opinion it should be remembered that there is no property in a witness. This means that although a party who chooses not to use an expert's evidence can claim privilege in respect of the expert's opinion given to that party he cannot muzzle the expert and other parties are entitled to subpoena the expert (subject to the procedural restrictions): see *Harmony Shipping Co. SA* v *Saudi Europe Line Ltd* [1979] 1 WLR 1380, CA.

13.1.3.7 Advance notice of expert evidence in criminal cases

The prosecution is obliged to disclose expert evidence to the defence on general principles (see the **Criminal Litigation and Sentencing Manual**). However, there used to be no obligation on the defence to disclose expert evidence even in cases where the defence carried a legal burden of proving a matter calling for expert evidence, e.g. insanity or diminished responsibility. This was changed, as regards Crown Court cases, by Crown Court (Advance Notice of Expert Evidence) Rules 1987 (SI 1987 No. 716) made pursuant to Police and Criminal Evidence Act 1984, s. 81 and see now Crown Court (Advance Notice of Expert Evidence (Amendment) Rules 1997. These, inter alia, require any party proposing to adduce expert evidence to furnish the other parties with a statement in writing of the expert finding or opinion. Such party then, *on request* in writing by any other party, must provide a copy of, or opportunity to examine, the record of any observation, test or calculation on which the finding or opinion is based. By virtue of Criminal Procedure and Investigations Act 1996, similar provisions now apply to expert evidence in the magistrates' court (see Magistrates' Courts (Advance Notice of Expert Evidence) Rules 1997 (SI 1997 No. 705)).

If the rules are not complied with the expert evidence can only be admitted with the leave of the court but a party may elect not to comply with the rules if that party has reasonable grounds for believing that compliance might lead to intimidation or attempted intimidation of an expert witness or to interference with the course of justice (but such party must give notice of the grounds for non-compliance to the other parties).

13.1.4 OPINION EVIDENCE AND THE HEARSAY RULE

13.1.4.1 In civil cases
In civil proceedings, hearsay statements are rendered admissible by Civil Evidence Act 1995, subject to ss. 5 and 6(2) of the Act. 'Statement' is defined in s. 13 of the Act for the purpose of civil proceedings as 'any representation of fact *or opinion* however made' (emphasis added). Accordingly, the fact that opinion evidence is presented as hearsay will not generally affect its admissibility in civil cases.

13.1.4.2 In criminal cases
By Criminal Justice Act 1988, s. 30:

> *(1)   An expert report shall be admissible as evidence in criminal proceedings, whether or not the person making it attends to give oral evidence in those proceedings.*
> *(2)   If it is proposed that the person making the report shall not give oral evidence, the report shall only be admissible with the leave of the court.*
> *(3)   For the purpose of determining whether to give leave the court shall have regard—*
> > *(a)   to the contents of the report;*
> > *(b)   to the reasons why it is proposed that the person making the report shall not give oral evidence;*
> > *(c)   to any risk, having regard in particular to whether it is likely to be possible to controvert statements in the report if the person making it does not attend to give oral evidence in the proceedings, that its admission or exclusion will result in unfairness to the accused or, if there is more than one, to any of them; and*
> > *(d)   to any other circumstances that appear to the court to be relevant.*
> *(4)   An expert report, when admitted, shall be evidence of any fact or opinion of which the person making it could have given oral evidence.*
> *In this section 'expert report' means a written report by a person dealing wholly or mainly with matters on which he is (or would if living be) qualified to give expert evidence.*
> *(4A)   Where the proceedings mentioned in subsection (1) above are proceedings before a magistrates' court inquiring into an offence as examining justices this section shall have effect with the omission of—*
> > *(a)   in subsection (1) the words 'whether or not the person making it attends to give oral evidence in those proceedings', and*
> > *(b)   subsections (2) to (4).*

The effect of this section (which applies to statements in the expert report of fact *and* opinion) is clear. It creates a hearsay exception specifically directed at expert reports. When the expert attends as a witness the report is admissible without leave. However where the expert is not available as a witness the court's leave to admit the report is required.

There is no *specific* provision applicable in criminal cases to out-of-court statements of opinion which are essentially a shorthand for facts (see **13.1.2**). However, it is probable that they would be admissible albeit hearsay if made or contained in a document falling within Criminal Justice Act 1988, ss. 23 and 24 (see **9.2.2.1**).

13.2 Judgments as Evidence of the Facts on Which They are Based

In the sense that a court judgment represents findings on matters of past facts, that judgment can be regarded as a statement of opinion. A typical example is the verdict of a criminal court that the accused is guilty of the crime for which he or she has been tried. It is, therefore, appropriate to deal with this topic in the same chapter as opinion evidence. The general rule (often referred to as the rule in *Hollington* v *Hewthorn*) is that such judgments are inadmissible if offered in later trials as evidence of the facts upon which they were based. Thus in a civil claim, alleging negligent driving, it is not possible to call evidence of the defendant's conviction for driving without due care and attention on that specific occasion in order to prove the facts on which that conviction was based: see *Hollington* v *F. Hewthorn & Co. Ltd* [1943] KB 587. The inconvenience of this general rule is obvious. The consequence was that proceedings in the civil courts were extended unnecessarily because unless the facts were admitted by the convicted party, the same issues had to be proved all over again. Not only that, but a further mischief was that some matters which had already been established beyond reasonable doubt were not established on the lower standard of proof, on the balance of probabilities. That inconsistency was a matter for serious concern.

An example is *Hinds* v *Sparks* [1964] Crim LR 717, where Hinds sued Sparks for defamation. Sparks had published a statement asserting that Hinds had committed a robbery some years previously. The law of defamation required the defendant, Sparks, to prove the truth of his assertion. In fact, Hinds had been tried for and convicted of the robbery and had appealed unsuccessfully to the Court of Criminal Appeal. The rule in *Hollington* v *Hewthorn* prevented Sparks from producing that conviction as evidence of Hinds' involvement. As he was unable to produce any other evidence to support his assertion, Hinds won his claim.

There are now several major exceptions to the rule in both civil and criminal proceedings (see **13.2.1** to **13.2.2**). The majority of these deal with the use of criminal convictions in subsequent trials.

A final judgment may have the effect of barring any parties to that judgment from relitigating any issues *between them* which were determined in that judgment. Where this bar applies (often referred to under the heading of *res judicata*), the judgment is not used as *evidence* in the subsequent proceedings: it has the more powerful effect of *stopping* the subsequent proceedings. (It may sometimes have a more limited effect — to prevent the re-opening of a specific issue which was decided in the earlier proceedings.) However, *res judicata* only affects subsequent litigation between the *same* parties. For example, a criminal trial involves the state prosecuting a defendant. If the same factual allegations arose in a civil claim between, say, the alleged victim of an assault and her assailant, the principle of *res judicata* would not apply. *Res judicata* is not dealt with in detail in this Manual. For more information, you should consult the practitioner texts concerned with cause of action estoppel or issue estoppel (in civil cases) and *autrefois convict* or *acquit* (in criminal cases).

13.2.1 WHEN JUDGMENTS ARE ADMISSIBLE IN CIVIL CASES AS EVIDENCE OF THE FACTS ON WHICH THEY ARE BASED

Sections 11 and 13 of the Civil Evidence Act 1968 apply only to criminal convictions (in respect of which the standard of proof is at its highest). Previous acquittals are almost certainly *not* admissible in civil proceedings to establish innocence of the offences charged. Also there is no *general* provision allowing for previous civil judgments to be used as evidence of the facts on which they were based. However, s. 12 of the 1968 Act, allows a very limited range of civil judgments to be used as evidence of the facts on which they are based.

13.2.1.1 Civil Evidence Act 1968, section 11

(1)   In any civil proceedings the fact that a person has been convicted of an offence by or before any court in the United Kingdom or by a court-martial there or elsewhere shall (subject to subsection (3) below) be admissible in evidence for the purpose of proving, where to do so is relevant to any issue in those proceedings, that he committed that offence, whether he was so convicted upon a plea of guilty or otherwise and whether or not he is a party to the civil proceedings; but no conviction other than a subsisting one shall be admissible in evidence by virtue of this section.

(2)   In any civil proceedings in which by virtue of this section a person is proved to have been convicted of an offence by or before any court in the United Kingdom or by a court-martial there or elsewhere—

(a)   he shall be taken to have committed that offence unless the contrary is proved; and

(b)   without prejudice to the reception of any other admissible evidence for the purpose of identifying the facts on which the conviction was based, the contents of any document which is admissible as evidence of the conviction, and the contents of the information, complaint, indictment or charge-sheet on which the person in question was convicted, shall be admissible in evidence for that purpose.

(3)   Nothing in this section shall prejudice the operation of section 13 of this Act or any other enactment whereby a conviction or a finding of fact in any criminal proceedings is for the purposes of any other proceedings made conclusive evidence of any fact.

(4)   Where in any civil proceedings the contents of any document are admissible in evidence by virtue of subsection (2) above, a copy of that document, or of the material part thereof, purporting to be certified or otherwise authenticated by or on behalf of the court or authority having custody of that document shall be admissible in evidence and shall be taken to be a true copy of that document or part unless the contrary is shown.

Civil Evidence Act 1968, s. 11, reverses the actual decision in *Hollington v F. Hewthorn & Co. Ltd* [1943] KB 587 (i.e. the conviction for driving without due care would now be admissible in the civil case to prove negligence) and, of course, creates a major exception to the general rule. Section 11 puts the legal burden of proof onto the party who denies that the person convicted of the offence in question did commit it (X). However, s. 11 does *not* create a *conclusive presumption*, but a rebuttable one. How X goes about rebutting the presumption has been considered by the courts on several occasions. See *Stupple v Royal Insurance Co. Ltd* [1971] 1 QB 50, *Taylor v Taylor* [1970] 1 WLR 1148 and *Wauchope v Mordechai* [1970] 1 WLR 317. The prevailing view is that it will not avail X to challenge the technical correctness of the conviction; X must prove either that he or she did not commit the crime or that it was not committed at all. In practice, s. 11 has made it extremely difficult for a party to challenge successfully the conclusion that the person convicted did in fact commit the offence in question. One need simply note the different standards of proof involved in securing the criminal conviction (beyond reasonable doubt) and in the civil trial (balance of probabilities).

In *Brinks Ltd v Abu Saleh (No. 1)* [1995] 4 All ER 65, Jacob J held that a convicted defendant must adduce fresh evidence which 'entirely changes the aspect of the case' in order to be permitted to contest a civil action based on the same facts. It has since been argued that this requirement to adduce fresh evidence which 'entirely changes the aspect of the case' is a very difficult one to surmount and if it were applied generally, the effect would be to prevent a convicted defendant from contesting a civil claim. That would be quite contrary to the intention of Parliament as enshrined in s. 11 and as interpreted by Lord Diplock in *Hunter v Chief Constable of the West Midlands Police* [1982] AC 529. This argument was raised in *J v Oyston* [1999] 1 WLR 694. Smedley J ruled that it was entirely legitimate for the defendant to seek to disprove allegations of rape and indecent assault, notwithstanding his convictions for both offences. The defendant wished to call evidence about the claimant/complainant which had not been produced at his criminal trial, although it had been put before the Court of Appeal when he appealed unsuccessfully against his convictions. Smedley J ruled against the claimant's assertion that to allow the defendant to do precisely that which s. 11(2)(a) permits him to do would constitute an abuse of process. Conversely, it seems that where a claimant seeks to re-litigate a matter which has already been determined against him or her by a criminal court (i.e. a convicted defendant seeks to challenge the correctness of the conviction by initiating a civil claim against the prosecuting authority), the claim is likely to be struck out as an abuse of process; see *Hunter* (and *cf.* Civil Evidence Act 1968, s. 13, below).

Section 11 only applies to subsisting convictions. When a conviction (which is to be proved under s. 11) is being appealed the civil proceedings should be adjourned until the appeal has been heard: see *Re Raphael* [1973] 1 WLR 998. A party seeking to rely on s. 11 should state this in the appropriate statement of case etc. including details of the conviction and the issue to which it is relevant. Section 11(4) allows a certified copy of the conviction, indictment etc. to be used to prove the facts on which the conviction was based.

13.2.1.2 Civil Evidence Act 1968, section 13

Section 11 would not prevent a party from seeking to use libel proceedings to reopen a criminal case which resulted in his conviction (because it only creates a rebuttable presumption). This specific difficulty is confronted by s. 13 of the Act, which creates an irrebuttable presumption:

> *(1) In an action for libel or slander in which the question whether a person did or did not commit a criminal offence is relevant to an issue arising in the action, proof that, at the time when that issue falls to be determined, that person stands convicted of that offence shall be conclusive evidence that he committed that offence; and his conviction thereof shall be admissible in evidence accordingly.*
>
> *(2) In any such action as aforesaid in which by virtue of this section a person is proved to have been convicted of an offence the contents of any document which is admissible as evidence of the conviction, and the contents of the information, complaint, indictment or charge-sheet on which that person was convicted, shall, without prejudice to the reception of any other admissible evidence for the purpose of identifying the facts on which the conviction was based, be admissible in evidence for the purpose of identifying those facts.*
>
> *(3) For the purposes of this section a person shall be taken to stand convicted of an offence if but only if there subsists against him a conviction of that offence by or before a court in the United Kingdom or by a court-martial there or elsewhere.*

The effect of s. 13 is such that an action in defamation based on the defendant's assertion that the claimant committed an offence for which he or she has been convicted would be struck out, i.e. in defamation cases a person convicted of an offence is *conclusively* presumed to have committed it. However, s. 13 does not give publishers *carte blanche* to make general attacks on the character of convicts: see *Levene* v *Roxhan* [1970] 1 WLR 1322.

13.2.1.3 Civil Evidence Act 1968, section 12 (as amended by Family Law Reform Act 1987)

> *(1) In any civil proceedings—*
> *(a) the fact that a person has been found guilty of adultery in any matrimonial proceedings; and*
> *(b) the fact that a person has been found to be the father of a child in relevant proceedings before any court in England and Wales or has been adjudged to be the father of a child in affiliation proceedings before any court in the United Kingdom;*
> *shall . . . be admissible in evidence for the purpose of proving, where to do so is relevant to any issue in those civil proceedings, that he committed the adultery to which the finding relates or, as the case may be, is (or was) the father of that child, whether or not he offered any defence to the allegation of adultery or paternity and whether or not he is a party to the civil proceedings; but no finding or adjudication other than a subsisting one shall be admissible in evidence by virtue of this section.*

> (2)   In any civil proceedings in which by virtue of this section a person is proved to have been found guilty of adultery as mentioned in subsection (1)(a) above or to have been found or adjudged to be the father of a child as mentioned in subsection (1)(b) above—
>
> (a)   he shall be taken to have committed the adultery to which the finding relates or, as the case may be, to be (or have been) the father of that child, unless the contrary is proved; and
>
> (b)   without prejudice to the reception of any other admissible evidence for the purpose of identifying the facts on which the finding or adjudication was based, the contents of any document which was before the court, or which contains any pronouncement of the court, in the other proceedings in question shall be admissible in evidence for that purpose.

The effect of s. 12(2) is very similar to the effect of s. 11(2), i.e. the legal burden is put on the party denying the facts on which the finding is based but the *scope* of s. 12 is very narrow. Section 12(5) provides that the phrase 'matrimonial proceedings' (used in s. 12(1)(a)) only includes matrimonial proceedings in the High Court and county court (not the magistrates' court).

13.2.2   WHEN JUDGMENTS ARE ADMISSIBLE IN CRIMINAL CASES AS EVIDENCE OF THE FACTS ON WHICH THEY ARE BASED

Until relatively recently the rule excluding judgments as evidence of the facts on which they are based was of general application in criminal cases. For example, where A was charged with handling stolen goods, it was not permissible to prove that B was convicted of the theft of the goods in question to show that the goods were stolen. This rule was changed as regards convictions by Police and Criminal Evidence Act 1984, s. 74. A distinction needs to be drawn between (a) convictions of persons other than the accused and (b) convictions of the accused.

13.2.2.1   Convictions of persons other than the accused

The Police and Criminal Evidence Act 1984, s. 74(1) and (2) provide:

> (1)   In any proceedings the fact that a person other than the accused has been convicted of an offence by or before any court in the United Kingdom or by a Service court outside the United Kingdom shall be admissible in evidence for the purpose of proving, where to do so is relevant to any issue in those proceedings, that that person committed that offence, whether or not any other evidence of his having committed that offence is given.
>
> (2)   In any proceedings in which by virtue of this section a person other than the accused is proved to have been convicted of an offence by or before any court in the United Kingdom or by a Service court outside the United Kingdom, he shall be taken to have committed that offence unless the contrary is proved.

By s. 75(1):

> Where evidence that a person has been convicted of an offence is admissible by virtue of section 74 above, then without prejudice to the reception of any other admissible evidence for the purpose of identifying the facts on which the conviction was based—
>
> (a)   the contents of any document which is admissible as evidence of the conviction; and
>
> (b)   the contents of the . . . indictment . . . on which the person in question was convicted, shall be admissible in evidence for that purpose.

The effect of s. 74(1) and (2) is very similar to the effect of Civil Evidence Act 1968, s. 11, in civil cases, i.e. it puts the legal burden of proof on the party who denies that the person convicted committed the offence in question (of course the *standard* of proof in a criminal case will vary according to whether that party is the prosecution or the defence).

Few could have anticipated the difficulties which s. 74(1) and (2) have caused in practice. In 1972, the 11th Report of the Criminal Law Revision Committee had recommended the abolition of the rule in *Hollington* v *Hewthorn* in criminal proceedings. The Committee apparently thought that it was recommending simply that the conviction be admissible in evidence to deal with the situation 'where it was necessary as a preliminary matter for it to be proved that a person other than the accused had been convicted of an offence' (see *R* v *O'Connor* (1986) 85 Cr App R 298, per Taylor J). This would ease the burden on the prosecution in the following situations, for example:

- In trials for handling stolen goods, to prove that the goods were stolen one proves the conviction of the thief.

- In trials for harbouring offenders, one proves the conviction of the 'offender'.

That seems quite straightforward. Difficulties began with the judgment of the Court of Appeal in *R* v *Robertson* (1987) 85 Cr App R 304. The Court considered the proper interpretation of the phrase in s. 74(1) 'where to do so is relevant to any issue in those proceedings'. Lord Lane CJ observed that this clearly encompassed an issue which is an essential ingredient in the offence charged; this is consistent with the thinking of the Criminal Law Revision Committee. However, Lord Lane continued 'The word "issue" . . . is apt to cover also less fundamental issues, for example evidential issues arising during the course of proceedings.'

Robertson itself involved the use in evidence of guilty pleas given by R's co-accused to several burglaries. All of the defendants were originally charged with conspiracy to commit burglary and R was tried on that allegation. The prosecution introduced the guilty pleas to prove that there was a conspiracy. The only live issue left was whether R had been a party to it or not.

The Court of Appeal said in *Robertson* that s. 74 was 'a provision that should be sparingly used'. Curiously, the Court of Appeal was still saying this in 1998 (see *R* v *Stewart* [1999] Crim LR 746) and in 2000 (see *R* v *Dixon* [2001] Crim LR 126). Perhaps this reflects continuing concern over the use to which s. 74(1) is being put, following the expanded definition of 'relevant to any issue' provided by Lord Lane CJ.

Since *Robertson* there have been several reported decisions of the Court of Appeal on the use of s. 74(1). Usually, the prosecution alleges that the accused was very closely involved in an offence, of which another person has been convicted already, and the prosecution wish to use that conviction as evidence that the offence was committed. It seems that the conviction is admissible subject to the discretion to exclude it under s. 78 of the 1984 Act. The most common reason for the accused to invoke s. 78 is that the conviction clearly and of itself implies the guilt of the accused then standing trial. This is not the purpose behind introducing the conviction so, if the trial judge agrees, then the conviction should be excluded. This situation is most likely to occur where there are only two alleged parties involved — the one who has pleaded guilty and the one who pleads not guilty.

In *R* v *Mahmood and Manzur* [1997] 1 Cr App R 414, the Court of Appeal held that in deciding whether evidence of a guilty plea should be admitted, the judge was required to apply a two stage test. First, he had to determine whether the plea was clearly relevant to an issue in the accused's trial. If it was, he had secondly to consider any prejudice to the accused in respect of the fairness of the proceedings. He then had to exercise his discretion accordingly.

M, M and L were charged with raping C one after another. L pleaded guilty. There were several live issues:

(a) whether C consented;

(b) whether the accused believed C was consenting;

(c) whether C was incapable of consenting.

The trial judge allowed L's guilty plea to be admitted. The Court of Appeal held the judge had erred. The main difficulty was that the court did not know on what basis L had pleaded guilty. There were several bases on which he could have done so which were consistent with guilt of the offence of rape, and it was essential that the judge should have had that information in order to be able to identify the relevant issue for the jury in the appellant's trial.

It should be noted that s. 74 only provides a shortcut for proving matters which otherwise may be proved by calling a witness. In other words, in cases in which there has been a guilty plea, the prosecution can call the former co-accused to testify for the Crown, in which case the accused can then cross-examine him, both as to the facts and his credibility. The trial judge may then give the jury a warning to take care when assessing the evidence of the former co-accused. By using s. 74 instead, the opportunity of cross-examination and the need for a care warning are removed. It is arguable that this situation could deny the accused a fair trial, contrary to the European Convention on Human Rights, Article 6.

When a conviction is introduced in evidence, the trial judge must be careful to direct the jury as to what issue in the trial it relates to and what the effect of the conviction is. For example, it is not conclusive evidence that an offence was committed by anyone; if the accused testifies that no such offence was committed, it is for the jury to decide which account to believe (see *R v Dixon*, *The Times*, 2 November 2000, CA). It is important for the judge and counsel to be clear on the exact issue that the conviction is said to be relevant to. If it is liable to misuse by the jury, then the judge should probably exclude the evidence using s. 78.

On the genesis and usage of s. 74. see also R. Munday, 'Proof of Guilt by Association under Section 74 of the Police and Criminal Evidence Act 1984' [1990] Crim ER 236.

13.2.2.2 Convictions of the accused

Police and Criminal Evidence Act 1984, s. 74(3) provides:

> *In any proceedings where evidence is admissible of the fact that the accused has committed an offence, insofar as that evidence is relevant to any matter in issue in the proceedings for a reason other than a tendency to show in the accused a disposition to commit the kind of offence with which he is charged, if the accused is proved to have been convicted of the offence—*
> > *(a)   by or before any court in the United Kingdom; or*
> > *(b)   by a Service court outside the United Kingdom,*
> *he shall be taken to have committed that offence unless the contrary is proved.*

This subsection has no effect on the general rule that the accused's previous convictions are generally inadmissible at his trial. Where, exceptionally, such convictions *are* admissible s. 74(3) will apply. The main problem in this context is created by s. 75(1) which deals with the way in which the facts on which a conviction is based can be established (for s. 75(1), see **13.2.2.1**).

Section 75(1)(b) provides that the contents of the indictment (information, complaint or charge-sheet) on which the accused was convicted 'shall be admissible' for this purpose. However, where a conviction is admissible to challenge the accused's credibility (e.g. where he is in breach of Criminal Evidence Act 1898, s. 1(3)(ii): see **7.3.4**) it is not *generally* permissible to prove the particulars of the conviction (because these are not relevant to the issue of credibility and may be prejudicial). It is assumed that despite the wording of s. 75 this approach will still apply.

Questions

OBJECTIVES

This Chapter is designed to ensure that you can:

(a) demonstrate a sound understanding of the principles underlying the general exclusionary rule in relation to evidence of opinion and the main exceptions to that rule, i.e. (i) where an opinion is a shorthand for several factual observations and (ii) where it is necessary to seek the opinion of experts;

(b) demonstrate a sound understanding of the special rules relating to the opinion evidence of experts — including the definition of an expert, the general form and content of expert evidence (secondary facts etc.), the status of such evidence, the requirements for advance notice (and the procedures to be complied with); and

(c) demonstrate a sound understanding of the rule in *Hollington* v *F. Hewthorn & Co. Ltd* and the exceptions to the rule created by Civil Evidence Act 1968, ss. 11 to 13 and Police and Criminal Evidence Act 1984, s. 74.

On the procedure regarding expert witnesses in civil cases you should cross-refer to the *Civil Litigation Manual*.

Question 1
Harvey is charged with being concerned in the supply of cannabis. His defence is that he acted under duress as a result of threats by Iain, his brother-in-law. The defence has consulted Jezebel, a psychiatrist, who says in her report that Harvey was subjected to various forms of physical and mental bullying during his childhood, and that this sort of childhood experience often leads to a condition in which the victim develops an increased vulnerability to threats. She adds that this is widely-recognised as a psychiatric condition in the USA, though not in Europe, and that in her opinion such a condition almost certainly led Harvey to react to Iain's threats out of fear for his safety. Consider the admissibility of Jezebel's evidence.

Question 2
You are appearing for Susan, who is suing Thomas for negligence, alleging that a bad fall she had had on a slippery patch on the floor of Thomas's shop, when she was 18 weeks pregnant, had caused a miscarriage five days later.

(a) After Susan has given evidence, you call her mother, Una, an experienced midwife, who testifies that Susan was extremely shocked and that her symptoms started the next day. Thomas's counsel objects (i) when Una states that such a heavy fall as Susan's bruises suggest must have caused the miscarriage and (ii) when she offers in support of her view an article in a medical journal, which she produces. How would you try to meet these objections?

(b) A shop assistant, Vera, who saw Susan fall, says it was a bad fall as the floor was so slippery and the fall must have affected the course of the pregnancy. Counsel for the defendant objects. Do you consider that you can successfully counter the objection?

(c) The defence calls Dr White, an obstetrician, who testifies that Susan's miscarriage would probably have occurred spontaneously, and that his experience totally contradicts the views expressed in the article cited by Una. He adds that Susan's evidence is quite untrustworthy because her grief at the loss of her baby must have affected her veracity and the reliability of her memory. Do you consider that you can successfully object to the admission of any of Dr White's evidence?

Question 3
Brian Laird and his brother Charles, together with three other men, have been jointly charged with conspiracy to obtain property by deception. It is alleged that all five men (who lived in the same block of flats) had obtained money from elderly house occupiers for whom they pretended to do substantial roofing work. Charles Laird will plead guilty but Brian and all the other co-accused will plead not guilty. Defence counsel are aware that at the trial, the prosecution, in reliance upon s. 74(1) and (2) of the Police and

Criminal Evidence Act 1984, will seek to admit in evidence Charles's conviction (of the offence charged).

(a) You are counsel for Brian Laird — what action will you take before the prosecution opens its case?

Make a note of the submissions you will make to the trial judge on the question whether this evidence should be excluded.

(b) You are counsel for the prosecution — make a note of the submissions you will make to the trial judge opposing the exclusion of this evidence.

FOURTEEN

PRIVILEGE AND PUBLIC POLICY

When is a witness entitled to decline to answer questions put to him or her or to refuse to produce documents or things (privilege)?

When should a judge rule that evidence should be withheld on the grounds that its disclosure would be likely to jeopardise national security, diplomatic relations or other state interests (public policy)?

14.1 General Introduction

It is a general principle that evidence which is relevant to the issues in legal proceedings should be admitted. However, this principle may give way where *either* there are doubts as to the reliability or probative value of the evidence in question *or* allowing the evidence to be proved might run counter to some aspect of public policy. In general the emphasis in this Manual has been on the first of these factors (although there are undercurrents of public policy in several of the areas considered already, e.g. competence and compellability of the accused and his spouse and the exclusion of illegally or improperly obtained evidence). This chapter is concerned almost exclusively with the second of these factors and the situations in which a person or body of persons can refuse to disclose information or documents (and, sometimes, prevent others disclosing such evidence) even though the evidence in question is reliable and clearly relevant to the issues in a particular case.

These situations can usefully be divided into two main categories: (a) *privilege* where a person has a specific right (privilege) in respect of non-disclosure, i.e. the public policy justification for upholding the privilege is presumed to exist, and (b) *public policy* where there is no specific right in respect of non-disclosure but it is nevertheless contended that the public policy justification for non-disclosure exists, i.e. the public policy justification is not presumed and a balancing of the conflicting policies is required. There are significant differences between these categories and they will be dealt with separately.

14.2 Privilege

14.2.1 PRIVILEGE AGAINST SELF-INCRIMINATION

In **Chapter 4** it was noted that an accused is (a) incompetent for the prosecution and (b) non-compellable for the defence. These rules are, in a sense, specialised aspects of the privilege against self-incrimination. However, the privilege is of general application and, broadly speaking, may be claimed by any person in any proceedings (civil or criminal) who would otherwise be obliged, by the general rules of compellability, to answer questions or disclose documents. Such persons when called upon to answer questions or disclose documents may refuse to do so on the grounds that they may incriminate themselves (assuming that this privilege applies). It is the general aspects of the privilege that are considered here.

14.2.1.1 Scope of the privilege

See *Blunt* v *Park Lane Hotel Ltd* [1942] 2 KB 253 per Goddard LJ:

> The rule is that no one is bound to answer any question if the answer thereto would, in the opinion of the judge, have a tendency to expose the deponent to any criminal charge, penalty or forfeiture which the judge regards as reasonably likely to be preferred or sued for.

The privilege also permits refusal to produce documents or things, to meet requests for further information, and to comply with search orders and orders for disclosure ancillary to freezing orders.

See also *R* v *Boyes* (1861) 1 B & S 311 per Cockburn J:

> The object of the law is to afford to a [person] called upon to give evidence in a proceeding . . . protection against being brought by means of his own evidence within the penalties of the law.

> . . . the court must see, from the circumstances of the case and the nature of the evidence which the witness is called to give, that there is a reasonable ground to apprehend danger to the witness from his being called to answer . . . The danger to be apprehended must be real and appreciable with reference to the ordinary operation of law in the ordinary course of things; not a danger of an imaginary and unsubstantial character. . . .

The scope of the privilege is further defined in Civil Evidence Act 1968, s. 14(1):

> *The right of a person in any legal proceedings other than criminal proceedings to refuse to answer any question or produce any document or thing if to do so would tend to expose that person to proceedings for an offence or for the recovery of a penalty—*
> *(a)   shall apply only as regards criminal offences under the law of any part of the United Kingdom and penalties provided for by such law; and*
> *(b)   shall include a like right to refuse to answer any question or produce any document or thing if to do so would tend to expose the husband or wife of that person to proceedings for any such criminal offence or for the recovery of any such penalty.*

Penalties imposed on companies under EC law can fall within the scope of the privilege: see *Rio Tinto Zinc Corporation* v *Westinghouse Electric Corporation* [1978] AC 547, where the House of Lords held that the privilege operated so as to prevent the production of documents which could have resulted in fines being imposed by the European Commission under Articles 85 and 86 (now 81 and 82) of the Treaty of Rome. The House of Lords held that 'penalties' included not just those imposed by court action, but also covered penalties imposed by administrative action and recoverable by proceedings under English law.

A claim to privilege will not succeed where the evidence against the witness is already so strong that whether or not he or she answers the questions or produces the documents will make no difference to the question of his or her being prosecuted. Equally, where the risk of exposure to prosecution or penalty can be removed, the privilege will not operate: see, e.g., *AT & T Istel Ltd* v *Tully* [1993] AC 45. This case concerned an order to disclose documents in a case of alleged commercial fraud. The order contained terms requiring that, *inter alia*, T should set out all his dealings with certain monies. There was also a term that no disclosure made in compliance with the order 'shall be used as evidence in the prosecution of the offence alleged to have been committed by the person required to make that disclosure or by any spouse of that person'. The Court of Appeal upheld the striking out of the terms relating to the disclosure of dealings on the grounds that it infringed the privilege against self-incrimination. However, on a successful appeal by the plaintiffs to the House of Lords, it was held that although the privilege against self-incrimination could only be removed or altered by Parliament, there was no reason to allow a defendant in civil proceedings to rely on it, depriving a plaintiff of his rights, where the defendant's own protection was adequately secured by other means. Having regard to a letter from the CPS (who were not a party to the proceedings) in which it was clear that they did not seek to make use of any of the material disclosed in compliance with the order, and to the original term in the order relating to not using disclosed material in a prosecution, it was held that this was sufficient protection, and as such the invocation of the privilege was rendered superfluous. The terms relating to disclosure of dealings were therefore restored to the order.

Such a term is unlikely to be included in an order unless there is clear agreement not to use the disclosed material in a prosecution.

However, once the court is satisfied that a 'forced' disclosure would tend to expose the witness to the risk of prosecution, the claim to privilege should be upheld (in the absence of specific exceptions): see *Rank Film Distributors Ltd* v *Video Information Centre* [1982] AC 380.

If a court wrongfully rejects a claim to privilege the witness's answer is not admissible in subsequent criminal proceedings: see *R* v *Garbett* (1847) 1 Den CC 236. However, as with other privileges, the privilege can be waived. Evidence disclosed whilst the privilege is waived is admissible (subject to other rules of evidence).

The privilege is subject to the following exceptions or partial exceptions.

14.2.1.2 Exception under Criminal Evidence Act 1898, section 1(2)

A person charged in criminal proceedings who is called as a witness in the proceedings may be asked any question in cross-examination notwithstanding that it would tend to criminate him as to any offence with which he is charged in the proceedings.

14.2.1.3 Exception under Theft Act 1968, section 31

(1) A person shall not be excused, by reason that to do so may incriminate that person or the wife or husband of that person of an offence under this Act—

(a) From answering any question put to that person in proceedings for the recovery or administration of any property, for the execution of any trust or for an account of any property or dealings with property; or

(b) from complying with any order made in any such proceedings;

but no statement or admission made by a person in answering a question put or complying with an order made as aforesaid shall, in proceedings for an offence under this Act, be admissible in evidence against that person or (unless they married after the making of the statement or admission) against the wife or husband of that person.

(2) Notwithstanding any enactment to the contrary, where property has been stolen or obtained by fraud or other wrongful means, the title to that or any other property shall not be affected by reason only of the conviction of the offender.

In *Renworth Ltd* v *Stephansen* [1996] 3 All ER 244 it was held that the fact that the witness might incriminate himself or herself in respect of a non-Theft Act offence (as well as a Theft Act offence) will not necessarily preclude the application of s. 31.

14.2.1.4 Exception under Criminal Damage Act 1971, section 9

(This provision is identical to the Theft Act 1968, s. 31(1) at **14.2.1.3**. The only differences relate to references to offences under the Criminal Damage Act 1971 rather than the Theft Act 1968.)

14.2.1.5 Exception under Children Act 1989, section 98

(1) In any proceedings in which a court is hearing an application for an order [relating to the care, supervision and protection of children], no person shall be excused from—

(a) giving evidence on any matter; or

(b)   answering any question put to him in the course of his giving evidence,
on the ground that doing so might incriminate him or his spouse of an offence.
(2)   A statement or admission made in such proceedings shall not be admissible in
evidence against the person making it or his spouse in proceedings for an offence
other than perjury.

Subsection 98(2) was widely interpreted in *Oxfordshire County Council* v *P* [1995] 2 All
ER 225 and *Cleveland County Council* v *F* [1995] 2 All ER 236 with the result that even
evidence revealed in advance of such proceedings was inadmissible in a subsequent
criminal case. In the *Oxfordshire* case a local authority initiated care proceedings in
respect of a baby who had suffered serious injury. The mother confessed to the
guardian ad litem that she had injured the child. The guardian then told the social
worker, who informed the police. The CPS wanted to rely upon the confession to prove
criminal charges against the mother, and obtained a witness statement from the
guardian. The mother applied to have the guardian removed from the care proceedings.
The main questions before Ward J were whether the guardian was at liberty to disclose
the mother's admissions to the social worker, whether the social worker was at liberty
to disclose to the police, and whether the guardian should make a witness statement
without leave of the court hearing the care proceedings. Ward J terminated the
guardianship and held that the privilege of confidentiality was a matter for the court
and the guardian should not have acted without obtaining the leave of the court.

In the *Cleveland* case a local authority instituted care proceedings in respect of five
children. The mother applied to the court for a direction that any oral or written
statement she might make either to the guardian or to a social worker would be
confidential to the care proceedings. Hale J followed the *Oxfordshire* case and held that
any incriminating statements which the mother might make to the guardian or a social
worker were adequately protected from disclosure by s. 98, although she declined to
make a declaration.

However, in *Re G (a minor)* [1996] 2 All ER 65 the *Oxfordshire* and *Cleveland* cases were
considered, and the Court of Appeal expressed the preliminary view that s. 98(2)
should not be interpreted so widely — it was doubted that subsection (2) could be
extended as far as Ward J and Hale J had suggested or that it would cover the
situations postulated in the *Oxfordshire* or *Cleveland* cases. It was recognised, however, that this view could not bind any criminal court seeking to interpret s. 98.

14.2.1.6   Exception under Supreme Court Act 1981, section 72

In *Rank Film Distributors Ltd* v *Video Information Centre* [1982] AC 380, the House of
Lords held that the privilege against self-incrimination applied to prevent discovery of
documents in an alleged case of breach of copyright. The effects of this case were soon
after reversed in part by Supreme Court Act 1981, s. 72.

(1)   In any proceedings to which this subsection applies a person shall not be
excused, by reason that to do so would tend to expose that person, or his or her
spouse, to proceedings for a related offence or for the recovery of a related penalty—
(a)   from answering any question put to that person in the first-mentioned
proceedings; or
(b)   from complying with any order made in those proceedings.
(2)   Subsection (1) applies to the following civil proceedings in the High Court,
namely—
(a)   proceedings for infringement of rights pertaining to any intellectual property
or for passing off;
(b)   proceedings brought to obtain disclosure of information relating to any
infringement of such rights or to any passing off; and
(c)   proceedings brought to prevent any apprehended infringement of such rights
or any apprehended passing off.
(3)   Subject to subsection (4), no statement or admission made by a person—
(a)   in answering a question put to him in any proceedings to which sub-
section (1) applies; or
(b)   in complying with any order made in any such proceedings,

shall, in proceedings for any related offence or for the recovery of any related penalty, be admissible in evidence against that person or (unless they married after the making of the statement or admission) against the spouse of that person.

(4)   Nothing in subsection (3) shall render any statement or admission made by a person as there mentioned inadmissible in evidence against that person in proceedings for perjury or contempt of court.

(5)   In this section—

'intellectual property' means any patent, trade mark, copyright, registered design, technical or commercial information or other intellectual property;

'related offence' in relation to any proceedings to which subsection (1) applies, means—

(a)   in the case of proceedings within subsection (2)(a) or (b)—

(i)   any offence committed by or in the course of the infringement or passing off to which those proceedings relate; or

(ii)   any offence not within sub-paragraph (i) committed in connection with that infringement or passing off, being an offence involving fraud or dishonesty;

(b)   in the case of proceedings within subsection (2)(c), any offence revealed by the facts on which the plaintiff relies in those proceedings;

'related penalty', in relation to any proceedings to which subsection (1) applies means—

(a)   in the case of proceedings within subsection (2)(a) or (b), any penalty incurred in respect of anything done or omitted in connection with the infringement or passing off to which those proceedings relate;

(b)   in the case of proceedings within subsection (2)(c), any penalty incurred in respect of any act or omission revealed by the facts on which the plaintiff relies in those proceedings.

(6)   Any reference in this section to civil proceedings in the High Court of any description includes a reference to proceedings on appeal arising out of civil proceedings in the High Court of that description.

14.2.1.7   Exceptions under various statutes relating to the investigation of fraud

The Youth Justice and Criminal Evidence Act 1999, s. 59 and sch. 3, has amended a number of statutory provisions which provide for the abrogation of the privilege against self-incrimination in relation to the investigation of serious commercial fraud so as to restrict the use of answers obtained under compulsion, in most cases prohibiting the prosecution in a criminal trial from adducing the evidence or asking questions about it, unless the accused himself or herself has adduced evidence or asked questions relating to it. The prohibition does not prevent the use of the evidence in proceedings for perjury or making a false statement: see sch. 3.

14.2.2   LEGAL PROFESSIONAL PRIVILEGE

There is no general privilege in regard to confidential statements made between a professional person and his client. However, legal professional privilege is a major exception to this rule. It attaches (a) to certain communications between lawyer and client and (b) to certain communications relating to pending or contemplated litigation between lawyer and/or client and third parties. The privilege is that of the client. Where the privilege attaches to a particular communication the client can insist on non-disclosure by the lawyer or third party in question.

14.2.2.1   Scope of the privilege

The scope of this privilege was laid down by common law. However, a guide is given in Police and Criminal Evidence Act 1984, s. 10 (relating to the limits upon police powers to search for and seize evidence) which was stated by Lord Goff in *R* v *Central Criminal Court, ex parte Francis & Francis* [1989] AC 346, HL, to be intended as an accurate reflection of the common law. Section 10 provides:

(1)   Subject to subsection (2) below, in this Act 'items subject to legal privilege' means—

(a)   communications between a professional legal adviser and his client or any person representing his client made in connection with the giving of legal advice to the client;

> (b) communications between a professional legal adviser and his client or any person representing his client or between such an adviser or his client or any such representative and any other person made in connection with or in contemplation of legal proceedings and for the purposes of such proceedings; and
>   (c) items enclosed with or referred to in such communications and made
>   (i) in connection with the giving of legal advice; or
>   (ii) in connection with or in contemplation of legal proceedings and for the purposes of such proceedings,
> when they are in the possession of a person who is entitled to possession of them.
>   (2) Items held with the intention of furthering a criminal purpose are not items subject to legal privilege.

The first head — *Communications between lawyer and client for the purpose of giving or receiving legal advice*

See Police and Criminal Evidence Act 1984, s. 10(1)(a) (*supra*).

Who is a lawyer for these purposes? Solicitors, barristers and foreign lawyers (*Re Duncan* [1968] P 306) and salaried, in-house lawyers (*Alfred Crompton Amusement Machines Ltd* v *Customs & Excise Commissioners* [1974] AC 405).

Which communications are privileged? In *Greenhough* v *Gaskell* (1833) 1 My & K 98 it was held that communication made before the lawyer/client relationship existed or after it ceased would not be privileged: see also *Minter* v *Priest* [1930] AC 558, where it was held that communications passing between a solicitor and a prospective client with a view to the client retaining the solicitor on professional business were privileged from disclosure, even if the solicitor did not accept the retainer.

In *Balabel* v *Air India* [1988] Ch 317 the plaintiffs claimed specific performance of an agreement for an underlease, and sought discovery of three categories of documents. These were: communications between the defendant and its solicitors other than those seeking or giving legal advice; drafts, working papers, attendance notes and memoranda of the defendant's solicitors relating to the proposed underlease; and internal communications of the defendant other than those seeking advice from the defendant's legal advisers. Upholding the defendant's claim to privilege in the Court of Appeal, Taylor LJ said:

> The test is whether the communication or other document was made confidentially for the purposes of legal advice. Those purposes have to be construed broadly. Privilege obviously attaches to a document conveying legal advice from solicitor to client and to a specific request from this client for such advice. But it does not follow that all other communications between them lack privilege.

For an interesting application of this test see *Nederlandse Reassurantie Groep Holding NV* v *Bacon & Woodrow* [1995] 1 All ER 976 in which it was held that communications between solicitor and client giving advice on the commercial wisdom of entering into a transaction (in respect of which legal advice was also sought) would be privileged. In *Hellenic Mutual War Risks Association* v *Harrison (The Sagheera)*, 18 October 1996, unreported, Rix J held that the practical emphasis when dealing with this first head of legal professional privilege must be on the purpose of the retainer (i.e. engaging the services of the lawyer). If the dominant purpose of the retainer is the obtaining and giving of legal advice, then, although it is in theory possible that individual documents may fall outside that purpose, in practice it is unlikely. If, however, the dominant purpose of the retainer is some business purpose then the documents will not be privileged unless exceptionally even in that context legal advice is requested or given, in which case the relevant documents probably are privileged.

Where one lawyer acts for two or more parties in respect of the same subject-matter, communications between lawyer and client X should be disclosed to client Y *but not to outsiders*: see *Buttes Gas & Oil Co.* v *Hammer (No. 3)* [1981] 1 QB 223 and *Re Konigsberg* [1989] 3 All ER 289.

The second head — *Communications between lawyer and/or client and third parties for the dominant purpose of use in pending or contemplated litigation*

See Police and Criminal Evidence Act 1984, s. 10(1)(b) (*supra*).

In *Wheeler* v *Le Marchant* (1881) 17 ChD 675 the Court of Appeal held that the privilege did not extend to letters which had passed between the client's solicitors and the client's surveyors at a time when no dispute had arisen. Moreover, it is not sufficient that litigation is in prospect if the dominant purpose of the communication is unrelated to such litigation: see *Waugh* v *British Railways Board* [1980] AC 521. In this case, the plaintiff's husband received fatal injuries from an accident involving a train collision, and sued for negligence. She sought discovery of a joint inquiry report relating to the accident. The heading of the report stated that it had finally to be sent to the board's solicitor for the purpose of enabling him to advise the board. A claim to privilege was rejected by the House of Lords on the ground that the purpose of obtaining legal advice in anticipation of litigation had been of no more than equal rank and weight with the purpose of railway operation and safety. In *Neilson* v *Laugharne* [1981] 1 QB 736 the plaintiff brought civil proceedings against the police and sought discovery of statements taken during the course of a complaints procedure instituted by the defendant Chief Constable Police Act 1964, s. 49 (which had resulted in a decision that there were no grounds for disciplinary or criminal proceedings against any of the police officers involved). Legal professional privilege was claimed, but this claim was rejected in the Court of Appeal on the ground that although the statements were taken for two purposes (carrying out the duty to investigate a complaint under the Police Act 1964 and also to be in a position to deal with the letter before action from the plaintiff's solicitors), the dominant purpose was to carry out the statutory duty to investigate. However, the court went on to hold that the statements were protected by public interest immunity (see **14.3**) and accordingly refused disclosure.

In *Re Barings plc; Secretary of State for Trade and Industry* v *Baker and others* [1998] 1 All ER 673 Scott J suggested that the test for this second head of legal professional privilege should not be divorced from the principle that underpinned it, i.e. that communications between an individual and his lawyers should be immune from compulsory disclosure. Viewed in this light this second head is merely a way of ensuring that the first head is not infringed when a third party becomes involved in connection with the provision of legal advice. However this does appear to add a new element to the test for determining whether the second head of privilege applies (i.e. whether production of the document might impinge on the inviolability of lawyer/client communications). Insofar as it does this it would seem to conflict with the Court of Appeal decision in *Re Highgrade Traders Ltd* [1984] BCLC 151. This case arose out of a suspicious fire at business premises. The insurers (Phoenix) commissioned reports from loss adjusters, fire investigators and accountants in order, as they claimed, to obtain legal advice as to whether to pay under the policy. These reports were obtained before any lawyers had been consulted. The Court of Appeal held that these reports came under the second head of legal professional privilege. In *Re Barings*, Scott J (although he was able to distinguish *Re Highgrade Traders* on its facts) observed that it was difficult to see how production of the reports in *Re Highgrade Traders* would have impinged on the inviolability of lawyer/client communications. Thus, although in the majority of cases application of the dominant purpose test will ensure that the underlying principle is observed, there may be cases where this is not so. This issue will eventually need to be resolved by the Court of Appeal.

The second head of legal professional privilege would be expected to apply to witness statements. However, in civil cases both parties are generally required to exchange witness statements (see **4.3.6**). The question arises as to what effect the exchange of witness statements has on the privilege. The clear answer is given now in CPR, r. 32.5(5): 'any other party may put the witness statement in as hearsay evidence'. In other words, the exchange of a witness statement is taken as a waiver of the privilege which would otherwise apply to it. For waiver see **14.2.2.7** below.

14.2.2.2 Duration of the privilege

The general rule is 'once privileged always privileged'. This means that once a communication becomes privileged it may continue to be privileged even though the original proceedings in relation to which the privilege was or may have been claimed have ceased, i.e. the client or his or her successors in title may still assert that the communication is privileged years after it was first made. See *Minet* v *Morgan* (1873) 8 Ch App 361 (letters by both the plaintiff and his predecessor in title, his mother, to their respective solicitors concerning the subject matter in dispute were held to be privileged), *Lee* v *South West Thames Regional Health Authority* [1985] 1 WLR 845 and *The Aegis Blaze* [1986] 1 Lloyd's Rep 203. But the privilege is that of the client and cannot be claimed by the lawyer or third party. See *Schneider* v *Leigh* [1955] 2 QB 195, where the author of a medical report prepared for a company for the purposes of defending a personal injuries case was not able to rely on the company's privilege to prevent an order for disclosure of the report when he was sued for libel allegedly contained in the report.

In *Re Molloy* [1997] 2 Cr App R 283 the question arose of the effect of the death of the client in a criminal case. The Court of Appeal confirmed that the privilege passes to the client's personal representatives. This, of course, means that the personal representatives are also empowered to waive the privilege if they are so minded. The position is probably the same in civil cases.

14.2.2.3 The nature and effect of the privilege

The privilege allows the client to prevent the lawyer and/or third party disclosing communications made for the purposes mentioned in **14.2.2.1**; it does *not* prevent the disclosure of all *facts* discovered as an incident of such communications. This may lead to the drawing of some fine distinctions.

Whether the lawyer or third party must produce real evidence, documents or copies of documents provided by the client

See:

R v *Peterborough Justices, ex parte Hicks* [1977] 1 WLR 1371. In this case a search warrant had been issued under s. 16 of the Forgery Act 1913, in respect of an allegedly forged document relating to the defence of the defendants. On an application by the defendants and the solicitors to quash the search warrant, the Court of Appeal, refusing to quash the warrant, held that the document was not privileged in the hands of the solicitors. Eveleigh J said:

> the solicitor holds the document in the right of his client and can assert in respect of its seizure no greater authority than the client himself or herself possesses. The client in this case would have possessed no lawful authority or excuse [a concept allowed for by s.16] that would prevent the document's seizure. In my view the solicitor himself can be in no better position. The solicitor's authority or excuse in a case like this is the authority or the excuse of the client.

In *R* v *King* [1983] 1 WLR 411, the prosecution had at trial been able to require a handwriting expert to produce samples of the defendant's handwriting which had been supplied when the expert had been instructed by the defence. The Court of Appeal rejected the claim that these documents were privileged, holding that in criminal cases the situation was no different from that in civil ones, that whilst legal professional privilege attached to confidential communications between the solicitor and the expert, it did not attach to the chattels or documents upon which the expert based his opinion, nor to the independent opinion of the expert himself. Again, the documents would not have been privileged if in the hands of the defendant himself. But *cf*: *R* v *R* [1994] 4 All ER 260 (facts which client would be entitled to withhold could not be disclosed by lawyer or third party — DNA sample obtained by *defence* expert should not have been admitted on behalf of prosecution).

Dubai Bank Ltd v *Galadari* [1989] 3 All ER 769 (a document which is not privileged in the hands of a solicitor's client does not become privileged simply by being sent by the client to the solicitor).

Ventouris v *Mountain* [1991] 3 All ER 472 (solicitor not obliged to produce *copies* of non-privileged documents obtained by the *solicitor* for the purpose of advising the client if this would reveal the trend of the advice).

Calling the lawyer or third party as a witness to facts
An expert can be called as a witness to facts even if his report is privileged: see *Harmony Shipping Co. SA* v *Saudi Europe Line Ltd* [1979] 1 WLR 1380, CA.

In *Brown* v *Foster* (1857) 1 H & N 736 a barrister acted for D charged with embezzlement before a magistrate. During the proceedings the barrister examined a ledger, and found no entry relating to a particular transaction (which it had been the duty of D to enter). The following day the ledger was produced again, this time containing an entry in the D's handwriting recording the transaction. The criminal charge was dismissed and D then brought an action for malicious prosecution. The defendant to the civil suit claimed that the entry had been added to the ledger by D after the first examination, and was allowed to call the barrister in the original proceedings to say that the entry in the book had not been there when first examined by him. When this ruling was challenged it was held that this evidence was admissible, as the barrister was being called to state what he himself saw, and not what was communicated to him by his client.

In *Conlon* v *Conlons Ltd* [1952] 2 All ER 462 the plaintiff in a personal injuries action wrote through his solicitors to the defendants' insurers offering terms of settlement. P later sued, and D claimed that the action had been compromised. This was denied by P, alleging that no compromise agreement had been made, and, if it had, his solicitors had no authority to enter into it. D administered interrogatories asking whether P had not authorised his solicitors to negotiate for settlement or to hold themselves out as having authority to do so, and whether he had not authorised them to offer terms of settlement. P declined to answer, claiming legal professional privilege. The Court of Appeal held that privilege did not extend to communications between a client and his solicitor which the client instructed his solicitor to repeat to the other party, for such communications were not confidential, and, therefore, P was bound to answer the interrogatories.

R v *Crown Court at Inner London, ex parte Baines and Baines* [1987] 3 All ER 1025 (lawyer could be required to reveal records of a conveyancing transaction but not advice relating to it).

In *R* v *Manchester Crown Court, ex parte R*, *The Times*, 15 February 1999, Lord Bingham CJ held that a record of the time of the accused's attendance at his solicitor's office could not be regarded as a communication and was not, accordingly, protected from disclosure by legal professional privilege.

The scope of the privilege
In *R* v *Derby Magistrates' Court, ex parte B* [1995] 3 WLR 681, the scope of legal professional privilege was considered. In 1978 a teenage girl was murdered. The applicant made a statement to the police admitting sole responsibility for the murder. Shortly before his trial he retracted that statement and alleged that although he had been present at the scene, his stepfather had killed the girl. The applicant was acquitted. In 1992 the stepfather was charged with the girl's murder and committal proceedings were commenced before a stipendiary magistrate. The applicant gave evidence for the prosecution and repeated his allegation that his stepfather had murdered the girl. The applicant was asked about the instructions he had initially given to his solicitors when admitting to the murder, but he declined to answer on the grounds of legal professional privilege. An application was made by the defence for witness summonses requiring production of the attendance notes and proofs of evidence disclosing the relevant instructions. The magistrate weighed the public interest in protecting solicitor and client communications against the public interest in securing that all relevant evidence was available to the defence, and issued the summonses.

The application for judicial review of the stipendiary magistrate's decisions was dismissed, but on a successful appeal to the House of Lords it was held that a witness summons could not be issued to compel the production of documents subject to legal professional privilege which had not been waived, since the principle that a client should be free to consult his legal advisers without fear of his communications being revealed was a fundamental condition on which the administration of justice as a whole rested. Notwithstanding the public interest in securing that all relevant evidence was made available to the defence, legal professional privilege was to be upheld in all cases as the predominant public interest, even where the witness no longer had any recognisable interest in preserving the confidentiality; and that, accordingly, the applicant had been entitled to claim legal professional privilege.

The rather sweeping pronouncements as to the absolute nature of legal professional privilege must be read subject to the following recognised exceptions.

14.2.2.4 Communications made in pursuance of fraud or crime

See generally Police and Criminal Evidence Act 1984, s. 10(2) at **14.2.2.1** and *R* v *Cox and Railton* (1884) 14 QBD 153. The principle is that if fraud or crime is the purpose of the communication then the lawyer has ceased to act as a lawyer, even if the lawyer is unaware of the illegal purpose.

The definition of fraud for the purposes of this rule was stated by Goff J in *Crescent Farm (Sidcup) Sports Ltd* v *Sterling Offices Ltd* [1972] Ch 553:

> Fraud in this connection is not limited to the tort of deceit and includes all forms of dishonesty such as fraudulent breach of contract, fraudulent conspiracy, trickery and sham contrivances.

In *Barclays Bank plc* v *Eustice* [1995] 4 All ER 511 the Court of Appeal held that if the dominant purpose of legal advice was not to explain the legal affect of what had already been done but to structure a transaction which was yet to be carried out so as to prejudice the interests of a creditor:

> The purpose of seeking the advice was sufficiently iniquitous for public policy to require that the communications between the legal advisers and their client in relation to the setting up of the transaction should be discoverable.

In *Dubai Aluminium Co. Ltd* v *Al Alawi* [1999] 1 All ER 703, investigative agents employed by the claimant were alleged to have, *inter alia*, committed trespass and conversion by going through the defendant's dustbin, as well as obtaining information about his bank account in breach of statutory rules. The defendant applied to discharge search and freezing orders, and sought discovery of the reports produced by the claimant's investigators. Legal professional privilege was claimed. Rix J held that criminal or fraudulent conduct undertaken for the purposes of litigation fell into the same category as advising on or setting up criminal or fraudulent transactions which had not yet been undertaken. Documents generated by or reporting on such conduct for the purposes of acquiring evidence in or for litigation were discoverable and fell outside the legitimate area of legal professional privilege. In the instant case, there was a strong *prima facie* case of criminal or fraudulent conduct in the obtaining of information relating to the defendant's accounts, and the application for discovery was granted. But mere civil wrongs would not give rise to loss of the privilege.

Where a lawyer is simply advising his/her client that a particular course would, if taken, involve fraud or crime, the communication remains privileged: *Butler* v *Board of Trade* [1971] Ch 680. For the privilege to be overridden the communication must be made *in pursuance* of fraud or crime: *R* v *Snaresbrook Crown Court, ex parte DPP* [1988] QB 532. The intention to carry out the illegal enterprise is the main consideration, but this can be viewed in hindsight. See *R* v *Central Criminal Court, ex parte Francis & Francis* [1988] 3 WLR 989, HL, where the police suspected an alleged drug dealer of hiding away drug money by buying property, using his family for that purpose. The police obtained an order for production by one of the family member's solicitors for all files in their possession relating to that member's dealings with the purchase of a particular property. The solicitors applied for judicial review to quash the order on the ground that the documents specified in the order were subject to legal privilege as defined in Police and Criminal Evidence Act 1984, s. 10 (see **14.2.2.1**) and so should be excluded from the order. This was refused and appeal was made to the House of Lords. A question of interpretation of s. 10 arose, with the appellants submitting that the natural and ordinary construction of s. 10(2) meant that the words 'held with the intention of furthering a criminal purpose' meant that the relevant intention must be that of the person holding the documents, which in the present case was the intention of the solicitors. There was no question on the facts of the solicitors having the intention of furthering a criminal purpose. The Crown submitted that the subsection must refer to the intention of the client, whether or not the solicitors were party to that intention, and that the intention could even be the intention of a third party who was using the client as an innocent tool in order to further his criminal purpose. By a majority, the House of Lords took the view that s. 10(2) was intended to reflect the common law position, and that the intention referred to could be that of the holder of the document or anyone else. See also *R v Governor of Pentonville Prison, ex parte Osman* [1989] 3 All ER 701, QBD.

14.2.2.5 Overriding the privilege in cases relating to the welfare of children (including wardship and Children Act 1989 proceedings)

In *Oxfordshire County Council v M* [1994] 2 All ER 269, the Court of Appeal held that, where the case relates to a child's welfare, the second head of legal privilege — usually relating to medical reports — can be overridden in the interests of the child. The Court of Appeal held that in care proceedings under the Children Act 1989 the statute required that the child's welfare was the court's paramount consideration, and that proceedings under the Act are not adversarial. Referring to the procedures of civil litigation which had given rise to the application of the doctrine of professional privilege in cases between parties, it was said (*per* Sir Stephen Brown P):

> Children's cases are not similar cases. They fall into a special category where the court is bound to undertake all necessary steps to arrive at an appropriate result in the paramount interests of the welfare of the child. If a party, having obtained the leave of the court, were to be able to conceal, or withhold from the court, matters which were of importance and were relevant to the future of the child, there would be a risk that the welfare of the child would not be promoted as the Children Act 1989 requires. In my judgment, the court must have power to override legal professional privilege in these circumstances.

This decision was approved by the House of Lords in *Re L (A Minor) (Police Investigation: Privilege)* [1996] 2 WLR 395. It was held by a majority that there was a clear distinction between solicitor-client privilege and privilege attaching to reports by third parties prepared for the purposes of litigation ('litigation privilege'). Care proceedings under the 1989 Act were non-adversarial and investigative and accordingly, not only was the notion of a fair trial between opposing parties of far less importance in care proceedings than in normal adversarial actions, but care proceedings were so far removed from normal actions that litigation privilege had no place in relation to reports obtained by a party which could not have been prepared without the leave of the court. However, it was suggested that when the Court of Appeal, in the case of *Oxfordshire County Council v M*, spoke of overriding the privilege, the better view was that litigation privilege never arose in the first place rather than that the court had power to override it. It was excluded by necessary implication from the terms and overall purpose of the 1989 Act. It was also made clear that the principle established in the *Oxfordshire County Council* case does not affect solicitor-client privilege.

14.2.2.6 By-passing the privilege (by resorting to secondary evidence)

The privilege prevents facts being proved in a particular way, i.e. through the client or through the lawyer or (where the second head of privilege applies) certain third parties. If a different or secondary route for the proof of the facts can be found, the privilege is not, as such, infringed. However, in civil cases it may be possible to obtain an injunction to prevent the use of privileged documents by persons who are not bound by the privilege.

In *Calcraft* v *Guest* [1898] 1 QB 759 the general principle was stated that the privilege could be by-passed, e.g., by obtaining *a copy* of the communication. This principle governs the position in criminal cases (unless there has been impropriety in obtaining the communication, in which case the court might apply PACE 1984, s. 78).

Criminal cases

In *R* v *Tompkins* (1977) 67 Cr App R 181, the Court of Appeal held that a note from an accused to his barrister found on floor of the courtroom was properly used by the prosecution to cross-examine the accused so as to expose his perjury.

In *R* v *Cottrill* [1997] Crim LR 56, C had given a written account to his first solicitor which was sent to the prosecution. The prosecution were allowed to use this document at C's trial (the defence having argued that it should be excluded under PACE 1984, s. 78). The Court of Appeal held that, in the absence of any impropriety or sharp practice by the prosecution, the judge had acted entirely within his discretion in refusing to exclude the document.

Civil cases

By CPR, r. 31.20, it is provided that: 'Where a party inadvertently allows a privileged document to be inspected, the party who has inspected the document may use it or its contents only with the permission of the court.' The obvious question arises — on what principles will the court decide whether to give consent?. It is likely that the courts will apply similar principles to those which were used before the new rules came into effect in deciding whether to grant an injunction in order to restrain the use of privileged documents.

In *Lord Ashburton* v *Pape* [1913] 2 ChD 469 it was held that in a civil case the court could award an injunction to restrain a party from by-passing the privilege. Pape (P) obtained by a trick letters which had been written by the plaintiff to his solicitor and were therefore privileged. P had those letters copied and proposed to use them in bankruptcy proceedings as secondary evidence of the contents of the letters which, owing to privilege, he could not produce. The plaintiff brought an action for an injunction to restrain P from disclosing the letters or the copies. On appeal the Court of Appeal held that the fact that the copies, although improperly obtained, might be admissible as secondary evidence in court proceedings (under the principle in *Calcraft* v *Guest*), was no answer to the claim for an injunction brought, before those proceedings, by the lawful owner of confidential information, and that the plaintiff was entitled to an injunction. This was a case where there was impropriety in obtaining the 'privileged' communication, but the use of injunctions is not confined to such cases. See *Goddard* v *Nationwide Building Society* [1987] QB 670, where a solicitor acting for the plaintiffs in connection with the purchase of a house was simultaneously acting for the defendant in respect of the grant of the mortgage. A dispute arose about the property, and the plaintiffs sued the defendant for negligence. Having been told of the proceedings, the solicitor sent the defendant a copy of an attendance note in which were recorded conversations which the solicitor had had with the first plaintiff. The defendant thereupon pleaded the substance of the contents of the note in its defence. The plaintiffs applied to have struck out the passages in the defence which were based on the contents of the note, on the basis that they were confidential and privileged, and sought an injunction restraining the defendant from using or relying on the copy and requiring it to deliver up the document and any further copies which it might have made of it.

On appeal, the Court of Appeal considered *Calcraft* v *Guest* and *Lord Ashburton* v *Pape*, and held that the principle discernible from those cases was that if a litigant has in his possession copies of documents to which legal professional privilege attaches he may nevertheless use such copies as secondary evidence in his litigation: however, if he has not yet used the documents in that way, the mere fact that he intends to do so is no answer to a claim against him by the person in whom the privilege is vested for delivery up of the copies or to restrain him from disclosing or making any use of any information contained in them. On the facts the Court held that the legal professional privilege attaching to the confidential communications recorded in the note belonged exclusively to the plaintiffs, and that they were entitled to the relief sought.

Whether an injunction can be ordered where there is no impropriety depends on all the facts, including particularly the extent to which it was obvious, to the party seeking to by-pass the privilege, that the communication was privileged and had been conveyed to that party in error. If the error is not obvious it is sometimes inferred that the privilege has been waived. In *International Business Machines Corporation* v *Phoenix International (Computers) Ltd* [1995] 1 All ER 413, P sued D in the UK for passing off and trademark infringement and also sued D's associated company on similar grounds in the USA. Because of the amount of documentation involved, the parties agreed that documents disclosed in the UK action could be used in the US action and vice versa. The parties agreed that P's solicitors would review the D's documents and copy relevant ones to P's US lawyers for the US proceedings. In the course of review P's solicitors found a number of invoices (including lawyers' bills) and a document from a US attorney giving legal analysis and advice. Although it was apparent to P's solicitors that D might have been able to claim privilege for these documents, they considered that they were free to use them and told D's solicitors of their intention to do so. D applied for an injunction restraining P from using the information contained in the documents and ordering their return on the ground that the documents were privileged and had been disclosed by a mistake that would have been obvious to the hypothetical reasonable solicitor. P argued that an injunction ought not to be granted unless the mistake was obvious to the actual recipient, irrespective of whether it would have been obvious to a reasonable solicitor, and that, on the facts, disclosure of the disputed documents had resulted from a deliberate decision rather than a mistake by D. Aldous J held that the general rule was that in the absence of fraud an injunction should be granted only if the disclosure of the privileged documents was the result of an obvious mistake, i.e. one that would be obvious to the hypothetical reasonable solicitor, the onus of proof being on the party claiming the injunction. The court had to decide whether it was satisfied that a reasonable solicitor, taking into account the extent of the claim to privilege in the list of documents, the nature of the documents, the complexity of the discovery, the way in which it had been carried out and the surrounding circumstances, would have realised that privilege had not been waived and that a mistake had been made. On the facts it was held that the reasonable solicitor would have been in no doubt that both the legal bills and the legal advice were privileged documents, that there was no good reason why D should have decided to waive privilege, and that disclosure had therefore been made by mistake.

For a case where an injunction was ordered: see *Guinness Peat Properties Ltd* v *Fitzroy Robinson Partnership* [1987] 1 WLR 1027. P, building developers, sued D, architects, for breach of contract and/or negligence. D inadvertently included in a supplemental list of documents a letter for which they had intended to claim privilege, and which expressed D's view on the merits of the allegation contained in a letter from P. Before serving the list D invited P's solicitors to inspect the documents: they did so, copied the letter and sent it to P's expert who referred to it in his report. On seeing the report, D realised the mistake and sought an order restraining P from making any further use of the copy of the letter and requiring all copies of it to be delivered up to them. P appealed against the granting of the injunction, and the Court of Appeal held that, by the manner in which the letter had come to be disclosed, P's solicitor and expert would have realised that there had been an obvious error on the part of D's solicitors in permitting them to inspect the letter and in including it in the supplemental list, and that, in those circumstances, the court had power to intervene for the protection of the mistaken party by the grant of an injunction and should so intervene for the protection of D who had moved promptly to seek relief as soon as they became aware of their mistake. See also *English and American Insurance Co. Ltd* v *Herbert Smith & Co.* (1987) 137 NLJ 148; *Derby & Co.* v *Weldon (No. 8)* [1990] 3 All ER 762.

For cases where injunctions were refused: see *Webster* v *James Chapman & Co.* [1989] 3 All ER 939 and *Pizzey* v *Ford Motor Co. Ltd, The Times,* 8 March 1993, where in a negligence claim for personal injury a point arose as to the admissibility of unfavourable medical reports which had been inadvertently disclosed by P's solicitor to D's solicitors. On appeal it was held that it was of the utmost importance that reliance could be placed on disclosed documents and it was only in the cases of obvious mistake or fraud that privilege could still be claimed. On the facts the Court held that a reasonable solicitor, on seeing the reports on discovery, would not have realised that privilege had not been waived.

(**Note**: Exceptionally, the principles of public policy exclusion will be applied in a civil case: see *ITC Film Distributors* v *Video Exchange Ltd* [1982] Ch 431 where the privileged communication had been improperly obtained.)

Paragraph 608 of the Code of Conduct for the Bar provides:

> A barrister must cease to act and if he is a barrister in independent practice must return any instructions:
>
> . . .
>
> (f) if having come into possession of a document belonging to another party by some means other than the normal and proper channels and having read it before he realises that it ought to have been returned unread to the person entitled to possession of it he would thereby be embarrassed in the discharge of his duties by his knowledge of the contents of the document provided that he may retire or withdraw only if he can do so without jeopardising the client's interests.

14.2.2.7 Waiving the privilege

The privilege is that of the client and he (but not the lawyer or third party) can waive it. However, he must take care to mark clearly the extent of the waiver. See *George Doland Ltd* v *Blackburn, Robson, Coates & Co.* [1972] 1 WLR 1338. The following points about this difficult area derive from the cases indicated:

(a) Where communications relate to the same subject matter an express waiver of privilege in respect of one communication may be taken as an implied waiver in respect of others (*General Accident Fire & Life Assurance Corpn Ltd* v *Tanter* [1984] 1 WLR 100 and *Clough* v *Tameside HA* [1998] 2 All ER 971).

(b) As regards documents, if privilege is waived for part of a document it is taken to be waived for the whole of the document unless it can be argued that 'the document' is in fact several documents each dealing with a different subject matter (*British Coal Corpn* v *Dennis Rye Ltd (No. 2)* [1988] 3 All ER 816).

(c) Privilege is not taken to be waived where communications are disclosed for a limited purpose (e.g. to assist the police with enquiries) (*Great Atlantic Insurance Co.* v *Home Insurance Co.* [1981] 1 WLR 529).

As to blanking out parts of a document disclosed on discovery, see generally *GE Capital Corporate Finance Group Ltd* v *Bankers Trust Co.* [1995] 1 WLR 172.

Where the accused calls evidence as to the reason for legal advice to remain silent when interviewed under caution, the accused is likely to be taken to have waived legal professional privilege: see *R* v *Condron* [1997] 1 Cr App R 185; *R* v *Roble* [1997] Crim LR 449 and *R* v *Bowden* [1999] 2 Cr App R 176, where D was charged with robbery, and made no comment in interview with the police. In the interview D's solicitor stated the grounds on which this advice was given. This part of the interview was not led in evidence by the prosecution, but was referred to in cross-examination by D's counsel. Prosecution counsel claimed that this amounted to a waiver of privilege, entitling him to ask questions about the advice given. The trial judge ruled that this was so, and the Court of Appeal agreed.

14.2.3 PATENT AND TRADE MARK AGENTS' PRIVILEGE

By virtue of Copyright, Designs and Patents Act 1988, ss. 280 and 284, in civil proceedings, privilege may be claimed in respect of communications between a person and his patent agent or trade mark agent for the purpose of pending or contemplated proceedings.

14.2.4   'WITHOUT PREJUDICE' STATEMENTS

In *Paragon Finance plc* v *Freshfields* [1999] 1 WLR 1183, the Court of Appeal (Lord Bingham) held that a client bringing an action in negligence against his solicitor impliedly waived legal professional privilege in respect of any communication between him and that solicitor relating to the case in question. However, this does not mean that the client has waived privilege with regard to other communications (e.g. made with other solicitors) relating to the case in question.

Generally communications between parties to civil proceedings are not privileged nor would they be 'protected' by legal professional privilege if the lawyers acted as intermediaries. However, it is obviously desirable that litigation should be avoided where possible by way of a negotiated compromise or settlement. In order to facilitate this, statements made as part of such negotiations are generally protected from disclosure (in those proceedings or proceedings relating to the same subject matter) as being 'without prejudice'. It is usual to mark the words 'without prejudice' on the correspondence but the fact that the words do not appear will not affect the position — the important point is whether the correspondence can fairly be said to form part of negotiations genuinely aimed at settlement: see *South Shropshire District Council* v *Amos* [1986] 1 WLR 1271. (If the correspondence does *not* fall into that category any 'without prejudice' heading is nugatory: see *Re Daintrey* [1893] 2 QB 116.) Once correspondence has fallen into the 'without prejudice' category a party who wishes to revert to open correspondence should signify this clearly: see *Cheddar Valley Engineering* v *Chaddlewood Homes Ltd* [1992] 4 All ER 942 and *Dixons Stores Group Ltd* v *Thames Television plc* [1993] 1 All ER 349. The protection can be waived but only if *both* parties to the correspondence agree.

If the negotiations are successful *the parties to the settlement* may then use the correspondence as evidence of the agreement (see *Tomlin* v *Standard Telephones & Cables Ltd* [1969] 1 WLR 1378). However, even then, the correspondence would not generally be made admissible in proceedings relating to the same subject-matter for any purpose other than proving the agreement (by the parties to it). Where the plaintiff sued D1 and D2 and settled with D1, the House of Lords held that D2 could *not* use the without prejudice correspondence which had resulted in a concluded agreement between the plaintiff and D1 (*Rush & Tompkins Ltd* v *Greater London Council* [1989] AC 1280, HL).

If the proceedings relate to a wholly different subject matter, or if the correspondence is relevant for a reason other than being a concession, the correspondence will be admissible: see *Muller* v *Linsley & Mortimer, The Times*, 8 December 1994.

An analogous rule applies to communications aimed at the reconciliation of parties to a failing marriage. Admissions made by either party cannot be used as evidence unless both parties agree. For the scope of this analogous rule: see *McTaggart* v *McTaggart* [1949] P 94, *Mole* v *Mole* [1951] P 21 and *Theodoropoulas* v *Theodoropoulas* [1964] P 311.

For the procedural rule that an unaccepted offer can be referred to in certain circumstances on the matter of costs: see the **Civil Litigation Manual** generally and *Calderbank* v *Calderbank* [1976] Fam 93, *cf. Singh* v *Parksfield Group plc, The Times*, 20 March 1996, where the Court of Appeal stressed that where a party can protect its position with a payment into court a simple offer to settle will not afford the same protection.

In regard to disputes over children which arise in relation to proceedings under the Children Act 1989 there is an exception to these general rules protecting attempts at settlement. This arises when the statement clearly indicates that the mother has in the past or is likely in the future to cause serious harm to the well-being of a child (it is for the trial judge to decide whether the public interest in protecting the child outweighs the public interest in preserving the confidentiality of attempted conciliation): see *Re D (minors)* [1993] 2 All ER 693.

14.3   Public Policy

14.3.1   GENERAL POINTS

Even where no private privilege applies there are many situations in which the disclosure of evidence would be damaging in some way to national interests including the effective operation of the public service and the administration of justice. In such cases the evidence may be excluded under the broad heading of public policy. However, it should not be assumed from the breadth of the heading that it is an easy matter to have evidence excluded in this way. The courts have in recent years tended to scrutinise such claims most carefully even when made by a Minister of State.

Although privilege and public policy are related topics there are important differences between them. Whereas privilege is a right which can only be exercised by the person(s) entitled to claim it, refusing to disclose evidence on the grounds of public policy is a duty as well as a right (which should, if necessary, be discharged by the court *proprio motu*). Moreover there can be no question of proving the facts by secondary evidence. It has often been said that the 'right' to public policy exclusion cannot be waived — see Lord Simon in *Rogers* v *Home Secretary* [1973] AC 388. However, the fact that the person or institution most obviously affected by disclosure (the relevant authority) did not seek to resist it might be a factor to weigh in the balance in deciding what was in the public interest. Moreover it is not accepted by the courts that the relevant authority has no responsibility for considering whether it is necessary in the public interest to object to disclosure: see *R* v *Chief Constable of West Midlands Police, ex parte Wiley* [1994] 3 All ER 420 and *R* v *Horseferry Road Magistrates' Court, ex parte Bennett (No. 2)* [1994] 1 All ER 289. If the relevant authority thinks it is not necessary to object it should not object (see below).

Many of the cases on public policy exclusion relate to the disclosure of documents in civil cases. In this context a distinction used to be drawn between cases where the objection was based on the contents of the document in question and cases where the objection was based on the argument that the document fell within a class of documents which should generally not be disclosed. See *Conway* v *Rimmer* [1968] AC 910. However the merit of the distinction (between class and contents) was doubted by Lord Woolf in *Ex parte Wiley* (see above). The Scott report suggested that, so far as government documents are concerned, a new approach was necessary. The Lord Chancellor published a statement about this new approach which is summarised in (1997) 147 NLJ 62:

> Ministers will in future focus directly on the damage that disclosure of sensitive documents would cause. The former division into class and contents claims will no longer be applied. Ministers will only claim immunity when they believe that disclosure of a document will cause real damage or harm to the public interest. Damage will normally have to be in the form of a direct or immediate threat to the safety of an individual or to the nation's economic interest or relations with a foreign state, though in some cases the anticipated damage might be indirect or longer term, such as damage to a regulatory process.

The nature of the harm will now have to be clearly explained on new style certificates which will set out in greater detail than before both the nature of the document and the damage its disclosure is likely to cause, allowing closer scrutiny by the court as the final arbiter.

The position is further complicated by the fact that in civil cases the court will only order production of any documents for inspection if it is of the opinion that the order is necessary either for disposing fairly of the cause or matter or for saving costs: see *Science Research Council* v *Nassé* [1980] AC 1028 and the **Civil Litigation Manual**.

Any attempt to establish separate categories for the cases on public policy exclusion is unlikely to be entirely successful. Even cases involving exactly the same type of document may result in different decisions about whether the document in question should be disclosed. This is because a balancing of the competing public interests is required and the public interest in disclosure will depend upon the relevance of the evidence and this will vary from case to case. However, the general area to which the evidence relates tends to determine the basic principles to be applied and the categorisation adopted here is intended to facilitate an understanding of these principles.

14.3.1.1 National security, affairs of state and the protection of international comity

National security

Asiatic Petroleum Co. Ltd v *Anglo Persian Oil Co. Ltd* [1916] 1 KB 822 (refusal to disclose letter containing details of the government's plans for the military campaign in the Middle East upheld).

Duncan v *Cammel Laird & Co. Ltd* [1942] AC 642 (refusal to disclose plans of the submarine *Thetis* which sank during trials upheld).

Affairs of state etc.

Burmah Oil Co. Ltd v *Bank of England* [1980] AC 1090 (bank's refusal, on government instructions, to produce confidential record of dealings between the bank and other businesses upheld).

Air Canada v *Secretary of State for Trade (No. 2)* [1983] 2 AC 394 (government's refusal to produce documents relating to government policy on landing charges in the UK upheld).

Buttes Gas & Oil Co. v *Hammer (No. 3)* [1981] 1 QB 223 (in the interest of international comity, company could not be forced to disclose communications with a foreign State relating to a border dispute with another State).

14.3.1.2 Journalists' sources

Contempt of Court Act 1981, s. 10:

> *No court may require a person to disclose, nor is any person guilty of contempt of court for refusing to disclose, the source of information contained in a publication for which he is responsible, unless it be established to the satisfaction of the court that disclosure is necessary in the interests of justice or national security or for the prevention of disorder or crime.*

In *Secretary of State for Defence* v *Guardian Newspapers* [1985] 1 AC 339 the House of Lords held that it is not necessary for the person resisting the disclosure to show that disclosure of the document in question will reveal a source of information, simply that it might.

Note: publication means 'any speech, writing, broadcast or other communication in whatever form, which is addressed to the public at large or any section of the public' .

Interests of justice exception

On the meaning of 'is necessary in the interests of justice' according to Lord Diplock in *Guardian Newspapers* this exception should be defined narrowly. In *X Ltd* v *Morgan-Grampian (Publishers) Ltd* [1991] 1 AC 1, the House of Lords decided that it will be contempt of court for a journalist to refuse to disclose a source (i.e. this exception *will* apply) if the information is required to enable persons to exercise important legal rights and to protect themselves from serious legal wrongs. (However, the European Court of Human Rights in *Goodwin* v *United Kingdom* (1996) 22 EHRR 123 arrived at a different conclusion on the same facts applying Article 10 of the European Convention of Human Rights. The test stated by the House of Lords was, however, applied in *Camelot Group plc* v *Centaur Communications Ltd* [1998] 1 All ER 251.)

In *Maxwell* v *Pressdram Ltd* [1987] 1 WLR 298 it was stressed that the appraisal of whether it is *necessary* to order disclosure would depend on the judge's view of whether knowledge of the source would significantly affect the ability of the party seeking disclosure to pursue an action (i.e. is the identity of the informant relevant?). Other relevant factors are the extent of damage which might be caused to the party seeking disclosure if disclosure is not ordered: see *Saunders v Punch Ltd* [1998] 1 All ER 234.

Prevention of disorder or crime exception

On the meaning of 'is necessary for the prevention of disorder or crime' see *Re an Inquiry under the Companies Securities (Insider Dealing) Act 1985* [1988] AC 660 and *X v Y* [1988] 2 All ER 648. According to these cases, disclosure of a journalist's sources may be required if it is necessary to help the fight against crime generally, not just the investigation of specific crimes.

Section 10 must now be read in conjunction with Article 10 of the European Convention on Human Rights, which provides as follows:

> 1. *Everyone has the right to freedom of expression. This right shall include freedom to hold opinions and to receive and impart information and ideas without interference by public authority and regardless of frontiers. This article shall not prevent States from requiring the licensing of broadcasting, television or cinema enterprises.*
> 2. *The exercise of these freedoms, since it carries with it duties and responsibilities, may be subject to such formalities, conditions, restrictions or penalties as are prescribed by law and are necessary in a democratic society, in the interests of national security, territorial integrity or public safety, for the prevention of disorder or crime, for the protection of health or morals, for the protection of the reputation or rights of others, for preventing the disclosure of information received in confidence, or for maintaining the authority and impartiality of the judiciary.*

In *Ashworth Security Hospital v MGN Ltd* [2001] 1 All ER 991, the Court of Appeal held that a court had jurisdiction under Contempt of Court Act 1981, s. 10, to order the disclosure of the identity of wrongdoers whenever the person against whom disclosure was sought had become mixed up in wrongful, even though not tortious, conduct that infringed a claimant's legal rights. The Court said that if this statement of the law was too wide, and it was necessary for the wrongful conduct to be tortious, that restriction did not apply where the defendant had been a party to the wrongdoing, instead of innocently mixed up in it. An order made in such circumstances did not infringe Article 10 of the Convention. The approach to the interpretation of Contempt of Court Act 1981, s. 10, should, as far as possible, (a) equate the specific purposes for which disclosure of sources was permitted with the legitimate aims set out in Article 10 of the Convention; and (b) apply the same test of necessity as that applied by the European Court of Human Rights when considering Article 10.

14.3.1.3 Information in the possession of police and revenue authorities etc. relating to the investigation of crime and revenue fraud (informant immunity)

The public policy in not revealing the identity of informants (so as not to deter people from informing the authorities of illegal acts) is generally upheld both in civil and criminal proceedings, see *Marks v Beyfus* (1890) 25 QBD 494; *Alfred Crompton Amusement Machines Ltd v Customs & Excise Commissioners* [1974] AC 405; *Rogers v Home Secretary* [1973] AC 388 and *D v National Society for the Prevention of Cruelty to Children* [1978] AC 171, HL.

But the public policy is not absolute, see in civil cases *Norwich Pharmacal Co. v Customs & Excise Commissioners* [1974] AC 133 and the **Civil Litigation Manual**. In criminal cases *R v Agar* (1990) 90 Cr App R 318; *R v Reilly* [1994] Crim LR 279; *R v Turner* [1995] 2 Cr App R 94; *R v Keane* [1994] 1 WLR 746. In the latter case, the Court of Appeal said that disclosure of an informant's identity should be ordered if it might prove the defendant's innocence or avoid a miscarriage of justice. In *R v Turner*, the Court of Appeal held that disclosure should have been ordered in a case where it was said that the informant may have *participated* in the events constituting, surrounding or following the crime. In many cases when disclosure is ordered the CPS will not proceed (so as to avoid disclosure). For the procedure in criminal cases for dealing with this sort of issue, see **14.3.1.4** below.

Regarding the extension of informant immunity by analogy

R v *Rankine* [1986] QB 861 confirms that the police may refuse to disclose the location of police surveillance posts which are located in premises; *cf. R* v *Brown* (1988) 87 Cr App R 52.

The following guidelines were given by Watkins LJ in *R* v *Johnson (Kenneth)* (1989) 88 Cr App R 131 at p. 139:

Clearly a trial judge must be placed by the Crown which seeks to exclude evidence of the identification of places of observation and occupiers of premises, in the best possible position to enable him properly in the interests of justice, which includes of course providing a defendant with a fair trial, to determine whether he will afford to the police the protection sought. At the heart of this problem is the desirability, as far as that can properly be given, of reassuring people who are asked to help the police that their identities will never be disclosed lest they become the victims of reprisals by wrong doers for performing a public service.

The minimum evidential requirements seem to us to be the following:

(a) The police officer in charge of the observations to be conducted, one of no lower rank than a sergeant should usually be acceptable for this purpose, must be able to testify that beforehand he visited all observation places to be used and ascertained the attitude of occupiers of premises, not only to the use to be made of them, but to the possible disclosure thereafter of the use made and facts which could lead to the identification of the premises thereafter and of the occupiers. He may of course in addition inform the Court of difficulties, if any, usually encountered in the particular locality of obtaining assistance from the public.

(b) A police officer of no lower rank than a chief inspector must be able to testify that immediately prior to the trial he visited the places used for observations, the results of which it is proposed to give in evidence, and ascertained whether the occupiers are the same as when the observations took place and whether they are or are not, what the attitude of those occupiers is to the possible disclosure of the use previously made of the premises and of facts which could lead at the trial to identification of premises and occupiers.

Such evidence will of course be given in the absence of the jury when the application to exclude the material evidence is made. The judge should explain to the jury, when summing up or at some appropriate time before that, the effect of his ruling to exclude, if he so rules.

These guidelines were applied and approved in *R* v *Hewitt* (1991) 142 NLJ 160.

14.3.1.4 Confidential/personal statements, especially those made in official reports and inquiries

This is probably the most difficult category of cases to deal with in that it is difficult to identify a dominant head of public policy. Moreover in some cases the decision will depend on the importance of the information to the party seeking disclosure. For various illustrations of the courts' approach, see:

Conway v *Rimmer* [1968] AC 910 (internal reports on a probationer police constable — disclosure allowed).

Gaskin v *Liverpool City Council* [1980] 1 WLR 1549, *R* v *City of Birmingham District Council, ex parte O* [1982] 2 All ER 356 and *Re M, The Times,* 4 January 1990 (social services reports and case notes — disclosure refused).

Science Research Council v *Nassé* [1980] AC 1028 (records and interview notes concerning SRC's employees not protected from disclosure).

Campbell v *Tameside Metropolitan Borough Council* [1982] QB 1065 (reports in possession of education authority about unruly pupil — disclosure allowed).

Lonrho Ltd v *Shell Petroleum Co. Ltd* [1980] 1 WLR 627 (evidence given in confidence to government enquiry into 'Rhodesian sanctions busting' — disclosure refused).

Brown v *Matthews* [1990] 2 All ER 155 (Court Welfare Officers report could be disclosed at discretion of the court which had ordered the report).

Evans v *Chief Constable of Surrey* [1988] QB 588 (report sent by police to Director of Public Prosecutions — disclosure refused).

R v *Hampshire County Council, ex parte K* [1990] 2 All ER 129 (Social Service Department's case records/files exempt from disclosure unless a judge specifically rules to the contrary).

R v *Chief Constable of West Midlands Police, ex parte Wiley* [1994] 3 All ER 420 (statements made by members of the public in inquiries into complaints against the police, under s. 49 of the Police Act 1964, were, until this decision of the House of Lords, generally given public interest immunity — see *Neilson* v *Laugharne* [1981] 1 QB 736. However, *Neilson* was overruled in *ex parte Wiley*, so that public interest immunity does not generally attach to such statements but it may do so depending on the contents of particular statements).

Taylor v *Anderton* [1995] 2 All ER 421 (reports and working papers prepared by *investigating officers* during investigations into police conduct pursuant to PACE 1984, s. 98 *were* entitled to public interest immunity).

14.3.1.5 Procedure for objecting on public policy grounds to disclosure in criminal cases
The whole area of disclosure has been considerably affected by Criminal Procedure and Investigations Act 1996 (see the **Criminal Litigation and Sentencing Manual** for details). At each stage in the disclosure procedure provision is made for the prosecutor to object to disclosure and apply to the court for an order that disclosure should not be made on the grounds of public interest immunity. As a corollary there is provision for the accused to make a counter application for the court to order disclosure. The procedure to be adopted to deal with these claims and counter-claims is now to be found in the Crown Court (Criminal Procedure and Investigations Act 1996) (Disclosure) Rules 1997 and the Magistrates' Courts (Criminal Procedure and Investigations Act 1996) (Disclosure) Rules 1997.

Questions

OBJECTIVES

This chapter is designed to ensure that you have a sound understanding of the principles of privilege and the exclusion of evidence on public policy grounds, and are able to apply them in a number of practical contexts.

Question 1
Consider the correspondence below in conjunction with the information given in the following separate situations and answer the questions posed in each case.

(a) *Ackroyd* v *Smithson*. In this case, which concerns a claim by the claimant for damages for negligence against the defendant arising from a motor car accident, the solicitors for the claimant are Adolphus & Ellis, those for the defendant are Carrington & Payne.

From Carrington & Payne

To Adolphus & Ellis

29 September 2001

Dear Sirs

Smithson ats Ackroyd

Further to our telephone conversation of 28 September, we confirm that we have instructions to make an offer on behalf of our client of £17,500 by way of compensation for the physical injuries suffered by your client, without prejudice as to liability. We also confirm that the special damages have been agreed at £377.25.

We look forward to hearing whether this offer is acceptable to your client.

Yours faithfully,

Carrington & Payne

From Adolphus & Ellis

To Carrington & Payne

3 October 2001

Dear Sirs,

Ackroyd v Smithson

We thank you for your letter of 29 September.

We regret that we do not have instructions to accept the offer of £17,500 but an offer of £20,000 would be very favourably considered by our client.

Yours faithfully,

Adolphus & Ellis

From Carrington & Payne

To Adolphus & Ellis

10 October 2001

Dear Sirs,

Smithson ats Ackroyd

We thank you for your letter of 3 October.

Our client is not prepared to offer more than £17,500.

Yours faithfully,

Carrington & Payne

No agreement is reached and the matter proceeds to trial.

     (i)   Is any part of this correspondence admissible in relation to the issue of liability?

     (ii)   Is any part of this correspondence admissible if the claimant seeks at trial to adduce evidence to show that the special damages to which he is entitled are in excess of £377.25?

  (b)   *Ball* v *Herbert*. This is a case which involves a claim by the claimant for damages for trespass to land and for an injunction restraining the defendant from parking motor cars on a field, the property of the claimant, known as Muddock's Square. The solicitors for the claimant are Carrington & Kirwan, those for the defendant are Ellis & Blackburn.

From Carrington & Kirwan

To Ellis & Blackburn

2 October 2001

Dear Sirs,

Ball v Herbert: Without Prejudice

We have now taken our client's instructions. The terms upon which he would be prepared to discontinue proceedings against you are as follows:

1. Mr Herbert will forthwith remove any motor vehicles remaining parked on Muddock's Square and will thereafter refrain completely from parking motor vehicles of any description there.

2. Mr Herbert will pay to Mr Ball £25 by way of damages for trespass to land.

3. Mr Herbert will pay to Mr Ball £50 as a contribution towards Mr Ball's costs in this matter.

Are these terms acceptable to your client?

Yours faithfully,

Carrington & Kirwan

From Ellis & Blackburn

To Carrington & Kirwan

10 October 2001

Dear Sirs,

Herbert ats Ball: WITHOUT PREJUDICE

We have taken our client's instructions and confirm that the terms set out in your letter of 2 October, for which we thank you, are acceptable to him.

We understand that no motor vehicles remain parked in Muddock's Square.

We enclose herewith our cheque for £75 in respect of damages and costs.

Yours faithfully,

Ellis & Blackburn

Some months passed without incident but now Mr Herbert has started to park vehicles once more on Muddock's Square. Advise Mr Ball.

(c) Explain the effect of 'Without Prejudice' in the following letter.

From Foster & Findlayson, Solicitors

9 Albert Square

London EC23

To Mr T Finkle

Glad Rags
Holborn
London WC1

6 October 2001

Dear Sir,

Re His-N-Her Clothing Ltd: WITHOUT PREJUDICE

We act for His-N-Her Clothing Ltd who instruct us that in March 2001 they entered into a contract with you for the supply to you of 600 pairs of jeans at a price of £3,000. The goods were delivered to you on 1 April 2001 but despite frequent requests no payment has been made by you.

We are instructed to commence proceedings against you without further notice if the sum of £3,000 is not paid to us within seven days of the date of this letter.

Yours faithfully,

Foster & Findlayson

(d) *Hayward* v *Wilson*. The following letter was written by a partner in the firm of Manning & Grainger (solicitors for the defendant) to a partner in the firm of Espinasse & Co. (solicitors for the claimant). The action concerned a claim by the claimant against the defendant for damages for wrongful dismissal.

From Manning & Grainger

To Ms Sharon Jackson, Espinasse & Co.

2 October 2001

Dear Sharon,

Wilson ats Hayward: Without Prejudice

Re: our discussions in Dieppe about this matter last weekend. I've taken instructions from Mr Wilson and he would be prepared to offer Mr Hayward £700, each side to pay its own costs.

Yours,

Charlene

From Espinasse & Co.

To Ms Charlene Laidler, Manning & Grainger

10 October 2001

Dear Charlene,

Hayward & Wilson: Without Prejudice

Many thanks for your letter but it looks as if this action will have to remain in an on-going situation at this moment in time. I've been in touch with Mr Hayward but no way will he accept anything less than £5,000.

Yours,

Sharon

Hayward v *Wilson* has not been settled but has not yet come to trial. The original of Ms Laidler's letter of 2 October has come into the hands of her husband. He wishes to use it as evidence in divorce proceedings which he has brought against his wife. He alleges as unreasonable behaviour on her part a lesbian relationship with Ms Jackson and he wishes to put the letter in evidence to establish that she was in Dieppe with Ms Jackson on the weekend referred to. May he do so?

Question 2
Brian claims damages in negligence from Cedric, alleging that Cedric had parked his van negligently on a slope with the result that it had run down the hill and damaged Brian's car and garden wall. Cedric denies negligence, claiming the van's brakes failed to hold it due solely to the exceptionally icy state of the road and its steep camber. Brian has pleaded *res ipsa loquitur*.

A copy of a letter from Donald, Cedric's solicitor, to Cedric, summarising counsel's advice on the claim, was in error included in a bundle of documents made available by Donald for inspection by Brian's solicitors. Advise Cedric.

Question 3
You are instructed for Country Farmers Ltd against Mammon Properties Ltd. Mammon Properties Ltd is the owner and occupier of land on which is constructed an irrigation work which, on 3 December 2001 flooded your lay client's farm. On 7 December 2001, your instructing solicitors intimated to Mammon Properties that their client would look to that company for compensation. Consider and advise whether the following documents can be obtained on discovery from the defendant:

(a) A report from surveyors, dated 1 January 2001, to Mammon Properties, advising that the irrigation work was prone to flooding and should be altered.

(b) A report from surveyors, dated 3 September 1989, to the Ministry of Defence tenants of the land before Mammon Properties. This report passed to Mammon Properties with the land.

(c) Advice from Mammon Properties Ltd's salaried solicitor as to the best method of evading liability for the nuisance by means of a tortious conspiracy with another of the company's servants.

INDEX